Strategic Business Planning for Accountants

Strategic Business Planning for Accountants

Methods, Tools and Case Studies

Dimitris N. Chorafas

AMSTERDAM • BOSTON • HEIDELBERG • LONDON • NEW YORK • OXFORD
PARIS • SAN DIEGO • SAN FRANCISCO • SINGAPORE • SYDNEY • TOKYO
CIMA Publishing is an imprint of Elsevier

CIMA Publishing is an imprint of Elsevier
Linacre House, Jordan Hill, Oxford OX2 8DP
30 Corporate Drive, Suite 400, Burlington, MA 01803, USA

First edition 2007

British Library Cataloguing in Publication Data
A catalogue record for this book is available from the British Library

Library of Congress Cataloguing in Publication Data
A catalog record for this title is available from the Library of Congress

ISBN–13: 978-0-7506-8132-2
ISBN–10: 0-7506-8132-2

For information on all CIMA Publishing publications
visit our website at http://www.cimapublishing.com

Printed and bound in The Netherlands

07 08 09 10 11 10 9 8 7 6 5 4 3 2 1

Contents

Preface xiii

Part 1: Delivering the Strategic Plan 1

1 Strategy is a Master Plan 3

1. Introduction 5
2. Strategic plans must be dynamic: case study with General Electric 7
3. Main components of a business strategy: case study with Hewlett–Packard 11
4. Positioning our Firm against market forces: an example with Cisco 15
5. The cost of doing business and of staying in business: risk is a cost 19
6. Standards setting, added value, and strategic planning 23
7. Reasons why strategic plans fail 27
8. Precious advice by Sun Tzu, Patton, and Walton: case study on AT&T 30

2 Examples of Leadership in Strategic Decisions 35

1. Introduction 37
2. Douglas MacArthur and the Inchon strategic decision 38
3. Strategic decisions in business: case study with Sprint 41
4. The nature of many strategic decisions depends on macroeconomics 44
5. Business strategy and the price of key commodities 46
6. The comparative advantage of knowledge workers 49
7. Strategic dimension under the new capitalism 52

3 Strategic Choices in Corporate Governance 57

1. Introduction 59
2. The choice of the product line: case study with Toyota 61
3. Strategic choices in the banking industry: a lesson from the 1990s 65
4. Strategic products: case study with Microsoft 68

5.	Strategic and Tactical Products Defined	72
6.	Strategic customers and Pareto's law	75
7.	Short-term *vs* long-term performance	81
4	**Establishing a Strategic Plan**	**85**
1.	Introduction	87
2.	Accounting for ambiguity in the development of a strategic plan	89
3.	How companies gain the high ground: case studies from Bloomberg and Bernheim	93
4.	Strategic planning at mean and lean organizations	97
5.	The importance of credit rating: case study with GM and GMAC	100
6.	Credit rating and strategic planning	102
7.	Strategic plans and capital allocation	105
8.	Developing alternatives to a strategic plan	108
9.	A methodology to support strategic planning	111
Part 2: Functional Effectiveness in Strategic Planning		**115**
5	**Forecasting**	**117**
1.	Introduction	119
2.	Prognostication is a difficult art	121
3.	The art of forecasting and its pitfalls	125
4.	Making forecasts: case study with Hurricane Katrina	129
5.	Forecasts must be realistic: case study with Hartford Insurance	132
6.	Models could help in prognostication: the case of unexpected losses	135
7.	Forecasts made public: case study with forward-looking statements	138
6	**Planning**	**143**
1.	Introduction	145
2.	Critical elements of the planning process	147
3.	Planning premises in the banking industry: a practical example	150
4.	Longer-range and far-out planning	154
5.	Challenges of shorter-range plans	159
6.	The role of policies in planning	163
7.	Management planning and business risk	166

7 Organizing and Staffing **171**

1. Introduction 173
2. A sound organizational principle taught by the Catholic Church 175
3. Case studies on the aftermath of reorganization: the Jack Welsh example 179
4. Emphasizing the role of the individual: lesson by Miyamoto Musashi 182
5. Leadership talent, knowledge assets and performance evaluation 186
6. Greed and glory in high paycheques: case study from NYSE 190
7. Establishing a rigorous training programme 193

8 Directing and Controlling **199**

1. Introduction 201
2. Professionals, experts, managers, and executives 203
3. Day-to-day tactical decisions 205
4. Unmanageable legacy costs: case study with Delphi and General Motors 208
5. Death by red ink: the abyss of bad management 211
6. Emulating the thinking of promoters: the ABC Management Teams 214
7. Management's controlling function, and internal control 218
8. Criteria for better corporate governance 222

Part 3: Strategic Financial Planning and Accounting **225**

9 Financial Planning **227**

1. Introduction 229
2. Money and the watch over money 231
3. Using derivatives in financial planning: case study with Fiat 234
4. The budget as a financial plan 237
5. Cash flow challenges 242
6. A company's liquidity obligations 247
7. Financing by equity or debt? The issue of financial staying power 249

10 IFRS and Strategic Accounting Principles **253**

1. Introduction 255
2. Why IFRS is a strategic accounting initiative 257

3.	Disclosure about capital and the need for standards	260
4.	Fair value, IAS 39 and corresponding US standards	264
5.	Hedging and hedge accounting	267
6.	A model based approach to assets and liabilities management	270
7.	Virtual consolidated financial statements	274
8.	The algorithm for credit equivalence	278

Part 4: Cost Control, Risk Control and Profitability **283**

11 Strategic Cost Control Is Good Governance **285**

1.	Introduction	287
2.	Cost control culture: case study on Sam Walton's experience	289
3.	Comparing cost performance to peer groups	292
4.	Cost control in banking and impact of overhead	296
5.	Deproliferating and cost cutting: case studies with MIT and Compaq	299
6.	An eye on survival: case study on IBM	302
7.	Applying the strategy of product capitalization	305

12 Accounting for the Cost of Risk **309**

1.	Introduction	311
2.	Concepts underpinning risk and uncertainty	314
3.	The cost of risk may be more than half the cost of capital	318
4.	The whole culture of looking at risk must be experimental	321
5.	A case study with Fidelity Investments' risk in 1994	323
6.	Monetization of risk and wealth management	327
7.	Credit, market, and operational risk in one cup: case study with Refco, 2005	330

13 Strategies for Sustained Profitability **335**

1.	Introduction	337
2.	Profit planning yardstick	338
3.	Profit planning in the banking industry	343
4.	Profit planning in the manufacturing industry	346
5.	Profitability analysis over the longer term	350
6.	Patterns of production: every country has its own characteristics	354
7.	Income-based profitability, added value, and time value	357

Part 5: Strategic Products and Markets 361

14 Research, Development and Product Planning 363

1. Introduction 365
2. Research and the knowledge economy 367
3. Research, development, and innovation 371
4. Product planning and product life management 374
5. The product planner's job in manufacturing 377
6. Product development in banking: case study with Morgan Stanley 383
7. Financial research and pattern analysis: case study with ECAPS 386
8. Critical evaluation of R&D deliverables 390

15 Strategic Decisions in Marketing 395

1. Introduction 397
2. Niche, unique product, and mass market 399
3. Strategies for market control: case study with Coca-Cola 403
4. Quantitative sales objectives and marketing savvy: case study with IBM 407
5. Marketing planning and sales force productivity 411
6. Sales office productivity and the experimental approach 416
7. Caring about the brand name: case study on 'Intel inside' 420

16 Know Your Customer 425

1. Introduction 427
2. Profitability analysis of a customer profit centre 429
3. Scrutiny should start at high level 432
4. Dependability and quality of service: case study with Six Sigma 435
5. Benefits derived from applying a rigorous management methodology 439
6. Statistical charts promoting the know-your-customer concept 444
7. Technology for managing customer profitability 449
8. General conditions characterizing a client's contract 451

Part 6: Strategic Mergers and Acquisitions **457**

17 Mergers, Acquisitions, Takeovers and Their Deliverables **459**

1. Introduction 461
2. Lessons from a quarter century of M&As 463
3. Mergers in the United States, UK, and Euroland 467
4. Friendly acquisitions and hostile deals 472
5. Big egos: case study on the RJR Nabisco takeover 476
6. A critical view of M&As and of some ironies behind them 480
7. Buyouts, leveraged loans, and commissions 483
8. Deferred tax liabilities: case study with Gillette 486

18 Case Studies on Mergers in Telecommunications, Computers, Oil and Air Transport **491**

1. Introduction 493
2. Strategy and aftermath of M&As in telecommunications 494
3. The acquisition of O_2 by Telefonica and credit ratings blues 498
4. An M&A that turned on its head: Pirelli's acquisition of Telecom Italia 502
5. Strategic switch towards services: IBM's purchase of Monday 506
6. 'One plus one' can be 'less than two': mergers in the computer industry 509
7. Giant mergers in the oil industry: but no new departures 512
8. Deregulation, consolidation, and shake out in air transport 516
9. The bankruptcy of Delta Airlines: a case study 519

19 Case Studies on Big Bank Mergers in the United States **523**

1. Introduction 525
2. Assets of US banks: case study with Citicorp 527
3. More growth, more mergers: from Citicorp to Citigroup 529
4. Chemical Banking and Chase Manhattan 532
5. JP Morgan Chase and Bank One 534
6. Acquisitions under distress: case study with BankAmerica 538
7. The merger of Citizen & Southern with Sovran: a case study on the downside of M&As 543
8. Mergers, acquisitions, and the regulators' nightmare 547

20 Case Studies on Big Bank Mergers in Europe **551**

1. Introduction 553
2. The takeover of HypoVereinsbank by Italy's Unicredit 555
3. Swiss Bank Corporation and the new UBS 558
4. Deutsche Bank and its investment banking ambitions 564
5. Dresdner Bank and the takeover of Wasserstein Perella 567
6. The ABN Amro and other merger strategies 570
7. Mergers and acquisitions in the EU: the BPI scandal 573

21 The Risk of M&As: Case Studies with Mergers that Went Sour **579**

1. Introduction 581
2. Reasons underpinning failed M&A deals 582
3. IBM's acquisition of Rolm and other mergers with cultural discontinuity 586
4. DaimlerChrysler: the merger of 'equals' and its unexpected consequences 589
5. Bank mergers may result in customer alienation 594
6. Fraudulent conveyance: a new thorn in M&As 596
7. Legal risk and social risk with M&As 598
8. The merger wave needs regulation to weed out seeds of disaster 601

Index **607**

Preface

As experienced hunters caution us, when stalking a flock of ducks overhead, aim at one. Strategic business planning is a general case – the flock of ducks. Therefore, the better way to address it is to focus on each particular subject, one at a time. This defines the mode in which this book is organized.

Written for professional accountants and for managers who have to make strategic decisions in the course of their work, the book is full of case studies based on an extensive research project. Members of the board, chief executives, operating officers, treasurers, financial officers, budget directors, auditors, product planners, marketing directors, and management accounting specialists – not only strategic planners – will find in this text practical examples helpful to their decisions and to their work.

Abiding by the principle of aiming at one duck at a time, the book divides into six parts. Part 1 focuses on the strategic plan. In four chapters it leads the reader from the concept of a master plan, through case studies on leadership, strategic decisions, and choices necessary in corporate governance, to how to establish a strategic plan.

Methods have to be developed and tools have to be used in increasing the functional management's effectiveness in the performance of strategic functions. The theme of Part 2 is precisely the management functions whose able execution makes the difference between success and failure in enterprise: forecasting, planning, organizing, staffing, directing, and controlling.

Knowing about the functions of management, and the way in which they should be performed, is a fundamental step in evaluating the quality of a company's practices. Typically, these practices involve both plans and contextual reviews of factors related to governance. The basic functions addressed in the four chapters of Part 2 are applicable globally and, as such, they fit a range of different corporate structures and organizational models.

Strategic business planning needs effective tools with which to quantify objectives, gauge performance, and undertake plan *vs* actual comparisons. The two chapters of Part 3 demonstrate that modern accounting rules, promoted by IFRS and US GAAP, not only assist in strategic financial planning but also provide a solid basis for management supervision and control.

Part 4 brings to the reader's attention the fact that costs matter. Strategic business plans that pay little or no attention to cost factors are doomed. Precisely the same statement is valid about risk factors. Risks being assumed should be monetized, because risk is a cost. Both costs and risks have a huge impact on profitability, as this text demonstrates.

The topic of costs, risks and profitability discussed in the three chapters of Part 4 is not a new one, but high-profile cases of bankruptcy, from Enron and WorldCom to Parmalat, and their negative fallout, have placed these issues at centre stage within the industrial and financial community. Indeed, while taking risks within the realm of business strategy is pivotal in capitalism, it also poses a unique set of challenges in ensuring that a company's assets are managed efficiently and prudently.

Part 5 addresses, in its three chapters, the issues associated with strategic products and markets. These range from research and development to market research, product planning, the able management of marketing functions, and sales effectiveness. This text also includes an issue that does not always receive the attention it deserves: Know Your Customer.

Additionally, some of the best case studies in strategic business planning revolve around mergers and acquisitions (M&As), the theme of the five chapters of Part 6. The text is full of practical examples on mergers, particularly among the bigger industrial companies and financial institutions. It also includes statistics that document that many M&As cost too much, and they don't always go according to plan.

Mergers, acquisitions, and takeover activity have accelerated sharply as corporates look for ways to put the excess cash on their balance sheets to work, or get deeply in debt for the glory of being bigger and bigger. Global deals amounting to almost 22% of the S&P 500 market capitalization have been announced in 2005 – although there is plenty of evidence that not all M&As add value for shareholders, as demonstrated by case studies in Part 6.

The importance of strategic business planning, like many of business life's essentials, is most evident when it is not available. This book examines the practice of strategic business planning, including its functions, methods, tools, and the way in which they are employed. It does so in a practical way through case studies, which help in demonstrating how to innovate in order to overcome obstacles and cover new and evolving challenges.

* * * * *

My debts go to a long list of knowledgeable people and their organizations, who contributed to the research which led to this text. Without their contributions this book the reader has on hand would not have been possible. I am also indebted to several senior executives for constructive criticism during the preparation of the manuscript.

Let me take this opportunity to thank Mike Cash for suggesting this project, Elaine Leek for the editing work, and Melissa Read for the production effort. To Eva-Maria Binder goes the credit for compiling the research results, typing the text, and making the camera-ready artwork.

Dimitris N. Chorafas

Part 1

Delivering the Strategic Plan

Strategy is a Master Plan

1. Introduction

Strategy is a master plan against one or more opponents. It is not just a list of smart moves, or of individual actions. Neither is strategy made in the abstract, independently of events taking place in the real world. Whether in industry, finance, politics or the military, the ground on which it is based necessarily involves *competition*, and this sees to it that competition is a fundamental ingredient in any strategy.

Strategy has been applied to war and to business. Also to other activities such as propaganda. In either case, strategy takes the longer view, in contrast to *tactics* which concerns moves in the shorter term. As such, it rests on much broader concepts than tactics, having implications in many areas of activity. Additionally,

- Strategy is not an object in itself
- There are several prerequisites to strategy formulation, and
- The able execution of strategy requires careful planning.

Strategic planning goes beyond the determination of basic long-term goals and objectives. It involves the adoption of a course of action that needs to be followed, and it includes the definitions and scheduling of projected activities. It also calls for proper allocation of resources necessary for carrying out plans. Usually, though by no means always, strategic decisions and the plans following them relate to:

- Expanding, maintaining or downsizing the firm's activities
- Responding to shifting market demands and tastes
- Capitalizing on new perspectives such as deregulation, globalization, and technological developments, and
- Counteracting the actions of competitors, positioning *our* company in a way to be ahead of the curve.

Decisions to enter a new market, launch a novel product, expand the volume of business, operate internationally, or become diversified, involve strategic choices based on forecasts (see Chapter 5) which are prerequisite to any plan (Chapter 6), and execution of plans being made (Chapter 8). An example is Wal-Mart's strategic decision to enter into retail banking (see also in Chapter 11 Sam Walton's strategic choice in cost control).

Wal-Mart's strategic plan capitalizes on the synergy of its current business and its clients' banking needs. Each week, in its merchandising activities in the United States, Wal-Mart processes more than a million financial transactions. Introduced in 2001, money orders account for the larger share of this volume. Another fast-growing activity, at Wal-Mart, is paycheque cashing, launched in 2004.

At no time is a company's strategy written in black-and-white. Usually it is revealed through its decisions and actions. In February 2005, Wal-Mart joined up with Discover, the plastic money processor, to offer a credit card with a 1% cash-back on in-store purchases. Some months later, in 2005, Wal-Mart applied to open an *industrial loan company* (ILC), based in Utah.

About a century ago ILCs were originally set up in America to help industrial workers take out small loans. Now, they are a favoured route for non-banks, allowing them to get into retail banking and side-step federal restrictions on the separation of banking and commerce. The forecasting element is reflected in the fact that pending US legislation *may* allow ILCs to offer business cheque-book accounts.

In this particular strategic move the stakes are high for Wal-Mart, because it has a low-income, blue-collar clientele, much of it without bank accounts.[1] The reader should appreciate that it is precisely through moves involving a high stakes business that an entity's strategy can be revealed to the careful observer.

A similar statement is valid about tactics though, as mentioned, tactics and strategy should not be confused with one another. One of the common elements shared by business strategy and tactics is that both must be flexible and adaptable to circumstances and they should be based on clearly defined goals and unambiguous assumptions.

No matter how good a company may be in its strategic plans, their able execution requires first class organization and lines of authority (see Chapter 7). Additionally, the adoption of a new strategy may bring along the need for new business skills, different infrastructural facilities, or changes in the business horizon of the firm.

Accounting for necessary support to strategic decisions, and projecting the aftermath of strategic moves, are integral parts of the strategic planning process. Prior to explaining objectives in concrete terms, and way ahead of developing long-term policies or establishing milestone plans, management should ask itself crucial questions:

- What do we want to reach?
- How can we go from 'here' to 'there'?
- What's *our* strategy for doing so?
- What are the goals and strategy of our opponents?
- Can our strategy overtake them? At what cost?
- What will be the reward if we are successful?
- Can we grow our resources so that we are able to support the strategic plan we are making?

These questions have to be answered in a factual and documented manner, prior to even thinking about possible strategic moves. It is not easy to provide such responses, and this is one of the reasons why strategy is the exercise of skill and forethought which, quite often, involves artifice but always requires first class governance of the enterprise.

2. Strategic plans must be dynamic: case study with General Electric

The fact that strategy is a master plan against an opponent means that strategic moves are not a list of individual actions. The able execution of a strategy requires synergy among all its component parts. It also needs worst-case scenarios, accounting for smart future moves of competition to counteract *our* strategy. Therefore, risk forecasting and risk management are basic ingredients of any strategic plan.

Every strategic plan involves risk, particularly so the plan of a company targeting its industry's No. 1 position. In the early years of Japan's calculator industry, Sharp had been the leading manufacturer, producing 34% of all calculators made in Japan. In the mid-1960s, Casio had only 10% of Japan's calculator market, but its management increased its production capacity and model variety while slashing its prices.

- Sharp grew at 100% per year,
- Casio grew at almost 200% per year.

Eight years down the line, by 1973, Casio had achieved the leading position in Japan, with 35% of the Japanese production of electronic calculators. Sharp's share had slid to 17%. The board and senior executives of a company whose market is growing at 200% a year must plan to triple production capacity *every year* just to maintain a competitive position.

- The original one plant must become three by year's end, and
- Three times three equals nine by next year's end, at least in terms of capacity (more on risk in section 5).

In order to establish the proper business perspective, elaborate ambitious but doable goals, and enable themselves to take sound, well-documented strategic decisions, the leaders of industry, commerce, and finance must be able to carry along the organization over which they preside. This should be achieved in spite of resistance by some of its members. Strategic plans cannot succeed without wider organizational support. Neither can they be successful if they fail to adopt a holistic approach to:

- Strategic planning premises, and
- Their effective, timely execution.

This is particularly important in a multidivisional or transnational organization where, typically, centrifugal forces are very strong. Every decision-maker should realize that in any company of a certain size there is no purely local, self-contained strategy. Neither does there exist a purely financial or purely marketing strategy. The need for a master plan sees to it that strategy is global and polyvalent, or there is no strategy to speak about.

Neither is it enough that strategy is based on clear vision and unambiguous choices. It is also necessary that all component parts come together in a harmonious aggregate. When management cannot make up its mind in terms of some of the goals, products or markets, there can be no success in strategy formulation and execution. Additionally, a strategy that is flexible and adaptable:

- Leaves no time for distraction by trivialities
- Helps senior management to concentrate on essentials
- Makes feasible a greater harmony of effort, because the goal is dynamic
- Sees to it that everything fits together in a comprehensive picture, and
- Assures that every contributor is playing his or her full part as a member of a team.

Even if companies feel more comfortable in keeping on the beaten track, their management should appreciate that sooner or later the law of unforeseen consequences will inevitably kick in. The flexible strategy that has been followed over the years by General Electric is an excellent example of what the board, CEO, and senior management must be doing in positioning the company against market forces.

- In the 1960s the GE strategy was defence contracting, which fuelled the company's growth.
- In the 1970s GE focused on its strengths and dropped unprofitable lines, like computers.
- In the 1980s it kept ahead of the curve by embedding microprocessors into its products.
- In the 1990s financial services took on the role of motor, propelling the company's turnover.
- In 2005 and beyond, GE's new strategy is *ecomagination*, which top management believes will develop into a lucrative business.

Ecomagination stands for ecological products and services that target both energy conservation and control of pollution. This new GE strategy is based on the prognostication that the company can double its revenues by betting on 17 well-defined clean technologies. These range from renewable energy to water purification systems, as well as cleaner aircraft and locomotive engines.

To get there, General Electric's management is doubling research spending on clean products, from $700 million per year to $1.5 billion, by 2010. This is a documentation of the fact that new strategy, as well as strategic switches, must be backed up by capital. GE can easily afford that increase in R&D expenditure as, most recently, its current total research budget stands at only 2% of revenues. In 2004, it was $3.1 billion with revenues of $152.4 billion.

The impact of this strategic switch in the company's priorities goes way beyond R&D. To become a leader in ecomagination and reach its goals, GE must radically transform itself and change its culture. The crucial question therefore is whether it can really transform its current approach to innovation, which has concentrated mostly on incremental improvements of well-understood products and their technologies. As a new strategy, ecomagination will be pursuing:

- Riskier objectives, and
- Less-proven technologies, like energy and hydrogen storage.

The challenge is not just one of business forecasting and of technological R&D, but also of human capital and of marketing. If IBM's experience in a strategic switch from electrical accounting machines (EAM) to computers is any guide,[2] GE will have not just to retrain but also to:

- Largely renew its sales engineering force, and
- Provide an interim solution of support to current sales engineers, like IBM did in the mid-1950s with the Applied Science department.

For many years environmentally friendly products have been a risk market. This is no longer true. During the past few years they have become *unique products*, a graduation in marketing perspective which is illustrated in Figure 1.1. (Chapter 15 discusses in detail the meaning of niche, unique product, and mass market – as well as their requirements.) Ecomagination eventually targets the mass market where:

- The sales potential is great
- But competition is tough, with innovation, quality, and *cost* being the keys to success.

To succeed in its first strategic switch of the 21st century, General Electric needs to excel in all factors stated in the second bullet. And it will also have to convince the financial community about the wisdom of its new strategy and its business prospects. This may not be too difficult.

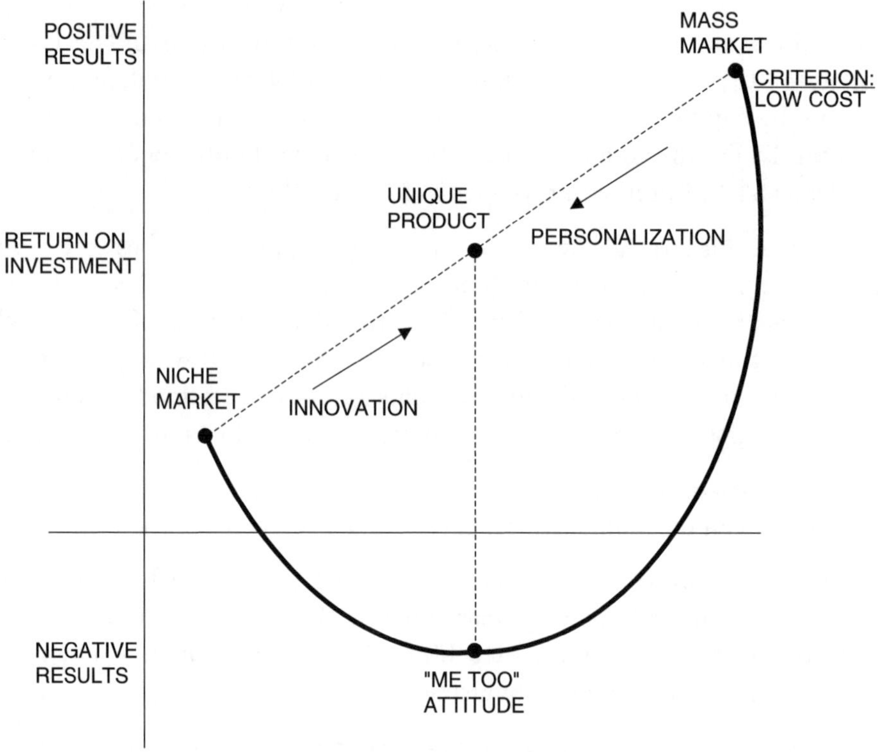

Figure 1.1 With ecomagination products and services General Electric is targeting a highly competitive mass market

According to one recent article in *The Economist*, Deane Dray of Goldman Sachs, the investment bank, endorses GE's business opportunity projections: 'Every one of the ecomagination initiatives looks commercially viable, even without the green angle,' says Dray.[3] Under the heading 'Rich Pickings', the same issue of *The Economist* suggests that US environmental industry revenues may reach $300 billion by 2010, of which:

- About 45% will be in services
- Some 35% will be in resource recovery and clean power, and
- The balance will be in all sorts of equipment serving the environmental planning and control sector.

Many of the products and services in every one of these sectors still waits to be invented; hence the R&D money. After that, it must be manufactured, sold, delivered, installed, and maintained at affordable cost. Provided the business opportunity projections are right, ecomagination might prove to be one of the most lucrative markets that have been imagined, developed, and exploited. This, however, is not certain. Therefore, the switch exemplifies the risk embedded in any strategy.

3. Main components of a business strategy: case study with Hewlett–Packard

If, as stated in the Introduction, strategy targets the longer term, *then* the question arises how, by means of current strategic moves, companies can secure long-term competitive advantages. The answer is that one of the major contributions of strategic planning is in positioning against market forces (see Chapter 3). The risk is that projected effects of a longer-term plan may be short-lived because:

- The business environment changes too fast, and
- Companies must steadily adjust to their unique circumstances, which requires first-class governance.

This is the Harvard Business School thesis, which further states that adjustments to strategic plans should not be haphazard. Strategic planning must be based on an organizational principle expressed by the so-called *experience curve*. What experience teaches is that the more a firm knows about its market, the more it can be in charge of its destiny.

Critics of the Harvard thesis say that the principle of the experience curve works only *if* we appreciate that needed knowledge and experience engender many crucial components which must be properly and timely developed. Because strategy is a *master plan* against one or more opponents, it has several important ingredients that must be nourished and made to work in synergy. In the majority of cases, strategic planning would integrate a plethora of issues relating to both *our* and our competitors':

1. Clients
2. Employees
3. Products
4. Markets
5. Financial, and
6. Technology.

As Solon (640–560 BC), the lawmaker of ancient Athens, was told by the Egyptian priests, whom he visited in his research on legal systems in the then-known world, there are too few really old men who can remember crucial points of the continuing, living history of humanity – particularly issues that, in their recurring present incarnation, are still shaping the world in which we live. This statement is just as valid in business and industry.

The experience curve is an empty shell without remembering crucial events of the continuing, living history of law, society at large, and of business. Sometimes experience is only imaginary or superficial, based on an exchange of opinions. At UCLA, Dr Harold D. Koontz, one of the best professors I ever had, often used to say that 30 years' experience is nothing more than 1 year's experience repeated 30 times.

This is Mandarin philosophy, and the emptying up of an experience curve. Real experience is based on a large number of actions and facts that can be analysed, tracked to their origin, studied in terms of their aftermath, explained, and critically discussed. That is why case studies are so vital to a book on strategy – and yet, while important, they are no substitute to real life experience.

People with real business experience appreciate that at any time, at any place, each of the main components of a strategy is confronted by limits to growth, which could be overcome only through a most significant effort, if at all. With Carly Fiorina at the helm, Hewlett–Packard (HP) grew to become an $80 billion enterprise, but at the end the CEO's strategic plan failed, and Fiorina lost her job. Critics say HP was:

- Simply trying to do too much too fast, and
- It lacked both resources and management skills to compete with the best of the best in nearly every technology sector it was present.

Critics also add that one of the risks Carly Fiorina should not have taken was that of misjudging HP's opponents. 'We have reckoned without the energy and guile of the old warrior. Perhaps we were unlucky. Perhaps maladroit,' said Jean Monnet, the French banker and 'father of Europe', after losing the fight for Bank of America to Amadeo P. Giannini – who had built up from scratch the institution and mastered the shareholders' loyalty.

Additionally, insiders suggest that, during her reign, Carly Fiorina continued to blame HP's woes on the company's culture rather than on prevailing severe management shortcomings. 'She didn't develop enough effective lieutenants,' said Stephen P. Mader, vice-chairman of Christian & Timbers, the headhunting firm that recruited Fiorina into HP.[4]

Employees and clients are a company's human resources. The chief executive should know them in depth, because knowing them is like knowing himself or herself. Nevertheless many entities don't always appreciate the importance of taking good care of their employees and clients and neither do they appreciate the wisdom of steady product development to satisfy demanding clients, although

- This sort of failure is very costly, and
- In the longer run it tears apart even the best business strategy.

Some years ago, I heard Christopher Reeves, then CEO of Morgan Grenfell merchant bank, say: 'Clients want to deal with people with original ideas. So new rules have to be created. We must not believe that rules are written in tablets of stone.' The people with original ideas are the entity's professionals and managers. Market perspectives should dictate the new rules:

- New products should be made for our chosen market(s), and
- Marketing strategies must be selected with plenty of attention paid to our competitors' strengths and weaknesses.

Moreover, it should be obvious that we cannot treat all our clients in the same manner, because they don't have the same needs, and they don't offer the same rewards. Neither do all of our products have the potential of providing the same return. But how many companies have studied, let alone established, a clear differentiation policy? How often do industrial and financial organizations take the proverbial long, hard look in examining their strategic decisions along the three-dimensional frame of reference shown in Figure 1.2?

Maybe Carly Fiorina failed in turning around Hewlett–Packard because it did not apply the dictum of the ancient Greek philosophers: 'Know yourself'; or at least she did not do so in a company-wide sense. Do we know what our people are

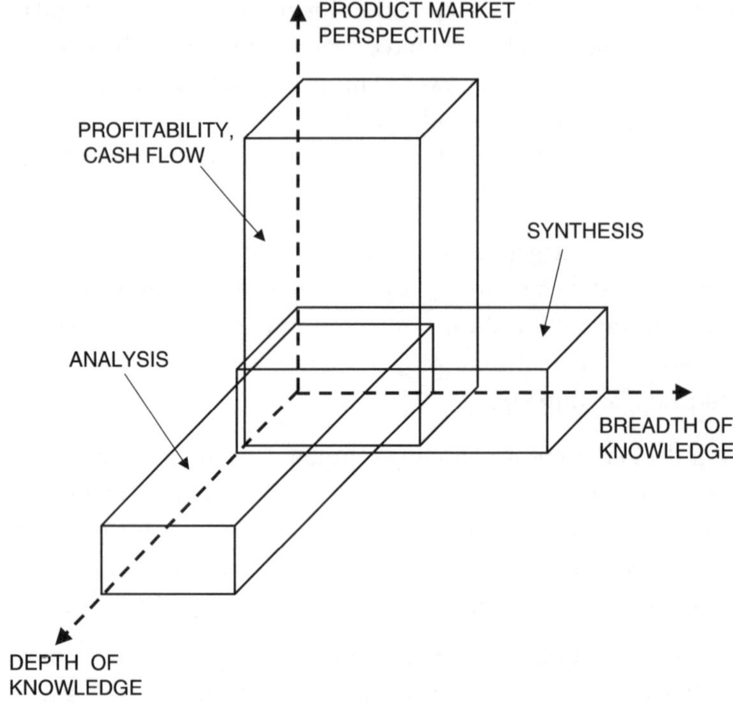

Figure 1.2 Strategy formulation, planning, and execution must be examined in a three-dimensional way

worth? Which are their competitive advantages? What is their contribution to *our* company's market appeal? Or, our products' profit margin? Their future costs? Their risks?

Applied to business, industry, and banking 'know yourself' means fully appreciating *why* our products and services are superior to those of our competitors. What exactly is our risk and reward when we sell them? What is the risk and reward competitors face with their products, which compete with ours? How much can we depend on *our* people to promote *our* business in the longer run? (We will be talking of human resources in Chapter 7, financial planning in Chapter 9, new product development in Chapter 14, and of the importance of markets and marketing in Chapter 15).

In relative, though never in absolute, terms the experience curve in an organization can be beefed up through an advanced technological infrastructure. Therefore, an integral part of a strategic plan is the attention to be paid to modernization of the company's infrastructure, which can be instrumental in maintaining its competitiveness. In a modern business environment the information system has at all times to be kept:

- Flexible
- Cost-effective, and
- Enriched with knowledge engineering.

As far as the infrastructure is concerned, the approach we adopt should allow migration into new solutions without having to improvise or reinvent in a rush. Projects in information systems and communications should not be done in a risky manner, or because 'that's what others are doing'. What others are doing is often at the bleeding edge. In this as in any other domain, a good project is when we can do with $1 a job for which our competitors need $2 and $3.

At the same time, however, high technology is not a goal but an enabling tool to support *our* strategic plans and reach *our* goals. Something similar can be said about financial resources. In principle, a company with innovative, low cost but high quality products, and with market appeal, does not have to be worried about finances, as Dr Louis Sorel, my professor of business strategy at UCLA, taught his students. On the other hand, Louis XIV, France's Sun King, used to say: 'The last Louis wins the war.'

By contrast, human resources, products, and markets are basic objectives that must be properly planned and developed. Andrew Carnegie, the Scottish-American king of the steel industry, was once asked if he would rather lose all his factories or all his people – and he answered: All my factories, because if I have my people I would rebuild the organization.

4. Positioning our Firm against market forces: an example with Cisco

The Introduction defined strategy as a master plan against an opponent. A master plan requires the exercise of skill, forethought, and artifice in carrying out specific plans to reach established goals. Strategic moves involve the interaction of two or more persons or entities. Each party's actions are based on a certain expectation of moves by the other party or parties, over which the first has no control. This more detailed definition of business strategy contains the three elements that set its plans apart from other plans, moves or actions:

- First, it states that it is a *master plan* not just a list of independent actions.

- Second, it contains the word *against*, hence, it involves competition which, as we saw, is a basic ingredient in any strategy.
- Third, it involves an *opponent*, another person, group, or organization, without which the competitive situation could not exist.

Taken together, these three elements lead towards a fairly complex system of approaches necessary for accomplishing objectives. Because of required foresight and sophistication, strategic concepts and plans are brought forward only by higher level organizations that have experience, and can present superior thinking as well as ability and ingenuity. An integral part of this ingenuity is information and intelligence, necessary to position *our* firm against *market forces.*

To a very significant extent, positioning ourselves against the forces of our competitors involves a number of tough choices that largely have to do with products and prices, as well as quality and marketability of these products. Take as an example Cisco, which has generally been considered a well-managed company. By late 2005, however, many analysts said it might have painted itself into a corner because of the dual aims which it targets.

- It can pursue either growth or profits, but
- It cannot do both at the same time because this would be like killing two birds with one, well-aimed stone.

Failure to choose between conflicting strategic goals may mark any entity's downturn. Some analysts suggest that Cisco finds itself at this crossroads. While in early 2005, John T. Chambers, Cisco's CEO, laid out a plan to boost revenues as much as 15% per year until 2008, a couple of quarters down the line it looked *as if* the company fell short of that mark. And this could continue unless it makes up its mind as to what is its top strategic goal.

- Cisco could target new markets, and slash prices in several markets to gain share and boost its top line.

This, however, will cut sharply into the company's current rich margins, which averaged 68% in 2004, and have been a key factor in boosting the price of its stock in that same year, even if Cisco pays no dividend.

- Or, with an estimated $16.5 billion in cash, it could pursue a policy of larger, aggressive acquisitions, as it did in the 1990s.

The challenge with this alternative strategy is that it would have to be adopted at the cost of the bottom line, which Cisco did not seem to be ready to do. Alternatively, management could give up the notion that Cisco is a hot-growth company, and start acting like a stable firm with steady cash flow, paying dividends to investors as Microsoft did. But this seemed to be anathema to its CEO.

Decisions of the type confronting Chambers are not 'one year' events. They have the nasty habit of showing up time and again; and they have long-term impact and repercussions. Because strategy addresses the longer term, Cisco's CEO has to position his firm against the forces of the next 5, 10, and 15 years. To do so, he must raise his eyes above day-to-day commitments, and face broader responsibilities affecting the company's future:

- Prognosticating the communications market's evolution
- Establishing and explaining further out-company objectives
- Defining long-term policies and milestone plans, and
- Guaranteeing a product's stream, cash flow, and continuing profitability, which is transparent to the market.

Practically every company faces the challenges outlined in these four bullets, and for every entity a properly studied and clearly established strategy is absolutely necessary in terms of market positioning and products offered to the market. This is a basic business principle, equally valid with both start-ups and long-established firms.

To a very significant extent, market positioning is inseparable from the able management of change. As centuries ago Heraclitos, the ancient Greek philosopher, said: 'Nothing is permanent. Nothing is a universal principle, but the intention expressed by an underlying principle of universal change.' Swiss Re, the Swiss reinsurer, applied this concept to the insurance industry. Most specifically to:

- The driving forces of the insurance industry's globalization, and
- The need for efficient management of change, in order to be ahead of the curve.

The results of the Swiss Re study are shown in a nutshell in Figure 1.3. The focal point is removal of barriers to market entry by insurers. As the reader can appreciate, the study focused on both push forces and pull factors which impact on market positioning, each one of these forces exemplified by its three major factors.

A different example, along the same frame of reference, is the making of strategic management decisions pivotal to the company's future evolution. After a soul-searching examination of strategic options, which took place in 1977, Bankers Trust decided to sell its network of branch offices in the State of New York, and concentrate on corporate banking. This decision was taken after a

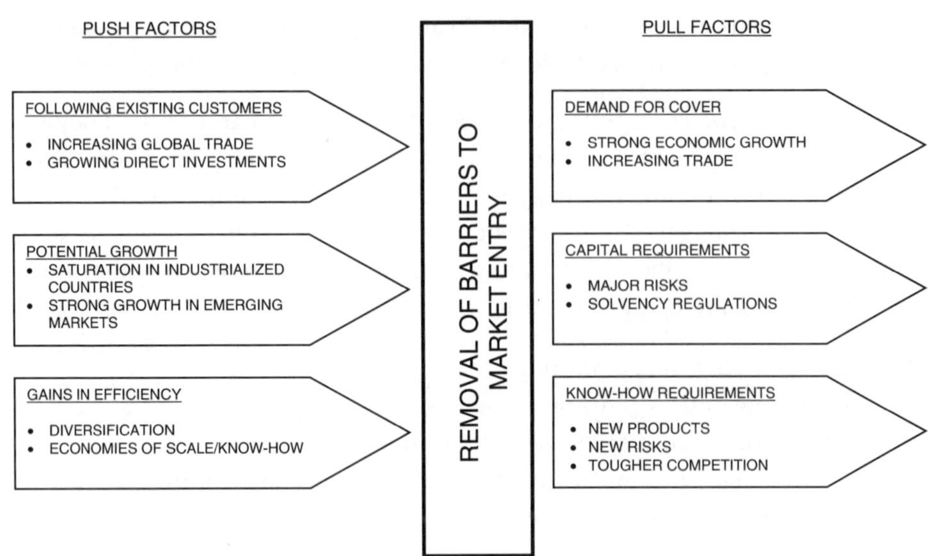

Figure 1.3 The driving forces of globalization in the insurance industry increase the need for able management of change (Swiss Re, *Sigma* No. 4/2000, by permission)

well-founded study, which documented that the bank was spreading thin its human and financial resources in trying to renew, restructure, and automate both

- Its retail branch offices, and
- Its corporate network addressing the wholesale business.

It is not easy to decide that part of the company has to be sold, but quite often in real life survival requires concentration rather than expansion. This Bankers Trust reference is also an excellent example of how and why strategic planning should precede investment decisions in all lines of business, including infrastructural issues related to computers and communications.

As section 3 has briefly shown, decisions about infrastructural renewal lead to financial commitments, and only tier-1 companies know how to control *investment risks*. The majority throw money to the wrong cause. Even if the technical study is sound, without pre-decided strategic options managerial decisions concerning infrastructural (or any other) investments will be misguided. Let's always keep in mind that when we are talking about investments in technology,

- We are not speaking about peanuts to feed the monkeys, and
- No matter what 'the trend' may be, we want to have a return for these investments.

Companies that are not able to assure good profitability, and associated cash flow, get lost in the dust of industrial history. Survival can never, ever, be taken for granted. Of the top 100 American industrial companies ranked in the early 1910s, the large majority have disappeared or have been taken over by other firms. Nearly a century down the line only one survives at the top of the list of US industrial enterprises: General Electric.

With innovation, deregulation, globalization and fast advancing technology, what companies need to position themselves into the market is to *gain recognition*. That requires development and marketing of products that the rest of the industry does not have. Novel products and services designed for a demanding market are key elements of strategic planning. No company can be a leader in all fields of activity, but if it is a laggard, this means that it has made the wrong bets.

5. The cost of doing business and of staying in business: risk is a cost

Good governance sees to it that strategic decisions are tested and evaluated prior to commitment through *simulation* and *scenario analysis*, as well as post-mortem by means of *walkthroughs* involving real life results. As is to be expected, such results are conditioned not only by the quality of the strategic plan, but also by *our* ability to implement it, the steadily changing business opportunities, and our competitors' moves. Hence the wisdom of repeatedly asking the questions:

- Can *our* strategy take advantage of new business opportunities?
- What sort of changes happened to the strategy of our opponents?
- Can our strategy cope with them under current and projected market perspectives?
- If not, what should we do to regain the high ground?

The message conveyed by these bullets is a different way of saying that every strategic plan must be sensitive to market factors, beyond current conditions that might change at a moment's notice. Strategic planners should always ask themselves:

- Is there an ongoing change in the market and its drivers?
- Which may be the more significant market shifts next year? In the 2–5 coming years?
- Are we equipped to confront these shifts? What should we do to improve our market position? Our products?

In the late 1970s, Walter Wriston, then CEO of Citibank, asked himself these questions and the strategic solutions he established gave a big boost to his institution. The results are documented through four years of statistics shown in Figure 1.4. Wriston applied in a masterly way the advice of his predecessor, who, when he chose him for the top job, had told him: Be brave to scare Chase, but not so brave to scare me.

To be able to follow a holistic approach which puts all costs and risks in perspective, and therefore improves corporate governance, all levels of management must be equipped with appropriate tools, which are easy to use and work in real-time. An example is Internet-based *dashboards*, putting executives in immediate and interactive touch with their business.

- They display critical information in user-friendly graphics, and
- Their deliverables are assembled in real-time from corporate databases, using knowledge-enriched software.

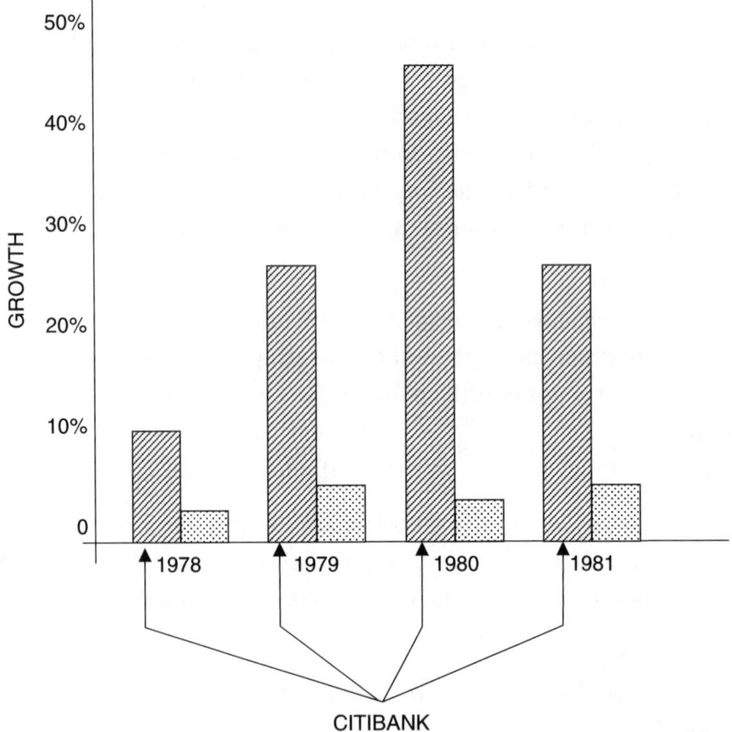

Figure 1.4 Planning for growth. Citibank *vs* the total banking market in New York in the late 1970s/early 1980s

Dashboard implementations have shown that the more successful real-time applications of executive information systems are those guided by managers and professionals. In terms of accuracy and update, the results are only as useful as the database behind them.

A holistic approach to product and market challenges sees to it that focused, critical questions have to be asked about every product or service: Which are the strengths and weaknesses of each of our products? Which are the strengths and weaknesses of our salesmen? Are we aware of where we lag behind? Are we capitalizing on our strengths? Where can we do better? Are we ready to exploit developing business opportunities? Can we accelerate their appearance? How can this be realized?

If an industrial, commercial or financial organization fails to take *immediate* advantage of its products and services, the market will pass it by. Management must always keep in mind that in an environment of fierce competition the market will not pay 'any price' for the products it needs. It will search for alternatives, and choose those which are more cost-effective. In a highly competitive environment only:

- The lower cost producer
- With top performance products, and
- A well thought-out strategic plan, can survive.

The cost to which reference has been made is not only that associated to production and sales. Able management is keen to differentiate between the cost of *doing business*, and the cost of *staying in business*. Direct labour, direct material, depreciation, amortization are examples of cost of doing business on the production side. Other examples are the marketing and sales costs, as well as overheads (see also the references made in Chapter 11).

The cost of staying in business is more complex and non-traditional. When it first appeared in management practice, in the years following World War II, it mainly related to the company's ability for innovation, and its research and development (R&D) budget (see the reference to GE in section 2, also the R&D examples in Chapter 14). More recently, a huge new factor has appeared, which can be expressed in two bullets:

- Risk being assumed in a transaction, and
- The control of inventoried exposures in the longer term.

Though there is a tendency to associate risk-taking only with transactions made by financial institutions, risk is an integral part of any business. In manufacturing and merchandising, for example, particularly among upper-medium size to bigger firms, treasuries run their department for profits. This is a far cry from the job of the treasurer taught at UCLA in the 1950s.

Management culture concerning *risk and its control* is at the crossroads of major change. What the board, CEO, senior executives, and all managers down the line should appreciate, is that today risk is taken in connection to every transaction and every position inventoried in the portfolio, no matter which the firm may be. *Risk is a cost.* We must stop thinking of risk as being balanced by return.

- Risk is the cost of yesterday when the commitment was made, and
- It is the cost of tomorrow; to be revealed at the transaction's maturity.

While accounting standards like US GAAP[5] and IFRS oblige companies to mark to market their assets, the risk so revealed is only an interim solution. Only when the marked position is extinct will we know for sure what has been its profit and loss (P&L). In the interim, however, the new accounting standards see to it that assumed risk is monetized.

Risk is an integral part of strategic business planning. In 1989, the Swiss Bank Corporation (SBC), which was at the time the third largest Swiss credit institution, set down a long-term strategy dubbed 'Vision 2000'. This strategy took a business view that was right on target – that capital markets of the 1990s would be driven by:

- Derivative financial instruments, and
- Risk management products.

SBC prospered greatly by capitalizing on this strategy. In less than ten years it absorbed the Union Bank of Switzerland (UBS), which was the top-most Swiss credit institution. (SBC and the old UBS have merged into United Bank of Switzerland – the new UBS – see the case study in Chapter 20).

Senior management should furthermore appreciate that the risk related to portfolio positions is not the only element that has joined R&D expenditures in the chapter of costs of staying in business. Malfeasance, severe professional errors, lack of ethics, and related-party transactions are other examples of risk-taking in daily business practices.

In 2002, Arthur Andersen, then one of the Big Five international auditing firms, disappeared from the business scene because of its involvement in the Enron debacle, the Baptist Foundation scandal, and some other scams.[6] As case after case demonstrates, limiting the cost of staying in business requires the presence of policies and mechanisms which assure that:

- Internal control is able to flush out and bring to the board's attention deviations from standards, and
- Senior management is willing and able to take immediate corrective action, rather than looking the other way in cases of malfeasance, or even condone them.

Much of the weight that sank Arthur Andersen was scams embedded in third party transactions. A recent publication by Fitch Ratings, the independent rating agency, has this to say on related party transactions: '[they] are a governance concern if their underlying purpose is to benefit the related part at the expense of the company's interests. Therefore, an important safeguard against potential abuse is for the company to assure such transactions are:

- Negotiated at arm's length
- Priced at competitive market terms, and
- Serve a viable economic purpose, (rather than) exploitative or fraudulent purpose(s).'[7]

To be in charge, and minimize that part of the cost of staying in business, senior management should consider whether the related party had any direct or indirect role in negotiating the terms of a deal on behalf of the company. Equally important is to critically evaluate the terms and conditions of the deal to see if they are negotiated at arm's length, or consistent with market pricing. Also, if they comply to:

- Company policies, and
- Regulatory rules and directives

The answers to be given to the challenging questions presented by business life should be subjected to an evaluation of their effect on the longer-term survival of the firm, not only on the shorter-term bottom line. What kind of profit and loss figures can we draw from an objective analysis of business opportunities is, and will remain, a most valid query. Additionally, such answers should not obscure the fact that hidden future cost can destroy the company even if current costs are contained and transparent.

6. Standards setting, added value, and strategic planning

The way an old adage has it: 'Work hard, and everything else will work out.' That is always true, but apart from working hard, we must also work intelligently, and be able to move ahead by establishing a name in the market, as well as having products that get solid acceptance. As a business case, solid acceptance by the market underpins the process through which 'de facto standards' are born.

A good example is the Toshiba/Time Warner video recording standard DVD, established in the mid-1990s. In the war of de facto standards for home entertainment, DVD has been most successful, while technical solutions advanced by Sony and Philips faltered, not because they were wrong but because they did not catch the market's eye and mind. The four topmost points characterizing the winners are that Toshiba and Time Warner did the right thing when they:

- Pushed the technology envelope to 10 billion bytes of storage
- Wooed other electronics companies with open licensing
- Prioritized films and games over computer applications, and
- Courted Hollywood aggressively, through an ad hoc advisory group.

Among themselves, these four points characterize the successful strategy used by Toshiba/Time Warner to win market control. Notice DVD is not the first de facto standard for home entertainment; it is the third. Its predecessor as first standard was the music cassette, and the winner was Philips. But Philips became big-headed, and lost the opportunity to establish the second home entertainment de facto standard, that for the video cassette. Its bet failed even if its technology was ahead of that of its competitors.

The winner with the video cassette was Hitachi's VHS, which carried the day against Sony's Betamax and Philips' technology because both companies lost the market's attention. In the second and third big battles for home entertainment de facto standards, wrong decisions haunted the losers, and led them to strategic blunders. Specifically in DVD's case, Sony and Philips followed a bumpy road by:

- Sacrificing capacity for compatibility with existing discs
- Slowing the development of their high capacity digital videodisc prototype
- Boasting of future recording capability, thereby raising copyright fears in Hollywood, and
- Presenting Hollywood with finished specs, instead of seeking advice.

In the strategy chosen by Toshiba/Time Warner, the 10 billion bytes of storage have been an *added value* which helped to sell the DVD project to potential users. Handholding with electronics companies and Hollywood provided the other players with the opportunity to appreciate the de facto standard in the making. Even so, its marketing might not have had a happy ending if there was no value differentiation associated to it.

The added value provided by the Toshiba/Time Warner solution should be a lesson. Classical banking products, for instance, are offered by almost every financial organization, as well as by non-banks (that is financial institutions outside regulatory control of the banking industry). This raises the question *what more* do we offer by way of added value? In the majority of cases, to answer this question in an able manner we must rethink the nature and role of *our* products and services. Added value is promoted through:

- Innovation in functionality
- High quality of service
- Low cost production, therefore competitive prices
- Very efficient marketing and client handholding.

As the DVD standard demonstrates, the added value which we embed into products and services can keep our company ahead of competition. Success in business is not just a matter of luck. 'Luck', a proverb says, 'is what happens when preparation meets opportunity.' The market provides many opportunities. But are we prepared to take advantage of them? Are we ready to turn on a dime to reach the business opportunity where it shows up?

Koji Kobayashi, former chairman of NEC, characterized as follows the process necessary for renewal, value differentiation, and management of change: It is important to create *stability within instability*. The goal of instability is to keep employees on their toes. Confronted with stiffening competition, we must make a new order to create wealth, says Kobayashi. To a substantial extent:

- This 'new order' is the result of a company reinventing itself and its products.
- But at the same time, the 'new order' is always subject to the law of unwanted consequences.

This is true both of enterprises and of the economy as a whole. After the reconstruction effort which followed World War II was over, industrial society gave way to post-industrial society. This largely took place in the 1980s, while in the 1990s, the *new economy* postulated novel criteria for global competition, including the axiom that adding value to financial instruments creates wealth.

Subsequently, the 21st century advanced the hypothesis that *service jobs* have more added value than manufacturing, further promoting the externalization of industrial activities. This led to a sharp reduction in industrial employment, down to 17% in Group of Ten (G-10) countries, while before World War II it stood well above 50%.

These are macroeconomic type changes, which have an evident impact on strategic plans established by enterprises. One of the major changes that has come with globalization is that companies in Western countries have lost pricing power. Any management that forgets this fact is in for trouble. Here is a practical example. Auchan, the French hypermarket, sells side-by-side two travel bags which look identical, both in construction and in quality.

- One is made in France and its price tag is 30 euro ($35).
- The other is made in China and sells for 7 euro ($8.3)

Guess which of these practically identical products most attracts the consumer's eye. It is not that the French travel bag manufacturers are greedy. Rather the raw material and labour costs they face in their country of origin (the latter augmented by an inordinate amount of social costs) are uncompetitive. To survive, and be able to compete with the Chinese in the *French* consumer market, French travel bag manufacturers are obliged to produce their goods in China.

- Travel bags are not high tech products whose added value is in steady innovation.
- The added value of common, bread-and-butter type products is the lower and lower price tag.

Not only bags but also Chinese textiles at large are a case in point, because China Inc. bought the best spinning machines and other equipment it could find in the United States, UK, France, Germany and Italy. Additionally, China Inc. trained its people in using these machines and then, capitalizing on the new rules of world trade, it flooded the Western markets with very low cost but rather good quality textiles.

As far as the Western companies are concerned, this has been a fairly significant failure in strategic planning. It is not the only type of failure, as we will see in section 7. This simple example talks a lot about what underpins the process of *outsourcing*.[8] Since the 1990s, industrial countries have become net outsourcers of labour-intensive jobs, while countries with an educated workforce, but low wages, offered themselves as *insourcers*.

Within this globalized outsourcing/insourcing environment, what high technology companies have done as a matter of policy is to keep the most advanced features of their products, as well as system assembly operations, in their country of origin. In high tech, these are the elements representing added value and a competitive edge. The rest, which in some cases is 85% of production or more, has been outsourced, often with questionable results in terms of target quality – or direct competition, which might develop some years down the line.

7. Reasons why strategic plans fail

A management failure lies behind every other failure connected to strategic business planning, as well as to day-to-day operations. For instance, this failure may be found in our product's obsolescence, or high cost. It could equally be of financial nature due to shortcomings in cash flow forecasts, or low credit rating, making it difficult to obtain loans. Moreover, management:

- May be unable to cope with uncertainties and market turbulence
- Fail to protect and grow economic resources, or have other shortcomings.

Alternatively, there may exist a major failure in marketing strategy connected to how to identify the growth part of our market, and develop a plan to reach it. Or, it may be a failure in business alliances as well as in outsourcing, because the company has not been able to establish what could be the services it could delegate to third parties. Other failures regard more generally products and services offered to the market, including:

- How to price them
- How to support them, and
- How to maintain a high quality, low cost position.

Still other failures often encountered in strategic business plans are of human resources type. For instance, how to identify and recruit key members of the management team, and how to train the organization's human capital to assure steady renewal and upgrade of know-how. There are also leadership failures, such as lack of impetus for keeping operations vibrant.

Tolstoy, the great Russian author, once wrote that every family feeling miserable is miserable in its own way. Paraphrasing this dictum, every company that fails in strategic planning is failing in its own way. Still, there are some more general background reasons for failures in business planning. The foremost which I have found in my practice are:

1. Lack of skill

This ranges from pure ineptness, to managerial and professional obsolescence. Also under lack of skill comes inability to focus and explore opportunities for able execution of a strategic plan. Nothing short of *lifelong learning* can correct this shortcoming.

2. Unclear objectives

These come in many forms. One of them is contradictory goals set by management; or goals that cannot be achieved at the same time. In practically every case, obscure or fuzzy goals suggest a senior management that has not sorted out its priorities, or what it wishes to accomplish.

3. Lack of market sensitivity

Past successes may mean that many big companies become blind of changes taking place in the marketplace, the shift in client requirements, and new competitors showing up. Yet strategy is a master plan against corporate opponents, and an integral part of it is positioning *our* company against market forces.

4. Product obsolescence

Many companies allow their product line to decay, either because of lack of market intelligence, too little investment in R&D effort, a cosy policy of being too late in bringing new products to the market, or by promoting products and services that simply cannot compete in terms of cost-effectiveness.

5. Low technology

Only top tier firms appreciate that, no matter what might be its product line, in a large number of cases the modern company is technology in motion. As a result, laggards fail to match the technology of their competitors, and this puts them at great disadvantage in terms of innovation, effectiveness, cash flow, profitability, or simply in dollars and cents terms.

Because technology moves so fast, being ahead of the curve opens up market perspectives. This is one more reason why management must be steadily on the alert. For instance, if we have a good production system but do not update it, it will become inefficient surprisingly fast. This will lead to a labour-intensive production floor compared to that of our competitors:

- Increasing our cost structure, and
- Making our products uncompetitive.

To determine the guidelines they should apply in developing a strategic perspective, Peter Drucker, one of the fathers of modern management, asks senior executives the question: 'What business are you in?' This pushes the executives he is talking to to critically examine their job. Another Drucker query is: 'What do you need to do your business better?', followed by: 'How can you translate to yourself the market information which you get?'

While these are mainly product-and-market oriented questions, answers given to them help to uncover a lot of human factors entering into decision-making. A straight human factor query is: 'Where are you going to be a year from now? In two years? In five years? In ten years?' It is surprising how few people can give a straight answer – mainly because they have not sorted out their priorities and their objectives.

Yet, to move from 'here' to 'there', from where we are now to where we should be 5 or 10 years hence, we must have in place a first-class process of selecting priorities, and of managing change. The problem is that the management of change is a process that runs contrary to the fact that many people and companies have fallen in love with the status quo.

Executives who made a name for themselves 'as turnaround artists' know from their personal experience that the only way for a company to survive is to overcome 50 years of management tradition in as many months. This cannot be done without strategic guidelines. Therefore, one of the first priorities in any turnaround effort is to establish a business planning process with appropriate guidelines that tell what should be done when:

- Competition toughens
- Protective barriers fall, and
- Business moves faster than ever before.

Equally important is to realize that strategic planning is not a linear process that can be relegated to underlings. Apart from requiring top management attention, and significant time contributions, strategic business planning involves primarily top management responsibilities: Setting objectives, collecting facts, ascertaining causes and effects, elaborating possibilities, developing alternative solutions, choosing among these alternatives, and outlining course(s) of action after assuring that they fit overall strategy.

Additionally, senior managers should appreciate that the relation between strategic plans and courses of action to be taken is two-way. The reason is that strategies have a great influence on operating decisions – and vice versa. Therefore, the possible aftermath of any decision must be examined in advance. Lightly studied strategic and tactical moves would have:

- Few of the results we want
- Many of the effects we do not want, and
- Plenty of other outcomes we do not know about.

In conclusion, top management leadership in strategic planning is not an option; it is a 'must'. Direct involvement by the board and CEO should determine not only laconic objectives but also such factors as quality and quantity of human resources, timetables of accomplishment, the nature of results to be obtained and, most evidently, the funding of plans and programmes. All this must be accomplished both in qualitative and quantitative terms.

8. Precious advice by Sun Tzu, Patton, and Walton: case study on AT&T

Two thousand five hundred years ago Sun Tzu, the great Chinese statesman and general, said: 'If you know yourself and know your enemy, you will not have to fear the outcome of one hundred battles.'[9] But then he added: 'To win one hundred victories is not the acme of skill. To subdue the enemy without fighting is the supreme excellence.' Two lessons can be learned from Sun Tzu's dual dictum:

- Invincibility depends on oneself, and
- Our opponent's vulnerability also depends on himself.

The master plan against our opponent(s) must be established by the CEO and the board. Both order and disorder are a function of internal organization and of leadership. Courage or cowardice often depend on circumstances; strength or weakness on tactical disposition. Skilled chief executives seek victory from the situation they are confronting, they do not just demand it of their subordinates. Closely connected to this are the merits and demerits associated to obtained results:

- Too frequent rewards indicate that the person in command is at the end of his or her resources.
- Too frequent punishments are evidence that the leader is in acute distress, not that he or she is tough and demanding.

Each of these bullets impacts on strategic business planning. As Sun Tzu had aptly suggested at his time, generally the best approach is to attack the enemy's strategy through a counterstrategy designed to overtake it. Strategy and counterstrategy have to be devised with the fundamental and long-term interests in mind, not just expediency. Emphasis should be placed on the salient problem, which is the problem the chief executive should address with top priority, always remembering that:

- The primary key factor is most decisive.
- A strategy should never be misled by complicated minor issues.

Speaking of his own experience as a very successful statesman and general, Sun Tzu said that it is much more complex to devise a strategy than to lay a plan for a battle which is made to serve the broader strategy. Additionally, he suggested that all warfare is based on deception. Therefore,

- When capable of attacking, feign incapacity, and
- When active in moving troops, feign inactivity.

If your opponent is of choleric temper, *then* Sun Tzu advises to try to irritate him. If he is arrogant, try to encourage his egotism. Behind such moves lies the fact that the opponent will lose his temper or his balance, thereby increasing his vulnerability. This is one of the basic elements a well-thought-out strategic plan should aim to achieve.

As the reader will recall from previous discussion, another crucial element is that of flexibility and adaptability. 'One does not plan and then try to make the circumstances fit those plans,' said George Patton, the best American general of World War II after Douglas MacArthur. 'One tries to make plans fit the circumstances. I think *the difference between success and failure* in high command depends on the ability, or lack of it, to do just that' (my emphasis).

Flexibility, adaptability, and readiness to switch out of the wrong path are keywords also in business planning. Sam Walton, one of the most successful businessmen of the post-World War II years, described in the following manner the way his mind worked: 'When I decide that I am wrong, I am ready to move to something else.' A project or process may prove unable to deliver what was promised, and as Walton aptly remarked on another occasion: 'One should never underwrite somebody else's inefficiencies.'[10]

Knowing yourself and knowing your opponent are not easy feats, but they are doable *if* one has initiative, patience and the right methodology. The same is true of keeping always flexible and adaptable. Yet, it is surprising how many companies, even big and mighty ones, fail to follow Sun Tzu's, Patton's, and Walton's time-honoured strategies. Such failure, and its aftermath, can best be shown through a case study.

AT&T's acquisition of NCR, the former cash register company which converted itself into computers, is one of the best examples of unpreparedness in strategic acquisitions, as well as a violation of the Sun Tzu, Patton, and Walton principles. It is also an unparalleled illustration of how a big company may plan not for success but for disaster. The highly paid AT&T top brass were not able to appreciate that:

- Industrial strategy should never be done on the run, and
- Strategy is by no means a way to solve a challenging but intractable problem.

Chapters 17 to 21 document through real life case studies that AT&T has not been alone in the mismanagement of mergers and acquisitions (M&As). Industrial history is littered with no-sense, ill-studied, or incompatible mergers, many of which have been done because of a big ego, or just to do something no matter what is its rationale. This has been precisely the case with the 1991 acquisition of NCR by AT&T.

To start with a reminder, after a court decision obliged AT&T to disinvest the Baby Bells, the operating telecoms in the United States, the formerly proud Ma Bell was struggling for a new identity to be expressed through a growth strategy. The pressure mounted in the wake of long-distance deregulation. Moreover, top management believed that telecommunications and computer technologies were converging:

- AT&T looked at NCR as a promising acquisition candidate, because reportedly it made a profit in computers, and
- An ill-documented study told the AT&T board that NCR would work in synergy with the existing product lines, since both companies shared a common vision and also a white-shirt style.

This argument has been, to say the least, absurd. The color of shirt or of suit executives wear is by no means what is meant by 'knowing yourself'. Strengths and weaknesses in management, and in the product line, are the focal point; and there is no evidence any one of them was properly studied – either on AT&T's or NCR's side. In violation of Sun Tzu's, Patton's, and Walton's strategic planning principles, the phone company's top brass:

- Thought of using its switch boxes as servers,[11] because since the 1980s switching centres have been digital, and
- Since client–server solutions need PCs, AT&T looked around for personal computers – which NCR had.

Speaking from an engineering viewpoint, the study of synergies between the two firms was, at best, superficial. Only after the merger, a *due diligence* process brought to light serious problems. Engineers from AT&T's Bell Labs assessed NCR's technology *after* the acquisition, while they should have done so ex ante. This post-mortem technical audit discovered:

- Substantial differences between AT&T's switching capabilities and basic PC technology, significantly reducing expected synergies from the acquisition, and
- To make matters worse, it was found that NCR was little more than a me-too assembler in personal computers. The acquired company was essentially a mainframer.

From a strategic perspective, as subsequent events demonstrated, even the hypothetical cultural similarities between AT&T and NCR proved practically non-existent. But there were rather pronounced management differences. NCR operated in a highly centralized, bureaucratic way. After its breakup by Judge Green, AT&T had become decentralized, and its subsequent attempts to flatten NCR's hierarchy, and cut overheads, backfired.

After having violated practically every principle in strategic planning, several years down the line, in 1996, AT&T spun off NCR. It is common knowledge that in doing so it suffered heavy losses. The fact that AT&T forbade its former subsidiary to manufacture and market personal computers speaks volumes of the fact its management finally learned that PCs are a cut-throat business. This late discovery did not change the fact that the master plan of AT&T was in shambles.

Notes

1 *The Economist*, 3 September 2005.

2 See also in Chapter 11 a case study on IBM's strategy in cost control, and in Chapter 15 a case study on IBM's quantitative objectives related to sales and marketing.

3 *The Economist*, 10 December 2005.

4 *Business Week*, 21 February 2005.

5 D.N. Chorafas, *IFRS, Fair Value and Corporate Governance. The Impact on Budgets, Balance Sheets and Management Accounts.* Elsevier, Oxford, 2006.
6 D.N. Chorafas, *Management Risk: The Bottleneck Is at the Top of the Bottle.* Macmillan/Palgrave, London, 2004.
7 Fitch Ratings, *Evaluating Corporate Governance: The Bondholder's Perspective*, London, 2005.
8 D.N. Chorafas, *Outsourcing, Insourcing and IT for Enterprise Management*, Macmillan/Palgrave, London, 2003.
9 Sun Tzu, *L'Art de la Guerre*, Flammarion, Paris, 1972.
10 Sam Walton, *Made in America: My Story.* Bantam, New York, 1993.
11 D.N. Chorafas, *Beyond LANs: Client–Server Computing.* McGraw–Hill, New York, 1994.

Examples of Leadership in Strategic Decisions

1. Introduction

In 1917, George F. Baker, then president of the prestigious First National Bank of New York, offered Jackson Eli Reynolds to join his inner circle in the corporate office of the credit institution. The proposal came out of the blue and Reynolds, a corporate lawyer and Columbia University professor, responded with a spontaneous burst of laughter.

'Have I said something funny?' the 77-year-old banker asked. 'It sounds to me,' Reynolds responded, 'as I am expecting a telephone call any moment from Paderewksi asking me to play a piano duet with him.' 'Banking is not as hard as piano playing,' Baker assured,[1] likely adding that there are some basic questions in the management of an enterprise which are universal enough that every leader should ask:

- What do we want to be, as a person?
- What do we wish to reach, as a company?
- Where do we choose to compete?
- Which are the services on which we are strong?
- How are we going to produce and deliver these services to remain competitive?
- Which are our cash flow and profit goals?
- How can we position ourselves to achieve these goals?

These are questions valid for every professional, and for everyone in senior management. Pity him or her who cannot provide valid answers. To respond to these queries, however, in a factual and documented manner, we must have a clear mind and unobstructed vision.

Able answers require making major choices, and therefore *strategic decisions*. Our goals should be tailored to the economics of the market(s) in which we operate (see section 4) and to the specific characteristics of our business. Chapter 1 made the point that goals that are too general or abstract are useless and they may be misleading.

The strategic decisions that we make, and the goals that we set, must be simple in character, expressed quantitatively and qualitatively, as well as easily understood. This may sound contradictory to the statement made in the preceding chapter, that strategy is a master plan and therefore tends to be complex. In reality there is no contradiction. Simplicity in strategic decisions means that:

- They should be stripped to their essentials, and
- Be phrased in a way that the degree to which they are realized is measurable and controllable.

Additionally, the quantitative metrics associated with strategic decisions should be directly related to the ongoing activities of the organization, not to far-fetched or imprecise events. An example of strategic goals is lowering production costs by, say, 10%. As we will see through practical examples in Part 4, costs matter.

- Low costs permit low prices, and
- Low prices associated to high quality attract and retain good clients.

Costs are important, as well, for another reason. Customers have become sophisticated and choosy. As a result, strategic decisions, including those connected to prices, quality, and delivery, are more *customer oriented* than ever before. Another aftermath of this trend is the strategic emphasis placed on research and development (R&D), which has become an important element of leadership in strategic business plans.

As we will see in Chapter 14, leadership in R&D requires research laboratories able to support a consistent, well-managed new product effort. In manufacturing, organized research is a development of the late 19th century, albeit at a timid scale. In banking, R&D began in the 1980s as securities markets and their instruments became the subject of steady innovation.

Research, development, and timely as well as effective marketing and implementation of research results are a product of the *knowledge industry*. Because a research project takes time to bear fruit, choices must be based on prognostication, which includes an element of risk. Therefore, before speaking of the impact of greater knowledge on strategic decisions, it is proper to examine how leaders make their bets.

2. Douglas MacArthur and the Inchon strategic decision

President Truman, and most Americans, felt that the late June 1950 unprovoked attack by North Korean forces against South Korea was comparable to the Japanese invasion of Manchuria in 1931 and Hitler's 1938 *Anschluss* with Austria. If the dictators were not stopped *then*, what would be next?

The decision to stop the North Koreans was topmost in the mind of the Truman Administration. The problem, however, was that in the preceding five years, those that followed the end of World War II, the United States had relaxed its defences. American forces in Japan and South Korea were only a skeleton of an army. As the invaders progressed, the South Koreans and their allies rapidly withdrew to the south of the peninsula till there remained only the Pusan enclave.

To get out of the limbo and have a good chance to claim victory, MacArthur's mind was firmly set on landing at Inchon, well in the north – rather than trying to roll over the North Korean and Chinese Red Army carpet. This was a strategic decision of utmost importance, and it had associated to it major risks. If successful, an Inchon landing would:

- Trap the invaders behind their extended supply lines, and
- Force a massive withdrawal of the invading army from the south of the Korean peninsula.

In Washington, the joint Chiefs of Staff had approved an ambitious landing from the moment MacArthur suggested it, capitalizing on US naval and air superiority. But they were not enthusiastic about his choice of landing place. To their thinking, Inchon was:

- Far to the north, from Pusan, and
- Its high tides, with their 12-hour cycle, would make landing difficult.

On 23 August 1950 a strategy summit was convened in Tokyo involving MacArthur; General J. Lawton Collins, Army Chief of Staff; Admiral Forrest Sherman, Chief of Naval Operations; General Lemuel Shepherd, Chief of the Marines; and a host of additional admirals and generals and their chiefs of staff. The purpose was to discuss the pros and cons of MacArthur's proposed Inchon operation.

Summing up the Navy's extensive, initial presentation, Admiral Sherman said, 'If every possible geographical and naval handicap were listed – Inchon has 'em all.'[2] His staff had delineated a number of them, including the horrible tides at Inchon, the two-hour window they left open for operations, and the fact the landing would be too close to Seoul.

Moreover, the generals and admirals from Washington said the main approach to the port of Inchon was a narrow, winding channel; the landings would have to be made in the heart of the city, itself; and the formidable Wolmi-Do Island fortress, which rose 120 feet above the water at the mouth of the harbour, could not be softened up by pre-invasion bombardment, because this would forfeit the element of surprise in the landing. Other objections were that MacArthur's plan called for extracting the First Marine Brigade from Pusan, weakening its defences, while MacArthur's troops moving out from Inchon would likely encounter heavy enemy resistance around Seoul, and could suffer an overwhelming defeat.

Given these weaknesses they saw in MacArthur's plan, General Collins proposed an alternative to Inchon – a landing at the west coast part of Kunsan, a city within 100 miles of what was then the Pusan perimeter – which would have both protected the forces at Pusan and bypassed its perimeter.

Quite likely, in his schooling, General Collins never learned that Frederick the Great had written in his *Instructions to his Generals*: 'Those generals who have had but little experience attempt to protect every point; while those who are better acquainted with their profession, guard against decisive blows at decisive points, and acquiesce in smaller misfortunes to avoid greater ones.'

A near-sighted approach to the risk being assumed in making strategic choices is an excellent example of the strategist's dilemma. It also provides evidence on the need to win over opposition to an imaginative but far-flung strategic move. Douglas MacArthur began his response to Collins by noting that the enemy had committed the bulk of his troops in deployment against the Pusan defence perimeter. He was therefore convinced that the North Koreans had not properly prepared Inchon for defence.

'The very arguments you have made as to the impracticabilities involved will tend to ensure for me the element of surprise. For the enemy commander will reason that no one would be so brash as to make such an attempt. ... Surprise is the most vital element for success in modern war,' said MacArthur. Then he went on to describe how, using the element of surprise, just as he intended to do, had carried the day in other major battles.

Turning to Admiral Sherman, MacArthur acknowledged the validity of his concerns adding, however, that he had developed a deep respect and appreciation for the exceptional capabilities of the US Navy during World War II. Therefore, he was confident that it was entirely capable of overcoming even the formidable obstacles being enumerated.

As for the proposal to land at Kunsan, MacArthur admitted that it would be less risky; but it would accomplish nothing of any strategic consequence: 'It would be an attempted envelopment, which would not envelop. It would not sever or destroy the enemy's supply lines or distribution center, and would therefore serve little purpose.' Nothing in war, or for that matter in business, is more futile than action taken just to do something.

As General MacArthur reassured the assembled US military leaders: 'If my estimate is inaccurate, and should I run into a defense with which I cannot cope, I will be there personally and will immediately withdraw our forces before they are committed to a bloody setback. The only loss then, will be my professional reputation.' But, he concluded in an earnest whisper, 'Inchon will *not* fail, and it will save 100,000 lives!'

Indeed, there was no room for failure. If the landing was repelled most of the men would be lost. MacArthur knew that and had not made his decision lightly. He had chosen a brilliant strategic move and he had confidence in his own military judgement. The now historic Battle of Inchon had the potential of unsettling all the strategic plans of the North Koreans, as well as of their Chinese and Russian supporters.

On 15 September 1950 the performance of the land, sea, and air components of MacArthur's assault force was incontestably brilliant on the day of the landing, and thereafter. It was MacArthur's victory not only against North Koreans, Russians, and Chinese, but also against the Joint Chiefs and a Truman Administration undecided about assuming the risks of the landing. The history of Inchon, including what preceded it, should be required reading at business schools.

3. Strategic decisions in business: case study with Sprint

Like any telecommunications company and, in a way, not unlike Alice in Wonderland, Sprint has to run fast in order to maintain its competitive position in an industry sector that, after nearly a century of slow motion, started to change very fast. Positioning required strategic decisions able to respond to the changing needs of the marketplace. For instance:

- Being more customer-centric than product-centric, and
- Restructuring the organization to mirror customer segments and needs, rather than products and services offered.

As the company's 2004 Annual Report points out, in executing these strategic moves Sprint found itself obliged to refine internal processes to reduce time and cost for the company and its customers. Senior management focused on re-energizing its brands, and devised ways to grow revenue faster than its competitors by data and multimedia:

- Doing so into the existing customer base, and
- By expanding scale and size of operations through wholesale agreements and key partnerships.

The strategic decisions Sprint has made, including its merger with Nortel, reflect the fact that the telecommunications industry is driven, like no other time before, by technology and competition. Also, that its customers are moving more and more to wireless and email substitutions. This has a profound effect on a carrier's long distance and local access services.

- Consumers are demanding more wireless data applications, such as broader band Internet access, gaming, and video streaming.
- Companies are pushing for more robust integrated solutions that improve their productivity, cut costs, and make their communications capabilities seamless to their customers.

At the same time, new entrants, like cable operators and entertainment companies, are eager to seize the developing new business opportunities. Their thrust into these telecoms markets is obliging existing telecoms to expand distribution beyond normal sales and geographic channels. They have to do so to remain competitive.

Additionally, telecom carriers cannot deliver true convergence without committing to a convergence business model, which they must develop and sustain in a way satisfying requirements posed by different market segments. For consumers, and many business companies, convergence delivers:

- Bundled wireline-wireless products where distance is not a barrier
- High-speed Internet access regardless of where one is, and
- The ability to easily assemble data, voice and video as part of an integrative solution.

In making its strategic planning decisions, Sprint took account of the fact that service integration must be features-rich, customized, and available anytime, anywhere. In turn, this requires major strategic choices in terms of technical solutions and investments made to support them.

One key element is financial stability, and staying power associated to it. To survive against growing competition, Sprint says that it took great strides to improve both its financial stability and flexibility, also focusing on costs and strong cash flow. A couple of strategic decisions in this connection have been to:

- Reduce debt levels significantly, and
- Bolster a stronger liquidity position than in previous years.

Crucial business choices of this nature have prerequisites revolving around the position management takes about developments in the longer run, which are often instrumental in providing answers to tactical problems. 'I have always thought of problems as challenges,' said Sam Walton, and while there may be room for mistakes, 'We had not made any mistakes we could not correct quickly. None so big that threatened the business.'[3]

Senior management should as well appreciate that strategic business decisions don't always lead to the hoped-for outcome because there may be reverses. But as Walton put it: '[I] have never been one to dwell on reverses. It is not just a corny saying that you can make a positive out of most any negative, if you work at it hard enough.' Good advice, which Sprint seems to have followed when it reabsorbed its wireless telecommunications subsidiary, Sprint PCS, after it had spun it off.

To survive, against competition and face the changing market whims, companies have not only to think up new things to try, but also to identify mistakes of the past and take corrective action. While they have to be innovating, experimenting, and expanding, they should not fail doing regular walkthroughs to establish if everything has gone according to plan. In a nutshell, this is what strategic decisions are all about:

- Being future-oriented is necessary but not enough.
- Another basic requirement is evaluating the plan's validity, as well as compliance to it.

There are many reasons why a strategy successfully followed in the past may have become counterproductive. In *The House of Morgan* Ron Chernow provides an example of lack of strategic decisions at a time when they were most crucial to adapt the company to a changing market. During the 1950s the Morgan Bank seemed to shrink, if only because its rivals grew so rapidly. To survive, it had to cobble together syndicates to serve large clients. But Henry Alexander, its CEO, stayed aloof from:

- Branch banking, and
- The spree of banking mergers.

'The old Wall Street,' Chernow said, 'vanished as musty, dignified old banks were snapped up by hungry retail giants. The First National Bank of New York – the bank of Pierpont's pal George F. Baker – was illustrative of the situation. Refusing to hustle for business and demanding client introductions, it was dying with dignity, and was acquired by National City' (more on this in Chapter 19).

At the same time, advertising, so far seen as subaltern and excluded from the world of finance, entered the banking business. This, too, was a strategic decision and some banks made it faster than others. Chase launched its advertising campaign with the slogan 'You Have a Friend at Chase Manhattan'. But as Chernow remarks, for elitist Morgan bankers, this was too much. 'You can't provide custom tailoring to a mass market,' sniffed Henry Alexander.[4] He was wrong.

4. The nature of many strategic decisions depends on macroeconomics

Whether we talk of manufacturers and merchandisers, telecommunications entities, like the example in section 3, real estate companies or, even more so, banks and other financial institutions, strategic decisions must account for current and projected state of the economy. Market psychology, inflation or deflation, the price of key commodities (see section 5), an ongoing bubble, as well as other factors that affect the outcome of a strategy, must be accounted for.

The evolution of an economy is the subject of studies in *macroeconomics*. Such studies are based on economic analysis, which is an arcane art whose results are indispensable in strategic planning. When top central bankers have independence of opinion and means, to carry out their job, they usually speak their mind freely, and what they say is vital input to senior management decisions.

In the 2005 annual symposium of the Federal Reserve Bank of Kansas City, central bankers and economists the world over paid tribute to Dr Alan Greenspan's 18 years as chairman of the Federal Reserve. In his speech, the boss of the Fed sounded a little worried about the economy's future, giving warning that an unusually long period of economic and financial stability:

- Might have encouraged investors to accept lower risk premiums, and
- This attitude contributed in inflating the prices of assets, such as shares, homes and some commodities.

'History has not dealt kindly with the aftermath of protracted periods of low risk premiums,' Greenspan said, adding that the 2001–2005 property boom was characterized by an imbalance. Prices of homes could fall, as happened in the late 1980s with real estate, and in 2000 with equity prices. Therefore, the chairman added, the Fed will need to pay more attention to asset prices.

In fact, not only the central bank, and its monetary policy-makers, but also companies and families will be advised to pay much greater attention to the way interest rates affect their decisions. The very low interest rates featured by the Fed during the first five years of the 21st century, indeed the lowest in nearly half a century, have been a motor behind this asset inflation in the housing market and in key commodities.

Another major contributor has been the very high liquidity, starting with the tragic events of September 11, 2001, following through in subsequent years. Companies that capitalized on high liquidity injected by central banks to keep the market from being nervous, must think ahead to what happens when monetary policy tightens.

The likelihood of plans turning on their head is faced equally by entities and investors whose strategic decisions are loaded on the side of cheap money. The fixed rate instruments hecatomb of 1994, an after-effect of tightening by the Fed on six consecutive occasions, is an ample example of how strategic investment plans – and even more so speculations – go astray.

As a reminder, the cheap money of the early 1990s, and consecutive interest rate increases in 1994, took place under Greenspan's watch. On the positive side of Greenspan's tenure has been his intellectual inflexibility, as well as his scepticism of economic models and forecasts. Another contribution was that of framing monetary policy as *risk management*. With this criterion at the top of the list of issues to watch, the Fed has been looking at the same time:

- At the most likely path for the economy, and
- At all possible paths it might follow, attaching greater weight to outcomes that could do severe harm.

A great deal of Dr Greenspan's contribution to the US and, by extension, global economy, rests on the fact that through his tenure he has followed no party line. He was not a member of a party clan and kept his own counsel. That is what every strategic decision-maker should do not only at national economic level but also at corporate level, in regard to company politics.

Independence of opinion is ethical behaviour's *alter ego*. 'The individual family member', says Antonio Ferreira, 'may know, and often does, that much of the family image is false and represents nothing more than a sort of official party line.'[5] One might add that this is just as valid of brand names and logos. But when this attitude reaches strategic business plans, it becomes self-destructive.

Independence of opinion is also a matter of culture, and it is to the credit of the Federal Reserve that its culture, which developed over nearly a century, is one of independence. (Woodrow Wilson was the Fed's founding president. With senator Carter Glass, in 1913, he shepherded the Federal Reserve Act through Congress.)

Members of the Federal Reserve Board have often shown their independence of opinion. 'It is not an easy thing to vote against the President's wishes,' said Henry Wallich, a Fed governor in the Carter years. 'But what are we appointed for? Why are we given these long terms in office? Presumably, it is that not only the present but the past and the future have some weight in our decisions. In the end, it may be helpful to remind the President that it is not only his present concerns that matter.'[6]

This is the policy every central banker should follow, and it is practically what Alan Greenspan did. Still, critics suggest that at his retirement from Fed chairmanship, Dr Greenspan has been leaving the economy unusually out of kilter, with record current account deficits and household financial debt. The early years of the new century have seen the biggest housing bubble ever in the United States. These are most important macroeconomic factors which, when left out of strategic decisions, can turn a business plan into shambles.

5. Business strategy and the price of key commodities

Theory says that market prices are established by supply and demand. While this can happen, it is by no means the golden rule applying in all places, and in all cases, for all commodities – particularly those most crucial to the economy which are also subject to other forces. The price of oil in 2005 provides a good example on how pricing a commodity comes unstuck from classical fundamentals and, over a significant amount of time, responds to:

- Lax monetary conditions
- Market psychology, and
- Market speculation, capitalizing on these two bullets.

Lax monetary conditions have prevailed, for instance, in both the United States and China who, in 2005, have been the two biggest oil consumers world-wide. Moreover, the United States kept the cost of money at rock bottom level, while China played on a highly undervalued currency and rules in giving loans to state firms which defied sound credit criteria. As the oil crisis deepened many experts suggested that high oil prices can partly be seen as a consequence of low interest rates.

- *If* this hypothesis is true,
- *Then* the price of oil and the price of money are inversely correlated.

Such a linkage in pricing crucial commodities, for example money and oil, has only recently been appreciated as a crucial reference in strategic decision. As a commodity, oil has taken over from gold both the role of regulatory instrument and of wealth refuge – becoming an issue whose price is highly exposed to market psychology and speculative action.

As far as commodity pricing is concerned, not everything is market psychology. There exist other fundamental factors to be accounted for in strategic decisions regarding the use of these commodities. For instance, rising oil prices are a signal that global economic growth has been more rapid than other variables characterizing existing financial conditions can sustain. In that sense:

- The rising price of oil is a way of constraining the world economy, helping to prevent it from overheating.
- Confronted with much higher prices, companies and consumers tend to change their behaviour, becoming more prudent.

Some experts say a better solution would have been to tighten global monetary conditions. Contrarians to this approach answer that a higher cost of money requires general policy agreement, and in some countries it risks puncturing the housing and borrowing bubbles which are going on. On the other hand, high oil prices have dreadful consequences for slower-growing economies in Africa, Latin American, part of Asia, and several countries in Europe, other countries benefit greatly from them.

Under these conditions what should filter into strategic decisions is the way the aftermath affects *our* company's fortunes. For instance, excessive growth in oil demand in America and China is imposing a tax on others by pushing crucial commodity prices higher. This is particularly true when price increases are fairly sharp: the price of a barrel of West Texas Intermediate (WTI) rose from $18 in November 2001 to $70 in early September 2005, and though it retreated from that height, nobody can be sure it will not surpass it in the future.

Nearly half an order of magnitude change in a key commodity should provide plenty of thought to corporate policy-makers. In terms of percentage increase, this is similar in scale to oil price jumps of 1973–74, 1978–80, and 1989–90, all of which were followed by:

- Worldwide recession, and
- Rising inflation in industrial countries.

Curiously, however, in 2005 inflation remained low. One reason is that developed countries use half as much oil per real dollar of GDP than they did in the mid-1970s, because of improved energy efficiency. And also, as a result of the shift that took place from manufacturing to services. The after-effect has been that a given rise in oil prices made a smaller dent in inflationary terms.

What has been stated in the preceding paragraph, however, is not true of most emerging economies, which are still big energy users. India and China, for example, employ more oil per dollar of GDP today than they did in the 1970s – but they also have very low labour costs, and they subsidize the pricing of their exports in order to gain foreign markets. It is a fact that the lesser developed economies which are currently growing faster than those of the industrial West tend also to be the least efficient users of oil.

- To produce one dollar of GDP, the so-called emerging economies use more than twice as much oil as developed economies, and
- Because governments are subsidising their oil price, consumers and companies burn more of it than *if* they had to pay full market prices.

Within the perspective established above, the International Monetary Fund forecasts that for the rest of this decade emerging economies could account for almost three-quarters of the increase in world oil demand. Since 2000, consumption in China has single-handedly represented more than one-third of the growth in global requirements in oil supplies. The United States remains the biggest consumer, roughly using one-quarter of the world's output.

The bad news is that with China's consumption per person still one-fifteenth of that in the United States, it is inevitable that its energy demands will significantly increase over the coming years. Will the global economy be able to withstand this shock, or are we now entering a period of stagflation? The good news is that so far in the 21st century stagflation has not yet taken hold, as it did two and a half decades earlier. As a reason for this, some economists suggest the impact of gradual adjustment.

- In 1979 the price of oil doubled in 6 months
- In 2004–2005 it took 18 months to multiply by 2.

According to this hypothesis, gradual adjustment had a favourable impact, giving companies and households more time to accommodate themselves with the new price levels, therefore doing less damage to their confidence – and, by extension, to economic activity. There is also the fact that even at $70 per barrel, in real terms the price is not as high as in the late 1970s. This is, however, small comfort.

Still another factor strategic planners should consider in connection to energy is that *if* oil prices are rising because of correlation to high money supply and strong demand, rather than being a supply problem, *then* they are likely to stay high for much longer. In past oil shocks, a rise in price as a result of temporary supply disruption caused oil consumption to decline. This has not happened yet in any significant way.

Because the costs of labour, raw materials and other commodities reflect themselves into all final cost figures, price volatility, and even more so an upwards trend, should not be taken lightly in strategic business plans. The best policy is to take a leaf out of the book of Japanese manufacturers. When the dollar/yen exchange rate turned against them, from a rather classical 100 to 125 yen to the dollar, down to 85 yen to the dollar, their strategic plans targeted remaining competitive with an even worse exchange rate, of 70 yen to the dollar.

6. The comparative advantage of knowledge workers

In the 19th century, economists developed the theory of *comparative advantage* to explain industrial location. Examples are possession of natural resources, availability of increasingly more skilled labour, abundance of capital to be invested per worker, and particularly benign climatic conditions that favour an industry like tourism, or some types of goods.

For instance, cotton was grown in the south of the United States because the climate and soil were right. But it was woven into cloth in New England, because that was where the water power and local skill existed. Steel was made in Pittsburgh, since this location minimized transportation costs given the rivers and the relative position of iron ore and coal deposits.

What the previous paragraph outlined is 19th century examples that explain why the big brown industries settled where they did. Knowledge-intense resources have different criteria and, moreover, the old capital and labour ratios don't hold any more; they have become fairly irrelevant as strategic decision milestones, because globalization, technology, and innovation have changed the rules of the game.

Classical industries are relocating to take advantage of *lower* labour costs. Financial capital has become widely accessible at a reasonable price. Human capital can be anywhere provided that:

- The educational system functions properly, and
- The population is characterized by personal initiative.

Today, even if lower costs are important, the raw form of unskilled and uneducated workers is less and less needed. At the same time, however, there is a fast-growing obsolescence of skills. Lifelong learning has become a 'must' in Western societies – where a large number of workers without a job are not simply unemployed – they are *unemployable*.

Knowledge is a competitive advantage with limited timespan. It decays not only if it isn't used, but also if it is not kept up. Therefore, it is not enough to develop careers for knowledge workers. These careers have also to be challenging, and a steady effort should see to it that lifelong learning refreshes people's know-how permitting them to remain competitive. The strategic element in this connection is that:

- Competitiveness is implicit in the nature of knowledge, and
- As knowledge workers become the central resource of the economy, society is bound to evolve only *if* it is constantly able to upgrade its people's skills.

Over the ages, there have been two schools of thought about knowledge which, to a substantial extent, contrast to one another. The first has emphasized what can be called *self-knowledge*, or the perfection of the individual by intellectual, moral, and spiritual means. The teachings of Socrates and Plato, but also of Taoists and Zen, find themselves on this wavelength, which is essentially *endogenous*.

The other school of thought promoted the type of knowledge that is *exogenous*, and has its origin in Protagoras and the Stoics, as well as Confucius. For Protagoras knowledge meant: logic, grammar, and rhetoric enabling a person to know *what* to say and *how* to say it. Both Protagoras and Socrates, however:

- Respected the skills (*techne*), which is not higher knowledge but necessary infrastructure, and

- They taught that the best way to master *techne* is through apprenticeship and learning by experience.

Apprenticeship amplifies what is taught in school because it provides hands-on experience. In turn, personal experience is supplemented, and in many cases augmented, through formal education. This interplay of formal education and apprenticeship is a strategic decision.

It should be noted, as well, that with every epoch the level of required literacy has changed. Today for *knowledge workers* the criterion is not alphabetism but literacy in computers, in research, industrial engineering, accounting, marketing, and the law. Taken together the extent and nature of required *techne* demonstrate that the new society of knowledge workers is a strategic development with its own particular characteristics. There is no definition available from the past, which fits:

- The current social description of knowledge, or
- The type of work knowledge workers are doing, and its evolution over time.

On the other hand, however, the knowledge society – and the new capitalism it brought along – have some easily detectable trends. Both brains and capital can go where they are appreciated, have great career opportunities, are provided with lifelong learning facilities, and are paid the most. Knowledge resources and financial resources have mobility.[7]

In the mid- to late-1930s the United States gained from Europe some of its best brains due to the suicidal policies of the Nazi government. In the early 1950s, Fullbright scholarships brought to the United States the cream of the young generation of European knowledge workers. Fullbright scholarships proved to be a very imaginative strategic initiative on behalf of the US government.

In the mid-1960s it was the huge budget and imaginative goals of the man-on-the-moon programme which created Europe's brain drain and America's brain gain. Twenty years later, in the mid-1980s, came the fourth wave. This time brains went to the United States from Asia, particularly India, Taiwan, and China.

What these four waves of knowledge workers have in common is their contribution to the real capital of the US economy. They have been attracted there by America's recognition of the competitive advantages knowledge workers bring along. It should, however, be appreciated that it is their knowledge which gave them the freedom to:

- Move across frontiers, and
- Be welcomed in the new country not as stage hands but as contributors.

Evidently, the knowledge capital one country gains, the other country loses. But losers don't have the knowledge necessary to appreciate what they have lost. None of their kings, or prime ministers, has taken the trail of King Minos of ancient Crete, who sailed after Daedalus, the greatest engineer of his time, to bring him back to his home country.

Up to a point, in our days, the spirit that best describes the concepts underpinning the knowledge society can be seen in the management philosophy of John F. Welsh. As far as human resources are concerned, in the years he led General Electric (GE), Welsh applied two strategic guidelines which are worth emphasizing:

- Employees who cannot adjust, do not belong at the new GE, and
- We want to create an environment where employees are ready to go and eager to stay.

John F. Welsh also set in motion other strategic initiatives which, over the years, became guidelines of the new capitalism. During the time of his tenure, GE personnel have been reduced by 100,000 workers out of 400,000, while revenues have grown 48%. At the same time, GE's executive development centre at Crotonville has been redirected to become the *change agent*, because without change organizations die from old age as their arteries clog and their brain closes down.

In conclusion, the most important problem our society faces is not one of race and religion, but of self-control and education. As De Tocqueville, the French philosopher, once suggested: 'The diffusion of knowledge is advantageous to all concerned. Ignorance leads to failure.' And ignorance is a very flexible theme indeed.

7. Strategic dimension under the new capitalism

While to a considerable extent the new capitalism of the late 20th and early 21st centuries can be seen as knowledge-based capitalism, it also has other ingredients of strategic importance. The purpose of this section is to bring them in perspective because of their impact on senior management decisions. Three issues of prime importance are the:

- Mobility of capital on a global scale
- Broadening horizon of wealth management,[8] and
- Impact of research, development, and innovation on corporate profits and survival.

All three are strategic factors favouring the industries promoted by the new economy. From finance, semiconductors and on-line entertainment, to education and health care, the new industries have grown much faster than the old, which actually are in decline. The only way old industries can survive and grow is through a thorough re-engineering. This is essentially what Sam Walton did with Wal-Mart, which started as a retailer before becoming a network of hypermarkets.

The financial industry, too, offers an example of re-engineering. Seen under the most recent perspective, the real product of the banking industry is knowledge. Practically all industrial sectors that have moved into the centre of an advanced economy, such as software, computers and communications, have as the infrastructure of their business activities research, production, and distribution of knowledge.

This is a totally different concept than the production and distribution of hard goods, with which most people are familiar. Without abandoning the strategic return on investment (ROI) criteria, in terms of making capital allocation decisions, the new capitalism has promoted new dimensions, which became its hallmarks. Figure 2.1 offers a bird's-eye view of the three pillars of the new system. Enlightened spirits have helped in bringing them into perspective.[9]

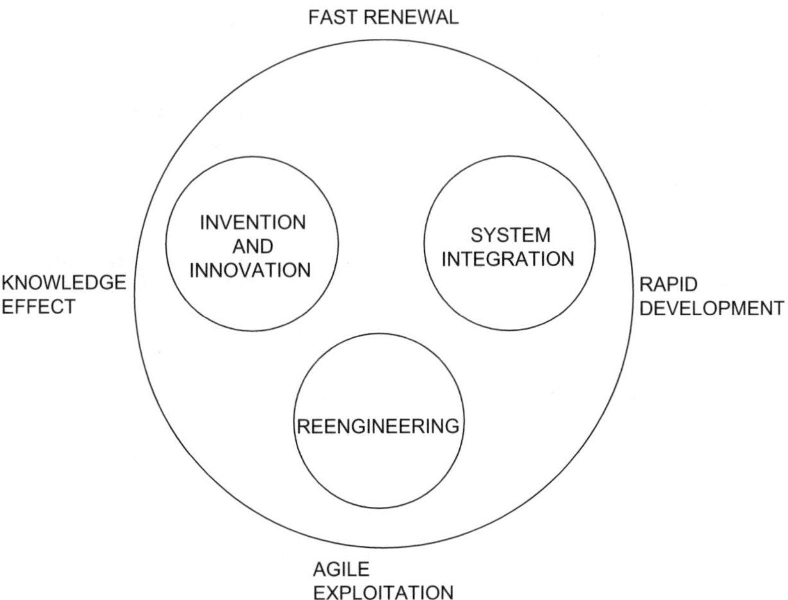

Figure 2.1 Measuring return on knowledge in the new capitalism

- The impact of invention and innovation is demonstrated by the success of life sciences and the strategy followed by high-tech firms.
- System integration is using information technology as the vector to create larger aggregates which cannot be built in a monolithic way.
- Re-engineering of an ancient concept like merchandising has been achieved by capitalizing on broadband communications, computer-based mathematical models, and the real-time enterprise.[10]

The first of these three bullets talks of a new strategic perspective in business and industry which has demonstrated its ability to serve the growing demand for advanced man-made products. By contrast, while the concept behind large-scale system integration is new, the components it brings together and makes work in a seamless manner, are already in existence.

As a strategic choice, system integration should not be confused with re-engineering. The latter does not create a new system. Rather, it significantly enhances an existing one through new objectives and novel departures promoted by the astute use of information and knowledge. Re-engineering provides a very useful platform for revamping old structures.

People who have not quite appreciated the strategic directives of the new capitalism tend to say that it is no longer possible to make big profits through industry. This is not true. As the late 1990s have shown with high-tech companies, it is always possible to create significant additional wealth – though high leverage eventually leads to a bubble, just as it has so often done in older times.

Peter Drucker is right when he says that we don't really fully understand the economics of knowledge, because we have not yet had enough experience to formulate an appropriate theory about it, and test it. What we do understand, however, is that today in order to gain competitive advantage we have to put knowledge into the centre of wealth-producing processes, as section 6 has explained.

More than that, tomorrow we will not be able to produce anything significant, and therefore survive, unless knowledge engineering underpins our the developments and applications. We also need to understand that a knowledge-based economy behaves in a totally different way than existing theories assume – including the prevailing economic theories.

Keynesian, monetarist, classical, and other economic theories that have had their day were made for a world where physical goods dominated, not for the service economy in which we currently live. In an economic environment where physical goods were the measure of activity, economists have based their theories on the concepts of:

- Perfect competition, and
- An efficient marketplace.

Both are alien to a service economy, where individual companies may be efficient but the market as a whole is inefficient. Not only have the concepts embedded in both of the above bullets been largely approximations, and do not hold true, but also in a knowledge economy these assumptions can be seen as quite plainly wrong. Let me repeat the previous statement. Both:

- Imperfect competition, and
- Significant market inefficiencies underpin the way the knowledge economy works.

Typically, with physical production the lead time to deployment of resources is relatively short, though a good deal of planning is necessary as the complexity of these resources increases. By contrast, in the service economy, where professionals dominate, the lead time can be significant. It takes years to educate a person into becoming a first class lawyer, expert accountant, imaginative researcher, or top-tier design engineer.

In the production of physical goods, the emphasis in investments is typically on fixed features: land, office buildings, factories, machines, and tools. In each country, the law then specifies how quickly these can be depreciated over a number of years.

By contrast, in the knowledge society strategic innovation works in a totally different way. Return on knowledge (ROK), and its intrinsic value, have to work in a rapid cycle and depreciation must be fast, preferably less than a year. Every night when the researcher or manager leaves his or her office to go home, the

Table 2.1 Frequency with which the strategic plan is matched or modified

Frequency	Use actual events to test strategic plan	Review strategic plan for possible modification
Monthly	20%	15%
Quarterly	25%	20%
Semi-annually	10%	15%
Annually	45%	50%

company for which he or she is working knows that tomorrow that person *might* work for a competitor. This radically changes the strategic dimension of competition in modern capitalism, turning many of our time-honoured notions on their head.

Notes

1 James Grant, *Money of the Mind.* Farrar Strauss Giroux, New York, 1992.
2 EIR, 10 December 2004.
3 Sam Walton, *Made in America: My Story.* Bantam, New York, 1993.
4 Ron Chernow, *The House of Morgan.* Touchstone, New York, 1990.
5 Antonio J. Ferreira, Family myth and homeostasis, *Archives of General Psychiatry*, 9: 457–63, 1963; at p. 458.
6 William Greider, *Secrets of the Temple: How the Federal Reserve Runs the Country.* Touchstone/Simon and Schuster, New York, 1987.
7 D.N. Chorafas, *The Knowledge Revolution*, Allen and Unwin, London, 1968, and McGraw–Hill, New York, 1969.
8 D.N. Chorafas, *Wealth Management: Private Banking, Investment Decisions and Structured Financial Products.* Elsevier, Oxford, 2005.
9 Peter F. Drucker, *Post-Capitalist Society.* Harper Business, New York, 1993.
10 D.N. Chorafas, *The Real-Time Enterprise.* Auerbach, New York, 2005.

Strategic Choices in Corporate Governance

1. Introduction

The message the final two sections of Chapter 2 provided to the reader is that there are excellent growth opportunities for companies that offer their customers significant productivity improvements, through knowledge-oriented solutions. The service society and its agents see to it that, while competition has greatly increased, the edge in overtaking corporate opponents is:

- Superior employees, and
- Proprietary body of expertise.

Human assets are more difficult for a potential competitor to duplicate than a steel mill or automotive factory. A company with proprietary expertise has a clear global competitive advantage, therefore knowledge-based processes and products are a good investment. This orientation, however, requires most important strategic choices by senior management; particularly choices which lie off the beaten path.

In 2005, Microsoft provided an excellent example. The launch of Xbox 360 in November of that year is a valid illustration of a well-managed company's advance into markets outside its original business. Making software for PCs and servers is still a lucrative market but Microsoft is not resting on its laurels.

- The original Xbox was a TV front-end, mainly oriented to gaming.
- But aside from its technical advances, the new Xbox 360 has greater ambitions, targeting the still open market of a hub for home cinema (more on this in section 4).

Besides gaming, Microsoft does its best to get its software into mobile homes and other non-PC devices. Every major industry today has come to a strategic crossroads, and choices currently being made have far-reaching effects. Chapter 1 brought to the reader's attention what characterizes winners and losers in a market that is more competitive than ever.

Through able strategic decisions, companies have to rise to the occasion, or stand by and watch their primary income sources shrink, while today's customers become tomorrow's competitors. If the board, CEO, and senior managers fail to take control of the company's future while there is still time to implement strategic alternatives, decreased profit margins, followed by red ink, will make the decision for them.

The challenge to the CEO and the board is not only the choice of strategic direction, and its able implementation, but also the need to be in charge of the risk being assumed – because risk-taking is inherent in every new departure. If R&D is the key ingredient in developing new value-added services, alert management supported by first-class methodology and technology is the most important means of risk control.[1]

Within the outlined perspectives, a vital responsibility of the CEO is to assure that the right strategic choices are not being delayed because of indecision, but that they are implemented at the right time. Two equally important duties are to oversee customer profitability and supervise the proper functioning of internal controls – so that the information flow is uninhibited up and down the organization.

When the responsibilities outlined in the preceding paragraphs are properly integrated into the system of governance, they give the organization a unique competitive advantage. The CEO is accountable for their development and their integration because the person who commands the enterprise is not a mere technician. He or she is the:

- Animator
- Promoter
- Planner, and
- Controller of the enterprise.

The role of animator and promoter is to see to it that the organization ticks like a clock. This role cannot be relegated to a committee because 'committees cannot drive a company, just like they cannot drive a car', as Henry Ford used to say. And Urwich, a well-known British consultant of the 1930s, added that committees have no soul to blame and no body to kick.

Both Ford and Urwich were very critical of committees, but committees do have a role to play and their contribution should not be underestimated. For instance, recent research suggests that in the long run committees are likely to take better decisions on interest rates than individuals.[2] Also, other things being equal, committees are better in choosing prize winners than individuals, who may fall into the nepotism trap.

When it comes to strategic choices, however, it is personal leadership, rather than the averages that come out of cumulative judgement that counts the most. The opportunities for good and bad strategic choices are many, as we will see in this chapter. Section 2 presents the reader with one of the best examples of what a well-managed company can accomplish.

2. The choice of the product line: case study with Toyota

As an old adage has it: 'What a man is doing, does the man.' This is just as valid for a company, government organization or any other entity. Hence, a most crucial question is: 'What do we want to be?' followed by: 'What are we now doing?' and 'Does it bring us to where we want to be?' The choices that we make and the awareness of the path we take are tantamount to:

- Redefining ourselves
- By managing out activities.

'In the past, we tended to run the company to occupy space,' Citibank's chairman and CEO John S. Reed told analysts in 1995. Having said this, he vowed that henceforth, 'We are going to run the company for performance' – implying that Citibank will no longer try to be in every market.[3]

A similar strategic choice connected to selectivity faces every company in the world. On and off, industry is carried along by a wave to diversify, which, quite often, is translated into spreading thin. The motor vehicle industry provides one of the best examples that can be found on both sides of the equation. That is:

- What should be done, and
- What should not be done.

Starting with the second bullet, Ford had an aerospace division that was fairly profitable. General Motors therefore bought Hughes Aircraft, when it became available. GM had also acquired Ross Perot's Electronic Data Systems (EDS). Daimler therefore had to buy a major consulting company, in Germany, to join the club of the irrational. Both Hughes and EDS have been disinvested some years down the line, when it became evident this was not what a (by then) poorly managed auto manufacturer should be doing.

- Toyota did not make that mistake in its strategic choices. It concentrated on what it knew best – autos, and
- It capitalized on its strengths rather than skating on thin ice by trying to be everything to everybody.

Which has been the better strategy is told by the outcome. As of 2005, both General Motors and Ford are at the edge of bankruptcy. And while in the past they could count on European profits to plug their American losses, now their European debts add to the general misery. GM has given every sign of getting tired of losing hundreds of millions of dollars in Europe with its Opel, Vauxhall, and Saab brands, which are continuously dogged by:

- Dullness, and
- Variable quality.

This did not happen 'just yesterday'. Because what is, by all the evidence, an incapable management has been feeding the company's weaknesses rather than its strengths, these brands have been losing money for years. Saab is a case in point. Its purchase by GM in 2000 was supposed to add to the company's stable a posh brand with better margins. But the result has been precisely the *opposite* than the one expected.

It is indeed surprising how highly paid managers cannot make up their mind about what the company for which they are responsible should or should not do. Experts say that the failure of GM's Saab investment, like that in Fiat, is just one of a string of bad strategic choices which, in the not too distant future, will see Toyota topple GM from the No. 1 slot among the world's auto makers. Today:

- Toyota makes a net profit far bigger than the combined total for Detroit's Big Three.
- Its global market share is growing towards 15%, a large number given tough competition, and
- Its market capitalization towers above its competitors, including Detroit's auto makers.

Like every other car manufacturer, Toyota's management is faced with tough choices because the worldwide car market is a very difficult one to be in. There is capacity in place to produce millions of cars and other light vehicles, like pick-ups and SUVs, every year, at a level well above current output. Capacity is estimated at 80 million vehicles while actual production stands at about 60 million a year. As a result,

- On average, factories are only three-quarters full in terms of capacity, and
- This gap is projected to increase as Chinese car manufacturing comes on-line, including exports. The launch took place at the September 2005 Frankfurt Fair.

What the writing on the wall says to everybody who can read it, is that the laggards in the global competition in auto manufacturing and sales are in for a very rough time. Interestingly enough, these were former industry leaders, like GM,

Ford, Chrysler, Fiat, and Volkswagen; even Mitsubishi Motors. But they have consistently failed to address their real problems. In particular:

- Sluggish product development,
- Unimaginative marketing effort, and
- Very poor financial discipline.

In most other industries, such significant management weaknesses would rather quickly bring the firm to bankruptcy, but autos are a special breed. For instance, Mitsubishi Motors is getting a lifeline of support from its *keiretsu* kin. And, after its failed effort to sell its car business to GM, Fiat got huge compensation from the American car manufacturer when the doomed deal went to the wall.

Moreover, like practically all mismanaged companies in Europe, Fiat receives lucrative subsidies from the Italian government (which can ill afford it). The Italian government is afraid of the massive unemployment that would be created by Fiat's bankruptcy. In all likelihood, GM made the strategic blunder to buy an option on Fiat because the formerly proud auto maker's management could not sort out its priorities. The bones of Alfred Sloan, a giant of industry, must be turning in the grave.

While the negotiations towards a financially painful disengagement between GM and Fiat were going on in early 2005, rumour had it that prior to paying the $2 billion dollar penalty GM had developed a strategic option. It played with the idea to buy Fiat Auto, declare it bankrupt, and shrink it to a specialist status dimensioned so that:

- It could make money, and
- Contribute a couple of brands to GM's own tired portfolio.

This strategic choice, however, came down in flames when both the Italian government and labour unions made it clear they would have none of this. This is an excellent example of the fact that strategy can never be made in the abstract. The stakeholders can be vigilant and, sometimes, violent in their response.

If GM, Ford, Fiat, and some of the other established brands provide insight into failed management decisions, what have been the strategic choices of the winners? Notably Japan's Big Three: Toyota, Nissan, and Honda. A first response is that they do not have magic answers; indeed, nobody does. But a more careful look reveals that they focus on *patient execution* of sensible, though ambitious, plans to expand their sales.

- They develop a steady stream of new models, making them with remarkable efficiency, and
- They don't go for takeovers or miracle cures. They are basing their strategy on relentless professionalism with novel design and high quality, rather than throwing money at the problem.

Particularly, in the case of Toyota, there is one extra ingredient: the company's strong corporate culture. Top down, every employee seems to know the 'Toyota way' of doing things. The board and CEO know how to do business on a global scale, and how to keep a steady watch on costs. The employees know that their duty is *quality work*, not just work. And they don't go on strike now and then, as French, Italian, and German auto industry workers do.

All these ingredients are important in enveloping the right strategic moves. They are particularly crucial in a global auto industry whose output has risen by about 3 million per year since 2000 – with half of this coming from Toyota alone. To reach such deliverables, the company has achieved dramatic growth all round the world, making more cars abroad than at home. Toyota:

- Has overtaken Ford in global production terms, and
- It is about to pass Chrysler in sales to become one of America's Big Three.

Additionally, among car manufacturers, Toyota is exceptional because it makes good returns consistently. This is evident in its market capitalization. Toyota is worth more than the traditional American Big Three put together, and more than the combination of its successful Japanese rivals, Nissan and Honda.

Having learned in the 1960s from the US auto manufacturers how to make modern cars properly, in the elapsed four decades Toyota has improved on its methods – while its American competitors fell behind. These improvements reflect themselves in the Toyota Production System (TPS), which, among other advances, pioneered *just-in-time* manufacturing.

To its credit, Toyota also learned a great deal from W. Edward Deming, the quality control expert who had played a big part in developing the principles and methods for highly reliable products. Deming's concepts helped Japanese industry tremendously while he was working on the staff of General MacArthur. At the core of quality assurance in Deming's method, and in TPS, is:

- Elimination of waste, and
- Absolute concentration on consistent high quality.

In Toyota's case, this has taken the shape of a process of continuous improvement (*kaizen*). Another competitive strategic choice has been the slick product development process that can roll out new models in record time. And there is, as well, a smart marketing strategy. As soon as Toyota bosses spot a gap in the market, or a good new product from a rival, they swiftly move in with their own improved offer. Strategic planning is not limited to words and vague statements. Its aftermath is measurable because plans are immediately put into action.

3. Strategic choices in the banking industry: a lesson from the 1990s

During the past three decades, strategic choices in financial markets have been promoted by globalization, technology, deregulation, product innovation, and institutional change that led to mergers, acquisitions, and restructurings (see also Part 5 for case studies). All these background reasons have increased the incentive for investors to:

- Take greater risks, and
- Move in a herd, buying at prices that have little to do with fundamentals.

Additionally, when interest rates are low, this behaviour is compounded by the search for yield, which leads to sailing in uncharted waters and makes financial booms and busts more likely. Nowhere have such significant changes had a greater impact than in the banking industry, reshaping its landscape.

While practically all major credit institutions moved in the same direction, adding to their retail and commercial banking, investment banking activities and derivatives trading,[4] those who were better managed looked for a competitive strategy – and they examined the choices that go with it. Among the questions senior management asked itself are:

- Would we like to be the acquiring entity or the acquired?
- Which will be our opponents in 5–10 years' time?
- Which new financial products can we offer to stay independent and prosper?

These were some of the critical issues confronted by credit institutions as market forces changed the banking industry in the late 1980s and early 1990s. For instance, are money funds among our big competitors? If yes, then let's devise a strategy that will give them a run for their money. Let's ourselves be much more efficient than they are.

Additionally, well-managed financial institutions have used competition as a stimulus in formulating strategic choices that could be instrumental in strengthening their position. In terms of products and services, many internationally active banks tended to organize themselves around six main business lines, of different levels of appeal and profitability:

- Lending, often oriented to senior debt
- Cash management and payment systems
- Investment advising, portfolio management, and private banking[5]
- Derivatives and associated services such as foreign exchange
- Retail banking in selected markets, and
- Investing in debt and equity on their own account, including securities lending.

The better-governed money centre banks appreciated that each of these main product lines requires not only first-class skills but also a rigorous risk management policy, procedures to see it through, and the technology necessary to support it. They also needed 'know-how' to provide a dynamic appreciation of exposure as both market behaviour and product prices change.

CEOs with experience in technology appreciated that computers, communications, and models can be used in an effective manner only when they are blended with good business sense. And good business sense suggests that as far as innovative products are concerned, rapid development timetables are the only answer to the maintenance of market competitiveness. This is also the focal point of financial engineering, namely:

- Developing new products and services
- Building added value to existing products
- Elaborating models for market tracking and evaluation
- Using pricing models to help in management decisions, and
- Establishing a first-class, company-wide system for cost control.

All this has been part and parcel of the effort to remain competitive in a fast-moving market. And the most advanced financial institutions in the world have proved they can do it through innovative approaches to a market as old as humanity. By contrast, projects that hang themselves to old concepts fail to account for the fact that business opportunity can best be exploited by being first or second in the market.

Market share can be gained by offering competitive solutions at reasonable prices. Dr von Rosen was right when he stated that, 'In the years to come, the losers will be those who use status-quo, restrictive legislation and other barriers to hide their weaknesses – rather than bring them to the open and *correct them*.'[6] Correcting them means:

- Changing the old culture
- Improving the human capital
- Restructuring the balance sheet, and
- Repositioning oneself against the market forces.

The early 1990s was the time when better-managed companies in the banking industry took the proverbial long, hard look in terms of their future. No two banks made the same strategic choices, as Tables 3.1 and 3.2 document. Table 3.1 presents the strategic perspectives of Citicorp and Table 3.2 that of J.P. Morgan. The careful reader would observe that, longer term, these strategic objectives have shaped the personality of the banks as we know them today.

At about the same time, early 1990s, at well-governed institutions senior management appreciated that real-time system solutions, for opportunity analysis and control of exposure, are vital. A senior bank executive suggested during our discussion that: 'Without risk management trading and investing in derivatives can be so bad in terms of exposure that the junk bonds of the 1980s will start looking like a good risk.'

In regard to strategic choices connected to restructuring of the branch network, also in the early 1990s some credit institutions opted for a dual approach: revamping their classical branches by using the best in technology; and instituting an R&D

Table 3.1 Strategic perspectives of Citicorp in early 1990s*

Overall objective	One year's goals
1. Provide all things financial to all people, using leading-edge technology where applicable	1. Improve loan-loss reserve
2. Express strategy as five 'I's – Institutional, Individuals and Investment banking, Insurance and Information	2. Increase presence in information business
3. Assure strong fee income growth, slower expense growth	3. Expand global investment banking activities
4. Improve consumer profitability	4. Improve return on equity (ROE)
5. Expand state-by-state in US	5. Make acquisitions

*Prior to the position taken in 1995 by John Reed, to focus rather than spread thin.

Table 3.2 Strategic objectives of J.P. Morgan in the early 1990s

Overall	Recent thrust
1. Serve large domestic and multinational corporations. Also: • Some middle market companies at home • Government and financial institutions on global basis	1. Develop non-credit services, as lending becomes more competitive
2. Profit from trading and funding skills in volatile markets	2. Selectively expand relationships with foreign multinationals and financial institutions
3. Retain good earnings visibility based on: • Strong net interest margins • Ability to leverage the balance sheet, to keep assets and net interest income growing	3. Enhance the ability to attract and retain some of the best financial minds in the world
4. Assure rapid expansion of fee income	
5. Remain flexible enough to adapt to changing market conditions	

culture. High labour content transactions were computerized to reduce costs, with investments in computers and communications judged by deliverables. And new perspectives were opened in product innovation.

Among the foremost institutions, newly established research labs were given the mission of developing an alternative line of financial instruments for client companies and high net worth individuals. These have been largely derivatives: options, futures, forwards, swaps, and exotic financial products. They were:

- Designed with the goal of exploiting the top of the client base, and
- Sold as 'risk management' instruments, which was a misnomer.

Banks that failed to protect their clients' capital invested in derivative financial products that they sold them, paid dearly for it. The legal risk hitting Bankers Trust provides the best example. A few years down the line, in 1998, the bankruptcy of LTCM provided another lesson: overleveraging is a bad strategic option; good governance requires that there is a limit to everything.

4. Strategic products: case study with Microsoft

Dr Louis Sorel, my professor of Business Strategy at UCLA, used to say that more companies fail because their products and services are out of tune with the market than for any other reason. And he insisted that product failure, not financial problems, are the topmost reason companies go bankrupt. Half a century of personal experience has proved Sorel right.

At a time when innovation is king, product obsolescence can be deadly. Quite often, obsolescence is slow in showing up. It becomes evident only after it gains in impact. International trade magnifies its risk, and failure to respond to market drives becomes lethal because competition is global and ferocious. The distance between decisions makers and the domain where the action takes place adds more to this challenge of product line upkeep.

Neither is obsolescence only a matter of lower functionality. Producing a good product at high cost, including overhead and commitments due to legacy costs (see Chapter 9), is just as destructive. When management is not in charge of cost control,

- This pushes the clients away from *our* firm, and
- Lands them in the orbit of our competitors.

No doubt, most of these considerations were on Bill Gates' mind when he decided to take the imaginative steps briefly described in the Introduction; namely, moving away from overdependence on software for PCs and servers. With Xbox 360 and gaming, Microsoft positioned itself as challenger to Sony's dominance of this industry sector. The question now is not whether Microsoft will eat into Sony's market share, but how much it will attain with its strategy.

To appreciate this strategic move, it is appropriate to remember that Microsoft has been trying for years to move beyond the PC, and into other products and services, including mobile phones and television set-top boxes. This has come in the aftermath of the company's strategic decision that the digital revolution was going to:

- Have a big market impact, and
- Present a business opportunity for which it had to be prepared.

An interesting observation which was instrumental in entering markets that looked *as if* they were off-stream is that, equipped with microprocessor power and often with low cost storage, more or less all electronic devices increasingly resemble computers. Hence Microsoft could sell software for these devices too. But at the same time, such devices offer new avenues for growth:

- Sales of non-PC gadgets are growing much faster than sales of PCs, and
- Controlling that market holds the promise that for the next 30 years Microsoft could be as successful as in the last 30 years.

In other terms, *if* the market moves towards using the set-top box as a hub to the digital home, *then* Microsoft wants to be there. The same concept applies to mobile phones, which outsell PCs by far, and start being regarded as universal instruments for businesses and for consumers.

Moreover, from a strategic planning viewpoint, moving into non-PC and non-server markets also provides a hedge against any future decline in the company's core business, such as Windows and Office software. And at the same time, Microsoft has a chance to rebrand itself as a younger firm. Hence, this strategy:

- Is more than hedging and diversification,
- It is one of gaining leadership in vibrant new markets and their offspring.

To master that new line of activity, Microsoft needs to acquire a new culture, and this is precisely what Bill Gates seems to be doing. It is interesting to note that contrary to the PC's basic software, which is sold once with each machine, gaming follows the model of the razor industry:

- Selling blades never ends, and
- This compensates even if the razor itself is given for free.

There is another interesting aspect of Bill Gates' new strategy – essentially a reversal of Microsoft policies prevailing in past years. To radically reduce *time-to-market*, the original Xbox was built from off-the-shelf parts. This way it was launched in just 18 months:

- This approach optimized timing, but kept costs relatively high.
- By contrast, the new Xbox 360 has been designed bottom up, with the dual goal of cutting costs while improving functionality.

In 2001, when it first came into the public eye, voice over Internet protocol (VoIP) was widely regarded as a technological advancement that would never reach mass-market commercial maturity. Even seasoned industry observers asked who would sit in front of their PC to talk to his or her friends. (Remember Jack Warner's question about who wants to hear actors talking?) But by now this question has been answered – and VoIP is popular.

Partly based on that experience, many experts now believe that the same query about IPTV will also be answered in the same way, and Microsoft is positioning itself for that day as platform provider. Gates is not alone in travelling that road.

Search engines like Google and telecoms from BT to Verizon are pumping financial and human resources into IPTV-related projects.

- Each has something to bring to the party, and
- Each has its own logical entry point to the IPTV market, which will probably flourish by the end of this decade, as Figure 3.1 suggests.

As this case study demonstrates, the products and services we offer must answer both current and future client needs, have a growing appeal to cerebral skills rather than manual skills, and be able to hold their own in the market as competition intensifies. Every one of the entrants into the IPTV market is facing a Herculean task. For instance, the challenge facing telecoms is dual:

- Entering a new market, and
- Defending their customer base using IPTV with broadband voice and data as well as with mobile links.

IPTV is a good example because it involves different players, each with its own likelihood they may gain or lose. Telephone companies, for example, have to thoroughly evaluate, and probably revamp, their existing capabilities in network infrastructure. And to succeed they will need lots of software to make content easily accessible.

Marketing studies indicate that at the end of the day IPTV will deliver returns only if it offers content that attracts consumers. This means that entrants to the IPTV market face plenty of challenges: providing the infrastructure, developing the software, creating or gaining access to a library of content, ensuring security

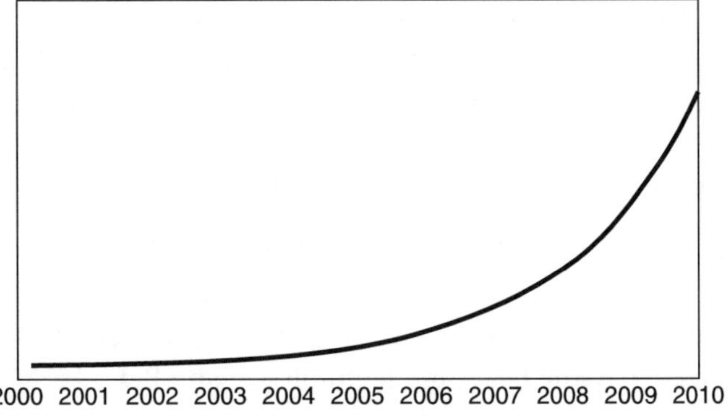

Figure 3.1 The growth in IPTV subscribers is projected to become exponential

and privacy, and protecting content rights while making it accessible through a platform that is reliable, fast, low cost and easy to use.

5. Strategic and Tactical Products Defined

In the mid-1990s, when it was launched, the 360 series of IBM was the company's strategic product. In the case of Digital Equipment, its strategic product in the late 1970s and early 1980s was Vax. In Microsoft's early history, the strategic product was MS DOS, followed by Windows and NT. As the history of all these references demonstrates,

- The strategic characteristics of a product fade over time,
- In a way, it is like the Tour de France and its 'maillot jaune' – a new winner – product comes in and takes the 'strategic' label.

Clearly, not all of a company's products can be fulfilling strategic requirements. Chances are that only a few will be characterized as strategic. Briefly defined, a *strategic product* is one on which *our* organization depends for its survival. Typically, it is:

- Longer range
- Views future needs, not only present ones, and
- There is a commitment to its continuation and further development.

Companies develop strategic products in order to continue being key players in the business to which they appeal. Such products usually require significant research effort and product design, which involves well-focused marketing perspectives. Strategic products are subject to wider advertising campaigns and communications support. Strategic products must be:

- Steadily evaluated in terms of their marketability
- Be ahead of competition and sometimes a little ahead of their time
- Be definitely customer-oriented answering properly defined requirements, and
- Act either as cash cows, prestige offering or both.

By contrast, *tactical products* are a different ball game. They are part of a shorter-range perspective, aiming to help today's business. Furthermore, they are usually, though not always, characterized by low cost production and distribution, and are not necessarily the best high technology can offer.

The market increasingly demands that both the strategic and tactical product are subject to customization, though this is more likely for the former than for the latter. Also, both should be adapted to evolving customer requirements in order to enhance their profitability. By contrast, policies for management and sustenance of tactical products are different from those used for strategic products.

Section 4 provided the reader with examples on policies followed by Microsoft in connection with the development of next generation strategic products. Tactical products and strategic products overlap up to a certain extent, as shown in Figure 3.2. Strategic and tactical decisions also overlap with policies developed for customization and more efficient marketing. At the core of this universe is found profitability.

This does not mean that tactical decisions are not challenging. At Microsoft the policy guiding difficult tactical decisions regarding the direction of product

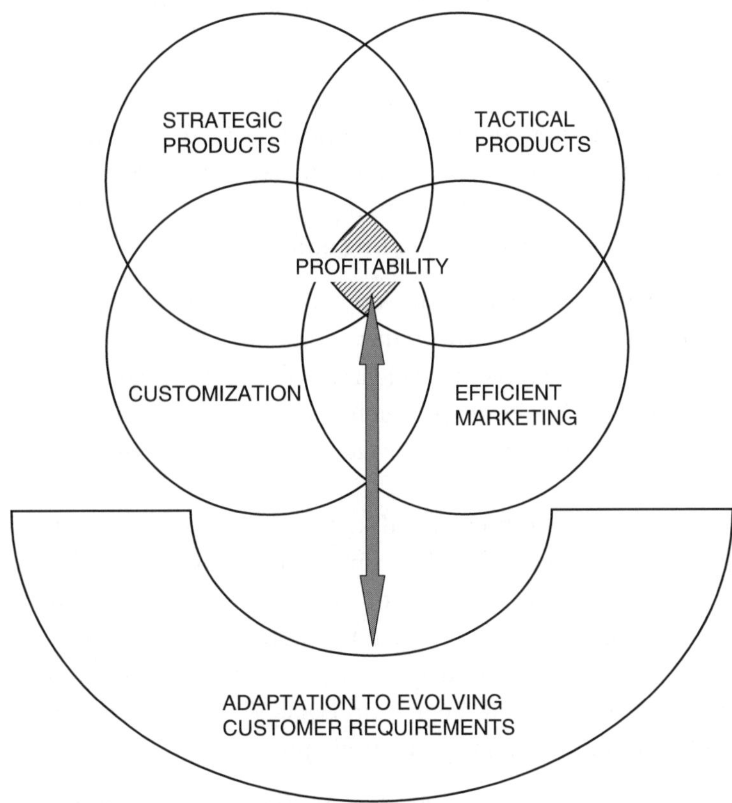

Figure 3.2 Both strategic and tactical products must be regularly reviewed for adaptation to customer requirements

development is referred to as *embrace and extend*. For instance, rather than inventing a whole new service to compete with the Internet, Microsoft would:

- Embrace current net standards, then
- Extend them, capitalizing on their general use.

If Netscape let Web browsers look at pages from around the world, Microsoft would let users look at Web pages from within familiar applications. If Navigator could play sound, Explorer would play quality sound. Because of this approach, although frequently second to market with its products, Microsoft wins by *out-featuring* its competitors.

The careful reader will observe that the examples in the previous paragraphs carefully avoided any associating a strategic product or a tactical one to an exclusive franchise. The reason is that with deregulation, globalization, and innovation, practically no organization today has an exclusive franchise, even if it thinks that it has one – as Microsoft found with Linux. What practically everybody does is try to be more *customer-oriented* than their competitors.

Loans, for instance, used to be a sort of exclusive franchise of commercial banks. But during the last quarter century capital markets took this product away from banks, by providing better terms of financing. At the same time, credit derivatives spread credit risk outside the banking sector, while loans inventoried in a bank's portfolio became subject to pooling and securitization.

As the exclusive franchise disappears, and capital markets as well as non-banks (such as GE Capital, GMAC, Ford Credit, and many others) are eating up part of the banking industry's pie, the more clear-sighted credit institutions understand that they have to innovate their products and services in order to be winners. Several characteristics help to describe the winners. Three of the foremost are:

- Efficient, low-cost producers and distributors of services, who know their costs and assure both value differentiation and quality of deliverables.
- Entities able to appeal to a selective client base, with solution selling and the ability to know risk and return by client and transaction.
- Management astute to market challenges affecting assets and liabilities supplementing strategic and tactical products, with modern, high-technology support and plenty of entrepreneurial spirit.

Behind these three bullets are crucial factors that assist in the evaluation of an entity's position in terms of products and services. As the previous two chapters underlined, one of the most important factors is management culture – particularly the ability to establish and implement a long-term policy in product development. Also important is to assure dynamic product line balancing, which takes account of the market's evolution.

Strategic and tactical products must also be examined in the perspective of *financial commitments*, since they will provide the cash flow needed to honour the company's obligations. Very important is each product's *profit pattern*, including the thread of growth or decline – month after month, and year after year – as well as its further out future perspective.

It is important to appreciate that products that are not strategic are not necessarily tactical, or vice versa. A company is obliged to also have *also-rans*, in order to present to the customer a full product line, even if these also-rans don't contribute to profits, or even represent a certain amount of losses.

- Few products will be strategic; many more will be tactical
- But taken together, these two populations would make about 15–20% of the total product line.

Marketing should watch strategic, tactical and also-ran products like a hawk – in terms of P&L. Every product should justify its existence. Key to the fulfilment of product-related requirements is the process of *product planning* (see Chapter 14). Product planning, which has been instituted by many organizations since the 1960s and 1970s, does not always work to perfection. To be successful, the product planner has to become faster than other professionals, and more entrepreneurial with:

- Specific goals in product development, and
- A fast track record of deliverables.

Strategic product planning processes should not only be very sensitive to market whims, but should also implement without loss of time what leading edge competitors have discovered that works (see the Toyota case study in section 2). The management of change is a basic ingredient of product planning and it must serve as the blueprint as we steadily revamp and restructure our product line.

6. Strategic customers and Pareto's law

Sections 4 and 5 underlined that, to a very significant extent, product strategy is conditioned by the market. The word 'market' however is too general, and this does not help in strategic planning. What we are really interested in is *strategic customers* – who may be individuals, companies, or whole sectors of the economy.

The way to bet is that these strategic customers will be demanding both innovation and high quality in products and services. They will also be able to identify and study alternative sources of supply, and will be tough in negotiating prices and conditions. But at the same time they will be contributing a high percentage of *our* company's turnover and profits.

A study I did in the 1990s with one of the leading financial institutions, which included nearly all product channels of universal banking – from asset management and portfolio management to wholesale banking and retail banking – led to the '20%/80%' rule regarding business done with counterparties:

- 20% of the clients
- Account for 80% of turnover.

The number of clients and amount of profit each relationship produces are characterized by a negative correlation. This is known as Pareto's law, named after the Swiss-Italian economist and mathematician who developed it after having found that about 35% of the Swiss population controlled more than 90% of the Swiss economy. Pareto's law is visualized on the left-hand side of Figure 3.3.

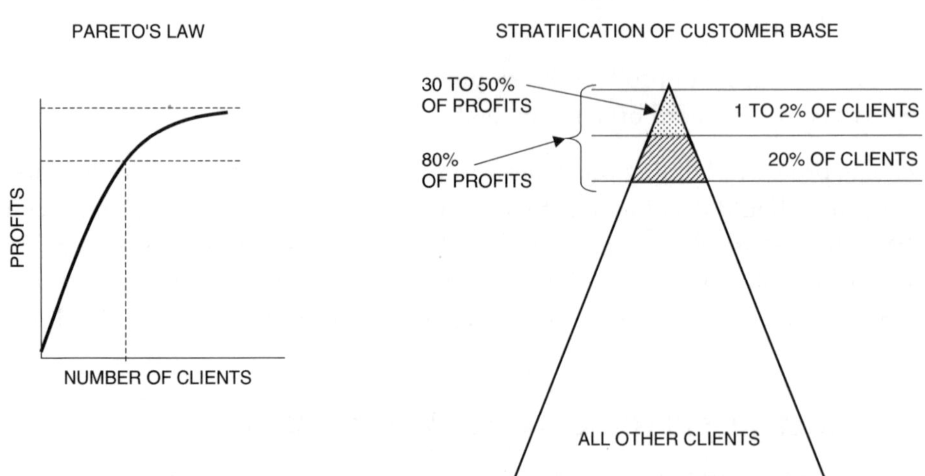

Figure 3.3 Pareto's law implies a stratification of clients according to business criteria with emphasis on product appeal, innovation, risk management, quality assurance, and potential profits and losses

In a similar manner, a business makes the larger part of its profits from a relatively small number of clients, as the right-hand side of Figure 3.3 shows. The study to which I referred above documented that in a credit institution:

- The top 1% of clients provide roughly one-third of annual profits. AT&T has found something similar in telecommunications.
- With the top 2% of its total client population, the bank makes about half its profits.
- The following 18% of clients, adding up to 20% of the total, bring the total profits for the bank up to 80%.

In my experience, Pareto's law is universal, and this can be proven through appropriate study. But the reasons underpinning it are individual to the firm.

After research, a Pareto chart should be constructed with the reasons underlying problems identified along the abscissa (horizontal axis of reference) and the frequency of location along the ordinate (vertical axis). For good governance purposes, this visualization must be complemented by the 'dashboard', which resembles a car's instrument panel, showing chosen critical variables pertaining to the product or service, and the customer relationship, including:

- The level of quality the customer is seeking, and
- How far the company is from meeting that requirement.

General Electric's Six Sigma will be an excellent tool in implementing this approach.[7] It includes *statistical quality control* charts, a *defect measurement method* that accounts for the number or frequency of defects that hit product or service quality, *chi-square testing* that evaluates the variance between two different samples, and therefore helps in detecting statistical differences embedded in variations.

Equally important analytical tools are: *experimental design*, that permits one to carry out methodologically *t*-tests of the mean, and chi-square tests regarding two populations (H_0, H_1); *root cause analysis* that targets the original reason for noncompliance or nonconformance, with specifications aimed at its elimination; and *radar charts*. Figure 3.4 presents an example of evaluating risk and return embedded in a strategic client account, due to derivative financial instruments in the client's portfolio.

Strategic clients, or 'dear clients' as Citibank called them, should have dedicated to them rich databases that are kept fully updated and are mined on-line. In one of our meetings in Tokyo, in the 1990s, the chief information officer

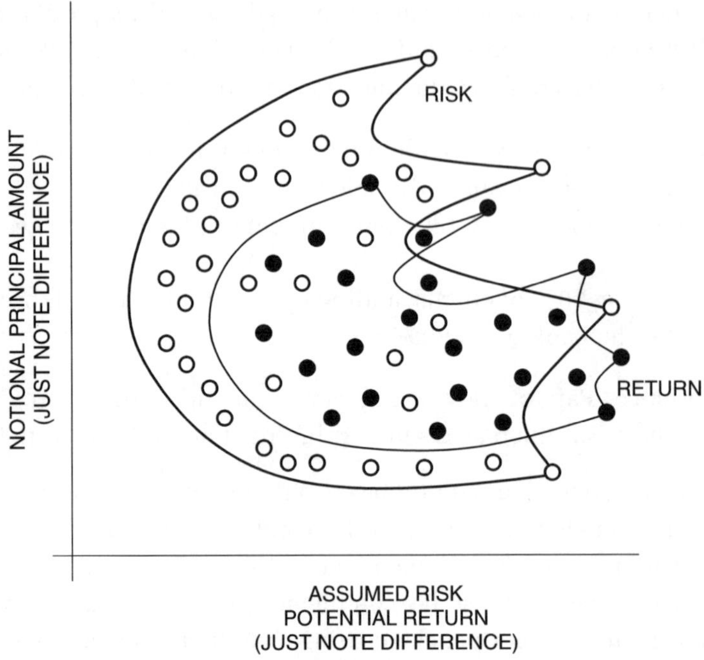

Figure 3.4 A radar chart can be used to visualize relationships concerning risk and return in derivatives exposure in strategic client accounts

(CIO) of Dai-Ichi Kangyo Bank said that his institution had dedicated databases for 20,000 of its clients – which represented 1% of its business client base:

- This top 1% posed very sophisticated requirements, but also provided roughly one-third of the bank's annual profit.
- As Figure 3.5 suggests, the next 1% of customers, or 2% of total population, produced about half its profit. These customers, too, could only be satisfied with significant effort.
- The requirements posed by the following 18% of clients, adding up to 20% of the total, called for innovation and customization, but this business, too, was lucrative to the bank.

The rationale behind this focused approach to the management of strategic customer relationships is that one should not treat in the same way things that are not the same. In banking, the strategic customer population is composed of institutional investors, high net worth individuals, and large multinational corporations, as well as their pension funds.

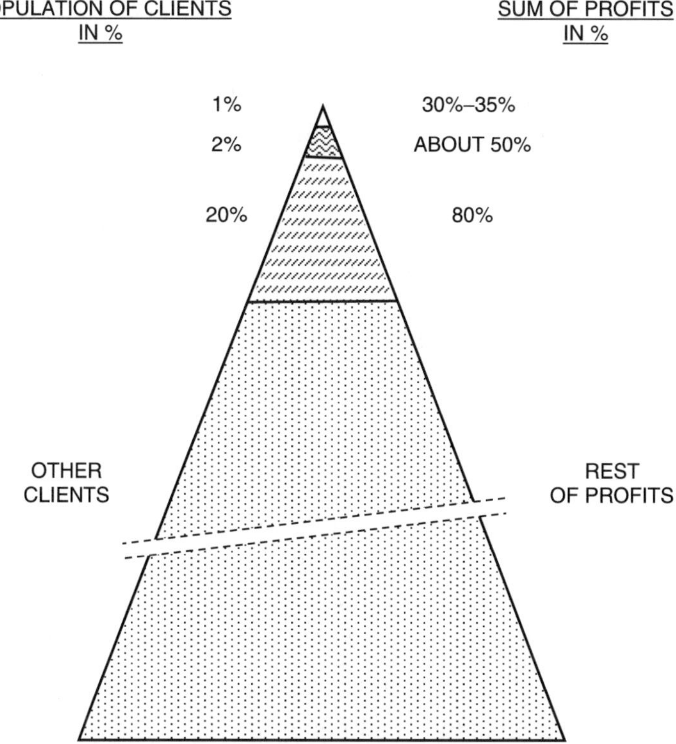

Figure 3.5 Some of the clients represent the lion's share of the profits

All three classes – 1%, 2%, and 20% – pose significant customer handholding and product development demands. But the returns are good. Not only my own analysis but also a number of other studies documented the wisdom of using client segmentation, placing emphasis on *strategic customers*, which means:

- The very selective client base, which is not always properly looked after.
- Crucially, the counterparties that are demanding in terms of novelty, quality, and short response time to their requests.

Speaking from personal experience, no bank can afford to disregard this market of strategic clients, which is highly competitive in every product line (including loans) as well as very selective. In 1980 AAA American companies had on average 36 banks to deal with. In the early years of the 21st century this number has been reduced to 7 and is still shrinking.

Selectivity is good for business because it enlarges the range of services being sold. Banks that continue to be retained by major corporations and institutional investors become a sort of assistant treasurer. And they remain in this position only as long as they are:

- Inventive in the type of products which they offer to their clients, and
- Able to keep ahead on terms of service quality, handholding skill, and technological know-how.

Because strategic customers place so much weight on the income statement, well-managed companies must reflect into their P&L both the rewards of sound governance and the aftermath of unsound product policies, poor handling, or undocumented premises offered to their clientele. A recent study has found that on the average:

- A 1% attrition in customer base
- Has a 7% impact on the bottom line.

Just as important is management's ability to avoid *strategic mistakes*. Some years ago, at Saatchi & Saatchi the crucial mistake was the decision to purchase a competing advertising agency in the United States whose biggest client happened to be in the same line of business as one of Saatchi's top customers. This is in disregard of the strategic client concept:

- Neither customer liked the conflict of interest which followed, and
- The more upset account opted to take its business elsewhere.

The switch of a strategic client to a competitor advertising agency meant a substantial loss of business to the acquiring company which resulted after the merger. The board and CEO will be well advised to ask for a thorough study on future conflicts prior to engaging in an acquisition (see also Part 5 on M&A).

All told, the identification of strategic clients is a research project not a matter of course or an exercise in looking up of customer files. The following example is revealing. In early August 2005, Space Adventures, a firm based in Arlington, Virginia, announced that it was offering a private trip to the moon for two fare-paying passengers – at the price of $100 million a seat. Who would pay that money? An article in *The Economist* suggested that at least 1000 people could afford to do so.[8]

In evaluating the existence of strategic clients and their contribution, market information must be examined in three dimensions – past, present, and future – with particular emphasis on repetitive business transacted with the client. For many years, continuing business relationships, for example, represented the 70% of IBM's sales – which is a totally different example than that of Space Adventure.

Both leadership and research are the best guarantees that strategic clients continue to need our company's services. Many other issues connected to account management are important for good governance, though less salient than those that have been mentioned in this section. (A salient problem is the one to which an able manager will devote first most of his or her attention.)

7. Short-term *vs* long-term performance

In terms of corporate management there is a crevasse between the American way of focusing on short-term results and, on the other side, the European and Japanese trend to look at the longer term. Yet, the American business philosophy of short-term financial performance makes US companies use their capital much more productively than their rivals in other countries. This tends to be documented by:

- The higher levels of productivity attained in most US industries, and
- The fact that American managers find themselves obliged to use their resources more effectively than their counterparts, in order to face market pressure for industrial results.

For instance, a 1996 study by McKinsey found that capital productivity was significantly greater in the United States than elsewhere because the market wants to see short-term deliverables. (*Capital productivity* is the amount produced for every unit of capital.) This leads to a virtuous cycle because higher capital productivity generates bigger financial incentives for further investments.

- Capital productivity is a two-way process, because
- Investors both accumulate more wealth and spend more.

McKinsey suggests that European and Japanese managers could do much better in their current business environments by paying more attention to productivity, including improvements in manufacturing quality and shorter time-to-market. Many German companies, for example, waste money by overengineering their products; and in Italy productivity has been stagnant for many years.

American managers cannot afford the luxury of taking it easy, because a primary objective given to them by the capital market is financial performance. In the United States capital market, investors overweight short-term results when making up their mind about where to place their money. This has two downsides.

One is that when the deliverables are positive, investors believe these will hold true in the long term.

- Many investors thought that the great returns of the late 1990s signalled that big gains would continue indefinitely.
- The opposite is also true. By 2002, several investors were just as sure that stocks will not rise again.

The second downside is that when the P&L results are not those that the company promises and analysts expected, many managers cook the books. Hopefully, the Sarbanes–Oxley Act of 2002 will drastically reduce this bad practice in financial reporting, but the push to show outperformance will not necessarily be swamped.

Outperformance and underperformance are both natural parts of complete market cycles. For example, between 1945 and 2000 the S&P 500 slid into 10 bear markets (declines of 20% or more). Reaching the bottom took from 3 months in 1990, to 37 months in 1948–49 and 2000–03 – well within historical precedent. After bottoming, the stock market has typically recovered in less than 20 months – but it took longer to do so at the beginning of the 21st century.[9]

These references are a reminder that one of the basic strategic choices top management must make is whether it wants its deliverables to be hedged by investors, and the market at large, in the shorter or in the longer term. Management's choice should be reflected in the strategic plan, which forgets neither the short-term nor the long-term objectives.

Strategic business planning is a balancing act between the shorter and longer term. Here is a real life example on what happens when this balance is disturbed. In the early- to mid-1990s Finsiel, a then quite important Italian software company, had a billion-dollar turnover and was one of Europe's biggest IT services firms. The company's problem has been that:

- Its business came almost entirely from lucrative IT contracts from Italy's then huge public sector, and
- Finsiel's tight grip on this market was forced open by European Union directives on competitive tendering.

There has also been a negative fallout from *tangentopoli*, the huge corruption scandal that rocked Italy's state industries and town halls in the mid-1990s. In the aftermath of these events, Finsiel's power in the Italian software market waned, and the Rome-based firm went into a long-term decline.

In March 2005, the fallen star of Italy's IT services industry finally found a new owner, Gruppo Cos, which specializes in call centres. Among other operations,

Cos, which overtook Accenture in the final round of bidding for Finsiel, had also acquired Telecom Italia's call centre business. Cos paid just 130 million euro to acquire the software firm through a joint venture with an Italian investment bank, a small fraction of what Finsiel was worth a few years earlier.

Making the shorter- and longer-term work in unison is a better strategic choice than betting exclusively on the one or on the other. For this, there is what I call the *4-P Prescription*: Plan, Power, Predictability, and Persuasion. What is targeted by *Plan* is the skill to: set a purpose; devise a scheme for reaching it; provide resources and schedule their usage; grow the available know-how; and program the actions necessary to sustain and renew the base of strategic clients (see section 6).

Behind the concept of *Power* is the ability to: control people and things; exercise influence; affect strongly; perform; and produce results. These results should be visible in the short term, but they should not be produced at the expense of longer-term survivability. The third *P* is *Predictability*, the quality of having a clear policy and sticking to it in the longer term. This, however, has the prerequisite of carefully evaluating the future cost of such policy.

Persuasion is the art of setting a firm conviction; promoting a particular belief; inducing adherence to it; and providing reasons for trust. Persuasion is the glue holding business alliances together. The strategy that we choose becomes that more persuasive to our counterparties, when we can:

- Create an image
- Explain, demonstrate
- 'Sell' the wisdom of a business venture
- Implement without upheaval, and
- Keep the product or service being sold attractive to the customer.

Any strategic business choice has many more chances to succeed when the organization behind it commits its resources to the attainment of goals it has established. This promotes the client's attraction to its products, and enhances the chance that capital investments will have a good return.

In conclusion, success in business strategy requires leadership, marketing clout, and innovation. Not just one of the three. While individuals and small companies can make a great deal of money out of good new ideas, the success of large established firms is generally based on factors such as:

- Their innovative spirit
- Depth of technical expertise

- Effective distribution capability
- Marketing skills and client handholding.

To properly flourish and bring home profits, marketing clout and innovation must benefit from the animator's contribution. The imagination of Walt Disney created a company that is still without parallel. General Electric was built on the extraordinary ingenuity of Thomas Edison, the Ford Motor Company on the abilities of its eponymous founder. The spirit behind IBM was Thomas Watson; Akio Morita of Sony occupies a similar place in the annals of modern business.

Notes

1 D.N. Chorafas, *Integrated Risk Management.* Lafferty/VRL Publishing, London, 2005.

2 *The Economist*, 3 September 2005.

3 *Business Week*, 11 September 1995.

4 D.N. Chorafas *Corporate Accountability, with Case Studies in Finance.* Macmillan/Palgrave, London, 2004.

5 D.N. Chorafas, *Wealth Management: Private Banking, Investment Decisions and Structured Financial Products.* Elsevier, Oxford, 2005.

6 At his lecture, at Edmond Israel Foundation, Luxembourg, 5 May 1992.

7 D.N. Chorafas, *Integrating ERP, CRM, Supply Chain Management and Smart Materials.* Auerbach, New York, 2001.

8 *The Economist*, 13 August 2005.

9 *Wall Street Journal*, 6 March 2001.

Establishing a Strategic Plan

1. Introduction

Chapter 1 presented to the reader the concept of strategy as a master plan. Chapter 2 contributed practical examples on leadership in strategic decisions, as on the impact of macroeconomics. The theme of Chapter 3 was strategic products, strategic clients, and choices that always have to be made in connection to corporate governance. With this background being acquired, the time has come to explain what is necessary in order to establish a sound strategic plan:

- The dynamics of a plan which can stand the test of time are this chapter's subject.
- The mechanics are discussed in Chapter 6, after having presented to the reader the prerequisite of forecasting in Chapter 5.

Stated in the simplest terms possible, a *strategic plan* focuses on achieving the basic objectives of the organization. As such, it encompasses all parts that enter into business strategy (see Chapter 1), ties them together, and makes sure that they fit well with the master concept as well as that they work in synergy.

Into the process of *strategic planning* integrate the decisions and actions that lead to a strategic business plan. This is not a once-in-a-lifetime event, but a steady continuous activity, which must be tuned in a way that helps the firm adapt to changing conditions. As a process, strategic planning is usually divided into logical steps, ranging

- From the determination of objectives
- To reports on execution, feedback, and evaluation.

A strategic plan allows the organization to take a pro-active role, aiming to have an impact on the environment before it feels its impact. Generally speaking, in business potential problems may be avoided if attacked early enough. The strategic plan must see to it that through proper actions competitors can be kept at bay, and the market can be influenced in the direction corporate governance has chosen.

The tools of planning are:

- Policies
- Procedures
- Priorities
- Programmes
- Budgets
- Timeplans
- Quality targets.

Another important tool is timely and accurate resource evaluation, including workforce, materials, and money. Among the means are research, development, production, and marketing, of methods and systems – including technological support. Planning premises require:

- Definition of resources needed to meet goals
- Appropriate allocation of resources, and
- Steady, objective evaluation of obtained results.

One of the reasons strategic business planning is so important is that knowing where the organization is headed is a good incentive to all employees, most particularly professionals and managers, to put up a better performance. Additionally, well-structured strategic plans can serve as a communications tool:

- Within the organization, and
- Between the company and its business partners.

This being the case, it is not surprising that companies look favourably on planning, even if the majority just practise 1-year financial plans (budgets) and short-range planning premises. Based on a study I did in the late 1990s, Table 4.1 presents percentages on the implementation of planning among industrial firms, by type of plan.

Aside from cultural issues, a basic reason why longer-range plans are not so popular is lack of appropriate tools for prognostication, and substandard information systems support. This is, however, changing; according to experts, the following critical phases will increasingly characterize the establishment and upkeep of a strategic plan in the coming years:

- Building up the information base
- Setting and revising longer-term objectives
- Exploding these objectives into component parts

Table 4.1 The practice of planning in industry and commerce: classification according to type of plans being prepared

Operating budgets	Short-range plans (up to 3 years)	Medium-range plans (up to 5 years)	Long-range (over 5 years)
99%	80%	70%	40%

- Elaborating each plan individually: human resources, product, market, financial, technological
- Assembling the component parts into a unified, coherent strategic framework, and
- Identifying planning gaps, analysing ways of closing them, and improving the plan's overall performance.

The development of strategic plans calls for information relating to environmental conditions that involve political, economic, and financial factors. A crucial role is also played by developments by competitors, their possible impact, and their strengths/weaknesses versus 'our' products. And also, our own organization's past performance and future outlook.

Both past performance and future outlook must be considered not only in a cumulative sense but also by product, business unit, region, and country of operations. Also, by important functional area, strategic customer, other grouping, and so on. Furthermore, the information used for strategic planning should be timely, accurate, and complete. It must also be compatible to that needed in preparing operational plans.

2. Accounting for ambiguity in the development of a strategic plan

Strategic plans are a practical exercise. As such, they must be tailored to the business requirements of the entity using them. That said, however, because the planning process is formal (see Chapter 6) strategic plans also have common characteristics – being flexible and dynamic is one of them.

Another common principle is that the strategic plan should help senior management to concentrate on *essentials*. This is achieved through the use of medium- to longer-range forecasting, which assists in making evaluations and developing transition plans, and also in making feasible a general harmony of effort, by having everything fit together. A sophisticated strategic plan would also allow – if the need arises – for the possibility to:

- Migrate into a larger (or smaller) structure
- Do so without having to rush or invent a transition path.

Within the perspective of the longer-range strategic plan, growth of business operations should be seen as an inverse pyramid structure. Usually, in a growth environment when management solves one problem it gets two, as the ancient Greek fable of Hydra stated so clearly. Moreover, modern business signified the arrival on the scene of a significant amount of uncertainty. Future events may be:

- Possible
- Probable, or
- Relative.

Globalization, deregulation and steady innovation have removed economic pillars of the past, which made some events more or less 'certain'. Therefore, the sophistication of a strategic plan can be judged through its ability to combine a clear description of a strategic path with the ambiguity of its likelihood. Laotse (c. 600 BC), an ancient Chinese philosopher, has phrased this ambiguity in the most perfect way:

> *For* is *and* is not *come together;*
> Hard *and* easy *are complementary;*
> Long *and* short *are relative;*
> High *and* low *comparative;*
> Pitch *and* sound *make harmony;*
> Before *and* after *are a sequence.*

It may sound curious, but the fact is that for managers who are worth their salt the existence of such ambiguity is a stimulus rather than a deterrent. The difference is made by properly capitalizing on ambiguity which enables a manager to get clearer vision, albeit in fuzzy sets. In turn, this helps in getting ready through better organization and a drive for efficiency.

Laotse was not the only ancient philosopher who spoke of ambiguity in human affairs. At around 600 BC, in ancient Greece, the Temple of Apollo was established at Delphi, which also gave its *chrisms* in fuzzy sets. In the 5th century BC, Herodotus, the historian, records how, by misinterpreting the fuzzy oracle of Apollo, King Croesus of Lydia went to war against Cyrus, the founder of the Persian Empire.

- The oracle told Croesus that if he crossed the Halys River he would destroy a mighty state.
- Croesus succeeded in doing so, but by failing to account for the ambiguity embedded in the oracle, the state he destroyed was his own.

To a substantial extent, the Apollo cult of Delphi was of the Sophists School, who taught that there is no basic truth; there is only opinion, nourished by sensitivity to events. Among Sophist philosophers was Protagoras (480–410 BC), a friend of Pericles. Socrates (470–399 BC) taught exactly the opposite; his method being a search for the truth through questioning.

As the late Dr Vittorio Vaccari, who is easily the greatest philosopher of modern Italy, once said, the civilization which we have developed in the 20th century is based on the School of the Sophists, not on Socrates' teachings. It is therefore inevitable that modern business is characterized by a significant amount of ambiguity, and this should be taken into account in every one of the stages designed to fulfil strategic planning requirements. Namely,

- Establishing the *primary objective* and associated secondary goals – which must be done by the board of directors, the CEO, and senior management.
- Elaborating the framework of an *overall* strategic plan, identifying its individual *components*, and assuring they work in synergy and serve the master plan.
- Putting in motion formal planning *procedures* which incorporate both operational planning and post-mortem control process, and
- Regularly re-evaluating strategic business planning premises to assure that they remain valid, adaptable and dynamic – as well as that they are executed as intended.

The last three bullets are the direct responsibility of the strategic planner and his assistants. Senior management, however, should keep a close eye on them, particularly so in regard to re-evaluations and post-mortems.

In research that particularly targeted the last of the four bullets, 60% of participating companies stated that they use actual events to test the validity of hypotheses used in strategic plans, while 80% have a policy of reviewing the strategic plan for possible modification, at regular periods – or more frequently in the case of major events.

Table 4.2 shows the frequency with which a strategic plan is matched or modified, within the aforementioned percentage of proactive action. There have been no significant differences on an industry-by-industry basis, but the better-managed companies were more prone to use actual events for testing strategic plans by integrating information from feedback channels.

One of the best case studies on how far the primary objective can change, and how when it changes it redirects the whole strategic plan, is offered by Julius Baer, the Swiss Private Bank. In early 2005 there was a disagreement among family members, successors of the founder.

Table 4.2 Frequency with which the strategic plan is matched or modified

Frequency	Use actual events to test strategic plan	Review strategic plan for possible modification
Monthly	20%	15%
Quarterly	25%	20%
Semi-annually	10%	5%
Annually	45%	30%
Only if something big happens	–	30%

- On one side were those who believed that the 115-year-old family firm could no longer compete against the goliaths of global banking. Hence, it should be sold.
- The diametrically opposite opinion was held by the other side, led by Raymond Baer, chairman of the bank. This clan wanted the bank to remain independent.

Raymond Baer won the day, and in September 2005 he took a big step forward in his effort to keep the bank independent. Julius Baer paid UBS, Switzerland's largest bank, 5.6 billion Swiss francs ($4.3 billion) in cash and shares for three private banks and the investment firm GAM, controlled by UBS. With this transaction, UBS increased its share in Julius Baer to 21.5%, but at the same time the transaction more than doubled Julius Baer's assets under management, to over 270 billion Swiss francs ($208 billion).

Critics, however, say that this strategic plan is not only ambitious but also ambiguous and flawed because the UBS deal does not solve a basic problem. Julius Baer has a small presence in Asia and other areas of growth for private wealth management. This way, the critics' argument goes, Baer is only delaying addressing the strategic question of an international presence – which is vital in a globalized economy.

While senior management at Julius Baer says that it plans to open marketing offices in central and eastern Europe as well as in Latin America, critics of the aforementioned strategic plan are not satisfied. Neither do they consider that an existing Julius Baer branch in Dubai and small office in Singapore can make the difference.

Where, these critics say, the current strategic plan may help Julius Baer is that the acquisition of three small banks and an investment firm increased UBS's stake; and this will deter a takeover attempt by a big international bank at least for some time. But they add that ultimately Julius Baer needs a proper global network of branches to:

- Attract wealth management clients the world over, and
- Participate in the growth of the global market for *wealth management*.[1]

Seen from this perspective, setting the primary goal is far more important than the other four basic steps enumerated in the preceding paragraphs. At the same time, however, the role played by top management's watch should never be underestimated. As Paul Kennedy has it: 'Without clear directives from above, the arteries of the bureaucracy harden, preferring conservatism to change, and stifling innovation.'[2]

3. How companies gain the high ground: case studies from Bloomberg and Bernheim

Today, the market of financial information providers is dominated by Bloomberg, whose terminals come with analytical tools that Reuters failed to offer it an early day. Reuters was way ahead of Bloomberg as information provider, but mismanaged its services and therefore lost market share. Bloomberg, for instance, makes available not just the price of a bond, but

- The bond's price history, and
- Its performance compared with other investments.

As a result of a market strategy based on product innovation, Bloomberg rapidly gained market share while Reuters' financial information business, which at its peak accounted for two-thirds of the company's revenues, had gone flat. Furthermore, the Reuters business was asymmetric as it made a disproportionate share of its money in Europe. Hence, apart from the failing in improving its service offerings, Reuters also had another gap in its strategic goals:

- After Europe's single currency came into being, European foreign exchange trading in what used to be different continental currencies withered, and
- The euro triggered more consolidation among Europe's banks and other financial institutions thereby reducing the number of client firms – which dealt Reuters another blow.

Considered from a strategic viewpoint, another basic problem for Reuters has been that for years it dominated the wrong side of the information providers' business. It was strong on trading floors, but as investment banks have merged the number of traders, and therefore the number of screens, has been falling rather than expanding as was originally forecast.

At the same time, the analytics Bloomberg provided on-line appealed to managers and investment professionals, beefing up that market. It needs no explaining that failure in strategic objectives, like this example with Reuters, is not usual. When it occurs, it quite frequently identifies senior management's inertia in prognosticating some of the crucial changes that sustain the business in the longer run, like:

- New product characteristics
- Evolution of market drives
- Seeds of strengths against competitors.

Sound governance requires that evaluations along the aforementioned frame of reference incorporate historical developments, effects of innovation, capabilities to match competitors' moves, supported functions, as well as weaknesses and drawbacks associated to one's own current product line. Senior management must always take a hard look at its strategic position, including ways and means for improving it.

One of the senior executives who participated in the research that led to this book, took the IT applications environment as an example of the missing, but highly necessary, proverbial long hard look: 'During the first 20 years [1955 to 1975], nobody projected the applications to match the power of the computer,' he said. 'Then, during the following 15 years [1975 to 1990] nobody designed systems solutions with an efficient use of the powerful database technology which was made available.' The result has been legacy IT applications that were, by and large:

- Limited in objectives
- Deficient
- Running on incompatible platforms
- Underutilizing available resources, and
- Constituting discrete islands of information.

Obsolete legacy IT is a pertinent reference in this case study, because it has been instrumental in Michael Bloomberg's decision to establish his own company, and endow it with first-class software. To do his job more efficiently in the investment bank of which he was senior vice president, Bloomberg had asked for a program able to provide interactively, on-line support in analytics.

Correctly, Bloomberg would not accept the argument by the firm's chief information officer (CIO) that he needed six months to do a feasibility study. This is the sort of argument so often heard by the unable, who is more tuned to do the unnecessary than produce wanted deliverables. Michael Bloomberg quit the investment firm and, as rumour has it, working together with a freelance programmer he produced in a couple of weeks the software that underpinned the services of his new firm.

This was the beginning. In terms of providing dependable, sophisticated and user-friendly customer service, Michael Bloomberg did not rest on his early laurels. Not only the on-line financial information, and associated analytics, continued developing, but he also personally kept a check on whether there was any disconnection of personal relationships, so important to the service industry.

During the Monte Carlo Investment Forum,[3] Bloomberg aptly suggested that automatic telephone answering services such as 'press 1, press 2, etc.' are counterproductive. Customers, he said, want to hear a human voice; otherwise, they take their business elsewhere. Therefore, his company reverted to a human answering service. He added that: 'We want people who ring us up to have somebody to help them:

- Give advice
- Provide handholding, and
- Explain what, why, when.'

This is a sound business principle. As far as lack of human contact is concerned, automation has gone a bridge too far because of wrong concepts. Another thing Michael Bloomberg underlined is that in the financial world (and, by extension, in any other industry) one has to provide a *seamless* interface to the client. This is the best way to keep the client calling back. Additionally, this has to be done in real-time with efficiency and security in mind.

The kind of original and interim decisions in the Bloomberg case study are instrumental in setting up the strategic plan and in revising it. Senior management must study in the right way not only the strategic plan's structure, but also its premises and its component parts. This means studying it very, very critically, always being ready to correct deficiencies in order to assure the best possible support to the business plan.

Neither is Bloomberg's overtaking of Reuter's an event that happens only rarely. Since the end of World War II the Sears chain of department stores has been in full expansion, having overtaken Montgomery Ward, its corporate opponent, in terms of merchandising strategy. But in 1993/94 it made a net loss on merchandising of $179 million. It also landed its parent, Sears, Roebuck, with a pretax charge of $1.7 billion to pay for a massive restructuring of the chain.

The opinion on Wall Street has been that, as a department store chain, Sears was mismanaged, and its strategic plan had fallen apart. Many analysts remembered that Sears, Roebuck was once an ambitious retailing and financial empire which built its fortunes in the post-World War II years by taking on Montgomery Ward. Not only in the late 1940s and 1950s but also in the 1960s to 1970s it continued to expand. But during the late 1980s it lost its speed. Subsequently, it substantially dismantled part of its operations:

- Selling Dean Witter, with its Discovery credit card, and
- Floating off 20% of its Allstate insurance subsidiary, which had already started to lose market favour.

This downsizing left Sears, Roebuck, as a group, hugely more dependent on its retailing arm, and retailing was not performing. New retailing empires, particularly Wal-Mart, had become masters of the market – with Sears suffering the fate it had once inflicted on Montgomery Ward. Like so many other companies, Sears was missing something much more precious than a concrete plan:

- The ability to believe in its strategic objective, and
- The power to see through the strategic goals management had established.

In his excellent book *Adventures of a Bystander*, Dr Peter Drucker mentions a story about Henry Bernheim, the man who started from nothing and, at the end of the 19th century, made one of the most important merchandising chains in the United States. Bernheim had sent his son to the then brand-new Harvard Business School to learn the secrets of management. 'But father,' said the son when he returned from higher education, 'You don't even know how much profit you are making.' 'Come along my boy,' answered Henry, and he took his son on an inspection tour, from the flagship department store's top floor to a sub-sub-basement, which was cut out of bedrock. There, at rock's edge, lay a bolt of cloth.

Contrary to what business schools teach, there were no statistics around, no balance sheets and no income statements. Just the bolt of cloth. 'Take away all the rest,' said the father, 'It's the profit. This is what I started with.'[4] Henry Bernheim had a strategic objective, a plan to see it through, and the will to do so. Hence, his was a success story.

4. Strategic planning at mean and lean organizations

'Mean' and 'lean' are relative terms, largely having to do with an entity's philosophy of management. But they are terms frequently used in present-day business. *Mean banks*, for example, have control of their pricing and revenues. Also of their investments, loans, and trades. When they are able to do so, they:

- Enjoy special competitive advantages
- Are able to sell value-added banking products, and
- Can occupy a particularly lucrative market share, or niche.

Mean organizations are keen to take advantage of any twist in legislation, integrating, ahead of others, its projected aftermath into their strategic plans. Table 4.3 provides, as an example, 12 key variables with impact on strategic planning in the banking industry. The statistics are the result of a study I did in the late 1980s following the deregulation of the financial industry.

Credit institutions that participated in this study, from the United States, UK, continental Europe, and Japan, suggested that the mean banking entities' strategy will not survive in the longer run if management has neglected other practices that can keep the institution ahead of the curve. Taken together, these practices characterize what are known as *lean banks* – meaning entities that have control of their costs. As such, they:

- Feature lower breakeven levels
- Focus on better earnings per share (EPS) than their industry peers
- Strive to steadily improve their competitive position through sound and thorough strategic planning.

Through cost reduction and earnings-enhancement initiatives, mean and lean organizations aim to lower their cost/income ratio to a level that compares positively with best-in-class competitors. They try to create 'unique' services, and target affordable pricing of their products when they compete in the mass market.

By capitalizing on their strengths, mean and lean entities develop a strategic business plan tooled around a policy to deliver top quality products to a premier client base. In parallel to this, in a cost-effective manner (see Part 4) they aim to bring their excellence in products and services to an ever-wider client base, while enhancing their offerings. They also aim to increase product choices by:

- Augmenting their in-house range, and
- Adding a quality-screened selection of third-party products.

Table 4.3 Twelve key variables in the banking industry with impact on strategic planning

	With regulated banking	With deregulated, globalized banking
Basic characteristics		
Number of financial products	Few	Almost unlimited, with brand differentiation
Content	Traditionally by common agreement	Open to innovation
Pricing	Uncompetitive, assured income	Potentially high, but possibly zero or negative income
Level of innovation	Very limited	Rapid and dynamic
Cross-product selling	Limited	Almost unlimited, but knowledge-based
Product life cycle	Long to very long	Short to very short
Mechanics of implementation		
Financial analysis	Traditional, with linear approaches	Non-traditional, real-time modelling, non-linearities
Introduction of new services	Regulated, by common agreement	Open to fierce competition
Means of delivery	Mainly paper	Mainly on-line
Distribution channel	Classical branch office	ATMs, POS, PCs and branches
Delivery point(s)	Proprietary	Proprietary or non-proprietary
Information technology	Legacy, unsophisticated, largely batch	High technology, intensive use of experimentation, real-time only

Behind these two points lie important issues on which the CEO and the board should excel: guiding the organization through a process of change, targeting the market segments, steadily developing the product line, seeking partners and forging alliances. Also assuring that their organization is and remains a high-quality, low-cost producer; and guaranteeing that technology is used in an effective manner to sustain the firm's cutting edge.

Another characteristic of lean and mean companies is that their policies account for possible obstacles to effective strategic planning. Starting with the most common, these are: lack of interest by top management in the plan's performance; lack of reliable data to gauge deliverables; improper organization of the planning function; unanticipated economic cycles; new government regulations; lack of trained personnel; or insufficient time for proper execution because competitors move faster.

In order to keep their competitors off-balance, mean and lean organizations use deceit, trying to destabilize the competitors and their plans, by keeping them guessing on the nature of their next move, as well as its timing. At the same time, they themselves move fast, targeting first or second position in the market – with the chief executive officer personally overlooking ongoing projects designed to keep subordinates on the run.

All this is done in appreciation of the fact that steady, rapid action is an indispensable characteristic of an effective strategic business plan. Not only does it oblige the company to keep up in performance, but it also has the benefit of throwing the enemy off-base. After all, as Chapter 1 emphasized, strategy is a master plan against one or more opponents.

One of the best examples of throwing the enemy off-base comes from the military and dates back to World War II. In August 1940, the Luftwaffe had made a concerted effort to knock out the RAF chain of home radar stations at Ventnor on the Isle of Wight. Its planes bombed the antenna and the transmitter shacks, damaging them badly, with heavy losses in men and material. The German command was not sure if the damage inflicted to the radar system was worth the several planes downed by the British air defences. So the next day they sent reconnaissance aircraft and their crude detectors showed that Ventnor was back on the air. Goering, the Luftwaffe commander, decided that if it was going to be that hard to knock out a radar site, it wasn't worth it, and the Luftwaffe stopped trying.

This, however, was a well-orchestrated deception. The British radar in fact was not working, but the technicians refused to admit that it had been knocked out. So they put some radar-frequency noise and oscillations into an amplifier, and pretended that it was a radar transmitter. Their bluff worked; the Germans fell for it.

Deception is a frequent ploy in business and war. In war it is a matter of self-defence and survival. In business, people say that companies practising deception have low ethical standards or they are truly mean. But is it really so? Judging from its widespread practice, deception looks like being a frequently used tool which has its limits.

President Lincoln once said that you can lie to some of the people all the time, or to all of the people some of the time. But not to all of the people all of the time. Additionally, companies and people practising deception must back it up with some hard facts. Otherwise, it will be a pure bluff, and chances are that it will be called.

5. The importance of credit rating: case study with GM and GMAC

Credit ratings are opinions expressed by independent rating agencies on the ability of issuers to repay punctually senior debt obligations. Typically, credit ratings also reflect a company's solid profitability and strong capitalization, the combination of which still sets a standard for identifying entities with good prospects in the future.

Companies take pride when independent rating agencies reaffirm an AAA or AA long-term rating, or change the outlook for the rating to positive, reflecting a stronger operating base and/or much better governance. Beyond this, higher credit rating means lower cost of funds – with an evident effect on the bottom line.

The turmoil through which General Motors (GM) has gone in terms of its financial stability, therefore its credit rating, and the possibility it may pull along with it into the abyss General Motors Acceptance Corp (GMAC) – a profitable entity – is a good case study on the importance of credit risk. Here is what a late November 2005 special study by Merrill Lynch had to say.[5]

GMAC, the world's largest prime auto finance company, as well as a 'top-10' residential and commercial mortgage lender, has been up for sale and, according to the investment bank, its solid profitability and meaningful market share should be attractive to buyers. In 2005 GMAC, ROA, and ROE were 0.93% and 13.1%, respectively, and a buyer:

- Could be able to reduce GMAC's funding costs to a mid-A level from BB− of GM

- Thereby, GMAC would be regaining access to similarly-priced unsecured debt markets.

With this, Merrill Lynch says, GMAC could generate visibly stronger returns, with positive economic value for the buyer. Over time, this could also improve the dividends to GM from its minority stake on its former fully owned subsidiary.

The information presented by the previous paragraphs is a testimony to the importance of higher credit rating. But Merrill Lynch adds in its study that the sale of GMAC is a complex operation because, among other reasons, the Pension Benefit Guaranty Corporation (PBGC, the US quasi-governmental pension plan insurer) would likely have valid claims against both GM and GMAC in the case of it becoming necessary to assume responsibility for GM's US pension plans.

PBGC is expected to do so after the likely bankruptcy of the world's No. 1 auto manufacturer, as has been the case after the bankruptcy of United Airlines and so many other firms. Moreover, even if only GM files for Chapter 11, it is possible that GMAC could also be pulled along as a result of having to:

- Make up unfunded pension obligations, or
- Avoid the attachment of PBGC liens.

Theoretically, default recoveries for bondholders and other borrowers would be much higher at GMAC than GM. Based on a previous analysis, Merrill Lynch believes recoveries for GMAC bondholders could exceed 90%, given a near-term bankruptcy filing, while recoveries for GM bondholders would probably be below 50%.

This is a way of illustrating that, if it were an independent entity, GMAC's credit rating would have been much higher than GM's. On the other hand, in practical terms the expected recovery for GMAC bondholders would be lower in substantive consolidation of GM/GMAC, than in a scenario where the two bankruptcy estates were administered separately – while for GM bondholders expected recovery would be enhanced.

Strategic plans, the shareholders' equity, and bondholders' debt exposure take a boost when the company's rating remains among the best of any major competitor. The message higher rating conveys is one of:

- Being well-capitalized
- Having a strong balance sheet, with steady cash-flow, and
- Featuring a cautious risk profile.

By contrast, the news to the business community is bad in the case of rating downgrade.[6] For instance, as the 2004 Annual Report by Sun Microsystems reported, on 5 March 2004, Standard & Poors lowered its rating on Sun to non-investment grade by two notches from BBB to BB+, but removed it from CreditWatch. By contrast, the two other rating agencies that follow Sun continued to rate it as investment grade.

- Rating from Fitch Ratings was BBB, on stable outlook.
- Moody's Investor Services gave a Baa3 rating, but on negative outlook.

In the aforementioned cases ratings reflected credit agencies' expectations that the intense competitive environment facing Sun in its core markets would continue, over at least the near-term, to challenge the company's sales and profitability. 'If we were to be further downgraded by these ratings agencies,' Sun suggested in its 2004 annual report, 'such downgrades could increase our costs of obtaining, or make it more difficult to obtain or issue, new debt financing.'

Successive downgrades also affect an entity's interest rate swap agreements that it uses to modify the interest characteristics of any new debt. In turn, any of these events adversely impact's a company's business and financial condition – and, by extension, its strategic plans. The contrary is true with upgrades as well as a stable outlook. Section 6 provides an example.

6. Credit rating and strategic planning

In its 2001 Annual Report, UBS had been jubilant that the three main independent rating agencies maintained a triple-A for the firm's long-term credit rating, as shown in Table 4.4. However, the Annual Report carefully noted that each of these ratings reflects only the view of the applicable rating agency at the time the

Table 4.4 Long-term credit ratings of UBS by independent rating agencies

	31.12.01	31.12.00	21.12.99
Fitch, London	AAA	AAA	AAA
Moody's, New York	Aa2	Aa1	Aa1
Standard & Poor's, New York	AA+	AA+	AA+

rating was issued, and any explanation of the significance of a rating may be obtained only from the agency itself.

Moreover, the 2001 Annual Report by UBS aptly suggested the presence of an element many investors (and some analysts) fail to appreciate in judging creditworthiness. There is no assurance that any credit rating will remain in effect for a given period of time, or that a rating will not be lowered, suspended or withdrawn entirely by the rating agency if, according to its judgement, circumstances so warrant.

What the previous paragraph outlined as uncertainties is precisely the strength of credit rating by independent agencies, which target company creditworthiness not only in the longer term but also in the short term – for debt that has an original maturity not exceeding one year. Issuers of debt and credit institutions providing loans look at Prime-1 (P-1) rating as identifying a superior ability for repayment of senior short-term debt obligations.

In plain credit rating terms, a P-1 repayment ability will often be documented by several characteristics, all of which directly impact strategic plans and, in turn, are being impacted by them as well as by their execution:

- Leading market position in an industry
- High rate of return on funds employed
- Conservative capitalization structure
- Moderate reliance on debt, and ample asset protection
- Broad margins in earnings coverage of fixed financial charges
- High cash generation internal to the business
- Well-established access to a range of financial markets
- Assured sources of alternative liquidity, rather than dependence on one channel.

According to some opinions, particularly those of major banks, reliance on rating agencies for evaluation of counterparties' credit risk is inversely related to the level of sophistication of the credit institution itself. Behind this argument is the notion that as far as large, internationally active institutions are concerned, rating agency information is used:

- As complementary to that of their own, or
- As a second opinion, along with other external information.

This, however, is a weak argument. Companies should always prize independence of opinion, because it protects them from future trouble. Beyond this, as we have seen with the UBS example, big global institutions are proud to get top rating by independent credit agencies. Moreover, many banks which publicly boast of having an unparalleled credit rating system for their clients:

- Have available only a coarse system of six or seven credit threshold classification.
- They are way behind the fine grid of 20 credit thresholds featured by independent agencies.

There is also the fact that rating agency information assists in strategic planning. Additionally, it is very important to medium sized and smaller banks, where it can have significant impact on their loans decisions.

Credit rating information is as well vital in the case of structured financial products,[7] where the role of rating agencies is considered important by nearly all banks – even if those more sophisticated usually complemented independent rating agency assessments with data from their own models. Beyond this lies the fact that, in a globalized market, rating agencies constitute a most necessary frame of reference, having a significant role to play in:

- How the market views a company's creditworthiness, and
- How the company itself can, or rather should, shape up its strategic plan to improve its creditworthiness.

The storm on Converium, the Swiss reinsurer, provides an example. Starting with the fundamentals, hurricanes like Jeanne, Charley and Frances, which wreaked devastation on Florida in 2004; or Katrina and Rita, which swept through the Gulf of Mexico and southern US states in 2005, have been always the nemesis of the insurance industry. But the storm that descended on Converium was entirely one of its own making.

Converium has been one of the world's top 10 reinsurers. In 2001, the company was spun off from Zurich Financial Services. By becoming independent, it had to convince investors to support a $420 million emergency rights issue. A bank consortium led by the CSFB and JP Morgan underwrote a deeply discounted deal. But this was only one step. Not only the rights issue had to be approved by two-thirds of shareholders, but also its outcome hinged on the absence of 'material adverse changes' to Converium's conditions – including its:

- Credit rating, and
- Financial stability condition.

US capital markets, as well as insurers looking for reinsurance, wanted reliable information on both points. At the time, US business accounted for more than a quarter of Converium's premium income: $1.2 billion out of $4.3 billion, and in the US the opinion of analysts was negatively weighted towards long-tail risks. (Long-tail risks are associated to insurance policies whose financial impact may only emerge years after being signed.)

The analysts were right. It was precisely this type of further-out risk associated to insurance and reinsurance contracts that triggered Converium's crisis. The rating agencies' assessment was not positive, and this influenced clients, particularly insurance companies seeking to cover their own risks. Many US insurers want at least an A-grade counterparty, and therefore they take a close look at creditworthiness.

As another example of the havoc created by a lower credit rating, when in 2003 the French reinsurer Scor dropped from A to BBB it lost more than one-third of its business. Gross premiums fell by 37% to $1.6 billion in the first half of 2004, compared with $2.67 billion in 2003, and the reinsurer had a hard time to repair its balance sheet.

It is also appropriate to notice that, to a certain extent share price and credit rating correlate. With Converium, the drop in equity price has been another indicator of trouble brewing. In late July 2004, Converium's equity price plunged 46%, on the initial news that big new reserves would be required to cover risks on US business. As shares dropped further after ratings downgrades by independent rating agencies, strategic plans had to be thoroughly revised, with downsizing of the company's operations high on the agenda.

7. Strategic plans and capital allocation

Seen from a strategic planning perspective, there are two sorts of capital which management should dearly care about. Taking the commercial banking industry as an example, there is *regulatory* capital, which buys a licence for the credit institution.[8] The new capital adequacy framework by the Basel Committee on Banking Supervision (Basel II) specifies the methods institutions should use in order to fulfil regulatory requirements associated to credit risks they have assumed.

The other sort is *economic* capital. Senior management assembles it to provide the company with financial staying power when confronted with assumed risks.

Management allocates economic capital to the company's business units to enable them to face exposures beyond regulatory capital. Such risks typically lie towards the long leg of the distribution of exposures assumed by the entity. This means that:

- Their likelihood is rather low
- But their impact, when they happen, can be quite significant.

Economic capital is essentially a message-giver to the market at large, and more specifically to the clients of the institution. Its existence and its appropriate allocation to business units has a significant impact on credit rating. As Walter Pompliano of Standard & Poor's suggested, 'We don't prescribe an economic capital allocation model. We evaluate what the bank has,' adding that:

- Market behavior cannot be modelled
- But modelling is useful as a discipline.

Not only is the allocation of economic capital one of management's most fundamental strategic decisions, but it is also an integral part of the company's business plans. Models help. One of the major contributions of modelling is that it forces the pricing of risk. The downside is that the bank's clients:

- May not pay the premium assumed risk requires, choosing to deal with a competitor, or
- Cannot afford to pay the premium because of their own rather poor economic condition.

Therefore, while a well-documented estimation of exposure, calculation of necessary economic capital, and its appropriate allocation, are indispensable components of a strategic plan, senior management should be able to make up its mind whether it wants to take on business whose pricing does not compensate assumed risk.

It is better not to take on a project than lose one's company because of it. The mission of economic capital is to cover well-studied risks and chance events – but not uncertain projects. The reader should notice that economic capital can be properly calculated only when risk assessment is factual and documented. This poses significant prerequisites. It requires a solid basis for:

- Identification of all risks
- Factual estimate of their frequency, and impact
- Comparison of risks by business unit and channel (product line)
- Choice of those exposures with the most favourable risk and return profile.

Experimental design, factor analysis to correlation of projected benefit and exposure, estimation of possible failure due to level of gearing, prognostication of possible spikes, and liquidity forecasts all contribute to a well-done study. Subsequent to these analytical activities comes the strategic need for aggregation at corporate level.

Comparison of projected exposure to available economic capital may indicate that the latter has to be upgraded; the alternative is to downsize the exposure. Additionally, risks being assumed must fit within:

- Guidelines set by strategic goals, and
- Limits established by the Board and CEO.

All risks should be managed in a rigorous way, which requires a close watch. A radar chart like the one in Figure 4.1 helps in visualizing the most important factors entering into the risk profile (see also the example on a risk and return radar chart in Chapter 3).

The strategic plan should also bring into perspective not only the allocation of economic capital to business units, to enable them in fulfilling their mission without starving the company in terms of liquidity, but also the strong and weak points of risk and return estimates. The process of economic capital allocation at business unit level, itself, has strong points such as:

- Providing transparency
- Promoting accountability

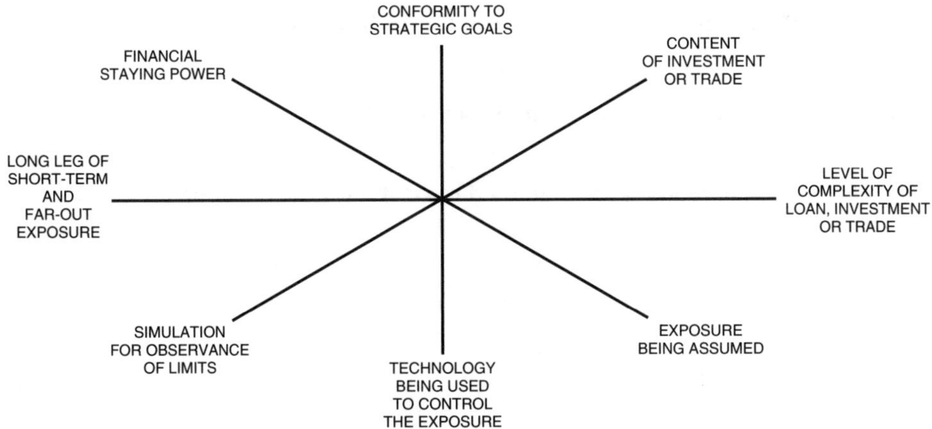

Figure 4.1 The most important dimensions linking the strategic plan to risk-taking and financial staying power

- Obliging the pricing of risk(s), and
- Increasing the focus on stress testing.

But this process of capital allocation also has weak points. Economic capital allocation to various units and channels is not a science. Even among better managed entities, it still uses:

- Ad hoc methodology instead of experimentation
- Rather obsolete and ineffectual risk measures, and
- Risk and return performance metrics which are largely detached from reality.

When this happens, the strategic plan being worked out is, to say the least, unrealistic. Apart from the fact that risk and return estimates must be rigorously documented, no two companies have the same economic capital requirements for their business units. Table 4.5 presents an example from the banking industry involving three different financial institutions.

In conclusion, companies that wish to be ahead of competition must provide themselves with skills and technology to study, analyse and experiment on risk and return, prior to formalizing their strategic plan and economic capital allocation which it entails. This approach is followed by well-governed organizations, along with the policy of developing alternatives to a strategic plan (see section 8) and having a sound methodology (see section 9). Without appropriate methodology, complexity could overwhelm any firm.

8. Developing alternatives to a strategic plan

As Nicolo Macchiavelli suggested in his famed book *The Prince*: 'Nothing makes a prince so much esteemed as great enterprises and setting a fine example. [But]

Table 4.5 Economic capital allocation by three different universal banks

	A	B	C
Corporate banking	20%	30%	30%
Investment banking	35%	20%	10%
Private banking	5%	10%	3%
Asset management	15%	2%	7%
Retail banking	20%	35%	48%
Other lines	5%	3%	2%

never let any administration imagine that he can choose a perfectly safe course.' Macchiavelli was right when he stated that prudence consists in:

- Knowing how to distinguish the character of troubles, and
- Having the power to make the choice of taking the lesser evil.

The 'lesser evil' is, for example, what was selected by John Kennedy when, during the Cuban missile crisis of 1962, he asked a group of 15 advisers to set out alternatives that were not all mutually exclusive. The six top options these advisers presented to the President were:

- Do nothing
- Use warning, diplomatic pressure, bargaining
- Try to split Castro from the Soviets
- Set up a blockade of Cuba
- Order an air strike against the missile sites, and
- Undertake an invasion of Cuba.

Prudence suggested the blockade alternative, as the lesser evil. Once this choice was made, there was no let-up. All sectors of the US government moved to reach the defined goal; this assured continuity and, eventually, success. It also fits well with Macchiavelli's dictum that 'One action must arise out of the other, so that men are never given time to work steadily against the prince.'

A lesson to be learned from President Kennedy's experience in the Cuban missile crisis is that on strategic occasions it is important to *list all possible alternatives* that come to mind – a process known as brainstorming. Then, to examine these alternatives on their merits and demerits, and through preliminary analysis choose two or three among them.

The next vital step in making a strategic plan is to provide a detailed examination of the retained options, and decide on one of them as the best course to follow. Before implementation, this option, and the process needed to implement it, should be fragmented into concrete, coherent, manageable steps – through a logical organizational approach (more on this later).

The existence of alternatives to permit an educated selection of the best possible solution is a vital element of strategic business planning. It is also part of the methodology every well-governed entity is using. The choice of an acceptable alternative has to fulfil at least two behavioural conditions:

- A *Feels Good* test, which provides a pattern of returns satisfying corporate goals.

'Feels good' is not a superficial estimate, but one to be backed by solid evidence. In addition to foreseeable *future* risks and liabilities a strategic choice must incorporate profit motives, cash flows, product offerings, and presence in certain market or industry sectors, unless the Board decides to move out of them.

- A *Sleep Well* test, which consists of a pattern of returns compatible with the risk being assumed.

To pass this test, economic capital allocation should address the entire path of returns over the investment horizon palatable to the company. Decisions must not focus exclusively on the short-term or end-of-horizon results. They must balance the quality of the journey with that of the destination, distinguishing between tactical and strategic aims.

Research in behavioural finance is a relatively recent development, which should be seen as a supplement to quantitative analysis. Its deliverables tend to keep separate mental accounts for different financial goals. For instance, most investors tend to sleep well and feel good about their allocations only if their mental account of projected income is dominated by cash flow producing assets. A rational investor would consider both:

- Risk aversion, and
- Liquidity preference

Then he or she would net out their effects on portfolio composition. This is an exercise requiring thorough methodology for developing and testing strategic alternatives. A general model of different phases being involved is presented in Figure 4.2.

- *If* the strategic plan is done first time around,
- *Then* it is wise to lower one's sights to the medium term.

This permits one to gain first-hand experience with goals that are more easily controlled. Every phase in Figure 4.2 calls for thinking and rethinking; projecting and correcting; as well as thoroughly revising and documenting what one does.

To gain input for rethinking, the strategic planner should ask prospective users of the plan to criticize it. He or she should restructure the plan after critique, and send it to operating department managers for a new round of feedback – attaching to it a concrete time schedule for implementation and action.

After implementation, the strategic plan should be followed up for plan/actual comparisons. Feedback requires a clear top management policy, one that leaves

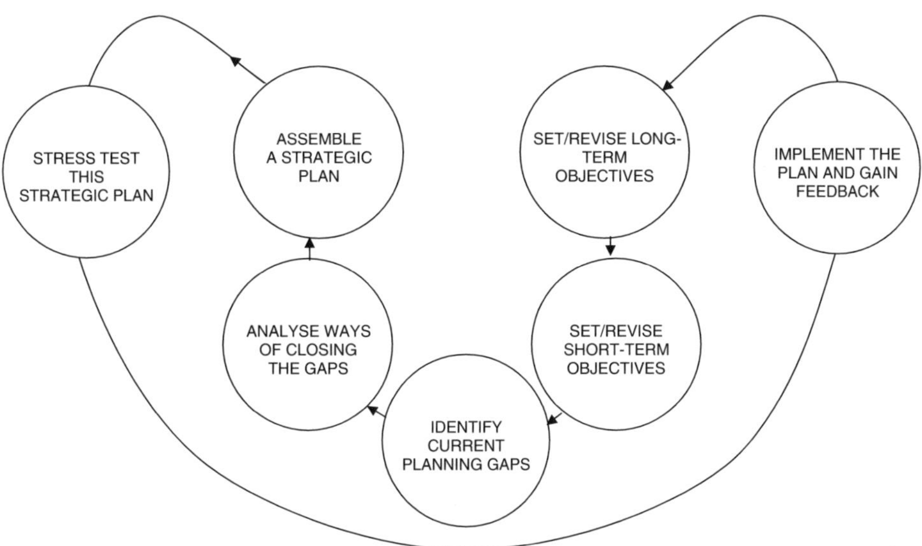

Figure 4.2 A general model of successive phases in strategic planning

no doubt in anybody's mind that internal control is a 'must'. Timely uninhibited feedback is absolutely necessary to every strategic business plan.

9. A methodology to support strategic planning

The strategic planning methodology will be somewhat different than the one described in section 8 when there is in-house experience from previous planning periods. Table 4.6 highlights, in a snapshot, the methodology I have applied for four decades, and its component parts.

Let me briefly discuss step 4: Criticize the plan. The principle is that for every strategic business plan being established, somebody at senior position, with conceptual capability and a very open mind, should be given the role of *devil's advocate*. 'Even if you are doing well, you risk becoming another big brown industry,' a senior bank executive said to me about a client firm. While strategic planning:

- Should use the momentum of products and services doing well at the present day
- It should also explore the downside of current products and of projected next big income earners.

Table 4.6 A rigorous methodology can greatly assist in strategic planning

1. Formulate the task
- Define the strategic objective(s)
- Identify reasons for it (them)
- Define the characteristics of the action sought
- Consider alternative approaches for reaching objective(s)

2. Develop the inputs
- Assemble the facts
- Position the company against its competition
- Forecast or postulate existing uncertainties
- Project alternative courses, and their likely outcomes
- Identify critical issues and conditions to be monitored for early warning
- Prescribe necessary performance standards

3. Evaluate the detailed alternative courses of action
- Convert retained alternatives to terms that can be compared
- Establish criteria for making a selection
- Compare retained alternatives against these criteria
- Prescribe performance schedule to be met
- Identify resources to be committed

4. Criticize the plan

5. Decide

6. Translate the decisions into statements of:
- Action being required
- Resources being involved
- Applicable milestones
- Consequences expected, and when
- Information required for feedback
- Control action to be undertaken, and criteria for it

The role of devil's advocate is not to inhibit action, but to promote it by making evident errors and shortfalls that should be corrected. If these are left untouched, a year on the initiative will be floundering – and the organization's willingness to move forward may cave in.

Criticizing a plan for its shortcomings is tantamount to increasing its opportunities, provided that these shortcomings are corrected. In fact, the search for new business opportunities is closely tied to refining our plans.

Pitfalls, shortcomings, and rough edges should be flushed out by the devil's advocate, in order to be taken fully into consideration. The same is true of weaknesses embedded into 'this' or 'that' aspect of a strategic plan:

- From hypotheses being made
- To mechanics and milestones being projected.

The devil's advocate should also be involved in post-mortem walkthroughs. To improve a strategic plan's performance, feedback from operations must be steadily used to update everything: from goals to means and procedures. Equally important is to feed into the walkthroughs recent research on markets, products, human resources and technological developments – including failures to account for research findings.

Finally, the devil's advocate should search to find inconsistencies among the strategic plan's component parts (product, market, financial, human, technological); audit the seriousness of alternatives, based on different major options; and do worst-case scenarios. Wise management is keen to learn about worst case before major commitments are made and the bad news builds a wall blocking off the company's future.

Notes

1 D.N. Chorafas, *Wealth Management: Private Banking, Investment Decisions and Structured Financial Products*. Elsevier, Oxford, 2005.
2 P. Kennedy, *The Rise and Fall of Great Powers*. Random House, New York, 1987.
3 Monte Carlo, Monaco, 30/31 March 2000.
4 Peter F. Drucker, *Adventures of a Bystander*. Heinemann, London, 1978.
5 Merrill Lynch, 'GM–GMAC', 22 November 2005.
6 D.N. Chorafas, *Managing Credit Risk, Volume 1: Analyzing, Rating and Pricing the Probability of Default*, Euromoney, London, 2000; D.N. Chorafas, *Managing Credit Risk, Volume 2: The Lessons of VAR Failures and Imprudent Exposure*. Euromoney, London, 2000.
7 Chorafas, *Wealth Management*.
8 D.N. Chorafas, *Economic Capital Allocation with Basel II: Cost and Benefit Analysis*. Elsevier, Oxford, 2004.

Functional Effectiveness in Strategic Planning

Forecasting

1. Introduction

'The plan is nothing,' President Eisenhower once said. 'Planning is everything.' *Planning* is the process that not only establishes and upkeeps the *plan*, but also sees to it that the plan is dynamic and adaptable to changing situations. A strategic plan is not done once and then put in a time capsule. Not only should planners match the plan to evolving conditions and events, but also regularly review it for possible modifications.

Plans are not made in the abstract. They have to be based on events in real life, and on the way in which they develop. This requires *forecasting*, which is a projection into the future. Forecasting is a prerequisite for planning, just like the setting of objectives is a prerequisite for information or strategy. In the business world, forecasting involves three major activities:

- A look into the future, including the evaluation of how the economy evolves (see Chapter 2).
- An estimate of trends in the industry in which *our* company operates and of how the market develops, which is the subject of *prognostication* (discussed in section 2).
- An expert evaluation of *our* company's standing in the industry and in the economy, including its current and future products and services (see Part 5).

Forecasting and planning need a structure, and a sound structure requires appropriate methodology, which involves all six basic functions of management. As shown in Figure 5.1, these range from forecasting to controlling. The able execution of each of these managerial functions needs skill, experience, the will to get results, and information that is timely and as accurate as possible – though it may be incomplete and involve uncertainties. At the top and bottom of the diagram in Figure 5.1:

- Forecasting provides prognostication as input to the plan.
- While controlling makes sure that activities are happening according to plan.

Even the best forecast and plans will turn to ashes without the exercise of management control. Effective control requires feedback and open channels for communications, as Part 1 underlined. In management literature as well as in practice, planning, analysis, and control have always been recognized as 'good things'. What is 'bad' is that quite often they are just admired rather than being effectively practised.

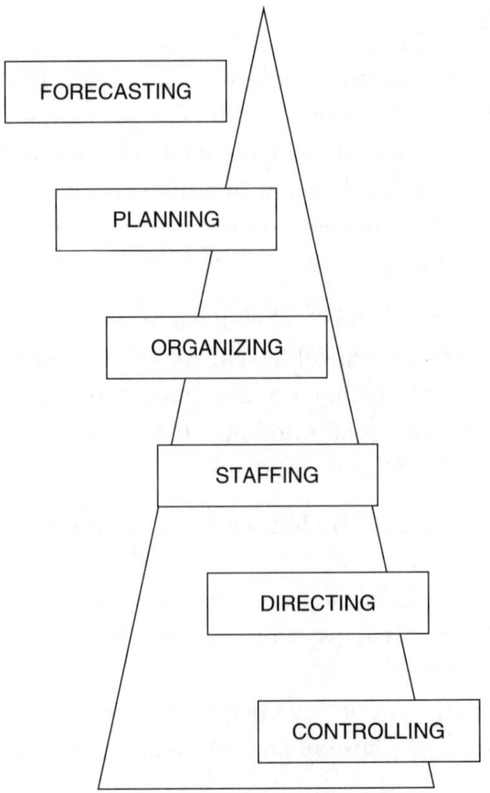

Figure 5.1 Pyramid of managerial functions necessary for corporate governance

Prerequisites to effective forecasting, planning, and control are not only skills and guts, but also independence of opinion and of means, which allows one not to compromise one's principles. The late J.P. Morgan, one of the best known investment bankers of the 20th century, once said: 'My job is more fun than being king, pope, or prime minister, for no one can turn me out of it, and I do not have to make any compromises with principles.'

Flexibility, too, is at a premium, because both exogenous and endogenous factors change. When asked why he changed his mind, Konrad Adenauer, the first German Chancellor after World War II, answered: 'What can I do, God makes me wiser and wiser every day.' And Lord Alanbrooke, chief of the British General Staff during WW II, used to say that he ate his words from time to time, and found them a nourishing diet.

Since, as Part 1 brought to the reader's attention, all management decisions are made in an environment involving uncertainty, it should be evident that not all forecasts materialize, not everything goes according to plan, and not all controls put the balances straight. There are several reasons behind the failure to forecast, plan, and control, beyond the fact that information may be neither complete nor unambiguous.

Both in the short term and in the longer term, one of the most significant reasons for planning and control failures is habitual thinking. Another is resistance to change. Both will eventually be downside effects. Most particularly, this will be the case:

- *If* 'time-honoured' methods and approaches are followed, without critically looking at them and testing them, and
- *If* a lax management permits lower efficiency and a certain degree of disorganization to carry the day, as well as allowing costs to escape control and products to fall behind competition.

Another major negative in strategic business planning which blurs management's vision is the culture of 'my problem is unique'. This makes management unable to adapt to market developments because it tends always to reinvent the wheel. In its essence, this kind of thinking about one's (or a company's) uniqueness in the problems being confronted is defensive, and it is most often a source of trouble.

Still another reason for failures in planning and control is reluctance to seek advice, and its opposite: getting the wrong advice. 'Wrong advice' is a common pitfall in industry, commerce, and banking, and also in government. Sometimes organizations mislead themselves willingly, because management:

- Has a big ego
- Does sloppy homework, or
- Is unable to clearly define its goals.

As the careful reader will recall from Part 1, a strategic business plan must have specific objectives, which should be reached within a defined timetable. But goals change over time, and the same is true of the means used to attain them. Moreover, a strategic plan encounters obstacles. The frequency with which the plan is matched or modified is important; and the same is true about the authority of executive(s) resetting the plan's sights and means used in its implementation.

2. Prognostication is a difficult art

Since forecasting is the first critical function in the realm of good governance, then it is also the first which must be done right. A legitimate question therefore is: How well is it performed? As the examples in this section document, the answer is not that positive. Even the leaders of industry make mistakes in their forecasts – and by a wide margin.

'I think there is a world market for maybe five computers,' said Thomas J. Watson, Sr, IBM's chairman, in 1943. Yet, he was a man of vision, albeit for a different epoch. 'But what ... is it good for?' asked an IBM engineer at the company's Advanced Computing Systems division in 1968. He was commenting on the nascent microchip. In fact, IBM engineers seem to have had an aversion even to transistors. When in the early 1960s they complained that transistors were unreliable, then IBM CEO Thomas J. Watson, Jr handed out transistor radios and challenged the critics to wear them out.

Watson, Sr was by no means the only pioneer of industry who eventually failed to live with his time. In 1977, Ken Olson, founder and CEO of Digital Equipment Corp. (DEC), another brilliant and, up to that time, very successful industrialist, made the profound statement: 'There is no reason anyone would want a computer in their home.' He paid for it dearly. By believing in his dictum he missed the PC revolution and eventually sent DEC to the wall.

'The telephone has too many shortcomings to be seriously considered as a means of communication. The device is inherently of no value to us,' wrote a Western Union internal memo in 1876. 'The wireless music box has no imaginable commercial value. Who would pay for a message sent to nobody in particular?' asked David Sarnoff's associates in the 1920s, in response to his prompting to invest in the radio as a consumer product.[1]

Failure in weather forecasting is one of the classics. Weather forecasting requires instantaneous combination of a lot of information, and it is a computing-intense job. The traditional job of a weather observer has been to launch wind balloons into the deep blue sky and plot synopsis maps. This, however, is too elementary to give valid results. Moreover, weather is an intriguing issue:

- Although it could be forecast,
- It could not be changed.

How much can computers and databases contribute to weather forecasting? From late 1958, when I was working in applied science with IBM, I remember an analyst from the Japanese Weather Bureau who came to Chicago to run a Fortran forecasting program on the 704 – one of the biggest scientific computers of its time, but a pigmy when compared to today's PC. The Fortran code the analysts wrote assembled beautifully:

- In programming terms it was judged as excellent,
- But the weather forecast was not that accurate.

To explain this dichotomy between program and forecast, practically everybody around said the 704 computer was not fast enough to produce a 2-day forecast. Therefore, everybody hoped for a still bigger machine that would be able to deliver. I have continued hearing this argument for the past 50 years, no matter that in the meantime computer power has increased by leaps and bounds.

- Weather forecasting models are too complex, because there are so many variables to take into account.
- As we try to simplify the problem we are faced with, we reduce the model's accuracy at the same time.

A similar statement can be made about a lot of other issues like, for instance, prognosticating the price of oil. Mid-September 2005, in its semi-annual 'World Economic Outlook', the International Monetary Fund (IMF) raised its oil price forecast for 2006 to $61.75 per barrel from $43.75 projected previously – a 41% increase. Some governments may need to adjust consumption subsidies, the IMF said.[2] This is too vague a statement, which also fails to explain the reason for a significant change in projected oil price.

Theoretically, forecasts should be objective and pragmatic. Practically, this is rarely the case. Many experts fail in their prognostication when it runs contrary to their stereotypes. This shows internal bias, which ends by depriving themselves, their firm, and their clients of the ability to know something in advance. Yet, a factual forecast is very important.

A judgement ahead of the facts concerning events for which there exist scant documentation and/or experience requires the skills so well described by Sam Walton, as the 'ability to turn on a dime'. This means lots of flexibility in making one's projections and decisions. Flexibility is as important in establishing business opportunity as it is in managing risk.

Risks have to be forecasted. There are always new types of risk to be confronted, as well as a metamorphosis of old ones, giving them much greater rigour. Barings, the venerable British bank, crashed in 1995 due to failure of market risk management, within a failure of operational risk control.[3] Barings management was a poor performer.

Facing the recasting of risks in an able manner requires action at both corporate and regulatory level. At corporate level, it is necessary to rethink and formalize risk management responsibilities, including the prognostication of evolution in exposure. Forecasts are not made just for the pleasure of doing something. Unless it is daydreaming, prognostication must lead to proactive concrete action.

Ex post, some biases that impact on forecasting appear systematic. They have been found to occur in empirical findings, and are more generally known as the *peso problem*. This term was coined in the mid-1970s when the Mexican peso, despite its peg to the US dollar and an economic policy that looked sustainable, was consistently traded at a discount on the forward exchange market. The reason seemed to be that market participants did not completely rule out a return to an inflationary Mexican monetary and fiscal policy, which would lead to the peso's depreciation.

- The term 'peso problem' has been used to describe situations in which market participants see the possibility of a discretionary change in the future, and therefore bias in one or more fundamentals.
- When this happens, it tends to lead to a subjective potential phase shift, whose influence makes itself felt. For instance, in future exchange rate decoupled from economic fundamentals.

The reader should appreciate that the peso problem is highly relevant in the general case of prognostication, and not only with exchange rates. For instance, every investor is interested in the timing and amplitude of a correction in the stock market, as well as in the chances of a recovery. Such predictions, which are usually based on extrapolation or inference with some sort of causality in the background, may however involve personal bias. To avoid such bias, we try to:

- Exploit a cause and effect relationship, or
- Find a sign, which might be an early indicator of things to come.

Some bias in prognostication may be the result of a prevailing culture. Others materialize when we confuse wishes with reality. Still others are the aftermath of lack of imagination. Since antiquity man dreamed of conquering the facility of flying, largely imitating the way birds flew. The story of Icarus is instructive in regard to the failures of a copying effort.

- Eventually man flew faster and further than the birds,
- But he also used a totally different technology to reach his goal.

The lesson is that *if* our hypotheses don't challenge the 'obvious', *then* we lead ourselves in the wrong direction – whether we talk of the economy or of some technical stuff we supposedly master. Here is, for example, Bill Gates, who in 1981 made the statement: '640K ought to be enough for everybody' (640 kilobytes of central memory). At one time or another, we all have had that sort of myopic vision.

If, as this section has demonstrated, so many well known people who have been pioneers in their business goofed in their prognostications about the future of 'this' or 'that' issue, *then* there is no reason to believe that you or I will do better in projecting the course of future events – independently of whether our estimates are optimistic or pessimistic. Still, in spite of this downside, we need to establish a valid system able to lead to acceptable accuracy in forecasting, as section 3 suggests.

3. The art of forecasting and its pitfalls

The way it has been defined in the Introduction, the art of *forecasting* focuses on future events. As the practical examples we saw in section 2 document, prognostication is a projection into the future based both on numbers and on hypotheses – and taking into consideration expectations. But we also saw why prognostications involve a fair amount of speculation as well as bias.

For all these reasons the forecasts that we do can turn on their head. In the late 1980s when Japan was the rising sun in the global economy, and its previous prognostications on computer developments had proved right, the Ministry of International Trade and Industry (MITI) projected the deliverables of a new project which it funded: Real World Computing. MITI's forecasts focused on results to be obtained ten years down the line; the highlights are shown in Figure 5.2. In a nutshell, this prognostication predicted an evolution:

- From the *computer world* of number crunching of the 1950s and 1960s
- And the *logical world* of knowledge engineering of the 1970s and 1980s
- To the ultimate goal of the *real world* which will characterize competitiveness in high technology in the late 1990s and beyond.

According to the MITI forecast, real world computing was expected to create a cooperative, close relationship between people and computers. It was also supposed to act as a catalyst in producing new, generic scientific and technological advancements. These were projected to significantly benefit the Japanese industry, providing it with a major weapon against its corporate opponents.[4]

Plenty of taxpayers money has been spent in a well-financed project aimed at fulfilling this forecast. To the MITI's experts, the project's strategic goals sounded

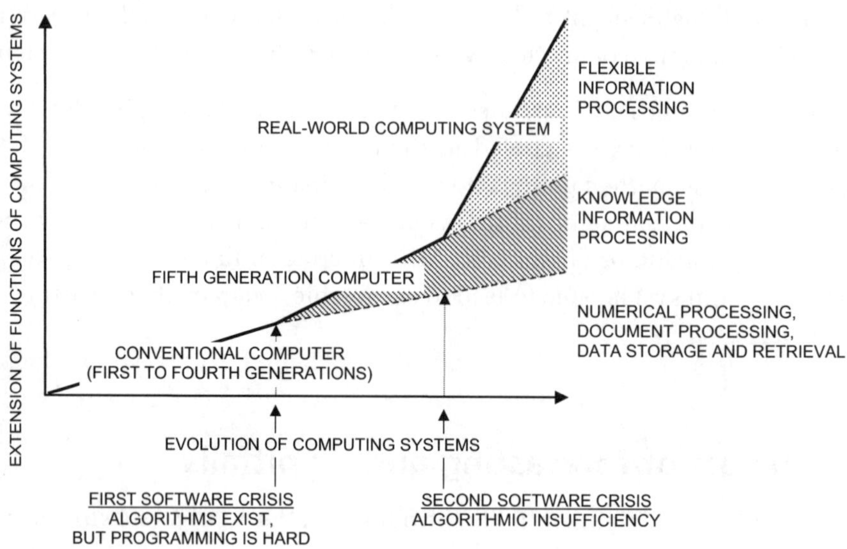

Figure 5.2 How the Real World Computing (RWC) project positioned itself in information processing technology

doable and reasonable. But after five years of frustration, the forecast on which this project was based proved wrong – and the high-tech Real World Computing project crashed, as its lavish financing was cut off.

In retrospect, several biases combined to doom this project, and the forecast made about its success. One of them has been that since (in mid- to late 1980s) Japan's economy was thought to be invincible, whatever it undertook had to give tangible results. The Real World Computing project, however, proved that this invincibility did not pass the real life test.

Another bias in forecasting was that all necessary skill would be transferable seamlessly from hardware to software computer technology. When this proved elusive, the Japanese involved a German computer research institute in their project – but by then it was too late. The third and fourth factors which worked against the forecast have been:

- The absence of clearly stated objectives in interim deliverables, including their milestones, and
- Lack of unity of command, as MITI executives, project management, and subcontractors fought over the turf.

Eventually, the environment that created a cooperative relationship between people and computers materialized through the *Internet*. Its software kernel, the

World Wide Web (www), was developed single-handedly by one person: Tim Berners-Lee, in 1992, while working at the European Centre of Particle Physics (CERN), in Geneva.

- With the Web, the network became the computer.
- As with Icarus, the Real World Computing project flew, but not in the way MITI bureaucrats had forecasted.

Much less grandiose industrial forecasts can also go down the tubes. The way a feature article in *Automotive Design* had it, by late 2005 the greatly heralded as 'the future' (i) remote vehicle diagnostics (RVD) and (ii) security systems had a penetration of only 7 and 9%, respectively. Navigation systems have achieved 23%, but that figure is expected to decline at a rate of 3% until 2010 this article says.[5] And rear-seat entertainment systems have contributed only 1.1% to the overall take-up of telematics and *infotainment* systems in 2004. Even in the upper luxury segments they remain just that – a luxury.

The statistics the preceding paragraph presented demolish previous forecasts that telematic functions, particularly navigation and entertainment information, will dominate motor vehicle design. What such forecasts forgot is the customer' response to rapidly increasing product costs. Many telematic functions:

- Are under huge price pressure from standalone aftermarket products, and
- There is a general perception among consumers that such devious systems are overly expensive.

At the same time, however, the fact forecasts can go astray, as the Real World Computing project and telematic gear in motor vehicles document, is no reason to shy away from them. Quite the contrary, these examples significantly reinforce the need for making forecasts. If things can turn wrong in spite of the analysis that goes into a prognostication, think of what will happen without the benefits of better vision which it provides.

On the positive side, a forecast done in an able manner represents the best estimate that can be made about a situation at the time of its preparation. Even though forecasts can never be as accurate as a watch, they should reflect learned assumptions about specific cases – and they should be tailored to fit the needs of the organization on whose behalf they are made.

Learning a lesson from the failure of Real World Computing and so many other projects, three rules can be instrumental in improving the success of a prognostication. First, *a forecast presumes a purpose*. The best purpose that I know connected to forecasting is not to predict the future precisely but to determine the effects projected results will have upon the:

- Specific scope
- Direction
- Risk, and
- Success of well-defined management decisions.

In this sense, a forecast is much more a predictor of future effect(s) of current management decisions than a prognosticator of major technological breakthroughs or epoch-making market switches. A key weakness of the Real World Computing forecast was that it aimed at reaping the benefits of an imagined colossal breakthrough, when there was nothing on hand to substantiate such a hypothesis.

The second rule of prognostication is that *a forecast should not be rigid or inflexible*. What it should do is to provide an identification of the probable course of coming events, including upside and downside. On this 'probable course' will rest the milestones in management decisions including:

- Timing
- Commitments
- Costs, and
- Expected results.

The third rule of prognostication is that *forecasts are made for planning purposes*. As we will see in Chapter 6, management planning paves the way for commitment of resources which might assure high returns, while taking account of the likelihood of headwinds in business conditions. To fulfil this goal in an able manner, we need different types of forecasts. For instance:

- *Short-range* forecasts of company sales are made every semester or quarter for the next 12 months.
- *Long-range* sales forecasts take a further-out time perspective, focus on trends, and are most often limited to 5 years.

Additionally, breakdowns of sales forecasts must be done by groups of products, often known as 'commodity groups', and by single product as well as by market. Forecasts are also necessary of inventory requirements for individual products by stocking period, taking into account product turnaround – which should be accelerated through appropriate marketing action.

In collaboration with the production planning department, corporate headquarters should make long-range forecasts of physical unit volume by manufacturing facility, leading to the definition of capital requirements for investments in plant and equipment. A global company must do so for its world-wide operation, keeping in perspective not only market-by-market needs but also currency exchange rates, political stability in different countries, labour costs, and evidently taxation. This must be a global plan that encompasses a whole family of forecasts.

4. Making forecasts: case study with Hurricane Katrina

A forecast presumes a purpose: for instance, a prospective evaluation of market demand, of our company's strengths and weaknesses, of its positioning of products and services within the perspective of developments in 'this' or 'that' market. As section 3 emphasized, the purpose of the forecast is not to predict the future precisely, but to determine the effects that a management decision, or projected market evolution will have upon the:

- Scope
- Direction
- Profitability, and
- Success of *our* entity.

The examples presented in the preceding section from the manufacturing industry document that forecasting is a projection into the future, which must take into consideration expectations. As such, the forecast involves specialization. Far from being a theoretical exercise, it must be a look into the future, including an evaluation of how the economy, of the market we appeal to or world-wide, is progressing; and how this evolution will affect future sale of our products and services.

Because prognostications must be adaptable to the developing situation, a forecast should not be rigid or inflexible. Its mission is to identify the probable course of coming events always keeping in mind the second rule of forecasting outlined in section 3:

- *Prognosis* is not concerned with future decisions.
- Its aim is to help in bringing into perspective the future impact of present decisions.

This is precisely why we are interested to learn about the *future course* of events – all the way from business opportunities to current and latent risks. On this probable future course will rest the milestones in decisions management makes, including commitments as well as their timing, costs, exposures, and expected results.

What the preceding paragraphs have outlined is the most basic characteristic of forecasts made for strategic planning, paving the way for the choice of actions aiming to ensure higher returns, while preserving the capital. The forecast that we produce should represent the best estimate that can be made about a good or bad situation, at the time of its preparation.

For instance, in the aftermath of Hurricane Katrina, Swiss Re, the world's second-biggest reinsurer, increased its estimated pre-tax losses from insured damages created by the hurricane from $500 million to $1.2 billion, or 7% of shareholders' equity. This was prognostication which told management it would probably have to dip into the company's reserves to meet the claims.

- Upgrading loss estimated from $500 million to $1.2 billion suggests that forecasts cannot be as accurate as a wrist-watch.
- Both the old and the new loss estimate reflect learned assumptions about this specific case: the damage from Hurricane Katrina.

To achieve this focused goal, a forecast has to be specific. It cannot be made in general terms. The same is true of model(s) written as supports to forecasting. Both models and forecasts should be tailored not only to fit the needs of the entity for which they are being made, but also a specific case – for example, Katrina. Only then can a prognostication lead to valid planning assumptions (more on this in section 6). Other things being equal,

- Predictive power is improved by exploiting the mountain of data on which a forecasting model draws.
- Powerful forecasting engines comb databases world-wide, painstakingly assembling statistics that can reveal cause-and-effect relationships.

When this is done, analysts take the distilled information and develop algorithms linking causes to effects, which are tested against historical figures in the database. By 'forecasting the past' it may be possible to identify relationships between circumstances and outcomes. This approach is akin to working out the physical laws that govern the behaviour of nature, which can be used in forecasting physical events.

The art of forecasting can be significantly assisted, in many cases, through timely and accurate data collection and on-line datamining. Thinking by analogy, this resembles a system of dedicated traffic-monitoring centres linked to networks of cameras and sensors, including traffic-spotting aircraft, as well as cars, trucks, and buses fitted with satellite-positioning gear. This way, not only is it possible to see exactly what is happening on the roads but one can also project traffic jams, warning drivers to:

- Switch from busy to quieter routes, and
- Avoid congestion with associated delays and pollution.

As we will see in Chapter 6, planning requires forecasting, even if made in the light of incomplete or uncertain information. When they are working in unison, forecasting and planning are most essential to business strategy, because the latter is in any case based on hypotheses made by management which require steady testing. As we have seen since Chapter 1, strategy and planning are not two separate processes but part of the same business task.

- Strategy makes choices, sets priorities, and gives a sense of direction on how to go From *here* to *there*.
- Planning establishes the detailed road map we use to get 'there', and this roadmap is based on forecasts.

Plans, and forecasts on which they rest, are much more than just a corporate activity directed at marketing, or any other standalone domain. Since strategy is a master plan, its individual component plans should be formulated at every level of the organization and for every area of activity. In the aforementioned case of Swiss Re this ranges:

- From prognostication about losses
- To management decision regarding payment of dividends.

As a sequel to its forecast about severe losses from Katrina, Swiss Re said that it would continue paying dividends *if* normal business development prevails for the rest of the year. But smaller reinsurers may be worse off. According to *Insurance Day*, a trade publication, the second-biggest maximum losses so far are at Montpelier Re, a Bermudian reinsurer, which expects a hit of up to $675 million or 46% of shareholders' equity.[6]

The estimate of future capital requirements is another important domain of forecasting. Because they foresee that losses from major events may escalate, as is their nasty habit, post-Katrina several reinsurers said that they would need to raise more capital. On the other hand, Lloyd's of London stated in September

2005 that it expected all its syndicates to withstand the blow – even if the prognostication is that the cost will be at the level of £1.4 billion ($2.6 billion).

Still another major contribution of forecasts is their impact on pricing products and services. In the follow-up to Hurricanes Katrina and Rita, energy insurance rates started rising, with increases of up to 25% reported for renewal premiums outside the Gulf of Mexico.

Sometimes a wrong forecast may be a boon to the bottom line. When in the mid-1950s IBM developed the 650 computer, senior management prognosticated its market potential was up to 50 machines, and the 650 was priced accordingly. But rather than 50, several thousand of the machines were sold, with IBM getting an enormous boost to its profits.

The nemesis of forecasts is that statistics from actual events don't necessarily match what has been projected. When this happens such statistics from real life results reveal discrepancies in planning, resources allocation, or pricing of products. For instance, in an early September 2005 estimate, some experts contended that in the past couple of years,

- The United States has accounted for about 75% of the world's natural catastrophe claims
- But capitalizing on high competition in the insurance market, US firms and other entities paid only about half of the premiums that should correspond to such a high accident rate.

There are also cases when conclusions reached by a given study assist in prognosticating what will happen next if nothing changes; or in trying to rebalance a system whose behaviour has become asymmetric. Whether prognostications are 'right' or 'wrong', the making of forecasts is a steady process, not a one-off event. Every time something changes, the forecast must be revised – sometimes in a fairly radical way.

5. Forecasts must be realistic: case study with Hartford Insurance

General Karl von Clausewitz once said that many assume half-efforts can be effective, but this is false. Half-efforts are sometimes made where a small jump is easier than a large one, and very few people are willing to cross a wide ditch without having crossed half of it first. Forecasting and planning, however, don't work through half measures. They require not only a broader view but also the crossing of a wide ditch. In turn this requires a clear, consistent, and flexible approach. This is precisely what many people and firms don't have. By persisting in the old ways under the cover of tradition they fail to notice:

- Whether the nature of the problem has changed, and
- That if it has, the old way may not improve upon the current situation, but rather make it worse.

The broad, and steadily enlarging domain of risk management is such a case. Take as an example forecasts about risk coverage made by insurance companies. An insurer does not make its money directly from premiums but on the interest, dividends, and capital gains it receives from investing that premium money.

- An insurance company might even be happy if its underwriting expenses and claims payments equal the premium.
- The problem is that the company never knows how great the total of claims will be against the policies written in any one year.

Moreover, particularly in the case of natural catastrophes and other major events, some of the claims are not paid out for several years. Hence, by law, the insurer must continue maintaining adequate reserves. If more or bigger claims come in than expected, or both, the insurance company must add to its reserves, reducing by so much its current year's net income. This is one of the cases where forecasting is king.

A real life example is the best way to explain the point just made. In his book on Harold Geneen,[7] Robert Schoenberg takes as an example Hartford Insurance. In 1971, its first full year with ITT, Hartford's income was $105.5 million, 26% of ITT's total. For income maximization purposes, at ITT's direction,

- Hartford started realizing much more in the way of capital gains than it had before, a measure that pumped up earnings,
- At the same time, Hartford's sales force was encouraged to go aggressively after more business.

In 1970 Hartford Insurance wrote $1.125 billion in premiums; in 1971 this grew to $1.335 billion, nearly 19% more. On paper, this compared well with a 10% industry average growth. In 1972 premiums were up another 14.5%. But in 1973 growth cooled to about 11.6%, with the total of earned premiums up to $1.733 billion.

The downside was not the cooling off of results produced by an intense sales effort, but the fact that much of the new business was in high-risk areas like product liability and medical malpractice. Time-wise, both have an especially long tail; risks do not develop for a few years (more on this later).

- Hartford had more premium money to invest, which it did mostly in equities characterized by volatility
- But losses started growing. In 1970 underwriting loss was only $13.7 million, or 1.2%. In 1973 underwriting loss climbed to $38.7 million, which was 2.2%.

Somehow senior management at corporate headquarters forgot to examine the correlation that exists between aggressive sales and extension of underwriting into high risk areas. The forecast was either flawed or missing. As a result, there was no prognostication made of likely increase in:

- Company losses, and
- Business risk (see Chapter 6).

Looking after only growth in sales is a half measure, falling under the dictum of Clausewitz. A realistic project cannot, and should not forget about the other side of the equation, which represents the growing exposure. In 1973 the underwriting loss climbed to a level that was not acceptable, and though in 1974 headquarters established less aggressive sales goals, it was too late.

As almost always happens when positive expectations turn on their head, at Hartford Insurance the past haunted the present. Claims rolled in and in 1974 losses soared to $123 million, a punishing 7.6%. As one misfortune seldom comes alone, the stock market collapsed, with Hartford's extra premium money in it.

- At the time, Hartford's portfolio stood at $880 million and showed a $240 million loss.
- That meant the insurer's readily liquifiable assets that protected policy holders looked insufficient, and state regulators wanted them increased.

Capital increases, however, don't come along just by pressing a magic switch. This is an excellent case study on the principle this chapter has underlined, that the main goal of forecasting is to examine the future impact of current actions; not to foretell the future at large. It is also a good documentation of the fact that forecasts must be focused and realistic.

Banks encounter similar problems in connection to assumed credit risk. As Figure 5.3 suggests, some events can be forecast statistically. These are known as *expected losses* (EL), and they have attached to them corresponding regulatory requirements. But there are also *unexpected losses* (UL) at the long leg of the risk distribution shown in Figure 5.3. Reference to tail events has already been made in connection to Hartford Insurance. The following section examines the kind of models that might help in prognosticating UL.

6. Models could help in prognostication: the case of unexpected losses

Models are tools that help in analysis and, sometimes, in decisions. When they are based on realistic hypotheses, are properly constructed, and are adequately tested, models can help in prognostication. These preconditions, however, are not always fulfilled. Therefore, quite often the use of models leads to a deception that might be stronger than reality. This is usually the case when:

- The hypotheses and assumptions being made are undocumented
- The modelling approach is off-focus, and therefore does not provide a proper response
- The people responsible for modelling try to hide the weaknesses of the artefacts being used, rather than bringing them out in the open for factual evaluation.

Take as an example of the modelling effort artefacts written for prognosticating exposure to credit risk beyond expected losses (EL). Unexpected losses (UL) can be computed through algorithmic approaches, provided the model(s) being used is (are) sound at the start, and continue being tested against real life returns. This is not the most frequent case. My experience documents that superficial approaches to modelling are worse than nothing.[8]

- They are misleading, and
- The forecast based on them is a fake.

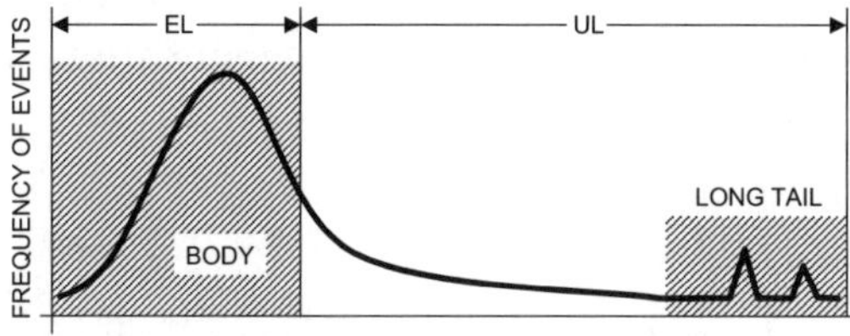

Figure 5.3 Expected losses, unexpected losses, and the long tail of the distribution

An example of a ridiculous model for UL is the so-called $VAR_{99.97}$ (value at risk at 99.97% level of confidence). I have explained its many weaknesses, indeed its total irrelevance, in my book on Basel II.[9] This is a model typically used by the unable, who has been asked by the unwilling to do the unnecessary.

The good news is that there are available today fairly good models to help in prognosticating UL, at least in terms of capital requirements. The reference to models in the plural is important because when we work near the edge of our knowledge we should use more than one model for forecasting, subsequently comparing results and identifying the reasons underpinning deviations. This helps in:

- Better focusing our prognostication, by looking at it from different sides, and
- Examining whether and how far discrepancies in results are leading to further investigation on model fitness.

For instance, an excellent model for pre-estimating unexpected losses is the UL algorithm developed by Deutsche Bundesbank:

$$UL_{BUi} = a \cdot s\ (\Sigma R_i w_i)\ A < K \qquad (1)$$

where:

a = constant, function of risk appetite
s = standard deviation of aggregate risk
R_i = outlier of unexpected losses at business unit i (BU_i)
w_i = weight, representing share of BU_i in the bank's total turnover
A = assets of the entity
K = economic capital of the bank

If the enterprise-wide sum of extreme losses is represented by R, *then* worst case is:

$$R = \Sigma_i R_i$$

because this means that the entity does not benefit from effects of diversification. If senior management thinks that current diversification will have a positive aftermath, then the result will be

$$R < \Sigma_i R_i$$

Notice, however, that the reduction of exposure is often subjective, and wishful thinking often plays a major role in it.

The algorithm in equation (1) can also be used for proactive purposes, as part of a system for economic capital allocation to business units (see also Chapter 4). In this case economic capital allocation to BU_i will be provided by $K_i = \beta_i \cdot w_i \cdot K$, where β_i is the internal beta (volatility) of a BU_i:

$$\beta_i = \frac{A_i}{s^2_{BR}} \Sigma w_i \, COV_{ij} \tag{2}$$

where:

A_i = assets of the business unit *i*
s^2_{BR} = variance of aggregate bank risk
COV_{ij} = covariance, returns of BU_i and of the bank

it is

$$\Sigma \beta_i \, w_i = 1.$$

In other terms, the sum of products of each business unit's internal beta multiplied by the weight representing its share in the bank, is equal to 1.

Another sound algorithm for estimating UL, which should be used in parallel to the Bundesbank's model, is one based on stress testing. The Basel Committee on Banking Supervision promotes this approach to prognostication of unexpected losses:

$$UL = SPD \cdot SLGD \cdot SEAD \tag{3}$$

where:

SPD = stress probability of default
SLGD = stress loss given default
SEAD = stress exposure at default

SPD and SLGD are percentages. SEAD is expressed in capital at risk. This approach to UL is a forward-looking measure – which contrasts to accounting for losses being incurred. The latter is post-mortem. Both ex ante and ex post metrics are important to good governance at large, and more specifically, to risk control.[10]

Contrary to equation (1), which addresses each specific business unit '*i*', equation (3) is a more general formula which can become personalized if it targets the SPD, SLGD, and SEAD of each unit under investigation rather than of the whole bank.

Another important personalization of equation (3) regards the level of stress testing. This is usually expressed by choosing the number of standard deviations, *s*, from the mean.

Statistical theory says that within ±3*s* from the mean is included more than 99% of the area under the normal distribution curve. This is true for one with a long leg. The level of stress testing is chosen by appropriately selecting the number of standard deviations at this long leg of the loss distribution – which is an important choice.

s = 5, is almost trivial
s = 10, is realistic
s = 15, is conservative

Since the UL algorithm is a development from the expected losses (EL) algorithm, some experts believe that, by assuring that it is implemented, supervisory authorities would eventually extend their jurisdiction into economic capital. In all likelihood, they will do so by exercising their prerogatives under Pillar 2 of the new capital adequacy framework (Basel II).

7. Forecasts made public: case study with forward-looking statements

Forecasts made for business purposes are usually kept close to the chest of the companies which they concern. An exception is the so-called *forward-looking statement* which contains no statistics but projections. Mainly this is a statement relating to the after-effect of implementation of strategic initiatives – in a particular product, country or world-wide. Also, to the development of new trading operations, or prognosticated future turnover and economic performance.

Forward-looking statements come in addition to a company's classical release of accounting numbers in annual or quarterly financial reports. Information included in them usually, though not always, includes issues relating to:

- Plans, objectives or goals
- Future performance or prospects
- Reasons potentially affecting future performance
- A certain number of contingencies, and
- Assumptions underlying other statements being made.

Since forward-looking statements are forecasts, words such as 'believes', 'anticipates', 'expects', 'intends' and 'plans' and similar expressions are used to identify the entity's thinking about projected future happening. In the general case, companies do not intend to update these statements, except as may be required by applicable laws.

By their nature, forward-looking statements have an inherent bias towards 'better news' – both general and specific. At best, they represent management's judgement and future expectations concerning the development of the company's business, as well as of risks, uncertainties and other factors that could cause actual results to differ materially from expectations. Such factors include, but are not limited to:

- General trends in the economy
- Changes in local and international markets
- Competitive pressures and technological developments
- Variation in financial position or creditworthiness, of customers, obligors and other counterparties
- Legislative and political developments including the impact of terrorist attacks
- The aftermath of management changes and of key factors that could positively or adversely affect the entity's financial performance.

There is always the risk that forecasts, projections, predictions, and other issues concerning outcomes described or implied on forward-looking statements, will *not* be achieved. A number of factors could cause end results to differ materially from plans, objectives, expectations, estimates and intentions expressed in forward-looking statements. These include:

- Market psychology and trend
- Interest rate fluctuations
- Volatility in exchange rates
- Strength of the economies of countries in which the firm conducts its operations
- Effects of, and changes in, fiscal, monetary, trade and tax policies
- Political and social developments, which upset established plans.

The reader can better appreciate the sense of these points if he keeps in mind that events described in forward-looking statements are not based on historical facts. They address activities or developments that the company *expects* or anticipates will, or may, occur in the future. This, however, is no excuse for making such statements lightly or misjudging business opportunities and risk factors.

Another problem with prognostication associated to forward-looking statements is that figures presented to the public may be far from being clear, or comparable to other figures being released. In the UK, on 4 October 2005 the FSA issued a warning to companies over their use of tailor-made profit figures. This was prompted by concerns that:

- Some entities may be confusing investors with the presentation in their financial reporting, and
- With the International Financial Reporting Standards (IFRS)[11] the change in accounting standards might have created loopholes certain companies are quick to exploit.

For instance, IFRS (see Chapter 10) allows companies to report additional earnings numbers that are not mandated in the rules. This seems to permit highlighting figures whose origins are vague. In the aftermath, FSA said that '[Companies] should make clear the basis on which numbers are calculated in order to avoid misleading investors.'[12]

Experts suggest that the issue of additional financial presentation has exposed a certain rule void within IFRS, creating scepticism over the validity of an earnings figure narrower than *net income*. Gaming the system already under way suggests that *operating profits* may not be a relevant reference, particularly when it is used as a way to twist other accounting notions.

At the same time, this operating profits issue casts doubt on the ability of regulators across the European Union to oversee the implementation of IFRS. Financial watchdogs correctly fear the credibility of the standards will be undermined if IFRS is applied and reported on inconsistently from one country to another. Such an occurrence will create an incentive for companies to:

- Bypass the new accounting standards, and
- Do as they please with their financial reports.

In France, the Autorité des Marchés Financiers, the local markets watchdog, said it is considering a reminder similar to the one by FSA, on the need for clear presentation. In the United States the Securities and Exchange Commission (SEC) is also monitoring implementation of IFRS, as well as its teething troubles, as it considers whether to accept IFRS accounts from European companies listed in the United States.

To ease the problem of cross-border coordination, the Committee of European Securities Regulators has already launched a data-sharing initiative to encourage national regulators dealing with accounting errors to compare rules with foreign counterparts. Moreover, the International Organization of Securities Commissions (IOSCO) announced a similar initiative with broader geographical scope.

As so often happens with the implementation of a new standard, the IFRS financial reporting problem comes from the fact that the new financial reporting rules do not contain a standard definition of *operating profit*. In practice, operating profit should reflect the underlying performance of an entity, but a growing number of firms choose to produce customized figures in their half-year results, screening out items such as:

- Pensions charges
- Stock option costs
- Changes in the value of derivatives, and more.

This confuses financial analysts, investors, and regulators, each group expressing concern that many companies are calculating their headline earnings differently from their industry peers. If such practices exist with established accounting standards, think of what may be happening with prognostications and projections. Therefore, the reader should be cautioned not to place undue reliance on forward-looking statements, which speak only:

- In their own language, and
- As of the day they are made.

There is also the fact that many events impacting performance are exogenous, therefore beyond management's control. In an era of globalization, examples of events external to the company which are instrumental in altering projections made in forward-looking statements include foreign exchange controls, expropriation, nationalization, or confiscation of assets in countries in which it conducts its operations. By contrast, examples of endogenous events and factors are:

- Management ability to maintain sufficient liquidity and access capital markets
- Operational factors such as system unreliability, fraud, human error, or failure to properly implement procedures.

Internal failures might also happen in connection to management's inability to be in charge of effects of changes in laws, regulations or accounting policies or practices; failure to forecast a spark in competition in geographic and business areas in which the company loses its market; inability to retain and recruit qualified personnel; or failure to timely develop new products and services. Still other management failures relate to mergers and acquisitions (see Part 6).

Notes

1 *Communications of the ACM*, November 1999, Vol. 42, No. 11.

2 *The Economist*, 24 September 2005.

3 D.N. Chorafas, *Operational Risk Control with Basel II: Basic Principles and Capital Requirements*. Elsevier, Oxford, 2004.

4 D.N. Chorafas, *Network Computers versus High Performance Computers*. Cassell, London, 1997.

5 *Automotive Design*, September 2005.

6 *The Economist*, 17 September 2005.

7 Robert J. Schoenberg, *Geneen*. W.W. Norton, New York, 1985.

8 D.N. Chorafas, *Modelling the Survival of Financial and Industrial Enterprises: Advantages, Challenges, and Problems with the Internal Rating-Based (IRB) Method*. Palgrave/Macmillan, London, 2002.

9 D.N. Chorafas, *Economic Capital Allocation with Basel II: Cost and Benefit Analysis*. Elsevier, Oxford, 2004.

10 D.N. Chorafas, *Integrated Risk Management*. Lafferty/VRL Publishing, London, 2005.

11 D.N. Chorafas, *IFRS, Fair Value and Corporate Governance: The Impact on Budgets, Balance Sheets and Management Accounts*. Elsevier, Oxford, 2006.

12 *Financial Times*, 5 October 2005.

Planning

1. Introduction

According to Simone de Beauvoir, the French author, a woman is not born, but *made*. The same is true about men, and evidently about companies, countries, and any other entity. But 'to be made' one needs a plan that establishes objectives and provides the means for coordinating decisions and actions.

Planning is the process of deciding what action should be taken in the future. The area covered by a plan may be a small segment of the entity and its operations, or it may be the whole enterprise. The decision as to whether the price of one product should be increased by, say, 3% is a plan; and so is a decision to merge the company with another firm (see Part 6 on M&As).

Planning, as we know it, grew out of the 'Gantt chart' originally designed in 1917 to plan war production. Slowly planning became sophisticated, using statistics and analytical tools, as well as employing the advantages provided by quantification to convert experience and intuition into:

- Definitions
- Information, and
- Diagnosis.

The plan is a framework involving different types of resources: human, financial, and material. Also time, as time is a key resource. The first essential characteristic of a plan is that it involves decision(s) about action to be taken in the future. Planning should therefore be distinguished from *forecasting*, which is an estimate of possible evolution. But as Chapter 5 explained, forecasting is prerequisite to planning.

Another essential characteristic of a plan is the *experience* required in making it and in putting it into effect. On his visit to ancient Egypt, Solon (640–560 BC), the Athenian lawmaker, was received by an old priest to whom he spoke with pride about his country of origin. The host interrupted him: 'You Greeks are like kids. There are no old people in Greece …' 'What do you mean?' asked Solon. 'You are young in spirit,' responded the Egyptian priest, 'because you have no really old traditions, no concepts whited by time …'

The essential point here is that, much more than the plan itself, it is the process of planning that must be 'whited by time'. Sound and efficient planning processes are a culture. Good plans are not made overnight, and the skill for making them is not being acquired on the fly.

A characteristic of sound planning is objectivity. Planners should not make their produce 'say' what they want it to say. My personal planning experience tells that the best plans are:

- Analytical and factual.
- They are also very well documented.

In his argument about being 'whited by time', the old Egyptian priest was right. Even if we take Pericles and his time as a reference (5th century BC) there is as much chronological distance between Pericles' time and ours, as there is between his time and that of the Pharaoh Djeser and his pyramid of Saqqara. When Herodotus, the historian, visited the Nile Valley, some 450 years BC, the pyramid of Cheops (2615–2550 BC) was already more than 2000 years old.

Experience in planning teaches that what is really 'whited by time' is the conceptual framework on which planning rests, and from which planning details evolve. During our September 2005 meeting, Wayne Upton, Director of Research of London-based International Accounting Standards Board (IASB) defined as follows the conceptual pillars on which IASB's plans and projects rest.

- The meaning of stewardship and accountability and their relationship to objectives of reliable financial reporting, and
- Relationships between qualitative characteristics of financial reporting information, and how they are used in building decision-useful financial reports.

Variations of these two pillars can be found nearly everywhere in the process of planning, particularly so when it addresses standards issues. *Stewardship* encompasses management's responsibility not only for the custody and safekeeping of assets entrusted to it, but also for their efficient and profitable use. This is a basic planning goal.

Accountability is a personal characteristic that has a great deal to do with authority and responsibility. Responsibility is never delegated. Only authority is delegated. The responsibility – and therefore accountability for decisions, plans, and actions – remains with the delegator at the top of the organizational pyramid.

In the course of our meeting at IASB, Wayne Upton also underlined that a financial reporting standards framework should clarify the nature and type of information useful for making investment, credit, and similar resource allocation decisions. This includes quantitative and qualitative characteristics of financial reporting information used to build decision-useful tools. A similar objective characterizes planning premises. Clear and unambiguous standards are prerequisite to the process of planning.

2. Critical elements of the planning process

Chapter 5 has brought to the reader's attention the fact that while *planning* requires forecasting, it is always made in the light of incomplete information. But even if this was not the case, in a changing business world plans must be flexible and adjustable. The flexibility and adaptability of planning premises is, also, the only way to minimize effects of the unknown.

Most of the unknown factors will be exogenous, while those that are endogenous are typically settled through management decision and action, if management is worth its salt. For instance, the *strategic plan* will detail goals and policies followed in making moves based on expectation(s) about moves by corporate opponents over which *our* company has no control.

- *Policies* are written to clarify the 'dos' and don'ts', thereby avoiding repetitive decisions on same or similar issues (see section 6).
- By contrast, strategies are never written. The opponent(s)' strategies are guesstimated by interpreting their policies and studying the moves being made in execution of their plans.

An article that appeared in *The Economist* following Swiss Re's acquisition of GEIS for $6.8 billion, compared Europe's top-two reinsurers: Munich Re and Swiss Re. Munich Re, this article said, is more diversified than Swiss Re, with a big interest in primary insurance, which tends to be more stable than reinsurance. By contrast, Swiss Re is focused on reinsurance.[1]

Based on these and other facts, which have become common knowledge, one makes the deduction that the strategy of Swiss Re is to become a premier company in reinsurance, well implanted in the US market where insurance policies are part of business ethics *and* consumer culture. Munich Re has a different strategy based on diversification of business opportunities and of risk.

While both goals and policies may be well-researched, in any domain of activity a strategy and the plan made to support it can have unwanted consequences. Letting Vietnam collapse, noted Melvin Laird, secretary of defence under Richard Nixon, in the November 2005 issue of *Foreign Affairs*, resulted in 2 million refugees, 65 000 executions and 250 000 people sent to re-education camps.

- The search for unwanted consequences is one of the responsibilities not only of strategic planning, but of corporate governance at large.
- A basic principle is that though plans have to be detailed and thoroughly tested, there are plenty of different reasons why results do not always conform to original plans.

These two bullets further explain why the planning framework briefly outlined in the Introduction is absolutely necessary. While strategies are based on intentions, implicit intentions are not good enough because they are not fully researched. Simply enumerating the goals cannot bring the focused and disciplined approach that is required. To focus on subjects, we need a master plan able to distinguish thoroughly and correctly between:

- What is essential, and
- What is only wishful or superficial.

The proper planning framework brings best returns when it is structured in a way that permits us to concentrate our thinking and our effort. In the 16 years I worked as personal consultant to Dr Carlo Pesenti, chairman of a large Italian banking and industrial group, I appreciated how much he was concerned about the ability of the presidents of his banks to *focus* on a subject.

Most managers judge their subordinates only in terms of deliverables. But while deliverables are important, Pesenti considered that focusing on a decision issue is even more important than the decision that is ultimately reached. His principle has been that lack of focusing will eventually destroy the enterprise (more on focusing in section 6).

- Experience teaches that this emphasis on focus and analysis is the golden rule in planning.
- Plans that lack concentration on details are full of contradictions, and they practically invite people to game them.

The need to focus, examine, analyse, justify, and provide detail is served by the planning framework's *structure*. In planning, structure is defined as the design of procedural steps through which decisions are made and the enterprise is administered. Structure also incorporates the information and knowledge flow through the organization's lines of:

- Authority, and
- Communication.

Information and knowledge flows are essential to assure the effective coordination and appraisal that must accompany the execution of plans. Also, in knitting together the total resources of the entity, including:

- Financial capital
- Products and services

- Marketing plans
- Human capital, and
- Technological infrastructure.

These five bullets identify major components of a strategic plan, as well as chapter headings of the means people will use to reach objectives. But structured dimensions as well as structural concepts change over time, and this impacts on the selection and setting of criteria used to guide decisions. Appreciating the fact that change is unavoidable is very important inasmuch as planning is fundamentally choosing among:

- Priorities
- Programs
- Budgets
- Timeplans, and
- Policies made to sustain corporate goals.

Problems of choice and of priorities arise when available resources are not enough to meet goals, or alternative courses of action, each of different weight, are being studied. Like strategies, plans must fit the objective(s) of the enterprise that makes them. By contrast, forecasts should not be made to serve objectives; they should be done with objectivity.

Budgets and time schedules are an integral part of strategic planning because every plan involves resource evaluation, including men, materials, and money. All resources entering a plan are subject to allocation (see Chapter 4); with the method supporting resource allocation being largely based on projected results. Plan *vs.* actual evaluation is a vital part of strategic planning. Figure 6.1 gives a synopsis of what is involved in this process.

Budgets are short-term plans expressed in financial terms. As the Introduction noted, planning has had its origin in time schedules exemplified by Gantt charts – a milestone in scientific management. Budgets and timeplans are two examples of strategic planning multiple dimension and of factors entering into the planning premises. The span of a plan is limited to the chosen planning period.

In conclusion, the search for alternative courses, formulation of derivative plans, choice among them, allocation of appropriate resources to meet the goals of the chosen plan and coordination of short-range with the long-range plans, are crucial elements of all planning premises – even if every industry

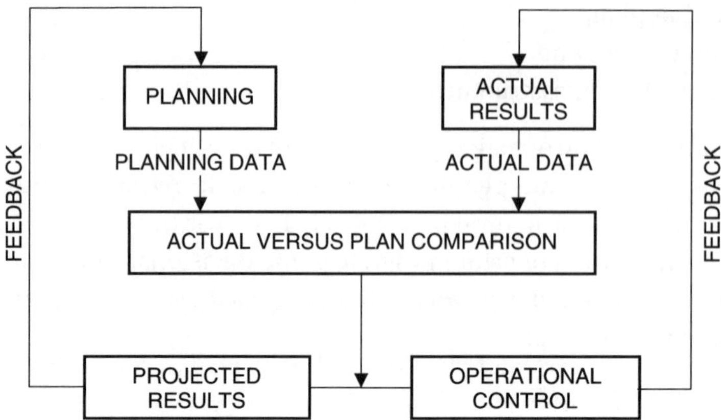

Figure 6.1 All plans must be made with consideration given to actual results, and they should be subject to management control

has its own prerequisites, as well as reasons for strategic planning. A good example is banking.

3. Planning premises in the banking industry: a practical example

A company is not like an oil well where all you have to do is hold a pan out and collect the oil, H.J. Stern once said. It is like a violin and you have to have what it takes to play it. As we will see in this section, the 'notes' to play with are provided by planning. (Stern was president of a gold mining firm and one of the first entrepreneurs to call on KKR for its advice.)

The need for having the right 'notes' to be a serious market player is exemplified through a case study in banking. Today in the banking industry strategic planning is so much more important than it used to be because the basic product of financial institutions is not really money but *services*, which are *derivatives of money*. These are:

- Increasingly more sophisticated financial services that must be planned well in advance.
- And they involve both business opportunity and risks; two reasons why the evolution in banking services must follow a strategic framework.

A flashback helps in appreciating this statement. In the 1960s, manufacturing companies hired bankers as treasurers. In the 1970s, banks returned the compliment by hiring industry experts in strategic planning. Though this strategic planning process started with major financial institutions, by the late 1990s it spread to medium-sized banks that wanted to hold their own against the giants.

During the last couple of decades strategic plans formulated by tier-1 banks have had four main components: building upon the company's profitable markets; designing novel financial instruments; developing the investment banking business to increase profits from fees; and controlling costs more tightly. Each bank is using its own criteria in prioritizing these objectives.

In the general case, in terms of choices, while the goal of novel financial instruments is aggressively followed by big banks, the other three objectives interest all credit institutions and their activities. Therefore, they have become critical components of their planning. Other goals, too, come into perspective. Among a retail bank's key markets are:

- The consumer business
- Mid-sized companies' portfolio
- Real estate, and
- Credit card operations.

The plan senior management develops will prioritize these goals, allocating resources to each of them according to its priority. This plan must also focus on salient problems in every chosen area of activity. Key questions are: What is the real significance of *product strategy* in the chosen channel? What will *our* organization do in 10 years from now in this line of business? From which other channel will the profits come? Moreover:

- Should our company be a product leader in every field of endeavour?
- If yes, what's the mission to be given to the product strategists? What should be their functions? Their criteria of success?

Another vital query that should enter the planning premises of a credit institution is whether there exists sufficient management to handle new products and new markets, given the prevailing rate of change. The answer to this query is by no means self-evident. A study done by Bank of Wachovia in the early 1990s documented that a banker who has not undergone steady training for 5 years loses 50% of his or her skills.

This finding is unsettling because the existence of management skills should always be reflected into the hypotheses and assumptions entering planning premises. An often-made assumption is that strength in the consumer, middle market, and special industries areas should enable the bank to enjoy above-average loan growth. Yes, but ... *if* the needed managerial and professional skill is not there, *then* this will be a self-defeating assumption.

If I stress the importance of skills and know-how it is because, as I know from experience, in banking, manufacturing and commerce companies pay much more attention to head count than to what is in these heads. This is turning the priorities on their head (see also the discussion on lifelong learning in Chapter 7).

In their strategic plans, credit institutions that wish to get out of their shell of services should keep in mind that their nemesis will be lack of professional skills and of managerial talent. Almost every board thinks that expanding the horizon of commercial banking:

- Is a good strategy, but
- Fails to account for the risks, and for the lack of human capital.

Less appreciated is the fact that:

- The more the business horizon expands, the greater the emphasis to be placed on know-how and on planning (see section 4 on long-range planning), and
- The more focused should be the planning procedures and premises; therefore the greater the amount of research and analysis which is necessary.

Moreover, business planning is conditioned by the assumptions senior management makes. Though most frequently (and correctly) these depend on prevailing business environment, some of these assumptions may not prove to be right; or alternatively they may not be reasonable. Either case obliges management to run after different events trying to catch up.

Additionally, quite often management finds out the hard way that the plans that were made were too ambitious. An example from banking is provided by institutions that tried to be all things to all people. Attempting to provide a wide variety of services to all customers does not yield the most profitable results. Therefore, after having lost time and money in ill-fated efforts, many of these banks decided to reconcentrate in sectors where:

- The promise of growth has greater appeal, and
- Return on investment stands a good chance to be higher.

In other terms, banks with appropriate strategic planning know-how pick out market segment(s) that they can serve well, rather than trying to capture the market by being everything to everybody – or by entering service domains where their expertise is slim. They also appreciate that as the market changes so do the institution's strengths and weaknesses.

Among key variables a strategic plan must consider are *cash flow* and *fair value*. Both are good measures of a bank's strengths, and they should be used as proxies in planning premises. A frame of reference that represents them is shown in Figure 6.2. The axes reflect the factors on which senior management should particularly focus.

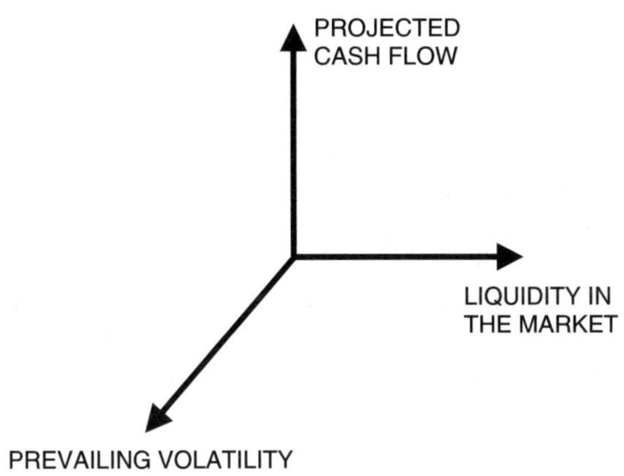

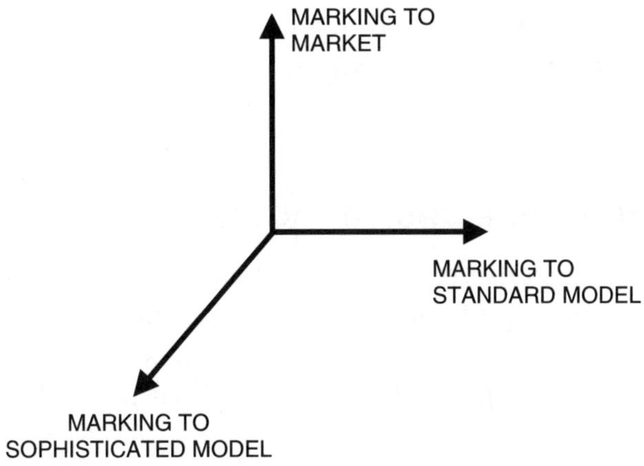

Figure 6.2 Senior management needs a frame of reference on which to focus, in evaluating the strength of the institution

Every serious plan in the banking industry should pay attention to current and projected market evolution. For instance, increased affluence has brought a change in preferences in (and new demands for) financial services. Many banks have missed their business opportunity because of failure to plan for the new priorities of companies and consumers. They worked on the notion that their staid, elegant image from past activities would bring in customers. That is not true at all.

Retail customers today no longer connect snobbery with where they shop. Rather they care about the product they purchase and its costs. As the range of options expands, it is very easy for a customer to lock onto an item considered upscale at a given moment and then buy it anywhere, including from a non-bank entity.

- In order to plan correctly, the credit institution needs to know the alternative options its customers, and potential customers, have.
- This is raw material for strategic choices that revolve around a focus on markets, customers, and products – and are made concrete through plans.

Some banks see to it that their products and services are plotted against two axes of reference: *strategic impact* and *strategic dependence*. The former gives a measure of marketing significance; the latter shows the level of dependence of one's business on market shifts.

Critical items in this approach are those placed high on both axes, as an enterprise is not only dependent on them for continuity, but also for the ability to add a competitive edge to its efforts. While at the end of the day board and CEO decide how the plan will be shaped to satisfy both present and future perspectives, this analysis enables them to prioritize where to allocate vital resources: people, capital, and time, to obtain the best return.

4. Longer-range and far-out planning

Part 1 has explained that plans may be short-range, up to a year; mid-range, up to three years; or longer-term, up to five years and beyond. Plans made with a 15-year perspective are characterized as far-out (see the General Electric example in the next paragraphs). The theme of this section is longer-range planning and beyond.

Statistics dramatize the need for a thorough long-range planning mechanism for any industry operating within a fierce competitive environment. The objective of this mechanism is to assure a framework for planning, and provide continuity in action. The longer-range plan helps in two most significant management duties:

- Clarifying in a factual manner long-range corporate objectives, and
- Linking together short- and medium-range plans with the further-out views by appropriately mapping resources and timetables.

Figure 6.3 shows in a snapshot the interconnection between longer-, medium-, and shorter-range planning premises, including necessary feedback and corrective action. Within the medium- to longer-term perspective, companies must be searching for ways and means to reinvent themselves and their policies, rather than hanging on to ageing concepts and products.

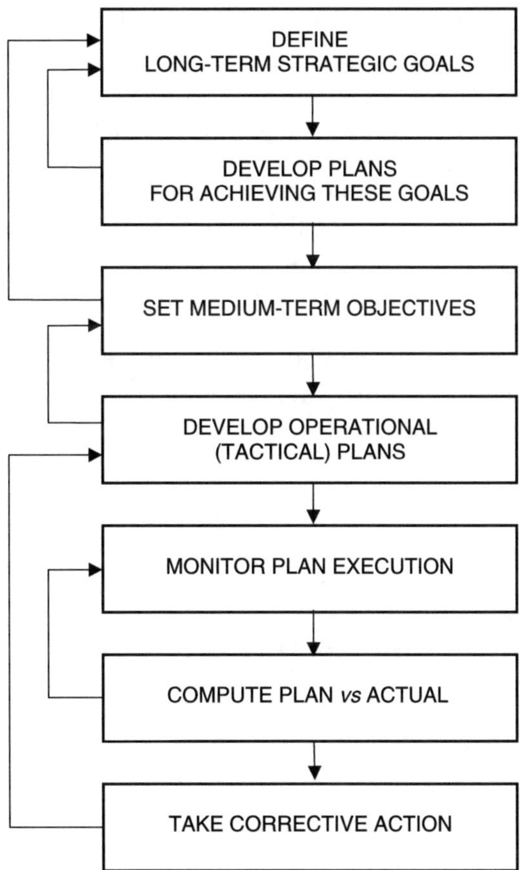

Figure 6.3 Long-range planning should be used as a mechanism for linking medium- and short-range plans

As for far-out planning, one of the best examples I have ever seen comes from General Electric, and dates back about four decades. This is a case study on how far-out planning enlarges the long-range plan's horizon, by forcing knowledgeable people to think of answers to crucial questions:

- What will our company be doing in the next 10–15 years?
- What is going to be our customers' profile 10–15 years from now?
- How fast and in which direction are the market's needs and requirements developing?
- How can *our* company be ahead of its competitors in answering such needs?

General Electric is one of the companies that has practiced far-out study and analysis in the most successful way. In the 1960s, it established a far-out planning laboratory in Santa Barbara, California, staffed with ex-general managers of its divisions – that is, with men who possessed the salt of the earth. Their mission was to define what GE would be doing 10–15 years down the line, and how it should transform itself to continue controlling the high ground.

Figure 6.4 provides the evidence of results from this transformation over a 10-year timeframe (1990–2000). By looking way ahead of events, the company has been able to change quite significantly over these years, nearly doubling the financial services supported by GE Capital, in the corporate total revenue pie.

This provides plenty of evidence that enables answers to the longer-term planning queries outlined in the preceding paragraphs, are instrumental in defining

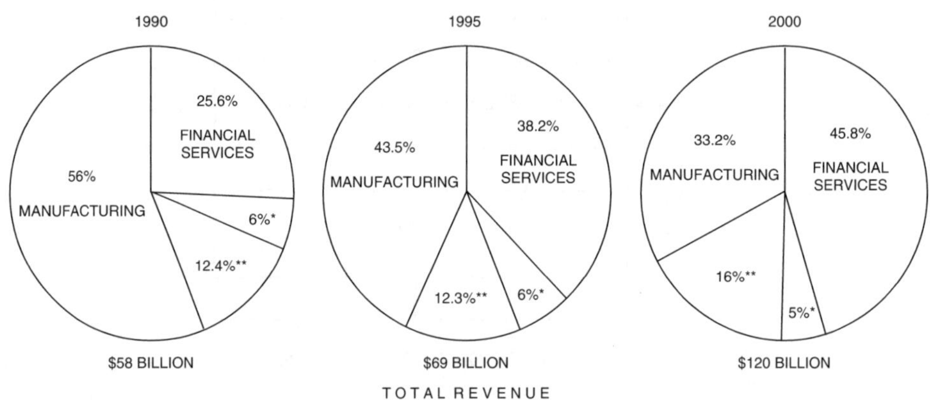

Figure 6.4 General Electric's transformation in 10 years. *Broadcasting. **After sales service

the type of products and services we should research, develop, and support. It also illustrates the moves necessary to get ahead of the competition, and the resources needed to satisfy our customers in an able manner.

An example is provided by *undated debt* as a means to beef-up a company's financial resources. Starting in 2004 and 2005, there has been a tendency towards long-term financing instruments. This is attested by the fact that some companies are issuing 50-year bonds, and they are also drawing on the capital market, through hybrid bonds.

Hybrid bonds are a novel instrument, essentially consisting of subordinated debt securities which have maturities of up to 100 years, are perpetual, or are *undated*. The debt securities are counted by rating agencies as partial capital substitutes. Undated debt instruments help to improve the debt ratio and other financial ratios of the issuing company. They also help in lowering its financing costs.

- The issuer has flexibility, because it can call in a hybrid bond after 10 years.
- Until the earliest call-in date, hybrid bonds typically have a fixed interest rate, while thereafter a floating rate is paid.

This shift to a floating interest rate means that these bonds correspond more closely to 10-year bonds than actual ultra-long bonds, like 50-year issues. Still investors may be locked into them for a long time, with all this means in terms of assumed credit risk and market risk.

Bonds with a maturity of 50 years were issued in Europe in 2005 for the first time in nearly half a century. France and the United Kingdom both placed 50-year government bonds and an Italian telecommunications company also drew on this segment of the capital market. The curious thing is that:

- Nobody can forecast ultra-long, or even simple-long, interest rates
- Yet, ultra-long bonds have been in great demand on the market, with demand exceeding supply.

The example of debt dated for out in time, offered in the capital market, is an issue which can turn investments on their head. How can high net worth individuals know what will happen 50 years hence?

The second example in this section regards longer range, but not far-out premises. When in the 1970s and 1980s Japanese banks invaded the US market, most particularly California, they took the longer view. They bought time by purchasing local banks, and paid plenty of money for market share. Contrary to US banks:

- These Japanese institutions did not care about their quarterly earnings.
- Their plan has espoused the longer horizon necessary for growing roots in the US market.

My planning experience suggests that *if* throwing money at the problem is to be avoided – which must always be the case – *then* the methodology to be used in connection to a long-term plan should be multifunctional. One of the functions is establishing market targets, with projected market share and price range of services examined from the point of view of direct competition.

Another crucial function of the long-range plan, to which company management should pay attention, is that of examining the dual aspects of *product image* and *company image*. The principle is that trademark and reputation take years to establish, but could be destroyed in a day. A careful policy includes the need to evaluate the impact of:

- Product novelty
- Product quality, and
- Pricing policies, from the longer-term perspective.

These three bullets lay a third function on the table: the study of the company's marketing capabilities in the longer term. Work on innovation, quality improvements and pricing strategy must always consider the long-term approach to marketing. Senior management's guidelines should definitely include a close look at:

- Sales training requirements, and
- Qualitative objectives against which it is possible to measure individual performance.

Solutions to be chosen must be competitive, and they should unquestionably be dynamic because both the market and competition change, and past marketing plans can turn on their head. Indeed, from R&D, to engineering, production, and sales, being ahead of the curve requires clear concepts and vision. Projections currently being made cannot be independent of the:

- Evaluation of further-out market evolution, and
- Positioning of our firm in terms of products and services.

If the longer-range planning study reveals warning signals, *then* coming up from under requires thorough redefinition of products and processes, including level of technological sophistication, adequacy of skills and cost factors. All this is part and parcel of the need for concentration and focus by senior management, of which we spoke in section 2.

In conclusion, in industries and markets that are technology-intensive, and this today means more or less in all industries, factual responses in connection to longer-term outlook assist in defining the goals our company should pursue. This statement is valid from R&D to client handholding. Special attention should evidently be paid to the level of technology literacy that allows one to get returns from investments well beyond that competitors achieve.

5. Challenges of shorter-range plans

Whether short-range or long-range, planning is always for the future. This emphasis is necessary in recognition of the fact that the future belongs to those who can create structures able to confront a changing and uncertain environment, in which the forms of traditional competition are substituted by new ones, for which a company must be prepared through the process of planning.

One of the challenging tasks confronting short-range planning is to assure the operational plans and budgets are aligned with longer-term policy expressed through the strategic plan. At the same time, the short-range plan should be based on the rolling year's goals and resources, which condition the course(s) of action. More precisely, the short-range plan itself should see to it that:

- Currently available resources are developed to fit the goals of a *rolling year*, which ranges between 12 and 24 months, and
- *If* initially resources are insufficient for goals being set, *then* the way to grow them should be outlined by the plan in its life cycle.

Because not only longer-range plans but also those of shorter range involve many assumptions, the hypotheses behind them should be clearly outlined. Additionally, they should be subject to periodic critical reviews – which help to evaluate and revamp them, as well as to ascertain their strong and weak points.

An example from personal experience comes from the 1980s and concerns IBM's H Series. At the time, many large firms promised the computer manufacturer that they would purchase far more 3081 mainframes than they ever intended to use. They did so to assure themselves of an advantageous position in the long list of orders.

- IBM planners based their assumption on H Series sales on these responses.
- Down the line, however, it was found that as a result of this attitude by clients, cancellations of H Series mainframes were substantially higher than expected.

The after-effect of forecasts failing to materialize has an impact all the way from budgets to production plans, inventory management, sales quotas, cash flow, and profitability. By being nearer to the salt of the earth given their rolling-year nature, shorter-range forecasts and associated planning premises are relatively easier to scrutinize and ascertain causes and effects than longer-range plans. Even if easier, this task is not trivial because scrutiny requires:

- Collecting facts
- Evaluating different possibilities
- Developing alternative solutions, as marketing and other information comes in.

Another more recent example on short-term worries concerns Parmalat, the Italian 'dairy products and hedge fund' company which went bust in December 2003.[2] Enrico Bondi, a most capable turnaround artist and special administrator of the bankrupt company, has been able to bring Parmalat back to life, part of the deal being money recovered from lawsuits.

Bondi planned to announce his retirement at the shareholders' meeting on 7/8 November 2005, but major shareholders asked him to stand for election as chief executive of the resurrected group. These investors, led by Lehman Brothers, the investment bank, were motivated by the fear that lawsuits Bondi has filed against Parmalat's former financiers would be shelved were he to retire. Bondi's thesis has been that:

- Banks and regulators should have spotted Parmalat's trouble much sooner, and
- On this basis he sued Italian and foreign banks for more than 13 billion euro ($16 billion) in damages and restitution.

The banks' answer has been that Parmalat's rebirth was possible only because they, as creditors, swapped some 20 billion euro in debt-related claims for equity. In fact, the irony is that some of Parmalat's big shareholders are the very entities being sued. Examples include Banca Intesa, Italy's biggest, as well as Citigroup and Bank of America.

In both of the aforementioned cases – IBM's H series and Parmalat – a medium-range recovery plan has been upset by short-term worries. In the first case these were due to overestimates of sales potential; in the second by the risk that if hefty lawsuits fizzled out the company's recovery (which counted on the proceeds to be obtained from them) may be in jeopardy.

The message both cases convey is that even if a prognostication has been made, initial results are good, and up to a point everything seems to go according to plan, returns may flatten at any time. Or a few undesirable consequences may emerge upsetting the shorter-term plans or even bringing a reversal. For instance, a merger projected to go smoothly may leave the surviving entity with:

- Conflicting organizational processes, and
- System complexity that places strain on operational efficiency and financial performance.

As we will see through case studies in Part 6, it is wrong to believe that mergers and acquisitions are long-term propositions. A merger will succeed or fail depending on what happens in short-term integration. Adverse effects are more likely when M&A plans, for instance, do not account for the fact that most acquired firms resist integration, and insist on operating with their traditional business structure. This makes it difficult to:

- Squeeze out unnecessary cost, and
- Present customers with value differentiation.

Not only in the longer-term but also in the short term, because competition is tough and there is a global squeeze on prices, companies cannot afford to have capabilities duplicated across product lines, with each business unit operating in its own way. Additionally, while it is thought to offer increased efficiency, the downside of vertically integrated supply chains is that they limit customer choice, leaving firms with:

- An undifferentiated value proposition
- Lower overall customer wallet share than originally thought, and
- Uncertainties about what tomorrow may bring in terms of turnover.

In his excellent book *My Years with General Motors*, Alfred Sloan makes reference to one of the two flat orders he issued during the long years of his reign over the large corporation. This was in the early 1930s, when the auto market was weak because of the Great Depression.[3]

Sloan wanted to collect his own facts about the pace of motor vehicle sales. To do so, he went coast-to-coast by train, visiting a large number of GM dealers. What he found was that their parking lots were full. His vice president of marketing had most likely also seen this, but took no action. The boss did not hesitate about what he should do. On his return to Detroit he issued the order to stop production.

Sloan's example brings into perspective another very important issue connected to short-term planning. The fact that there is a budget, therefore a short-term financial plan, for production or for any other purpose, does not mean that it has to be used. In fact, well-managed companies see to it that:

- Budgets are no authorization for spending money, and
- Even major expenditure has to be specifically approved by senior management.

This is one of the lessons I learned in the years I was associated to General Electric. A great amount of attention should also be paid to short-term plans concerning operations, and projects such as the implementation of new regulatory rules. An example from the International Financial Reporting Standards (IFRS) by IASB is hedge accounting – which in the large majority of cases has been a short-term implementation project.

Figure 6.5 presents in a nutshell planning for project management in connection to the implementation of IFRS.[4] As the reader can appreciate, the first major component of the plan is analysis of requirements followed by a first integrative study, coordination of subprojects, problem resolution, and on-line databasing/datamining. Other key component parts have been:

- General accounting
- Hedge accounting
- Management accounting
- Risk management
- Information technology
- Documentation and monitoring.

These examples bring to the reader's attention the fact that short-range plans are made not only for financial and operational purposes but also for other reasons – for instance, reasons intended to comply to new regulations, or to create shareholder value.

On several occasions I was called to advise on crash projects intended for revenue diversification, by expanding the revenue base through additional

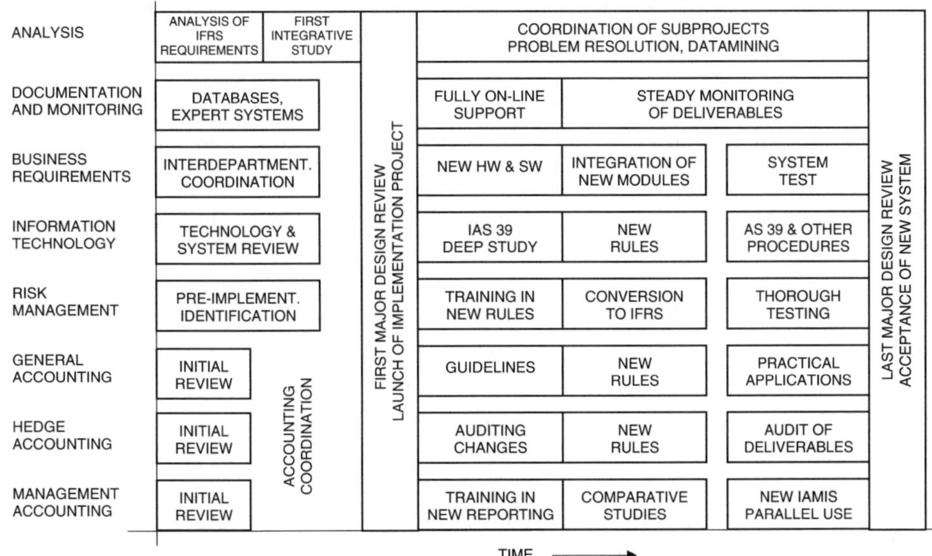

Figure 6.5 Project management planning for IFRS implementation

sources of noninterest income. Another crash project has been risk reduction by means of securitizing loans, as well as other assets sitting on the books. Still another is consolidation by capturing economies of scale. All these are short-term planning challenges. Projects that take three years to materialize are dead ducks.

In conclusion, failure to regularly re-evaluate and to update short-range plans, including the hypotheses behind them, can lead one into dire straits. It is therefore no surprise that well-managed companies are moving away from the notion that major projects should take nearly a lifetime. Even so, with 'pluses' and 'minuses' continuously shifting to different parts of the value chain, many firms are struggling, unsure which areas of their business matter and uncertain where they should be headed. Only a properly focused plan can help in easing such constraints.

6. The role of policies in planning

Because organizations are made up of people, what is said about entities is valid of its executives and of the plans they make. Whether or not an entity uses models and datamining, at the end of the day people make the decisions. Section 2 brought to the reader's attention the importance of focusing on management decisions leading to plans and their execution; for instance, plans that:

- Target those products and customers best suited to its operating model
- Address incremental revenue processes by examining every business component
- Evaluate the element constituting best-in-class capabilities, and associated efficiencies.

Focused management decisions enable the entity to develop new products faster than its competitors; customize its products to fit targeted needs justifying a price premium; integrate new resources rapidly, thereby achieving synergies sooner; or aggregate data across the organization, turning it into useful information for further action.

The more important, and more far-reaching, of these decisions will be expressed through policies that are typically established as guides to specific actions. As we have already seen, policies are guidelines with resilience, helping to avoid taking repetitive decisions on the same or similar issues. Policies are also employed for the purpose of interpreting or shading the emphasis and meaning of strategies and plans.

- Policies are not plans
- But they do help in planning.

Usually, though not always, policies will aim to create a responsive and resilient entity. Rigorous risk management policies will make an entity that knows its exposure to market, credit, and operational risk in real-time; effectively controls its limits to exposure; and is most careful in its choice of strategic partners based on their quality of risk management.

Policies are necessary for many purposes. One of the not so often appreciated is a policy on what must be done to recover quickly from operational disruptions caused by unpredictable external factors. Another policy must outline for the business units how to build robust, self-healing organizational capabilities to face adversity when it comes. Still another policy elaborates on the need for controlled cost structure (see Chapter 11).

A good example on rigorous policy that provides the basis for planning economic capital requirements is offered by the KBC Group, a major bank holding company in Belgium. Typically, financial holding companies (FHCs) own at least one bank plus insurance and broking subsidiary.

By looking at economic capital as required *risk capital*, KBC established a policy instituting a new book:

- Available financial resources (AFR).

According to KBC's policy, these financial resources must be about 20% larger than risk capital because of strategic reasons, evolving business opportunities, effects of information latency, as well as model risk. Model risk is present in all businesses using models, but only the best managed recognize it as such.

Rigorous policies and short- to medium-term planning premises, promises that reflect a focused responsive and resilient approach, help senior management to concentrate on essentials. They make feasible a general harmony of effort, and see to it that everything tends to fit together, with all contributors playing their part. A prerequisite is that:

- The board and CEO are able to define long-term policies and
- Establish procedures are in place that permit verification of whether established policies are followed everywhere in the organization.

Policies concerning products, and the product line at large, are a good example on how they help to distinguish one company from the next. A major planning decision concerning the product line is always: Shall we be 'first' or 'second' in 'this' or 'that' income earner? Quite often the answer is situational, and there are cases where accidents can strike gold.

In the early 1950s IBM's refusal to buy Univac when its developers offered it to Thomas Watson, Sr led to an intensive internal computer development effort and a premier educational strategy. Also to a change of management, as Thomas Watson, Jr succeeded his father at the helm. Coming up from under:

- Eventually IBM overtook Univac, who had become a division of Remington Rand.
- By helping in educating its customers in computer technology, and in assisting them on enlarging their applications domain, IBM developed a strategy that has been instrumental in gaining No. 1 position for nearly three decades.

As far as product strategy goes, including policies and planning premises associated to it, 'first' or 'second' decisions are instrumental in establishing what we will do in the market. This requires us to assess how well our enterprise is able to maintain a position as innovator, how far it has moved in market appreciation, and whether existing processes, human skills and financial resources permit a leap forward.

While in the 1950s and 1960s IBM policies were in tune with their time, two decades later, in the 1980s, they came unstuck. This should serve as a reminder that, like plans, policies do not serve forever. A thorough analysis of current policies in terms of their pertinence and impact helps to gauge whether *our* firm continues to be a dynamic enterprise.

Stated in different terms, an integral part of the policy-making and planning effort is their evaluation. Are they still pertinent as industry changes? Or are they becoming obsolete or irrelevant? Policies should be scrutinized for their ability to serve as a catalyst for further evolution of our company's activities.

In conclusion, senior management must identify the areas of business activity that need to benefit from the guidance provided by policies. These may be in different lines of competence: R&D, production, inventories, sales, distribution, infrastructure, IT, risk control, financial management, and personnel. Senior management also needs to establish performance indicators for its policies, and assure their adaptability to market conditions.

7. Management planning and business risk

Whether management speaks of longer- or shorter-range planning, *business risk* is rarely taken into account in a way commensurate to its importance. Yet it is omnipresent in all industrial, commercial, and financial activities. Many companies look at business risk under a narrow perspective, as something of residual value and with cyclicality, often expressed through:

- A fall in margin, or
- Loss of market clout.

In reality, it is much more than that. Moreover, while intimately relating to business risk, *reputational risk* has its own important characteristics, some of which have to do with market discipline. Business risk and reputational risk do overlap, but not completely so.

A major uncertainty befalling business risk is that there are no clear guidelines on how exactly a company enters into it. Currently, many cognisant people believe that business risk has the status of operational risk in the 1990s. They also point out that, for planning purposes:

- Business risk must be measurable in order to treat it adequately, and
- It will become measurable only after its definition is properly settled, it is generally acceptable, and there are conventions regarding its management.

'One of the crucial queries is how far business risk, industry risk, and management risk correlate,' Alastair Graham, senior vice president of Moody's Investors Service, told me. In fact, industry risk and management risk correlate not only with business risk but also among themselves, as Figure 6.6 shows.

Graham took Rover, the British car company, as an example of how far industry risk and management risk overlap with the result that endogenous factors of one company may become exogenous factors in one or more other firms. This linkage is provided by the fact there is *contingent risk*. When Rover went bust, hundreds of other companies suffered. The same has been true, in 1995, with Delphi Automotive.

Alastair Graham is right in his assessment. Because contingent risk is omnipresent, it should be fully accounted for in our strategic plans. Both overconcentration and a false sense of diversification can spell disaster. Hence, the queries:

- Is client diversification part of the perceived business risk?
- *If* yes, *then* what is our strategy in keeping it under lock and key?

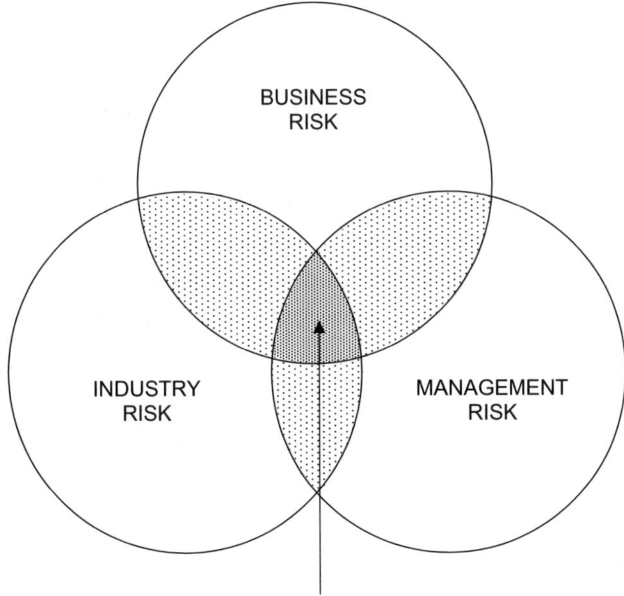

Figure 6.6 Business risk can be found at the junction of industry risk and management risk

Similar questions can be asked about legal risk and reputational risk. The challenge for every board of directors is to appreciate these correlations, obliging the CEO and his immediate assistants to integrate them into the corporate plan. At the same time, the challenge for every risk manager is to perform the most severe and imaginative criticism of business risk and reputational exposure – and do so before either gets out of hand.

In the seminars I give for senior management many participants ask: 'How can business risk be quantified?' There is no unique answer to this question, but there exist alternative approaches. A good example is presented through the road taken by Crédit Suisse, which accounts for business risk by reducing by 60% the goodwill on its balance sheet. At Crédit Suisse management reached this decision because goodwill is the area that would suffer the most from business risk events.

Another good example, one that is more analytical and takes costs into account, comes from Barclays Bank. The approach Barclays has chosen computes business risk through an algorithm that accounts for turnover, margin, fixed costs, variable costs, and business volume:

$$\text{Business Risk} = \text{Annual Turnover} \cdot \text{Margin} - \begin{Bmatrix} \text{Fixed Cost} + \\ \text{Variable Cost} \cdot \\ \text{Revenue Volume} \end{Bmatrix}$$

At Barclays Bank, experimentation connected to the business risk algorithm has included historical turnover volatility, margins, costs, and revenues. Turnover studies have been done over a 20-year timeframe. Barclays also does Monte Carlo simulation, selecting values from business risk's lognormal distribution, and applying last year's margin.

The inclusion of fixed and variable costs makes sense because business risk-type losses may come from costs that have escaped management's attention and steady vigilance. It will be the wrong assumption to think that the more we spend on a service, the higher will be its quality. My experience tells me that quite the opposite is true. In fact:

- Because of high production and distribution costs our company may drive itself out of the market.
- At a time when only low cost producers and distributors can survive, high internal costs are an important contributor to business risk.

The argument that high quality costs too much money is nonsense. In terms of business risk control, the only way to improve quality is to use a rigorous quality assurance system, like Six Sigma.[5] An analytical approach will also take a careful look at correlations between strategic risk and business risk, which depends:

- On type of organization
- The way it is being managed, and
- The market(s) in which it is active.

In 2005, HSBC wrote off $5 billion connected to losses of its Household Finance subsidiary in the United States, an entity that specializes in lending to low net worth individuals. The strategic decision by HSBC to make this acquisition had taken place years earlier. Through Household Finance, it bought market share. But the $5 billion in red ink wiped out a quarter of HSBC's $20 billion profit in that year.

How are rating agencies handling the business risk companies take? Charles Prescott, group managing director of Fitch Ratings, told me, 'We don't specifically put business risk in credit rating,' adding that business risk is a function of:

- Endogenous factors that relate to quality of management, and
- Exogenous factors, including the economy, important business facts, unemployment, physical disasters.

In the opinion of other executives with know-how, still another basic factor underpinning business risk is spikes resulting from events like major frauds, legal risk, and other crucial variables. In September 2005 an American judge approved legal settlements returning $6.2 billion to investors who lost money in the Worldcom scandal. Citigroup and J.P. Morgan Chase, underwriters and traders of Worldcom securities, had to pay $2 billion each.

Since business risk is omnipresent, a milestone in effective economic capital allocation is that of choosing the tools and the benchmarks. In the final analysis, benchmarks must be sufficiently sophisticated, represented by a function that (if need be) can be scaled up or down, and able to provide means for establishing a pattern of results.

In a world where business risk is rising, and with globalization it can gain worldwide dimensions, a most legitimate question is how much capital should be allocated to it. We have seen two examples. The Crédit Suisse approach is ex ante; that of Barclays, ex post. But is a goodwill discount enough as capital provision? If not, how much money should companies be allocating to business risk?

- Deutsche Bank is said to allocate 3% of its economic capital for business risk.
- Danske Bank, a much smaller European regional credit institution, allocates 21% of its economic capital.

These percentages look lopsided, but at the same time much depends on what the bank puts into business risk, and which are the drivers guiding such capital allocation. Also, how is capital allocation made between competing risk factors, and where will the money come from to pay for each one of them? All these are queries which, for the time being, are answered individually by each institution. The time will come when regulatory authorities will establish a capital adequacy framework for business risk.

Notes

1 *The Economist*, 26 November 2005.
2 D.N. Chorafas, *The Management of Equity Investments*. Elsevier, Oxford, 2005.
3 Alfred Sloan, *My Years with General Motors*. Pan Books, London, 1967.
4 D.N. Chorafas, *IFRS, Fair Value and Corporate Governance: The Impact on Budgets, Balance Sheets and Management Accounts*. Elsevier, Oxford, 2006.
5 D.N. Chorafas, *Integrating ERP, CRM, Supply Chain Management and Smart Materials*. Auerbach: New York, 2001.

Organizing and Staffing

1. Introduction

Organization is one of the vital management tasks. The able execution of organizational duties requires determining the kind and extent of departmentalization, and hence of specialization, that should characterize the work of the business unit. It also requires establishing two-way communications channels, which are the information arteries of the entity. A most important organizational duty is that of defining:

- Authority, and
- Responsibility.

Also part of organizational chores is coordination of activities, which in turn requires setting structural issues, delineating proper relationships, establishing lines of accountability for performance, and elaborating positional qualifications. Still another organizational duty is defining the appropriate liaison to promote closer collaboration between different units.

Books on organization say that lines of authority and responsibility should be formal. However, in parallel to the formal organization there is an informal one, the *grapevine*, and some chief executives know how to use it to their advantage. Ken Olsen, the chairman of DEC, often employed the grapevine strategy to prepare the company's personnel for oncoming change. In the general case:

- Rumours can do a good preparatory job
- But at the same time they may exercise psychological stress and destabilize the organization.

The reader would do well to notice that as far as formal organization is concerned no structural dimensions are set in stone. Usually, structure changes over time along with changes in the concepts underpinning it, or with organizational upheaval. An important tool I have used in my professional work in studying structural issues is the *span of management*. It measures the manager's ability to run the organization based on four criteria:

- *Span of control*, that is, how many managers report to a superior.
- *Span of knowledge*, which identifies the spread of know-how in a business unit or department.
- *Span of support*, specifically being provided by the infrastructure.

- *Span of attention*, regarding each manager's capabilities for directing and controlling operations under his or her authority.

In each of these four dimensions, a greater span has important after-effects in making the organization more lean, as well as better able to respond to changing situations. Another of a greater span is that of reducing overhead (see Chapter 11).

The engine behind the structure being developed would be human resources. Therefore, staffing is another vital management function. Its execution calls for recruiting qualified personnel; providing lifelong training to counter human obsolescence; effectively managing this personnel to higher levels of productivity, and assuring career planning.

Other staffing functions involve assigning qualified people at each position, continuing the development of a valuable human inventory, and helping in the improvement of attitudes and skills. Personnel policy should take account of the fact that some 70% of all jobs in the Western world require cerebral skills rather than manual skills.

Persons as well as organizations will be out of business if they cannot adapt to this knowledge-intense landscape. Today, capital buys brainpower, not just land, tools, and equipment. When in June 1995, IBM put down $3.5 billion for Lotus Development, it was not just buying a company but was also acquiring the vision of Lotus Notes architect Ray Ozzie, and scores of other creative minds working for the firm.

The importance of staffing with people possessing the best available knowledge can be appreciated when we account for the fact that many, if not most people in high-tech companies have their compensation linked to the success of their entity. This is a good way to make them understand that their future is tied to the willingness of investors:

- To take a chance on a good idea, and
- To earn a fair rate of return for that risk.

While this type of personal involvement is usually associated with start-ups, the management of settled traditional companies needs to recognize the impact of brainpower, and to develop a policy reflecting it. No company can afford to remain transfixed in organizational and staffing issues by the vision it sees in the rearview mirror.

2. A sound organizational principle taught by the Catholic Church

Stated in the simplest possible terms, organization is the current arrangement of lines of authority and responsibility within an entity, usually valid for medium-term and day-to-day application. In the longer term, structural solutions become obsolete and all organizations change.

In terms of rules and principles, in general, an entity should be organized in the manner that will best implement the strategy established by the board and CEO. The line of command should work in synergy with the objectives. This is doable because strategy should precede organization, though in practice this is not always the case. Strategy and organization are closely related, and the way to bet is that a good strategy with poor organization will fail – though the opposite is not true.

The problem with organizational principles in daily practice is not different from that presented with all others. While principles are often enunciated, they are rarely observed. The frequently encountered fact that organization lags behind strategy means that structure is based on a business model:

- That is no longer in existence
- Or is in the process of going out of use.

The most glaring reference is to a model developed in the industrial economy, which has significant weaknesses when applied in the service economy in which we live today. This is known as the hierarchical model of organization, with a small span of control, as in the one shown on the left side of Figure 7.1.

A long hierarchy is an ineffectual structure that puts the company at disadvantage against its better-organized competitors, by making it insensitive to market changes, clogging the arteries of communication, and increasing the overheads. By contrast, a large span of control leads to a flat and cost-effective organization.

Table 7.1 provides documentation on what has been stated in the previous paragraph. By increasing the span of control (see definition in the Introduction), from five to eight, five organizational layers handle an entity of over 32 000 people – while it takes seven layers to do so with a span of five; and there are companies which use a span of two or three.

The whole issue of span of control revolves around management structure, and the entity's ability to avoid centrifugal forces. Theoretically, the role of smaller

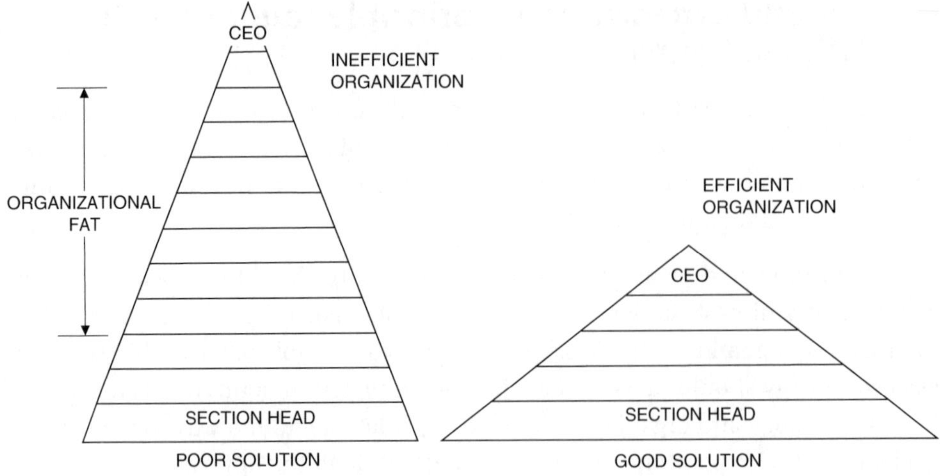

Figure 7.1 A long hierarchy puts the company at a disadvantage and increases overheads

Table 7.1 Effects of a broader span of control on the layers of an organizational structure

Organization layers	Span of control		
	5	7	8
1	5	7	8
2	25	49	64
3	125	343	512
4	625	2 401	4 096
5	3 125	16 807	32 768
6	15 625	117 649	262 144
7	79 125	823 543	2 097 152
8	390 625	5 764 801	
9	1 953 125		

span of control is to hold together the organization and limit breaches of accountability. Practically, this is nonsense, because the technology we have available can succeed in reaching the objectives just stated with a wide span of control.

True enough, controls are needed on the organizational side to help offset weaknesses caused by lack of segregation of duties – which is another organizational objective but is never perfectly done. But it is equally true that some of these controls can be effectively executed through expert systems. Knowledge artifacts provide a computer-supported capability to:

- Detect and prevent accidental errors
- Flash out fraudulent manipulation, and other adverse occurrences
- Digest news and provide on-line reporting.[1]

Properly used, technology helps in enhancing the sense of hierarchy even within a flat organization. This is important inasmuch as every organization – industrial, financial, religious or government – has a hierarchy. The challenge is to structure this hierarchy in the most effective manner. By definition, a hierarchy is a classification according to rank and/or authority.

- The greater the number of reporting levels in an organization, the more 'hierarchical' it is in the old pyramiding way.

Apart from the other negatives we have seen, the downside is that a very hierarchical solution is bureaucratic, characterized by a long vertical dimension of structure and short span of control.

- The less the number of reporting levels, the lower the managerial overhead and the more restrained the time spent on trivia and administrative duties.

The Catholic Church provides an excellent example of a flat organization, which has been able to hold itself together for two thousand years. The modern company has much to learn by studying the structure of a successful organization, and the way in which it works.

In fact, a reason why the Catholic Church provides an excellent example of flat structure is that it has only three levels: Pope, cardinals, bishops. The bishops are foremen with priests being the workers. Few, if any, business corporations are as flat as the Catholic Church. Usually industrial organizations follow the now classical General Motors model.

Looking back at the origins of this currently most widespread organizational structure, we see that it was in the 1920s that Alfred Sloan developed it at General Motors: His was a decentralized operation combined with centralized policy and financial control. This happened more than one and a half centuries after the start of the industrial revolution in England. An earlier, fully centralized organizational model was implemented in mid-19th century, in France, by Henri Fayol.

In industry, bureaucratic organizations flourished because it has been generally considered that span of control should be between four and six. Beyond that, most senior managers believed (without much evidence) that the amount of attention a boss can pay to each subordinate is not enough to enable him or her to do a decent job. This meant that when too many people are reporting to an individual, an intermediate level of supervision should be inserted, with the result that:

- The span of control shrinks, and
- The hierarchy increases, and along with it, the bureaucracy.

This is both counterproductive and unnecessary. Today we have the technology to create flat organizations with a wide span of control – like the one on the right side of Figure 7.1 – without being subject to centrifugal forces, and without hiding vital information from the top layers of the organization, as happens in bureaucratic settings.

Business and industry is currently transforming the Sloan model of organization, using it as precursor to a different model, sometimes referred to as *mass customized organization.* For instance, in the GM Sloan model, corporate planning and financial control are centralized, while operations are decentralized around a product division structure.

- Each product division is treated as a complete business.
- Yet, at the same time, it is a part of the larger corporation.

In looking back in organizational practice, one would notice that the next milestone in organization and structure has been provided by the *business unit* (BU) developed in the 1950s by General Electric. The BU is defined as a smaller identifiable self-governing whole within the larger entity, with criteria for determining it:

- Resources applied to meet a goal
- Market needs to be fulfilled close to their origin, and
- Products and services addressed to the market and matched against those of competitors.

This is the distributed paradigm shown in the left side of Figure 7.2. Authority flows from the centre to the periphery. By contrast, the right side shows a totally different organizational solution: the federated organization, which works through *inverse delegation* of authority – from the periphery to the centre.

Virtual organizations with huge outsourcing contracts fall between the two types, but nearer to federated organization structure. Virtual companies, which tend to multiply, have nothing to do with hierarchical settings. Through a mixture of

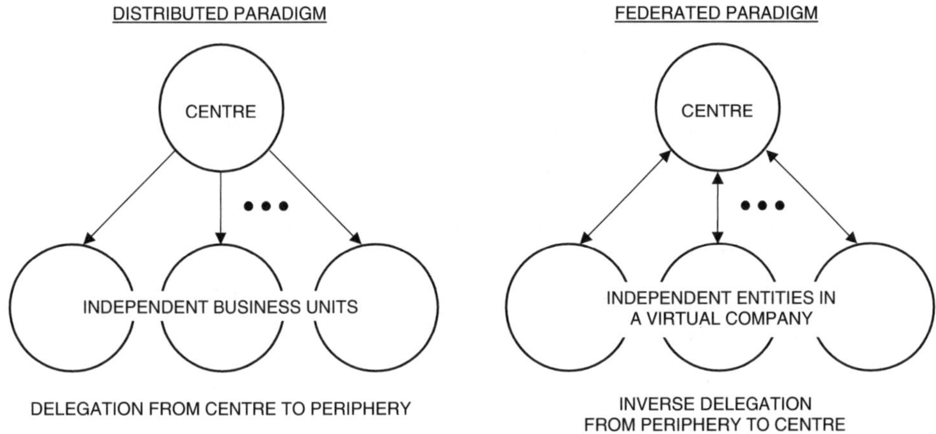

Figure 7.2 There is an essential difference between decentralization and federation of independent entities

direct and inverse delegation they labour to manage resources including those which directly affect their products, markets, information, know-how, and capital.

In a book published two and a half decades ago, Charles Handy aptly comments that organizations used to be perceived as gigantic pieces of engineering, with largely interchangeable human parts. These structures were viewed as systems of inputs and outputs with local and central controls. By the end of the 20th century, however, organizational monoliths started dying like the dinosaurs did ages ago.[2]

In all likelihood, decentralized organizations have been nothing other than a phase of transition. Independent business units with their own cultures, knowledge, products, markets, and networks held together by a common interest, have become rather commonplace. However, the challenge of taking over control of the organization remains, as we see in section 3.

3. Case studies on the aftermath of reorganization: the Jack Welsh example

Theoretically, organization and structure should be set independently of the people who would fit managerial and professional functions within it. This is what most textbooks say. Practically, this is rarely if ever the case. Organization and staffing correlate in more than one dimension.

One of the chief reasons for this correlation, is that in every company there is room for the CEO to initiate organizational change, using at any time and place the method that suits him or her best. There is no general rule about reorganization. Sometimes, it takes years of lead time for structural change to evolve and mature. In other cases, restructuring is done in no time.

The same is true with human resources. When Lee Iacocca became chief executive officer of a nearly bankrupt Chrysler, he found in place 35 vice presidents. Two years down the line only one of them was still working at Chrysler. Iacocca not only restructured the company, but also filled the top jobs with his own people.

As Dr Pier A. Abetti of Rensselear Polytechnic Institute notes, to assert himself and prove that he is fully in charge, a leader consolidates his power by seizing the few neural centres where power is exercised. Then he gradually conquers the entire organization. Abetti takes as an example Jack Welsh at General Electric, who started by eliminating at headquarters the complacent, overstaffed offices that might offer passive resistance. Welsh,

- Removed 167 of the 200 members of headquarters senior staff
- Then, he added 67 new senior managers who were loyal to him personally.

Corporate-wide, to slim down GE and cut overheads Jack Welsh laid off 80 000 employees in the first year of his reign, and 42 000 in the next two years. By preference he concentrated the downsizing on the older, more bureaucratic and more expensive personnel. These are also the people less inclined to change.

Restructuring did not end there, because the new CEO wanted to change the way people worked at headquarters and in the field. Classically, GE had a policy of establishing strategic plans by 65 different business units. Each of these strategic plans featured 100 or more pages. Welsh changed that practice. His strategy as CEO was not to read pages of printed material but:

- Look into the hearts and minds of business units' leaders
- Evaluate their skill and their drive, and
- Check the way they supported their arguments, by responding to his queries.

To tight-size the company, Welsh regrouped GE's 65 business units into 13, which he supervised directly, greatly enlarging his span of control – and proving that this is doable. He also instituted the 20–70–10 principle in connection to staffing. Initiated in the late 1980s, GE's policy under Jack Welsh has been:

- The 20% of personnel, the most productive, must be adequately compensated for its efforts.

- The next 70% should be led and trained to significantly improve its deliverables, and
- Management should let the bottom 10% go, so that the company steadily renews its human resources, based on the best elements working at business units and headquarters.

GE and Chrysler are by no means unique examples. In well-managed companies management does not let organization and structure be out of tune with the entity's operation. Neither does it allow operating expenses to be out of line with predetermined cost standards. In organizational terms, crumbling structures are due, in great measure, to the confusion arising from:

- Overlapping functions and responsibilities
- Costly duplications of effort
- Complexity resulting from uncontrolled growth, through the company's national or multinational operations.

As an example, in an industrial organization which I prefer not to name, the executive vice president responsible for *operations* had seven vice presidents reporting to him. They were in charge of research, engineering, production, marketing, and three regional (world-wide) divisions. The vice presidents of finance, information systems, personnel, purchasing, industrial relations, and transportation, were reporting to the other executive vice president of the firm in charge of *staff*.

Both executive vice presidents reported to the president, which made the span of control at top management equal to 2. Since these EVPs competed for the top job, they withheld vital information from one another, obliging the other party to duplicate numerous functions. The result was:

- A mixture of costly corporate activities.
- These were working in an almost air-tight relationship, without adequate management controls.

Eventually, realizing that this problem of miscoordination was present not only at headquarters, but company-wide because the subsidiaries emulated the parent firm's structure, the CEO was able to persuade the board of directors on the need for reorganization. This led to an executive board with 14 people reporting to the CEO. One of the EVPs had responsibility to run the international business operations. The other EVP quit the firm.

Looking in retrospect at the results of this reorganization, after nearly a decade, the redefined functional areas were able to accomplish cost and performance goals, significantly reducing general management expenditures. They were also able to feed back reliable information to measure operating results against goals, with the aim of immediate corrective action. Additionally, a more cost-conscious central management improved its own performance in:

- Setting up workable master budgets
- Receiving and analysing financial and operational reports, and
- Recommending actions based upon overall evaluations of results obtained against plans.

In parallel to these changes, a thorough organizational study developed a comprehensive and effective answer to accountability objectives along structural and product lines. At business unit level, management was given a yardstick to measure results through:

- Responsibility accounting reflecting budgetary performance, and
- Exception monitoring for custom-made interactive reporting by domain of responsibility.

While the outlined solution passed successfully the test of time, it is appropriate to emphasize that there is no unique answer to organizational problems. Neither is there a single organizational chart that can fit the requirements of every enterprise, other than the general framework which is shown in Figure 7.3.

Last but not least, with restructuring it is wise to install a new management mindset that promotes competitive analysis; adaptation to short product life cycles; improvements of costing and pricing methodologies; and open communications channels. All this identifies a domain where organization and staffing merge, as the following section documents.

4. Emphasizing the role of the individual: lesson by Miyamoto Musashi

Miyamoto Musashi was one of the most famous Japanese Samurai, whose techniques were based on an inner-directed speaking to the soul of an individual (more on this later). Study, meditation, and mental preparation were the Musashi approach. 'My way of strategy is the sure method to win when fighting for your life, one man against five or ten' says his *Book of Five Rings* – a 17th century manual for Samurai sword combat.[3]

Musashi's dictum is akin to the concentration needed for a prayer, or in making autosuggestions. As such, it is a principle that has greatly influenced the way

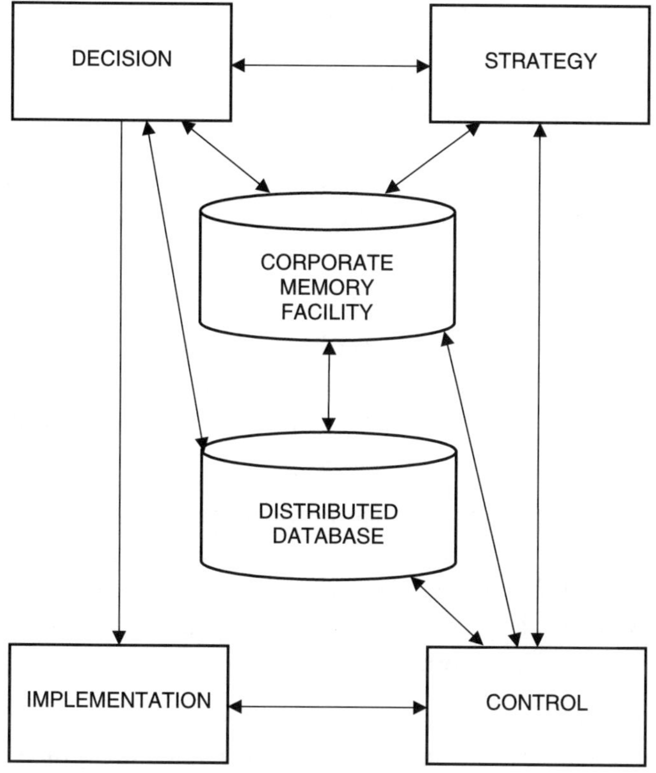

Figure 7.3 Organizational structure common to all industrial and financial organizations

human capital develops – from training for leadership to religious extremists. At the end of the day, the CEO (and in many cases the boss of the independent business unit) will be fighting with (if not against) five or ten business partners who may be corporate opponents at the same time.

Senior executives able to behave like a Japanese Samurai are not formed overnight. It takes years of experience, and plenty of troubleshooting to develop that type of knowledge and skill. Well-managed organizations recognize this. Hence the dictum that:

- If the best people are not entering at the bottom of the pyramid, then
- They will not find themselves at the top when needed.

What works against this principle is the fact that the interests of recruiters and students are not identical. Recruiters favour schools that provide a reliable stream of recruits. Students want schools where they get the most job offers.

Schools have their own criteria. When asked by what criteria he would like his school to be judged, Kim Clark, who was the Dean of Harvard Business School until the end of July 2005, said 'the achievement of its alumni'.[4] This is, however, a lagging indicator.

Miyamoto Musashi's approach is a leading indicator. It is also generic because it talks of a culture, not just of individual behaviour. But the individual behaviour is also very important. In modern business, to help in defining what a manager or professional has to do, we elaborate job descriptions for each position emphasizing:

- *Responsibilities*, which are longer lasting
- *Indicators* of performance which change more frequently, and
- *Objectives* set annually and reviewed at regular intervals against performance – or at least once at the year end.

Every year, in the mid-December executive board meeting, Brainard Fancher, the CEO of General Electric-Bull to whom I was consultant, started by presenting his EVPs with a copy of the annual objectives they had presented to him the year before. Each vice president had to explain how well he had met his self-established goals in front of every other EVP.

Then, the vice presidents of R&D, engineering, manufacturing, marketing, personnel, finance, information systems, handed to Fancher a draft of their objectives for next year. These were discussed in the executive board meeting to assure that they were within the strategic plan, and that they worked in synergy. When finalized:

- They became annual goals of the executive position, and
- Everybody knew that a year hence he or she had to explain in an open session what had been delivered as compared to the plan.

An example of what is involved in Responsibilities, Indicators, Objectives – this triple approach to job description – is provided in Table 7.2. As a matter of principle, job description elements must be very few, very clear, and very brief. Long descriptions don't help.

- They confuse the reader, and
- They provide too many loopholes for avoiding accountability.

Annual goals must be subject to open review and discussion. To make these efficiency reviews factual and documented we must establish quantifiable measures of performance. By contrast, qualifying criteria help in defining liaison lines to facilitate coordination. Lack of coordination always has a negative effect on deliverables.

Table 7.2 Job description of chief executive officer

Responsibility	Indicators	Objectives
1. Assure long-term survival of the enterprise	1.1 Establish strategy 1.2 Focus on market goals 1.3 Select strategic products 1.4 Assure low cost production	
2. Manage effectively corporate resources to increase profitability	2.1 Product innovation 2.2 Market development 2.3 Control of risk exposure 2.4 High return on investment	Annual goals (5 to 10)
3. Handle government and major client relations	3.1 Lobby government for industry support 3.2 Keep in close touch with authorities on tariffs 3.3 Handhold with the top 1% of clients 3.4 Participate in design reviews of client-specific projects	

In the 1960s IBM was the leading company in the computer business. It was also one of the best managed enterprises. One of its basic policies at the time was the annual review of deliverables of every executive position. This review was not done by just one person, the boss at the top of the hierarchy, but by two. This way there could be dissension, which helped in checking one-sided opinion.

At General Motors, Alfred Sloan had set a corporate-wide policy of *developing dissension*. In his book *My Years with General Motors*, Sloan recounts how, as chairman of the board of GM, he never accepted an important proposal without having dissension. This allowed:

- Critical discussion about the project's merits and demerits.
- It also permitted examination of details and hidden sides to issues that might escape a less critical review.

For his part Dr Robert McNamara, former president of Ford and of the World Bank, advises never to go ahead with a major project unless one has examined all the alternatives. 'In a multimillion dollar project you should never be satisfied with vanilla ice cream only. You should have many flavours,' has been McNamara's suggestion.

Fancher's, the Watsons', and McNamara's Western culture blends well with Musashi's Eastern personal development principle, and its impact on the individual. The underlying issues lie in the junction of organization and staffing, because:

- They rest on intellectual probing, and
- Bring decision-making back to its roots.

Management commitment and the drive for obtaining concrete results also characterizes the thesis of Karl Maria von Clausewitz. His view has been that strategy of warfare is predetermined by one's position and ability to exploit a foe's weakness. This concept has been carried over to the business world almost intact. Musashi's *A Book of Five Rings* does not really refute Clausewitz, even if it reflects an entirely different world-view.

In his work, Miyamoto Musashi associated with the individual certain mystical objectives as 'the way of strategy'. These amount to a craft of self-fulfilment to be mastered, just as 'the way of Buddha' might be pursued.

- The way Clausewitz categorizes the various types of strategy is peculiarly logical.
- By contrast, Musashi's techniques are inner-directed, speaking to the soul of an individual.

Clausewitz's theories focus on a general's ability to command an army. Most of Musashi's principles are addressed to the sword wielder in single combat. In both cases, the individual can and does make a difference. The challenge rests in passing on to the individual values and initiatives. A basic Musashi advice is not to become complacent from success in a protected environment. Therefore, he advises that 'If you learn "indoor techniques", you will think narrowly and forget the True Way. Thus you will have difficulty in actual encounters.' Indoor contests follow formal rules and rituals not observed outdoors where the true contests are happening.

5. Leadership talent, knowledge assets and performance evaluation

Qualifying and quantifying the leadership talent is the first step toward developing plans to bridge the gap that so often exists in corporate leadership. Both training and experience should be used to prepare qualified personnel, able to face the coming challenges, whether these are in:

- The market
- The product line

- The delivery process, or
- By the sum of them all, at general management level.

The debate on whether leaders are born or self-made by exploiting circumstances and opportunities as they present themselves, is as old as mankind. This is an ongoing argument which has not reached thus far any factual and documented conclusion, and it is doubtful if there will be one.

Most likely, both inborn qualities and the 'whiting' by long-term effects of the sum of experience – as the ancient Egyptian priests had it – play a role. Leadership talent is a very complex issue, involving many factors, with domain knowledge being one of them. This knowledge tells the leader when to move, and when it is better to stay put. Ancient wisdom can be a most helpful guide. Sun Tzu states in *The Art of War* (written 25 centuries ago): 'To fight and conquer in all your battles is not supreme excellence. Supreme excellence consists in breaking the enemy resistance without fighting.' This is not just a military principle; it is equally true of finance and industry.

Knowledge of the weak points and of the strong points – our own and those of our opponent(s) – is a principle valid both in business competition as in armed conflict. The same is true about the ability to set goals and develop strategic plans, as well as:

- The way to manoeuvre
- Tactics for special situations, and
- Dealing with different types of opposition.

Sun Tzu had this to say on how leaders decide when to fight and when not: 'The commander stands for the virtues of wisdom, sincerity, benevolence, courage, and strictness.'[5] Also, by his powers of decision, and his knowledge of the value of time. Rushing into a situation is a prescription for disaster. Sometimes, power of decision:

- Is more than a demonstration of leadership talent
- It is a proxy of leadership qualities and power at large.

Knowledge is power of a different kind. It is not the exercise of force to oblige a certain action by someone else. It is not hitting people over the head. Rather, it is a tandem trial of organizational relationships where individuals guide other individuals in practical and proper terms.

The ability to call any number of knowledgeable people and say, 'I have a problem. Can you help me in such and such a way?' is a demonstration of power, says

Moira Johnson. Power at large has prerogative, but also preconditions. If someone cannot stand the pain, he or she should not be in management. 'If you cannot stand the heat, get out of the kitchen,' Harry Truman used to say. Management is a case about power, its use, abuse, and eventually legal action.

In her book *Takeover* Johnson recounts an interesting legal example. A court had said that a corporate board had the right to assume extraordinary powers, seizing them from the shareholders without approval. 'That decision was just wrong,' Irving Shapiro believed, 'and I predict that time will show the decision was in error.' Shapiro added that 'The court never explained what the source of that power could be.'[6]

The CEO exercises power when he asks his immediate assistants: 'What are the strong and weak functional areas in our firm?' or, 'Are all managers training their replacements?' or, 'How does value added per employee compare with the competition figures?' Power is embedded in management control of individual productivity, as well as in implementing the principle of personal accountability.

This exercise of power, however, can either be done by brute force, the effect of which is often ephemeral, or through using superior knowledge and information in evaluating conditions. The latter helps in developing the company's culture, and involves:

- Ideas
- Experiences
- Statistics, and
- Analytical processes.

A knowledgeable staff is an asset, because knowledge is used by people to design, manufacture, sell, install, and support products and services; it is also used to torture information in the database so that it reveals its secrets. Knowledge assets are intangible by excellence. They cannot be found in:

- Physical inventories
- Real estate
- Bank balances, or
- Straight accounting ledgers.

But they do exist in the minds of the company's people, derived from their background and experience, as well as the information they accumulated over the years. Knowledge assets are precious because a service economy requires cerebral skills rather than manual skills. Examples of knowledge-based business are R&D, consultancy, finance, marketing, journalism, and teaching.

Knowledge is an investment. The more precious knowledge assets become, the greater is the attention companies have to pay not only to hiring knowledge workers, but also to their productivity. This is a challenging task because improving the knowledge base requires significant changes in organizational structure and in society as a whole. It also calls for cultural after-effects:

- Softening resistance to an acceptance of new ideas and new procedures
- Redefining the role of knowledge workers and their compensation
- Creating a policy of multiple careers in a lifetime to broaden personal opportunities
- Establishing firm criteria that make it possible not only to strengthen responsibility but also to assure personal accountability

As Peter F. Drucker aptly remarks: 'A business that does not show a profit at least equal to its cost of capital, is socially irresponsible. Power must always be balanced by responsibility. Without responsibility, power degenerates into non-performance.' With this, the productivity of knowledge becomes dismal.

No two knowledge workers are productive in the same way; and knowledge productivity varies tremendously from firm to firm, as Table 7.3 demonstrates. Based on 1988 statistics, published by *Business Week*, this table shows that down to the bottom line of profits per employee, the productivity ratio of professional workers ranges from 1 to 6.6.

Since management is a knowledge business, this reference to the need of judging the productivity of knowledge workers is valid in terms of strategic evaluation of top executives performance. At GE, Jack Welsh held annual 'Session C' meetings

Table 7.3 Earnings per employee among investment banks

Banks	1987 pretax profits ($ millions)	Profits per employee ($ thousands)
Morgan Stanley	364	56.0
Salomon Brothers	225	37.5
First Boston	120	22.0
Merrill Lynch	391	9.0
Paine Webber	110	8.5

Source: Based on statistics published in Business Week.

during which he personally evaluated the performance of GE's top several hundred managers. These top level evaluation meetings included general managers of major business units, as well as senior engineering, manufacturing, sales and marketing executives. The performance evaluation goal has been to extend GE's boundaries by analysing careers and deliverables; linking bonuses to new ideas, customer satisfaction, sales growth; priming cost-cutting and efficiency; and spending billions to fund 'imagination breakthrough' projects that extend the company's business horizon.

6. Greed and glory in high paycheques: case study from NYSE

While the quality of staff must be steadily and significantly improved, its number should be reduced for the same amount of work by increasing individual productivity. On their own, however, numbers don't tell the whole story. Intangibles count for a great deal, and the same is true of the staff's drive and synergy.

Reductions in staff and change of roles, as well as properly studied reward systems, based on bonuses dependent on performance rather than on years of service, act as catalysts to greater returns. A similar statement is valid regarding a policy of no employment security. In a free economy, the company may dismiss anybody, any time, regardless of length of service – while employees who found better jobs in other companies are free to leave without being considered disloyal. Contrary to what its critics say:

- Hire and fire creates employment, because companies are more at ease in hiring new employees.
- If it were not so, the unemployment figures would not have been 4.5% in the UK and 5.0% in the United States while they are 9.0% in France and 11% in Germany.

Improving one's employment opportunities and bettering one's career requires ability and brain power, but also steady training as well as adaptation and flexibility in fulfilling job requirements. Ideally, companies look for people able to fill vacant jobs at a moment's notice. Keeping pace with job requirements has its own prerequisites. J.P. Morgan was proud of the fact that he could sit at the desk of any of his employees and finish the work the other person was doing.

In modern business, internal, intensive training programmes (see section 7) are a much better staffing strategy than buying wholesale skill from the outside. On the one hand, intensive internal training permits a more efficient, streamlined organization that reduces bureaucracy and motivates employees to achieve improved results. On the other hand, it costs less than buying knowledge workers working for competitors. Facts document this statement:

1. In 2000, CSFB earned $358 million for underwriting $5.4 billion of technology initial public offers (IPOs).
2. Staffers in the CSFB technology group kept about 50% of net fees they generated as their tangible incentives.
3. But at the same time, Crédit Suisse First Boston is believed to have spent $300 million, or 60% of the profits left to the firm from these IPOs, to lure back a team of 40 bond dealers headed to Barclays.

The amount of money Wall Street and City of London investment banks pay to pirate each other's key personnel is a story of greed and glory. In many cases, top management is doing just the same for self-gratification. Indeed, outrageous pay, exceptional bonuses for average work, and other sorts of self-gratification have added their lot to the string of scandals that hit business and industry in recent years – from Enron, to Global Crossing, Adelphia Communications, Tyco, and WorldCom.

As *The Economist* aptly noted in an article, outrageous paycheques 'have revealed senior executives apparently plundering their companies with little regard to the interest of shareholders or other employees'. In *The Economist*'s words, 'not only does it seem that bosses are being fed bigger carrots, but also if the stick is finally applied to their backside they walk away with yet another sack full of carrots to cushion the blow.'[7]

Lavish options the CEO and his or her immediate assistants shower upon themselves, with the approval of a rubber-stamp board, have become the shame of the free enterprise system.[8] Sometimes, however, the wheels of justice start turning to right the balance. In *The Economist*'s feature article (referred to in the preceding paragraph) the former boss of the New York Stock Exchange, Richard Grasso, is taken as an example of a CEO who went:

- From a sort of folk hero
- To a symbol of excess almost overnight, when it was revealed that he was due to receive $188 million in 'accumulative benefits'.

On 24 May 2004, Eliot Spitzer, New York State's Attorney-General, filed civil charges against Grasso, demanding the return of at least $100 million, about half of what he seems to have received in his final years at the top of the NYSE.

Grasso said he deserved every penny, demanded an apology, and made vague threats of a counter-suit.

Joining Grasso as a defendant has been Ken Langone, former chairman of the NYSE's compensation committee. The Attorney-General's office reached settlements with Frank Ashen, former head of the NYSE's human resources and a firm, Mercer Human Resource Consulting, which had analysed Grasso's pay for the board. Both have admitted providing inaccurate information.

Spared from being the direct target of litigation were the members of the NYSE's board, other than Langone, which includes many of Wall Street's top brass. But though other board members were not called to the defendant's table, their actions were likely to be closely scrutinized in the trial.

Grasso's compensation reflected a 'paradigm for misbehavior' by a board, and a 'fundamental breakdown of corporate governance', said Eliot Spitzer.[9] The case against Grasso rested largely on allegations that his pay package violated New York's Not-for-Profit Corporation Law, which governs NYSE.

- The law states that executives pay should be 'reasonable' and 'commensurate with services provided'.
- Grasso's salary and bonus for the four years from 1995 were $17.8 million; but in the following four years they were $80.7 million – an unwarranted 453% increase.

One of the most damaging allegations, which applies to many CEOs, concerned how Grasso ran the exchange. According to the filed complaint, not only did he have the authority on the Compensation Committee but he also regulated most of the other committees of NYSE. This amounted to conflict of interest allowing NYSE's CEO to:

- Influence directors who might have wanted to pay him less, and
- Reward directors who would pay him more.

Looking a little further, the prosecution's argument has also alleged that bankers on the committee appointed by Grasso paid him large sums in return for which he helped smooth regulatory problems. Conflict of interest is one of the not so transparent major pitfalls in staffing.

Increasing liberalization of global markets and the arrival of competitors hungry for first-class staff has an inevitable effect on human resources policies, pay, premiums, and their misuse for glory and for greed. Knowledge productivity is a 'must', but what companies get in terms of knowledge workers is not always commensurate with what they seek.

In this respect, pedigree is not a guarantee of suitability. Here is an extract from a letter to *The Economist* published on 11 November 1995: '[Our] company enlisted the guys from Harvard – management consultants with brains but no scar tissue. "One-piece kids in three-piece suits", someone called them. They were sincere, and what they knew they knew well. They had the support of top management. But they were over-challenged by the job at hand.'

This letter continued with other references not pertinent to this discussion, but the last one is a jewel. 'One late night, our day having been extended by the necessity of attending yet another management seminar, somebody remarked on a newspaper article which claimed that the cost of maintaining a convict in the California prison system was equal to that of putting a kid through Harvard Business School. Whereupon someone else said that the world would be a lot better off if we took all the kids out of Harvard and put them in prison.' It would have been a solution of practically equal cost.

7. Establishing a rigorous training programme

A rigorous programme designed to steadily upgrade human resources must be established by the CEO and the board. One that finds its origin further down the line is not going to succeed. Such a programme starts with selection of personnel intake. Pier Abetti points out that at GE Jack Welsh's criteria for selecting future leaders were very similar to those for selecting elite members of the German general staff. Clausewitz classified all potential candidates as smart, stupid, eager, or lazy. This leads to different combinations.

- The smart and eager may be the best choice, but there are not enough of them.
- Therefore, many companies are populated by 'smart and lazy', and the challenge is how to get them on the move.

The best approach is to motivate them to get going. If they do not respond, they will fall into the lowest 10% of Welsh's classification (see section 3). A challenge for organizations is what to do with the stupid and eager. They are the worst combination because they cause all kinds of trouble with their zeal, which is empty of appropriate skills and background. What you get is bureaucrats.

It is not easy to manage the human inventory in an effective way. Assuming an organization can attract and retain the right employees, management should ensure that they always keep up their skills. Yet, although millions of dollars are spent on training, in a great number of cases it is questionable how effective this training really is.

- Organizations are quite poor at measuring the return of different types of training, and
- They do even worse when they try to establish its impact on the workplace.

Of course, it is easier to measure training effectiveness in manual jobs than in mental ones. But there is a learning curve whose general trend line is shown in Figure 7.4. The abscissa is time under training and work practice. The ordinate can be time to execute a job, or number of errors being made. Statistical quality control charts provide good metrics at the workplace, including office chores.[10]

An example helps in appreciating the effect of schooling. From the collapse of the Roman Empire until about the 14th century, the centres of culture were monasteries. But in 1455 Johannes Gutenberg's invention of printing changed all that. It made feasible wider dissemination of information, particularly in those

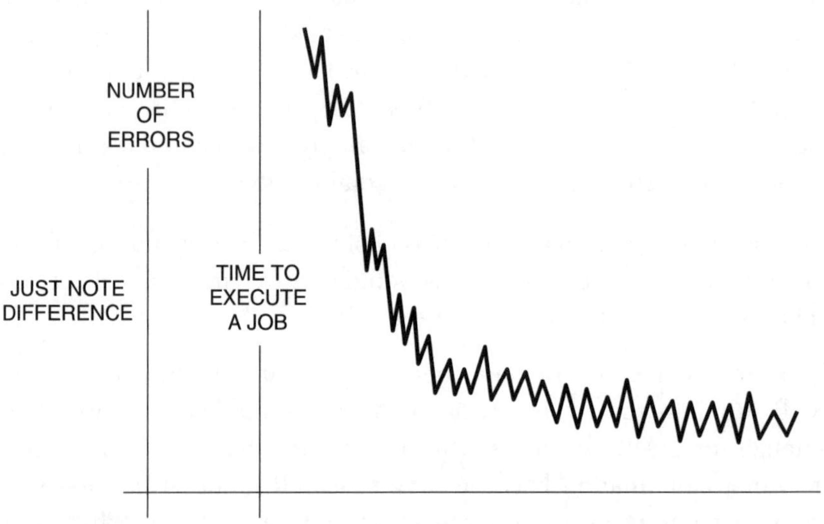

Figure 7.4 The learning effect must be weeded out as fast as possible to reach cruising speed and performance

countries, religions, and cultures that did not resist the printed word, as for instance has been the case in Islam.

Since antiquity, books have been not only the depositories but also the pivotal points of knowledge. Hence, their spread increased its diffusion. Formal schooling started as primary, then secondary education. Universities were attended by the intellectual elite. Company training was unknown at the time of the industrial revolution, and even management conferences had no appeal. The first management conference was organized in 1882 by the German Post Office; but according to the records nobody turned up.

- The art of management was not part of the 19th century culture, and
- Learning beyond one's relatively narrow realm was considered unnecessary, a loss of time.

All this changed in the 20th century's interwar years, and even more so after World War II. Under Thomas Watson, Sr, training became IBM's secret weapon for decades, while the majority of companies, both in the United States and in Europe, had nothing similar to show as a training track record. By the 1960s, however, many chief executives realized that they must invest in human capital just like they invest in plant and equipment. The need to train every manager, every professional, and every other employee in the firm manifested itself along with evidence that a significant part of training effort should be driven by future:

- Strategic goals, and
- Business perspectives.

Sales training is an example of these two bullets. Two research projects I did world-wide in the mid-1960s for the American Management Association documented that as knowledge started to be considered as the capital of a developed economy, knowledge workers became a pivotal group in setting the society's standards and norms.

For more or less the past 40 years, training has propelled the transformation of Western economies, allowing companies and countries to do something that traditional economic theory said could not be done: that is, to become efficient at short notice.

A great deal of what has been accomplished over the decades in scientific breakthroughs and managerial innovations represented the application of knowledge to work. Training, particularly lifelong training, promoted innovation. It also filled the gap between development and implementation.

- Accelerating the application of new discoveries and engineering designs.
- But also penalizing people and companies who do not innovate – the former their skills, the latter their products and processes.

Because training of human resources is strategic, among other goals it pursues it must focus on performance. The sense of deliverables and need for them has to be built into knowledge work done in the enterprise. Performance must also be built into products, markets, and their management. It also has to be continuously improved as well as:

- Measured, and
- Judged in pragmatic terms.

Some professional associations have seen the strength of such a policy, and took good notice. Since the late 1980s, for example, the American Federation of Teachers has demanded that teachers be held accountable for the learning performance of pupils, and be paid accordingly. Also, that non-performing teachers be dismissed rather than protected by tenure.

This is an eyes-open strategy on teaching and learning that should be widely generalized, the more so as the very nature of knowledge changes fast. Daily practice in doing something new or different is also very important. Arthur Rubinstein, the pianist, was once asked why he practised every day and he answered: 'If I don't practise for a month, the public will notice it. If I don't practise for a week, my friends will notice it. If I don't practise for a day, I will notice it.'

In a similar manner, from the CEO all the way down the organization, training and practice is one of the keys to success. To enforce the Six Sigma culture[11] at GE, Jack Welsh made clear that nobody would be promoted unless he or she was a trained and certified 'black-belt' team leader. He then started a similar campaign for digitization, e-commerce, and other major projects.

In lifelong training programmes everyone should have the opportunity to act both as a trainer in one area and as student in all others. Delivering higher levels of literacy is based on the ability to keep on learning and the desire to do so. In the knowledge society there is no such thing as a completed education. Professional survival requires that even people with advanced degrees come back to school to learn more and more.

This is a basic principle in staffing, and it is the cornerstone in avoiding people's obsolescence. Automation or no automation, the bottom line is that the difference is made by people. An example from military experience helps in dramatizing this point. Right after the Korean War, two US Airforce colonels, John Boyd and Chuck Yaeger,[12] demonstrated on the basis of combat-skill results in Korea, that:

- What a fighter airplane could do – climb, roll, dive – was less important in combat.
- More important was how quickly it could change from doing one thing to doing something else.

A slower and theoretically less capable plane could often beat a 'better designed' plane, *if* the pilot's skill, and the plane's original specs, permitted it to switch quickly from one manoeuvre to another. This was instrumental in taking its enemy by surprise.

Yaeger and Boyd provided convincing in-flight evidence that a similar principle applied to combat on the larger scale. It did not really matter whether an army attacked by land, by sea, on the flanks, or from the air. What mattered was whether it could change its behaviour more quickly than its adversary. Similar arguments can be made on the implementation of technology. Whether in the military, in manufacturing, merchandising, or finance,

- Success is never assured in competition
- It can be gained through hard effort, and
- The advantage lies with the side that proves to be more adaptable.

If the managers and the professionals are unwieldy and unrealistic in defining the nature of problems involving complex activities with numerous moves, and if they are hard to work with, the whole organization becomes inflexible and stagnant in its deliverables. Even the decision processes fail to give much insight into how the conclusions are related to the assumptions being made. When this happens the company gets into a tailspin.

Notes

1 D.N. Chorafas and Heinrich Steinmann, *Expert Systems in Banking*. Macmillan, London, 1991.

2 C. Handy, *The Age of Unreason*. Arrow Books, London, 1980.

3 Miyamoto Musashi, *A Book of Five Rings*. The Overlook Press, New York, 1982.

4 *The Economist*, 24 September 2005.

5 Sun Tzu, *L'Art de la Guerre*. Flammarion, Paris, 1972.

6 Moira Johnson, *Takeover*. Bantam Books, New York, 1987.

7 *The Economist*, 11 October 2003.
8 D.N. Chorafas, *Management Risk: The Bottleneck is at the Top of the Bottle*. Macmillan/Palgrave, London, 2004.
9 *The Economist*, 29 May 2004.
10 D.N. Chorafas, *Reliable Financial Reporting and Internal Control: A Global Implementation Guide*. John Wiley, New York, 2000.
11 D.N. Chorafas, *Integrating ERP, CRM, Supply Chain Management and Smart Materials*. Auerbach, New York, 2001.
12 The American pilot who broke the sound barrier.

Directing and Controlling

1. Introduction

Directing means much more than simply administrative-type duties. It includes delegating, motivating, stimulating creativity, watching for improvements in productivity, coordinating, and managing change. Still, to a significant extent directing is a day-to-day activity that has a great deal to do with overcoming obstacles and differences, as well as pulling efforts together into winning combinations.

As section 2 explains, directing involves leadership (discussed in Chapter 7), particularly in the sense of inspiring the subordinates and, at the same time, assigning authority commensurate with responsibility and demanding accountability from everybody. Both delegation and accountability (for delegated authority) are crucial elements in assuring attainment of company goals.

While the exercise of leadership has always been a basic component of directing, the management of change is a new one. Every good thing stands moment by moment on the razor's edge of change, says H. Ross Perot, of EDS and GM fame, when explaining his principles of management. Therefore, every good thing and every goal must be fought for. Perot is a proponent of entrepreneurship, not of bureaucratic-type directing. The way he puts it:

- The entrepreneur is an irritant to the bureaucracy, because he stirs things up.
- The doer's nature is to be a proponent of push, push, push – and harder, harder, harder.

Individuals responsible for directing an enterprise, a project, or any other activity must be doers. The business of doers is not that of providing a 'social service' for those who don't care to move. Harold Geneen, of ITT fame, was an excellent example of a doer. Having the company run his way was to him something essential. According to Robert Schoenberg, his biographer, it was the validation of his life's work. Nobody could run Geneen's company in Geneen's way. But after his retirement, the board told new ITT CEO Lyman Hamilton he should run the company as he saw fit. 'We'll handle the Geneen matter,' they said. Hamilton thought they meant it and would stick to it, and on this assumption set about changing the canon on which Geneen had built ITT.[1]

The Geneen-to-Hamilton changeover is a good case study because the most profound change was in corporate direction. Geneen's dedication had always been to growth. Hamilton stressed profitability and return on equity (ROE). It was not all or nothing on either side. It was an issue of emphasis and on priorities, and for this reason it constitutes a great paradigm on directing.

For instance, after he took over as CEO, Hamilton tented to discard the less promising IT subsidiaries collected by Geneen. Of the 250-odd businesses in the company, about 50 were judged inadequate performers. But many of these, Schoenberg says, were Geneen's pets.

- He had acquired them and he judged them still valuable.
- He would keep them in the stable no matter how they looked to less practised eyes.

This was in step with the business principles of the old CEO. 'We don't sell our mistakes at ITT,' Geneen had often said. 'We fix them.' With his successor, however, selling was the policy, and it made Geneen boil. Formally speaking, the new CEO was right in taking his own counsel. What to keep and run and what to sell is one of the chief executive's prerogatives – part of what is meant by directing.

As contrasted to directing, *controlling* is the process through which management assures itself, as far as is feasible, that what the company does conforms to plans and policies. Controlling involves feedback, through *internal control* as well as informal channels, plan versus actual, analysis and other means for judging:

- Compliance, and
- Performance.

It takes guts to implement rigorous control. Accounting information, particularly cost accounting, is most useful to management in evaluating whether the company is a lean enterprise, and also the efficiency of employees in doing their jobs (more on this in Part 3). *Merits* assigned in the aftermath of appraisal of performance may result in salary increase and/or promotion. *Demerits* may lead to reassignment, corrective action of various kinds, or even dismissal. Crucial questions are:

- How much was accomplished?
- How good was quality compared to specifications?
- How well were timetables observed?
- How much did it cost? Was it within budget? Within cost standards?

The answers to be provided to these questions have *qualitative* and *quantitative* components. On the quantitative side, accounting information assists in the appraisal process, even if an adequate basis for judging individual performance cannot be obtained from accounting records alone. Organizational activities also require reliable personal evaluation and control action. Several aspects of management control can be done only by being on the spot.

2. Professionals, experts, managers, and executives

Professionals are office workers directly responsible for creating or handling knowledge and information while carrying out the functions they have been assigned in an organization. Alternatively, professionals may be freelancers. Engineers, attorneys, writers, planners, accountants, foreign exchange dealers, other traders, marketing experts, are professionals.

Experts in any walk of life, or profession, are persons who know not only the subject on which they work but also how to research on other subjects, and how to recognize their mistakes early enough. Additionally, real experts have the vision and courage to take immediate corrective action. Experts may be generalists or specialists. The way a joke has it:

- A specialist knows more and more about less and less, till he or she knows everything about nothing.
- By contrast, a generalist is one who knows less and less about more and more, till he knows nothing about everything.

True experts are generalists with broader vision, and specialists with deeper knowledge, at the same time. Though an expert may be specializing in a given field, he is always on the alert for understanding and working on interdisciplinary subjects, and ready to not only keep up and upgrade but also to expand the horizon of his or her know-how.

Professionals who have learned how to sharpen their expertise, perform analytical and other creative functions, resulting in a tangible product. This product may be a design, or an opinion. It may also be documentation contained in a report, other manuscript, or a specific proposal they have been asked to provide.

By contrast, a *manager* handles people and information for the purpose of planning, organizing, directing, monitoring, or controlling the business functions under his or her authority. Theoretically, the job a manager performs is closely related to direction. This is, however, a misconception, because a manager's basic functions are not one but six – as defined in Chapter 5.

Another confusion existing both in literature and in organizations is in the sense of the words *manager* and *executive*. A very simple way to distinguish them is that managers use information to take action whereas executives use information to make policy decisions. The concept of policy has been introduced in Chapter 6 as a guide for thinking and acting; a mental framework on which the planning process will be built.

The jobs of both managers and executives are, so to speak, perpetual – at least as long as they hold their assignments. Opportunities for action, and for control of actions, present themselves many times per day. Like strategies, policies are not to be set once and then put in a time capsule. As:

- Formal statements expressing a relationship between information and decision patterns, and
- Means for highlighting certain issues vital to the enterprise, policies are in need of steady and timely evaluations.

At the same time, by being general statements, policies are never too specific. To channel their decisions and actions in accordance with corporate policies, subordinates must *interpret policies*. This interpretation is, most often, done by the managers.

While executives are policy-makers, they are not necessarily managers in that form. They may be, for example, outside board members. By contrast, managers are an organizational element internal to the firm. And they are not necessarily executives. The CEO is both a manager and an executive; but the CEO's immediate assistants are not necessarily executives.

Managers interpret and implement policies elaborated by the board of directors. But to perform their work, they establish *systems* and *procedures* that should not be confused either with policies or with plans. Procedures are means of action, more detailed in their making than policies and, also, better controllable. Systems are aggregates of components united by some form of regulated interaction:

- To form an organized whole, and
- Work in synergy in order to reach an objective.

An assembly of operations, procedures, men, machines, and other components by which a specific task is accomplished, forms a system. A system may also be a group of equipment which is integrated to perform a certain function. A fire-control system includes the tracking (sensor means), monitoring computer, and missile (or gun) batteries.

To keep the enterprise competitive and ahead of the curve, a major function confronting executives and managers is that of organizing for knowledge management. In the post-World War II years businesses deal more and more with information and know-how, and this has created a new challenge in a managerial sense expressed by the dichotomy between:

- Power based on position, and
- Power based on knowledge.

If the organization sticks to old-fashioned position power to make all of its decisions, *then* chances are decisions would be made by people unfamiliar with the skills, products, processes, and technology of the day. In general, the faster the change in know-how on which the business depends, the greater the dichotomy between knowledge power and position power.

Executives, managers, and professionals contribute to organizational life either individually or through committees. In larger companies, for example, the board may feature several committees: Finance, Audit, Compensation, Governance, Compliance being examples. Other committees exist at several levels of the organization – their presence reflecting the system of governance practices prevailing in the firm.

- Board committees concern themselves with longer-range plans (see Chapter 6).
- Management committees are typically shorter-range oriented in their views and in their decisions.

The type of decisions taken by committees varies with the committee's goal, but usually they concern budgets, service objectives, priorities, and coordination of interdepartmental activities. Some committees are consultative. Others are given the mission to steer a particular effort like information systems support, and ensure effective coordination – including communications and resource utilization.

Committees may also be set up to control costs or streamline operations. Alternatively, their objective may be to create a higher level management group which involves users of a service like computers and communications, set direction, or review systems projects aiming at overall corporate integration. This will be the goal of a steering committee.

At middle-management level, for example, a committee may be set up to elaborate a plan for procedural realignments, improve interdisciplinary flow of information, or create a level ground where functional business viewpoints can be properly weighed. These are among the goals of directing day-to-day activities but, as the reader is already aware, management by committee has severe limitations.

3. Day-to-day tactical decisions

As it has been explained since Chapter 1, management decisions may be strategic or tactical. Both are made in the face of uncertainty, with more or less insufficient information; and both must meet relatively tight deadlines. Tactical decisions typically:

- Deal with allocation of finite resources.
- Aim to preserve resources or increase them in execution of daily duties, and
- Target specific shorter-term deliverables within the environment defined by strategic decisions.

Tactical decisions are inseparable from directing activities. Usually, strategic decisions are preceded by deliberation, calculation, and thought. Managers making tactical decisions don't have that leisure. Most often they must respond on the spot. This type of decision is an integral part of the managerial function; probably it is the most difficult and challenging part.

Often, though not always, the need for decisions originates from communications received from higher authority in the organization; cases referred to by subordinates; problems arising with business partners; competitors actions that require commensurate response; or initiatives of the manager involved in that decision. In all cases, decisions must be:

- Pertinent to the subject at hand
- Clear, so that subordinates can understand them
- Made in a timely manner
- Executable, which means realistic, and
- Within the authority of the person making the decision.

Management decisions may concern themselves with solving a given problem, implementing planning premises, providing support in a certain domain under responsibility of the manager making the decision, or have other objectives. No matter which may be their origin, decisions being made risk not being executed down the line. One of President Truman's biographers stated that one of the US chief executive's main frustrations was to give an order, wait for results, and see that nothing happens.

Managers, therefore, must always be on the watch that their decisions are followed by actions. It is advantageous if an *action list* is associated to a management decision, with the aim of identifying the work to be done and the person responsible for *deliverables*. Also, when specific results are due. Leadership is a basic ingredient both in making decisions and in seeing that they are executed. Within the realm of directing:

- The best decisions are a matter of concentration and focus.

The way to bet is that sound decisions will promote the elements of strength. A person, an organization, a whole society gets rewards only for strengths – not for weaknesses. Performance today is largely the result of the capabilities, or lack of them, management has demonstrated in years past and of the decisions it made. Decisions have a forward-looking character. Even in terms of day-to-day activities:

- The future is determined by the goals we establish for *tomorrow*, not by those for yesterday.

Decisions also have a significant human component because things are done through people. More precisely, decisions and their execution have to do with the attitudes of people. People and organizations who were 'yesterday' successful, tend to be defensive. They try to keep yesterday alive, thereby missing tomorrow. This brings into perspective the need for management appraisal in decision-making:

- Is the director of an activity able to hold on to the reins in times of rapid change? Of turbulence?
- Is he or she able to prognosticate coming trouble? To face tomorrow's challenges?
- Can incumbent management lead the way in intellectual effort and in focus, required for increasingly more complex decisions?

Behind all three of these bullets lies the fact that today more intellectual effort must be organized around the problem to be solved, rather than around traditional functions such as production or marketing. Sections 4 and 5 provide the reader with case studies from the US automotive industry, where:

- Drifting in management decisions, and
- Failure to evaluate ahead of time the aftermath of commitments, leads the firm to its downfall.

Persons responsible for directing business activities must appreciate that, like resistance to change, failure to look ahead makes adaptation to the business environment much more expensive. As a result the company will suffer because planning failures would lead to rush decisions; while resistance to change will not slow down the process of change itself.

Moreover, to face the challenge of tomorrow in an able manner, the act of directing should always be ready to feed on business opportunities. Even tactical adaptation calls for a steady process of evaluation and modernization of products, plants, sales offices, and human resources at large. Every concept, every product, every factory ages – and eventually becomes obsolete. The same is valid of management practices.

Sometimes, managers' decision-making ability gets confused because of rapid business growth. Growth is an inverse pyramid structure: when management solves one problem, it gets two. Another test of a manager's ability in directing operations is whether or not he or she can thrive with ambiguity, or is unsettled by its existence. As the preceding chapters emphasized, the dawn of modern science, signified the arrival on the scene of the:

- Possible
- Probable, and
- Relative.

Because the act of directing finds itself in an environment characterized by tonalities of grey rather than by black *or* white colours, modern management requires more thinking and concentration than ever before. Particularly, analytical thinking. It also calls for faster reactions and, to achieve them, decision aids become a 'must'.

Last but not least, day-to-day directing makes it mandatory to keep cool under fire. Today's managers are much more often under fire than their predecessors were. But even so, they must be thinking ahead, examining alternatives and options in detail prior to making a decision. This is the case even if many decisions must be taken in an increasingly shortened space of time.

4. Unmanageable legacy costs: case study with Delphi and General Motors

Most decisions constitute irreversible commitments for the firm. The curse of decisions made 'this day' for directing purposes can cast a long shadow into the company's future. Tactical decisions taken without the proverbial long hard look Chapter 5 defined as forecasting, become *legacy commitments* the company has to live with. And they may make impossible new, more rational strategic initiatives.

In October 2005, the bankruptcy of Delphi, the largest automotive components company in the world, drew attention to the plight of its former parent, General Motors. GM had guaranteed some of Delphi's pledges to retirees when, in 1999, its former subsidiary was spun off. This was the wrong decision, which became a legacy cost, and it was preceded by other similarly wrong decisions.

- In 1955, at the time of its glory, GM had 650 000 workers, the large majority of them in the United States.
- Half a century down the line, GM has fewer than 200 000 American workers, but nearly 1 million retirees and dependants.

Very bad management decisions in directing the formerly proud company, which span over five decades, saw to it that General Motors' $15 billion stock market value has become only half the size of its unfunded pension liabilities. And even this huge legacy commitment is dwarfed by an estimated $70 billion of unfunded health care liabilities. ('Unfunded' means the firm has failed to put aside enough money to meet such obligations.)

What has become known as *legacy costs* is a crippling burden for old industrial companies, as they struggle to compete with much more efficient and relatively unburdened rivals. GM has tried to redimension itself by laying off workers and shutting down factories. But the United Auto Workers (UAW), and other trade unions, have been so obstructive to the effort of (belatedly) finding a solution that workers are often expensively idled rather than let go.

At the same time, GM management's care for the so-called 'shareholder value' also made its contribution to bad tactical decisions. Under stock market pressure GM paid out billions in dividends and share buybacks. This has been money it definitely needed for investments and factory renewal.

Delphi's bankruptcy is a good case study on what can happen to other mismanaged companies. In the 1970s and 1980s when fast-growing health care costs and lavish retirement benefits were not written in the balance sheet, the top brass of GM, and of its subsidiaries, found a fast and dirty way out of threatened strikes:

- Wrong-way decisions bought labour peace by mortgaging the company's future
- But when the US GAAP accounting rules changed, in one year GM lost nearly $25 billion, of which $24 billion was the write-offs because of commitments in pensions and health care.

Worse yet, GM management learned no lesson from its gigantic failure and the wrong-way decisions, and policies on which they were based continued. Proof is that in 2004, despite Delphi's annual revenues of $28 billion, losses mounted because the market was increasingly being served by low-cost workers in Asia, while raw-material costs continued to rise.

It does not take a genius to understand that, under these conditions, past lavish worker and management benefits are no longer affordable. When in October 2005 Delphi went bankrupt, its future pension obligations, alone, were valued at $8.5 billion with some $4.3 billion of that unfunded.

The United Auto Workers attitude is just as incompetent as that of GM's and Delphi's top management. UAW has for many years been inflexible and stubborn.

This attitude is self-destructive, because it ends by the company, and its future, being held hostage by the labour union – a state of affairs that damages everybody's interests – including the workers.

Even a blind man can see that Delphi's and eventually GM's bankruptcy has most painful consequences for its workers, and even more so for its retirees. Under Chapter 11, the US bankruptcy code:

- Both would see their benefits most severely slashed, and
- The company would restructure liabilities hoping to become profitable again by significantly shrinking legacy costs.

As proof of the absurdity of the current situation, at GM legacy costs add up to some $1500 for each car being made. This is about 3% of the firm's revenues. Health insurance and retirement cost for over 1 million former personnel are the largest item in a car's production budget – larger than steel.

Neither is GM alone in this plight into which it led itself. Ford and Chrysler also face massive financial problems from legacy costs. The same is true of four of America's leading airlines, which are now flying whilst bankrupt. America's steel industry also went through a similar process of financial restructuring a few years ago, by getting rid of commitments by means of bankruptcy.

As plenty of examples from car manufacturers, steel, airlines, and other companies document, the sense of accountability in directing an entity's future has seemingly been abandoned, and all stakeholders have contributed. Also everybody will be burned, as companies become noncompetitive in a globalized economy because of the synergy between legacy costs and third-class management:

- Shareholders fear the aftermath of bankruptcies on their equity investments.
- Workers are nervous as they lose benefits that they have been counting on in old age.
- The government is uneasy of having to fund retirements, albeit greatly scaled down.

Some experts think that supporting retirees in the aftermath of a rash of bankruptcies could become the next Savings & Loan crisis, which in the late 1980s ended in a $800 billion black hole and $200 billion bail-out by taxpayers. The US government and the firm's own stakeholders are afraid that GM could become the world's biggest bankruptcy. And America's second largest car manufacturer, Ford, could follow suit.

In the past, the US government-backed insurer of company pension plans, the Pension Benefit Guaranty Corporation (PBGC), agreed to take on an unprecedented $6.6 billion in unfunded pension liabilities from bankrupt United Airlines, prompting allegations that companies dump pensions schemes on taxpayers. In the aftermath of this and similar safety net actions:

- PBGC's liabilities exceed its assets
- This makes PBGC technically insolvent, though nobody doubts the government will come to the rescue.

The message the reader should take from this case study is that decisions made in connection with day-to-day directing of company activities may have far-reaching after-effects. Unbearable legacy commitments are not a worst-case scenario. They have become daily business, and while their weight on the company's future is negative, their size and frequency can send the whole economy into a tailspin.

5. Death by red ink: the abyss of bad management

The bankruptcy of big companies, and even worse of whole industries, because of persistently poor management decisions, is the negation of everything that has been written so far about strategic business planning. It also has high-stake consequences in the physical economy, and it could tear apart the financial system.

Delphi buys $14 billion worth of goods annually from 3800 nationwide suppliers in the United States. When the company's CEO announces, as in the 11 October 2005 issue of *Business Week*, that Delphi has delayed payment to suppliers as part of bankruptcy, this means that thousands of suppliers are under stress. Such financial stress can snowball.

- Many of these suppliers are small, family-run machine-tooling shops of 20 workers or less.
- For some of them the bankruptcy of a big client can be the tipping point.

To appreciate the impact the bankruptcy of the US automotive industry may have on corporate America, and on the world economy, it is appropriate to recall that traditional US automotive manufacturing reached its peak in profitability in the 1955 to 1963 timeframe. In 1963, the combined industrial operating margin of GM, Ford, and Chrysler hit a remarkable 16.9%.

- This impressive prosperity was the result of massive consolidation, led by GM.

- A good deal of such consolidation began in the Great Depression, resumed in the post-World War II expansion, and is now likely to happen once again.

By the 1960s, the American auto industry was synonymous with General Motors. In 1965, GM had 50% of the US passenger car market, holding up a price umbrella that made Ford profitable. Ford and Chrysler had copied GM's successful business methods, and in the process they became scaled-down copies of GM. This was a major failure in Ford's and Chrysler's strategic business planning.

General Motors reached its turning point in good management with the retirement of Alfred Sloan from its board in the early 1960s. Because the rest of the US auto industry followed the GM model so closely, Ford and Chrysler also started down the slope. In a way, this resembles the way IBM headed for bankruptcy after the retirement of Thomas Watson, Jr.

The similarities between poor management in GM and IBM go beyond their sticking to legacy products. In their flawed business strategies, both appeared to shift their priorities from growth to maintaining the financial status quo. At GM, the design, engineering, product development, and marketing functions declined in the 1970s and 1980s, and the same thing happened at lots of other firms in the United States and Europe.

At the same time, attracted by high margins plenty of new competitors entered the market. In the automotive industry when the energy crises hit in the early and late 1970s, consumer preferences shifted rapidly from Detroit's dinosaurs to smaller, more efficient cars produced by Japanese and European firms. In the 1979 to 1981 recession:

- Chrysler and Ford almost failed, and
- GM had its first loss in decades, but nothing changed in the way management directed the firm's fortunes.

Yet, torrents of red ink made GM a pale copy of its past image, and independent rating agencies continued to downgrade its debt. A rare positive spike came in October 2005 when GM succeeded in putting a welcome spin on its dismal third-quarter financial report. The shaving off of $1 billion of its annual health care bill of $6 billion, through a deal with the unions, was a kind of achievement that was good news, but the truth remained that:

- GM still lost $1.6 billion in the third quarter of 2005, and
- This brought annual losses to $3.8 billion over only nine months.

Even if top management promised to shave another $1 billion off GM's product development bill, analysts said that there were plenty of reasons for scepticism about the company's future. A major negative was that the company was saddled with billions in additional pension and other costs, as a result of Delphi's bankruptcy.

Additionally, poor management decisions showed up in many areas, including product strategy. The increase in oil and gas prices turned many buyers away from the sport-utility vehicles (SUVs) that long supported Detroit's balance sheet. The costly re-launch of full-size SUVs, such as the Chevrolet Tahoe, is an example of a tactical and strategic blunder happening at the same time.

Faults in product strategy have been augmented by supply chain mistakes. Because when management falters in its decision process, one piece of bad news never comes alone, even after the 1999 spin-off General Motors' car production remained highly dependent on Delphi. The result is that Delphi's bankruptcy, and inability to deliver parts, can shut down GM's assembly lines.

Conscious of these facts and their impact, on 11 October 2005 Standard & Poor's downgraded GM bonds to BB-, which is three levels below the better-off investment grade. Earlier, on 5 May 2005, S&P's first downgrade of GM into junk bond territory:

- Set off a violent disruption in the derivatives (hedge fund) market, and
- Put several hedge funds under stress.

Wall Street insiders said that billions of dollars of hedge fund capital was wiped out. Pension funds and other institutional investors also suffered severe losses with the downgrade in creditworthiness. As in the case of AT&T and Lucent Technologies, GM has been a blue chip and its debt was sought after by serious bond investors.

On Wall Street, some analysts suggested that this is not necessarily the end of the bad news as various ratings agencies have signalled the possibility of further downgrades in GM debt. Neither was the auto market, at large, at high prosperity. Merrill Lynch, the investment bank, rated the US domestic auto industry conditions as being characterized by:

- Leveraged balance sheets, especially including legacy liabilities
- Deteriorating domestic OEM performance and mounting supplier failures
- Upward pressure on capital spending, necessary to beef up competitiveness
- Poor quality of demand, essentially propped up by incentives
- Rising labour tension and great input costs affecting raw materials and labour

- Rising costs of vehicle ownership because of energy and interest rates
- Changing consumer preferences, towards high fuel economy and low emissions.[2]

As if the goal were to push the shaky corporate America represented by the auto industry into the abyss, General Motors received subpoenas from the Securities and Exchange Commission over pension accounting. This put another cloud of uncertainty over the company's future. SEC has been seeking information about the methods the company uses to determine its pension obligations. Both GM and Ford were asked to provide data on their pension assumption.

In the aftermath, GM's 8.385% bond due in 2033 fell 1.75 cents on the dollar to 75 cents. The yield rose to 11.3%, according to Trace, the bond price reporting system of the NASD. This fact alone speaks volumes about silly investors, including pension funds, who paid good money to buy GM's 30-year bonds, at a time when they knew already about the company's deteriorating finances. How investors can know about what will happen to a company 30 years down the line is beyond my comprehension.

6. Emulating the thinking of promoters: the ABC Management Teams

To a very significant extent, the blunders made in directing a company's operations (and fortunes) are an after-effect of the bureaucracy that has set in to company management. By so doing, it has turned formerly prosperous entities into third-class joints. As a remedy, some experts suggest a return to fundamentals by emulating the thinking and decisions made by the *animators* and *promoters* of industry.

In the first stage of development of the modern corporation, there was always an innovative and dominant personality: Rockefeller at Standard Oil, Ford at Ford, Sloan at General Motors, Firestone at Firestone, Watson Sr at IBM, Dupont at Dupont, Avery at Montgomery Ward, Rosenwald at Sears, Giannini at Bank of America, Trippe at PanAm, Walton at WalMart, Gates at Microsoft. These animators and promoters became originating names whose existence can be identified with nearly every one of the Fortune 500 corporations in manufacturing, merchandising, transportation, or finance. At the second or third stage, however, 'me too' bureaucracy took over. (Sometimes, as in the case of Henry Ford, this has been strongly resisted by the original entrepreneur – but in the end professional management, and the legacy costs it brings along with it, prevailed.)

The main argument presented by professional managers in defence of their doings is that the requirements for decisions, both tactical and strategic, have become too demanding and too diverse for one person. This is a lie that will not run. One of the leaders of industry to whom I was consultant for 16 years held together his empire, which ranged from manufacturing to banking and insurance, practically single-handed.

- To clear his mind on important decisions, he depended on five people whom he called his collaborators.
- And he distinguished between this small select group and the thousands of other managers who worked for him.

But at the same time, the industrial leader I refer to here worked past midnight and he was up daily before 6.00 a.m. His were practically 18-hour days at the rate of 7 days per week. Some of the company presidents who award themselves lavish options, and run their firm to its knees, don't work even a quarter as much.

To make up for wanting work ethics, second- and third-rate managers create an immense bureaucracy of 'experts' and 'specialists' who protect their turf by stonewalling. Low-grade CEOs justify this approach by saying that any important action calls for a large range of specialized knowledge. Therefore:

- Formal organizational structures have to be developed, and staffed, and
- This is done even if, at the following stage, they get rusty and the system is grounded under the weight of unnecessary costs.

Invariably this leads to decline. Restructuring tries to correct past errors and refocus objectives. But this does not always work. Organizations are made of people, and therefore corrective action should put the human component at the No. 1 position. This is what the so-called 'ABC Teams' solution tries to do.

Underlying this concept is the notion of a knowledge-intense organization with a novel command structure and well-defined teamwork. The whole approach can be classified into the three layers, as shown in Figure 8.1. We will call these layers A, B, C.

Team Level A is a relatively new type of top management. Contrary to the hierarchical line and staff organization, it is a tightly integrated board of management structure, the way Vorstand operates in Switzerland, Germany, and Austria, or the president's office in the United States. Peter Drucker uses the tennis-doubles team to describe how this level functions, its size being a low one-digit number.

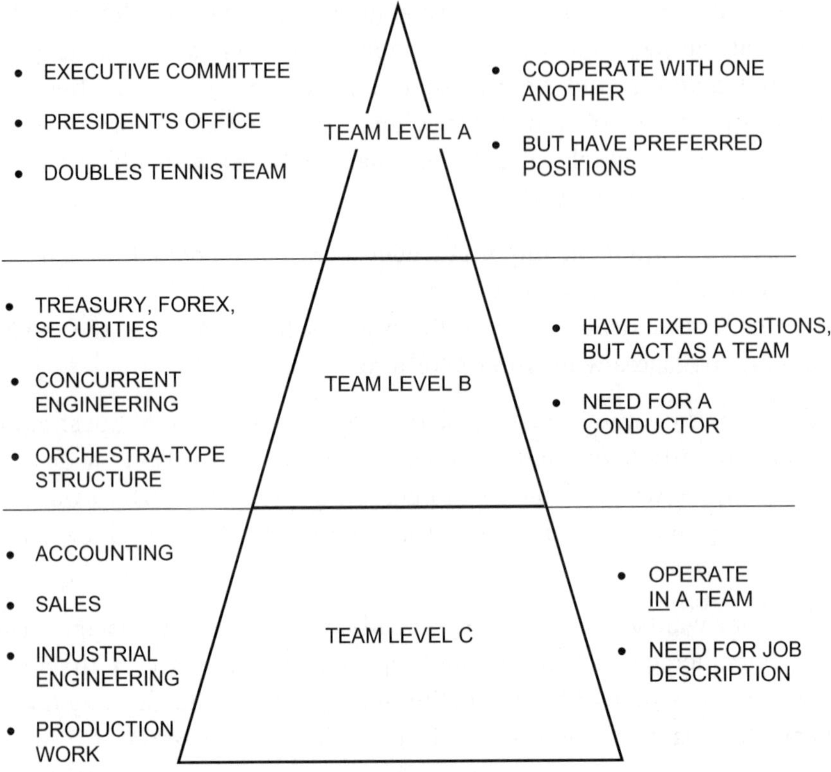

Figure 8.1 Three team levels in an ABC organizational structure

Here is a real life example. Back in the 1960s Nestlé had two chief executive officers: The one was in charge of strategic plans, the other of day-to-day decisions and operations. The great innovation was that they switched jobs every two years. Even if the board of management is of a bigger size – say of five or six people – the players have a dynamic rather than a static, fixed position.

- They complement one another in terms of functions, and
- They adjust themselves to the strengths and weaknesses of each other. Sometimes they even switch jobs.

The Team Level A effort works best when interdisciplinary adjustments become a conditioned reflex. This is essentially what happens in a tennis team. To be winning, its performance must be significantly greater than the sum of its individual parts. This type of solution however:

- Requires enormous self-discipline by all of its members

- Must feature dissent in terms of opinion as well as debate, till there is a sense of the meeting, and
- Can only consist of people with unconventional and innovative ideas, able to provide stimulus for change as well as to manage change.

Arguably, with human nature being what it is, this is not always possible. Company politics may lead Team A members to cover one another, with the result that this process may end up by featuring all the negatives of management by committee, with none of the positives of the promoter's approach which it tries to emulate. In short, Team Level A is no miracle solution.

As Figure 8.1 explains, in Team Level B are the professionals. Typically in a banking environment they work in the forex money market, securities trading, wealth management, loans and other departments. In manufacturing companies characteristic work at Team Level B is concurrent engineering, new design solutions, quota-based sales, and so on.

While the members of Team Level A have preferred positions but in essence they complement each other, and at times they switch jobs, the members of Level B have rather fixed positions – but switching between specialties can be a rewarding experience, as well as preparation for Team A. Indeed success at Level B requires rotating managers and professionals, to:

- Promote a diverse talent base
- Prompt everybody to contribute new ideas, and
- Foster exchange of information and know-how.

While at Level A the team members are semi-equal, even if they have a speaker who expresses the opinion of all of them, at Level B there has to be a conductor or manager, who however has a very wide span of control (see Chapter 7). This:

- Contradicts the classical notion of a narrowband structure, which is most prominent today, and
- Leads to an organization which, as Drucker puts it, resembles an orchestra with, say, 40 instruments, a few virtuosi and one conductor.

One of the differences between Levels A and B is the way in which technology is being used. Both should benefit from wideband communications among team members and with on-line databases. This makes it feasible to hold together Level A and Level B, in spite of the broad span of control characteristics. A broad database bandwidth is necessary both between levels and within levels, but:

- Team A people are mainly database *miners*
- While Team B are more database *feeders*.

In a responsibility-based organization, like the one described in this section, accountants, salesmen, industrial engineers, loans officers, and other professions, rather than working as a team *are* in a team. This is Team Level C. Some of its members are knowledge workers. Others are service workers. But they all operate within a structured information environment, with each team bringing its own speciality into play.

The members at Team Level C occupy, over a certain period of time, fixed positions because they have been given specific tasks to perform. These can be measured by fairly crisp performance scores; a job that is more difficult at Level B, and even more so at Level A.

Accountants have legal obligations to fulfil. Salesmen have a territory and must deliver their quotas. Industrial engineers should be busy with efficiency studies for daily work of their own and of other professionals. Every team must recognize that its success depends on the programmes executed by the preceding teams – offering, therefore, full collaboration.

Senior managers who put this approach into practice say that it leads to interesting results. One of the senior executives I interviewed stated that in his company the best professionals are the askers and note-takers, because they are the more efficient learners. Additionally they:

- Appreciate that they can learn from everybody, and
- Keep in perspective that, near or far, there is a challenger to their company and its future.

The ABC Team Levels is not a fantastic breakthrough but an approach worth trying. In practically every business, uniqueness most often comes not from once-in-a lifetime breakthroughs but from accumulation of thousands of tiny enhancements that have been done first by somebody else, probably in some other market. Yet, when they are adapted, improved, and integrated to *our* mainstream, they help in creating uniqueness and therefore product leadership. For Team A this leads to better governance, as we will see in section 8.

7. Management's controlling function, and internal control

Control is the sixth capital function of management. Its mission is to ensure progress towards objectives, conformity to plans, ability to ascertain the extent of deviations taking place. All these are prerequisites to an effective route to corrective action. A byproduct is provision of means for adjusting plans to changing business conditions.

Among the functions of control are to ascertain whether the company continues being a lean, decisive, and effective organization, while on a personal level it treats each customer with dignity, consideration, and respect; also, whether the firm's employees take pride in working as a team – at all levels and across all boundaries – bringing all of their diverse skills and resources to bear in solving client problems.

Effective management control requires a steady, accurate, reliable feedback mechanism. In well-managed organizations this is provided by internal control (more on this later). Another prerequisite to control action is the existence of performance standards, as yardsticks against which to measure results. Still, other prerequisites are:

- Exception reporting, with open communications channels
- A common language, generally understood in all corners of the organization, and
- Well-timed evaluation procedures, with rewards and disciplinary action associated to them.

The latter is the carrot and stick approach. There should also be merits and demerits, because without them the wheels turn slowly or even come to a complete stop.

Dr Harold D. Koontz, my professor at UCLA from whom I learned the most, taught his students that no other crucial function of management is more closely associated to corporate culture than controlling. This is true because corporate culture is the sum of what people in the organization believe and think, how they work together as colleagues, and how they conduct themselves as individuals.

- While corporate culture is by nature undefinable
- In essence it begins and ends with planning and control principles that characterize the business and its individuals within the corporate governance framework.

Precisely for this reason, everybody in the organization should understand and appreciate the intent and impact of management control. This function is not only concerned with deviations from plans. Among other responsibilities, it aims to identify fraud, failures of compliance, legal risk, and other exposures being assumed; also knowledge gaps in one or more fields, which one day would haunt the firm. Control should also answer questions such as:

- *How well* is the projected solution to the salient problem executed?
- Are the steps being taken *consistent* with the overall corporate objectives?
- What's the *impact* of market changes and new product designs on staffing requirements?

Product and market changes affect a long list of company functions: manufacturing technology, marketing policies, salesman training, client support, maintenance costs, and a horde of others. Their impact is usually appreciated when the company's future is at the mercy of incompetent staff – but by then it is too late.

It takes an iron hand to change senior management, and this is not always around. Therefore, Dr Neil Jacoby, another of my professors at UCLA, used to say that the best way to get rid of a CEO is to give him enough cord to hang himself. Management control is more effective when it looks proactively at every indication of possible failure. Deviations from plans and sloppy handling of business activities can upset:

- Timetables
- Budgets
- Product marketability, and much more.

The information network necessary in achieving the required supervisory results is generally known as *internal control.*[3] The intelligence it provides is instrumental in enhancing management's effectiveness; this, however, is true only when internal control channels are open and functioning at all times – thereby providing a fast response capability.

By definition, internal control is a dynamic system covering all types of risks and deviations from policies and plans as well as other mischances which, from time to time hit an enterprise. To do so, it requires policies, organization, technology, and adequate training of human resources. When this is achieved, internal control:

- Helps in assuring transparency
- Makes possible reliable financial reporting (see Chapters 9 and 10), and
- Assists in ensuring not only compliance but also that there is no cognitive dissonance at any level.

The chairman of the board, directors, CEO, and senior management are accountable for the organization's internal control, and for its focus on preservation of assets.

Theirs is also the responsibility for timely and rigorous corrective action. In many companies, however, internal control is weak or altogether nonexistent.

After the Barings, Daiwa, and Sumitomo debacles happening in quick succession one after the other, in the mid- to late 1990s equity investors injected a new risk factor – *weak management controls* – into their valuation of risk. This has been an interesting addition because, until then, the concept was that:

- The main risks were external, related to counterparties and countries with which the company did business.
- But after Barings and the other scams, including Enron, WorldCom, Parmalat, etc., solid evidence has been provided that some of the top risks are *internal* to the firm.

There have been too many false financial statements challenging management integrity and its ability, or even willingness, to protect the company's reputation whatever the cost. Yet business reputation is the bedrock of a firm's prosperity and its pride. Both can be lost at short notice, taking along with them the life of the firm – as Arthur Andersen documents.

Take as an example KPMG's alleged involvement in client tax evasion. A total of 19 people, including KPMG's former chief financial officer, have been charged in what is thought to be the biggest-ever criminal case of tax fraud.[4] Clearly, the company's internal control system was not functioning.

These tax shelters operated between 1996 and 2002, and they cost the US government billions of dollars in lost tax revenue. The way it has been reported in the press, the shelters went by the simple, quirky names of FLIPs, BLIPs, SOS, and OPIS, but in reality they were sophisticated and complex – often sold to clients who had received large one-off payments and wanted to reduce their taxes, but also involving false tax returns and hiding of information from the Internal Revenue Service.[5] KPMG's top management had failed miserably in its internal control function.

As a company, KPMG, one of the 'Big Four' global auditors, settled this tax fraud case with the US government. At the end of August 2005, if left to follow its path, the scam might have led KPMG down the same path as Arthur Andersen. The US government claimed that over the six-year timeframe, in exchange for $128 million in fees,

- KPMG arranged dubious tax shelters, and
- These allowed rich individuals to claim over $11 billion in phony losses and avoid $2.5 billion in taxes.

KPMG agreed to pay fines of $456 million and accepted a long list of other conditions, including further monitoring and the end of its tax-advisory business for private clients and corporates. The US government's prosecutors let the company off the hook – but of its former employees, seven ex-partners have been charged with fraud and are now facing the likelihood of large fines and long prison terms.

8. Criteria for better corporate governance

The quality of both directing and controlling shows up in corporate governance. The Organization for Economic Co-operation and Development (OECD) defines corporate governance as relating to internal means by which corporations are operated and controlled. As such, it involves many relationships between:

- A company's management
- Its board of directors
- Its shareholders and other stakeholders.

Corporate governance provides the framework through which the objectives of the company are set, and the means of attaining them, as well as ways of monitoring performance, are determined. Sound corporate governance:

- Facilitates effective monitoring, thereby encouraging firms to use resources more efficiently, and
- Provides proper incentives for the board and senior management to pursue objectives that are in the interests of the company and its stakeholders.

'Poor corporate governance practices can be either a cause or a symptom of larger problems that merit supervisory attention,' says the Basel Committee on Banking Supervision, adding that 'The proactive practices that need to be in place [should] be evaluated by supervisors who must also assess the quality of banks' internal controls.'[6] This statement is valid not only for banks but for every corporation.

The Basel Committee further suggests that 'The board and senior management can enhance their effectiveness by requiring that internal control reviews include not only *core* banking businesses, but also activities ... that lack transparency.' Therefore, internal control is cornerstone in determining that individual banks are conducting their business in such a way as not to harm depositors. Indeed, supervisors view corporate governance as one element of depositor protection.

Because illegal, unethical or questionable practices can have a detrimental impact on any company's reputation, sound corporate governance suggests the need to establish internal procedures promoting the communication of material concerns directly (and confidentially) or indirectly to the board. This, the Basel Committee advises, should be done in a way independent of the internal chain of command. Direct access is important inasmuch as:

- Corporate governance considers the interests of *all* stakeholders, and
- Sound corporate governance is the best way to evaluate the board's, CEO's, and senior management's effectiveness.

It is however true that evaluating the governance quality of companies with complex holding structures poses unique challenges. The web of interlocking subsidiaries and affiliates makes it difficult to evaluate the firm's:

- Decision-making ability
- Lines of authority and responsibility, and
- Worth of company assets and amount of its liabilities.

From this perspective, a fundamental issue to explore is the underlying reason or motivation for the complexity of organization – which may or may not have a viable business rationale (usually, it does not). For example, it can be the result of mergers or acquisitions activity without the benefit of integration and streamlining (see Part 6).

A study by Fitch Ratings points out that sometimes the reasons for complexity have no economic basis and are not explained clearly to investors. When this happens, governance concerns should be raised. Discerning the true motivation behind a complex structure is not always straightforward, Fitch suggests.[7]

To help in analysis and evaluation, different organizations have tried to develop indices for better corporate governance. At the end of 2004, Institutional Shareholder Services (ISS) teamed up with FTSE, the London Stock Exchange index provider, to launch corporate governance indices that will rank more than 2000 global companies. Ranking is to be done against best governance practice criteria.

- Companies will be rated at a scale of one to five, and
- The higher scores will identify those that are best governed.

The development of a *quality of governance* index was prompted by demand from investors and fund managers. Both have been facing mounting pressure to put their money in well-governed companies, following a wave of corporate scandals which rocked the financial and business world in the early part of the 21st century.

Notice that technically, the ISS–FTSE index has become feasible because of a global change in attitudes towards corporate governance over the past years. Companies and investors now co-exist in a substantially different business world, in which corporate power is gradually shifting towards the big shareholders. One of the entities instrumental in shifting the investors' sights toward corporate governance has been Calpers, the California-based largest US state pension fund.

Moreover, the globalization of the world economy has resulted in a large increase in cross-border investments. For instance, US-based investors now own nearly 20% of the UK stock market, and there is also cross-border fertilization of ideas.

Another area of investor interest in evaluating the quality of corporate management are the governance conferences taking place across the world. Interest in such events has been the silver lining of scandals at Enron, Global Crossing, Adelphia, and WorldCom in the United States, Parmalat in Europe, and China Aviation Oil in Singapore – among many others. This torrent of corporate scandals has heightened shareholder concern that companies in which they invest are not being run soundly.

Notes

1 Robert Schoenberg, *Geneen*. W.W. Norton, New York, 1985.
2 Merrill Lynch, *Life Cycle of Industrials*. 1 November 2005.
3 D.N. Chorafas, *Implementing and Auditing the Internal Control System*. Macmillan, London, 2001.
4 *The Economist*, 22 October 2005.
5 *The Economist*, 3 September 2005.
6 Basel Committee on Banking Supervision document: 'Enhancing Corporate Governance for Banking Organizations' (Consultative Document), BIS, Basle, July 2005.
7 Fitch Ratings, Special Report 'Evaluating Corporate Governance The Bondholders' Perspective', London, 12 April 2004.

Part 3

Strategic Financial Planning and Accounting

Financial Planning

1. Introduction

One of the most important elements of sound corporate governance is the system designed for financial planning and control. Vital components of such a system are long-range planning, asset management, budgeting and budgetary control, cost control, profitability analysis, and cash flow projections. Each of these major component parts can be further analysed into its constituents. For instance, cost control requires:

- Cost standards
- Watch over overhead
- Optimum scheduling of productive resources
- Fast inventory management
- Automation of labour-intensive jobs, and other functions.

Cost elements are important in financial planning. As the reader will recall from Chapter 6, to a significant extent *planning* is based on forecasting and standard costs help in computing unit prices. Like all, financial planning plans presuppose the existence of goals, an important one being the maintenance of adequate capital to meet projected financial obligations which is done by the budget.

Assets and liabilities (A&L) management (see Chapter 10) is a good example of mid-range financial planning. Another important financial goal is tax treatment analysis both in regard to next year's operating plans and in conjunction with investment studies. Section 3 provides an example on ingenuity in investment practices – albeit at the border of acceptable financial strategy. This is a case study on position-taking at Fiat, the Italian motor vehicle manufacturer.

Financial planning connected to operating plans revolves around gross and net financial income. A company's efforts must be directed at establishing a sound financial position. Tight debt control and efficient use of resources are examples of tactical moves. Figure 9.1 shows an example on projected net financial income from one of the better-known global manufacturing firms. Another fundamental aspect of financial planning is the development of contingency options supported through careful and steady:

- Financial position monitoring, and
- Reconciliation of financial analyses done in different sectors of activity

Budgeting (see section 4) is the process of established shorter-term financial plans, designed to meet definite goals by making available adequate financial resources to match projected activities. Executives of well-managed companies appreciate the budget is a plan; not an authorization to spend money.

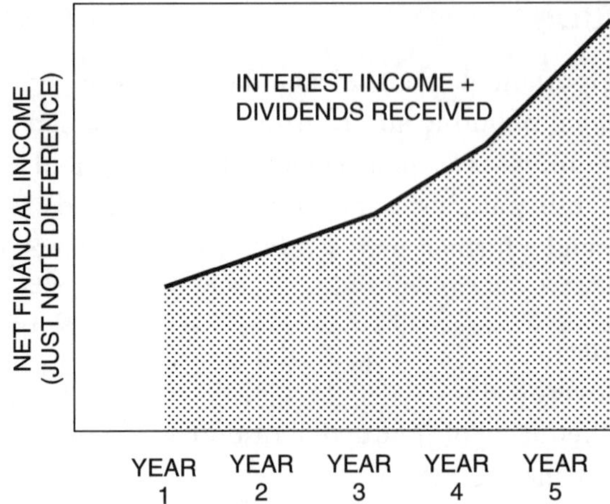

Figure 9.1 Net financial income over a 5-year timeframe of one of the best-known manufacturing companies

Cash flow estimates (see section 5) should definitely cover the budget's 1-year or rolling-year period, including accounts receivable from the company's sales and other income such as from patents and investments; also from extraordinary items like sale of property. In the longer term, cash flow is a function of income from products and markets. In the short to very short term (90–180 days), the cash flow makes the difference between liquidation and survival.

Cost control (see Chapter 11) is a pillar of good governance. It involves both planning activities such as standard costing and the steady accumulation, analysis, interpretation and reporting of detailed unit cost and performance data. Within the cost control domain, *inventory control* aims at minimizing the capital tied up in all sorts of inventories, while the company is ready, at all times, to meet production and customer demand. Prerequisites are:

- Sales forecasts
- Supply chain characteristics
- Maintenance of accurate records
- Development of inventory targets, and
- Timely reporting of inventory status at every level of reference.

Profitability analysis provides senior management both with a prognostication, which helps in establishing profit targets, and with a feedback on what has been achieved. The sustenance of profits calls for continuing review of costs and sales targets, as well as of actions taken to ensure a realization of management objectives.

Miscomprehension and misinterpretation are enemies of financial planning. Many people, including people in management, can never grasp the difference between sales and profits. When they say *revenue*, they mean either one. This is near-sighted because it deprives decision-makers of clearly established financial planning and control tools.

Finally, financial planners must steadily pay attention to fund strategy and asset allocation to meet maturity-matching and other requirements. They must also document the pricing of internal funds transfer to provide improved coordination of asset-liability management decisions. All business units of the enterprise are in need of funds. Financial planning must not only assure provision of funds but also optimize their allocation.

2. Money and the watch over money

Money is raw material in financial planning. It serves as a means for transacting business and as a means of exchange, a substitute to barter agreements. Money is also a store of value; the value of money derives from the fact that it is limited in supply. Additionally, money is a unit of measurement, providing metrics and reference values for accounting reasons. Therefore, reporting on money should be based on accounting standards (see Chapter 10).

Money is also raw material for the banking industry. Without it, credit institutions cannot act as financial intermediaries. Moreover, money is the key ingredient of the system that makes up the *economy*. As such, it is the object of a monetary policy as well as of government controls. The basic equation of money supply (MS) is:

$$\text{Money Supply} = \text{Monetary Base} \cdot \text{Velocity of Circulation of Money}$$

$$\text{MS} = \text{MB} \cdot v \tag{1}$$

Money supply is the total of money available to the economy including the amplification of the monetary base (MB) by the banking system, due to current account deposits, loans with a relatively low reserve, and other transactions. Loans are a main ingredient in the velocity of circulation of money (v), mainly regulated by changing the level of required reserves.

The monetary basis consists of printed money and coins, the latter roughly representing 7% of MB. Because the velocity of circulation v is positive, MS is greater than MB. There is practically no limit to the amount banks can expand the financial system, said Marriner Eccles, chairman of the Federal Reserve in the Roosevelt years.

In addition to the role which it plays in the economy, for a company money provides the standard measure for accounting in its balance sheet – including reference to cash, accounts receivable, accounts payable, inventory, current assets, current liabilities, salaries payable, short-term loans payable and taxes. All this will all be expressed in monetary values.

As a means of exchange, money, first as coins and then paper, substituted for a large part of transaction previously made through barter agreements, but not all of them. According to some estimates, today more than 20% of world trade is conducted on what is known as a *countertrade* basis, such as:

- Barter
- Counterpurchase
- Buyback agreements, and
- Other arrangements.

As a result, companies active in the global market have to be experienced not only in money management but also in countertrade, and be ready to do barter-type business while still keeping their accounts in money terms. Financial instruments known as 'barter bucks', have opened the doors for increased trade without the legal tender provided by money.

For instance, such instruments permit the making of loans directly to project applicants, bypassing government bureaucracies. At the same time, some sorts of barter bucks based on derivatives are used to beautify the balance sheet. The *prepays* Enron had contracted in its heyday with JP Morgan and Citigroup are an example.

Novel financial instruments, such as derivatives, alter the now classical types of money-based transactions. Because these products are (usually) highly leveraged, they should attract the close attention of board members. The board has the responsibility to evaluate the company's transactions and other operations most critically and objectively:

- Assuring that the firm pursues reasonable financial objectives, and maintains its access to funding, and
- Promoting an environment of proper corporate conduct that helps to preserve and enhance the company's reputation.

Indeed, one of the ways of assessing the quality of a company's board of directors is how active, committed, and knowledgeable its members are in performing their fiduciary duties. Gaining a sense of a board's effectiveness involves the contextual analysis of qualitative factors such as expertise in novel financial instruments and the risks embedded in them not only of quantitative factors mainly represented by auditing.

For instance, one critical money-based question the board should study (and answer) is whether investments with maturities beyond one year may be classified as short-term, based on their liquid nature, and what should be the case if these are derivative instruments – which, by definition, means illiquid. Another query is that of value of collateral and/or security interest determined upon the:

- Underlying security, and
- Creditworthiness of the borrower.

Still another capital query for the board, in its fiduciary duty over money, concerns investments considered to be impaired when a decline in fair value is judged as other-than-temporary. Well-managed companies employ a systematic methodology, usually on a quarterly basis, that considers available quantitative and qualitative evidence in evaluating potential impairment of their investments.

Other money-related issues for board-level decisions concern the use of derivative instruments to manage exposures to foreign currency, equities price, interest rate, and credit risks. The company directors should be able to evaluate operating management's stated objectives for holding derivatives, such as reducing or eliminating the economic impact of different exposures.

- Derivative instruments must be recognized as either assets or liabilities, and
- They must be measured at fair value under both IFRS and US GAAP (see Chapter 10).

Moreover, transactions between senior management, or major shareholders, and the company merit close review by the board. Time and again, *related party* transactions give rise to potential conflicts of interest. In fact, in many cases, the primary motivation of a related party transaction is to enrich the CEO and other senior managers, at the expense of shareholders. The cases of Adelphia Communications, Tyco, WorldCom and many other companies document this argument.

A rubber-stamp, lax or insider-dominated board might neglect to carefully examine financial transactions that create potential conflicts of interest between management and the company. Adam Smith, of *Wealth of Nations* fame (published in 1776), is often credited as being the first in identifying some of the weaknesses of professional management connected to money matters: 'being the managers rather of other people's money than of their own, it cannot be well expected that [the directors] should watch over it with the same anxious vigilance with which the partners in a private company [their daily business]. Negligence and profusion, therefore, always prevail.'

Taking a page out of the book of Adam Smith, self-respecting boards and the company's executive management cannot afford to lower their oversight. When this happens, both the reputation of the people involved and of the firm itself get damaged. All business is based on confidence, as Demosthenes, the great orator of ancient Athens, used to say.

3. Using derivatives in financial planning: case study with Fiat

A basic philosophy in management, which should guide the hand of decision-makers, is that 'Every good thing and every acquired asset stands moment by moment on the razor's edge of change.' Ownership, or alternatively, financial control, of a firm provides an example. To face new developments in ownership and in money matters, which may come at a fast pace, we must:

- Be ready to think the unthinkable
- Challenge the obvious, and
- Adjust swiftly to market realities.

The late 18th century, most precisely 1797, provides interesting evidence about thinking the unthinkable. That was one of the most curious times in history. In one year, the British invented income tax and the French implemented military conscription for the first time – both being alien concepts to the known world.

Another example of thinking the unthinkable dates from 2005, and it is provided by Fiat, IFIL and Exor. These three Italian entities are related. Fiat, Italy's largest industrial firm, has been the stronghold of the Agnelli family for three generations. IFIL is the financial holding of the Agnellis, and Exor Group, IFIL's sister, is held 70% by the Agnelli family.

- Through a cascade of companies the Agnellis control IFIL Investments.
- IFIL is a quoted company, which is in turn Fiat's controlling shareholder.

For most of 2004 and early 2005 Fiat had found itself in financial difficulties that would not go away. Investment experts, and no doubt its owners, wondered if the company could survive. Nobody really seemed sure which financial plan would bring the venerable firm back up, at least in the mid-term – particularly at a time when the US auto giants were themselves in deep trouble (see Chapter 8 on General Motors).

For Fiat, the first *deus ex machina* was General Motors. In February 2005, helped largely by a nearly $2 billion divorce settlement from GM (which GM itself could ill-afford), Fiat got a new lease of life. Short-lived as it may be, this turnaround followed total pre-tax losses of over $10 billion since 2001.

Two billion dollars looks like lots of money, but for a company that had lost $10 billion over a few years, it was not enough. In late April 2005 Fiat announced that it would not repay a $3.7 billion convertible loan from a consortium of banks. With credit institutions being paid in equity rather than cash, it looked *as if* IFIL might lose control of the Italian auto maker. Converting $3.7 billion in loans into Fiat shares, on 20 September 2005:

- Would give the banks a 24% share of the company, and
- This would dilute IFIL's holding of Fiat from 30% to 23%.

The mathematics of this transaction describes what equity analysts thought of the Agnelli family's financial plan. But was it really so? By mid-September 2005, a short while prior to equity payment to the banks, a second *deus ex machina* delivered its goodies. IFIL said it found a way of avoiding both:

- Dilution of equity, and
- A mandatory offer.

Assisted by Merrill Lynch in an advisory capacity and in a trading role, the financial plan of IFIL was indeed ingenious. As the banks converted their loans, IFIL simultaneously acquired sufficient shares to retain control. The amount was about 7% of Fiat's voting capital:

- It was acquired at 6.50 euro a share,
- Compared with the market price of 7.30 euro.

The seller was Exor, which bought the shares on the same day from Merrill Lynch at $5.60 a share under an equity swap, a derivative financial instrument which is ahead of the regulators and of the taxman. This also is a good example on the assistance new instruments can offer to people who know how to use them.

On all the evidence, the American investment bank signed the swap on 26 April 2005, the very day Fiat announced the conversion of the banks' loan into equity. At that time, Fiat's shares sold at around 4.50 euro, its bottom price for years. The deal made Exor a profit of 74 million euro ($92 million). But was it at IFIL's expense?

One of my professors at UCLA taught his students that to really understand what is happening one has to read the fine print, as well as between the lines. Strategy, including financial strategy, is never written in big block letters. Consob, Italy's stockmarket regulator, required disclosure (and published certain details) of the transaction. They are revealing on the way a modern financial plan can be constructed by:

- Using derivative financial instruments, and
- Exploiting loopholes in legislation, as rules and regulations are always behind their time.

Under the equity swap, Merrill Lynch was to buy 90 million Fiat ordinary shares by 7 June 2005. The broker bought them for 495 million euro ($610 million), an average of 5.50 euro per share. According to the agreement, Merrill was to sell the underlying shares on the swap's expiry in December 2006, or sooner, if Exor requested early settlement.[1]

- If the proceeds exceeded the stated cost of 495 million euro, Merrill would send Exor the surplus in cash, less its funding costs.
- If they were below 495 million euro, Exor would pay Merrill in cash for the difference, thereby covering the deficit and the investment bank's funding costs.

The beauty of equity swaps and associated two-party agreements is that they are novel, imaginative, practically legal, but also able to run way ahead of the stock markets' thinking. They are also designed in a way to insulate the counterparties from some of the risk. In this case, the brokerage firm was protected from any risk relating to Fiat's share price. This is a first class example on how new financial instruments:

- Deconstruct old structures
- Increase manoeuvrability, and
- Reconceptualize financial functions.

However, to be ahead of the curve companies must carefully evaluate how financial innovation affects themselves and their clients. As far as IFIL, Exor, and Fiat are concerned, post-mortem analysts said that the equity swap's original cash-settlement terms were an ingenious plan to avoid informing the market. Some experts commented that the losers from the manoeuvre were all investors who sold Fiat shares when the shares underlying the swap were being bought. Critics added that therefore:

- Investors would not feel comfortable putting their money in a quoted company that uses such financial tricks.
- While regulators, and the authorities at large should learn a lesson and close the loopholes in financial transactions opened through derivatives.

Merrill Lynch is off the hook. From the advisory and brokerage point of view, there was no financial difference between settling in cash and physical delivery. On the other hand, for Exor there was a big difference. The construction of the financial plan saw to it that it wanted the shares themselves, not cash representing an increase in their value over 495 million euro.

Notice that when on 15 September 2005 the two firms agreed to revise their swap contract to enable the broker to sell the shares themselves to Exor, this required disclosure under the law. As it was legally required to do, Merrill Lynch declared that its stake in Fiat had crossed the 5% and 10% thresholds on 15 September. This was done according to the equity swap contract, and there is no evidence the regulators reacted at the time. IFIL, Exor, and Fiat carried the day.

4. The budget as a financial plan

Sound financial planning premises and cost discipline are the pillars on which a good budgeting policy rests. Prerequisites are factual and documented projections on business activities, reliable evaluation of this year's (or the rolling year's) commitments, possible constraints on financial obligations (based on estimated cash flow, profits, and other variables), and standard costs. Other indispensable elements are consolidation of budgetary results, and plan versus actual evaluations done post mortem.

No budget should ever be made on the run. Every position should be analysed and documented. Budgeting may be a short-term financial plan, but it is a crucial part of implementing a company's strategy. Indeed, one of its objectives is to translate other key planning assumptions into account representations about products, markets, and resources.

- The company should always know what it makes and what it loses with each product.

- Sales targets embody the company's strategy about markets.
- The capital allocated to responsibility centres reflects the choice about resources, and
- When budgeting is properly done, its entries are benchmarks for management control.

Seen from the perspective of these bullets, a budget must perform much more than the function of informing about financial provisions to fund the company's activities. It should provide opportunities for making estimates about necessary financial resources, and serve as a base for comparisons between project figures and actual performance – to be performed post mortem.

The budgetary methodology must reflect the fact that the company's master budget is a numerical expression of forecasts of the organization's projected activities. In a way, this is combining income statement, balance sheet, and cash flow. To arrive at these aggregate figures, budgeting considers all the business that will finally be accounted for, incorporating:

- The *cost of doing* business, which practically includes all operating costs, and
- The cost of *staying in business*; that is, the money the firm must be investing in research and development.

When the operating costs get out of control, as so often happens, they leave precious little to be invested into the mission of staying in business. Therefore, an integral part of the budgetary process is management control done through Plan/Actual calculations and walkthroughs. The three-dimensional frame of reference presented in Figure 9.2 can be instrumental in doing such analyses.

R&D, too, can go astray. In 50 years of hands-on experience I have seen many research projects whose timetable has been overrun many times over. My advice is that it is better to kill a project than allow this go-slow culture to become a policy in R&D.

Additionally, there should be some crucial ratios to guide the board's hand when evaluating the R&D budget. Table 9.1 provides an example of quantification of goals for basic research, applied research, and development for a major manufacturing company for whom I was consultant to the board. Though precise targets cannot be revealed, what is written provides guidelines.

The reader should also notice that the constitution of an R&D budget is polyvalent. Not all the money for staying in business will be spent in the laboratory.

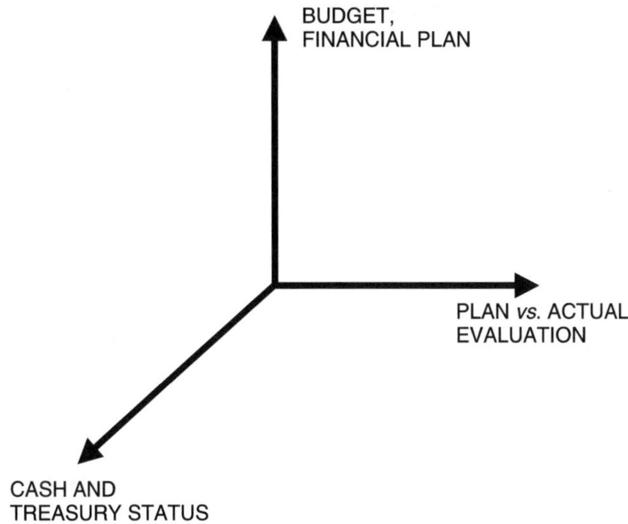

Figure 9.2 A frame of reference for budgetary evaluation and walkthroughs

Table 9.1 Deliverables of basic research, and applied research and development

Basic research	
Goal:	Scientific discovery
Budget:	10–15% of total R&D budget
Hit ratio:	Less than 5%
	Also running: 5–10%
	Expected failures: about 85%
Applied research and development	
Goal:	Technological leap and productization
Budget:	85–90% of total R+D
Hit ratio:	60–80% technical successes
Particular characteristics:	Tough design reviews and accountability for timetable
	Quality and cost of deliverables

Table 9.2 is based on real life projects that I audited in the computer industry. As the reader can see, marketing takes the lion's share of a new product's budget.

Money allocated to the cost of doing business, and the cost of staying in business, through the annual budget, must have a return. Therefore, cornerstone to any sound budgetary process is the identification of *deliverables*, which tell what we

Table 9.2 Relative costs in launching a new product

• *If* R&D =	1	cost unit
• *Then* manufacturing =	1½	cost units
Thus, total hardware technology =	2 ½	cost units
• Software developments, including some applications =	2 ½	cost units
Thus, software and hardware technology =	**5**	**cost units**
• Marketing: sales, training, systems support, maintenance =	**5**	**cost units**
• Total =	**10**	**cost units**
Hence, on 10 cost units, about 50% is marketing		

expect to gain from the money we plan to use. Moreover, there should be in place a computer-based, interactive *budgetary model* integrating:

- Cost standards, which should underpin all budgetary exercises, and
- Quantitative as well as qualitative descriptions of projected deliverables.

These are some of the dynamics of a budgetary methodology. It needs no explaining that the mechanics are equally important. The making of a short-term financial plan should start at the bottom of the organization to co-involve lower management at each business unit. In so doing, it should be made clear to everybody that budget is not an automatic authorization to spend money.

As the annual financial plan reaches the top of the business unit, it should be refined. The same is true about reaching the level of corporate headquarters. In essence, the so-called *bottom-to-top* and *top-to-bottom* approaches are part of the same methodology – because budgeting is an interactive process.

A logical starting point in elaborating a budget is the sales forecast prepared by marketing. On this basis of projected sales figures, the production and distribution financial plan as well as human resources procurement and the capital budget have to be analysed and constructed. A sound policy is *flexible budgeting*, necessary to:

- Provide a realistic and adjustable basis for financial planning, and
- Do away with the policy of spending outside a given authorization, which characterizes many firms that find their budgets too restrictive.

Because of the premise that, for control purposes, budgets must link closely with the costing system, flexible budgets rely on the cost figures and on cost drivers. These are reflected in the organization's internal accounting system, as well as in forecasts of business activity and their amendments. The rules characterizing flexible budgeting must, however, be clearly spelled out.

For instance, the *interest budget* can be made flexible by targeting a central interest rate projected over the year, then accounting for ±100 and ±200 basis points around the central line. This reference to the interest budget needs explaining. Every industry has its own jargon. In commercial banking, a distinction is made between the:

- Interest budget, and
- Non-interest budget.

The first is the interest the bank pays all the way from deposits to money bought from other institutions. The second includes everything else: administrative costs, real estate, utilities, personnel (the major chapter), information technology, and other expenses associated with operations.

Regarding budgetary jargon, it is important to bring certain distinctions existing in budgeting into the perspective. *Line-item* budgets refer to solutions that allow spending of a fixed maximum amount on specified items. This prevents managers from making overly bold moves in substituting between budgeted items. Some companies have discovered the perpetual motion machine, by serving themselves freely with money allocated to other expense chapters.

A sound policy is that of *lapsing* budgets. Companies should not allow the carry-over of unused funds into the next budgeting period. This makes budgets irrelevant. A lapsing budget allows tighter controls on managers and on spending habits – which is a rewarding policy.

A *zero-based* budgetary policy questions the very core of last year's financial allocations. Zero budgeting sees to it that every activity is financed from scratch. This helps managers to think creatively about their activities, thus reducing slack within the organization.

In conclusion, budgets are an important mechanism for financial planning and control. The number of separate budgets that have to be drawn up depends on the design of profit centres and cost centres. The number of iterations in establishing a budget depends on the complexity of reconciliation, budgeting technique being used, internal culture, and corporate environment. Choices made in accordance with these references add up to a budgetary methodology.

5. Cash flow challenges

Textbooks usually write that a company's *cash flow* is equal to its net income plus depreciation. This statement is technically correct, but too simple to describe (in modern business) the complexities of funds inflow, and its management. A more realistic definition than the textbook one that cash flow consists of net income plus non-cash expenses (such as depreciation) would take that cash flow figure:

- *Adding* deferred taxes and changes in working capital, and
- *Subtracting* the earnings of unconsolidated subsidiaries, that are reported but not remitted to the parent company.

This gives *operating cash flow* (OCF), or what is available before debt servicing and taxes come into play. In the 1990s, investing in companies based on their price-to-OCF multiples has often been a rewarding strategy, and one that can be significantly assisted through financial analysis. The algorithm is:

$$\text{OCF} = \text{Cash Flow} + \text{Inter} + \text{Income Tax Expense} \qquad (2)$$

Interest expense is added to the simple cash flow to get the broadest possible measure. In case of takeovers, *income tax expense* is added because it will not have to be paid if the new owner has suffered hefty losses.

Another important indicator is *free cash flow* (FCF). It is quite popular because it tells how much cash is uncommitted and available for other uses. Its algorithm is:

$$\text{FCF} = \text{Cash Flow} - \text{Capital Expenditures} - \text{Dividends} \qquad (3)$$

Another interesting approach to cash flow estimates is to start with the concept of *funds inflow and* outflow, which occur more or less continuously in the current assets and current liabilities accounts (see also Chapter 10). When receivables are collected, cash is increased. When goods are purchased or wages paid, cash is decreased.

- This cycle occurs over and over again in the course of normal business.
- For this reason, current assets and current liabilities are often called *circulating capital.*

Other funds tied up in land, buildings, equipment, and other noncurrent assets, are known as *permanent capital.* Both permanent capital and circulating capital are reflected in a company's *funds flow statement.* Well-managed firms look carefully at cash flow, and tune capital expenditures to cash flow forecasts. An example is given in Figure 9.3.

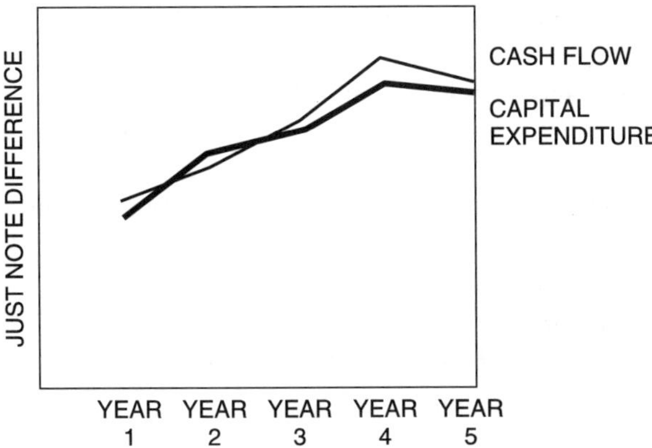

Figure 9.3 Capital expenditure correlated to cash flow at a major manufacturing firm

For instance, in response to an adverse market environment, investment in plant and equipment related to expanding production may be curtailed, bringing capital expenditure down. This may be a temporary measure, while overall the company intends to continue with a policy that emphasizes a commitment to capital spending directed at modernizing operations.

A fundamental challenge with estimates related to funds inflow and outflow is that the amount of capital a company needs is related to the financial riskiness of its business. This defies the boundaries of a standard methodology, and it has to be measured by volatility of:

- Its income, and
- Its cash flow.

The funds flow statement shows changes in the total amount of circulating capital, but not necessarily volatility in individual items comprising it. For management accounting purposes, however, it is important to look at the detailed flow of funds amounts. This is done through a *cash flow statement*, which tells how much cash is uncommitted and available for other uses. Its computation takes the operating cash flow and adjusts certain balance sheet items, subtracting current debt and capital expenditures.

- Table 9.3 presents a detailed cash flow statement from a major financial institution.
- By contrast, a presentation centring on main chapters only, is shown in Figure 9.4.

Table 9.3 Cash flow statement from a major financial institution

1. Cash flow from and used in operating activities

1.1 Net income

1.2 Adjustments to reconcile net income to cash flow from and used in operating activities

1.2.1 Non-cash items included in net profit and other adjustments:

- Depreciation of property and equipment
- Amortization of goodwill and other intangible assets
- Credit loss expense/recovery
- Equity in income of associates
- Deferred tax assets
- Net loss/gain from investing activities

1.2.2 Net increase/decrease in operating assets:

- Net due from/to banks
- Reverse repurchase agreements, cash collateral on securities borrowed
- Trading portfolio including net replacement values and securities pledged as collateral
- Loans/due to customers
- Accrued income, prepaid expenses and other assets
- Accrued income, prepaid expenses and other assets

1.2.3 Net increase/decrease in operating liabilities:

- Repurchase agreements, cash collateral on securities lent
- Accrued expenses and other liabilities

1.2.4 Income taxes paid

2. Cash flow from and used in investing activities

- Investments in subsidiaries and associates
- Disposal of subsidiaries and associates
- Purchase of property and equipment
- Disposal of property and equipment
- Net investment/divestment in financial investments

3. Cash flow from and used in financing activities

3.1 Monetary transactions:

- Net money market paper issued
- Net movements in treasury shares and treasury share contract activity
- Capital issuance
- Capital repayment by par value reduction
- Dividends paid
- Issuance of long-term debt

(*continued*)

Table 9.3 (*Continued*)

	• Repayment of long-term debt • Issuance of trust preferred securities • Dividend payments to/and purchase from minority interests
3.2	**Net cash flow from and used in financing activities** • Effects of exchange rate differences
3.3	**Net increase/decrease in cash equivalents** • Cash and cash equivalents, beginning of the year
3.4	**Cash and cash equivalents** • Cash and balances with central banks • Money market paper • Due from banks maturing in less than three months

The first box in sources of cash in Figure 9.4 is net income. For management accounting purposes some companies take *operating income* and the gain or loss in the value of assets and liabilities. This means marking-to-market and passing gains or losses into the income stream.

These are the mechanics. As far as the dynamics of cash flows are concerned, what it basically means is financial staying power. For instance, by telling how much of the generated capital is uncommitted, free cash flow indicates how much is available for other uses fulfilling the firm's objectives.

Notice, however, that there also exist many misconceptions associated with cash flow. One of them is the use of depreciation as source of funds. Depreciation is cash because it affects taxable income. In some companies, from time to time depreciation actually exceeds net profit. But in the general case cash from depreciation is a half-truth. As an expert accountant put it:

- Depreciation should be sued for non-support.
- It does *not* provide funds or any other assets for replacement of property.[2]

Additionally, safety margins should be established in connection to estimates of cash flow from sales of the company's products and services. These may be influenced through price wars; changes in product design leading to repricing; the industrialization of a service company's production activities with commensurate decrease in costs; and policies able to assure that not only the company is competitive but also remains so.

In conclusion, every entity has an interest in improving the accuracy with which cash flows are estimated. Any asset or liability that has an expected

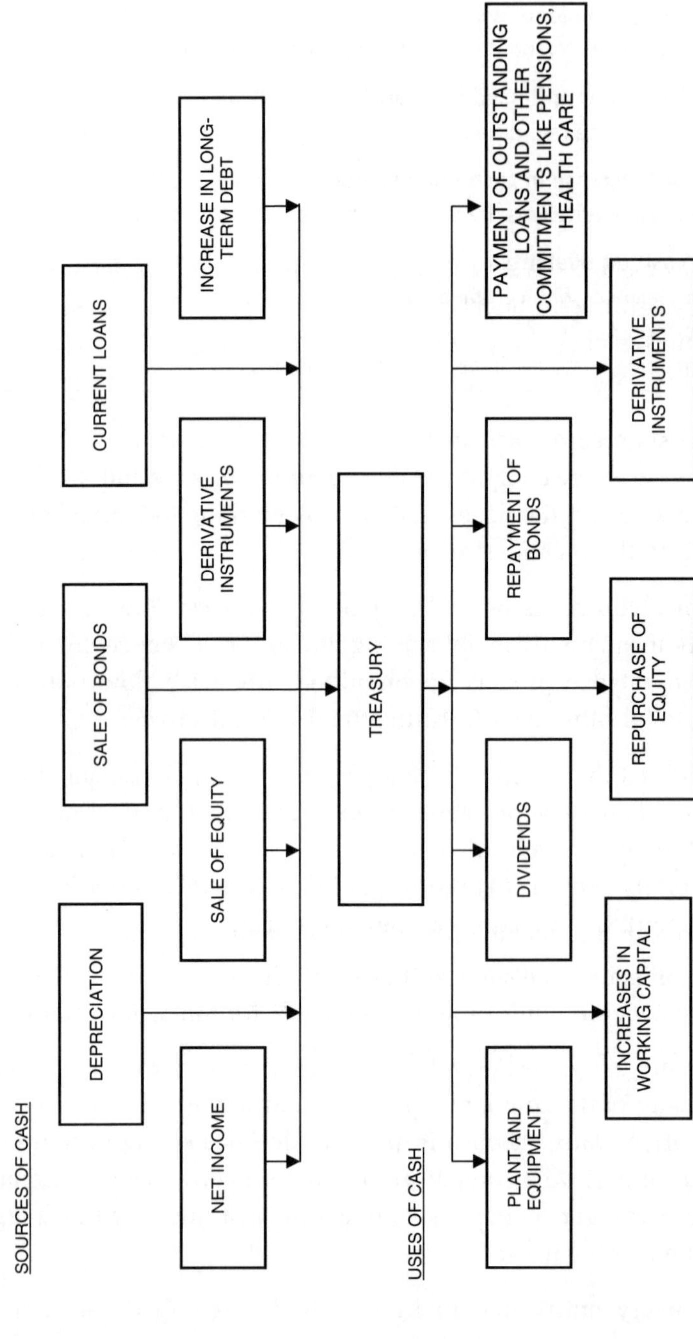

Figure 9.4 The cash flow statement is one of management accounting's pillars

future cash flow should be discounted to the present day. Positions can be tested in terms of their cash flow contribution by discounting or marking-to-market. This is particularly true of derivative financial instruments. A good example is provided by cash flow practices at the Mitsubishi Bank. For trading and risk management purposes, swaps and futures are classified into two major categories:

- Generic, and
- Non-generic, or irregular.

This decision has been taken on the basis that the number of derivative securities is practically unlimited, but there must be *one* basic pricing which reflects the market and makes possible planning and control. 'The only valid one is *cash flow*,' said a senior executive at the Mitsubishi Bank during our meeting in the early 1990s.

6. A company's liquidity obligations

Liquidity refers to an entity's ability to meet its current obligations. Therefore, liquidity is a relative concept having to do with size, frequency, and relationships of liabilities due; and with current assets that presumably provide the source of funds to meet such obligations. By contrast, *solvency* talks of an entity's ability to meet interest cost, repayment schedules, and other obligations in the longer term. The most important elements in judging a company's solvency are:

- Debt capital, and
- Equity capital.

Debit capital is a different name for liabilities, particularly those of the medium to longer term. Failure to meet debt capital requirements usually leads creditors to taking legal action, which may force the entity to bankruptcy. *Equity capital* is much less risky to the firm, because shareholders receive dividends only at the discretion of the board (more on this in section 7).

- Theoretically, liquidity and solvency are different notions.
- Practically, under certain conditions they merge, as Dr Gerry Corrigan, then chairman of the New York Fed, pointed out to Dr Alan Greenspan in September 1987.[3]

As far as both liquidity and solvency are concerned, companies must be able to meet their obligations when they fall due. In commercial banking, for example, such obligations mainly comprise deposits at sight or short notice, term deposits, bought money as well as commitments to lend, including unutilized overdraft facilities, and commitments due to derivatives losses.

In any period of time, existing obligations and their incidence vary between different entities, but the maintenance of an assured capacity to meet them is an essential principle of sound governance which is common to all firms. The responsibility of assuring liquidity and solvency lies with the board, CEO, and senior management. For liquidity reasons, the company must hold sufficient immediately available cash or liquefiable assets subject to:

- The provision that marketable assets vary in quality and in terms, and
- The estimation of the prices at which such marketable assets are capable of being sold is subject to uncertainty.

Senior management must also be able to secure an appropriately matching future profile of cash flows from maturing assets, always accounting for shortfalls if borrowers are unable to repay. While shortfalls can lead to serious problems, abundant liquidity that is unwanted results in lower profits.

Sometimes abundant liquidity is the result of management's failure to closely watch appropriate liquidity ratios. In other cases, it is a symptom of the attraction presented by cash and interest-bearing money. High liquidity may also represent deferred spending, or it may be needed to supplement falling income.

In the banking industry, for example, a valid liquidity strategy is that of maintaining an adequately diversified deposit base in terms of both maturities and type of counterparties. Depending on the individual counterparty's standing, and on the general liquidity situation in the financial system, this might add up to a hedging policy that can provide the ability to raise fresh funds without undue cost.

Classical measures of liquidity have involved a comparison of deposit liabilities, in part or in total, with the available stock of certain assets generally accepted to be *liquid*. The benefit from this approach is simplicity, but the classical method:

- Does not account for factors that are non-traditional, such as derivative financial instruments
- Does not reflect the fact that many accounts are not sharply liquid or non-liquid, but have tonalities of grey, and
- Does not benefit from the development of asset and liability management techniques, for controlling liquidity through cash flows.

Neither are legacy methods for liquidity management accounting for a bank's creditworthiness as perceived by depositors, its position in the system of credit institutions, or the current financial conditions. Analyses that differentiate for these issues are more in touch with the real underlying liquidity condition.

Another example where a more analytical approach is advantageous is when distinctions are drawn between different types of deposits, for example between retail and wholesale deposits – and within retail demand between deposits and savings, including constraints associated to withdrawals from savings accounts. The stability and diversification of the deposit base should always be given due weight.

Additionally, known firm commitments to make funds available on a particular date must be incorporated in the appropriate time band at their full value. Liabilities should include any significant non-deposit commitments, which mature within the time span of the measurement, such as tax liabilities. Assets, too, should be measured by reference to their maturity and fair value.

Within the perspective of a liquidity study, the treatment of marketable assets must take account of the extent to which they can be sold quickly for cash, or used as security for borrowing. Quick liquefication means no fire sale, but quite the opposite: incurring little or no cost penalty.

Credit risk and market risk, which may impact on the assets' potential value, should also be accounted for. It is important to assure that the market for the asset is sufficient and there is stable demand for it. An important factor in fair valuation is the willingness of the central bank to use the assets in its normal market operations.

Different considerations affecting asset value are recognized in calculation of net worth and cash flows by applying varying discounts, normally against the market value of marketable assets. Assets known to be of doubtful value must be excluded from the general liquidity measurement, being treated on a case-by-case basis with considerable discount. In the general case, the further ahead a bank's assets mature, the more difficult it is to estimate confidently credit, market, and other risks which will characterize them at maturity.

7. Financing by equity or debt? The issue of financial staying power

In my book on *Economic Capital Allocation with Basel II*, I have treated quite extensively the wisdom, and lack of it, of the Modigliani–Miller hypothesis on using debt rather than equity for company financing.[4] The thesis behind doubt in regard to the Modigliani–Miller model has been that:

- Debt financing has inflated leveraging, and
- It has significantly contributed to financial instability in a downturn.

The reason why the equity *vs.* debt theme is once again brought into perspective in this text, is that it closely correlates with equity capital and debt capital, discussed in section 6 in connection to a firm's liquidity and solvency. It also impacts most significantly on the market's appreciation of a company and of the quality of its governance.

- Beyond a certain point of gearing, worried bondholders see to it that the cost of the firm's debt rises sharply.
- This pushes down the entity's credit rating, as independent rating agencies are watching out for market signals – and rightly so.

Modigliani and Miller have not been the only people to like debt. 'Debts are assets,' Henry Kaiser openly declared. 'It is through debts that you get the money to meet payrolls and buy the plant and equipment. Then, you finish the job and pay off your debts and everybody is happy.'[5] This fits well with the product cycle of a builder, but not with every business. Neither does it make sense when one is confronted with the policies of chronic debtors.

Kaiser looked upon entrepreneurial activity as a game with all the excitement of both winning and losing. From his early construction days, he knew there would be some jobs where he would make money, and other jobs where he might lose his shirt. The challenge would always be to come up with enough good-paying jobs to help his weathering the bad times.

- This is the principle underpinning investments, and
- It might be sound if one, as Kaiser states, is weathering a bad time, rather than accumulating more and more debt.

Tax laws promote indebtedness. Companies take on debt in order to benefit from the fact that interest payments are tax-deductible (at least in some countries, while dividends are taxable. (In fact, they are doubly taxable.) They also issue debt to profit from discrepancies in market value; but this should be done within limits.

For instance, a firm whose true value is underestimated by the stockmarket might do better by borrowing funds than by issuing more equity at undervalued price. Also, some managers assume that by replacing equity with debt their firm can boost shareholders' returns on the remaining shares. This, however, is not an unchallenged principle.

Some experts are of the opinion that a shrinking value of equity has certain advantages. It makes it cheaper to own a significant part of a given company's shares. It also allows shareholders to give management an equity stake at lesser cost, and enables a small group of shareholders, who increase their equity stake, to monitor company management and its performance. But there are also negatives. Therefore, corporate financial theory suggests that the choice between debt and equity should depend on four key factors:

- The rates at which debt and equity are taxed
- The likelihood that leveraging leads to default
- The potential costs of bankruptcy, and
- Conflicts of trust between managers, shareholders, bondholders, and other creditors.

For historical and cultural reasons, in many countries rational choices are not feasible in a global market sense. For instance, the above four factors are distorted in emerging economies, where several government policies, including nepotism, encourage companies to use either more equity or more debt depending on the whims of different politicians and ill-conceived protectionism.

Therefore, an analysis of the company's financial condition should take place both by country of operations, and on the basis of its consolidated statement. A rather classical measure the board and senior management can use to avoid high

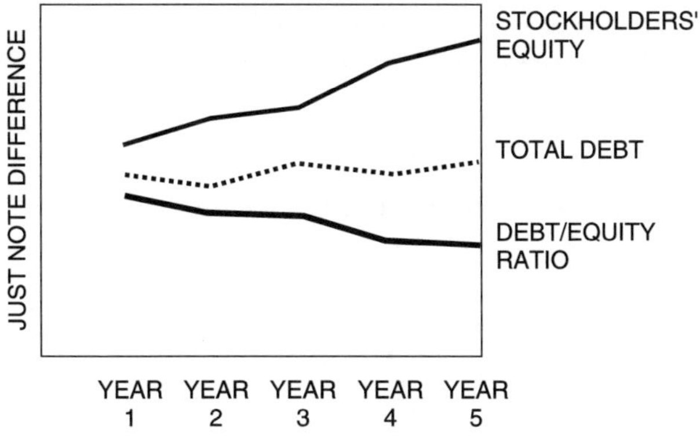

Figure 9.5 Debt/equity ratio: 5-year trend lines of a company with excellent governance

gearing is the trend in *debt/equity* ratio, also known as capital/equity ratio. The downside is that this ratio can be defined in two different ways.

- One definition of debt/equity includes current liabilities.
- The other definition excludes them.

Therefore, the user of this ratio must always carefully ascertain which is the intended meaning. This difference in regard to current liabilities is confusing, though some experts argue that in specific situations it is less so because a company may account for current liabilities in liquidity management – and they set their benchmarks accordingly.

In the general case, companies that concentrate on maintaining and strengthening their financial soundness, with the emphasis on debt management and enhancement of stockholders' equity position, have a shrinking debt/equity ratio. As a result of holding total debt more or less steady, but raising stockholder equity, this ratio moves south. The trend lines in Figure 9.5 come from a manufacturing company with top-tier management.

In conclusion, the objective of performing a contextual review of the company's debt *vs.* equity practices is to address important elements of corporate governance that are not readily captured through other forms of quantitative analysis. Another goal is to ascertain the firm's financial staying power, which is weakened through leveraging. Also, to examine the rationale of different practices and attributes in the way they affect the company's overall quality of governance.

Notes

1 *The Economist*, 15 October 2005.
2 Robert N. Anthony, *Management Accounting*. Richard D. Irwin, Homewood, IL, 1964.
3 Bob Woodward, *Maestro: Greenspan's Fed and the American Boom*. Simon & Schuster, New York, 2000.
4 D.N. Chorafas, *Economic Capital Allocation with Basel II: Cost and Benefit Analysis*. Elsevier, London, 2004.
5 Albert P. Heiner, Henry J. Kaiser: *Western Colossus*. Halo Books, San Francisco, 1991.

IFRS and Strategic Accounting Principles

1. Introduction

From January 2005, listed companies in the European Union must comply with the rules of the International Financial Reporting Standards (IFRS) elaborated by the London-based International Accounting Standards Board (IASB). Companies that are unlisted but have listed debt must comply with IFRS by 2007. For all companies, and most particularly those accustomed to old accounting standards, this is a challenge.[1]

Boards, CEOs, senior managers – in fact, all company employees – must appreciate that top-quality financial reporting is a hallmark of good governance. With about 80 countries implementing, or planning to apply, the new rules, IFRS has become a strategic accounting system on a global scale. Implementers must appreciate that:

- Generally acceptable sound standards provide a dependable view of the company's financial position and fundamental risks, and
- Viable and accurate accounting statements are critical not only to investment decisions of stockholders and bondholders, but also to decisions of the firm's own management.

To the contrary, publishing intentionally inaccurate or misleading accounting statements is evidence of deeper flaws in an entity's governance framework, and in its ethical standards. Creative accounting techniques subvert the spirit of fair play. They are designed to mask fraudulent activities undermining:

- Investor confidence, and
- A company's value as a whole.

Sound governance of the accounting process is an important safeguard in protecting the integrity of a firm. Beyond public disclosure, a rigorous and reliable accounting system provides management with critical information on which to base factual decisions that affect the company's future.

Accounting, as was said in the course of our meeting a senior executive of the US Financial Accounting Standards Board (FASB), is not a science that obeys strictly quantitative terms. In his opinion, which is well-founded, accounting is very much *qualitative* and *judgemental*. Who is to say:

- What is the appropriate allowance for bad debt?
- The proper reserve for legal risk, which may hit at any time?
- The right presentation of accounting results for planning and control reasons?

Precisely because the rules that should guide accounting and financial reporting are not self-evident, standards boards have taken on the mission of defining them. This is a never-ending job because accounting standards must always be reviewed in the light of changes in the business environment, as well as of violations to existing financial reporting rules, as these arise.

At Enron, for example, management was upfronting gains without any market evidence that gains exist. To stop such practices FASB is strengthening the statement of Financial Accounting Standard (SFAS) 133, taking account not only of Enron's, but also of WorldCom's and many others' violations and novel 'creative' practices in financial reporting.

A major conceptual difference between US GAAP, by FASB, and IFRS, by IASB, is that the former is very prescriptive, while the latter keeps its accounting rules at general lines. 'Our accounting rules are like the Ten Commandments,' said Wayne Upton, IASB's director of research. By contrast, US GAAP has several hundred pages of implementation guidance.

According to Upton, IASB is constantly on the watch for the ability of people and companies to structure a series of transactions through solid accounting rules. By contrast, prescriptive details are a matter of implementation at each jurisdiction adopting IFRS. This is a sound strategy given:

- The many legal and regulatory differences existing among the many nations adopting IFRS, and
- The procedural and cultural issues arising in these nations, given the diverse historical precedents in accounting and reporting regulations.

Many experts believe that, in the longer run, IFRS will have a positive influence on management practices. It will impact not only goodwill and accounts for pensions, but also major governance issues. For instance, how companies recognize revenue. 'At the end of the day what is important is the free cash flow', said Alastair Graham, senior vice president of Moody's, 'Not just the cash flow or EBITDA.'

To account for the impact of IFRS on the financial statements of the companies it covers, Moody's Investors Service has introduced eight adjustments normalizing the presentation and interpretation of financials. Examples are: inventory, share options, marking to market, and consolidations (see section 7). Generally, all corporate codes in Europe and America advocate that financial statements have to be accurate. The question is: 'Under which rules?' And, moreover, rules alone are not enough. The 'do's' and 'don'ts' must be properly updated and steadily controlled by supervisory authorities.

2. Why IFRS is a strategic accounting initiative

Disclosures about capital and risk associated with financial instruments are useful to all stakeholders – regulators, investors, and entities that deal with, transact and hold financial instruments of another entity – not only to banks for their loans, underwriting of securities, and derivatives activities.

Deregulation, and most particularly innovation, has made it very difficult to satisfactorily differentiate novel derivative instruments from one another, regarding their aftermath. The case study on Fiat's derivatives in Chapter 9, provides an example.

Whether for investment reasons, liquidity management purposes, wealth management or any other objective, transactions of a financial nature must be very transparent, and such transparency should be reflected in financial statements. Users of financial statements need information about not only capital levels but also in regard to risks arising from a transaction or portfolio position, including credit risk, market risk, operational risk and business risk (see Chapter 6).

Not only investors and regulators, but also the company's board, CEO, and senior management need to know the ability of the firm and its counterparties to identify, measure, monitor, and control assumed risks. Therefore, disclosure standards must see to it that clear and consistent reporting requirements apply to all entities so that:

- They operate on a level ground, and
- Users receive comparable information about capital, transactions, and risks being incurred.

These two bullets tell why financial accounting and management accounting converge in their objective. They also explain why it is to the advantage of all entities to follow the same rules. Additionally, good governance would suggest that the same IFRS rules and regulations are used both for financial and for management accounting.

By definition, the primary objective of *financial accounting* is that of providing financial information to people and entities outside the company: shareholders, bondholders, bankers, regulators, and other parties. To a considerable extent the techniques, rules, and conventions according to which financial accounting figures are collected and reported reflect the requirements of these outsiders and, as its title implies, IFRS is primarily oriented to their information needs.

By contrast, *management accounting* is concerned with accounting information that is useful to the firm's own management for its plans, decisions, and control action. Whether financial accounting and management accounting should base themselves on the same rules is an important recurrent theme.

The answer is 'yes', because the most crucial problems are no different. In terms of management accounting, a crucial issue concerning the board, CEO, CFO, and all of the company's management levels is use of accounting figures in:

- Recognition, and
- Timely solution of operational problems.

Furthermore, at the same time the company's managers are responsible for the content of financial accounting reports. It follows that governance can be improved if the same principles, rules, and conventions are used for financial accounting *and* management accounting – which means that IFRS could, and should, be made a strategic initiative for the entity's own internal accounting management information system (IAMIS).

As advice based on a recent experience, this strategic initiative should capitalize on the five pillars of IFRS: derivatives, goodwill, intangible assets, pensions, stock options. Here is a brief explanation of what comes under each of these headings:

- *Derivatives*: The company's balance sheet must show the current market value of all derivative instruments which it contains. This is the *fair value* principle (see section 4). Accruals has no meaning with derivatives.
- *Goodwill*: Companies can no longer amortize goodwill from acquisitions. Instead, they must conduct an annual impairment review, taking charge if the asset's value falls – no matter what may be the reason.
- *Intangible assets*: Management must both disclose and quantify the value of assets like patents, software, customer lists, trademarks, research, and development projects. These can no longer be lumped into goodwill.
- *Pensions*: Companies must appreciate the financial impact of pensions. For this, they need to account in full for pension liabilities and assets on their profit and loss statement of the year. Pension liabilities must be funded.

- *Stock options*: Management can no longer bury the cost of stock-based compensation as notes to financial accounts. In its financial statements, the company must show full value of all options granted to employees.

While every pillar implies changes in at least some of the established practices, the biggest one is the switch from historical cost accounting, where all items on the financial statement are based on accruals reflecting their original cost, to fair value accounting. The fair value method recognizes gains and losses in value on an ongoing basis, based on marking to market.

Additionally, IFRS rules unveil items that many European companies either buried as footnotes in their financial reports or simply did not reveal at all. Examples are pension liabilities. These and other changes in financial accounting have profound effects on balance sheets and P&L statements of 7000 listed European companies that have to switch their books to IFRS. Still, some experts reckon that:

- It will take up to two years before analysts and investors fully come to grips with what the changes mean in terms of company valuation, and
- When this happens analysts and investors will have a much better understanding of a company's financials, because IFRS forces every entity to disclose more information than ever before.

Not everybody, however, sees it this way. Many companies fought IFRS tooth and nail, most specifically International Accounting Standard (IAS) 39 (see section 4), and its fair value requirement. To put it mildly, this has been a case of distorted self-interest because, as the preceding paragraphs documented, the greater is the detail and accuracy of financial accounting and IAMIS, the better is the quality of governance.

The task faced by IASB, in establishing the new rules and regulations, has been substantial. 'One of the difficulties we encounter is dealing with the other prudential regulators,' said Wayne Upton during our meeting of 20 September 2005, meeting. 'Supervisory authorities usually have different priorities, as well as a large range of agendas.' Some of the differences lay in a long cultural tradition.

Many regulators are fully supportive of transparency. An example is regulators of Nordic countries. Others, however, think they should have information the market must not have. This is a largely paternalistic approach. The surprise is that even the US Federal Reserve, which is known for its open mind, has taken a view which recommends much less transparency in regard to hedge funds. Yet,

- The thin red line dividing regulated banks from unregulated hedge funds is becoming less and less visible, and
- If the world's financial system blows to pieces, the way to bet is that the reason would lie in the most leveraged financial industry – namely the hedge funds.

There is also a significant difference in the structure of regulatory bodies, from country to country, which finds its way into their response. In the UK, nearly all supervisory functions of a financial nature are integrated under the Financial Services Authority (FSA). In the United States there is the Fed, the Office of the Controller of the Currency (OCC), Federal Deposit Insurance Corp (FDIC), Office of Thrift Supervision (OTS), 52 state regulators (including District of Columbia and Puerto Rico), and 52 insurance regulators.

As far as regulatory bodies, and their functions, are concerned, beyond this comes the fact that some supervisors are endowed with direct authority, while others have to work by inverse delegation. In the general case, globalization has seen to it that the regulatory agenda includes a wide variety of frequently unspoken local agendas, as well as an enormous range of competencies. At the end of the day this:

- Provides different interpretations, by jurisdiction
- Aggravates the home–host problems in terms of regulatory coordination, and
- Makes difficult global integration of supervisor activities, which affects negatively companies operating transborder.[2]

Legal, cultural, and procedural differences that exist by jurisdiction inhibit effective coordination, which is quite worrisome in a global market. Take a loan's front fee as a case in point. If, for example, the loan is $10 000 at 4%, the front fee may be $200. The client gets $9800, but pays 4% on $1000. Some 20 years ago, in the United States, Statement of Financial Accounting Standards (SFAS) 91 normalized this practice. IAS 39 did so in 2005. But in many jurisdictions, who adopted IFRS, this is an alien concept which they now have to apply.

3. Disclosure about capital and the need for standards

IFRS rules reflect the International Accounting Standards Board's belief that information about *capital* is useful for all companies, investors, regulators, and other parties, as evidenced by the fact that several entities now set internal capital requirements. Also, industry norms established for some sectors, for instance banking, require capital levels defined by regulators. In a similar manner, the Insurance Advisory Steering Committee has proposed, in its draft statement of principles, that capital disclosure requirements should be introduced for insurers.

The best example on the evolution of general capital requirements in the globalized economy is provided by Basel I (of 1987) and Basel II (1999–2006). Both have been elaborated by the Basel Committee on Banking Supervision. With Basel II, the Basel Committee has upped the Basel I regulatory capital adequacy requirements, making them:

- Sensitive to risk being assumed, and
- Dynamic in their computation, as well as in the message they convey to the market.

This reflects more rigorous accounting standards, and is influenced by their need. Therefore, IASB correctly concluded that there should be norms on how information about capital is disclosed by companies. And, moreover, such disclosure should be set in the context of the firm's objectives, policies, and processes for managing capital and for controlling risk.

To better appreciate this statement the reader should keep in mind that even the most elaborate accounting standards are not cast in stone. Their application requires:

- Hypotheses, and
- Interpretations.

When preparing financial statements, management usually makes estimates and assumptions that affect the reported amount of capital and other assets, as well as the amount of liabilities, revenue, and expenses. Provisioning for some of these expenses involves uncertainty. An example is impairment of goodwill.

While the different parochial accounting standards that preceded IFRS differed from one another, sometimes significantly, nearly all of them treated in roughly the same way goodwill and other intangible assets.

The tool has been depreciation, which is a well-known method. By contrast, *impairment* is not only new but also involves uncertainty – and accounting for uncertainty requires a cultural change.

Of course, hypotheses and interpretations associated to accounting have been always present; particularly so in financial reporting. But IFRS requires that these are made at a higher level of confidence, and that they benefit from justification. This is a different ballgame than *historical costs*, typically involving balance at the beginning of the year, additions, write-offs, and balance at the end of the year. Such a fairly linear approach was followed in *accumulation* of goodwill and intangibles to reach net book value. IFRS does not work like that.

The estimation of impairment is not an exact art; the good news is that there is precedence to its usage. In the United States, SFAS 115, *Accounting for Certain Investments in Debt and Equity Securities*, and SEC's SAB 59, *Accounting for Noncurrent Marketable Equity Securities*, have already provided guidance on determining when an investment is other-than-temporarily impaired. For this purpose, companies must review their investments quarterly for indicators of such other-than-temporary impairments:

- Their determination requires significant judgement, and
- In making such judgement, management should employ a methodology that considers available quantitative and qualitative evidence in evaluating potential impairment.

If the cost of an investment written in the books exceeds its fair value, management must evaluate, among other factors, general market conditions, the duration and extent to which the fair value is less than cost, and its intent and ability to hold the investment. These factors have a great deal to do with available capital, but, by necessity, many are subjective.

This is not new to the reader. The Introduction already brought to attention the fact that, in large measure, accounting rules often require judgemental interpretation. The presentation of results is itself an art, whose heterogeneity can reach significant proportions. By contrast, decisions on how to present accounting entries require a level of homogeneity; hence the need for standards based on:

- Research and analysis
- The ability to reach a certain consensus, and
- The virtue of describing in a comprehensive manner what is being reported.

Achieving general acceptance for a given standard, and maintaining support for the process of standards-setting, has become particularly crucial because of the speed our economy moves. In terms of standardization, in the United States FASB is constantly deliberating far-reaching norms that are connected with financial reporting models. It also devotes time to practices concerning some of the mechanics of the financial accounting profession itself.

Such initiatives by the Financial Accounting Standards Board rest on the understanding that accounting standards are essential beyond disclosure about capital, all the way to the proper functioning of the economy. Decisions about allocation of financial and other resources rely heavily on credible, concise, and comprehensive accessing information – even if, as stated, assumptions and hypotheses are always present.

A multinational may manage capital in a number of ways and be subject to different capital requirements by jurisdiction. An example provided by IASB is that of a conglomerate which includes entities that undertake both insurance and banking activities, and operates in different geographical regions. The way to bet is that solely an aggregate disclosure of capital requirements, or of about how capital is managed,

- Cannot provide useful information, and
- It can even distort the user's understanding of a financial statement.

If this is the case, *then* the company must disclose information on its capital base separately, in a way that enables users of its financial statements to evaluate its capital and other crucial variables. IFRS specifies that every company shall also disclose qualitative information about its objectives, policies, and processes for managing capital. This should include a description of what it regards as capital, its status, and its adequacy in connection to its assumed obligations. Also:

- How it is meeting its objectives for managing capital
- When it is subject to externally imposed capital requirements, and
- What is the nature of these capital requirements, as well as how they are incorporated into the management of capital.

To be complete, this mainly qualitative information should be accompanied by quantitative data about capital targets set by management. Another qualitative input is the consequences of non-compliance *if* and *when* the entity has not complied with capital targets set by regulators and other authorities.

As is documented by this evolution in reporting standards, standards setters consider any significant areas of deficiency in financial accounting that might be improved through new norms. They are also watching over international comparability of accounting standards concurrent with improving the quality of financial reporting.

As in the case of technology standards set by the International Standards Organization (ISO), the American Standards Institute (ANSI), and other standards bodies, references provided by financial and accounting standards constitute a conceptual framework. This helps to establish reasonable bounds for judgement in reporting information that is sound and useful, and in increasing understanding of, as well as confidence in, the contents of reports being released.

4. Fair value, IAS 39 and corresponding US standards

International Accounting Standard 39 has been the most controversial of all IFRS rules. Fair value accounting requires that for each class of financial assets and liabilities a firm must disclose value in a way that permits it to be compared with the corresponding carrying amount in its balance sheet. By definition, *fair value* is the value paid by a willing seller to a willing buyer under other than fire sale conditions.

Fair value accounting is by now second nature to American companies and to those foreign companies quoted on US stock exchanges, and therefore using US GAAP. The concept of fair value accounting was introduced in 1999 with SFAS 133. But this notion is rather new to other firms. As such, it represents significant cultural change requiring:

- Marking to market inventoried derivatives and other instruments for fair value reasons, and
- A departure from the classical accruals method leading to book value, which can be quite inaccurate.

Under IAS 39 some of what is currently shareholder funds will be classified as liabilities. For instance, if a bond pays no cash but shares, it should be seen and reported as a liability. As far as the banking industry is concerned, this can have significant impact on the method of meeting Tier-1 capital requirements.

For financial instruments such as short-term trade receivables and payables, when the carrying amount is a reasonable approximation of fair value, no disclosure of fair value is required. Otherwise, like SFAS 133 in the United States, IAS 39 expands the use of fair value for measuring and reporting on:

- Financial assets
- Financial liabilities, and
- Derivative instruments.

IAS 39 also provides for limited use of hedge accounting (see section 5), but sets criteria for recognition and derecognition. This comes beyond IAS 32, which calls for compound instruments such as embedded derivatives, to be split into their components, and accounted for accordingly.

Volatility in fair value is primarily, but not exclusively, due to market risk. For instance, currency exchange risk arises on financial instruments that are denominated in a currency other than the functional currency of the entity. Other examples of fluctuation in fair value are commodity price risk and equity price risk. (In fact, equity itself is a commodity.)

The rules of IFRS require that, in disclosing fair value, a company must group financial assets and liabilities into classes, and offset them only to the extent that their related carrying amounts are offset in the balance sheet. Moreover, in its financial statement an entity shall disclose:

- Method and assumptions applied in determining fair values of financial assets and financial liabilities, and
- Other hypotheses, such as estimated prepayment rates, rates of projected credit losses, interest or discount rates, and so on.

Behind these requirements lies the need outlined in the preceding two sections: that every entity must disclose information enabling users of its financial statements to appreciate its capital and evaluate the nature and extent of risks arising from financial instruments to which it has been exposed:

- During the period, and
- At reporting date.

As contrasted to US GAAP, IAS 39 integrates seven or eight different SFAS standards by FASB; not only the better known FAS 133 which addresses derivatives. For instance, part of IAS 39 are some procedures prescribed by FAS 91 regarding accounting for new loans. References to this broader coverage have been made in a meeting at IASB. It is proper to bring to the reader's attention, however, that in the United States several agencies develop reporting rules. For instance, the 2005 Annual report by Microsoft states: 'We account for the licensing of software in accordance with American Institute of Certified Public Accountants (AICPA) Statement of Position (SOP) 97-2, '*Software Revenue Recognition*'. The application of SOP 97-2 requires judgment, including whether a software arrangement includes multiple elements, and if so, whether *vendor-specific objective evidence* (VSOE) of fair value exists for those elements.'

Microsoft's 2005 Annual Report further states that changes to the elements in a software arrangement, the ability to identify VSOE for those elements, the fair value of the respective elements, and changes to a product's estimated life cycle could materially impact the amount of earned and unearned revenue. It also points out that judgement is also required to assess whether future releases of certain software represent:

- New products, or
- Upgrades and enhancements to existing ones.

The same Annual Report underlines that Microsoft accounts for research and development costs in accordance not with one but with *several* accounting pronouncements, including SFAS 2, *Accounting for Research and Development Costs*, and SFAS 86 *Accounting for the Costs of Computer Software to be Sold, Leased, or Otherwise Marketed*. SFAS 86 specifies that:

- Costs incurred internally in researching and developing a computer software product should be charged to expense until technological feasibility has been established for the product.
- But after technological feasibility is established, all software costs should be capitalized until the product is available for general release to customers.

Judgement is, most evidently, required in determining when technological feasibility of a product can be established. And as the reader is aware from section 3, judgement is also present with practically every interpretation and implementation of accounting and financial reporting rules.

Finally, an interesting case to bring to the reader's attention is that of fair value of debt. The fair value of a company's debt is determined using pricing models that reflect one percentage point shifts in appropriate yield curves. The fair value of investments is determined through a combination of:

- Pricing, and
- Duration models.

For starters, duration is a linear approximation that works well for modest changes in yields and generates a symmetrical result. In 1938, Frederick Macaulay developed the duration algorithm that bears his name. Its output can be used as a proxy for value over the length of time a bond investment is outstanding.[3]

Over the years, the duration algorithm has evolved different versions. Modified duration, with greater price sensitivity, is an example. Another is average duration, assumed for positions that fall into each time band. More sophisticated pricing models are reflecting the convexity of the price/yield relationship. As such:

- They provide greater precision, and
- Take account of asymmetry of price movements for interest rate changes in opposite directions.

The impact of convexity is more pronounced in longer-term maturities and low interest rate environments. As this example demonstrates, modern financial reporting and management control not only involve assumptions that may be subjective, but also require appropriate choice of models. This brings into perspective *model risk*. The reader should keep these references in mind when evaluating an accounting system's dependability, as well as the action of its implementers.

5. Hedging and hedge accounting

The *Oxford Popular Dictionary and Thesaurus* defines a *hedge* as a fence of bushes or shrubs. Or, alternatively, as avoiding giving a direct answer or making a commitment. Neither definition is fully applicable to financial hedging but, ironically, both have a bit of truth in them.

In banking, finance, and treasury operations, the objective of *true hedging* is the reduction of risk being assumed. For instance, hedges are made for physical commodities using futures and options. But while a hedge may reduce the *price risk* in the physical commodity market, the hedger becomes subject to *basis risk* and hedging expenses. *Basis risk* is the difference between the:

- Cash price of the commodity being hedged, and
- Futures market price providing the hedge.

In principle, hedging aims to reduce the risk on a *hedged* instrument by combining it with a *hedging* instrument. The latter may be an option, forward, future or swap. Theoretically, through hedging value changes in instrument 'A' are offset by value changes in instrument 'B'. Practically, this is never the case because the behaviour of the hedged and hedging instruments is most often asymmetric.

Particular conditions existing at the time of initiating a hedge will be chief determinants in the choice of hedge instrument, and of the scenario to be followed. For instance, a chosen hedging strategy may exploit seasonal and inter-commodity price patterns in two ways:

- As a guide to selecting the hedge vehicle, and
- In the evaluation of a chosen hedge programme.

However, the historical pattern of the direction of a commodity's price volatility, or extrapolation of futures prices from current spot price, is not a reliable guide to the pattern spot prices will actually take. An underlying seasonal variation in prices, the market's perception of a different direction of price, or other reasons, can see to it that the investor's (or speculator's) hedge turns on its head. Also, quite frequently, hedging gives asymmetric results.

These are important background notions in a discussion about hedging. If standards setters and regulators are so careful in spelling out hedge account rules, it is because they know that when talking of hedging nothing is set in stone.

Take as an example current-earnings accounting which uses derivatives designated as *hedges of fair value exposure*. This means hedges of firm commitments, whether assets or liabilities. For financial reporting purposes, the gain or loss on such transactions should be included in the profit and loss account. Also to be recognized and included in earnings is the offsetting loss or gain on a firm contract.

For most commodities and transactions, a sound *hedging* policy requires a global market viewpoint rather than a more limited consideration of trends in prices and/or in industry sectors. Moreover, as far as decisions on hedging are concerned, a great deal depends on the intended use of the hedge and resulting designation.

For a derivative instrument designated as a fair-value hedge, the gain or loss is recognized in earnings in the period of change, together with the offsetting loss or gain on the hedged item attributed to the risk being hedged. For a derivative instrument designated as a cash flow hedge:

- The effective portion of the derivative's gain or loss is recognized in earnings when the hedged exposure affects earnings.
- The ineffective portion of the derivative's gain or loss is also recognized in earnings.

A hedge frequently done among multinational firms concerns foreign currency risk. Current assets and inventoried transactions, as well as projected transactions and assets, are exposed to currency risk. Therefore, companies monitor their foreign currency exposures daily and try to protect themselves against current volatility.

Options are often used to hedge a portion of forecasted international revenue for up to three years in the future and are designated as cash flow hedging instruments. For US companies this falls under SFAS 133, *Accounting for Derivative Instruments and Hedging Activities*. IAS 39 also provides rules for hedge recognition.

Hedges are also made for equities price risk, because equity investments are subject to market price volatility. Some companies, as well as individual investors, use options to hedge fair values and cash flows on certain equity securities. They determine the security selected for hedging by evaluating:

- Market conditions
- Up-front costs, and
- Other relevant factors.

A very frequently done hedge is for interest rate risk. Even if the fixed-income portfolio is diversified and consists primarily of investment grade securities to minimize credit risk, market risk is omnipresent. Many firms use exchange-traded option and future contracts, as well as over-the-counter swap contracts (which however are not designated as hedging instruments under SFAS 133) to hedge interest rate risk.

It should be fairly obvious that, in all these examples, *if* different accounting valuation methods are used for the different instruments, such as historical cost and accruals for the hedged item and marketing-to-market for the hedging, *then* the result will be significant volatility in the profit and loss account. Hence the interest in employing a specific accounting treatment, known as *hedge accounting*. Hedge accounting works in two ways:

- It either defers the recognition of losses
- Or, alternatively, brings forward the recognition of gains in the profit and loss statement.

In this manner, gain or loss from the hedged instrument is recognized at the same time as the offsetting gain or loss from the hedging instrument. To avoid situations where hedging relationships are identified as ex post to deliberately massage profits and losses, the International Accounting Standards Board laid down a number of specific requirements, which must be fulfilled to qualify for hedge accounting. The most important are:

- Hedging relationship clearly identified and documented at inception
- Evidence that such relationships are effective, and
- The requirement that a hedge's aftermath must be highly probable, if this is a forecasted transaction.

The message these three bullets conveys is that a hedge can only qualify for hedge accounting if it passes an *effectiveness test*. For instance, changes in the value of the hedged item and the hedging instrument, should almost fully offset each other at designation. In addition, actual results realized over the life of the hedge must remain within a narrow margin in order for it to continue to be considered effective. Effectiveness is a precondition for hedge accounting.[4]

6. A model based approach to assets and liabilities management

As part of their assets and liabilities management (ALM) programme, financial institutions, and other corporations, enter into various interest rate and foreign exchange contracts. Many of them are derivative instruments, including interest rate swaps (IRS), forward rate swaps (FRS), cross-currency swaps, as well as forwards, futures, options, caps and floors.

- The goal is to manage overall interest rate, foreign currency, and other market risk exposures.
- Eventually, the aftermath of all these transactions will show up in the consolidated financial statement.

Prior to the implementation of IFRS, at many European credit institutions ALM contracts have been accounted for on an accrual basis. For instance, swap income and expense were reported in *interest revenue* or *interest expense*, applicable to the related assets or liabilities. Yield-related payments or receipts associated with swap contracts were accrued over the terms of the contract. Gains (losses) realized on other ALM contracts:

- Were deferred and amortized over the term of the related assets or liabilities, and
- Were included as adjustments to interest revenue or interest expense.

While with IFRS the accruals method of accounting has been, so to speak, put to rest, the methodology top-tier companies have developed around it, including models and expert systems, is still valid, albeit with some updating. Particularly interesting in connection to a sophisticated ALM methodology is the family of models written to support assets and liabilities type management decisions. An example is provided in Figure 10.1.

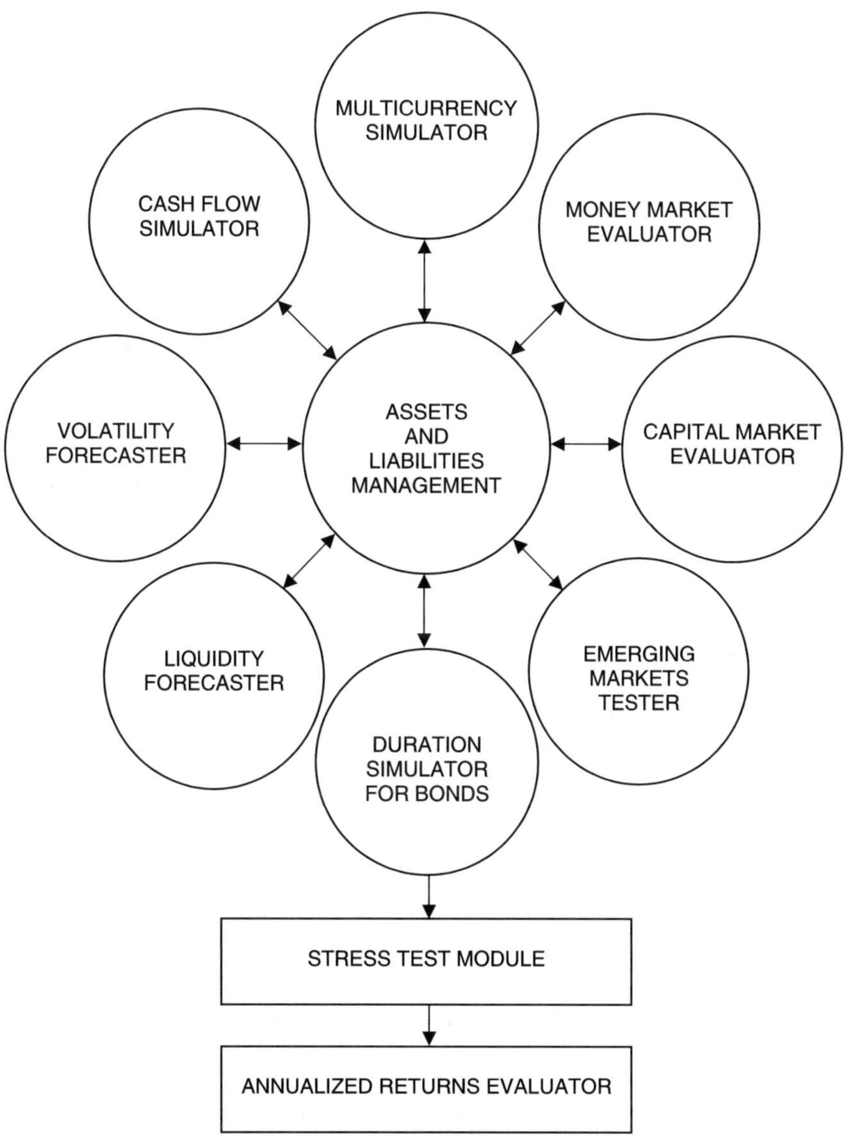

Figure 10.1 A family of portfolio management models for ALM

In this solution, the money market evaluator addresses two key variables which, up to a point, correlate: market liquidity and interest rate risk. The capital market evaluator targets fair value of equities, including available-for-sale securities. An expert system assists in the judgemental aspect of accounting for equity investment. This process involves determining whether an other-than-temporary decline in value of the investment has been sustained. Conversion to IFRS led to a change in this module:

- First determining whether an investment has sustained an other-than-temporary decline in its value
- Then, in case the answer is 'yes', writing down the investment to its fair value by a charge to earnings.

This is a good example of an application that cannot be handled effectively through legacy type computer programmes. It requires expert systems and, more specifically, *fuzzy engineering* which permits one to integrate uncertainty into the model – and therefore the outcome.

While deterministic models, characterized by algorithmic solutions, have their place, their domain of applicability is constrained by the judgemental processes (to which I have been making reference), as well as by the need to:

- Include a growing number of qualitative factors, and
- Integrate data on economic, social, demographic and other trends and their patterns.

Chapter 5 has explained the processes that enter into forecasting. The analyst, and by extension the banker and the investor, must be an extrapolator of trends. This often includes speculative visions embedded into scenarios. Scenarios force people to relate events to one another in narrative form.

Scenarios that involve important qualitative factors do not rely on computers but on *discussion* and *imagination*. Their primary tool is talk. The best scenarios, along this frame of reference, begin with a surprise-free pattern of development, imagining the changes that are most likely to occur in the absence of unforeseeable events. Then, they bring into the picture possible though unlikely types of economic, financial, and political turmoil.

This approach goes beyond what has become by now institutionalized quantitative models like, for instance, value at risk (VAR). An integrative qualitative and quantitative evaluation is dependent on both likely and unlikely specific facts and circumstances. For example, factors considered in determining whether an other-than-temporary decline in value has occurred include:

- The market value of the security in relation to its cost basis
- Financial condition of the investee, which impact on his or her decision to sell
- Further-out intent and ability to retain the investment for a sufficient period of time to allow for recovery in its market value.

In evaluating the above factors for available-for-sale securities, a sophisticated model would experiment with a decline in value to be other-than-temporary if, say, the quoted market price of the security is 20% or more below the investment's cost basis for a period of six months or more. Or, the quoted market price of the security is 50% or more below the security's cost basis at any quarter end. In experimental finance:

- The first is known as the *20% criterion*
- The second as the *50% criterion.*

There may however be instances in which impairment losses are recognized even if the 20% and 50% criteria are not satisfied. For instance, there may be a plan to sell the security in the near term if the fair value is below its cost basis. Other factors indicative of an other-than-temporary decline include recurring operating losses, credit defaults in connection to debt instruments, and subsequent rounds of financing at an amount below the cost basis of the investment.

The services provided by the stress module shown in Figure 10.1 address themselves to the whole constellation of ALM models in that aggregate. Stress testing also puts severe demands on selected crucial factors – for instance, the firm's solvency, by assuming that the pattern in the 50% criterion applies in a range of inventoried positions.

Both liquidity and solvency (see Chapter 9) must be stress-tested because high demand for capital by big and thirsty industries may siphon off funds for other investments having macro-economic impact. When this happens, available financing is decreasing. In the application that lies in the background of this discussion, a knowledge engineering module tests interest differential on interest rate swaps:

- Accrued over the lives of the contracts, and
- Recorded in trading account profits and commissions.

If not closely matched with offsetting swaps, such contracts are marked to market, with changes in market value recorded in trading account profits and commissions. Fees on interest rate swaps are deferred and amortized over the lives of the contracts.

Additionally, because model risk is omnipresent in the specific case of the application under discussion, auditing has been enriched with staff able to exercise model control through appropriate testing. Another element of the adopted ALM solution is test for compliance, mainly based on scenario analysis reflecting cases that in the past escaped management control.

Work currently under way targets an improved method for ALM, including knowledge engineering bridges to a virtual consolidated statement of financial position. This is based on fair value accounting, incorporating guidance provided by IASB to assure some uniformity in procedures. A policy followed by the entity that informs this case study, is to:

- Address the standards issue by level of complexity, and
- Establish a hierarchy of complexity control to test the accuracy of fair value estimates.

This approach is based on the understanding that the knowledge on which an investor, or other decision-maker, must act is never likely to meet strict standards of financial, legal or scientific proof. Therefore, one must be forthright about the nature of uncertainty.

The fact that in real life we must deal with cases that are plausible but less than certain of full proof, combined with the need to have order of magnitude estimates as guides to decisions, has led to *virtual consolidated statements* of financial consolidation. The underlying concept is no different from that underpinning a virtual balance sheet,[5] aiming at rapid production of financial reports, albeit at reduced level of accuracy. For IAMIS reasons – but not for regulatory reporting – a 3–4% error rate is admissible.

7. Virtual consolidated financial statements

As has been explained in preceding sections, the preparation of a financial statement in conformity with IFRS, or US GAAP, requires management to make estimates and assumptions that affect the reported amounts of assets and liabilities, as well as of contingent A&L, at financial statement date. Therefore, actual results could differ from those estimates, even in regulatory financial reporting and certainly in virtual consolidated financial statement (VCFS) of financial condition, which include the accounts of a company and its subsidiaries. In principle:

- Material intercompany balances and transactions are eliminated in consolidation.
- But client transactions are recorded on a settlement date basis, as with a financial statement for regulatory reasons.

Securities borrowed and securities loaned are recorded at the amount of cash collateral advanced or received. Adjustments that result from translating foreign currency financial statements are reported as a separate component of stockholder's equity. A general form of a consolidated statement of financial condition is shown in Table 10.1.

The level of leverage embedded in these positions can be appreciated through different indices that are not difficult to interpret. For instance, securities sold under agreement to repurchase may be nearly half the total liabilities, and the repos alone may represent seven times or more stockholder equity. (This example about 'seven times' comes from an analysis of the statement of a highly geared company.)

Securities purchased under agreements to resell and securities sold under agreements to repurchase, are collateralized financing transactions. They are carried

Table 10.1 General lines characterizing a consolidated statement of financial condition

Assets

- Cash and cash equivalents
- Cash and securities segregated under prevailing regulations
- Securities purchased under agreements to resell
- Receivables from brokers and dealers
- Receivables from clients
- Other assets

Liabilities and stockholder's equity

Liabilities:

- Drafts payable
- Loans payable
- Securities sold under agreements to repurchase
- Payable to brokers and dealers
- Payable to clients
- Securities sold but not yet purchased
- Accounts payable, accrued expenses
- Other liabilities

Subordinated liabilities

Stockholder's equity:

- Preferred stock
- Common stock and additional paid-in capital
- Accumulated deficit
- Cumulative foreign currency translation adjustments

at their contract amounts, plus accrued interest; and they are subject to both credit risk and market risk – an exposure that may be fairly significant and of which the board, CEO, and senior management must be steadily updated through VCFS:

- *Assets* recorded at market or fair value include cash, securities owned, and cash & securities segregated under prevailing regulations.
- *Liabilities* recorded at market or fair value include securities sold but not yet purchased.

In the virtual (as in the regulatory) consolidated financial statement, instruments recorded at amounts that approximate market value generally have variable interest rates or short-term maturities. Accordingly, their market values are not materially affected by changes in interest rates. Assets that are recorded at amounts approximating market value:

- Consist primarily of short-term financial instruments, and
- They include agreements to resell securities borrowed, and certain other receivables.

Short-term liabilities, which include agreements to repurchase, loans payable, securities loaned and certain other payables and accrued interest, are also recorded at amounts that approximate fair value. Because with IAMIS management should not lie to itself, it would be a false belief to think that market risk is mitigated by:

- Hedging transactions, or
- Static trading limits.

The most important contribution of VCFS is to bring home the point that the company faces an outstanding exposure *even if* it thinks its positions are hedged. Because derivatives risk can turn the most carefully prepared financial plan on its head, good governance also suggests the wisdom of preparing interactively, on request, a report with both:

- Notional principal amounts (NPA), and
- Demodulated NPA to the level of assumed risk, also known as *credit equivalent* amounts (see section 8).

Because nothing is static in business, hedge effectiveness must be measured steadily by comparing the change in fair value of each hedged position at applicable market rate. This continuous monitoring is as necessary for currency risk as it is for interest-rate risk, and the price of every other commodity (see also Chapter 14 on the need for pattern analysis).

The fact that a company enters into interest-rate swap agreements to manage its risk between fixed and variable interest rates, does not mean that the positions it has assumed are free of risk. The same reference is valid about hedging the future value of our produce:

- Theoretically forward sales protect from price pressure.
- Practically, if the market turns around, forward sales become a drag to profits, and sometime a serious one.

In the 1990s, gold mines got into the habit of selling forward their produce every time the price of gold, which had long been stagnant, edged up a bit. This worked well for a number of years, but those gold companies who were 'star hedgers' got burned when in 2005 the price per ounce soared, as shown in Figure 10.2.

Whether upward or downward, a trend in the price of a commodity holds many surprises. In the last week of November 2005, for example, the gold price jumped $10 per ounce to $496, continuing to build upon its gains. December 7 took bullion to a 28-year high at $514 per ounce. Prior to that spark, bullion had peaked at $503 on 14 December 1987 – 18 years earlier.

The irony is that gold producers who were 'best hedged' in an environment of depressed price per ounce were precisely those who felt the most pain when the good news came. A December 2005, study by Merrill Lynch identified Bema Gold Corp, Northgate Minerals, and Buonaventura as the companies with most exposure to the price hike in terms of *lost profits*. They lost money precisely

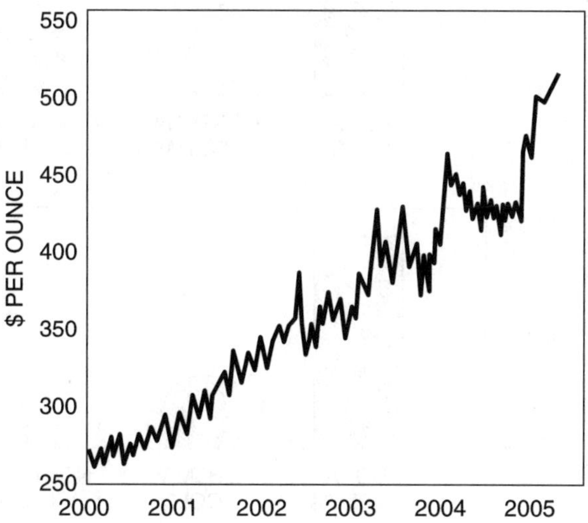

Figure 10.2 The upward trend in price of gold bullion and the 2005 spike

because of their hedging.[6] The pattern of income that went down the drain is different by company. As Figure 10.3 shows:

- Bema Gold had 'hedged' nearly 50% of its 2005 forecast production, but 'only' 7% of its reserves.
- Buonaventura had hedged over 30% of its 2005 production, and a whopping 18% of its reserves.

It needs no explaining that hedging proved a disaster to the companies, which found themselves so deeply committed that they could not benefit from price upswings. Their shareholders were unhappy. Boards, CEOs, and senior managers should not be found sleeping when it comes to *hedging risk*, and a virtual consolidated financial statement available in real time is the best way to keep them steadily awake.

8. The algorithm for credit equivalence

One of the better methods for the control of derivatives risk is to focus on *credit equivalence*, which is essentially morphing market exposure into a corresponding credit risk. An effective algorithm for doing so is to *demodulate* the notional

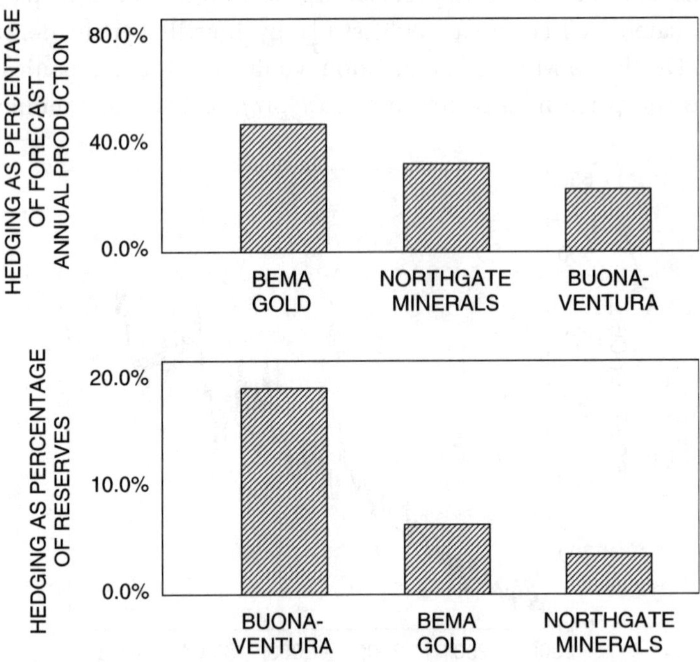

Figure 10.3 Hedging strategies on gold bullion that turned on their head in 2005

principal amount (NPA) of derivatives exposure in portfolio positions, down to the level of real money at risk – which is a sort of toxic waste.

Demodulation can be done individually by type of instrument, which is the better method. Or, it can be calculated on the basis of an envelope of possible replacement values, during the lifetime of the contract under derivatives positions. The challenge in terms of risk management is to bring this notional amount to the level of pure risk.[7]

With an approach that addresses each type of instrument, the NPA must be divided by a factor that is, principally, a function of the volatility of the instrument to which it applies, but at the same time accounts for prevailing market volatility and market liquidity. Variables such as high gearing, transparency in the entity's financial information, and market psychology, also have an impact on the value of the demodulator. Other things being equal:

- *If* the derivative instrument is leveraged or exotic
- *Then*, the divisor of the notional principal amount will be smaller, giving a higher value of money at risk.

Moreover, the greater is market volatility and/or liquidity, the smaller should be the divisor. Another criterion in terms of risk is the duration of the inventoried instrument following the derivatives transaction. Prudence advises that the majority of inventoried derivatives positions should have short-term duration:

- With a large share maturing within 3 months
- While another large percentage matures within a year.

However, management may or may not exercise a prudent policy. If it does not, it increases the amount of assumed risk. Also, the uncertainty prevailing in the market reduces the demodulator and, in consequence, increases the credit equivalent amount corresponding to the same notional principal. This is how the market works in times of crises, let alone panics – a reason why the demodulated notional amount is called *toxic waste*.

The rationale for this approach lies in the fact that in derivatives trades assumed exposure is usually less than the notional principal – a term borrowed from swaps, and representing a contractual amount not to be paid or received but used as a level of reference. But there are exceptions. In some cases, such as with binary options, the risk being assumed is equal to the notional principal amount specified by the contract.

- Binary options, and other instruments, provide discontinuous payoffs.
- The buyer will pay or receive the notional amount as cash flow, *if* a specific threshold is reached.

The alternative to an instrument-by-instrument computation of the divisor, based on the amount of risk involved in each portfolio position, is to take a weighted averaged of all inventoried derivatives. This will give a demodulator to be applied to total NPA exposure, reducing the accuracy of the result but at the same time facilitating a real-time response – which is very important with virtual financial statements, whether or not they are consolidated.

It is not necessary to calculate the demodulator every day, but it does have to be updated from time to time, as the composition of the portfolio changes and market conditions evolve. Once a reliable computation has been conducted, it makes sense to adopt the levels of dynamic inspection required to face market conditions and/or the firm's own state of business. For instance, the demodulators might be:

- 25 for reduced inspection
- 20 for normal inspection
- 10 or 15 for tightened inspection
- 5 or 6 depending on the severity of a worst case.

Stress testing should use a demodulator of 6 or less, based on historical statistics such as those derived from two rather recent crises. The first of these arose when the Bank of New England (BNE) collapsed in the early 1990s. It had a portfolio of derivatives with a total notional principal amount of US$36 billion. Eventually, after a year, the Fed of Boston tried to unwind the BNE portfolio, and final losses on derivatives trades amounted to US$6 billion. This meant demodulation by a factor of 6, which is providing a useful example for stress scenarios using historical values.

Another example of worst-case conditions is the meltdown in East Asia that started in mid-1997. Credit institutions in Thailand, Indonesia and, above all, South Korea were heavily loaded with derivatives. Some of the east Asia banks that went through this crisis found that the demodulator between notional principal amounts and derivatives losses was 5.

Financial products for which the described demodulation procedure is appropriate include interest rate swaps, interest rate options (caps, floors), swaptions, and other fixed-income options. Also futures, forwards, and exotic instruments. The calculations can then be used to:

- Build a credit equivalence envelope of present value for different time buckets, and
- Develop a risk and return curve for the portfolio of derivatives.

The level of inspection briefly outlined in the preceding paragraphs should always be kept in mind. Decisions about inspection should be based on exogenous factors such as market psychology, liquidity, volatility, and historical time series; as well as endogenous variables like amount of leverage, level of transparency by the treasury department, and effectiveness of the company's risk control.

In cases of wanting transparency, or weak internal control, because the board is lenient, a stress test should be performed with a demodulator equal to 2, *as if* half the derivatives portfolio was invested in binary options. A good stress test would also account for loss of capital due to counterparty risk over and above market risk. The likelihood of operational risk must also be accounted for because it is omnipresent.

Notes

1 D.N. Chorafas, *IFRS, Fair Value and Corporate Governance: The Impact on Budgets, Balance Sheets and Management Accounts*. Elsevier, Oxford, 2006.
2 D.N. Chorafas, *After Basel II: Assuring Compliance and Smoothing the Rough Edges*. Lafferty/VRL Publishing, London, 2005.
3 D.N. Chorafas, *The Management of Bond Investments and Trading of Debt*. Elsevier, Oxford, 2005.
4 D.N. Chorafas, *IFRS, Fair Value and Corporate Governance: The Impact on Budgets, Balance Sheets and Management Accounts*. Elsevier, Oxford, 2006.
5 D.N. Chorafas, *The Real-Time Enterprise*. Auerbach, New York, 2005.
6 Merrill Lynch, 'Global Precious Metals', 1 December 2005.
7 Dimitris N. Chorafas, *Stress Testing: Risk Management Strategies for Extreme Events*. Euromoney, London, 2003.

Part 4

Cost Control, Risk Control and Profitability

Strategic Cost Control Is Good Governance

1. Introduction

From the end of the 19th century until his death at the age of 93 in 1920, George F. Baker – chief executive of New York's most prestigious institution the First National Bank – wrote memoranda on used envelopes. If a clerk brought him a statement on a sheet of paper and the message covered only half the available space, he could send for the writer and thunder at him about wasting paper.

Another Baker characteristic, of which the reader should take notice, was to challenge the obvious. Sam Walton, who built the largest merchandising empire, did the same. One of his greatest strengths has been that he was unpredictable, always his own person, totally independent in his thinking. As a result, Walton was a far-sighted owner/manager. He never rubberstamped anything for anyone.

Being thrifty and being independent-minded correlate among themselves and with the sense of *personal accountability*, a most important business trait. Personal accountability must be enhanced through concrete measurements and metrics; and it must be supported by cost accounting procedures. It is good management to be always able to compare the *cost* and *revenue* involved by:

- Employee
- Product
- Process
- Production facility
- Distribution channel, and
- Client account.

Costs matter. Managers who know how to exercise cost control as a strategic process, appreciate that without formal planning they cannot support in an able manner both profitability and the wiping out of expenses. And formal planning must focus on costs. This concept underpins *cost-effectiveness*, which is an attempt to identify the alternative that:

- Yield the greatest effectiveness, and
- Do so in relation to the incurred cost.

The notion underpinning cost-effectiveness is that each management decision, each programme, each project uses resources that could otherwise be put to some other more profitable purpose. Cost in any programme represents effectiveness foregone elsewhere. Therefore, underlying cost effectiveness is an attack on the relevance of cost.

Because organizations are made of people, profitability, cost control, and risk management (see Chapter 12) all rest on individual initiative. The problem is that the larger is the organization, the worse is the management of its profitability, cost, and risk. Also in principle, the bigger the company, the more likely the average employee will be average. This is a serious matter because companies who are satisfied with mediocrity are bound to get into trouble and eventually disappear under the weight of:

- Runaway risks, and
- Uncontrollable costs.

Under the title 'Wachovia Profit Surges 32%', a report of 17 October 2005 by the Stanford Financial Group had this to say on the bank's leap forward: 'Chief Executive Ken Thompson has been trying to cut costs while expanding existing businesses and entering new markets.' Results have shown up in the expense to revenue ratio:

- Revenue rose 19% to $6.7 billion
- Expenses rose 9% to $4 billion, at a ratio of nearly 60% to revenue.

A better ratio would have been less than 50% of revenue, as many well-managed companies do. In the 1950s and 1960s, during IBM's great years of rise to global power, the rule was that costs must increase at less than half the increase in revenue. This is an excellent rule on cost control, to keep always in mind.

Another interesting reference is provided by a mid-2005 report by the Bank of New York, 'Future Leaders in Investment Management: Survival of the Fittest'. This focused on factors investment managers consider critical for success, and it has shown that managers rank cost-performance above all else, with corporate culture at second place.

For every company, a factual and documented cost control should be a strategic policy. Figure 11.1 suggests how to go about its implementation in order to remain a low cost producer. In 1979, Chrysler had to sell 2.3 million cars and trucks to break even – and it was selling about 1 million vehicles. In 1982, the new management reduced the breakeven point to 1.1 million, and it increased the level of sales to 1.4 million, thereby giving a new lease of life to the firm.

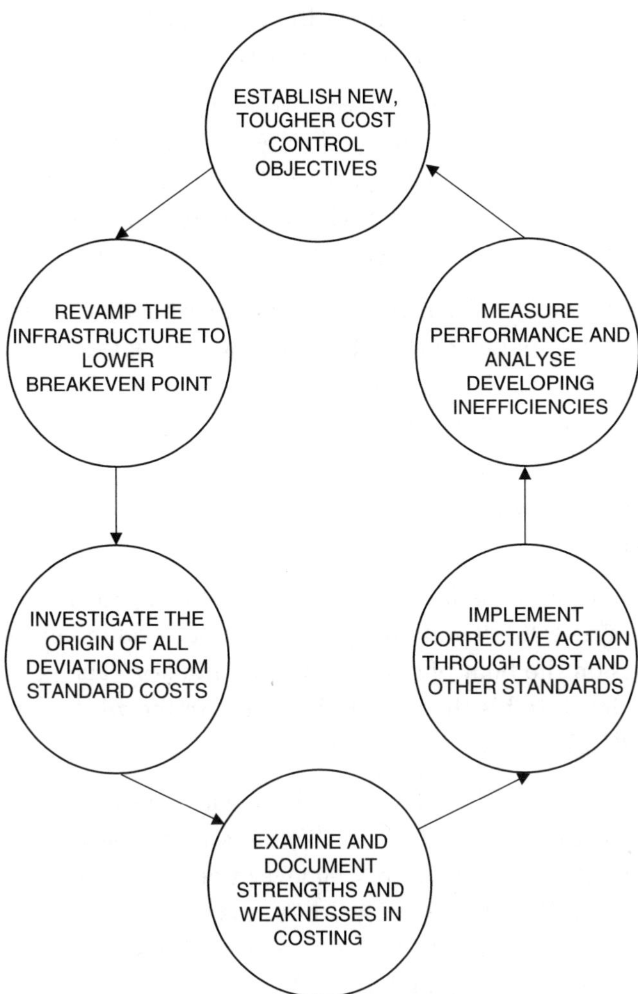

Figure 11.1 Developing and implementing a strategy for cost control

2. Cost control culture: case study on Sam Walton's experience

In the general case, the different myths about managers and management are created by people who are more interested in the study of vague notions of sociology than they are in recognizing the realities of industrial and business life. There are, however, important exceptions to this statement:

- Some leaders of industry have become a recurrent paradigm for future generations, and

- Their way of going about running their enterprise both provides evidence of *foresight* and creates an excellent *precedent.*

It has been a deliberate choice to take Sam Walton and his cost control policies as an example. As he states in his book *Made in* America,[1] in the early days of empire building he tried to operate on a 2% general office expense structure. Two per cent of sales were enough to carry Wal-Mart's buying office, its general office expense, his own salary, the district manager's salary, and that of several other company officers.

As business grew and Wal-Mart became a top merchandising firm, Walton saw to it that it kept to its policy of operating at a low percentage in office overhead; in fact, a lower one than it did in the early years. And that includes tremendous expenses for computer support and distribution centre expenditures.

- This 2% is an excellent benchmark
- But it takes iron will on behalf of the boss to implement a low ceiling in expenses.

As Sam Walton says in his book, in recounting his cost control experience: 'I remember one time I didn't want to spend any money on motels, so we all slept in sleeping bags on the floor of one of our guys' houses.' The person who wrote these lines has been, in his time, the richest man in the world, with a net worth estimated at $25 billion.

Neither has success changed that attitude towards swamping costs. After he became the richest man on earth, Sam Walton was to suggest: 'A lot of people think it is crazy of me to fly coach whenever I go on a commercial flight, and maybe I overdo it a little bit. But I feel like it is up to me as a leader to set an example. It is not fair of me to ride one way and ask everybody else to ride another way. The minute you do that:

- You start building resentment, and
- Your whole team idea begins to strain at the seams.'

If the first ingredient of a successful cost control strategy is to establish a clear policy, to be respected by everybody in the organization, the second is to elaborate the method for applying it. No strategy, even the best would ever work if management does not come up with a sound method for implementing it and for controlling it. As Walton suggests: 'You have to double check to see that people did what you told them to do.'

This is precisely what the milestone of a 2% overhead did in terms of quantification. The lesson it taught to all Wal-Mart employees was about learning to value a dollar, and swamping expenditures is all about. 'It is great to have the money to fall back on. But if you get too caught up in that good life, it is probably time to move on – simply because you lose touch with what your mind is supposed to be concentrating on: serving the customer,' says Walton.

Cost control is very important, but swamping expenditures should be done by increasing efficiency, not by reducing the quality of service or by cutting corners. Commenting on how and why companies fail, Walton suggested that: 'Their customers were the ones who shut them down. They voted with their feet. Competitors offered better quality at lesser cost.'

Notice the emphasis being placed on both quality and cost. This accent is important because in many cases industrial engineers, purchasing managers, and accountants, measure their success by reduced billings they are able to show. These do not always tell the full story, and sometimes they may be a *false economy*. Mercedes Benz learned this the hard way as quality dropped during a disastrous period when lowest price carried more weight within the organization than highest standards of engineering.[2]

'Better quality' and 'lesser cost' work in tandem. Selling the one for the other is a very bad policy. The effort to uphold quality, and indeed improve it, sees to it that the proper cost study should start with a thorough organizational review.

- Where are the opportunities for cost savings?
- Does the current system reflect these opportunities?
- Are our production and distribution costs the lowest in our industry?
- Where lie our weaknesses in cost control? Who is holding them up?

The early 1960s saw the development of a cost control method in engineering design known as *value analysis*. I applied it in connection to the evaluation of cost-effectiveness of refrigerators made by a major international firm. The method consisted of buying comparable products of our main competitors, dismantling them, hanging their components on the wall of an old empty factory, and patiently analysing every one of them in terms of quality, functionality, and cost. This meant concentrating on serving both:

- The customer through greater functionality, and
- The company by finding ways and means of reducing costs.

With both new and old industrial products, the challenge starts in engineering. Designers have to rethink the approach they took in establishing the specifications. Every component must be put in active status. The designer must be imaginative, objective and very critical – including his or her own work. In order to survive, the market's test:

- Every product or service must be tested for cost-effectiveness.
- This means repositioning itself in the market in terms of added value to the customer.

As designers, we must develop a uniqueness, and capitalize on it. But also we should steadily maintain that uniqueness, otherwise, it will be overtaken by our competitors. If our business is going to prevail, and remain competitive, we have to get accustomed to the idea that we have to change our approach once it has proved to be not so successful, or the market itself has shifted.

Chapter 1 made the point that in order to survive in a highly competitive market, we have to adapt to changing conditions. Procurement has been one of the areas where Sam Walton was extremely careful in his commitments. The way he put it, he has always resented paying anyone just for the pleasure of doing business with him. Wal-Mart's suppliers learned that:

- They couldn't bulldoze its management like they did with other customers, and
- Walton and his assistants were completely serious when they said they wanted to form a personal opinion of the supplier's quality and cost base.

In a way not so different from what happens with governments, corporate level bureaucracy is the No. 1 promoter of inefficiency and high costs. Really, it is a pretty simple philosophy, advises David Glass (a former president of Wal-Mart). What you have to do is just draw a line in the dirt and force the bureaucracy behind that line. And then know for sure that a year will go by and it will be back across that line and you will have to do the same thing again.

In his book, Sam Walton reinforced that concept by stating that: 'A lot of bureaucracy is really the product of some empire builder's ego. Some people have the tendency to build up big staffs around them to emphasize their own importance. As CEO, Walton never allowed any of that at Wal-Mart, and he was always on the look-out for big egos.'

3. Comparing cost performance to peer groups

Other business leaders, too, have risen against bureaucracy and chopped away at booming costs. When he was the boss of Primerica Corporation, Sanford I. Weill obsessively eschewed such bureaucratic hallmarks as organization charts and memos. Unlike many financial services monoliths, Weill ran his sprawling conglomerate *as if* it were a small family business with the owners' money on the line. Like Sam Walton, in spite of being a billionaire, Sanford Weill has been ruthless in paring expenses.

- He set up precise reporting systems, so he could calculate profitability down to the level of individual officers, and
- He rooted out extravagance in cost-effectiveness metrics, having designed a system that measured productivity only on the basis of factors that line managers can control.

At Primerica Weill had attained a high degree of cost-effectiveness when compared to peer groups. Banking is not renowned for being keen in controlling expenses, as we will see through practical examples in section 4. Yet, it should be always kept in mind that overcoming costs is a basic responsibility of senior management; and it is also evidence of good governance. As John D. Rockefeller, Jr, once suggested: 'I believe that:

- Every right implies a responsibility
- Every opportunity an obligation, and
- Every possession a duty.'

After KKR took possession of Safeway, the food chain, cutting costs became the top priority of Henry Kravis and George Roberts. They slashed executive perks, taking away 350 company cars. They also cut headquarters staff by 25% to 850, saving $15–20 million a year.

Kravis and Roberts also used a sharp knife in cutting down the monetized perks. In 1993, Safeway required the company's top five executives to give up the bonuses they had already earned for 1992, when profits fell 20%. 'When shareholders lose, managers should lose,' said Steve Burd, Safeway's new chief executive officer, who instituted a revamped bonus plan tightly tied to performance.[3]

Cost cuts at the top, Steve Burd acknowledged, are largely symbolic. But symbolic sacrifice has been crucial in wrestling concessions from labour. Burd threatened to close all 84 Safeway-operated stores in Alberta, Canada, unless the union agreed to concessions. The union gave in to longer hours and lower pay. A cashier who earned $638 for a 37-hour work week had to work 40 hours to earn $608. Those wage rollbacks added up to annual savings of $40 million in the first year.

Redressing the cost structure at Safeway is a good example because, like banks, many supermarkets are known to be poor at cost control. An effective way to demonstrate to all stakeholders the need for a tight rein is comparisons to peer institutions, particularly those best managed. To be meaningful, however, peer comparisons:

- Must be based on entities whose financial and operational characteristics are essentially similar
- Should spread out over time, usually three to five years, and
- Should be both quantitative and qualitative, as far as the peer group costing tests are concerned.

Additionally, peer-to-peer comparisons should demonstrate the ability to relate cost to performance for each activity under study, and for the entity as a whole. They should also be able to exploit, to full extent, the possibility to apply financial ratios in different expense categories, with each ratio expressed as peer group median and percentiles. Patterns are an effective way of comparing cost distributions.

Administrative expenses is one of the areas where peer group studies provide interesting results. Properly exploited peer group data on overhead expenditures add a badly needed dimension to the management process, by making feasible a better understanding of competitors' strategies in terms of swamping costs, and the success these may have. They also:

- Offer an external standard to complement internal standards utilized in cost and profitability reporting, and
- Help in documenting the analysts' evaluations of management effectiveness, thereby presenting an incentive for better governance at *our* side.

Not only the handling of overhead requires tough decisions at board, CEO, and senior management level, but also the cost of doing business often escapes executive control (see Chapter 1 for cost of doing business). As an example, in the late 1980s a report by McKinsey and Salomon Brothers dramatized the breakdown of expenditures associated to securities trading. The statistics were startling:

- Backoffice and settlements represented 65% of the budget
- Trade support, consumed another 25%, and
- This left only 10% for analysis, product research, and market development.

Yet, the areas of activity in the third bullet point were those with highest potential returns to an investment banker. A comment made at the time in regard to the McKinsey/Salomon Brothers findings was that these regrettable results were due to the fact that with information services the approach was basically numeric therefore involving considerable labour costs. By contrast, the true automation of payments documents required image lifting.

The lesson to learn from studies revealing just how much money is going down the drain is that research and analysis of undermining causes must be done with a sharp eye on deficiencies, but also with objectivity. Objectivity does not reside in theory-free perception. Rather, it lies in the flexibility to reject an established concept, or theory, when:

- Anticipated observations cannot be affirmed
- A perception of contrary meaning dominates, and
- Findings reveal that management is not in control.

To a significant extent, the better answer lies in experimentation, which allows us to identify weaknesses – our own, and those of our products. But if we do not cast our experimental net widely enough, we will not see what lies before our eyes, because the necessary conceptual tools will be unavailable to us:

- We would not query events properly, and
- As a result, we would not understand the prevailing patterns and forms.

Cost, like risk, forms a pattern that helps in appreciating both trend and magnitude. One of the major benefits of peer studies is that they often help to make this pattern clearer and better comparable to *our* results. When presented with this evidence, alert management knows which road it has to take, though there is always the problem of political interference in cutting costs.

A case of cost control which is most challenging is that of redimensioning when business opportunities wane. In the mid-1990s, a study of the British Post Office reckoned that up to 20% of the business could be at risk from competition over the next years of that decade and, with it, 30 000 jobs as well as the closure of up to 5000 post offices. Overall the Post Office estimated that it loses 1500 jobs for every 1% of lost volume.

That 1995 study proved to be a fairly good predictor of things to come. The business perspective of Post Office services did not improve, but employment did not cave in as projected because the taxpayer (unwillingly) came to the rescue. And over and above overemployment come social costs. Happily for British taxpayers, the contribution to social security as a percentage of salary is not as high in the UK as in France and Italy; but it is a high multiple of what happens in Denmark.

4. Cost control in banking and impact of overhead

Like the British Post Office, and so many other state-run services, all banks are overstaffed and overbranched, though some are more so than others. In research I did some years ago, a major French bank estimated it could do business with 50% of its people – while a British bank said 60% of its staff would have been plenty.

A German bank reckoned its ongoing business could be effectively handled with about two-thirds of current employment. An Italian bank considered three-quarters of its personnel to be more than enough. A Swedish bank found that significant personal reductions were feasible because 75% of all staff activities revolved around:

- Low value services, and
- Simple transactions.

Overstaffing hurts because it sees to it that productivity is low, while costs are being artificially kept high. In the financial industry at large, between 65% and 75% of all non-interest budget costs are human costs – while two-thirds of all human costs are managerial and professional. This roughly means that 50% of all non-interest costs are at the managerial/professional level.

As far as the bottom line is concerned, the effect of labour costs in the banking industry is akin to that of fuel cost in airlines. Since deregulation, for nearly a quarter of a century US airlines find it difficult to survive because:

- Price wars have ravaged their bottom line, and
- Sharp increase in fuel costs in 2005 made the chances of their survival even slimmer.

As of October 2005, a major casualty has been the formerly proud Delta Airlines. Investors and financial analysts believe that both busted airlines, which sought protection under Chapter 11, and those still afloat, have to trim their expenses as never before, shedding aircraft, routes, destinations, and employees. For banks, the way to cost-cutting is shedding excess staff and branch offices.

Another trend fairly common in the banking and air transport industry is the growing weight given to outsourcing – with the added feature that airlines also engineer significant cuts in employee plans. In an effort to reduce fixed costs, Northwest outsourced its entire plane cleaning and maintenance operation in October 2005, at the start of the mechanics' strike during which the airline declared bankruptcy. Delta announced a large cutback in flight service:

- Eliminating its air parcel freight service entirely, and
- Making the point it will default on its next planned contribution to its employees' pension plan.

Banks have not taken such drastic cost cutting measures, though they do try to flatten their organizational structure, accounting for the fact that managerial expenses are *overhead*. Overhead costs are indeed a tough issue in banking. Financial institutions with experience in cutting overhead advise that the best strategy for bringing it under control can be expressed in three bullets:

- *Show it*, don't hide it
- *Charge it*, don't spread it, and
- Make it highly *visible* in the institutions profit and loss account.

A most interesting commentary on the leadership low overhead can provide appeared in *The Economist* in connection to the North Carolina National Bank (NCNB), then a regional bank, which acquired the first Republic Bank of Texas, a much bigger entity: 'NCBN's greatest strength has been its ability to control costs.'[4] Controlling costs is a sign of good governance.

At about the same time as the article in *The Economist*, another article in *Business Week* had this to say about France's Société Générale: 'S.G. Warburg Securities estimates that overhead eats up a hefty 66% of the bank's earnings only the troubled Crédit Lyonnais, at 71%, is worse off among French lenders.' Because such high expenses left Société Générale behind other global competitors, its CEO mounted a tough campaign to shed thousands of the bank's 24 000 branch employees in France, while increasing its lending and securities trading in the United States, Eastern Europe, and Asia.

The message is that financial institutions that treat overhead as a sacred cow should know that any study done for cost control purposes, even the best of studies, will be de facto invalid with its effectiveness undercut by runaway overhead expenses. Usually high labour costs are the aftermath of years of:

- Over-manning
- Weak management, and
- Political interference with the slimming down of the organization.

Sometimes, political interference knows no borders. In October 2004, General Motors announced that it would close one of its European plants: either in Rüsselsheim, Germany, or Trollhättan, Sweden – depending on which wins the bid to jointly produce its Saabs and Opel Vectras more cheaply. With this:

- The two GM subsidiaries were put in competition to one another.
- This competition, however, was short lived, because labour strikes that simultaneously took place in Germany and in Sweden saw to it that GM had to abandon its Darwinist solution.

Plenty of examples document that not only in banking but in the manufacturing industry, too, the cost of overstaffing accounts for a large portion of product costs. This is a financial weight that has dramatically increased within pensions and health care for retirees, as we saw in the case of Delphi and GM. Moreover, the allocation of overhead costs, if not done methodically, may misalign product price and profitability estimates.

- The thicker the overhead of the firm
- The thinner the dividend that goes to shareholders.

Being in charge of overhead, as well as of any other cost chapter, in no way means across the board cuts on a percentage basis, or any similar metrics. Across the board cutting costs is a prescription for failure. The first step of a sound approach is to find out where our weaknesses lie. Some years ago, during our meeting, J.M. Williamson, former deputy chief executive of UK's APACS, said that:

- 70% of a British bank's real resources are tied up in transaction processing, and
- This leaves only 30% to be devoted to banking proper.

High transaction costs is a major weakness. A prerequisite to keeping on top of personnel costs is thoroughly revamping systems and procedures by using the best services technology can offer. Together with this comes collaboration among banks in developing and sharing financial networks (devolution); and commitment to industry-wide standards to help reduce the unit cost of a transaction.

In parallel to action involving the whole industry sector, we should study *our* own institution's strengths and weaknesses in efficiency terms. The personnel division of a major bank calculated a statistic on how much time the average employee works. The answer was 3 hours per day. A different financial institution examined the aftermath of a major catastrophe and close-down of the computer centre. How many days after the disaster was the bank no longer able to handle the clients' accounts? The answer was 3 days.

Here we have two different issues that should definitely attract top management's attention. Productivity can, and must, be dramatically increased. Steady upgrading of skills as well as organization and technology can play a significant role in increasing productivity. Technological solutions and their specific personnel requirements should, however, be studied in a way that will improve reliability, so that management does not need to shut down operations when the system fails.

5. Deproliferating and cost cutting: case studies with MIT and Compaq

Some years ago, at MIT, a Leaders for Manufacturing team tackled the task of *deproliferating* spendable parts for General Motors. The results of this study were eye-catching. Composed of interdisciplinary skills and analytically minded persons, the team found that GM could save millions of dollars by *modularizing* options offered to clients throughout its North American Trust Platforms (NATP) group.

The MIT research team calculated that GM offers its truck customers more than *one trillion* possible option combinations. For example, GM customers can choose from 131 different rear axles on a full-size pickup. The problem is that to sustain this vast array of options:

- Each manufacturing plant has to be prepared to build any and all of them, and
- This is a demanding and highly costly proposition.

While a wide array of options looks attractive from a marketing point of view, it can have a deadly impact at the cost side. Moreover, the sheer complexity of the products puts limits on manufacturing capacity, affects scheduling and overburdens both engineering and marketing. Additionally, as the MIT research team has found, the competitive advantage is very limited. At the time of the study:

- Each GM plant built about 200 000 trucks a year, but 70% of all truck orders came from retail dealerships.
- The customers bought trucks off the dealer's lots and rarely placed custom orders.

Based on these findings, the MIT research team approached the issue of axle rationalization by categorizing its features, analysing sales data, and exploring manufacturability as well as modularity. Examination of sales trends pinpointed option combinations that were not selling. A thorough analysis demonstrated that GM did not need to offer eight different axle combinations for any given truck family – what it needed was only two.

The team also found that 67 axles could be taken out of production, yielding millions of dollars in annual savings in labour, rework, quality, freight, and inventory storage costs. Deproliferation also created significant savings from engineering. This is the sort of fundamental studies necessary for:

- Tracking in a factual manner cost cutting issues, and
- Leading to strategic decisions that sustain (or improve) market appeal, while simplifying product line management.

Sometimes a poorly studied product strategy leads to an unwarranted proliferation of wares and options. Alert management knows this. Back in the early 1990s, one of the first priorities of Eckhard Pfeiffer, when he became chief executive of Compaq, was to cut costs and prices – not to come up with some brilliant new engineering feat.

- Compaq also spend lavishly on market research before developing a new product, and
- The new rule has been that marketing must come up with a price target when the product started in design, not after the first prototypes were available.

That is the formula Compaq used in 1994 to develop the ProSignia VS server. Marketing saw an opportunity for a server costing only 5–10% more than a desktop PC. To meet that target, engineering and manufacturing scrapped expensive features, such as high-end graphics, while adding critical software to manage networks.

'A ground rule,' said Pfeiffer at the time, 'is to set very aggressive cost goals to get very attractive entry-level products.'[5] The No. 2 rule has been that shipments must soar, but hiring should be kept under lock and key. And the No. 3 is that when a product or marketing approach is not paying off, kill it fast. Quality of management made the difference, and when management quality slumped, Compaq went under.

In his heyday, Pfeiffer had an expression for his strategy: '*The cost-leadership mode*'. In practice that means increasing output to meet demand while keeping a close eye on cost figures, and at the same time finding new ways to run factories more intensively. With a one-word vision – *Survival* – Compaq also developed other modern management techniques. To make its manufacturing operations leaner:

- It re-engineered its production processes, and
- Adopted a design-for-manufacturing approach, with common components, which is an example of deproliferating.

An example helps in documenting the deliverables of that approach. In 1994, the company's computer servers used one-third fewer parts and screws than they did in 1989. The new management also introduced *activity-based costing*, an accounting technique that allowed it to apportion overheads more accurately than before to individual products.[6]

As a result, Compaq's combined labour and overhead costs per computer fell about 75% over a two year period, with labour accounting for as little as 2% of some of its products' total costs. At the same time, also in its heyday, Compaq designed into each product the potential for a 25% price reduction during its life-cycle a wise move since everybody knows that price competition with computer products is intense.

Another of the characteristics of good governance is the senior executives' willingness and ability to challenge the obvious. An example of how much imagination and moving away from the beaten path can help in business efficiency has been offered by upbeat PC manufacturers who took on their big competitors and won by:

- No longer stockpiling countless versions of PCs, printers, and other gear in warehouses.
- But, instead, stocking components and software at distribution centres, combining them at the last minute to match each customer's order.

Such changes to established 'obvious' practices have driven operating expenses to a record low, something the big companies with their bureaucratic approach to long-standing policies cannot match. Inability to change methods while there is still time led to a death spiral for high-cost producers who failed to read the signals of the market. This death spiral:

- Cost Digital Equipment Corp. its life, and
- Led IBM to sell its PC division to a Chinese competitor.

Careful studies often reveal plenty of subjects that can be corrected, while such failures are not evident at first look. To be effective cost-cutting requires new people at the helm and new departures. After Japan's Bridgestone bought Firestone Tyre & Rubber in 1988, labour relations were downright friendly. But the cosiness vanished after Firestone posted a total of $1 billion in losses by 1992. This brought:

- A new cost-cutting strategy
- A change in management to Bridgestone/Firestone
- Tough measures to redress the situation, which led to a strike.

To be able to honour its delivery commitments, Firestone bought 500 000 tyres from rival Cooper Tyre & Rubber, and parent Bridgestone agreed to supply another 3 million tyres from its Japanese factories to develop a war chest inventory. Thereafter, management demanded that the United Rubber Workers (URW) labour union break with the contract it ratified with Goodyear Tyre & Rubber, which called for a 16% increase over three years.

In its place, Bridgestone asked for *12-hour shifts*, pay hikes tied to productivity goals, health co-payments, and lower new-hire pay – all to overcome big cost disadvantages against competition. (The big three auto makers of Detroit should have taken a leaf out of this book.) And though the union went on strike, Bridgestone's stockpile, and production from its other factories unaffected by the strike, allowed it to keep most major customers supplied. It was almost like the strike never happened.

Then, on 4 January 1995 Bridgestone announced it had hired 2000 permanent replacements. The move struck a nerve in the Clinton Administration, which supported a law to limit employers' ability to replace strikers. Then Labor Secretary Robert Reich, who had intervened in six major strikes, tried to get the two sides talking again. Instead of quietly agreeing, Bridgestone rebuffed Reich, saying its president was unavailable and offering its labour chief instead. Cost cutting carried the day.

6. An eye on survival: case study on IBM

Throughout the 1960s and 1970s, years of IBM's market glory, up to the middle-to-late 1980s, when its share price ebbed, IBM was considered to be one of the best managed companies, as well as a barometer of what was happening in American business. Analysts even saw it as a proxy for the stock market itself.

At over $150 stock price, IBM loomed large in the market because of its size in *market capitalization* – a term which in this connection means the total value of IBM stock (not to be confused with product capitalization discussed in section 7). At the time, IBM capitalization stood at $92 billion, which was nearly 2.5 times that of Exxon and greater than the total capitalization of all companies traded on the American Stock Exchange in the United States, or in the Frankfurt stock exchange in Germany. Indeed, IBM has a market value larger than the stock markets of France, Switzerland, Italy, the Netherlands, or Australia.

Then, because of consecutive years of poor governance, which left the company depending on mainstreams well after the 'big iron' market caved in, fortunes changed. With the downturn, IBM's shareholders lost nearly 75% of their capital, as the stock dropped to the low 40s. Louis V. Gerstner, Jr, the new IBM CEO, admitted that the company's biggest mistake was waiting too long to address the client-server market.[7]

To make a turnaround possible, Gerstner not only took the proverbial long, hard look at IBM's product line, but also instituted tough cost-cutting procedures that hit every function within the global IBM empire, from order-taking and delivery to warranty management. With costs looked at as public enemy No. 1 the company has been able to see a significant turnaround.

Insiders say that some cost control measures, however, preceded Gerstner, and they were the aftermath of the company's sharp fall in market share, particularly in Europe. IBM had got so close to the edge, it really shook up management at headquarters and William E. McCracken, the IBM US distribution chief, was dispatched in early 1991 to 'fix' Europe.[8]

What McCracken found was that inefficiency prevailed in many quarters. For instance, in Greenock, Scotland, costs were running high – despite Scotland's low-cost and highly skilled labour force. Greenock used to cobble together PC motherboards for all its models on a single line, with the result that switching from one model to another could idle production for up to eight hours. To remedy this situation:

- The production line was split into six minilines, one for each product family
- With this, total manufacturing and testing time has been slashed from five days to less than eight hours, while quality rose 10%.

Greenock also instituted a new flexible manufacturing that can quickly shift from one model to another. This made it feasible to build only what was at the time in demand, and kept critical parts from sitting around in unsold systems. As a result of these measures:

- Inventory of completed systems plummeted 90%
- While sales increased by 42% over the same period.

Similar improvements were made in distribution, where costs were reduced from $200 to $45 per computer. Other cost cutting strides have come from paring inventory to the bone. By shipping finished goods daily to customers directly from Greenock, therefore bypassing 14 country warehouses, IBM further slimmed down its cost structure.

As personal computer prices continued to drop, IBM figured its most cost-conscious approach would give it an edge in Europe over rivals like Dell Computer and Compaq. At Greenock, towards the end of 1993, the plant began preloading software for customers for about 25% less than local dealers, who traditionally provide that service.

The lesson IBM learned from this experience, and can teach to others, is that companies can compete in global markets only *if* and *when* they become low cost producers compared even to their most far-away competitors. This means that:

- One must do a lot to get the cost base in line, and
- Has to continue doing so, because competitors have the nasty habit of catching up very fast.

That means a continual war on costs, including internal efficiency measures as well as discussions with suppliers on slashing prices while upholding quality and delivery standards. At headquarters, for example, information technology (IT) costs must be controlled even when resources are available for fairly significant investments.

- *If* the rationale behind technology investment is to improve a company's share price, which it should be
- *Then* IT strategy could aim to align business drivers with money spent on technology.

High performance companies are always thinking about those drivers, and they match investments to them by emphasizing strategic choices. By contrast, when they think of IT, too many companies are focusing on back office activities which are not aligned to:

- Strategic objectives, and
- Share price growth.

A similar point can be made about any line of enterprise, from R&D and manufacturing to sales and maintenance. Production scheduling is an example where greater efficiency pays dividends. An efficiency study at Ford, made in 1990, has shown that a good part of the delay in delivering a car was caused by the need to draw up and reconcile two different production schedules.

- The marketing department did one production schedule, which concentrated on sharing out best-selling cars in short supply.
- But the production department did a different schedule, which concentrated on sharing out production facilities in short supply.

Doing one schedule that accounted for both criteria would have been simpler and quicker. But building an organization that knows about both market demand and production facilities, as well as being able to balance the two, took time.[9] Many companies face similar problems, at all sorts of levels. Automating the supply of parts is a case in point.

In conjunction with its 1990 efficiency study, Ford found glitches in machine-to-machine communication between headquarters and parts suppliers in connection to computer-based ordering. In the aftermath, the motor vehicles manufacturer specified, for suppliers of key parts, exactly which computer-aided design system to buy.

- That way, Ford engineers could load new designs straight into suppliers' computers, and
- Those suppliers had to decide what to do with their own suppliers, too.

What this broader supply chain study has revealed is that simple price reduction becomes less important than the broader perspective of evolving new products, and their components, in harmony with the client's changing product views. The new emphasis on flexibility and design skills went way beyond costs, and it found within it new weaknesses to be corrected.

7. Applying the strategy of product capitalization

Applying a strategy of *product capitalization* to all production chores is a good way of keeping up cost-consciousness in the organization. The concept underpinning it is simple. IBM defines *product capitalization* as the sum of direct labour (DL) plus direct material (DM) embedded in manufacturing its goods. In short, it is the money invested into the product before depreciation, amortization, interest paid, overhead and other factors are accounted for. The algorithm is:

$$PC = DL + DM \quad (1)$$

In its years of market dominance, IBM had made the *strategic* choice to keep product capitalization at 15% of its wares list price. Product capitalization is an important concept in all manufacturing industries where management has to keep tight control over costs. To this basic cost reference should then be added to other elements that weigh on final product cost.

Dr Harold D. Koontz, my professor of Management Planning and Control at UCLA, taught his students that capital investments are nearly irrevocable commitments which are made for the medium to longer term – and their cost has to be carried even if the factory turns at only 50% of capacity. Contrary to these longer-term commitments, decisions on product capitalization:

- Are short term, and
- They should be subject to dynamic planning and control action.

Figure 11.2 presents three trend curves, from 1997 to 2003, of cost of materials, depreciation, and labour costs in Germany (based on statistics by the Deutsche Bundesbank). As these statistics document, the trend curves of labour cost and depreciation correlate, while the cost of materials has zoomed. This is one more reason for bringing product capitalization into perspective in all decisions concerning a production plan.

The concept of product capitalization also helps in managing the *transfer price* concept. Industrial firms like IBM and John Deere, the farm equipment manufacturer, have organized the whole entity into two major profit centres. The one centres around engineering and manufacturing, with emphasis on cost of goods *to be* sold. The other around marketing and sales.

At the cost of goods to be sold side, are R&D expenditures, manufacturing engineering, investments in machines, new tooling, depreciation (factories, machines), manufacturing overhead, and other technology-oriented costs. The total of these costs makes up a *transfer price*. In a multinational company this is also influenced by other considerations like: transportation, insurance, custom duties, and taxation. (Notice that the cost of goods to be sold should not be confused with the cost of doing business discussed in Chapter 1, which is a different notion).

An important advantage multinational companies derive by using product capitalization as measurement of engineering and manufacturing cost efficiency, is

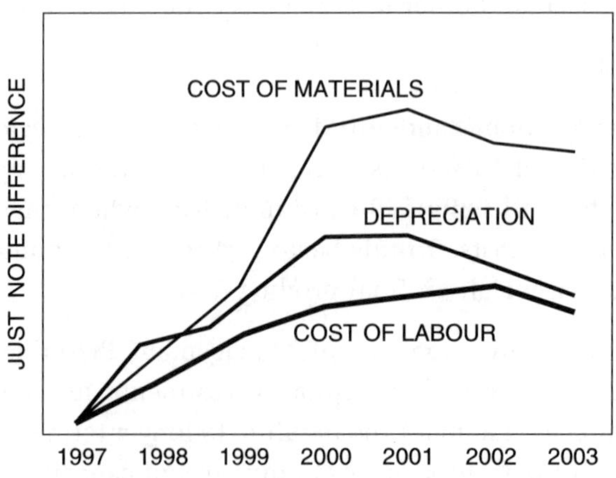

Figure 11.2 Six-year trend of cost of materials, labour costs, and depreciation in Germany (Deutsche Bundesbank, Monthly Report, October 2005)

country-by-country comparison of labour costs. Not only do no two countries have the same labour cost structure, but also, quite often this is overburdened by an inordinate amount of so-called *social costs*, as Table 11.1 demonstrates.

In fact, even in the same country labour costs may vary significantly from one area to the other. When towards the end of the 20th century, BMW studied the US labour market in order to decide where to build its US manufacturing base, it found that labour costs in unionized Michigan were 50% higher than in the Carolinas. Even so, labour costs at Detroit were well below those in Bavaria – which is evidence of the sorry state of the German labour market, snowed under beneath unbearable social costs.

On the marketing and sales side are other types of expenditures, like marketing costs, advertising campaigns, salary and commission of sales engineers, warehousing, and other non-chargeable expenses such as sales overhead. Between the technology and sales sides come administrative expenses, including management overhead and human resources training programmes if paid for by the corporate budget.

All expense chapters have to be budgeted (see Chapter 9), with costs carefully planned and controlled. Product capitalization, however, continues to be the kernel of the cost structure, because a company lives and prospers on the sale of its products and services. This concept of capitalization originated at IBM with accounting machines and mainframe computers because in the 1950s they were rented or sold in a proportion which varied by:

- Type of equipment
- Country, and
- Industry (banks tended rather to buy).

Table 11.1 Social cost contribution to social security as a percentage of salary

	By companies	By workers
Denmark	1	18
France	57	19
Italy	38	8
Japan	16	14
Ireland	13	6
UK	13	11
USA	10	10

Source: La Republica, 18 May 2005

By and large, in the 1950s and much of the 1960s, rental represented for IBM some 75–80% installed value. It follows that the lower are manufacturing costs, and more particularly direct labour plus direct material, the better the company stands financially due to the carrying charges of its rented property.

It comes therefore as no surprise that IBM policy not only specified that product capitalization must be controlled very closely, but also that the way it compares to list price is most important (the aforementioned 15% principle). Additionally, this provided a milestone to decisions concerning the product's redesign. *If* the 15% became 20% or 25%, this meant that the product and/or the process were:

- Obsolete, and
- No longer competitive.

Precisely because in a global market practically no manufacturer has pricing power, the 15% rule of capitalization as a percentage of list price is a great strategy. Notice that while this is not a typical ratio in every industry, every industry has a representative ratio which only Tier-1 companies can deliver. In others, product capitalization rises and rises, totally out of control.

In conclusion, the challenge is that product design, supply chain management, industrial engineering, advancing technology, a steady effort, value analysis, and unrelenting management pressure must keep product capitalization well below a pre-established ceiling. When this happens, it provides the company with a comfortable operating margin, allowing it to spend more money on marketing, further promoting shareholder value.

Notes

1 Sam Walton, *Made in America – My Story*. Bantam, New York, 1992.
2 *European Automotive Design*, October 2005.
3 *Business Week*, 18 October 1993.
4 *The Economist*, 6 August 1988.
5 *Business Week*, 11 July 1994.
6 *The Economist*, 2 July 1994.
7 *Business Week*, 11 July 1994.
8 *Business Week*, 13 December 1993.
9 *The Economist*, 16 June 1990.

Accounting for the Cost of Risk

1. Introduction

We must stop talking of risk as being balanced by return. Risk is a cost. It is the cost of yesterday when the commitment was made; and the cost of tomorrow, at the transaction's maturity. Additionally, many risks are assumed in the course of doing business, without a specific return attached to them, and financial institutions are discovering that this sort of exposure is on the increase.

Prior to its merger with Chemical Banking, which subsequently merged with Chase Manhattan, JP Morgan and Bank One, the former Manufacturers Hanover Trust Bank (MHTC) had done an intraday risk evaluation of assumed exposure, and found astonishing results.[1] Just one customer, General Motors, was running every working day at 2:00 pm a $2 billion to $2.5 billion overdraft.

- This was big money in the 1980s, with no direct counterpart other than the client connection, and
- Since then has been added the major weight of exposure with derivatives without a firmly defined return.

As with open lines of credit to major clients, derivatives transactions may involve risks that make small game of commissions and fees. The rules of IFRS (see Chapter 10) require fair-valuing the inventoried derivatives trades. When marking to market is not feasible, marking to model is used – requiring:

- Powerful algorithms to project on positions
- High performance computing for number crunching
- Knowledge engineering for handling qualitative issues, and
- Other sophisticated technological supports like interactive visualization.

Moreover, there is model risk, database insufficiency, and steeply changed time series. Mega-risks hitting insurers from a growing frequency and amplitude of both natural and man-made catastrophes, provide an example. Table 12.1 shows the 23 hurricanes to strike the United States over four decades, nearly approaching $300 billion in damages (if the two 2005 big events overrun their estimates). Notice that 9 of the 23 mega-risks took place in the first years of the 21st century, which means:

- Nearly 40% of catastrophic events
- Took place in 12.5% of the time covered by Table 12.1.

There may also be legal risk awaiting its turn, as Crédit Suisse found to its dismay. In early October 2005 Parmalat Finanziaria brought a lawsuit against

Table 12.1 The 23 billion dollar hurricanes to strike the United States during the past 40 years

Hurricane	Date	Category	Damage ($ bn)	Inflation adjusted October 05 ($ bn)	Estimated damage ($ bn)
Katrina	Sept 05	5			$30 to $50
Rita	Oct 05	5			$30 to $40
Wilma	Oct 05	4			$20 to $30
Andrew	Aug 92	5	$26.5	$43.7	
Charley	Aug 04	4	$15.0	$15.0	
Ivan	Sept 04	3	$14.2	$14.2	
Frances	Sept 04	2	$8.9	$8.9	
Hugo	Sept 89	4	$7.0	$12.3	
Jeanne	Sept 03	3	$6.9	$6.9	
Allison	June 01	Tropical Storm	$5.0	$5.8	
Floyd	Sept 99	2	$4.5	$4.5	
Isabel	Sept 03	2	$3.4	$3.6	
Fran	Sept 96	3	$3.2	$4.5	
Opal	Oct 95	3	$3.0	$4.3	
Frederic	Sept 79	3	$2.3	$6.3	
Agnes	Jun 72	1	$2.1	$11.3	
Alicia	Aug 83	3	$2.0	$4.4	
Bob	Aug 91	2	$1.5	$2.6	
Juan	1985	1	$1.5	$3.1	
Camille	Aug 69	5	$1.4	$8.9	
Betsy	Sept 65	3	$1.4	$10.8	
Elena	Sept 85	3	$1.3	$2.6	
Georges	Sept 98	2	$1.2	$2.3	

Crédit Suisse First Boston for damages worth 7 billion euro ($8.4 billion). This was part of Parmalat's efforts to recover money after it went bankrupt two years earlier. The lawsuit is the twelfth case Parmalat brought against banks that sold bonds for it before it collapsed. Crédit Suisse said that the allegations against it were unfounded and it will be vigorously contesting the claim.

Legal risk hitting after a delay is no longer an exceptional case, like asbestos. Part of the strategy of Enrico Bondi, the administrator of Parmalat, has been to recover a total of 50 billion euro ($60 billion) from the company's former lenders, including Deutsche Bank, UBS, JP Morgan Chase and many other banks, alleging that they contributed to the dairy company's collapse when they sold bonds on its behalf before 2003, the year of the company's bankruptcy.

Theoretically, legal risk is part of operational risk.[2] Practically, it is a big issue on its own; it is real and biting heavily into a firm's treasury. In Parmalat's case, as a first instalment Bondi obtained more than 300 million euro ($360 million) in settlements from Morgan Stanley and the fund management unit of Banca Intesa, the large Italian bank. These have been operational risks.

The effectiveness of legal risk defences is unpredictable. Merck, the US pharmaceutical company and maker of Vioxx, appealed its conviction of 19 August 2005 when a jury in Texas awarded an unprecedented $253 million in damages to the widow of Robert Ernst, a 59-year-old marathon runner who died from an irregular heartbeat caused, so the jury concluded, by Merck's now infamous anti-inflammatory drug.

The risk Merck took with a product, which has been withdrawn from the market, does not end there. The jury's decision was the first ominous verdict in more than 4000 lawsuits the company faces over Vioxx. These reflect a dramatic decline in the fortunes of one of America's most respected pharmaceutical companies, prompting questions about its ability to survive the Vioxx crisis, at least as an independent firm.

What these and plenty of other cases suggest, is that with assumed risk – financial, legal or any other – responsibility on exposure should be assumed at board level, including the need to establish the firm's risk policy and *risk appetite*, which means the willingness of investors and other market participants to bear risks. There should be an independent risk reporting function within the overall risk management framework, with individual accountability for managing risk not only at corporate level but, also:

- At business unit level
- By major product area, and
- By geographic domain of company operations.

Another very important ingredient of rigorous risk control is a corporate culture fostering the identification and reporting of losses due to risks being assumed, as well as a robust programme for corrective action. Essential to the fostering of successful risk management, and fundamental to the survival of any firm is the practice of *looking at exposure as a cost* that should be budgeted and controlled.

2. Concepts underpinning risk and uncertainty

Risk is the chance of injury, damage or loss; a hazard. Quantitatively, risk is expressed as probability of loss. Its likelihood, however, is not a question of mathematics, but of the type of loss which is involved; the nature of exposure involved in a transaction, or inventoried position; the magnitude of damage that could be created, and its limits (if any); and the risk control measures taken in order to be in charge of assumed exposure.

Risk management experts appreciate that they must analyse and cost every risk being assumed. In so doing, they keep in mind that, as stated by Heisenberg's *Uncertainty Principle*, the act of studying a problem, let alone attempting to correct it, can fundamentally alter the nature of the problem itself. This is true throughout science – and it is just as valid in finance, where well-managed companies are keen to know their exposure:

- At any time
- For any instrument
- With any counterparty
- Anywhere in the world.

Uncertainty (noun, singular) is the quality or state of not being certain; a situation characterized by doubt. Uncertainties (noun, plural) are things not exactly known, not well determined, unsettled, or involving contingencies. Uncertain hypotheses or statements characterize an environment in which many of us have been operating for long years.

- Business people appreciate that something is vague, if it is not clearly or precisely defined.
- What they appreciate less is the amount of risk they, and their companies, assume in such situations.

Risk events are uncertain in the sense that they do *not* have a well-defined or sure pattern, or outcome. In principle, risk events imply that loss or danger is apt to be substantial. Hence, financial and other transactions should not be calculated on face value, but on the basis of assumed exposure, and likelihood of its magnitude. A well-known model, Risk Adjusted Return on Capital (RAROC), helps in doing so with credit risk.

The concept of risk – and therefore that of assumed exposure – is closely related to the idea of an *outcome* that may be probable but *not* certain. Risks can be said to be under control, *if* there is a system that flushes them out every time they exceed set limits, either individually or in a consolidated form. Risk values cannot be established once and for all, they have to be dynamically recomputed, which means that we need:

- A policy for setting and adjusting risk *limits*, in function of our risk appetite, the economy, and the market.
- *Tolerances*, which identify which deviations from set values might be acceptable.
- A *system* able to track risk in real-time, across our domain of operation, alerting senior management on exposure.

It is inevitable that some of the risks being assumed will be better defined than others. Figure 12.1 presents examples of risks associated to five different investment strategies. Typically, each type of assumed exposure evolves over time as the characteristics of its component parts change. For instance:

- Credit risk may vary by country, operations, industry sector, and individual counterparty
- Investment risk associated to bonds and equities is subject to market liquidity, interest rate changes, stock market volatility and fluctuations in exchange rates (for global investments).

Market volatility and the proliferation of financial instruments make it difficult for any single individual, even the most talented, to follow exposure by a given portfolio unassisted. Global interactions between financial institutions and investors must be properly analysed to prognosticate likely developments (see Chapter 5 on forecasting).

Innovation, deregulation, and globalization have seen to it that market complexity increases most significantly. Sophisticated investment experts (and their customers) appreciate that it is not possible to control risk without improvements

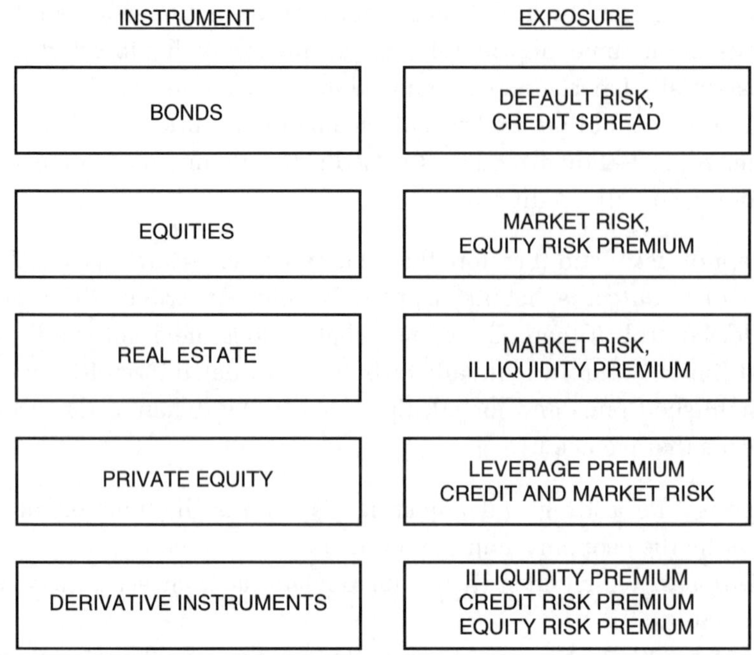

Figure 12.1 Risks associated to broad classes of investments and transactions

in technology, methodology, and organization. Interactive approaches are at a premium. There is a fundamental difference between:

- Looking at a loan on its own, and
- Examining what we get when this loan is seen as an integral part of a portfolio.

As far as the control of risk is concerned, we are also interested in how assumed exposure impacts the balance sheet and income statement. This type of analysis must be done from a lot of viewpoints, as expected profit is too summary to permit an informed decision and subsequent control. Moreover, two or more risks, and their interaction, may be present in any one transaction.

The presence of cumulative risk factors has changed the rules of the game of finance. To face evolving challenges, our grid of capturing exposure must be much finer than ever before, permitting us to capture events by risk category, class and subclass; identify operating departments where such risks originate, detailing the product (or products) entering into these transaction(s); and keeping track of the client for whom a given operation is carried out.

Additionally, special attention must be paid to package deals that may involve many products in different currencies, countries, and counterparties; as well as different conditions. And because risks accumulated through financial operations are volatile, we need an *exposure evaluation system* that focuses on patterns, with top management receiving alarm signals when:

- Risk limits are exceeded, and
- Risk patterns change.

Alarms should be activated and the calculation of trends should be always made in real-time. Graphics, like quality control charts, which are easy to understand and interpret, must be employed to assure effective visualization of obtained results.[3]

Whether by variables or by attributes, statistical quality control charts have been well established in manufacturing industry since the World War II years. Their qualities see to it that they can be effectively used as tools for *risk assessment.* Quantifying dangers, and their patterns, permits responsible executives to decide, without loss of time, *if* a particular risk is worth running further.

Statistical quality control charts and other tools like analysis of variance and experimental design, as well as sophisticated information technology, underpin *interactive computational finance.* Its goals are not only to analyse but also to help management to decide where to draw the line in terms of committed positions, credit risk, liquidity, maturity, derivatives risk, and more – with dependable estimation of exposure being the focal point. Expert systems and simulators assist both in analysis and in optimization.[4]

Here is a practical example. In the leveraged buyout (LBO) of Avis Europe by Avis USA, General Motors, and a Belgian holding company, the analysts of Lazard Brothers, the investment bank, took notice of the fact that each of the 12 countries in which Avis Europe operated had significant differences in legal issues, and in taxation. These differences greatly affected rules governing:

- How much debt can be assumed by a local subsidiary, and
- How much interest will be allowed to be deduced from corporate taxes.

To facilitate the Avis transaction, Lazard Brothers analysts designed a simulator able to figure out the optimal placement of the debt to minimize taxes; experiment with and maximize the effect of lower interest rates in some countries and currencies; and avoid falling foul of corporate laws on currency and dividend outflows. In turn this capped the risks involved in the LBO.

3. The cost of risk may be more than half the cost of capital

Product characteristics, pricing, cash flow, projected performance, and most evidently risk, have to be thoroughly investigated prior to making a commitment. This must be done under different market conditions. Additionally, prior to handling the mathematics of a complex financial situation and the exposure which it involves, the financial executive, banker or investor has to settle the concepts and policies on which the risk control system will rest.

At top of the list of priorities is settling the *cost of risk* (which will be exemplified through the Fidelity and Refco case studies, respectively in sections 5 and 7). The cost of risk comes over and above the so-called *free-of-risk cost of capital*, which is an opportunity cost. At root, the cost of capital can be seen as consisting of at least two layers:

- Free-of-risk, and
- Needed risk-premium to face all aspects of exposure.

Free-of-risk is the return that could be obtained in a secure investment that is similar in duration to capital tied up in the project. For instance, an investment in US Treasury bonds. To this riskless cost of capital should be added the cost of risk which is specific by instrument, transaction, counterparty, market, and so on – therefore much more difficult to calculate than the free-of-risk cost component.

For instance, a major component of the cost of risk with a debt instrument is *inflation*.[5] Inflation is market risk of a special type. Government deficits feed inflation, Arthur Burns, a former chairman of the Fed, used to say to his students at Columbia University. Government deficits and government mismanagement, too. The two correlate. Beyond inflation, which reduces by so much the fair value of capital embedded in a fixed interest rate instrument, investment decisions are subject to:

- Credit risk
- Other market risks, and
- Operational risk associated to transactions.

Many firms have been developing different models to account for cost of risks but, as George Soros suggests, one of the major problems with current financial models is that they are generally constructed on the assumption of efficient market theory. That theory is in conflict with the fact of imperfect understanding of the market, which sees to it that the models break down.

Soros, for instance says that even if the model's failure is only 1%, this is a reason for being concerned. In his words: 'I see a certain systemic risk that cannot be encapsulated in those assumptions that generally assume a continuous market. I am particularly interested in discontinuities and I find that those measurements are of little use to me.'[6]

George Soros is very generous in his reference to 1% model failure. If the models to which he makes reference were working even 90% of the time, it would have been great. But this is not the case. There are not many valid models at the present time which address in a rigorous way the calculation of risk premium, providing accurate enough results for a growing array of circumstances.

While models and simulators are useful, model risk is omnipresent, even if many practitioners refuse to admit its existence. They would use any irrelevant model in the most counterproductive manner, just to say that 'they use models'. In a seminar I gave in London on Basel II, in late September 2005, a few of the participants got very nervous when I said that $VAR_{99.97}$ is simply ridiculous.[7]

- Not only did they use it regularly to calculate unexpected losses
- But they also believed in the (unreliable) results $VAR_{99.97}$ was giving, without any cross-validation.

As an example on model failure, George Soros uses the case of interest exposure. Usually, when we deal with interest exposure, we reduce everything to the equivalence of a 30-year bond. So we convert even a T-bill to a 30-year bond equivalent, and we are willing to invest our capital along the three axes of references shown in Figure 12.2.

This is, however, a relatively simple model which does not account for the fact that some of these stated risks reinforce each other. And there is also still greater amplification of assumed exposure, as N after-effect of *leverage*, which is a fourth dimension not shown in the axes of reference in Figure 12.2.

It is appropriate to notice that this three-dimensional presentation is by no means the simplest approach possible. Indeed, it is one that gives a much better view than the classical one-dimensional presentation of exposure, or the equally traditional two-dimensional graph. The point is that, to increase accuracy of our risk evaluation, we must map an n-dimensional space by introducing other key variables such as *leverage* – which cannot be handled through the now classical models.

'Leverage', Soros suggests, 'gives us much greater flexibility than if we operated with a two-dimensional portfolio. Managers of bond funds, if they have a positive

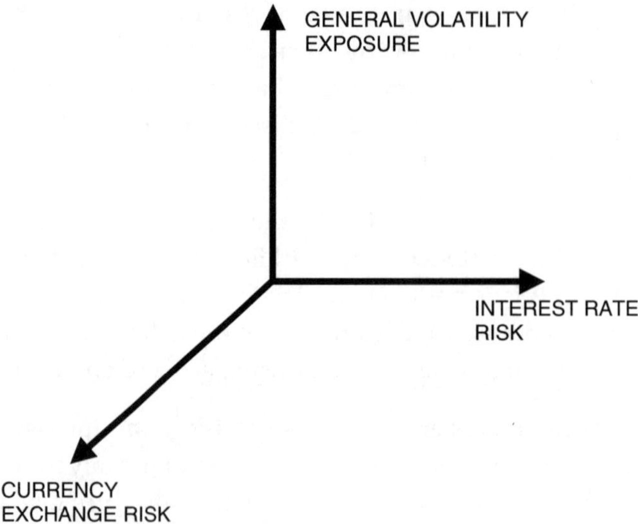

Figure 12.2 Risk-premium analysis in a coordinate system that might permit better visibility

view of interest rates, can lengthen the maturity of their portfolio to, at most, 15 years. When they have a negative view, they can keep the average maturity very short. We have much greater freedom to manoeuvre. When we are bearish, we can sell short; when we are bullish, we don't have to buy long maturities. We can buy short maturities but use a lot of leverage.'[8]

Leverage, the Hungarian financier advises, permits us to position the fund to take advantage of larger trends. This has become known as *macroinvesting*. Within those larger trends it is possible to pick stocks and stock groups. Moreover, *if* derivative instruments are used, *then* this fourth dimension is magnified. A reliable model must also include *time* as a fifth dimension, or more precisely *duration*. Risk estimates can be meaningless without accounting for duration.

- A capital of $100 million invested in Treasury bills has a much different risk factor than $100 million invested in 30-year Treasury bonds.
- Additionally, investors who are in the derivative business need quite elaborate risk calculations because, for any practical purpose, they take a huge exposure without knowing it.

The message these paragraphs aim to convey is that the now classical financial models do not allow operation on many different levels of reference, like the n-dimensions we have been examining. They have been largely designed for traditional portfolios which were fairly flat, and for less sophisticated people than present-day leaders in finance.

A leverage portfolio, as most of them are today, needs advanced modelling techniques, plenty of experimentation, and steady testing. With skill, it becomes feasible to construct a four- or five-dimensional structure: for instance, models of instruments using equity capital as the base supported by the collateral value of the underlying securities, equity and leveraging credit risk or market risk exposure. A horde of uncertainties involved in that structure must be reflected into the modelling of cost-of-risk. Otherwise the result will be half-baked. This is what greater sophistication in modelling is all about.

4. The whole culture of looking at risk must be experimental

One of the mistakes often made with funding cost is that projects are valued using the interest rate payable by the company, but without reflecting the risk of the investment. The main reason behind this approach, which is wrong, is that the large majority of bankers and investors have not yet changed their mental framework, even if the instruments they use are much more complex than in the past.

For instance, many investors believe that earnings per share is something independent of how sound the company is. Bankers make a similar mistake when they approve loans, in spite of all the talk about credit rating. This has been the case in the international lending boom, which, other things being equal, had the effects of:

- Significantly lowering credit standards, by dissociating lenders from their customers, and
- Leading to the eminence of independent rating agencies, as third parties that can provide a factual opinion about creditworthiness.

One of the fallacies believed by many bankers, has been that debt ratings they used to determine the borrowing capacity of sovereign and industrial borrowers were independent of their borrowers' strategic goals and means to achieve them. When bankers, treasurers, and investors operate without reference to strategic plans of counterparties, their moves become unstable, and such instability is cumulative:

- The longer this trend to lesser prudence lasts
- The more unsettled the market becomes, and
- The more risks companies and people are taking.

Moreover, in spite of US GAAP and IFRS reporting standards, many activities are still guided by book values, not by market values. Therefore, quite often treasurers, bankers and investors are following the wrong signals. Not only are companies accustomed to work according to old bookkeeping requirements, but also the supervisory authority has a great deal of training work to do as far as their own personnel are concerned.

One of the senior executives who participated in the research that led to this book suggested that it is simply impossible to dance to the tune of bureaucracy (whether corporate or governmental) and at the same time dance to the tune of the market. He also pointed out that, moreover, one of the main uses of derivatives is their ability to circumvent regulations, adding that:

- Regulations are absolutely necessary. Without them, there will be chaos.
- But because of derivative financial instruments, successful regulations can no longer be of a purely accounting type.

This expert is right. A new and better approach to regulation should be *experimental*; the 'show me' type supported through interactive computational finance. In fact, since the late 19th century, work by Leon Walras and Vilfredo Pareto has focused not only on mathematical approaches but also on experimentation as such – whose concept originated with the seminal work by Claude Bernard on experimental medicine, in the mid-19th century.

An experimental approach is not only the best; it is the only rigorous way to factor into a model the *risk premium*. For instance, in studying the exposure assumed when we take positions – long or short – in currencies or index futures, it is wise to experiment on how specific positions reinforce each other over time.

- Today, as George Soros says, usually two days, one up and one down day, are sufficient to tell how the fund is positioned.
- Tomorrow, with the mounting complexity of financial instruments and transactions, two days would be utterly insufficient for forward-looking experimentation.

The concept of experimentation is well known from the physical sciences. In finance, experimentation permits us to gain insight on risk-premium. This should not be difficult to understand. If it seems difficult, it is because the concept of experimentation is alien to most bankers and investors.

Yet, market forces have become globalized and this led to a mutual self-reinforcing interaction between values that guide people and the course of events. Because this is done on an international scale, models that assume efficient markets and near-equilibrium conditions are incapable of mapping:

- The diverse and colliding real world, and
- The value systems of market participants.

Another problem with simplistic approaches to risk management is that, quite often, what investors believe to be fundamental values turn out to be wrong bets. Wrong bets are also made when we don't sort out our priorities, or fail to clearly define our goals. This is particularly true in a market environment characterized by instruments that are at the same time:

- Polyvalent, and
- Ambivalent.

For instance, index futures are being used sometimes for hedging purposes, and sometimes to gain market exposure either on the long or the short side. 'We don't use options very much,' says George Soros, 'because we don't know how to fit them into the exposure we are willing to live with'[9] – and in his book he explains the reasons why:

- When you buy options, you pay the professionals a hefty premium for providing a leverage that you can create cheaper yourself by borrowing against your securities, and
- There is more risk in taking an actual position in a stock and borrowing against it, than in buying an option; but you can match your risks better when you are dealing with actual exposure than when you have options.

Conversely, when one sells options, assumed exposure does not necessarily mix well with the risks inherent in a leveraged portfolio. Therefore, a better approach is discounting a capital investment project at rate of return, including both components of cost of capital: risk-free and taking account of risk being taken, not only the riskless rate of interest. Never forget the *risk premium*.

In conclusion, no project is ' riskless' and therefore none should have its cash flows discounted at risk-free rate of interest. But no risk premium should ever be based on averages and guesswork. This is a very poor way to proceed and it can be awfully misleading. The recommended way is modelling and experimentation, with stress testing an integral part of the experimental approach.[10]

5. A case study with Fidelity Investments' risk in 1994

Fidelity is the largest independent investment management organization in the world, with a network of fund management operations in the United States and in Europe. The company traces its origins to 1930, when Andersen & Cromwell, a Boston money manager, established the Fidelity Fund as a vehicle to manage clients' investment accounts. In 1942, the fund was acquired by Edward Johnson who, three years later, established the Fidelity Management & Research Company to provide investment advice to the Fidelity Fund and other mutual funds launched under the Fidelity name.

Fidelity prospered in the rolling stock markets of the 1950s and 1960s, capitalizing on the skills of its investment managers. By 1972, when Edward Johnson III assumed managerial responsibilities, assets under management had grown from $3 million in 1943 to over $3 billion – by three orders of magnitude in an equal number of decades.

A decline was experienced by the mutual fund market during the 1970s, the years of 'stagflation'. However, a combination of new products, innovative marketing and the fund manager's knowledge, enabled Fidelity to continue to prosper. Its speciality has always been managing equity funds.

- The long bull market of the 1980s was particularly advantageous for the company, and
- In 1990, it became the first investment firm to manage assets in excess of $100 billion.

Adversity, however, struck in December 1994. Subsequently, risk management controls at Fidelity saw to it that investments in emerging markets, which have been frequently used by the mutual fund's managers to beef-up performance, became subject to a *liquidity framework.* The company's risk management worked on:

- Ways to measure the safety of fund investments, and
- Means for evaluating liquidity concerns when the funds make big bets.

In principle, any fund manager is supposed to be able to pick the right time to switch between equities and/or markets. Switching between markets is supported to enable investors to take advantage of globalization. That is, however, theory. Evidence suggests that investing through global funds involves risks that can be and should be monetized.

At Fidelity, management tried to cut down on the pack mentality that leads so many managers into the same stocks. For instance, it halted the internal distribution of *daily night sheets* listing the prior day's trading records of all portfolio managers, which enabled others of the firm's portfolio managers to piggyback on one another's trading.

There were also other problems. Since the early 1990s critics have been saying that size was beginning to hinder the Fidelity funds. Managers were finding it increasingly difficult to manoeuvre their huge holdings in and out of the stock-market. And the company's prominence has led to an extraordinary level of scrutiny by the Securities & Exchange Commission (SEC).

In 1994, Fidelity had $8 billion invested in emerging markets. But SEC had no charter to tell the funds to stay at home. Had that happened, it would have been against the prevailing current, as financial advisers and the finance press in the United States have been urging Americans to place some of their investments overseas. As an expert investment adviser put it at that time, it is also a function of:

- Where one is in one's development as an investor, and
- Losses can happen with investments in the home market as well.

That investment adviser was right. In 1994, aggressive investments by some Fidelity professionals and managers, combined with rising interest rates, produced dreadful results and, according to some sources, major losses. Most embarrassing were hits to the firm's most conservative short-term funds, which had been the vehicles investors counted on never to lose money.

On 6 December 1994, Fidelity Investments announced that its Magellan Fund would probably have no year-end distribution, rather than the $4.32 per share previously estimated. Fidelity said the change was part of the normal review and verification process, and did not reflect any recent portfolio activity. But financial analysts suggested that this underscored the notion that top-calibre investment funds may report disappointing results. On Wall Street,

- Many observers generally attributed those losses to rising interest rates.
- While others suggested that the fate of leveraged portfolios is uncertain, particularly in a highly illiquid, end-of-the-year market where few of them are traded.

At the time, the Magellan Fund was valued at $36 billion and, among investment experts, some wondered if Magellan's losses were due to derivatives. On the hypothesis that the losses suffered by Magellan took care of the $4.32 dividend featured the previous year, this money was taken as proxy of the *monetization of risk*, which was assumed, down to the level of the individual investor. Further losses, which were not made public, could be treated the same way on a per share basis.

There has also been an aftermath in the market at large. In the United States, as the troubles at Fidelity Investments and Orange County bankruptcy news hit the market, some bonds were reportedly out for bid, and traders said someone appeared to be testing the market's response. This was a plausible hypothesis, which extends to monetization of risk to the ask-bid spread level.

Moreover, the Magellan Fund news reverberated worldwide, causing anxiety in London about the stability of mutual funds in the United States and the UK. Such news was viewed as problematic for European stock markets, because it provided yet another incentive, along with jitters about interest-rate increases, for scrutinizing not only losses in P&L figures but, also, withdrawals by fund clients.

As shareholders pulled out hundreds of millions of dollars, in late January 1995, Fidelity took a proactive stand. The Boston-based fund group responded to its investors' concerns by sending them an educational pamphlet explaining the kinds of derivatives used by its portfolio managers. Fidelity's swift action helped reassure most of its clients, but at the same time this pamphlet surprised some investors.

- They had thought that their bond fund invested in US Treasuries, German bonds or British gilts.
- But they discovered that it also used structured notes,[11] interest-rate futures, currency forwards, and other (then) exotic products.

Investors also discovered that among mutual funds, Fidelity is not alone in using derivative financial instruments. Most fund managers had been using derivatives as tools supposedly 'to reduce risk'. In reality, many of them used derivatives aggressively to increase returns, *if* their view of interest rates, equity market movements, or commodity prices was right. In their defence, fund managers said that investors have contradictory goals, leading them to wonder:

- How they can balance performance with conservatism in investments, and
- How they can employ great caution in their investment strategy and still come up with two-digit annual returns.

The irony, these investment managers commented, was that if *they* pulled back too hard, their investors would suffer. If they go too conservative, they would be likely to recuperate losses, or to show high returns in the years to come. Critics, however, had a different view than that of investment professionals.

After the Magellan debacle of late 1994 critics said that at Fidelity Investments, as elsewhere, a major part of the problem has been that the ground of professionals' and managers' compensation system generates handsome annual performance bonuses *without* accounting for risk. This pushes the traders towards more risk-taking not only for higher profits, but also for higher commissions. The market made its message clear, as Fidelity lost 11% of its bond-fund assets.

While this is now past, and a dozen years down the line it has been largely forgotten, it is always a sound policy to remember past lessons, and the investors' pain associated with them. Risk has a price that should be fully accounted for in every investment decision. The challenge is how to integrate it with the strategy of an investment portfolio, when the individual investor is in the dark about risks assumed by fund managers.

6. Monetization of risk and wealth management

Any organization aiming to survive in times of turbulence must spend significant time and effort in studying the risks it has assumed, and those risks that new transactions bring in. Out of the results of analytical risk studies evolve business strategies that are flexible and dynamic, and therefore adaptable to changing:

- Circumstances, and
- Exposure profiles.

This is a principle valid for practically every company that confronts, on a daily basis, the uncertainties of the market. It is even more so for financial institutions whose functions have become very different than those of classical banking – for instance, institutions whose main theme is the *management of wealth* rather than deposits, loans, and securities trading.

The able management of wealth involves not only handholding and the provision of products and services that are increasingly personalized, but also accurate and efficient risk control. Investors are becoming more and more inquisitive about how their wealth is handled, as the alumni disgruntlement at Harvard Endowment has shown.

- This 2005 alumni revolt concerned performance bonuses paid in the past to the fund's managers.
- Asset management and other investment advisory services, however, will do well to look at it from a broader perspective – because it is a forerunner of things to come.

Featuring AAA credit rating, tax-exempt status and long-term investment outlook, the Harvard Management Company (HMC), the entity investing that university's $25.9 billion endowment, is a good place for asset managers to exercise their skills. But while HMC's high visibility is attractive, its limited compensation by lowering the cap of bonuses (in the aftermath of the alumni reaction), made it difficult for Harvard to attract wealth managers.

Nobody can really tell what's the ' right' compensation for an investment professional. Neither do all investors appreciate how much they pay in wealth management fees. Additionally, most investors don't appreciate how much risk they assume which is not converted into the cost of the investment, as should be the case (see section 3). And while fees can be negotiated (though few investors care to do so), the risks assumed by wealth managers are there to stay.

Starting with the fundamentals, wealth management is a fairly complex task that requires a great deal of expertise. Wealth managers prefer to run discretionary accounts, where the client gives them full power to make decisions. Savvy investors, on the other hand, mainly ask for advice and information, using their know-how to make investment decisions for themselves.

Professional investment advisers see their mission as one that goes well beyond picking stocks and bonds. They include in it the task of hedging the client's unwanted risks, but also of acquiring new risks that suit their chosen investment profile. This involves not just trading and recordkeeping but also analytically:

- Unbundling,
- Transforming, and
- Repackaging risks.

Along the principles section 2 outlined, this mission should also involve costing each risk, which is far from being the general case. Yet, as it has been explained, the monetization of assumed risk is the best strategy in keeping the investor informed on the status of his or her wealth under management. Tier-1 brokers do so by marking to market the client's holdings in their monthly reports – and ad hoc, on request.

Wealth managers who don't follow this approach advance as an argument that, in the majority, investors don't have the necessary skills to extract from their marked to market accounts the elements necessary for monetizing the risk they have assumed. Yet, this is fairly easily done by computing the mean and standard deviation of reported fair value:

- Short term, over one year, and
- Medium term in a three- to five-year timeframe.

The implementation of this approach to quantification of every position's volatility is instrumental in providing the investor with a clear vision of risk assumed with financial products, in the market environment within which these products exist. Wealth management vision can be improved by technology, which should not be a problem as the new generation of investors is most agile in on-line datamining and in visualization.

My experience in the banking industry has convinced me that financial institutions have an embedded interest in promoting the risk management skills of their clients, because in this evolving global financial market *wealth accounts* have become a key currency. Today, the better-governed companies, and more sophisticated individual investors, hold their assets and liabilities in readily, interactively accessible accounts – with risk being a transparent quantity.

In the years to come, investors will still hold financial instruments such as stocks, bonds, and derivative products, as well as physical wealth like buildings, farms, and vehicles. But model-based interactive financial systems will continuously track each item in one's individual wealth account:

- Constantly mark it to market (or to model), and
- Try to make it liquid under fair value conditions.

Fair valuing is an excellent test, because *if* an investment position can only be liquefied through fire sale, *then* the risk that has been assumed is most significant. Stress testing is another 'must', as it helps to reveal the effect on a portfolio's value of a significant increase in market risk or credit risk.

The way to bet is that coming development will magnify the interest in fair value tests and stress tests. Some of the banks that invest a great deal in forward planning and research talk of a coming development of individual *wealth cards*. With them, one can pay, for instance, for a new car by instantly drawing on part of the wealth inherent in, say, a vacation house anywhere in the world. These wealth cards will essentially be a subset of one's wealth account.

At the same time, derivative financial instruments already see to it that virtual assets and virtual liabilities are traded globally at any time, in any currency, anywhere in the world. Virtual money transactions are facilitated by exchanges that become increasingly electronic bulletin boards, the medium through which buyers and sellers post their needs and execute transactions. Ongoing studies indicate that, in the future, the majority of financial transactions will be different from those we know today.

- Starting with forward and other derivative financial instruments, the trend will be *mass customization*.
- With high technology, many financial products can be tailored to a client's need at a reasonable price, the challenge being that of properly costing assumed risk.

On all evidence, this trend will increasingly include highly personalized services from financial companies selling to market segments, made up not just of giant institutional investors but also of single households, or a single individual investor. It is not for nothing that Wall Street firms are engaging more and more experts in mathematical modelling of financial phenomena who explore:

- Portfolio opportunities
- Asset pricing algorithms
- Option pricing heuristics, and
- Market *inefficiency* theories.

All four bullets identify issues prominent in non-traditional research. One of the goals of these studies is customized products and services. A second objective is innovation to gain market advantage. A third is the early identification of transient market opportunities where profits can be made but the opportunity window is short-lived.

Scandals, however, can turn all these projections on their head, and they are a sort of risk not so easy to monetize in advance. Refco, one of the United States's largest futures brokers, and its biggest retail commodities broker, provides an example (see section 7). It also gives evidence that financial scams include a cocktail of credit risk and market risk, which can be lethal not only to investors but also to the financial entity itself.

7. Credit, market, and operational risk in one cup:[12] case study with Refco, 2005

Phillip Bennett, Refco's chief executive officer, has been charged by Federal prosecutors with defrauding investors in the firm's initial public offering (IPO), which took place in August 2005. Allegedly, he did so by hiding hundreds of millions of dollars in loans to another company that he controlled.

This is an excellent case study on operational risk, compounded by credit risk, because of the CEO's lack of accountability. It is a case of operational risk that also brought market risk into the cocktail of exposures, after traders got wind of what was going on at Refco. Indeed, operational risk is a polyvalent issue that originally centred on fraud and on errors in payments and settlements, but currently identifies all sorts of management weakness.

- Organizational deficiencies
- Wanting professional skills

- Substandard internal control
- Unreliable auditing practices
- Defective execution methods
- Substandard fiduciary and trust activities
- Defective security solutions
- Serious gaps in infrastructure
- Obsolete technology and model risk.

Many of the risks outlined in the preceding bullets correlate with one another, and merge into the much broader perspective of an ever-growing legal risk. Within a week after the Refco scandal broke into the open (more on this later) several lawsuits had been filed. At the same time, accounting experts said it was almost inconceivable that:

- A debt of $430 million could remain hidden for an extended period of time, and
- *If* that happened, *then* Refco's CEO used very sophisticated means to cover the alleged shifting of money between firms.

Nor was the legal risk of this case contained only within the walls of one company. In fact, two class actions against Refco also named Grant Thornton, the company's principal auditor, as a defendant, while the certified public accountant maintained that it was the victim of 'purposeful deception' – which itself is another operational risk.

Prosecutors became aware of a possible scam when, in early October 2005, Refco announced the findings of an internal review. This showed that Bennett had borrowed $430 million through another company. While the money was repaid on the day of the announcement, and Bennett placed on leave, the news triggered a sharp reaction in the financial markets:

- Refco's share price fell more than half in two days, and
- The company's equity lost even more the day after Bennett's arrest.

According to Federal prosecutors, since late 2004 Refco's CEO had actively participated in a scheme to hide as much as $545 million, with the money cleverly repaid just before routine audits. Moreover, an initial internal review found a receivable owed to Refco by a firm controlled by Bennett, largely consisting of uncollectable historical obligations owed by unrelated third parties to Refco.

When Refco filed for bankruptcy on 17 October 2005, some analysts said that its sheer size made its collapse an important test of the resilience of the industry.

The company was a major market player, possessing $654 million in derivative contracts in the year to February 2005, more than:

- The Chicago Board of Trade (CBOT)
- Or the New York Mercantile Exchange.[13]

Several equity investors who joined the Refco bandwagon when it went public in August 2005 have been licking their wounds. The IPO was at a little above $20 and the equity's price rose to $30 over a two-month period. As is to be expected, after the scandal it collapsed to $8.

Creditors, too, have been nursing losses after Refco's fall. At top of the creditors' list was an Austrian bank that lent 350 million euro ($418 million) to Bennett to repay money he owed Refco. Other major creditors included Wells Fargo, a US fund, and a Moscow hedge fund. Also firms in the Bahamas, Italy, and Venezuela.

Beyond this, a good deal of uncertainty surrounded the fate of customers, many of them hedge funds, whose accounts were frozen when now defunct Refco Capital Markets, an unregulated entity that specialized in off-exchange trading (primarily in foreign currency), suspended operations on 13 October 2005. It was *as if* these client hedge funds had found their nemesis.

Refco is one more example documenting why, as the Introduction underlined, we must stop talking of risk as being balanced by return. Credit, market, and operational risk are *costs* – as Refco's creditors, shareholders, and clients found out the hard way. And more costs may be on the way. According to some experts, the defunct company's client funds faced two potential problems:

- Inability to manage their strategies, and get investors' money out
- A fall-off in the liquidity Refco provided to the market, which in turn forces leveraged investors to liquidate assets.

On Wall Street, experts said that, quite likely, entities that will be most affected are small hedge funds that did not have more than one clearing firm for their trades, and did not count risk as a cost. Moody's Investors Service suggested that at least 87 transactions in collateralized debt obligations (CDOs) that it had rated had been affected by Refco's bankruptcy.

- All these were cash transactions, and
- Therefore, most were likely to be tied to Refco Capital Markets.

Had the former chairman of the Securities and Exchange Commission (SEC) succeeded in his efforts to have hedge funds registered and supervised, the fallout of Refco's bankruptcy might have been less acute. But in April 2005, Donaldson was fired by George W. Bush as big hedge funds:

- Complained that regulation was against *their* best interests, and
- Had the political muscle to throw the top regulator, a former investment banker who knew his business, out of SEC.

The silver lining was that the timing of the Refco scandal has been perfect. Ironically, it occurred as American lawmakers were conducting a regular review of the regulation of commodities and futures industries. As with the Enron scandal, which resulted in the 2002 Sarbanes–Oxley Act, the Refco scandal could be instrumental in leading legislators along the right path.

The Chicago Mercantile Exchange, and other exchanges, urged Congress to bring off-exchange trading in currency derivatives, in which Refco Capital Markets was engaged, under the authority of the Commodity Futures Trading Commission (CFTC). To the contrary, the International Swaps and Derivatives Association (ISDA), which represents firms in the derivatives industry, claimed that such rules would dampen volume. Big banks and SEC under its new boss were also against extending the regulator's authority. That is wrong, because as everybody should appreciate:

- Business is made on confidence, and
- When confidence disappears, business opportunity goes with it.

In the aftermath of the scandal, Refco stated that financial statements, including that of 2002, cannot be relied on, and that questionable transactions may date back as far as 1998.[14] Credit institutions, hedge funds, and other counterparties that used Refco's services in different trades and were therefore affected by the fallout should be the first to realize that confidence in any system is badly shaken by scams.

Notes

1 Statistics from a personal meeting with MHTC in the course of a research project.

2 D.N. Chorafas, *Operational Risk Control with Basel II: Basic Principles and Capital Requirements.* Elsevier, Oxford, 2004. Operational risk is also discussed in section 7 and in Chapter 16.

3 D.N. Chorafas, *Reliable Financial Reporting and Internal Control: A Global Implementation Guide.* John Wiley, New York, 2000.

4 D.N. Chorafas and Heinrich Steinmann, *Expert Systems in Banking.* Macmillan, London, 1991.

5 D.N. Chorafas, *The Management of Bond Investments and Trading of Debt.* Elsevier, Oxford, 2005.

6 G. Soros, *Soros on Soros: Staying Ahead of the Curve.* Wiley, New York, 1995.

7 The reasons are explained in D.N. Chorafas, *Economic Capital Allocation with Basel II: Cost and Benefit Analysis.* Elsevier, London, 2004.

8 Soros, *Soros on Soros.*

9 Ibid.

10 D.N. Chorafas, *Stress Testing: Risk Management Strategies for Extreme Events.* Euromoney, London, 2003.

11 D.N. Chorafas, *Wealth Management: Private Banking, Investment Decisions and Structured Financial Products.* Elsevier, Oxford, 2005.

12 Operational risk is discussed in Chapter 16.

13 *The Economist*, 22 October 2005.

14 *The Economist*, 15 October 2005.

13 Strategies for Sustained Profitability

1. Introduction

The financial and industrial events of the 1990s and early years of the 21st century have forced on boards, CEOs, and senior managers a greater concern about *profitability* than ever before in the post-World War II years. This has been translated into:

- Better strategic choices of business lines
- Faster new product offerings
- A more rigorous cost control, and
- Improvements sought after in risk management.

The crumbling of the Soviet Empire, new leadership in Eastern Europe and in Russia, as well as a change of heart in China's rules, saw to it that during the 1990s the profit motive was in the ascendancy. Early 21st century privatizations pushed in the same direction. At the same time, experiences with state control of the economy helped in enforcing the conviction that social freedom is not possible without economic freedom.

Not everything taking place in the profitability domain is, however, positive. Unwilling to change past habits and restructure their social safety net, many countries have tried to substitute mass for purpose, only to find out that in the longer run this never really works. Fundamentally:

- Greater profitability is based on better performance, and
- Performance requires concentration on goals, setting precise objectives, working smarter, establishing priorities and sticking to them.

Whole countries, not just companies, fall into decline when their management is unwilling or unable to establish, and put into effect, a strategy that can provide a quantum leap in performance. Argentina hit the skids in the 1990s. Today Italy seems to be taking a similar course, lagging way behind the European Union average, as Table 13.1 shows, in:

- Productivity, and
- Added value in products and services.

For a company, profitability is a function of a complex equation of productivity improvements, innovation in products and services, market appeal, earnings, expenses, and risks. Earnings must be increased while expenses and risks must be put under lock and key. Tough cost control should take care of the expense side, as we saw in Chapter 11. And risks should be monetized, as Chapter 12 has explained.

Table 13.1 Italy versus the European Union average

Indicator	Italy	EU
Industrial productivity	+0.7%	+2.1%
Added value in industry	+0.8%	+1.8%
Productivity in services	−0.1%	+0.9%
Added value in services	+2.5%	+3.4%

Source: *La Republica*, 18 May 2005

Together with first-class management, *profitability* is one of the top criteria financial analysts use in order to evaluate an organization's present and future business perspective and trustworthiness. For this purpose, they assess the quality of each entity's earnings, and they adjust the results being reported by the firm when these differ from their own estimates about a company's ability to produce profits.

Not only stockholder value but also the interests of every stakeholder in the enterprise see to it that profitability should be examined under both longer-term and shorter-term perspective. A number of studies have explored earnings performance, in an effort to establish links between profitability and various aspects of operating decisions. Their consensus is that:

- In the shorter term, cost control is the most important factor in achieving higher profitability.
- By contrast, in the longer term profitability is best sustained by rigorous forward-looking risk control.

Focused on a relatively longer period of time of a decade or so, quality of governance makes the difference, with the ability to be in charge of risks as key determinant of profitability. A first-class management will also be keen in reducing operating inefficiencies through reorganization and restructuring, within the framework of the strategic business plan which the enterprise has adopted.

2. Profit planning yardstick

A primary goal of many businesses is to achieve maximum continuing return on invested capital, while preserving the capital base. The issue of profits starts right there. However, without the proper profit planning methodology and coordination, results sought after will be elusive. Furthermore, the way to bet is that growth and profit goals will be set either above or below the entity's ability to produce results. Another pitfall is that business plans are separated from market reality. Therefore,

- Planning for future profits from existing business units (BU), and product lines, should be done by the heads of these units.
- Planning for new sources of earnings beyond the normal scope of existing business units and product offerings should be done at headquarters (HQ), which also has coordinating responsibilities.

Whether at BU or HQ level, invested capital must be managed effectively. Within limits, this can be done in a variety of ways among asset categories. Capital allocation to business units, and their profit centres, must aim to optimize resulting profitability.[1] Profits do not come about incidentally. They must be *planned* years in advance, to materialize in a sustainable manner.

Establishing profit objectives at corporate and business unit level will provide senior management with a factual background for capital allocation decisions. Profit strategies help in defining the means of accomplishing longer-term goals. It is probable, but not certain, that increased profits could be obtained from:

- Rapid product innovation
- Greater market penetration
- More aggressive marketing strategies
- A just-in-time inventory structure (more on this later), or management initiatives.

In connection to the first two bullets, profit planning interlocks with product planning and market planning, the third bullet is addressed by the entity's marketing strategy; however, keep in mind that product and market strategies correlate. Underlying the fourth bullet are efficiency measures affecting product capitalization (which has been defined in Chapter 11).

Strategic decisions cover the whole domain discussed in the preceding paragraph. In a static industry technically superb products are made to last, while the organization of product innovation, process modernization, and financial review is given no place worth mentioning. By contrast, in a dynamic industry, which is the general case today, market sensitivity and product innovation are given priority – flanked by financial planning.

Because planning and control work in synergy, financial planning is prerequisite to financial accountability, which should not focus on historical information alone.

- 'History' concerns the details of what has happened.
- Accounting data should be examined not only as numerical information, but also as support for qualitative inference.

Unless a specific study is undertaken to learn lessons out of the past, historical detail ends by snowing management under the weight of past numbers, thus losing the opportunity of looking forward. By contrast, a basic requirement of good governance is the ability to look forward and make reasonable hypotheses about the future course of profitability.

In a research project I held on this specific issue, the controller of the Scandinavian operations of General Motors phrased his thoughts in the following way: 'Much of the controllership today, is forecasting. The actual accounting is taken for granted, mostly. Besides, management does not want yesterday's date. It wants action forecasts.' *Action forecasts* must be made for every business unit, every market, every product, and every project, from beginning to end.

Because business units compete for funds, senior management has to resolve a number of conflicting issues. The business units themselves should clear their mind on their policies – beyond products and markets. For instance, an easier collection policy might produce more sales but it would also increase:

- The investment in working capital, and
- The risk of bad debts.

Other issues, too, should be thoroughly examined in all their facets, including inventory management (see section 4), product innovation (see Chapter 14), and market appeal and market response (see Chapter 15). A larger inventory of finished goods might sometimes result in quicker delivery, but more inventory means more investment in product capitalization and lower turnover. Moreover, this goes against the *just-in-time* (JIT) strategy followed by competitive firms.

A brief historical reference is the best way to appreciate the contribution of JIT. In the late 1930s, Toyota began the development of what has become known as the just-in-time system – which has been considerably improved in the 1960s, becoming popular as the best way to manage inventories. However, simply regarding JIT as a way for inventory reduction is a serious underestimation of its importance, because:

- JIT changes the fundamental economics of manufacturing, and
- Alters the basis of competition in many industries, *if* management capitalizes on its potential.

To clearly see the system's impact, it is appropriate to recall that the Toyota production system was born out of the need to develop a new way of manufacturing automobiles, of many different types, in small volumes but at high cost/effectiveness. JIT is the result of a strategy aimed at overcoming the disadvantage inherent in a smaller size firm. (At the time Toyota was smaller than Nissan, its key competitor in Japan.)

As the system developed in sophistication, JIT included *level scheduling*, a process in which product schedules are progressively refined in the months prior to their execution. This permits a master production schedule to be done way ahead of time, while the final production schedule is frozen only for two to four weeks. During this period no changes in the schedule are permitted.

J.C. Abegglen and G. Stalk, Jr take Yanmar Diesel as an example on how Toyota's manufacturing strategy, and JIT technology, has helped other firms.[2] In 1975, the Japanese economy was in deep recession and demand for Yanmar's diesel engines and farm equipment was severely depressed; so were profits. But while Toyota was caught in the same recession as Yanmar, it was profitable. Toyota management credited the efficiencies of the firm's unique production system for enabling it to weather the recession. Yanmar began a crash program converting to JIT, and the results were that:

- Total labor productivity in the factory almost doubled
- Work-in-process inventories shrank by 66–80%, and
- The production volume required for the factory to breakeven fell from 80% of capacity to 50%.

As these references demonstrate, profit responsibilities involve issues that concern every manager in every one of the company's divisions. Profit planning must be seen as a yardstick. Much of an executive's failure to protect the profit ratios of his or her area of responsibility can be traced to wanting management skills.

A study in commercial banking I conducted some years ago provides a good example on this yardstick reference. This study concentrated on statistically valid samples of high and low return on equity (ROE). Those credit institutions were examined that were in the higher or lower 30% of all listed banks for at least 7 out of the preceding 10 years. This criterion was chosen to assure bank samples characterized by:

- Relative consistency
- But, a distinctly different earnings performance.

The study presented an interesting insight in the banking industry's profit potential. Contrary to the often heard argument that leveraging helps produce zooming profits, the analysis of profitability data documented that high-earnings banks are significantly *less* leveraged than banks in the low-profit sample. (More on this in section 5.) Additionally:

- Higher operating expenses were recorded by the low-earnings banks
- While no differences were observed in the ability of the two bank samples to utilize the prevailing tax laws.

It is also interesting to notice that the more profitable banks tended to record lower monetized risk costs (see Chapter 12) as a percentage of total revenue than their low-profit counterparts across a number of expense categories. Additionally, high-earnings banks registered lower ratios of interest on subordinated notes, debentures, and provision for loan losses to total revenue, than the lower earners.

Among other findings, the low-earnings banks held a greater percentage of capital in subordinated debt, though this also reflected rising difficulty on the part of the lower earners in raising equity. On the other hand, the balance sheet structures of the two bank samples did not present dramatic differences, leading to the hypothesis that balance sheet variations do not provide an explanation for the operating expense differences observed between the higher and lower profitability bank samples.

In the service industry at large, and most particularly in banking, personnel expenses represent a major cost item chapter. Salaries and wages over total revenue had a ratio of 15–17% for high-earnings banks; versus 18–22% for low-earnings banks. A major problem with personnel expenses is that they are non-linear in behaviour.

Other studies have come to fairly similar conclusions. Table 13.2 shows some US statistics on selected operating expenses on total revenues. These ratios suggest that operating cost differences are a principal discriminator between high- and low-profit banks. Unfortunately, these statistics don't address the issues of whether observed cost differences reflect differences in management skill, or in risk appetite between credit institutions.

Because when they escape tight control personnel costs tend to increase exponentially, expenses incurred last year may not be able to provide a basis for current estimation of future overhead. A basic principle in management is that costs can be efficient or wasteful.

Table 13.2 Statistics on selected operating expenses on total revenue among US banks (average ratio per year)

	High earners	Low earners
Salaries and wages / total revenue	15.5	20.0
Interest on deposits / total revenue	31.7	32.5
Expense of federal funds purchased / total revenue	7.4	9.6
Interest on other borrowed money / total revenue	0.8	1.2
Interest on subordinated notes and debentures / total revenue	0.2	0.9
Provision for loan losses / total revenue	2.3	3.8
Other expenses / total revenue	17.0	22.5

- Efficient costs are associated with income-making activities
- Wasteful costs are those that do not contribute to action, production, or profit generation.

Given the impact of all cost chapters on final profit figures, a system for personal accountability is a complex set of procedures and records integrated with the company's operations. Cost control is part of the company's internal accounting management information system (IAMIS) designed to accomplish objectives not directly associated with balance sheets and disbursements.

An expert who looked up the aforementioned statistics, and tentative conclusions, came forward with an interesting insight: that economic rents provided by regulators may be sufficient to secure the longer-run position of relatively incompetent management. *If* such regulation were significantly relaxed, as part of a substantial pre-competitive deregulation of the banking industry, *then* the low-profit banks and their managers could well be forced out of business by competitive pressures. (More on the analysis of long-term trends in section 5.)

3. Profit planning in the banking industry

Cash flow and quality of profits have become an increasingly important concern in banks' boardrooms, the offices of bank regulators around the globe, as well as among analysts and investors. The great variance in cash flow streams and in profits brought home by credit institutions, as well as huge discrepancies in assumed risk, led the Basel Committee on Banking Supervision to adopt an 8% capital standard for international banks (Basel I). Established in 1988, this took effect in 1992.

To comply with the 8% requirements of Basel I, many banks have been trying to build up their capital bases. Evidently, those that made the most profits were able to boost their capital faster than their competitors. Not all credit institutions, however, were able to restructure their balance sheet because:

- Their governance was wanting
- Their profits margins were dismal, or
- They had overextended their hand in terms of assumed exposure.

The squeeze on credit institutions' profit margins came only partly because of disintermediation. Disintermediation saw to it that banks lost part of the chain that passes money from original depositor (or, more precisely, lender) to ultimate borrower. The difference has been made by factors internal to the firm whose management was substandard. Figure 13.1 presents a list of endogenous factors, which are often found to be wanting.

Figure 13.1 also shows the exogenous factors that impact on an enterprise. Some of them are novel. For instance, while competition at large is as old as business, more recently credit institutions got competition from the capital markets and

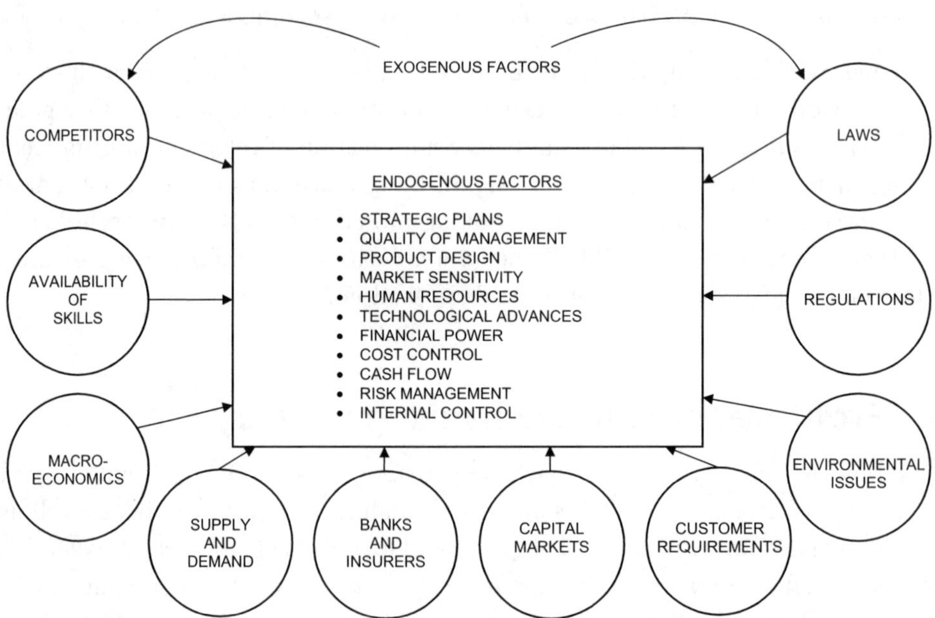

Figure 13.1 Any company feels the impact of internal and external factors that influence its course

from their own clients – which had an impact on their profits. Large companies buy one another's commercial paper, and make loans:

- This swells their balance sheets by increasing financial assets
- But it also augments their gearing, as such assets are matched by financial liabilities.

With deregulation, capital markets have entered the financing business, formerly reserved to credit institutions. And because a capital market is more efficient than a bank, in terms of cost of financing, the *net interest margin*, an important yardstick of a bank's profitability, is under siege.

Throughout the banking industry, net interest margin is a strategic important ratio because it indicates how well the spread between interest paid and interest earned is managed. One of the metrics connected to this spread, or margin, is the yield to break even. This calculation involves:

- Computing total interest earned on a tax equivalent basis, and
- Subtracting total interest expense, including interest on savings, time deposits, bought funds, and other borrowed money like capital notes and debentures.

Capitalizing on deregulation, and in order to compensate for business lost because of disintermediation, banks engage in types of loans where the capital market has not been that active: Real estate loans, leveraged-buyout (LBO) loans, as well as loans to oil firms and emerging economies are examples. In the late 1980s, however, failing property prices and a weak energy market saw to it that many banks:

- Had write-offs rather than profits, and
- Their attention was redirected to trading, particularly in derivative financial instruments.

This led to largely increased market risk, and in 1996 the Basel Committee advanced the market Risk Amendment to Basel I, requiring daily reporting on exposure. Subsequently, in mid-1999 the Basel Committee produced new rules for capital adequacy, particularly in terms of credit risk, where assumed exposure is being modelled and taken into account. Implemented in 2006 (or 2007 for big banks) Basel II:

- Changed the rules of the game, for the better, and
- It has conceptually altered the simple algorithm of Basel I based on a flat capital adequacy rate.

Even prior to this, banks that understood their interest in keeping a low risk profile looked for leadership in the more classical product lines of their industry. For instance, Citibank bought in Germany a small retail banking institution, Kundenkreditbank (KKB), and turned it into one of the most successful retail banks in Europe. In 2004, KKB's return on equity was 39%. Citibank knew what it was doing:

- It moved KKB upscale
- Thoroughly trained its personnel
- Enriched its operations with expert systems
- Provided it with a real-time technology, and
- Made its performance a 'how to' case in retail banking, in order to gain market leadership.

In terms of strategic business planning, other credit institutions looked at the development of private banking; or re-enforced their asset management activities, as the way to boost their profits. Credit institutions able to position themselves as leaders in the fee-making business saw to it that today 60% of their income comes from *fees*, while at most big banks this figure is down to 30% or less.

To the contrary, among those banks that chose to become big derivatives players, 70–75% of revenues come from trading, while interest sources like ordinary loans account for only 20%. These statistics tell a most interesting story about the divergence of business strategies among credit institutions. No two banks are the same in their strategic choices.

Whether they chose private banking, asset management, trading, loans, or retail banking as the domain of their major thrust, well-managed banks set clear parameters for profitability: they also put limits on their exposure; observe standards in pricing their products competitively; know their costs and control them; and do their best to be in charge of assumed risks. Fairly similar principles prevail in manufacturing and merchandising.

4. Profit planning in the manufacturing industry

As far as regulatory financial reporting is concerned, revenue and income follow the same frame of reference in practically every industry. There is, however, a certain confusion in terminology, with terms such as revenue, operating profits, profit before accounting change, and so on, used almost interchangeably. In fact, differences in terms being employed exist not only between industries but also among companies – particularly so when these terms are used for internal management accounting reasons.

Practically every entity has its own art of measuring profits, and the fact there are several different ways for doing so does not provide grounds for homogeneity. Additionally, each term has merits depending on company goals and what the market accepts. Key metrics of corporate profits are: operating profits, net cash flow, pretax profits, aftertax profits, and earnings before interest, taxes, depreciation, and amortization (EBITDA).[3]

Another measure of company profitability is the so-called *economic profits*. This is defined as aftertax profits adjusted for inflation, inventory valuation, and capital consumption. People and companies promoting this measure say that it allows management to view results from operations as a competitive weapon.

This kind of dispersion in regard to metrics and terminology makes the work of analysts and investors very difficult. It is always advantageous to use the same matrices for regulatory reporting and management accounting and, in my judgement, *operating profits* is the best measure of performance.

Operating profits tell the difference between yearly business and main cost chapters. In manufacturing firms, these cost chapters include: cost of goods sold, research and development, sales and marketing, general and administrative expenses. Personally, I would classify all these expenditures into two large classes:

- *Cost of doing business*: production, inventory, distribution, sales, investments, and overhead.
- *Cost of staying in business*, which includes research and development, and should also feature lifelong training of human resources.

Profit planning in manufacturing industry should target the optimization of all cost chapters falling within these bullets. In a pragmatic way of thinking, optimization means doing the same job at lesser cost, or more and better at equal cost. 'More' at 'lower cost' is a jump in two directions and is doomed to failure.

Inventory management provides a good example on profit planning in manufacturing. One strategy is just-in-time; another is inventory–shipment (I–S) ratio, which is used as a measure of industrial health, all the way down to the single company. Provided inventories are efficiently managed, in times of economic expansion the I–S shrinks. When growth expectations disappoint, and/or inventory management is poor, one usually sees a rise in the I–S ratio.

- When demand falls short, typically companies find themselves with excess inventory, and
- When the I–S ratio rises, the economic aftermath is that inflation expectations and bond yields tend to decline.

From a strategic business planning point of view, with rising I–S ratios credit spreads and supply chains come under pressure, with negative consequences for corporate cash flows, as well as for industrial pricing power. Moreover, with earnings growth set to slow, risk appetite also starts to deteriorate.

Proactive inventory management helps the bottom line, but also has its risks which, as Chapter 12 has explained, should be monetized. Take supply chain management as an example. In December 2004, Nissan Motor found itself short of steel for its four car manufacturing plants in Japan and had to suspend production temporarily at three of them.

- Nissan had reduced the number of its steel suppliers from five to two in the first years of the 21st century.

That streamlined costs, but it left the company's supply chain vulnerable, when unexpected strong demand for its new models caught it on the wrong foot.[4]

Other manufacturing companies, too, found themselves squeezed in steel supplies, and their predicament came as a wakeup call to industrial entities that have extended supply lines around the world, and run tight order management and inventory control systems. As in the case of finance and banking:

- The more sophisticated are the systems we develop and use
- The greater are the risks we assume.

Globalization has introduced new risks, which are ill-understood by the majority of companies. For this reason, risk analysis studies focusing on profit planning in manufacturing, are practised only by Tier-1 companies. Yet, they are of critical importance to all firms, because they help to evaluate the impact of major procurement decisions on manufacturing facilities. For example decisions like:

- Introducing a new product
- Adopting a new technology
- Using dynamic scheduling
- Reducing manufacturing lead time

- Cutting inventories
- Consolidating operations.

Profit planning yardsticks (see section 2) should be used in connection with each of these bullets to help in documenting their 'pluses' and 'minuses'. Such input is crucial in strategic decisions about production capacity, machine utilization, work-in-process, inventory targets, lead time, and more. Manufacturing management should be keen to evaluate trade-offs between critical elements at all stages of an industrial environment's evolution. Experimental models should be on hand, taking as input:

- Identification of work centres
- Information about current facilities
- Characteristics of product families
- Process routings, and associated operation data.

Experimenting on profit planning alternatives allows selection of the best before commitments are made. Very important in this experimentation is the ability to translate operating costs into capacity costs, work-in-process costs, inventory costs, and product family costs.

Implementing the capitalization strategy, we studied in Chapter 11 how we should differentiate between direct costs, leading to the concept of product capitalization, and other costs. We should also examine costs by work centres where they are incurred. An expert system which I developed several years ago for manufacturing operations has been using four criteria to analyse existing production facilities:

- Completeness check
- Utilization check
- Queuing heuristics, and
- Quality tracking.

The *completeness check* warned if planned utilization exceeded 100% (minus a margin) at any workcentre. In conjunction with the *utilization check*, it also helped to determine how to modify production capacity, to keep utilization below 100% – also what is the cost of such changeover and how much time it will take to recover it.

Queuing heuristics employed production capacity, scheduling, routines, operation processing time, and weekly release data to determine work-in-process inventory and lead time. A *simulator* was selectively employed to check the output queuing heuristics, as well as to permit experimentation on the ability to reach profit planning targets at the manufacturing end.

The *quality tracking* module integrated quality control charts, by attributes and by variables already in place throughout the production floor. Its contribution to added value has been the holistic view of quality, as well as the fact of pinpointing (and reporting) the standard deviations around the mean, and distance of manufactured product characteristics from limits established by tolerances. (In this sense, this application was a forerunner to Six Sigma.)[5]

5. Profitability analysis over the longer term

Many studies have explored earnings performance, in an effort to establish links between profitability and various aspects of operating policy and practice. The downside shared by several of these studies has been that they focused on one or two years – too short a timeframe for valid conclusions. Few analyses have been done on a longer-term basis. Yet, the best way to protect the bottom line is to take it as a long-term concept.

While long-, medium-, and short-term profitability criteria do not necessarily coincide among themselves, several studies tend to confirm that careful *expense control* is the most important factor in achieving higher profitability, in both the shorter- and longer-term. From this starting point, we can test expense control as a longer-term determinant of profitability.

Experience teaches that the main area where cost control should be addressed is operating expenses. Because operating expenses cannot be discussed in a meaningful way 'at large', we will take the banking industry as the first target. There are many characteristics unique to the financial business that make measuring profit contribution more difficult than in manufacturing.

This is a job requiring several assumptions. Economic theory may be good as general background, but it will *not* help much in profitability analysis. For instance, there is no great use that can be made of its premise that 'over time competitive pressure should reduce operating efficiency differences'. A more effective approach is to divide financial institutions into two groups:

- One with high rates of return on equity (ROE)
- The other containing banks that perform poorly, in terms of ROE.

Several analysts follow this path and the more sophisticated look at return on equity (ROE) trends. The problem is that there is nothing like universal ROE ratios. Every country tends to have its own standards. One of the most pronounced differences is between the United States and Japan. The snapshot presented in Table 13.3 makes very interesting reading. While Japanese entities are characterized by higher leverage than the United States, their:

- Return on equity, and
- Return on assets lags way behind.

A classification of high- and low-profitability banks is often based on annual ratios of *net income to equity*. However, while annual financial data can be taken from bank reports of condition, and from income statements, some editing may be needed because of differences in the manner of reporting income and expenses of foreign operations. In my experience, the most important ratios to be examined are:

- Net income equity
- Net income before taxes, including securities gains and losses/total revenue, and
- Total assets/equity.

Among the best performing banks, which should be the target of investment decisions, net income to equity tends to be much higher. On average, it is 40–80%), above that of low-profitability banks. Net income before taxes, including securities gains and losses, over total revenue also tends to be higher, by 100–150%. This suggests much better management of the enterprise. By contrast, the ratio of total assets to equity tends to be lower, by over 50%.

Sorting according to these criteria will lead to a differentiation between high- and low-earning banks. It is, however, proper to underline that ratios provide a quantitative, not qualitative, basis for judgement. While very different portfolio

Table 13.3 Snapshot on major differences in corporate profitability between the United States and Japan

Performance measure	US		Japan		
	Average	Best	Latest	Average	Best
Operating margin	10.1	12.0	2.5	3.8	4.8
Net margin	6.0	7.5	0.8	1.2	2.0
Asset turn (times)	1.1	1.3	1.0	1.3	1.4
Return on assets	6.4	8.0	0.8	1.2	2.0
Leverage (times)	2.4	3.4	3.5	4.5	6.0
Return in equity	14.8	22.0	2.7	6.0	13.0

structures could yield equivalent gross rates of return, some of these portfolio structures may well be much better than the others in regard to:

- The rationale of investment decisions being made, and
- The amount of leverage and exposure which has been assumed, and which may turn back to bite the investor.

As I have explained in my book on *Wealth Management*, there is a huge difference in philosophies – and in strategies being chosen – between traders and investors. The trader is a short-term operator; while the investor must care for the longer term. To help in understanding the behaviour of a portfolio in the longer term, one needs to explain differences in net rates of return characterizing different portfolio structures.

A different way of making this statement is that qualitative criteria should always be used in conjunction to profitability analysis over the longer term. For instance, it will be useful to test for differences in asset and liability composition between high- and low-profitability portfolios (as well as banks). An analytical study made along this path found that:

- High-earnings banks are significantly less leveraged than banks in the low-profit sample, and
- Poorly managed banks that try to offset their high cost structure through leverage are getting a risk exposure they cannot afford (as we saw in Chapter 12, risk is a cost).

Let me repeat this reference to assure it is properly understood. In the longer run, poor governance manifests itself in two ways: through much greater risk, and by means of run-away costs. The better net rates of return obtained by the high-profit banks derive primarily from:

- Registering lower operating costs per dollar of total revenue, and
- Being in charge of all the risks they are assuming.

As a reminder of concepts discussed in Chapter 11, a good way to address cost control issues, in the longer term, is to examine differences in balance sheet structure that may account for observed differences in operating expenses. Table 13.4 presents a model for assets structure, liabilities structure, and capital structure, which can help in analytically evaluating an entity's performance.

Last but not least, measuring the profit contribution of individual business segments is essential to the continuing profitability of operation. Given the increasing breadth of products and services offered and the high level of competition

Table 13.4 Balance sheet ratios for analytically evaluating bank performance among US banks

1.	**Asset structure**
1.1	Cash and due from third parties / total assets
1.2	State and local securities / total assets
1.3	State and local securities / total assets
1.4	Other securities / total assets
1.5	Federal funds sold / total assets
1.6	Total loans / total assets
1.7	Wholesale loans / total loans
1.8	Business loans / total loans
1.9	Retail individuals / total loans
1.10	Real estate loans / total loans
1.11	Agricultural loans / total loans
1.12	Venture capital investments / total loans
1.13	Other loans / total loans
1.14	Derivatives classified as assets / total assets
1.15	Foreign assets / total assets
1.16	Other assets / total assets
1.17	Monetized risk exposure / total assets
2.	**Liability structure**
2.1	Total deposits / total liabilities
2.2	Demand deposits / total deposits
2.3	Time and savings deposits / total deposits
2.4	Money market funds / total deposits
2.5	Deposits of state and local governments / total deposits
2.6	Deposits of other financial institutions / total deposits
2.7	Deposits of other financial institutions / total deposits
2.8	Federal funds purchased / total liabilities
2.9	Current liabilities / total liabilities
2.10	Equity / total liabilities
2.11	Derivatives classified as liabilities / total liabilities
2.12	Foreign liabilities / total liabilities
2.13	Other liabilities / total liabilities
2.14	Monetized risk exposure / total liabilities[a]
3.	**Capital structure**
3.1	Acid test: current assets / current liabilities
3.2	Capitalization (as proxy of assets / total liabilities)
3.3	Subordinate notes and debentures / total capital accounts[b]

[a] Other liabilities include other liabilities of borrowed money, deferred income taxes and miscellaneous other liabilities.

[b] Total capital accounts includes equity plus subordinated notes and debentures.

from both within and outside a given segment of industry, knowledge of both qualitative and quantitative factors characterizing products, services, and customers is vital in planning for the future.

6. Patterns of production: every country has its own characteristics

As section 5 brought to the readers' attention, in a globalized economy there are no unique ratios to characterize high profitability and low profitability credit institutions or any other entities. While the United States and Japan tend to be at the two ends of the spectrum, and ratios in other countries fall somewhere in-between, existing differences are so significant that averages mean nothing.

Table 13.3, in section 5, presented a snapshot on the major difference in corporate profitability prevailing between the United States and Japan. The pattern in Figure 13.2 dramatizes the most significant differences, over a 15-year timeframe, between US and Japanese companies – in terms of operating margin. Several reasons can be found behind such huge discrepancies.

While on the surface these reasons change over time, there are always strategic and cultural differences in the background. This statement is valid in banking and merchandising as much as in manufacturing industry. Notice that two-thirds of the 15-year period in Figure 13.2, essentially the first 10 years, are those when

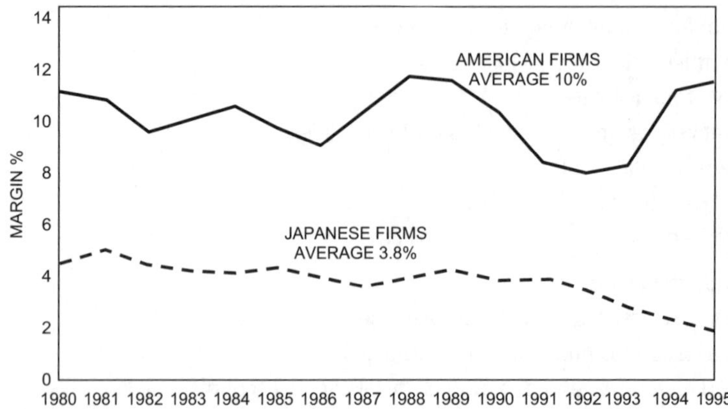

Figure 13.2 Operating margin of US and Japanese companies over a 15-year time frame

Japanese companies rode high in the global market. Still, they featured less than 40% of the operating margin of US firms.

During the last five years (1990–1995) in the Figure 13.2 pattern, the global economy went through a crisis. In the aftermath, the operating margin of US companies dropped more than that of Japanese; but by 1994 operating margins had risen for US companies while they continued deteriorating for the Japanese, who achieved post-war lows.

These results are visible at the financial end. What we should also account for is the prevailing patterns of production, which vary most significantly from one country to the next. Take the services sector as an example, which accounts for about 75% of total production in the United States, 68% of Europe and only 61% of Japan. Yet, all three areas are highly developed economies.

The industrial sector, including construction, accounts for just below a third of the total activity in Euroland. This percentage is higher than in the United States, but somewhat lower than in Japan. Primary production, such as agriculture, fishing, and forestry, is similar in all three economies; and it is limited to around 2% of total output.

With regard to world trade, Euroland has the highest share, with a ratio of exports to total global exports, at around 19.5%. This is well above that of either the United States' 15% and Japan's 8.5%. Another important criterion related to trade is the degree of *openness*, as measured by the average of exports and imports of goods and services as a percentage of gross domestic product (GDP).

- In Europe this is standing at 16%
- In the United States, at 12%, and
- In Japan, at 10.5%.

What such statistics don't say is that most trade originating in Euroland countries takes place with other Euroland countries. In this sense, from an area-wide perspective, Euroland trade is internal trade and hence unaffected by exchange rate movements of the euro *vis-à-vis* other currencies. Prior to monetary union, individual member states of Euroland were considered:

- Small or medium-sized open economies
- With significantly higher average ratios of export and import of goods to GDP.

International trade left aside, patterns of production in the three aforementioned areas – United States, Japan, and Euroland, are characterized by differences in productivity, capital investments, wage policies, and impact of the social net. Greater productivity derives from management's drive for better efficiency, advanced methods, high technology and, most evidently, capital investment.

Capital expenditures (capex) mirror, in large part, decisions of management regarding expenditures on plant and equipment, as well as in organization and infrastructure. In turn, capital expenditures are influenced by economic factors, sustainable market demand, cash flows, and the cost of capital. Capex is volatile. Its volatility in the United States, expressed as percentage of corporate profits, is shown in Figure 13.3.

An interesting comment made by a Merrill Lynch study of August 2002[6] is that in mid-2005 market liquidity was driven by the fact that corporate capex-to-cash-flow ratio was flirting with 30-year lows. Such liquidity is rarely seen in a low cost-of-capital environment. Economists consider it to be a symptom of lingering excess capital. At that time, capacity utilization rate in finished goods manufacturing stood below 78% in the United States.

For a given level of productivity and capital investment, the other important patterns of production expenditures are materials and labour costs. Proxies of

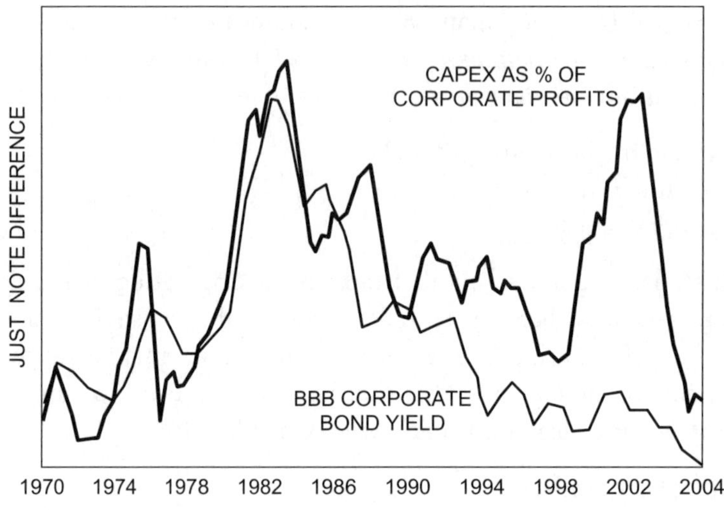

Figure 13.3 Capital spending as a percentage of corporate profits (4-quarter moving average), versus lower investment grade corporate bond yield (12-month moving average). (By permission of Merrill Lynch)

labour costs are salaries, wages, and social costs. Notice, however, that the latter do not reflect the relative productivity of labour.

- The high cost of labour weighs heavily in a global market, and social costs are outright liabilities.
- Accounting for social costs is indispensable to any analytical approach to profitability, particularly to one pinpointing weaknesses that are determinant to the bottom line.

France, Germany, and Italy are examples of countries where the pattern of production is distorted, in terms of cost/effectiveness, because it is snowed under heavy social costs. And voters make politicians say what they want to say about the maintenance of the status quo. No major changes in restructuring the social net can take place if everybody opposes them – even if they are no longer affordable.

In other terms, on the other hand, while productivity gains are critical because with globalization businesses have lost pricing power, they are not everything. Wrong way risks taken in the national economy weigh as much as productivity, or more. Additionally, failures in the quality of governance also contribute to margins being squeezed.

7. Income-based profitability, added value, and time value

At the marketing side of *our* company's products and services, value differentiation is a good strategy for boosting profitability. Developing an understanding of where value is added, as opposed to caring only where cost is incurred, is prerequisite to a sound business strategy that operates at both ends of the profitability spectrum.

Boards and CEOs of well-managed companies appreciate that it is crucial to invest in those product characteristics necessary to gain and hold a lead over rivals. This is true of all key activities in which a company participates. Income-based profitability can only be sustained by creating an edge and by continuously re-inventing the value chain. It needs no explaining that:

- Profits are far from automatic consequence of doing business, and
- In competitive environments profits are hard won and hard to sustain.

Companies that do not benefit from specific advantage in pivotal activities that impact upon their products and markets, and that do not pay enough attention to the evolution of value chains, make only modest returns. Practically they make the returns their more powerful rivals allow to make. As a result, they find themselves dictated a course of action.

Economic history teaches that profits accrue to people and firms in a powerful position. This can be created by having the foresight to invest in building up capabilities particularly important to a marketplace undergoing inevitable, though possibly gradual, restructuring. As far as the individual company is concerned, its restructuring should be characterized by:

- High market sensitivity
- Steady product innovation
- Uninterrupted cost control, and
- Focus on timely, effective risk management.

All four bullets bring forward the role of sound corporate governance, which pays plenty of attention to added value, and is not afraid to take a critical look at the company's prior performance. Strategic planning for income-based profitability requires establishing new, higher performance objectives, and (if necessary) *reinventing* the firm.

Evidently, this type of business strategy requires tough decisions. Mere words would not turn an entity into a high performer: nor will they make its products big income earners. Senior management must be willing and able to pinpoint problem areas and identify corrective action needed to acquire higher performance characteristics.

An example is management's ability to understand the combined impact of competitors' actions, and respond to market changes with a firm hand. Experimentation on the ways in which related variables affect each other is a most helpful aid prior to commitment. Experimentation also helps in keeping a sense of balance. For instance, when management targets a particular manufacturing objective, its aftereffects on other, previous goals should be properly considered. Failure to do so may have negative effects on overall performance. This is true whether we talk of:

- New product planning
- Increase in sales quotas, or any other issue.

Part of the experimental effort should be devoted to financing. Any change in current policies, including changes targeting value differentiation, require funding. Therefore, their impact must be appropriately studied. If such changes are frequent, a committed liquid assets chapter should be instituted to include all coming financial requirements resulting from present day management decisions.

What has been stated in the preceding paragraph is part of a *time phasing* strategy in financial planning, which helps to provide better visibility of the issue of inheritable assets and liabilities. Time phasing must also characterize managerial estimates regarding reallocation of resources.

The existence of an experimental facility helps in examining the aftermath of different assumptions – which is the essence of forecasting, as we saw in Chapter 5. Moreover, because important commitments are rarely short-range, their time phasing should show, in time increments, what is needed to proceed smoothly towards achieving stated objective(s). Methods can vary; two of the best are:

- % Time–% Cost (PTPC). It accounts for time leads and lags with respect to different phases of a certain project.
- Phasing Expense/Revenue Curves (PERC). Cumulative expense curves can be drawn to include R&D, manufacturing, marketing, with results contrasted to projected income curves.

Notice however that the uncertainty surrounding original estimates is *not* necessarily changed by such presentations, which break a long-term project, or management plan, into a series of time-phased projections. What is gained is better visibility and consistency in resource commitments, which make feasible a total appreciation of the situation which otherwise could be (and usually is) largely obscure.

Like any scheduling effort, this approach must benefit from steady feedback for re-evaluation. No plan can be considered worthwhile unless updates are feasible, and comparisons are steadily made between planned figures and actual results. Moreover, a plan involving financial resources must be based upon the notion of cost behaviour, including longer-term commitments.

Finally, profitability evaluations should be based upon a planning period able to anticipate recovery of the investment. Conversely, a *recovery-of-cost plus* principle can help determine the span of the planning period, while observing established return on investment (ROI) criteria. *Prospective payoff* of a project or plan of action can be evaluated by the drawing of proforma financial statements, and responding to queries such as:

- What major tasks are required to carry out the plan?
- What is the needed financial commitment?

- What is the estimated financial payoff?
- When can this payoff be expected?
- How does it measure against the company's performance goals?
- What potential problems and opportunities are created by this project or plan?

Able, punctual answers to such questions help reveal the company's anatomy of management planning, and its effectiveness. The purpose of forward-looking appraisals, and of post-mortem reappraisals, should be to monitor the internal and external environment of the firm in search of greater effectiveness. This helps to sharpen management's judgement as to whether the current business strategy holds, or a new one is called for.

Notes

1 D.N. Chorafas, *Economic Capital Allocation with Basel II: Cost and Benefit Analysis*. Elsevier, Oxford, 2004.

2 James C. Abegglen and George Stalk, Jr, *Kaisha: The Japanese Corporation*. Basic Books, New York, 1985.

3 D.N. Chorafas, *Management Risk: The Bottleneck is at the Top of the Bottle*. Macmillan/Palgrave, London, 2004.

4 *Total Telecom Magazine*, January 2005.

5 D.N. Chorafas, *Integrating ERP, CRM, Supply Chain Management and Smart Materials*. Auerbach, New York, 2001.

6 Merrill Lynch, 'Interest Rate Outlook', 1 August 2005.

Strategic Products and Markets

Strategic Products and Markets

14 Research, Development and Product Planning

1. Introduction

A key factor affecting a company's growth and survival is steady, unrelenting innovation. Globalization has given the issue of innovation a global dimension. In our society, research, development, and product planning are strategic issues; no company can do without them. The coming innovation from R&D is anchor business, requiring that senior management:

- Makes long-term commitments, and
- Considers a wide spectrum of options and projects.

Part 4 brought into perspective these issues, and their financial aftermath, when it advised that a distinction should be made between the cost of doing business and the cost of staying in business. Research, development, product planning, and market planning are part of the cost of staying in business.

What has been stated in these paragraphs is true not only of companies but also of nation-states. Take Italy as an example. The country faces a worrying loss of exports, and a major reason is the fact that its high-tech exports make up only 12% of total exports. That's half the European average.

- Italy spends only 1.1% of its GDP on research and development, and
- This compares poorly with the EU average of almost 2% and as much as 3.2% in Japan.

Moreover, Italy's market liberalization is incomplete, the country's infrastructure is poor, and social costs that push up labour costs are among the largest in Europe. Taken together, all these reasons work against creating the right conditions to attract investments, while falling behind in R&D discourages the new initiatives and new thinking that promote innovation.

Take information technology as an example. With Olivetti, Italy had one of the global players, but poor management saw to it that Olivetti went to the wall. This is bad for competitiveness, because the markets for hardware platforms, basic software applications, and tools are continuing to grow. This is fed through innovation in products and services projected to appeal to the unique requirements of specific markets, with:

- Products designed to be readily available and affordable
- Technologies that offer greater value in meeting many targeted customer needs, and
- Any-to-any communications that integrate the best available current solutions.

Being ahead of the curve, however, requires considerable investments in basic and applied research. As a generic term, *research* is the process of investigating, exploring, and enquiring, as well as fact-finding, scrutinizing, examining, probing, analysing, and experimenting. In science, research divides into:

- *Basic*, which aims at uncovering physical laws, principles, facts, and materials
- *Applied*, which targets practical application of basic research findings, leading to new product development.

The process of *development* aims to bring forth more advanced or more cost-effective products, services, and systems. In this sense, development means evolution, advancement, evolvement, and is therefore a fundamental ingredient of progress in:

- Industry, and
- Society at large.

When properly managed, the money spent on research and development, as well as in marketing and sales (M&S) positively impacts on revenues, income, and earnings per share. Figure 14.1 presents a snapshot of evolution in the key variables of corporate performance from one of the leaders in the global software business – over three consecutive years.

To be effective, the development effort must be directed towards specific product (or process) goals. This is true in all industries, from manufacturing to banking and insurance. No industry sector can allow itself to fall behind in R&D, because eventually this leads to oblivion. Every company needs a thorough studied R&D strategy which, as Table 14.1 suggests, has to focus on both:

- Strategic, and
- Tactical products.

'Most of the products we have now were built gold-plated,' said a senior executive of London's Lloyd's, the major insurance entity. 'Now we see that many customers have much simpler needs and require down-to-earth innovative products, with much broader appeal.' The Lloyd's executive pointed out three characteristics to describe the insurance products he had in mind. They must be:

- Relatively simple
- Offered at lower cost
- But with build-up capability.

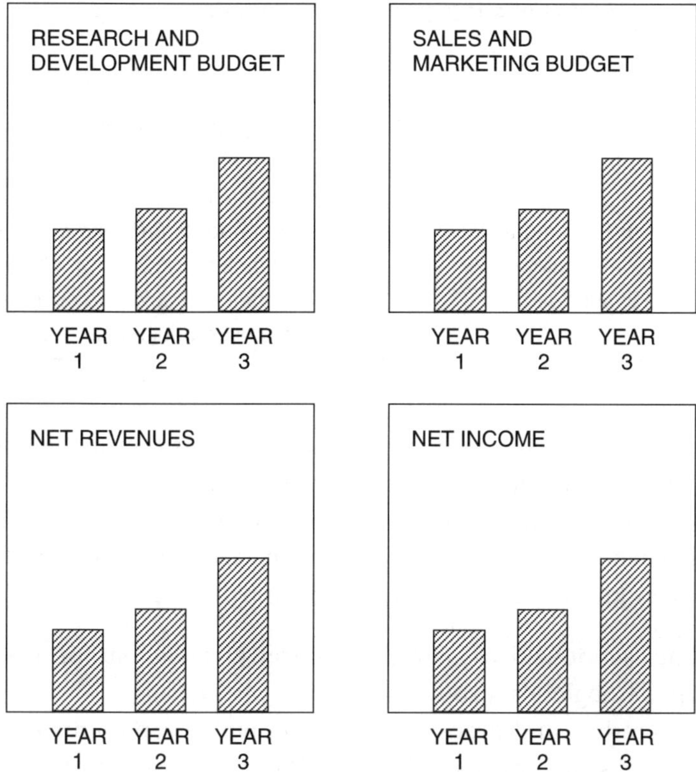

Figure 14.1 Impact of R&D and marketing / sales investments in revenues and income (just note the difference)

Having found that there is a market outside its classical clientele, Lloyd's introduced the 'Starter Account'. It also rethought the pricing policy, which will make its revamped products appealing to the market. Behind these decisions lies the fact that sound product management, good service, and cost-effectiveness in pricing are the basic ingredients of a sound strategy. They are also the mission assigned to the product planner.

2. Research and the knowledge economy

In 2005, Booz Allen Hamilton, the consultancy, made a comprehensive study assessing the influence of R&D on corporate performance. This study concluded that there is little relationship between R&D spending and the primary measures of economic or corporate success. What matters most is not how much money is spent on R&D, but *how* it is spent.

Table 14.1 Characteristics of strategic and tactical products

Strategic	Tactical
• Selected few which must get most management attention	• Many products under P+L evaluation
• Longer range	• Shorter range
• In-house R&D, with fast time-to-market	• Both in-house R&D and bought licences
• Commitment to continuation	• Under steady review for weeding out
• No money spend in subsidies	• May be given at lower cost to catch a client
• Pricing freedom	• Low cost production and distribution

R&D has a goal: the launch of new products and processes propelled by advances in technology. The most important criterion is the deliverables – the visible and tangible results of R&D investments. Precisely the same reference applies to the economy as a whole, and its participation in significant events affecting the global market. A knowledge economy is driven by two motors:

1. Brilliant service ideas which practically come out of nowhere. For example: Google, Amazon.com, EBay.
2. Steady product and process innovation, which represents a fast-growing share of gross domestic product (GDP) in many Western countries.

The Introduction made reference to what Japan and Italy invest in R&D. Adding to this the expenses for education, a recent *Business Week* article suggested that the United States is investing $1.5 trillion per year – measured by budgets for research, development, and education. This is nearly 12% of the GDP of the United States; a large figure indeed.[1]

The budget's origin is also most interesting. Of this huge amount of money, roughly $1.0 trillion for R&D and education comes from businesses; another $0.25 trillion comes from governments – also for R&D and education; and $0.25 trillion from households as parents invest in their children's future through higher education.

There is practically no counterpart for this quarter trillion contribution by households in European countries, as everything (including university education) is paid for by the government. At the same time, however, governments are chronically short of funds (which explains the sorry state of many schools and universities. It is wrong to think that students get something for nothing.

Beyond all this, the United States also benefits from huge inflows of human capital, estimated at $0.2 trillion per year, as many young people from the educated elite of other countries flock to the United States to make a career. Notice that as of recently this has included many young French people who have finally overcome the language barrier and now find top jobs in the UK and the United States.

The deliverables, and more precisely the end result, is what counts. The point these reference make is simple. Globalization has broken down the obsolete country barriers and events seem to favour those countries which are 'on the go'.

- Scientists flock to where they are appreciated, and
- Plenty of those left behind are those unwilling or unable to provide creative work.

Scientific immigrants (and I consider myself an example) are motivated to make great efforts, and move ahead, because they can only depend on their brains and their produce. This pushes out the frontiers of innovation. For instance, most of the innovation on pharmaceuticals these days comes from small new entities, while R&D activity in big pharmaceutical firms concentrates a great deal on identifying and doing deals with small, innovative firms.

Curiously enough, many of the better-known laboratories have proved sterile in recent years, while marketing departments have become a hive of creative activity by forging alliances. Additionally, the post-World War II giant labs have disappeared in a most radical redistribution of R&D effort. The giants in the early 1950s were the Bell Labs and General Motors Laboratories. Today, both are dwarfs, and the same is true of others of the top 10 of the 1950s. Judged by the number of patents obtained in 2005, the top 10 now are:[2]

- IBM, with 2941 patents
- Cannon, 1828
- Hewlett–Packard, 1797
- Matsushita, 1688
- Samsung, 1641
- Micron Technology, 1561
- Intel, 1549
- Hitachi, 1271
- Toshiba, 1258
- Fujitsu, 1154

This means four US, five Japanese, one Korean – but no European creative lab in this number of patents. It also should be appreciated that all these top 10 are global firms, and their R&D budget is directly linked to implementations – innovative products that address the global market. The reader should also keep in mind that today most of the big spenders in R&D follow a polyvalent strategy, aimed to assure a flow of new ideas. For instance, Motorola has four main sources from which it hopes to draw concepts of innovation:

- Universities, where it funds research in areas of interest to it
- Government bodies, to which it applies for research grants
- Small and medium-size enterprises, from which it licenses or buys new ideas, and
- Its own in-house venture capital fund, which promotes and finances start-ups of interest to the firm.

But while financing of research, development, and innovation is necessary, by itself it is not enough. Innovation is too important for the future to be left to its own devices. It must be properly managed – and non-conventional development methods are at a premium.

Planning, control, and organization for R&D has itself been the subject for innovation. A great deal of Motorola's Razr mobile phone, a big market hit, was developed in a new laboratory that the company set up in downtown Chicago, 50 miles from its main R&D facility. The building and its workspace are very different from Motorola's classical offices, with lots of:

- Rigorous schedules
- Dividing walls, and
- Bright colors.

This emerging new R&D organization pays more attention than did its predecessors to the environment in which people work – as well as to the quality of communication between researchers and other professionals. In a way, it is a descendant of Lockheed's *skunkworks* and its people who worked on a project outside the company's classical R&D culture to produce the U2 spy plane in record time.

In the new culture of R&D researchers are not just left to make pure intellectual contributions, they are constantly brought into contact with designers, as well as experts in marketing, production, finance, and accounting. This way, at the end of the day, they emerge with products that make their competitors jealous, and customers wanting to buy them.

3. Research, development, and innovation

The financing of research, development, and innovation is a strategic decision, but R&D is not an investment from which immediate results should be expected. Though every effort must be made to steadily shrink the *time to market*, and pass from development to implementation, there is lead time in R&D. There are also goals to meet. An example is given by Johnson & Johnson where:

- Management policy sees to it that not every new product has to be a blockbuster.
- But the hundreds of new products that are introduced over the years must account for a growing share of annual sales.

One of the innovative industrial companies which, year-in and year-out, has been generating 25% of its annual sales from new products, is 3M. Innovative firms encourage their people to take risks, creating a corporate culture where even mistakes could be a badge of honour – because mistakes are an inevitable byproduct of the process of innovation.

Government policy should be supportive of research not only through minimizing red tape and promoting tax allowances, but also by means of financial contributions to worthy R&D projects. In the post-World War II years, in the United States, investments in science and technology began a long-term growth period which, experts suggest, will be still going strong in the next decades.

Critics, however, say that government funds continue their drift toward applied research, cutting the money going to basic research which is the springboard of new discoveries. Industry, too, focuses on applied research and development, increasing its reliance on precompetitive cooperative research with other companies, as well as with the government and nonprofit laboratories.

Because so much depends on research results, and the R&D domains are expanding, the 21st century has seen a surge in licensing agreements which, for many companies, are an important source of income. According to a 2004 survey by McKinsey, the consulting company:

- Between 2000 and 2002, 54% of US firms saw growth in licensing of between 10% and 50%, and
- 75% of executives say they expect to buy as well as sell more licences over the next 2–5 years, and
- 43% expected a dramatic increase in their licensing revenue, as currently the licensing market is still at an early stage.

One of the newest entrants to the intellectual property market is Microsoft. The software giant has reshaped its entire strategy around innovation and patents. Bill Gates reportedly asked Marshall Phelps, father of IT patent licensing, about the strategy to follow with intellectual property and Phelps told him that he had three options:

- Keep the firm's intellectual property within its confines but make no ancillary revenue from it
- Assert the company's patents against others, and in the process face lawsuits by regulators and rivals, or
- Create an intellectual property licensing strategy, with good income from cross-licensing deals.[3]

By all the evidence, Microsoft chose the third strategic alternative, which is also the most forward-looking. Not only does licensing create a good cash flow and income stream, but it also leapfrogs regulatory or antitrust court actions, since the company does not refuses to release its intellectual property. It releases it, but for a fee.

This switch toward licensing is an interesting factor, given that in the coming years intellectual property will be king, as competitive advantages will increasingly rest on innovation. In that environment, embedded knowledge represents a growing share of product costs. Valuable lessons in R&D can be learned from the pharmaceutical industry, where value is added primarily in three ways:

- Clinical and regulatory clearance is necessary prior to the launch of a new drug
- Service activities like drug development require carefully constructed patent and legal defences, and
- Effective drug retailing and distribution systems should form a well-knit network, to promote the company's sales.

With production costs a small portion of a drug's value, the strategy of leading companies concentrates on specialized activities, within their chosen value chain. For example, Merck focuses on a powerful research-based patent position, while Glaxo targets rapid regulatory clearance of drugs. In research, development, and innovation, as in any other business activity, success is the result of:

- Sound, professional management of long-term investments, and
- Well-established relationships with hospitals, doctors, pharmacists, and ultimate customers.

A long-term strategy requires a policy of constant research in discovering, structuring, and marketing new products and services, and in finding better processes for running the production and distribution activities. These are fundamental steps in a culture designed to promote new developments whether innovation concerns:

- New products
- Greatly improved existing products
- Business process redesign, or
- Paradigm shifts, including changes in the rules that govern a particular activity.

All four types bring commendable results if we are able to anticipate developments and predict customer needs. Anticipation is necessary in order to be in the right place at the right time, with innovative products and services. The ability to anticipate enhances dramatically the chances of success. It also makes easier needed paradigm shifts.

Another important input in connection to research, and new product development, is the amount of marketing effort needed to promote them (more on this in Chapter 15). In principle, no two projects get the same market response after being launched. As an example, Figure 14.2 shows two broad categories:

- Products that got rapid market acceptance, and
- Others that, while very successful, took a much longer time to reach market maturity.

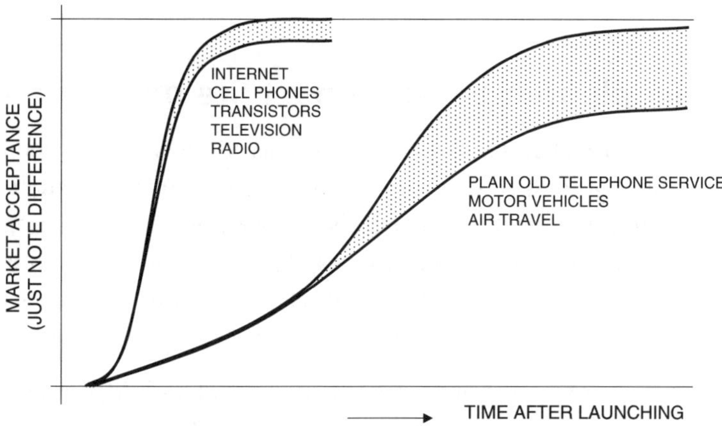

Figure 14.2 Product acceptance and market growth for killer applications and longer-term products

It is appropriate to notice that both the rapid rise and slower growth classes have been characterized by major shifts in design, and in appreciation on the customer side. Businesses, and their managers, who continue working *as if* nothing changes in the market place, and show no interest in anticipating future market shifts, are missing the beat of the market.

Somewhere between the proactive and reactive companies are those at a loss on what to do. After a problem arises, they try to solve it but have no experience in troubleshooting. Part of their inability to plan ahead in regard to future contingencies is due to inertia and to the tendency to follow the beaten path. When we are in the middle of a known paradigm it is hard to imagine any other.

- The set of rules we follow establishes boundaries for behaviour, and
- Those boundaries confine us to viewing a problem from only a single viewpoint – which is wrong.

Defensive attitudes reinforce this culture of staying behind, because new paradigms put the old and known ones at risk. At the same time, however, the more successful one is at practising the 'old way' the greater the inertia; and inertia eventually amounts to loss of opportunity.

In conclusion, research, development, and innovation work in a proactive way. The keyword is *anticipation* and this requires first-class strategic-type studies. Rather than waiting for a trend to develop, we should constantly monitor paradigm shifts through early indicators, which allow us to account for lead time and capitalize on it. The mission for doing so is typically given to product planning.

4. Product planning and product life management

The dictum of architect Mies van der Rohe was 'God is in the detail'. This is product planning's golden rule in answering strategic questions such as: What's our product line? What are the special characteristics of each one of our products? Do we know strengths and weaknesses of each product? Which is the direction the market is taking? Will our products continue to be appealing after projected market shifts? Are we aware of where we may lag behind?

The answer to these queries should not only be factual and documented, but also account for what is demanded by our company's strategic plans. This is no intermittent duty, but one requiring a holistic approach characterized by a *product life management* (PLM) methodology. Product life cycle management is one of the newest developments focusing on the able implementation of strategic plans. Because computer support is vital, PLM software is becoming integral to the operation, growth, and profitability of many big companies. Its goal is to help manage the life cycle of a product or service:

- From concept and design
- To production, marketing, and even recycling.

One of the benefits of using PLM software to engineers designing a new product or system, is that they can reuse parts of previous designs and so keep to a minimum the number of new parts and suppliers. The process also ensures that old and new components fit well together. Other benefits include:

- Lower prototyping costs
- Reduced time-to-market for new products
- Improved product quality, and
- Less overall waste in materials and labour.

Interactive datamining ensures that changes to a product's plans are quickly visible to the development team; also to industrial engineers designing the production line on which the product will be built.

- PLM approaches target the mechanics of product development.
- The process of product planning, however, is broader because it addresses the dynamics of product management.

Product planning looks at the future of our company's product and market strategy, including the far-out future. When the microprocessor was invented in the early 1970s, General Electric's Far-Out Planning unit in Santa Barbara, California asked itself and answered the questions: How many of the GE products can benefit from the microprocessor? When will microprocessors be integral parts of the majority of GE products?

Far-out product planning is by no means the exclusive province of industrial companies. The US Navy is setting a course 50 years ahead in planning future platforms. This long lead time is vital because while technology changes fast, weapons systems don't swing from the laboratory into the fleet at a similar pace. Some likely features of the Navy in the middle of the 21st century include stealth technology – now being used to help warplanes evade radar detection – applied at sea.

For instance, according to projections, war ships will be built in rounded shapes of non-metallic composite materials. They will also move faster, being built like catamarans, with twin hulls, cruising at 60 knots (about 11 kph), compared to top speed of just over 30 knots today. Lasers and particle beams will use intense heat to destroy incoming missiles, while robots will be extensively employed in place of crew members.

- Because industrial companies will be building these ships, naval shipyards should also be doing far-out product planning.
- The same is true of electronics firms, which will be called to equip the naval ships of the future.

Quite often product projections materialize much faster than product planners think. Returning to the GE example of far-out planning, ten years down the line, in the early 1980s, microprocessors entered into GE products. That was the time when expert systems started being applied in business and industry by leading Japanese manufacturers:

- From photo companies
- To refrigerators and washing machines.

The messages these examples convey are that prudent product planners look far ahead. They do not limit themselves to the near future. Moreover, they ask themselves probing questions in connection to processor capacity and intelligence embedded into their products. Answers to such queries are essentially educated guesses, but even so they are critical to *our* company's ability to face future competition:

- Which will be our strategic products in 10 years, 15 years hence?
- Are we capitalizing on our strengths in developing them? If not, what do we need to do?
- Can the products we have in the pipeline respond to coming market requirements?
- Where should our further-out innovation drive be directed? Our new effort in research?

A precondition to responding to the queries is close coordination with marketing, because the products we develop must have market punch. There should be handholding between product planning and marketing from the level of market research (see Chapter 15), to that of product development, to product pricing, and product launch. There is synergy between design and sales.

There are no 'Ten Commandments' in product planning. No two companies have exactly the same product planning structure or job description of the product planner's job (more on this in section 5). But at root, the core activities are fairly similar from one firm to the next. A leading manufacturer of computer equipment defines the various planning activities within each phase of a new product programme, as outlined in the following three tables:

- Table 14.2: Product idea evaluation
- Table 14.3: Technical product definition
- Table 14.4: Product programme development.

These three tables can be instrumental in developing a methodology for product planning. An integral part of a sound product planning methodology is the sharing of skills between key activities: research, development, production, quality control, after sales service, should be collaborating quite early on in product design. Figure 14.3 dramatizes the loss of reliability experienced by engineering products when R&D, manufacturing, and field service work in airtight departments, as so often happens today.

5. The product planner's job in manufacturing

To be regarded as an adviser to top management on matters concerning the company's product line, and its future, the product planner must first give evidence that he or she feels responsible for solving two types of problem: One is related to product innovation; the other to product obsolescence. The product planner should also be able to demonstrate sound judgement as to how well the company and its products appeal to clients and how they compare with those of competition:

- What kind of products will customers be asking for?
- Which characteristics must these products have?

Table 14.2 Product idea evaluation

Identification	Planning job
Product idea	Find out 'pluses' and 'minuses' about a new product idea, falling within the company's objectives
Marketing and competitive research	Study the projected product(s) in conjunction to market drives, customer needs, and competitive performance
Business opportunity analysis	Select among competing product ideas the most promising for further consideration through integration of research, engineering, marketing and finance into an Opportunity Analysis

Table 14.3 Technical product definition

Identification	Planning job
First systems analysis	Determine functional specifications, including matters relating to initial industrial design, and price target
First engineering report	Prepare a preliminary engineering proposal, and general estimate on probable schedules and costs. Include all other pertinent factors to the design under analysis
Original definition report	Formulate overall product plan, including timing. Integrate engineering, manufacturing, marketing, and financial data
Original first profit forecast	Compare estimated costs with projected 'market potential' times 'price', and formulate a profit forecast for the product in question
Product programme authorization (PPA)	Integrate tentative definitions and estimates of the plan for a proposed product, provide a well-thought-out basis for decision. Define opt-out procedure for discontinuing product programme
Reliability report	Proceed with a statistically significant reliability study. Use simulation to construct non-existent subsystems
First marketing plan	Following the PPA, establish together with marketing the general lines of the sales and promotion plan which marketing should then study to detail
First service plan	Based on PPA, work out with field maintenance the first approach to service requirements, and ways and means of meeting them. Assure field maintenance is *not* the weakest link in the chain
Applications support	Establish the nature, extent and cost for applications support. Analyse whether it should be done internally or externally; estimate costs and delays; project a budget
First competitive evaluation	In collaboration with marketing develop concrete estimates on where the competition will stand in one, two, five years in regard to the new product. Project on likely competitive strategies

Table 14.4 Product programme development

Identification	Planning job
Engineering/manufacturing specifications	Initiate work in engineering specifications; also, manufacturing engineering study for process development
Final competitive analysis	Formulate a final competitive intelligence and analysis report. Show probable strategic moves by competition and the company's ways and means for counteracting them
Appraisal report	Conduct appraisal studies for product design and manufacturing engineering. Flush out possible discrepancies. Record realistic cost estimates for work to be done
Final P&L plan, and price approval	Prepare a detailed profit forecast based on firming-up data and on market analysis. Obtain final approval of product price structure, including range
Manufacturing order	Initiate the manufacturing work (first series) with objective timely, high quality deliveries within budgetary limits
Final marketing plan	Formulate the proper, detailed marketing work, launch information and demonstration sessions; work with advertising in building momentum for product support
Information plan	Develop informative literature, programmed instruction simulators, exercises, working out thoroughly all assistance requirements
Final service plan	Establish a definite schedule for training of field support. Study organizational and administrative requirements

- How are competitive products comparing to *ours*?
- What kind of competition will *our* company's products face in the years to come?
- What quantities of products under development can be sold, at which prices, over which periods?

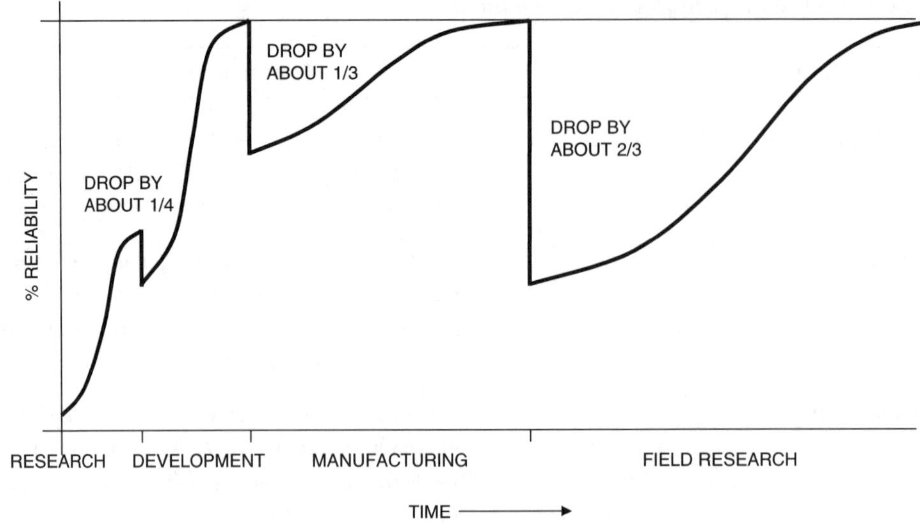

Figure 14.3 The old way of working in airtight departments of research, development, manufacturing, and field service is detrimental to overall dependability

Some of the answers must be elaborated in collaboration with engineering; others with marketing; and the majority with both departments. The best responses are not given in the abstract, but in a factual way, within the current and projected competitive environment. Other crucial questions are: Are other manufacturers likely to enter the market with products similar to ours? Can other companies bring out a seriously competitive programme quickly?

Questions about internal costs and pricing power should also be at the top of the product planner's list. Can our product compete favourably on a price basis with similar products at the competitors' price line? Which are the elements creating value differentiation for *our* products? In the early 1950s, at one of the graduate seminars at UCLA, colleagues asked Dr Ralph Barnes, our professor of production management and former senior executive at Ford, how Ford established its price list. Barnes answered that:

- Ford did not establish a price list.
- It read the price list of GM and tried to do better in cost-effectiveness by 5–10%. Otherwise it did not sell cars.

Some years ago, an article in *Business Week* characterized as follows Gillette's hold on product innovation, and on the market: 'Since 1990, Sensor and Sensor Excel have grabbed a leading 27% share of the US market. The lessons:

spend whatever it takes to gain technology supremacy in a category, and then produce innovative products that will capture consumers, even at premium prices'.[4]

Through a methodological approach to the analysis of business opportunity, product planners should be capable of comparing resource requirements to business opportunity and expected benefits. In doing so, they must relate the firm's capabilities to the market's drives, and evaluate the required level of performance in order to be ahead of competition. This will require lots of:

- Market research, and
- Internal company soul searching.

Among other advantages, results from well done market research will be instrumental in deciding whether to propose to top management the need for a crash programme in product development. A consolidated statement on product-market opportunities may indicate that a crash programme is necessary – otherwise competition would be skimming the cream off the market.

Market research and an analytical evaluation of internal capabilities will allow the product planner to draw the connection between business strategy and his responsibilities for deliverables. They will also help him or her to foresee how a competitive environment may promote or limit product innovation choices, as well as product life cycles (see section 4).

Our understanding of the factors outlined in the preceding paragraphs impacts on our choice. Market research can also provide a documented basis for estimating the impact of uncertainty on funding options in connection to alternative projects targeting innovation. The product planner may use websites, virtual areas, and other novel techniques to collect intelligence on user requirements. Connected to this is the concept of *customer gateways*, which aim to focus on opportunities for:

- Acquiring superior customer knowledge, and
- Evaluating not only products and concepts but also delivery channels.

Inputs from engineering and marketing will help the product planner in appreciating the contribution of *incubators*, alliances, and other non-traditional development approaches. For instance, corporate venturing efforts. Incubators help in establishing ideation processes and innovation streams, by generating and collecting different ideas. Venturing efforts might contribute non-traditional approaches enabling the design of mass-customized products and services.

Using the so-called *lead user* method of bringing innovations to market, product planners can more effectively tap into the sources of innovation, as well as help them identify more quickly better opportunities for innovations – or, alternatively, for:

- Significant cost reduction, and
- Global distribution of manufacturing and procurement activities.

Some years ago, when running high as a motor vehicle manufacturer, Ford defined a *world product* as one whose parts are being manufactured in the four corners of the globe. Table 14.5 gives Ford's distribution of manufacturing at a glance – and at the same time it identifies the planning challenges faced with that distribution.

In conclusion, the success of the product planner's job depends a great deal on proactive information collection, analysis, and screening. The results help in more effectively anticipating both articulated and unarticulated customer needs – particularly so in a changing landscape of product design. Therefore, he or she must be an artist in integrating:

- Technical
- Business, and
- Competitive intelligence.

And should do so while keeping in perspective the organization's decision-making processes and strategic thinking. Included in this reference are the ability to use

Table 14.5 Ford's 'world product'

Eight countries, besides the United States, supplied parts for Ford's 'Escort' model. In alphabetical order:

- Brazil: rear brake assembly
- Britain: steering gears
- France: hub and bearing clutch assembly
- Italy: engine cylinder heads
- Japan: the manual transaxles
- Mexico: door lift assembly
- Taiwan: wiring
- West Germany: valve-guide bushing

The Escort was assembled in three countries, with the US version containing parts from all nine origins.

competitive technical intelligence to identify products he or she should investigate and track. Other necessary information centres around the ability to forecast changes that impact on *our* company's product innovation effort, and their disruptive effect if senior management fails to meet its targets.

6. Product development in banking: case study with Morgan Stanley

Thomas Alva Edison invented the stock market ticker tape before he got around to inventing the light bulb. The stock market ticker tape has been the first technology on record to impact on the financial industry, but product innovation in banking dates back a thousand years. In the 1100s *lettres de faire* were introduced, specifying the delivery of goods at a later date; they were first used at fairs in Lyons and Champagne, France.

More recent, by a few centuries, are exchanges. In 1570, the *Royal Exchange* opened in London. This was the first place in the world at which contracts for goods could be bought and sold all year round. During the 17th century organized *futures trading* began in Japan. It was from the 19th century onwards, however, that development of new financial instruments really took off.

American Express (Amex) was established in 1850, when three independent express companies merged. In 1882, Amex issued its first, and most successful, *money order*. In 1891 the Amex *travellers cheque* was born. M.C. Berry designed both instruments – and his product designs remained virtually unaltered till today.

Diners Club was incorporated in 1950, establishing the principles of the *worldwide credit card* industry. Amex plastic cards came shortly after, being introduced in 1958. *Visa* was also launched in 1958, evolving from BankAmericard. In 1966 Bank of America began to license other banks on Visa; in 1974, Ibanco was formed to control the worldwide operation of all licensed cards; and in 1977 the Visa debit card was introduced.

In 1967 the Interbank Card Association was incorporated with seven founding members. In 1969, Interbank acquired the Master Charge trademark, and eleven years later, in 1980, changed the name to Master Card. A hierarchy of card privileges was established with the Premium Gold Master Card, introduced in 1981.

The year 1968 saw the birth of Eurocheque, aimed to provide a standard procedure for cheque encashment. Credit for its creation goes to Dr Eckart van Hoosen, of Deutsche Bank. Eurocheque was enhanced in 1974, when banks from six countries agreed to replace their local guarantee system with uniform procedures. Today Eurocheques constitute a standard procedure in many European countries.

The common background linking all the preceding references to credit cards, debit cards, and travellers cheques is that they are banking *products*. This is significant inasmuch as today bankers *think products*. They see themselves as inventors and sellers of financial solutions, involving innovative instruments which:

- Produce a stream of new services
- Generate new income sources for the bank
- Stimulate alternatives to conventional debt, and
- Open up a range of investment opportunities.

Innovative forces in the international financial markets are currently creating a steady stream of *new instruments*. Also, the spread of communications, computers, and expert systems brings forward unprecedented opportunities for new product developments. Like the product planner in the manufacturing industry (see section 5) the product planner in banking must:

- Identify those factors that most affect a new product's value
- Project cash flows that are real rather than wishful
- Model the risk which is embedded in every financial instrument
- Prognosticate how risk will affect the bank in financial and business terms.

Why the product planner? In a way not dissimilar to that which characterizes new products in engineering and in the manufacturing industry at large, in the early days many new financial instruments were the outcome of one-man's effort. But while individual initiative is very important, depending on one-man efforts is no longer a good solution, particularly when innovation becomes the means for survival. The answer is:

- Organized research laboratories, and
- Formal functions needed to underpin new product development.

Since the mid-1980s, research and development has been a keyword at Morgan Stanley. The investment bank's management firmly believed that in the coming years the only real money would be in innovative instruments and in packing banking services for a wider clientele. To reach such a goal, evidently required using some of the best analytical skills and capabilities available.

'You cannot divide trading, execution, and control from R&D activities,' said Dr Nunzio A. Tartaglia during our meeting in mid-1988. Tartaglia was managing director of Morgan Stanley's Advanced Systems Group (ASG), which he characterized as a research laboratory like the Bell Labs – only smaller size. At the time, this was exceptional in the banking industry because it was quite unique to find an R&D laboratory in a major bank – even more so one with some 50 people working in it. And:

- ASG was a well-to-do profit centre
- Its annual contribution to the P&L of Morgan Stanley was about $50 million.

Times have changed. Today, research is a keyword in the financial industry. Twenty years of experience with R&D in banking demonstrate that while the tendency is to orient research activities towards the most sophisticated future product, no banking service should be really excluded from the R&D spotlight:

- From the simplest short term credit
- To the most complex leveraged buyout, or project financing activity.

The product planner's role is important because an organized research effort has to be managed at product development end. The different stages of product development (discussed in the earlier sections) have to be handled boldly – whether we talk of engineering or of finance. The task of managing them must go to the root of problem, and it should be set on permanent foundations.

One of the missions given to the product planner of financial instruments and services is to rank-order projects when too many proposals are on the table, funding is scarce, or he or she only has the resources to do some of the wanted new developments. Moreover, to get senior management approval, he or she must use pragmatic and financially sound arguments to sell a project, which brings into perspective the need to explain what is the risk and the reward.

Innovation in banking primarily depends on the ability of managers and professionals to become market oriented, conceptualize new developments, invest in research (which as we saw is part of the cost of staying in business), and see to it that researchers and designers of new instruments come up with proposals that, hopefully, might cream off the market. Product planners, and senior managers, should however appreciate that new products are not only born; they also die because the market shifts, and competitors come up with better offerings.

7. Financial research and pattern analysis: case study with ECAPS

In the communications, computers, and software industries, some 80% of revenues come from products that did not even exist 2 years earlier. In banking, a growing stream of income comes from novel products. In the software business, more than a third of new product ideas spring out of customer demand, as shown in the statistics in Figure 14.4. This is not the case in banking, where success depends more and more on internal research (see section 6). In all of the industries mentioned in this paragraph:

- The course to new product development is unrelenting, and
- The domains to which research in finance addresses itself continue to expand.

An example of a 2005 new financial product is the so-called *Enhanced Capital Advantaged Preferred Security* (ECAPS). In a way fairly similar to the instrument designed by Merrill Lynch for Fiat, which we studied in Chapter 9, ECAPS addresses itself to tax optimization (to put it mildly). Part of its competitive advantage is that it finds itself a long way ahead of what tax authorities can decipher.

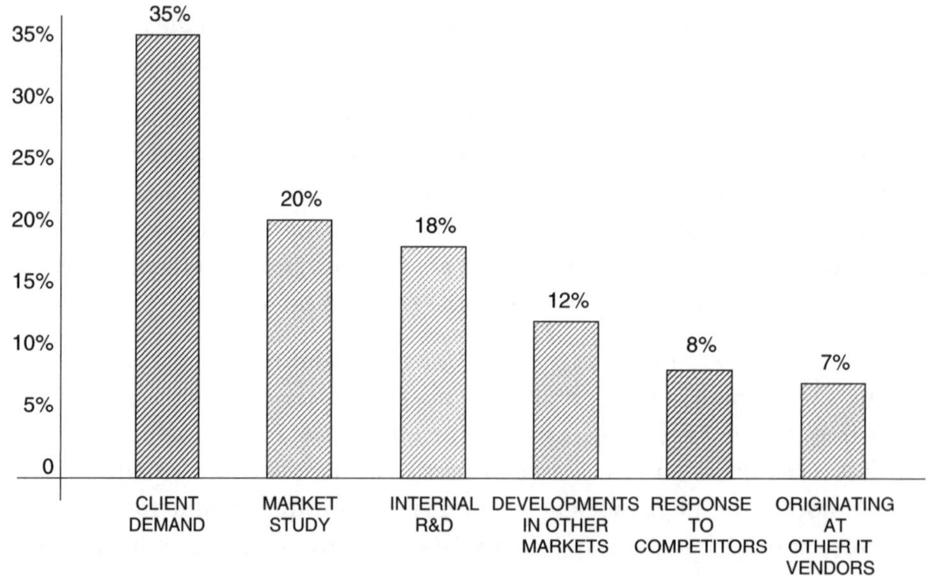

Figure 14.4 Origin of new products in the software industry

Behind the new instrument lies the argument about whether companies and investors should bet on *equity* or on *debt*, which is as old as the financial markets. In modern times, because interest payments are tax-deductible, debt is appealing. The downside is that it constitutes a liability that has to be repaid even when times are hard.

Equity does not have to be paid back. But dividends are paid after taxes and, even so, they are taxed again at the investor's side. This plus the risk that equity investors are at the front line, decreases equity's appeal. Essentially, equity offers investors less protection than debt, and costs companies more.

The sense of this argument is that there is no ideal security. But what about a derivative instrument that looks like equity to credit-rating agencies, and debt to the tax office? This is what Lehman Brothers designed in mid-2005, when it issued a $300 million security – the aforementioned Enhanced Capital Advantaged Preferred Security. ECAPS, analysts say, has taken months of work by tax experts and product developers on Lehman's side.

Like debt, ECAPS carry routine payments and have finite though long maturities: 60 years for Lehman's offering. This long but finite maturity was chosen because guidance from the Internal Revenue Service suggests that debt securities must have a redemption date.

On the other hand, ECAPS offers something like dividends on shares at least in a negative sense: The interest payments can be deferred in times of financial stress. They can also be met by issuing extra shares at maturity. Based on these characteristics, Moody's agreed to treat the Lehman security *as if* it were 75% equity. A similar, but not quite the same offering by Morgan Stanley, will be treated *as if* it were 50% equity.

We shall see how investors react. The pattern these hybrid debt-and-equity instruments will establish in the market will be most interesting to analyse, because it will be revealing of their clients' longer-term response. The pattern of ECAPS behaviour can be revealing. The careful reader will remember that a good example of pattern analysis was given in Chapter 10, section 7, in connection to the volatility in price of gold.

Not only equity/debt hybrids but also many other areas open to financial research effort are in trading and investments: floating exchange rates, options, futures, forwards, interest rates, and currency swaps, to name a few. Another research domain is the mix of equities and debt in portfolio management. A different area of research activity focuses on efficiency in the bank's distribution functions. Within the realm of these examples, crucial questions in defining R&D priorities are:

- What does it take to create a successful innovation effort?
- How can we improve our procedures for choosing products that are likely to succeed?
- How can we manage in the most able way the risk associated to a product's life cycle?

All three bullets emphasize the interest placed on products, and the reason is self-evident. Whether we look at manufacturing or at banking, the No. 1 reason for company failures is lack of *top products*. In all industry sectors that invest in *research and development*, the aim is to bring new products into the pipeline and to the market. However,

- To sell them, we need first-class marketing.
- The trouble is that, classically, both R&D and marketing have often been underestimated in the banking business.

Bankers should appreciate that clients, and most particularly the sophisticated clients everyone is after, don't always go to the bank. Rather, it is the bank that should go to them and try to bring them home, as King Minos, of Crete, did with Daedalus – the great engineer of the antique world – when he left his home country for Sicily.

Another area R&D and marketing come together is in assuring a fast time to market, and good earnings while the novelty of the product lasts. New banking products are not patented. There is no copyright in the banking business. As a rule, new products offer the institution that developed them competitive advantage only for a short time period. Therefore, marketing must move fast.

- Opportunities to excel have to be found and exploited without loss of time, and
- As cannot be repeated too often, great attention has to be paid to the risk new products implicitly or explicitly imply.

If risk is not given the weight it deserves (see Chapter 12) the resulting exposure may outstrip the benefits. Many cases document that this *is* the case – from penalties by regulators to very expensive settlements connected to class actions and huge losses of capital. Unless we keep our mind constantly on exposure and our eyes open to its presence:

- Risk events will crowd one upon another, and
- The institution's profitability will deteriorate.

One fact product planners should appreciate is that product development cycles in financial industries are much faster than in manufacturing. The lifespan of many new products is measured in weeks or months, not in years; and some are developed to satisfy just one deal. We are living in an era of customized financial services, which calls for:

- Specific client orientation, e.g. Fortune 1000 companies
- Response to *future*, not just present, client requirements, and
- Close collaboration with specialized departments, because many new products are polyvalent.

Product planners in the financial industry know that, in the global market, a bank's reputation as leading trader and investment adviser is built on its ability to arrange sophisticated currency, interest rate, and credit risk mitigation transactions is an innovative way. More often than not, this includes considerable leverage.

Financial research is incomplete without analysis of the pattern of leverage involved in new financial instruments being sold, as well as in those inventoried in the portfolio. Expected *return* must always be measured against *risk control* principles. Any study that pays no attention to leverage will be fraught with contradictions.

- Leverage is almost the alter ego of present day banking and novel instruments.
- But at the same time, it is an issue that is presently devoted to it.

Optimists look at leverage as the balance between what they desire to spend and what they can afford; or, as a way of trading off a lower tax bill against higher risk connected to their cost of capital. Realists compare net debt to book capital employed and judge the results on whether or not they are acceptable. Pessimists say that there is risk of misinterpretation because debt is book value, and book value can be arbitrary:

- Underestimating the effect of debt covenants
- Paying no attention to the fact that financial conditions change.

Some research-minded financial experts suggest that a good alternative is *interest cover*, defined as underlying operating profit divided by net interest. This captures both the interest rate paid and, using depreciation as a proxy, maintenance reinvestment. A cover of 6 is very low; 10–12 is more acceptable; 20 is good. The many aspects of leverage must be appropriately analysed when:

- Designing a suitable issue for clients: debt, equity, takeover
- Going through appropriate regulatory channels

- Facing challenges associated to risks way ahead of their aftermath
- Exercising diligence to assure all relative information is provided to investors.

Analyses of this type are an incredibly dynamic process, quite often requiring non-traditional research, as well as a great deal of database mining and pattern studies. For starters, non-traditional research includes: *non-linearities* encountered in economics and finance; *fractals theory* developed by Dr Benoit Mandelbrot; *chaos theory* by Dr Edward Lorenz and Dr Mitchell J. Feigenbaum; study of the *butterfly effect*, focusing on aperiodicity and unpredictabiliy; *chance, uncertainty, and blind fortune* theories by Dr David Ruelle.[5]

Fractals theory, for example, is an excellent tool for the study of patterns. The Securities and Exchange Commission (SEC) was the first on record to use pattern analysis, to uncover illegal trading schemes. The Federal Loan Mortgage Corp (Freddie Mac) worked with two supercomputers on risk management in connection with securitization of mortgages and their patterns. The Federal Reserve Board also used two supercomputers for pattern analysis of money flows to detect abnormal financial transfers, such as those taking place for money laundering and speculative reasons.

8. Critical evaluation of R&D deliverables

Research, development, and implementation (R,D&I), and technological leadership, determines who wins the next round of global competition. However, companies sponsoring research must appreciate that not every project that goes into R&D results in a marketable product. In the manufacturing industry there is an 85–10–5 rule, which says that:

- 85% of research money leads to dead ends and abandoned projects
- 10% results in products which roughly break even in the market
- But products coming out from the remaining 5% of R&D money are the business's future.

The 10%, of breakeven type projects helps in broadening the product line, even if the products are not big hits. This is important for a number of reasons – one of them being that *breadth* of range represents more alternatives; while *depth* of a product line provides a greater number of options.

Essentially, however, it is the 5% of successful deliverables that blossom into strategic products for the coming years. Their market appeal provides the company's future cash flow and underpins its profitability. The challenge in reaching that aim is that they should be properly managed in terms of marketing and sales (more on this in Chapter 15).

I underline the importance of the marketing angle because it is by no means sure that new products will be given the attention they deserve. One of the reasons is that they are too often evaluated apart from their *environment*. Either market research did not do its job properly, or the sales organization has been deficient.

Quite often, after having spent a small fortune on R&D management wrongly decides to make economies in the marketing budget. Or, the new product calls for lots of customer training to increase its appeal, but senior management does not allocate the appropriate budget. Yet, this is a strategic decision.

- IBM was a master in customer training.
- Univac decided to move that way only after it lost ground to its No. 1 competitor.

Another reason for new product failures is that too little consideration has been given to competitors at the product planning stage. As a result, negative surprises kill the product. Still another negative factor is a long *time to market*. When new products stay too long in the lab, the result is disaster. In spite of this, very often the factor of *timing* is neglected or, even worse, a timetable is set that is simply wrong.

Even big companies who should know better don't appreciate that timing is a *key factor of success* in their business. An example that sticks in my mind dates back to the mid-1990s. The stated goal of the August 1995 reorganization at General Motors had been:

- To speed development of new models by 25%, to 36 months,
- To slash engineering costs by 30%, and
- To restore pizzazz to GM's bland brands.[6]

But on Wall Street financial analysts were quick to point out that, in hallmark fashion, GM's efforts to both renew and simplify itself have created an ever-more complex structure. Neither has the way these goals have been presented pleased them.

GM's targeted 36-month time-to-market compared poorly with Toyota's already-achieved 30 months. Additionally, while this 36-month period was three-quarters the 1995 average of 48 months for GM, it was silly to go for a target that was not below what Toyota was already doing. The time to market target, some analysts stated, should have been 20 months or less.

Post-mortem, the years that have elapsed since the 1995 reorganization of GM have demonstrated that time-to-market is a moving target. In a globalized economy, it is whoever is able not only to produce the best product but also to deliver under conditions the customer appreciates, that wins. Toyota carried the day and in little over a decade down the line, in December 2005, it became the No. 1 auto manufacturer in the United States.

There were other disapproving voices on Wall Street concerning the 1995 GM reorganization: 'GM has too many cooks making the stew,' said JP Morgan analyst David Bradley. 'It's a disaster.' 'Why did they have to make it so complex?' wondered Lehman Brothers analyst Joseph Phillippi. 'Why not just have one chief engineer with profit and loss responsibility, like Toyota?'[7]

This look back into the 1990s is most useful because the elapsed years document beyond any doubt that it was not the GM top brass but the analysts who were right. Not only the 1995 and subsequent reorganizations led nowhere, but they also made matters worse. By October 2005 there was talk that it is not unlikely, following in the steps of Delphi, that GM may declare bankruptcy and Chapter 11 protection.

Yet, another reason for product failures is wrong-way pricing. Products should be priced right, which means they should not price themselves out of the market, neither should they spoil the market. I am against price wars to win market share. These are gains that don't last long. But what might be the right price? In principle:

- There are no formal rules about pricing, and
- Diversity in prices is a characteristic of a competitive industry.

It is precisely this diversity in prices for similar products that makes the market. Management should appreciate that in the globalized economy companies have lost their pricing power. As global competition intensifies:

- *If* costs have increased
- *Then* margins are necessarily reduced.

Which turns our discussion to my earlier message that tough cost control is good governance (see Chapter 11). For every product our pricing should be commensurate to the strategy we have chosen; and this pricing should reflect the sort of adopted market strategy. *Specialization* provides greater depth, clarity of offer, higher quality, and differentiated style, allowing premium prices. But *superstore* type marketing of products and services means three things: low cost, low cost, and low cost. If, for any reason, this is not doable, *then* superstore type marketing can turn the company on its head.

Notes

1 *BusinessWeek*, 13 February 2006.
2 *The Economist*, 14 January 2006.
3 *The Economist*, 22 October 2005.
4 *Business Week*, 19 January 1998.
5 D.N. Chorafas, *Chaos Theory in the Financial Markets*. Probus, Chicago, 1994.
6 *Business Week*, 14 August 1995.
7 Ibid.

Strategic Decisions in Marketing

1. Introduction

In the short term markets, and most particularly the financial markets, are moved not by economic expectations, but by *flows of money* and the cumulative response generally known as *market psychology*. Contrary to what is generally thought, security markets respond less to improved profits and lower government borrowing, and more to the amount of funds seeking an investment home. This is what makes markets tick.

Not only during normal times but also at times of stress, it is liquidity that carries the day. And because many consumers buy on credit, if low interest rates prevail, and there is a positive wealth effect, the sales effort goes so much further. At retail level, part of the liquidity is provided by plastic money. Much of the growth in spending is being financed by credit cards. This explains the surge in consumer debt in many Western countries, and also hints about slowdowns as lower net worth families run into credit buffers.

On the wholesale side, a great deal of the marketing effort focuses on winning business contracts, participating in supply chain agreements, and serving asset management accounts.[1] This, and the preceding paragraphs, provide a framework within which marketing operates. They also describe an environment that can be (and usually is) massaged through advertising, and organized by means of a methodology based on three pillars:

- Positioning
- Differentiation, and
- Market segmentation.

Positioning requires market and product know-how; education, and training in sales methods; information dissemination and direct client contact; rational, competitive pricing (see Chapter 14); and able client account management. It also requires a marketing budget that sustains a first-class sales effort, including longer-term client handholding.

Market differentiation focuses the company's efforts on its strengths, which put it ahead of competition. Effective client handholding is crucial in market differentiation, which calls for: relationship marketing, personalized sales orientation, high quality services, client counselling, and other means of sustaining the client relationship. Training, both of the customers and of the sales force, is a way to market differentiation.

Market segmentation is based on research that addresses demographic and other factors; business opportunity analysis; customer classification according to needs for products and services; customer classification regarding the amount of business done with them; as well as design, pricing, and marketing of products directly related to each market segment. Also, intersegment complementarity of services, and profitability analysis of segment-linked offerings.

In connection to all three pillars – positioning, differentiation, and segmentation – marketing decisions must deal effectively with the firm's internal and external policies. They should also overcome organizational barriers, structural impedances, status symbols standing in the way, and information insufficiencies. Success on all these axes is instrumental in picking up a marketing strategy. Equally important is to manage the risk inherent in testing out new sales concepts, in a way that has a positive impact on obtained results.

Modern banking, for example, is characterized by two main drives: market segmentation and value differentiation. In financial services, the process of segmentation rests on recognition that very few institutions can attempt to be all things to all people – and succeed. In many cases, positioning is attempted by means of specialization.

Companies that have decided to become and remain market leaders share the following six principles:

- New products must be constantly introduced to continue the cycle of market appeal, price reduction, market share gain, and control of business risk.
- Price is the principal competitive weapon to gain and hold market share; therefore, prices must decline steadily by swamping costs.
- Market share is a key index of performance in a high-growth market; by growing faster than the market a company overtakes its competitors.
- At least two-thirds of the sales force's salaries must be quota-based, and the quotas regularly reviewed.
- The sales force must be steadily trained, informed on new products and design changes, and believe in the company's effectiveness and their own.
- Investment in skills and facilities must exceed the growth of the market regardless of short-term impact on profit and loss; falling behind is not an option.

In any industry, value differentiation is based on the rationale that competitiveness can increase by performing in an environment where product line, pricing, delivery system, and promotional activities are markedly similar among banks. Hence, Tier-1 credit institutions and manufacturing companies aim to:

- Offer added value to their clients, and
- Stand out from the crowd by capitalizing on their brand name (see section 7).

Also, in practically all industries, marketing management must be on guard for product maturity, which means that its demand is tapering off; and for a market that is at saturation, meaning that market potential starts falling. Both maturity and saturation are reasons behind the steady R&D effort discussed in Chapter 14 – which has also explained the role of the product planner and his or her functions, falling half-way between engineering and marketing.

2. Niche, unique product, and mass market

Like living systems, markets exhibit aspects of birth, growth, development, mutation, crossover, ageing, and decline or death – hence history. There are market changes resulting from new opportunities, as well as from shocks and other reasons induced by trends, mass response, or individual advance knowledge. It is questionable whether markets ever learn, but this aside, all the other reasons can alter the breadth and depth, as well as functions and structure, of markets. For instance, new, advanced products can broaden business opportunities:

- Like species, products and markets are real entities.
- They are characterized by points of origin, duration, but also by changes during their life cycle, all the way to extinction.

This is essentially what we mean when we say that markets *are dynamic*; therefore we must be able steadily to update and upgrade the solutions we build to answer market needs. This includes not only products and services but also marketing plans and their execution, as well as the selection, training, and directing of sales forces, providing them with needed supports.

This is tantamount to saying that a marketing effort must be organized and staffed (see Chapter 7). It should also be working as a system, with the other staff departments and business units. Figure 15.1 shows a frame of reference that incorporates marketing and sales with technology and solution development. Attention should also be paid to supporting functions: logistics, performance measurement (including quotas), quality control, cost control, and customer satisfaction through high quality after-sales maintenance.

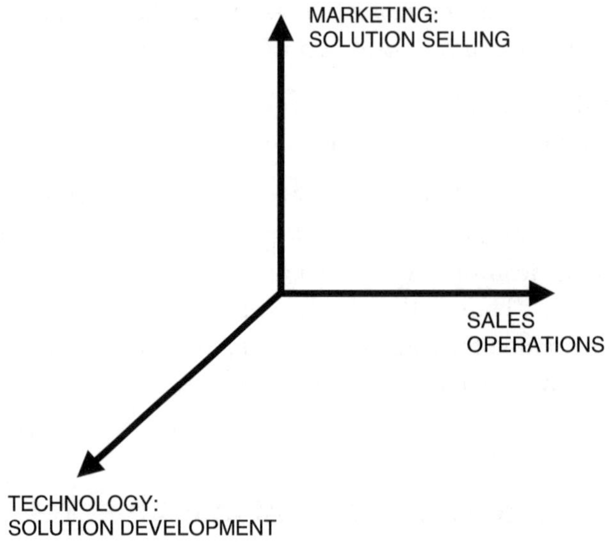

Figure 15.1 A frame of reference for marketing and sales of a portfolio of products

This approach has been adopted by several firms for large accounts requiring individual attention. The gearing of the sales organization is done by incentives associated to deliverables. Judging the sales agents on the basis of *their* deliverables requires giving full profit and loss responsibility to the salesman. Additionally, organizing for relationship management means providing:

- A system able to mirror all business relations, and their development.
- Ways and means to preserve the existing customer base, and acquire new clients.
- Customer mirror services (see Chapter 16), enabling evaluation of what a customer costs and what the company gains from the relationship.

Usually, though not necessarily always, account management orientation requires market segmentation and targeting (discussed in the Introduction), which must be critically evaluated in terms of effect on the bottom line. Cluster analysis is a valuable method in testing quality of segmentation,[2] provided we are developing customer clusters that are meaningful and actionable.

In terms of supporting technology, neural networks have been used for customer targeting in direct marketing campaigns, and proven to achieve higher targeting performance than classical approaches such as linear regression analysis. The use of fuzzy logic allows pattern analysis and helps in optimizing the configuration of sales effort to meet demands posed by customers and market segments.

Self-sufficient databases mined on-line, by profit centre, product, and account being managed, are a 'must'. As a policy, however, prior to choosing specific support tools the board, CEO, and senior management should decide on the marketing strategy the company wishes to follow, and the best way to implement it. The broader strategies to choose from are:

- Niche
- Unique product
- Mass market.

Niche product strategy makes no attempt to challenge the whole market. With few exceptions, such as the case of exploiting a global niche, it requires a local or regional rather than global view of doing business. What a niche strategy does is to resegment and exploit pockets of low competition. By so doing, it provides management with a certain degree of pricing power, because competition is low and, in all likelihood, the product will be fairly advanced.

Notice, however, that a niche can also be served by established products for which there is demand, but nobody wants to make in quantity – or can compete price-wise. A niche strategy may fail because of lack of clear understanding of what a niche *is* and *is not*; defective product/market orientation; pricing that is not affordable to the user; or substandard preparation of:

- Product(s) appealing to the niche, and
- People selling the niche products.

Other reasons for failure (which also apply with unique products) are efforts disconnected from market trends, and/or insensitivity to shifts in the niche, its contents, its customers, and what it takes to appeal to them. The good news is that, other things being equal, the niche will not prove to be a commercial disaster, though it may eventually become extinct. But the way to bet is that:

- The investment will not be so big, and
- The company can pull out of the niche without losing too many feathers.

Business conditions are different, with an orientation towards unique product. By definition, a *unique product* is one competitors are not ready to offer; typically one somewhat in advance of its time or requiring special skills. A unique product strategy calls for long, sustained commitment to innovation; it involves (in many cases) a relatively moderate risk. Policies aiming to capitalize on a unique product tend to:

- Redefine the current market, and
- Create a new customer base.

A unique product strategy may also try to hold on to the existing customer base through special projects. In this case, assumed risk increases significantly. Talking from my experience at AEG Telefunken, and other companies, many 'specials' end up recorded in red ink. Moreover, steady innovation is a demanding concept. It is usually disruptive, unpredictable, and upsets organizations that are resistant to change. Unique products raise a swarm of questions, among the most important being:

- How can management implement successful innovation practices in the face of internal opposition?
- How can the CEO protect early-stage developments from being dismissed by the organization, because they appear 'too complex' or too much out of tune with slow-moving practices?

As briefly stated in Chapter 1, a well-executed unique product strategy can be much more lucrative than a niche, though less so than the mass market – which, however, is a very tough cost critic. Customers would pay high prices for products they need and cannot find anywhere else. Or, when they find them are of dubious quality, uncertain delivery schedules, and low dependability (see also Chapter 16). Still, a unique product market is not large; when it expands significantly, it becomes a mass market.

The third major marketing strategy which, when properly executed has positive results, is that of appealing to the mass market. Here, the rules of the game change. The 2004/05 onslaught by Chinese textiles in Europe and the United States is an example of how mass markets can be conquered. Today, *mass market* strategy is global, based on being a very low cost producer and distributor of products and services. Additionally, a 21st century mass market strategy demands:

- Customizing products while addressing the total market
- Managing change by keeping everybody on the run
- Making compulsory the meeting of objectives, which are steadily redefined, and
- Building longer-term strategic advantages, as well as capitalizing on them.

My experience suggests that trying to merge the unique market and mass market strategies becomes an unmitigated commercial disaster, because 'uniqueness' alone is not enough to persuade lots of people to pay to cover the vast costs of that uniqueness. This means that the board, CEO, and senior management must be very specific in their choice of strategies, and after this is done:

- Stick with the marketing strategy they choose, and
- Do their best to make it profitable, rather than always being in doubt whether they made the right choice.

As a last bit of advice, the choice should be *internal* to the company rather than a copy of what somebody else has done. The copycat is also a marketing strategy, and one which, in the short run, could pay dividends, but in the longer run it is the worst possible choice. 'Me too' is the decision of the unable, who cannot make up their mind about what they want to do and how to go about it.

3. Strategies for market control: case study with Coca-Cola

Marketing evolved as a result of applying management concepts to the tasks of distribution and selling. By the mid-1920s and early 1930s, marketing pioneers like Thomas Roebuck began to question the way manufacturing was organized, and particularly the lack of anticipating how the market behaves and what one should expect in 2, 3 or 5 years. Roebuck and others also concluded that the assembly line was a short-term compromise. They thought that, despite its tremendous productivity, Henry Ford's method was poor economics because of its:

- Planning inflexibility
- Difficulties in engineering changes, and
- Less than optimal use of human resources.

One of the business leaders who revolutionized marketing was Thomas Watson, Sr, of IBM (see section 4). But Watson did not particularly address the manufacturing side. It was left to the Japanese to restructure the manufacturing process along flexible lines, promoting teamwork through quality circles and the information-based organization, as the way to impact on human nature. Every one of the aforementioned managerial innovations represented:

- The application of knowledge to work
- The substitution of systems and information for guesswork, and
- The fact of replacing working harder with working smarter.

Chapter 14 has already explained that market research has proved to be of invaluable assistance in shaping product plans. The same is true of its effect on marketing efforts. In the global market place, customers are tough critics of the companies whose products and services they buy. Research contributes a great deal towards increased market sensitivity.

Much can also be learned from policies followed by well-run companies. Hitachi, one of the better-known Japanese electrical and electronic equipment manufacturers, uses as criteria of success of its marketing effort annual sales growth at home and abroad. Also, most significantly, the R&D to sales, and return on sales ratios. The trendlines on the upside over a period of four years in the case of Hitachi is shown in Figure 15.2.

To appeal to increasingly more sophisticated and demanding clients, manufacturing and merchandising companies must solve the marketing and sales problems they face with abundant energy and singleness of purpose. The board must appreciate that – from information collection, to analysis, and experimentation – nothing should be left to chance.

- A company should never consider its business adversaries to be petrified in their habits, thoughts or decisions.

ANNUAL SALES GROWTH RATES IN %

JUST NOTE DIFFERENCE

SALES OVERSEAS

SALES AT HOME MARKET

YEAR 1 YEAR 2 YEAR 3 YEAR 4

R&D TO SALES AND RETURN ON SALES

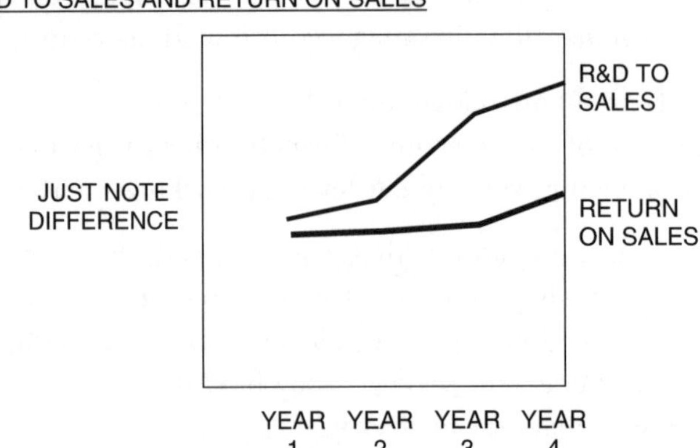

Figure 15.2 Hitachi's trend lines identify the marketing effort of the manufacturer. Notice the R&D to sales ratio

- Instead, top management should appreciate that those competitors who count are the most flexible, adaptable, and able to turn on a dime to satisfy customer needs.

This has for long years been the strategy of Coca-Cola, which defines marketing as anything it does to *create* consumer demand for its brands (see in section 7 the discussion on branding). To achieve this aim, management focuses on continually finding new ways to differentiate the firm's products, and build value into all of its business lines.

According to Coca-Cola's management thinking, marketing spending enhances consumer awareness; it also increases consumer preference for the company's brands. This produces growth in volume, greater per capita consumption and an increase in the company's share of worldwide beverage sales. The Coca-Cola strategy is to heighten consumer awareness and product appeal for its trademarks, using integrated marketing rather than a lone wolf approach. Through strategic alliances with independent bottlers of its products, it implements these programmes worldwide:

- Conducting product and packaging research
- Establishing brand positioning
- Soliciting consumer feedback, and
- Developing effective consumer communications.

To maximize the impact of its advertising expenditures, Coca-Cola assigns specific brands to individual advertising agencies. This makes it possible to increase each individual firm's accountability, and it enhances each brand's global positioning. The policy also provides a basis for documented comparison of the different outsourcers' advertising effectiveness.

As is to be expected, other companies have adopted different strategies in terms of advertising their brands. One of them is known under the jargon term *exclusivity incentives*, which includes forms of payment like joint promotion or advertising subsidy, in exchange for a commitment not to deal in the goods of a competitor. Alternatively, the exclusivity deal may take the form of a market-share discount.

Typically, *market share discounts* increase when the distributor gives the manufacturer a greater share of its business than it offers to competitors. Critics say that this tends to drive weaker competitors out of the market. Quite often, market share discounts take the form of *slotting fees*, which are widespread in the food and beverage industry, and are sometimes used to purchase exclusive shelf space at supermarkets.

Examples of other offers by vendors to their distributors are *bundled rebates.* They come into effect when the distributor purchases more than one product from the vendor's product line. Bundled rebates make sense if one of the goods in the rebate bundle is in exceptionally high demand. This strategy is tantamount to *tying* – a marketing practice where a manufacturer makes the sale of a product in high demand conditional to the purchase of a second and third product which may not be so popular.

- *If* these two or three products are connected to one-another and they are priced together
- *Then* the marketing practice is known as bundling. The terms of the agreement may be flexible, involve quotas, pay premiums, or use other marketing tools.

One of the marketing strategies that has been extensively used in a number of cases, particularly in connection to motor vehicles, is that of exclusive *dealerships.* Sometimes, the practice of dealerships is carried too far, because they are allowed to multiply, with the result of eating into each other's territory. As a reaction, this has brought a consolidation drive. Consolidation of a manufacturer's dealership network is a relatively new phenomenon based on the premise that:

- It will create larger, more appealing and more profitable dealers, who
- Will do a better job of moving products to the market, and acquiring customers.

Consolidation is the antithesis of proliferation of dealerships, the two processes, however, also complement one another. Since 1990, automotive manufacturers in the United States have been slowly trying to remake their distribution system through consolidation of dealerships, many of which have been damaged by Japanese competition. The process of consolidation is not easy, and the going has been tough. For example, in 1990, General Motors implemented plans to:

- Relocate some dealers and merge others
- The goal being to shrink its dealer count in the United States from 9500 in 1990 to 7000.

The consolidation of dealerships is a costly project. In GM's case, this has been a $1 billion project. It was officially launched in 1990, but it did not really progress till 1995/96, after a new GM sales and marketing chief, Ronald L. Zarrella, made the dealer overhaul a central part of his push to create distinct brand images for GM's models and divisions.

A couple of years down the line, by 1998, GM executives said they were delighted with results, stating that the Zarrella plan accelerated the consolidation pace, and gave new life to the dealerships. In Bergen County, NJ, for example, sales rose 42% in 1997 after half of the eight GM dealerships there were upgraded or moved.[3]

Japanese competition in motor vehicles aside, what GM did was to catch up with population shifts by moving stores out of small towns, and declining cities, and into bustling retail zones along suburban highways. At the same time GM pushed dealers to reconfigure their holdings in order to increase their performance.

Also in the mid- to late 1990s Ford Motor launched a similar initiative in dealership consolidation, starting with tests in Tulsa and San Diego. A part of repositioning the dealers' goals has been to pare costly overhead and inventories, as well as eliminate many expensive body shops, while offering customers better service and a wider selection.

Seen with the hindsight of elapsed years, GM's and Ford's efforts left much to be desired – not because the concept of consolidation of dealerships was wrong, but because on its own it cannot produce much in terms of results. As has been stated on previous occasions, strategic business planning, and the marketing chores, start at the drafting table. It is too late to develop a marketing strategy when the cars are already at the dealer's parking lot.

4. Quantitative sales objectives and marketing savvy: case study with IBM

From Day 1, even before the IBM logo was adopted, marketing was the topmost strength of Thomas Watson, Sr. On several occasions, his company has been behind in product design: for example, in the mid-1950s with computers *vs.* Remington Rand Univac; in the mid-1960s with scientific computers *vs* Control Data Corp.; and in the mid-1970s with minis and maxis *vs* DEC. But IBM's marketing strategy has been so far ahead of its competitors, that the latter were not able to exploit the gaps.

Another of IBM's strengths in marketing was the quantitative sales objectives, or *quotas*, assigned down to the single salesperson level. Commissions were planned in a way that a good IBM sales person would make more money, and in cases much more money, from quotas than from base salary. Money made the sales force run faster.

'What sort of guidelines could we follow in establishing quotas?' I was asked by the CEO of a company of which I was consultant to the board. To respond to this query, in the course of a project centring on quotas, together with the CEO and his immediate assistants, we established that besides quantitatives objectives there are other basic considerations that should be taken into account in elaborating individual sales targets:

- Sales force training, which must be sustained
- Product-mix of the equipment the individual is given to sell
- Orientation of the sales effort towards more effective client handholding
- Support provided to the sales force in fulfilling their duties, and
- Compliance of sales effort with the company's overall product and market strategy.

The product and market strategy, for instance, may be that the majority of sales come from the established customer base; and next to it, priority is given to installations or unit sales to customers won over from competitors. For instance, BMW rewards its dealers with an extra premium if they sell a car to a person who, until then, drove a Daimler – Benz.

Getting the most out of the established customer base requires close coordination between R&D and marketing, often provided by product planning. When properly executed, this is a rewarding strategy. In IBM's case, for example, about 70% of annual sales came from the existing client base.

Marketing experts should never underestimate the salesman's training as well as the salesman's qualities including drive, age, and personal characteristics. IBM was a master in training, regarding both quality and quantity, that went into this process – with the result that the company had a first-class sales force. In the years I was with IBM (the late 1950s) about 24% of the sales representatives' and system engineers' time went into training and information sessions. This ratio continued until the mid-1960s, as a research project I did with the American Management Association (AMA) documented. By the 1970s, however, it ebbed, and IBM's fortunes ebbed with it.

There are further lessons that could be learned from IBM's hey-day in terms of marketing and sales effort. For instance, the scheme the company had developed to compensate sales results. Originally, IBM calculated the sales force commission on the basis of a point system (a point was a dollar in monthly rental of equipment).

- For *new* accounts the salesperson got a commission equal to $1.0 per point
- But for sales to existing accounts the commission was only half as much, and rightly so because this was (so to speak) a captive market.

In the case of equipment sales, half the commission the salesman received was paid on signing the contract; the other half on installation. When rented equipment was being taken back, its rental value was flatly subtracted from the rental value of the newly installed equipment, and commissions were only paid on the difference. Over time, of course, quotas and commission systems became more complex as:

- The products being sold multiplied
- The unit cost (for instance, per bit of storage or instruction per second) dropped dramatically
- The market expanded unevenly, and sales territories varied substantially as to their potential.

Many of these changes left a footprint in the quota and commissions system, with commissions influenced by four factors: quota level, territory, productivity, and years on the job. Adjustments were also made to avoid cases where salesmen made a small fortune and then left the firm. This happened because of big commissions – a windfall which came by applying accounting machines' commission levels to high computer sales prices.

Instrumental in the marketing results IBM achieved, next to intensive training, quotas, and commissions, was the support provided to the sales force. In the case of computers, this ranged from applied science (later, system engineers) to the restructuring of sales offices. For instance, following the product evolution that took place in the 1970s, in 1980 IBM organized new marketing channels and services aimed to:

- Improve customer contact, and
- Reduce its own support costs, which started to get out of control.

For example, *retail product centres* for office machines and small computers were opened in Baltimore, Brussels, Cordoba (Argentina), Philadelphia and Stockholm. Slowly, the number of such outlets worldwide was brought to 12. For some years these stores proved to be a cost-effective way to attract new business.

Business computer centres were organized where customers could see demonstrations of small systems and make purchases. Those were opened as a test at six locations. Subsequently such centres have been operating in 50 cities in the United States, and 30 cities in other countries. Along with this a new systems management programme was established aiming to provide IBM marketing and service teams with a comprehensive, structured approach for helping customers manage their computer systems more effectively.

Another marketing initiative has been *customer support centres*, whose objective was to provide users and prospects for IBM's intermediate-size computers with sales, education, and installation support. In the first and second instalment, they were operating in more than 100 IBM branch offices worldwide.

Still another marketing service has been *direct mail and telephone selling*, which targeted lower cost products such as typewriters, dictation machines, computer terminals, small computers, office products, and also data processing supplies. Customers were provided with toll-free telephone ordering, using major credit cards. This service was expanded by IBM worldwide with the aim of:

- Enhancing contact with the customer, and
- Improving IBM sales productivity.

Existing *quick-response telephone services* were both expanded and enhanced to help customers obtain software information at any hour, seven days a week. Such toll-free services significantly reduced time and cost of calls at customer sites by IBM personnel. Figure 15.3 give a glimpse of the integrative ability of on-line interactive services.

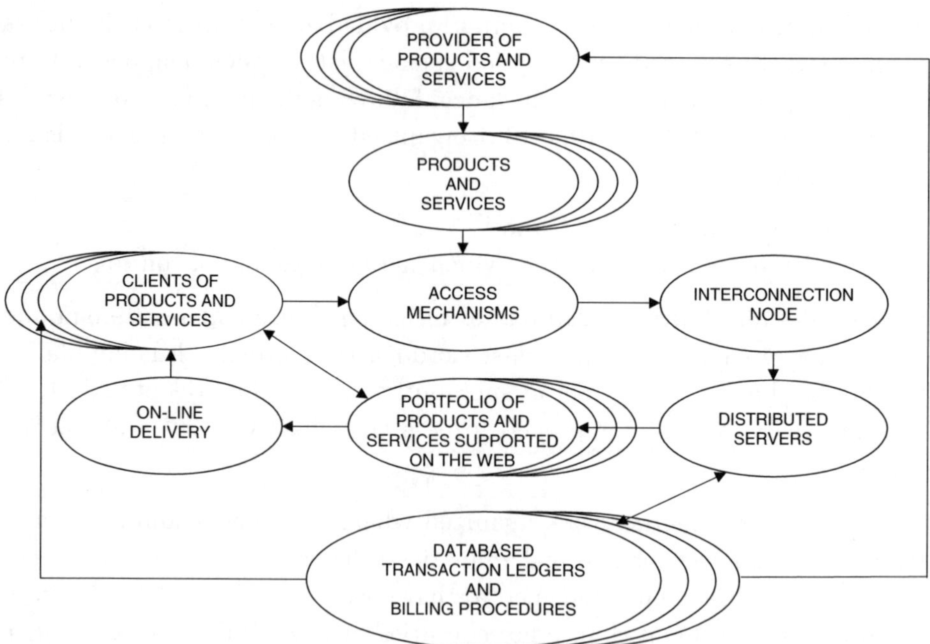

Figure 15.3 Internet commerce integrates a number of support services that were previously standalone

Notice should also be taken of *application information centres,* established by many customers with IBM assistance. Their goal was to enable employees not trained in data processing to develop their own computer programs for many tasks, such as managing files and preparing reports, with improved productivity at the customer site.

Moreover, as a forerunner of IBM's change towards being a software-oriented company, *software distribution* to customers in the United States and 32 other countries was expanded by 25% in 1980. As these examples demonstrate, there can always be a 'new way of marketing' – but it took new management with the will to enforce change to produce the largest turnaround in IBM history in the early 1990s. Still, the examples from the 1980s are valuable because they show the road to sales force conversion from a primary hardware to a basically service and software sales orientation.

5. Marketing planning and sales force productivity

The case studies we have seen in sections 3 and 4 leave no doubt that marketing has to be planned. No important function can, or should, be left on its own to grow like wild cacti. Sales productivity, too, should be the subject of rigorous planning. Short of this, the results would be a hammer blow to the company's bottom line, and senior management would bear the responsibility.

Next to product definition and development, which has been the theme of Chapter 14, one of the most critical questions for marketing planning is what's the percentage of market share *our* company wishes to attain? Are we planning to be leaders or followers? In what product(s) do we really want to lead? Are we ready for product leadership? For how long will our estimates of holding the high ground be valid?

Closely associated to the answers to be given to these questions is what's the sales volume *our* market targets represent? Which are the markets and products we expect to perform best? How much investment will be needed to reach *our* targets? And most evidently, what level of profit margin can we sustain given:

- Cost of goods sold
- Marketing and sales expenditures
- Transportation and duties, and
- Administrative costs.

Factual and documented answers have to be provided to these queries, not only in connection to our company's traditional markets but also in regard to new markets we plan to enter. Also, how are we going to perform in these new markets? Will we have our own sales network or work through agents? Closely related to these queries is the issue of investment that will be required:

- What's the return on investment we are projecting?
- Is this above or below the industry standard?
- What will be the asset turnover ratio? Is this a satisfactory target?

Another important marketing planning question is, how can our company increase its influence in the market? Is the increase projected by a new marketing plan commensurate with our strategic goals? Is profit improvement part of the increase? How much profit improvement is planned from cost reduction? How much from expansion of sales? No marketing effort will be worth its while without commensurate improvement profits, but at the same time the entry price may be high.

No marketing planning effort will be worth its salt without paying due attention to ways and means for growing the quality (and possibly quantity) of human capital dedicated to sales. Hence, the queries: What new skills must be obtained in sales? In sales support? How fast? At what cost? Do the profit estimates being made take account of available human resources? Of those to be acquired?

Comparative studies that focus on sales productivity, and compare our sales productivity to that of the competition, can be revealing. They also provide a benchmark against which to judge our own results. Invariably, the question is raised how can *our* sales efficiency be improved? Do we control our sales costs? Can we initiate distribution improvements? Is the general marketing effectiveness acceptable?

Time and again, as a consultant, I found sales productivity lagging because management did not really know how to go about improving it. Yet, IBM's example with quotas and commissions, which we discussed in section 4, can be an excellent guide in this direction – provided senior management has the vision and guts to apply it. In my experience, as far as sales productivity is concerned, the first most crucial question regards planning and control action:

- Is management in charge?
- What is a salesman doing if his sales numbers are below average?
- What is management doing if the sales force's deliverables are below target?

The answer may involve a long list of measures to be taken, both at organizational and at individual salesperson level. Probably sales personnel may be planning poorly, or not at all, their approach to customers. May be they lack the proper know-how on how to manage time and territory (this is still problem No. 1 for many salespeople). Or, the company fails to help every member of its sales force in doing a proper job in terms of:

- Time and market planning
- Product promotion
- Customer handholding.

To help in promoting the focus and efficiency of sales people, Table 15.1 presents a list of questions that every sales organization should be able to answer affirmatively. If not, then something is wrong with senior management, not only with the sales managers and their people.

As the milestone queries outlined in Table 15.1 document, closely associated to marketing planning is the evaluation of sales results, and of sales productivity. Based on an audit I did in the business systems division of one of the better-known

Table 15.1 Ten questions every sales organization should ask itself about sales force performance

1. Have we properly selected our sales personnel on their ability to present their subject and handle people?
2. Are we steadily training our sales personnel on products, markets, and sales techniques?
3. Have we ever made an organized study of how our sales personnel use their time?
4. Do we determine in advance how many calls to make on an account in a given time?
5. Do we decide how long each call should take? And how often it should be repeated?
6. Do our sales personnel report on execution of call schedules? Do they report on every call they made?
7. Do our sales personnel use flair to qualify a planned sales presentation?
8. Do we have a system of classifying and assigning accounts according to their potential?
9. Do our sales personnel rework and optimize prescribed routing patterns in covering their territory?
10. Are sales objectives and profit objectives set for each account? Do we review these objectives and compare them to actual results?

electrical and electronic engineering companies, Table 15.2 quantifies the available salesmen at one of the firm's major sales offices, by product line.

To better appreciate this distribution of the sales force, the reader should know that the auditing of sales organization, and of sales results, took place in 1972. At that time, data systems was a new, non-traditional product line for the particular firm referred to here; and 1972 also saw the initiation of office automation.

One of the problems confronting the data systems division was the definition of its market, which consisted, nearly 50–50, of accounting applications and office automation (OA) solutions. Up to a point sales for accounting applications hurt the calculators' sales. This was a rather minor overlap, as this company was not in the business of electromechanical accounting machines.

Where data systems sales hurt the firm's own classic lines was in office automation. To a significant extent, these data systems sales decreased the top end of typewriter sales – because engineering had failed to produce new models that would integrate into OA solutions.

Typewriter sales representatives, however, took heart from the fact that the data system division, which was operating as an independent profit centre, had failed to put in perspective the specific characteristics of its market.

Table 15.2 Personnel in a major sales office of a business equipment manufacturer

	Typewriters	Copiers	Calculators	All classical lines	Data systems	Total
Salesmen	10	9	10	29	10	39
Sales support	1	1	1	3	9	12
Sales support/ sales personnel	0.10	0.11	0.10	0.10	0.9	0.36
Maintenance	37	21	32	90	39	129
Secretarial assistance				16	3	19
Others, including management				30		30
Total	**48**	**31**	**43**	**168**	**61**	**229**

Table 15.3 presents the sales statistics by individual sales personnel, for all 10 people, relative to units sold during one single year. (Value is written in dollars, to hide the origin of the firm. This was *not* a US company.) The following observations can be made on the basis of these statistics:

1. While the average $ yield per sales person per year stands at $502 000, the range is too wide: between $64 000 and $1 800 000.

Sales quotas could help in better planning and controlling sales results, but there was a lack of quality management in this division. Its aftermath is documented by this huge discrepancy in performance among individual members of the sales force.

An interesting statistic in Table 15.3 is the performance of 'B' and 'E'. They both sell at the same average cost per product, but the marketing effort of 'B' is nearly eight times more effective than that of 'E'. The performance of 'G' is also dismal.

1. While an average of $502 000 was reasonable at the time such statistics were collected, in reality the $ billed per sales person per year in this sales office meant little in terms of profitability.

Table 15.3 Sales statistics by individual sales representatives of data systems technology

Sales representative	$	Quantity in units	Average price
A	1 800 000	38	47 368
B	504 000	63	8 000
C	248 000	12	20 666
D	847 000	93	9 107
E	64 000	8	8 000
F	300 000	27	11 111
G	97 000	6	16 166
H	255 000	20	12 750
I	687 000	35	19 628
J	258 000	19	13 578
	5 060 000	**321**	**16 138**

Average price per unit	$15 538
Average units per salesman	32
Average sales per sales representative per year	$502 000
Range/price per unit	$8 000–$47 368
Range/units per sales representative	6–93
Range/sales per sales representative per year	$24 000–$1 800 000

This is due to the way this company worked. To gain a share in the data systems market, the company made huge discounts. And its costs were too high, partly due to technical factors, which should have been taken care of a long time ago.

Very thin profit margins saw to it that even at half a million dollars per year for the product line under consideration (office products and systems), this average per sales person was too low. A careful study followed to identify ways and means to improve these results, and drop those pieces of equipment with a negative profit margin which could not be fixed.

1. The average price per unit sold is $16 138.

This relatively low average price, coupled with the low number of units sold by many sales persons, had the effect of loading the direct sales budget to over 33% of the list price for this expense alone. This compared very badly with competition, and contributed to the fact that the company's business system division was typically in the red. To survive, this division needed to reinvent itself, but management was too weak and unwilling to undertake major restructuring.

6. Sales office productivity and the experimental approach

The performance of a sales office depends not on one but on all major players – from its manager, supervisors, and sales engineers to its system engineers (in the case of computer equipment), maintenance personnel, as well as secretarial and clerical assistance. The sales office manager and his salesmen are responsible for:

- Handling the client base, and
- Opening new market opportunities.

Section 4 brought to the reader's attention the importance of *quotas*, as quantitatively expressed commercial objectives down to the level of the single sales person; also the associated incentives (carrot) and quota control system (stick). Contrary to each individual's performance, however, branch office productivity and profit figures are a group effort, which should account for *market forces* indicating the direction on which to base marketing parameters such as: human capital, planning, organization, inventories, product availability, and internal control.

Each sales office director is a crucial element in the organization's performance, in terms of obtained results. *Market potential* is a function of: direction of customer choice, as well as handholding; competitive intelligence, which also accounts for the force of competitors; product to sell to the customers, and their margins; available skills to fill present and developing customer needs; and the way in which the marketing effort, as a whole, is managed.

Part and parcel of current sales office management functions is the supervision of activities. When this supervision is wanting, as in the case study discussed in section 5, the results are dismal. Next to able management, the most important factor is training of personnel, from project managers to sales engineers, systems analysts, maintenance specialists, and more. The branch manager also has other responsibilities, like top customer handholding, building up market potential, exploring sales opportunities, and establishing proactive policies. All these duties have to be effectively performed, along with the top-most responsibility of always being sensitive to market shifts.

The exact manner in which the sales office will be managed depends, among other factors, on the type of industry it serves, the products it handles, and the personality of its leader. Industries such as banking, air transport, steel, cement, lamps, autos, computers, electromechanical equipment and electronics do not have the same requirements in terms of:

- Type of branch office
- Supported services, and
- Approach to the market.

By contrast, they all need to calculate the potential business in the territory for which they are responsible, enlarge their market penetration, and identify ways and means to gain control of important customers. All these functions should be the subject of careful marketing planning.

The branch office manager will run the operations under his or her authority through sales meetings and person-to-person meetings, which include account managers, representatives from headquarters, sales force, product planners, persons responsible for inventory control, and field maintenance service representatives. Key questions in many of these meetings are:

- What does it takes to improve our bottom line?
- How fast can we build up market potential?
- What are our strengths and weaknesses?
- Why is sales productivity slackening?
- Why did we lose 'this' important customer?
- How can we best feed our opportunities and starve our problems?

If the sales office has attached to it a warehouse from which it makes delivery of goods sold, *then* warehouse management becomes an important responsibility of the branch director. Able execution of this duty may have several aspects, ranging from inventory replenishment to warehouse organization.

The strategy to follow is *fast flow replenishment* (FFR). Twenty years ago, FFR was 'the future' for the retail industry. Today, it is an absolute 'must': companies who don't use FFR are behind the curve – but able execution of fast flow replenishment has prerequisites, as well as dramatic organizational consequences.

- FFR's particular characteristic is implicit dependence on shared information. It is a partnership between retailers and their suppliers.
- In this, fast flow replenishment closely resembles *just-in-time* (JIT) inventory management in manufacturing.

Sales office and sales warehouse organizational duties can make good use of analytical studies and experimentation. Based on a study on warehouse reorganization and restructuring which I did for Osram, the global lamp manufacturer, in the late 1960s, Figure 15.4 dramatizes the results that can be obtained. The specific theme in this figure is error rates, which are always present in warehousing. Error rates:

- Lead to higher costs and returns by the client, and
- Negatively affect the business, because in the background of returns is customer dissatisfaction.

At the time this study was made (late 1960s) the error rate at Osram's warehouses was half the European average, but Professor Prinzing, the CEO, correctly decided it was not good enough for a premier firm. Getting much better results required the design of a new classification and identification system for all products and processes.[4] It also called for warehouse reorganization.

The next question that came up was how to judge the success of this reorganization effort. Experimental design permitted the evaluation of results of a new control methodology against the approach that has been classically followed in regard to operational risk management. The objective was to quantify and qualify the reduction of errors and its effect on operational risk management.

- At warehouses A and B the new method was implemented, which, over a three-month period (September to November), succeeded in significantly reducing the error rate.
- The worst performer in this experimental design was warehouse C, used as a control group, which continued to utilize the old method during the experiment.

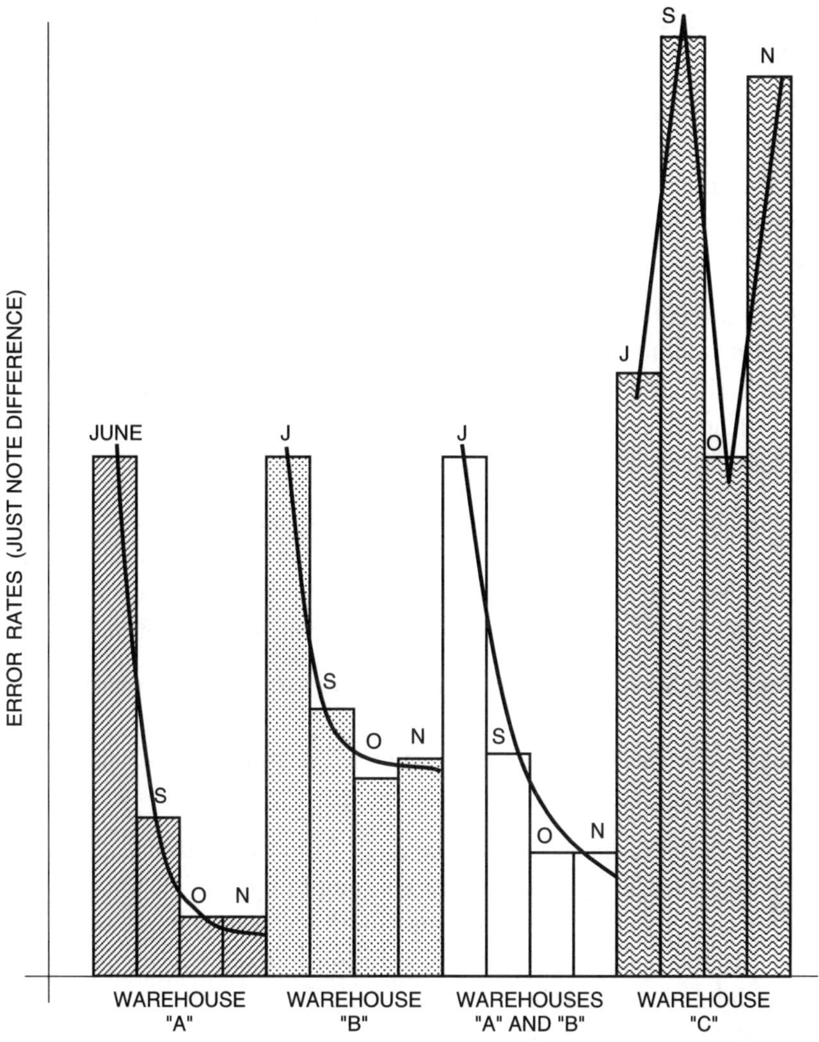

Figure 15.4 Experimental design done to evaluate operational risk control at warehouses A and B using a new method, versus the old method at warehouse C. (June, September, October and November)

The striking improvements brought by the new method as compared to the old have been shown in Figure 15.4. This is a good example of what it takes, in terms of studies and operational risk control, to improve performance – and therefore the bottom line. Good governance requires that both the marketing division, as a whole, and each branch office individually must have profit and loss responsibility and in this are included metrics such as error rates.

7. Caring about the brand name: case study on 'Intel inside'

'Lipstick', 'eyeshadow', and 'make-up' are terms that were popularized years ago by Max Factor. They are words whose power lies in the fact that they are composed of a simple meaning that is easy to understand and, most importantly, easy to remember and associate with a product. This is precisely what a *brand* wants to achieve.

'Make-up in a second, look lovely for hours,' was the headline in a typical Max Factor advertisement. For millions of ordinary women, the cosmetics firm simplified the fairly complex task of *looking*, or at least feeling, good. In the process, this simplification helped to create the first major international cosmetic business – a brand everyone would recognize.

The concept of *branding*, and by extension of remembrance advertising, has become a pillar of marketing. From manufacturers to merchandisers, retailers and service industry agents (like banks), many think that the cornerstone of successful marketing is the development of brand concept. Therefore:

- They drive for own-brand products, which promote the company's image, and
- Look at brands as a means to produce improved margins, while increasing pressure on competitors.

The banking industry has taken this concept from merchandising, where brand management is seen as the way to create strong identities not only for perfumes but also for cars, trucks, cornflakes, and toothpaste. Few companies, however, understand that whether we talk of banking products or minivans, the pivotal point of brand management is to:

- Stop chasing your competition, and
- Start chasing your customers.

This must be done in a planned and coordinated manner. A sound approach would ensure that the brand manager's pay is linked to the brand's success, while activities ranging from advertising to pricing are handled in a serious, well-studied way by persons responsible for them. At the same time, product pricing and brand management should not mix.

Good governance requires that the CEO is keen to avert the risk that competing brand managers end up brawling among themselves, as they vie for fame, management attention, and marketing money. Conflicts of duties among professionals are a downside which, in 1988, led Procter & Gamble to abandon brand management.

- P&G decided that its system was pitting brands like Camay and Ivory soaps against one another, and
- It switched to *category management* in which responsible executives oversaw whole product categories.

Other companies, however, stick to the brand concept at company level, product level or both. An example is MS Windows, which identifies both the product and Microsoft, as a company. To enhance brand recognition, several entities also associate to the brand management accounting standards, such as:

- Return on sales
- Return on assets, and
- Leadership in the industry.

In high technology, for instance, Cisco shares with Microsoft and Intel the distinction of being ranked in the top five among Fortune 500 companies by return on sales and return on assets. Some financial analysts say that Cisco is obsessed with getting brand recognition – more specifically something like an 'Intel inside' trick (more on this later).

Like Intel, the strategy Cisco has followed is to turn the company name into a brand name for all of its products. It did so by capitalizing on the fact of being market leader. The company already has close to a 70% share of the market in its router business and furthermore:

- Cisco is either first or second in every other market in which it operates, and
- It has a long-standing policy of buying any company that has a technology it fancies.

A December 2005 example is Cisco's acquisition of Scientific-Atlanta in a $6.9 billion deal. The move combines Cisco's business in networking equipment with Scientific-Atlanta's set-top boxes. This would enable the acquiring company to better address the consumer market, branching out of its current high ground in corporate networks.

Many high-tech firms now feel that serious brand-building is important because big information and communications technology contracts are increasingly being awarded at board level, rather than by IT managers alone. Microsoft, Intel, Cisco, and others believe that their future will increasingly be influenced by boards of firms that operate far beyond the confines of the technology industry. Because of this:

- Brand recognition can help to win the attention of non-technical executives, and
- At the same time it is raising the barriers to smaller, less known rivals, the way IBM once did.

Intel, which makes the microprocessors found in 80% of the world's PCs, provides one of the best examples on branding that can be found in the past few decades. In 1992 it began its 'Intel inside' campaign, which at first met with scepticism both outside the company and within it. The logo made sense because Intel's footprint can be seen all over the market. Today:

- Intel's brand outstrips that of any PC manufacturer, and
- 'Intel inside' has become a *trustmark*; that is a trademark that consumers regularly put their faith in.

Originally, Intel's customers were PC manufacturers who did not need a fancy brand to tell them what kind of performance and value they were getting from the company's chips. But that did not deter Intel from pushing its brand, a non-reaction assisted by the fact the chip maker also had the bright idea of contributing directly to the PC makers' advertising campaigns – as long as they promoted its processors.

Seen under this perspective, 'Intel inside' is a double hit: it is branding, but also a way of franchising a brand name. Other companies followed suit.[5] As 1997 came to a close, AT&T considered a novel and less costly way of entering the telecommunications market more quickly than building its own infrastructure.

- The move has been to franchise its brand name to local and wireless carriers.
- These targeted carriers were directly connecting to the AT&T network and billing systems.

The concept behind this and similar branding plans is to enable the brand owner to quickly widen the brand name's coverage. For instance, in AT&T's case the adopted strategy brought wireless and local services to long-distance clients. This branding strategy contrasted to that of other firms. An example on an opposite strategy is that adopted in the mid-1990s by MCI, which operated cellular service in 50 major markets although it did not own the facilities. Essentially, MCI:

- Bought transmission from local companies, marketing it as an MCI service, and
- It bundled this transmission facility with other business services it was already providing.

Among the benefits provided by that strategy is that customers received one comprehensive bill. Another strategy has been that of Sprint, which had a US-wide footprint, licences to reach 100% of the US wireless market, and operations in 75 markets in the United States. Sprint originally spun off its wireless operations, then reabsorbed them, merged with Nextel, and set a policy on concentrating on wireless.

A possible downside to renting the brand is a damaged reputation. For instance, AT&T had a widely respected name for high-quality service and customer care. *If*, however, its franchisers failed to uphold the high standards direct AT&T customer expected, *then* AT&T could be hit. Therefore, franchisers of brand names need to exercise steady quality control and vigilance. This is precisely what McDonald's is doing.

Notes

1 D.N. Chorafas, *Wealth Management: Private Banking, Investment Decisions, and Structured Financial Products*. Elsevier, Oxford, 2005.

2 See D.N. Chorafas, *Statistical Processes and Reliability Engineering*. Van Nostrand Co., Princeton, NJ, 1960.

3 *Business Week*, 23 February 1998.

4 D.N. Chorafas, *Integrating ERP, CRM, Supply Chain Management and Smart Materials*. Auerbach, New York, 2001.

5 Even if in December 2005 Intel decided to change its logo, in order to broaden the market to which its adds appeal.

Know Your Customer

1. Introduction

Know your customer (KYC) is what companies and their managers most frequently fail to do. For instance, banks call many of their customers, particularly those in private banking 'Dear Client', but they don't really know enough of them to justify the word 'dear'. A same statement is valid for companies in other industrial sectors.

Additionally, 'know your customer' is a polyvalent expression, widely ranging in terms of meaning. For example, in the case of private banking, KYC ranges from the customer's investment profile, his or her risk appetite, quality of required service, intensity of necessary handholding, to a number of other variables. The latter include the bank's own individual account management strategy and its profitability analysis policy, which is the main theme of this chapter.

In my experience, the best way of looking at the individual customer is as a *profit centre* with relationship requirements that must be managed in an able manner to contribute to the bottom line. This is valid for all industry sectors, from banking to manufacturing, merchandising and beyond. The careful reader will remember that in banking 20% of clients represent about 80% of the bank's turnover.

Pareto's law, that a small percentage of one variable represents a big percentage of another, also prevails in manufacturing. As the statistics in Table 16.1, from a major cement manufacturer, show, 2.5% of clients represent nearly 40% of the firm's annual business; indeed, one client absorbs 10% of annual production volume. By contrast, the turnover corresponding to the 86% of clients is only 22%.

Apart from reconfirming Pareto's law, these statistics suggest that KYC is so much more important with the bigger clients. The most broadly spread method to measure individual customer profitability is *account analysis*. Its

Table 16.1 Turnover by client population segment in the cement industry

	Percentage of clients	Percentage of business	Profits
End user companies	86.0	22.0	Positive
Distributors	9.0	24.0	Very positive
Manufacturers of prefabricated	2.5	15.0	Rather negative
Concrete production centres	2.5	39.0	Rather negative

algorithm is fairly simple. In performing the analysis, the account executive must determine the:

- Revenue represented by an account
- Cost incurred in serving this account, and
- Effect of special conditions made to keep the account.

Revenue is computed by classifying all transactions in homogeneous groups, multiplying their frequency by their number, and summing up the partial results. The expense of servicing the account is computed by multiplying the number of times a given activity or service is utilized by the cost providing the product or service (Standard cost is a preferable approach, if it has been implemented.)

The nature of special conditions varies with the company, its products or services, and the customer to whom these are addressed. Both competition and established customer relationships play a major role. Special conditions are usually deviations from price list(s), and as such they impact the revenue side.

- But they may also be higher quality services, affecting the cost side.
- Additionally, a special condition may be assumption of credit risk, as in a bridging loan – and as Chapter 12 has explained, risk is a cost, sometimes bigger than other costs.

The difference between income and expenses represents the estimated profit the company derives from the specific client relationship under study. However, while account analysis is an important step in determining the profitability of a *customer profit centre*, it does not measure total customer profitability. The latter may be higher or lower depending on qualitative factors not included in a quantitative analysis.

For instance, in the banking industry the quantitative account analysis generally focuses on operations for which compensating balances are maintained and/or corresponding activities are billed. For instance, current account maintenance, cost per item deposited or withdrawn (differentiating between teller cost and automated teller machines – ATM), ledger entries, wire transfers, currency exchange rates, and fees. Banks, however, rarely enter in the customer profit centre account the cost associated to them, like credit risk and interest rate risk with loans, and legal risk with trust services, to name but a few.

This is a major failure in terms of profit centre accounting. The omission of the weight represented by credit risk, market risk, operational risk, and legal risk, may turn a profitability analysis on its head. It is, therefore, not surprising that a growing number of credit institutions have adopted the monetization of risk as an indicator of the biases existing in estimating profit and loss from servicing customer relationships. The following sections demonstrate what a properly done profitability analysis should involve.

2. Profitability analysis of a customer profit centre

The first step in establishing a customer profit centre consists of its acquisition. This is a focal point of many marketing models because, as marketing experts suggest, it costs between 4 and 10 times as much to acquire a profitable customer as it does to retain one. A customer acquisition strategy must be preceded by appropriate selection. As we saw on a number of occasions, a narrow segment of customer base typically accounts for 80% or more of revenue.

The next step is solid execution of customer relationships. It is up to relationship management to handhold and work so that established profit centre targets are fulfilled. In this process the emphasis is both on customer retention and on extension of product and service sales. The two constitute the driving force of relationship marketing.

- Customer retention is less dependent on traditional marketing tools than many people think.
- Basically, it is more oriented to the value perceived by the customer during every interaction he or she has with the company.

This is particularly true in the service industry, insurance and banking being examples. Customer relationship management permits business actions in response to, and in anticipation of, actual customer demands, and other characteristics of customer behaviour. From a strategic perspective, this is a process of:

- Allocating organizational resources to those activities that have the greatest return, and
- Measuring the impact profitable customer relationships have on the bottom line, then taking steps to improve it.

From a technological viewpoint, relationship management requires us to capture, analyse and share all the facets of the customers' activities with *our* company and, therefore, each customer profit centre's contribution to growth and survival of the business. The profit centre's contribution should be judged under a triple perspective, in the:

- Shorter
- Medium, and
- Longer term.

The evaluation of a customer profit centre should be based on proper metrics and methodology. The tools and measures should be the same for all accounts. By this principle, *profitability reports* should provide the way for management to judge operations under its authority. In a banking environment, for instance, these may be deposits, loans, investments, trading or other. Evaluations must never be based on averages but on:

- Each specific product and service being offered
- Individual transactions pertaining to a product or service, and
- The way these transactions and services affect the profit centre account.

The strategic perspectives mentioned in the preceding paragraphs converge in requiring activity-based costing, detailed transaction data on customers, and real-time updates of account information, which must be available on request to every authorized executive. This means that effective customer relationship management calls for a fairly sophisticated systems infrastructure, and for a reporting system able to:

- Document how much money we make or lose from a given client relationship, and
- Permit examination of whether *our* products and services leave a profit margin, given the way they are priced and handled.

Every industry has its own criteria on how to apply these principles. In financial services, for example, the focus on customer profitability is driven by real business issues such as the declining effectiveness of traditional marketing, an increasingly competitive environment, rising customer expectations for new services, the after-effect of technology, and the impact of deregulation and globalization. All these reasons have been leading to:

- Customized products
- Multiple pricing options, and
- New distribution and communications channels.

Participants in the research that led to this book aptly commented that, while this strategy is doable, handling the customer as a profit centre poses significant challenges to the organization. Among them are cultural issues, as well as an urgent need for financial metrics and models to differentiate between:

- Short-term customer profitability, and
- Long-term customer lifetime value.

This observation reflects a sense of good governance. A profit centre is not made for the short term, but at the same time it is expected to produce short-term results. Therefore, both the short term and the long term are integral parts of profitability analysis in its effort to overcome some of the shortcomings of the more traditional account analysis, by means of considerably more focused statements.

- The longer-term view is provided by the meta-layer of the client relationship, which is macroscopic.
- The short-term view is served by the lower layer in Figure 16.1, which is microscopic, detailed, and with information elements that can be recombined by functional area.

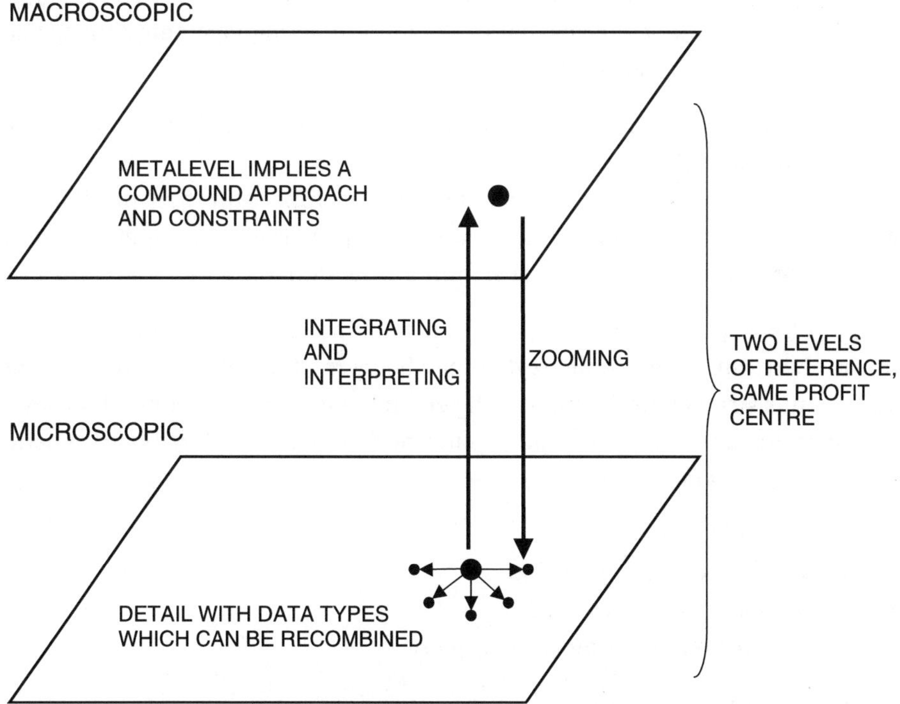

Figure 16.1 The meta-layer is based on longer-term macroscopic knowledge, while the lower layer contains shorter-term detailed information

The meta-layer in customer relationship is a knowledge engineering concept, which implies a compound approach, and at the same time imposes constraints. The latter help in channeling the behaviour of the relationship as well as in integrating the provision of services, and in interpreting customer responses. In Figure 16.1, top to bottom detail on the customer profit centre's activities is obtained by zooming – for instance, looking at day-to-day details of multiple accounts maintained for a single corporate relationship, which will be consolidated at meta-layer level. Such consolidation will also show whether losses on one customer sub-account are being offset by profits on another sub-account of the same customer entity, and therefore profit centre. This is a theme further elaborated in section 3.

3. Scrutiny should start at high level

One of the main issues affecting an entity's profitability is how rigorously the board questions, or dissects, management's evaluation of customer profit centres – including both cost and risk factors. In forming an opinion on this matter, one should ascertain the key queries that directors pose to management during board meetings, particularly those related to:

- Changes in business strategy, such as a noticeable shift in the company's customer orientation
- Overdependence on some customer relationships, and their profitability
- Negative events affecting the company's operations, like operational failures, poor financial results or pending litigation.

This line of analysis of customer centre behaviour can be instrumental in providing early warning on problems that may be facing the entity. It can also reveal management's strategy for dealing with sensitive situations. A contextual review should also focus on whether the agenda of topics covered at board meetings reflects a proper balance of:

- Key strategic goals
- Client selection and retention
- Operational challenges, and
- Risk environment facing the company.

While the chairman of the board should exercise leadership of this process of questioning, all individual board members are responsible for participating in discussions revolving around the theme of knowing your customer. From a governance standpoint, it is important that customer account management reflects an appropriate examination of:

- Corporate actions that require board review or input, and
- Current and projected financial performance, including key emerging risks or competitive issues.

Every one of the factors outlined in the foregoing paragraphs can affect longer-term strategy and economic value of the entity. Another element in assessing board effectiveness is the amount of time and energy directors devote to their responsibilities, in both preparing for and participating in board meetings. Good governance requires that the board and its key committees hold enough meetings of sufficient duration to:

- Discuss the company's performance, and
- Form a view on its strategies, its clients, and key risks it faces.

Considering the individual customer as the ultimate profit centre is most helpful in decisions concerning capital allocation to the entity's business units, their activities, and their risks. In the case of a credit institution, capital allocation and net funds employed is macroscopic information (see section 2). By contrast, loan interest, loan fees, earned credit in deposit account, and service charges are examples of microscopic information.

Customer acquisition cost is macroscopic because the acquisition of new customers should be seen as a long-term relationship. The same is true of assumed exposure in connection to customer relations and of the process(es) necessary to keep it in control. Key elements in reviewing risk and return associated to customer-related transactions include the presence of:

- Policies that assure transactions are properly negotiated, and
- Mechanisms to ascertain they are priced at competitive market terms, and serve a viable economic purpose
- Knowledge-enriched processes that permit one to measure risk and return of each transaction and customer profit centre to which it applies.

One of the board's roles is that of reviewing or approving major commitments; also, most evidently, any shifts in product policy or customer orientation. Another important responsibility of the board is that of assuring that cost control has the upper ground and senior management is responsible for ensuring it stays that way.

- Administrative cost is running cost and, therefore, it is microscopic.
- Transaction *cost* is also microscopic, but any transaction can have a *risk* aftermath years down the line – and this is macroscopic.

Cost control awareness is one of the criteria of good governance. Some years ago Dr H.H.F. Wyfells, then chairman of Rabobank, made the point that the cost of a customer operation at the bank's teller (cashier) is 6 florin per transaction. With 100 million teller transactions per year at Rabo, this amounted to a cost of florin 600 million (about 270 million euro, or $314 million today). This is the human and infrastructural cost:

- The risk associated to teller transactions is mainly operational
- By contrast, a bridging loan has a major credit risk component and, depending on the convention governing this loan, it may also have plenty of market risk.

The earnings, expenses, and most specifically exposures associated with loans and other fee services not typically considered in a classic customer account analysis should definitely be included in a profitability statement. Such a statement must provide its reader with clear evidence on anything concerning the client profit centre *and* the bank's own organizational unit where transactions originate. Rather than emphasizing only activity charges, profitability analysis must focus on:

- The function, and
- Its characteristics, which help in determining customer profitability.

Specific methods of measuring customer profitability differ significantly from one industry sector to another – even within the same sector, for instance, among banks. But the general formulae being used tend to have rather similar characteristics. Bank income on a relationship is often computed by adding interest received on loans, interest earned on the customer's deposit funds and various fees paid to the bank by the customer. Expenses include charges for such items as:

- Activity service
- Cost of funds loaned
- Loan handling expenses
- Cost to the bank of supporting services.

Missing from this classical approach is the monetization of risk assumed with the client, which can turn the aforementioned cost accounting approach on its head. For instance, with loans assumed exposure is not only the customer's credit risk but also market risk associated with the value of collateral and other exposures which find themselves on the long leg of the risk distribution.[1]

For this reason, the statement that the differences between income and expenses is profit is at best superficial – and generally totally wrong. It remains wrong even when related to some artificial base representing the size of the relationship; including net funds borrowed, gross loans, total revenue, cross-channel sales, or whatever.

Equally wrong is the policy of many credit institutions to estimate client profitability in a way mainly influenced by loan terms, such as compensating balances, interest rates, and associated fees; extending all this to a plan to meet a minimum profit goal for the bank. This sort of approach tends to highlight the most profitable aspects of customer relationships, which is evidently a partial view. Therefore, they give:

- A distorted overall picture, and
- A misleading evaluation of a customer profit centre's profit and loss.

Instead of the classical approach to potential profit evaluation, where multiple loans to a customer are first consolidated to obtain average total loans outstanding and then these averages are used to estimate profit margins, the approach should be much more analytical. It must address cost, risk, and return transaction by transaction, including its specific characteristics like:

- Cost of funds
- Exposure being assumed
- Costs of the transaction itself, and
- Margins pertaining to this transaction.

An analytical methodology would relate the profit on a customer relationship directly to the return on capital, since with every loan a portion of the bank's capital must be allocated to that relationship. It will also account for interest rate risk, credit risk, and operational risk, as well as market risk connected to collateral. By including all other expenses related to the transaction, an analytical approach to profitability can provide much more realistic estimates of the contribution of every customer profit centre to the bottom line than the old method.

4. Dependability and quality of service: case study with Six Sigma

Curiously enough, *quality of service* (QOS) is one of the issues that has often taken a back seat in strategic business planning. This might have been excusable when, prior to deregulation, many banking services were provided for free. At that time banks were making their profits from the difference between interest rate charged and interest rate paid for funds. This is, however, no longer the case.

- Today banks are charging for their services.
- Therefore, quality of service should be given top-most position in strategic plans.

The fact that financial services are sold to the customer at a price ensures that banks have a major obligation in assuring quality of service and in minimizing operational risk.[2] Concomitant to this requirement is to know the customer's needs for products and service more profoundly than in the past, which is part of the KYC principles discussed in the Introduction. To appreciate the importance of quality of service, it is appropriate to recall that companies typically enjoy two kinds of *strategic advantages*:

- One is transitory, the result of being in the right market, with the right product(s), at the right time. This means riding a favourable tide, as long as it lasts.
- The other is more fundamental, and comes from having in place first-class products and processes and management able to mobilize the organization and keep it under control.

Beyond the advantages to be gained in terms of quality of service, over and above relationship management in its usual form, what has been stated in the second bullet is a prerequisite to assuring the *dependability* of an organization towards its *business partners*:

- Its clients
- Its supervisors, and
- Its own personnel.

Both in the manufacturing and in the service industry there must be in place a system of *total quality management* (TQM), and it has to be tuned in a way that it delivers first-class results. Additionally, a well-delivered total quality function must be supported by *internal control*. Total quality assurance is very important both in engineering and in finance. Japanese banks, for example, are masters of *quality control circles*, which were originally an American invention. Since World War II:

- In the manufacturing industry quality assurance has been immensely assisted by statistical quality charts.[3]
- Among financial companies implementation of quality control charts is more recent – a cross-fertilization from manufacturing.[4]

Additionally, because costs, returns, and quality have a lot to do with one another, this mission of quality of service extends its reach all the way into return on investment (ROI). The CEO and members of the board should be very interested to know what the company is doing in terms of dependability and quality of service, as well as to assure that it delivers much better than its peers and its competitors in terms of quality results. This means that the board should be:

- Establishing firm guidelines
- Doing proactive supervision, and
- Attracting new talent which appreciates the importance of quality.

Speaking from personal experience, higher quality is a catalyst to an attractive work environment; and this adds a great deal to the firm's reputation. Apart from the evident effect on the firm's clients, motivated technical talent wants to work on high quality projects because *the work a person is doing defines his or her self-worth.*

Dependability in deliverables, reputation, product quality, cost containment, fast time to market, and a challenging work environment:

- Lead to improved job performance, and
- Create a virtuous cycle that increases personal satisfaction.

It is no secret that successful companies are careful to populate their ranks with employees who uphold work quality and are eager to contain costs. By doing so, they gain an advantage over their competitors and ascertain their survival, which is in the interests of all of their employees in the first place.

For instance, as manufacturers prepare to introduce the next generation of products – and in these days of rapid innovation products, follow one another in quick succession – they must not only adapt to changes in methodology and technology, but also improve cost control and quality performance. Firms that will not or cannot do so are condemning themselves because they are not going to be around for long as independent entities.

To bolster performance and improve quality of service, prior to their merger both JP Morgan and Chase Manhattan implemented General Electric's *Six Sigma* methodology. The Morgan Bank did so through 300 Six Sigma projects that boosted quality and squeezed costs out of everything. Channels under scrutiny ranged from results contributed by research to selling derivatives.

What is special about Six Sigma? Starting with the fundamentals, over time income, costs, risks, any variable, have a characteristic distribution. Figure 16.2

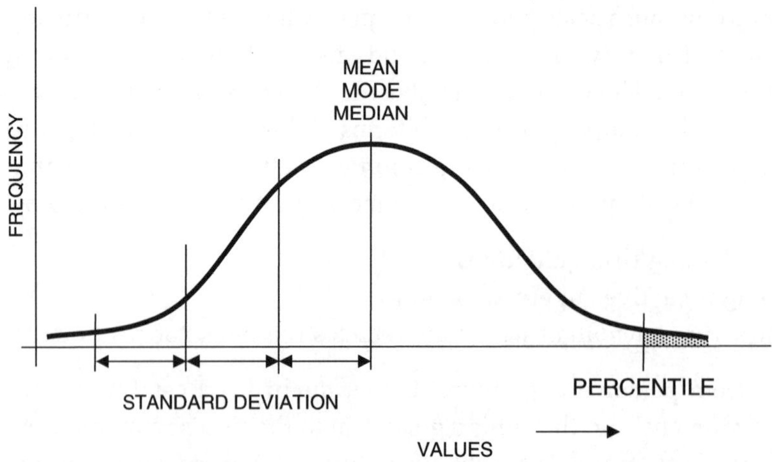

Figure 16.2 Normal distribution, mean, mode, median, and standard deviation

provides an example of a normal distribution curve. The first moment of a statistical distribution is the *mean*, or central tendency. The second moment is the *variance*, which defines the spread. (There is a third moment, *skewness*, and fourth moment, *kyrtosis*. Neither is the theme of this book.)

The standard deviation of a distribution, σ or *sigma*, is the square root of the variance. As a statistical term this measures how far a given process deviates from the *mean*, which is expected value. The idea behind Six Sigma is that if one can measure the number of defects in a product or process, one can systematically figure out how:

- To eliminate them, and
- Get close to zero defects.

Apart from statistical measures, this evidently requires a thorough, well-structured methodology. In a normal distribution curve, like the one in Figure 16.2, within ±3 standard deviations (or 3σ) from the mean lies 99.73% of the area under the curve. The outliers are in the remaining 0.27%, and this percentage becomes extremely small towards the long leg of the distribution – but spikes can happen.

- Six Sigma is essentially a process of self-assessment based on statistical notions.
- Standard deviations reflect status and performance of a quality programme that helps in identifying concrete actions, and in estimating their most likely aftermath in terms of keeping a process under control.

In connection to the Six Sigma methodology, General Electric has developed and implemented an entire set of tools revolving around the statistical control concept. GE management has good reason to claim that this methodology changed the company's DNA – in everything it does and in every product or service it designs and markets. The basic tools underpinning Six Sigma include, but are not limited to:

- *Statistical process control* methods that analyse data, helping to study and monitor process quality, capability, and performance
- *Other control charts* that monitor variance in a process over time, and raise an alert to unexpected variances that may cause defects
- *Process mapping*, which illustrates how things get done, by visualizing entire processes and their strengths and weaknesses
- *Tree diagrams* that graphically display goals broken into levels of detailed actions, encouraging creative solutions
- A *defect measurement method* that accounts for the number or frequency of defects hitting product or service quality
- *Chi-square testing*, a powerful tool for evaluating the variance between two different samples, detecting statistical differences in cases of variation
- *Experimental design* that permits one to carry out methodologically mean and variance tests regarding two populations (H_0, H_1)
- *Root cause analysis* targeting the original reason for noncompliance or nonconformance, leading to specifications aimed at its elimination
- A *dashboard* that maps progress toward customer satisfaction – for instance timely delivery, fill rate, billing accuracy, low per cent defective, and so on
- A *Pareto diagram* which exhibits relative frequency or size of events, such as 20% of the sources cause 80% of any problems.

Most evidently, tools and methods will not provide deliverables on their own. The will should come from the board, CEO, and senior management. GE was very successful with Six Sigma because Jack Welsh, its CEO, stood solidly behind it.

5. Benefits derived from applying a rigorous management methodology

Able solutions to management problems, including the most important know your customer issue, require support from technologically advanced systems, all the way from mathematical tools to platforms able to store and manipulate massive amounts of detailed data. One of the challenges is integrating disparate information elements from multiple operational sites:

- Distinguishing types of transactions
- Tying this data to individual customers, and
- Understanding the entire context of each customer relationship.

Many organizations fail to appreciate that this should be an accurate and focused enterprise. It is also a process requiring significant change to traditional practices and culture in both account management and the sophistication of technological support.

The major cultural change in the KYC strategy is to understand that the *customer* and not the product, or business unit, is the ultimate profit centre. This is a new departure in corporate management, which cannot be served by legacy approaches to measuring and understanding internal profitability. *Legacy* practices bear little relevance to *needed* practices.

All functions within the enterprise – finance, treasury, loans, forex, securities, accounting, and auditing – must put *customers* at the top of their decision-making processes. Traditional product-oriented management may not be able to scale up to handle this more complex information-intensive environment:

- Measuring activities across multiple product categories, and
- Handling in real-time diverse channels and constantly changing decision points.

Next to customer focus comes product focus, where the methodology discussed in section 4 finds a vast terrain of applications. Statistical quality control charts focusing on locating defects are so much more effective when we are breaking a product's or process's quality management requirements into manageable tasks. An interesting case of Six Sigma in action comes from Camco, GE's Canadian appliance subsidiary.

The company had tried conventional approaches to solve a problem connected to lack of rigidity in some of its units, which was leading to high scrap rates. Industrial engineers tried different approaches during assembly that seemed logical, but the problem persisted. Then, using *experimental design*, engineers tested ten possible cause-and-effect combinations. They were analysed in 14 versions of the experiment. Subsequently, graphical presentation of obtained results allowed the GE engineers to pinpoint the source of variation. After the source was localized, the trouble spot was detected by hanging the parts in the oven during successive steps of the enamel-baking process, and analysing the ratio of enamel on the top and underside. By tightly controlling the corresponding processes, it was possible to solve some outstanding quality issues while at the same time:

- Reducing costs, and
- Improving yields.

This excellent example by GE on deliverables of experimental design should be used as a paradigm for other similar applications, including those of managerial or financial type. Whether the industry is manufacturing or services, many companies work on the false premise that their customers do not see the quality defects; but they are utterly wrong on this account. Customers are not stupid. Industry leaders know that, and they do their utmost to increase customer satisfaction while keeping costs under control.

Quality, as measured by customers, will be the biggest differentiation between manufacturing entities, as well as between service providers. The concept behind this statement is exemplified in Figure 16.3, which visualizes how the concept of Six Sigma allows one to meet customer specification requirements in an able manner. Based on statistical inference, quality engineering teaches that:

- The smaller the standard deviation of products from a production process, the higher the quality being assured.
- Therefore, the challenge is to fit six or more standard deviations between mean value (or target) and customer specifications.

In the upper part of Figure 16.3, high quality is exemplified by 6σ. The lower part depicts the usual case of 3σ between target and customer specs. CEOs and managers who think '3σ is enough' are mistaken. Much more than the company's reputation, and its profit figures, are at stake. The market is changing rapidly and it demands higher and higher product quality.

In principle, the more impersonal Internet commerce becomes, the more the brand and reputation of a company will depend on the quality of its product. Ironically, this impersonal characteristic of e-commerce promotes the need for customization of products. E-commerce is not only an equalizer but also a promoter of greater competition, and companies have to face up to this challenge by emphasizing three keywords:

- Quality
- Cost
- Risk.

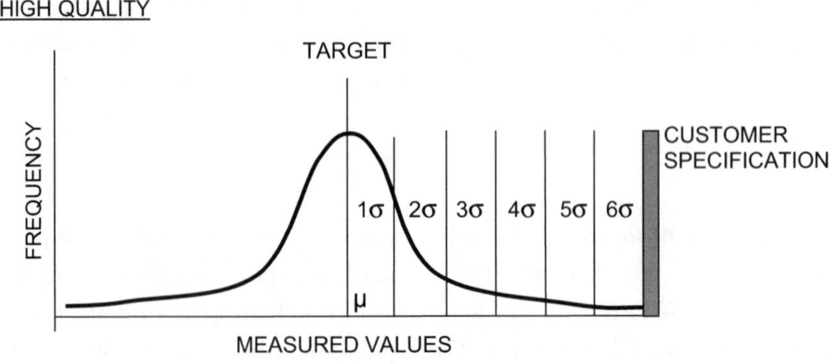

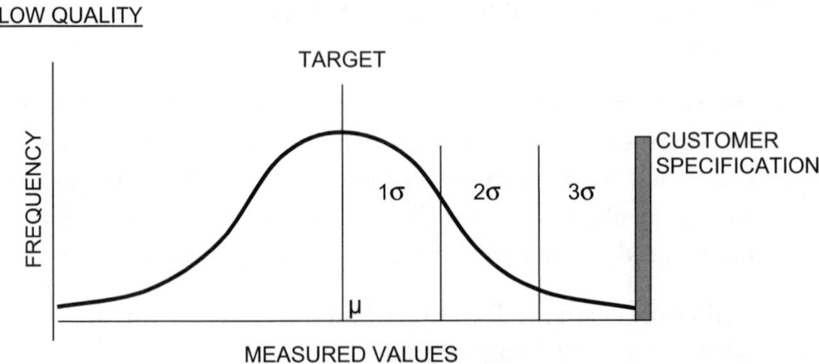

Figure 16.3 The measure of standard deviation, therefore of variance, is a good proxy of the probability of defect. (By permission of General Electric)

The use of a rigorous analytical discipline, like the one described in the preceding paragraphs, is not only the better method, it is the only one currently available *if* we wish to get *results*. Take, as another example of quality assurance through Six Sigma, GE's Medical Systems' Performix CT X-ray tube. Medical Systems is a process-intensive, high-technology industry with $20 million per year scrap and rework; hence, there is significant possibility of important savings.

In this case, the Six Sigma project focused on increasing tube life. Additionally, one of the goals has been zero per cent dead on arrival (DOA, meaning that on delivery the tube is out of action). By reaching this objective there is no patient rescheduling at the hospital end, among other benefits. Still other goals have been guaranteed tube availability, and an order of magnitude reduction in what

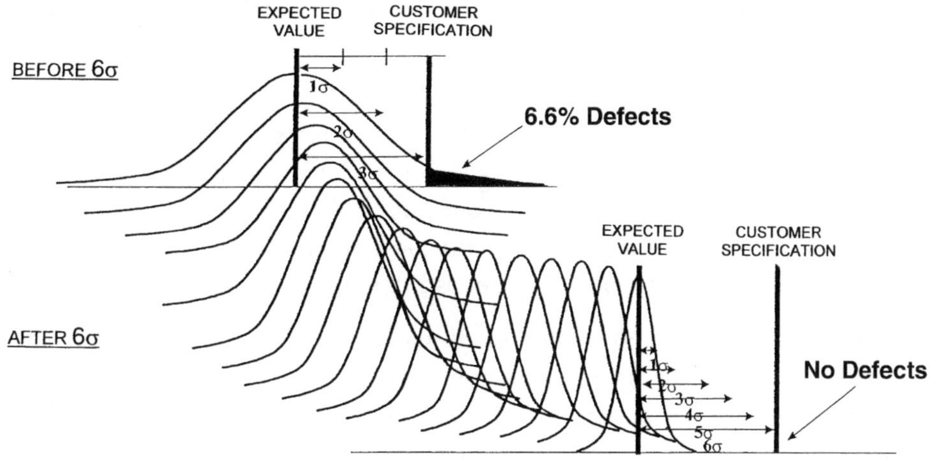

Figure 16.4 Three standard deviations usually fit between quality control target and customer specifications, but this is not enough. (By permission of General Electric)

GE calls *unquality cost*. Each of these aims is food for thought to practically every industry – from manufacturing to banking.

The sequential steps in reaching the goals are dramatized by the torrent of normal distributions in Figure 16.4 (from a practical Six Sigma implementation, reproduced with the permission of GE). The reader should appreciate that it is not possible to go from 6.6% defects to 0.0% defects overnight. Such improvement is doable over a period of time, after:

- Identifying, qualifying, and quantifying all factors that are critical to quality (CTQ)
- Co-involving customers in pinpointing those aspects of product service deemed crucial from a quality perspective, and
- Establishing a process that permits steady quality improvements with the goal of no defects.

The method we have examined is part of the armoury necessary to truly know your customer. It is also the only valid approach in protecting our company's bottom line. Notice, however, that even the best method and most sophisticated tools will be powerless *if* the board, CEO, and senior management don't stand 100% behind their implementation.

6. Statistical charts promoting the know-your-customer concept

Statistical quality control charts help management to track measurements and plot them against a given standard, which, for example, may be engineering specifications, tolerances, or an acceptable level of error. Quality tracking may be done by *variables*, as in the case of continuous measurement of an important variable characteristic of a product or process; or by *attributes*. An example is go/no go; a certain quality exists or it does not exist.

One type of control chart by attributes, known as *p* charts, tracks defects per unit in a quality control process. In many applications, below a given level, per cent defective constitutes a measure of good performance. Beyond that level, the process being measured is of poor performance.

- In production, for instance, a *p* chart measures and maps quality performance of a manufacturing process.
- Applied in an office environment, the *p* chart measures errors made in paperwork, such as documentary credit.

Per cent defective charts work equally nicely on the production floor and in the office, and they have proved to be a very good tool for controlling general quality levels. A *p* chart can be effectively used on individual parts and assemblies, but also in accounting – for instance, for evaluation of errors made in accounts. Its flexibility makes it an ideal tool all the way from manufacturing and merchandising to banking and finance.

An example is provided in Figure 16.5, which presents an operating characteristics (OC) curve for per cent defective. OC curves are powerful tools for quality control and for dependability measures, such as level of confidence, α. The statistics behind the curve in the *p* chart come from the computer industry.

- The *ordinate* is the probability of acceptance of each lot, P_A.
- The *abscissa* is the quality of lots coming into the sampling plan, expressed in per cent defective, *p*.

Not only is the level of quality clearly shown by this type of chart, but also the chart indicates if there are any trends or changes of which management should be immediately aware. In the general case, the per cent defective is obtained by dividing the number of defective units by the total number of units inspected, the quotient being multiplied by 100.

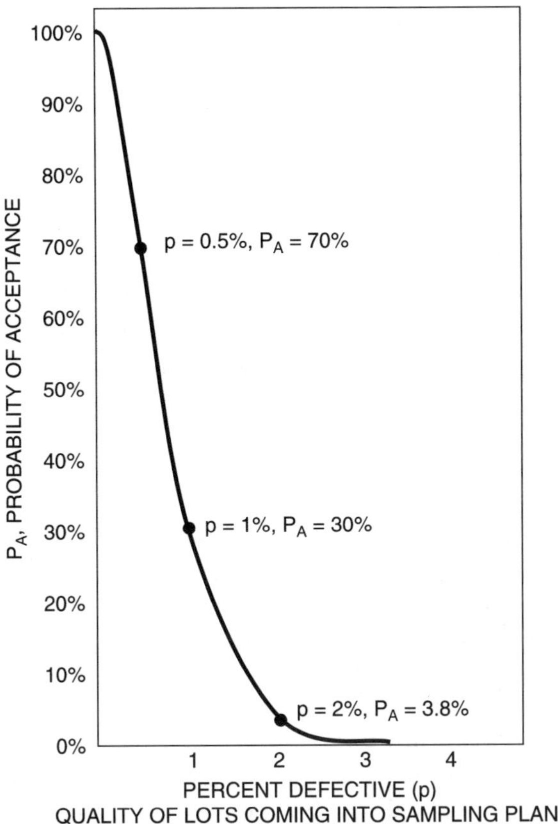

Figure 16.5 Operating characteristics curve for per cent defective

Sometimes individual *p* charts are kept by office function, *if* this function has important characteristics or significant costs. In other cases, *p* charts are applied to track one critical dimension, such as the result of go/no-go testing used in control by attributes. As such, they can be both a complement and an alternative to the accept/sample again/reject procedures in connection to quality control by attributes. An excellent example of OC curves by attributes is the risk-adjusted return on capital (RAROC) application. In principle:

- All pertinent data must be noted on the chart, so that the pattern of a complete written history can be obtained.
- Like any other statistical quality control chart, the *p* chart has control limits, computed from well-established formulas.

A chart can be plotted for whatever time unit is practical. Department or group performance is usually plotted daily. Where it is imperative to exercise close control of quality, per cent defective should be tracked intraday. For instance, *p* charts on the quality of production of individual parts or assemblies are often plotted hourly. New limits should be calculated as:

- Improvements are made to the controlled process, and
- The per cent defective changes, indicating conditions under stress.

Indeed, one of the important roles of statistical quality control *p* charts is that they can serve as early warning tools, flushing out abnormal per cent defective situations. Outliers indicate out-of-control conditions. The *p* chart can also be used as a gauge of the consistency of inspection. Companies that employ per cent defective quality control charts found them to be excellent yardsticks on progress towards quality of service.

In the financial industry, for example, one of the major fields where institutions have been successful with the implementation of per cent defective charts is accounting and auditing. In practically every case, obtained results have strengthened the company's position in areas such as financial planning, budgetary control, overhead analysis, cost control, and detection of fraud – among other operational risks.

Operational risk is present in every enterprise no matter which is the industry sector to which it addresses itself, and it is a pervasive issue because it incorporates under one roof many types of exposure.[5] Figure 16.6 provides a snapshot by categorizing operational risks into three classes:

- *Classical*, such as legal risk and fraud
- *Modern*, such as management risk[6] and organizational risk
- *Technology*-oriented, which range widely.

Many operational risks are internal to the company, starting at the highest level. Examples include the presence of important affiliations or business relationships between members of the board and key company executives; integrity of the firm's nomination process; background and ability of directors to understand the business; and financial implications of the company's:

- Strategies, and
- Risk appetite.

Still other operational risks centre around the flow of information between management and the board; rigour of the questions or issues the board poses to executive management; processes for determining important subjects covered at

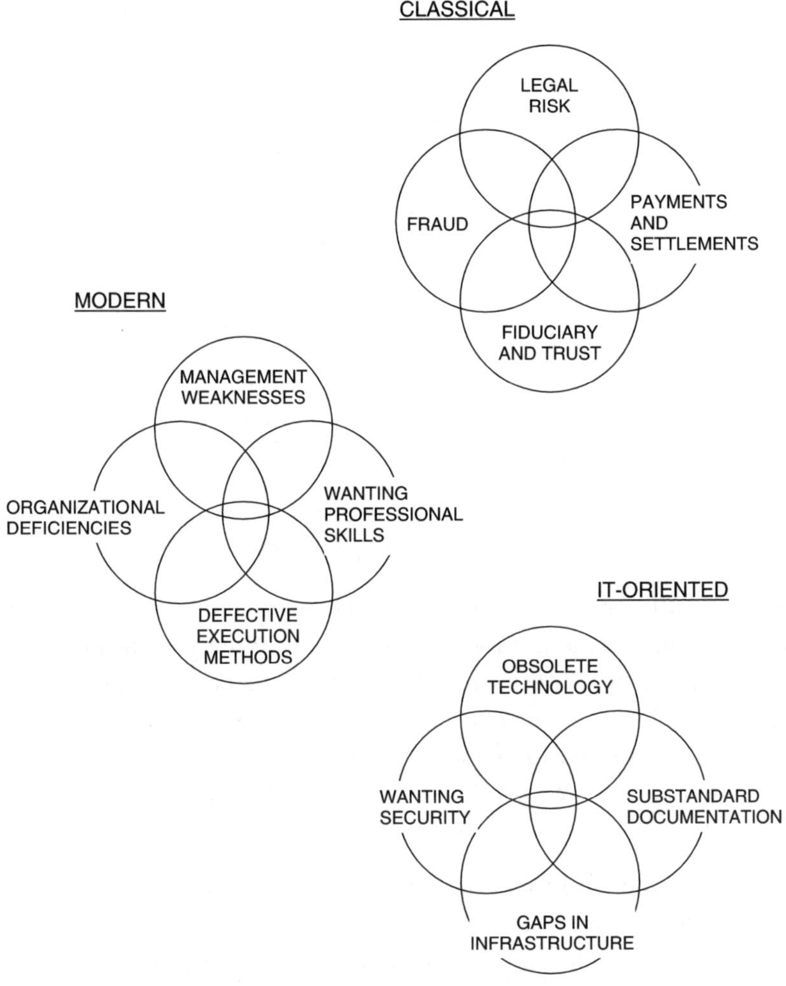

Figure 16.6 Three different groups of operational risk present in practically every organization

board meetings; depth of coverage; and amount of time and energy the directors devote to their responsibilities in:

- Preparing for, and
- Participating in board meetings.

Particularly vital in connection to the topics covered in this chapter is how often, in what sense, and to what degree board members keep watch on applications of the know-your-customer principle. For instance, they may interfere with KYC by asking for favours connected to client accounts, or pressing for opening new accounts that otherwise would not have qualified.

Operational risk is also present because of the fact that KYC calls for sophisticated statements on profitability by what has been discussed as the *customer profit center*. A dependable profitability statement must list the major sources of income derived, cost paid, and risk faced by the entity in connection to each customer relationship – its positions, and its transactions.

Errors made in this connection can be effectively tracked down by means of a $\overline{p}$ % defective chart, like the one shown in Figure 16.7. The pattern is in control as the $\overline{p}$ statistic never crosses the upper control limit. When that happens, then the process is out of control, and corrective action is necessary.

The tolerance limits and control limits to be established will be set by process definition. The problem is that, quite often, this definition is incomplete. For instance, what banks usually write down as entries –

- Interest accruing on loans during the analysis period, and
- Interest inputted on loanable funds supplied by the customer –

is absolutely insufficient, even if required to give the customer income credit for compensating balances maintained. Other listings under income are also characterized by insufficiency; these include any amount paid directly to the bank, such as a service charge; or fees for loan commitments, data processing and trust services. All these information elements are important, but they are not enough. Quality control charts are of assistance when the process is well done, not when it is incomplete.

In fact, well managed banks feel that an accurate picture of the profitability of a customer relationship can be obtained *only if all* income and expenses from products and services sold are included. Their practices also demonstrate that determining the appropriate interest rate to use as an earnings allowance in deriving the income represented by a customer's compensating balance can also be a demanding issue.

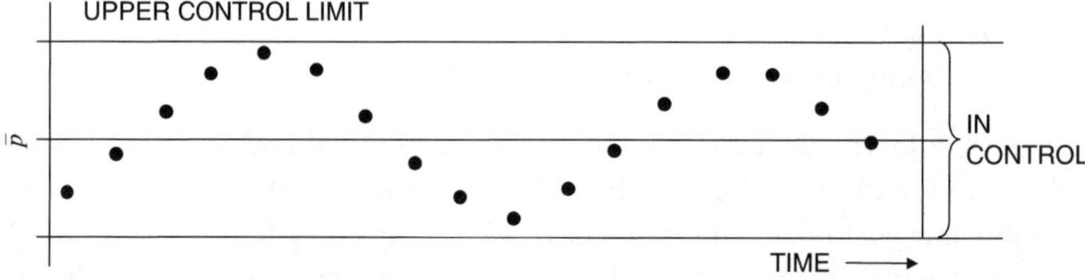

Figure 16.7 $\overline{p}$ per cent defective chart: monthly performance in a large backoffice operation

Numerous practices are followed, including using a rate equal to the bank's cost of funds; average return on loans and investments; inputs comparable to the cost a bank would incur in obtaining funds from alternative sources; or a rate the customer could earn if the funds had been invested directly in the money market. Which approach should be employed is up to the bank to decide. Implementation of the planning and control methodology discussed in this chapter makes sense only after management has made up its mind on the policy it wishes to follow.

7. Technology for managing customer profitability

Competitive companies win by thinking smarter. That is what the implementation of Six Sigma and other modern management tools is all about. The directives given by the chairman, board members, and CEO of companies characterized by good governance, to executive management, serve to tune technology to business needs – rather than the other way around, as uncompetitive firms do.

For instance, without the benefit of datamining a rich database oriented to customer profit centres, management cannot say for sure how many clients produce profits and how many customer relationships result in losses, all risks included. A major financial institution which asked itself this query on customer profitability found out that there were no exact statistics on how many, and what type, of accounts a client profit centre had. Senior management 'guessed' that the most likely answer would be:

- The 16 million accounts on the banks books
- Represent 8–9 million customer profit centres, at an average of about two accounts each.

More precise measurements were made after the customer database was pruned, a new client account identification was introduced, and accounts belonging to the same client entity were integrated. Through them, it was established that the answer was 7 130 000 customer profit centres.

The careful reader will appreciate that this average of 2.2:1 does not mean much. What management was really after was profit and loss with business entities, a subset of the aforementioned client population, and there the ratio between accounts and profit centres was found to be 7.5:1.

It is simply not possible to study customer profitability, if (i) we do not properly identify the customer profit centres, and (ii) we cannot integrate all information pertaining to a customer profit centre. As has been explained in the preceding sections, this requires a conversion from account-based files to a client-oriented database. Failure to do so is part of operational risk associated with information technology (particularly the obsolete 'legacy' systems) and with a methodology out of tune with current business requirements.

As a statistic, management's guess of 8–9 million customer accounts was not that wrong, but this is of no value to the study of individual customer profitability. While the average was 2.2:1, the number of accounts per client entity ranged from 1 to more than 20, and most of these 20 had no linkage to one another. As a result, the guesstimated profiles of this customer base were way out of focus. Under these conditions:

- Management was at a loss in evaluating customer profitability
- No effective marketing action could be taken, and
- No effective control of risk, specific to each customer profit centre, was feasible.

Another aspect of operational risk associated to technology and methodology is failure to appropriately train people to the implementation of a holistic approach to the management of customer accounts and their profitability. This starts with strategic decisions involving the organization of customer profit centres, and monetization of risk.

The next important step is to design a system solution that provides real-time response to queries related to each customer profit centre. This exercise, however, will be void of substance if it does not include costing and pricing of the risk component of all products, services, and transactions relating to each client – including estimation of overhead and calculation of direct and indirect product costs.

As these paragraphs have documented, there is not just 'one' but many prerequisites and ingredients in customer profitability analysis. For instance, among on-line databases which are needed for a properly functioning client profit centre profitability analysis system are:

- *Control audit*, containing images of controls that have been exercised.

An image(s) must be created reflecting the activity performed during control action.

- *Customer profit centres* – identifying companies and those individuals among the top 20% income earners for *our* firm.
- *Transactions* – storing pointers to all transactions related to the top 20%, no matter with which functional department or branch they are done.

- *Other account activities* – containing all products and services for client accounts other than transactions (For instance, asset management).
- *Other relationships* – relating to the 'other 80%' of customer accounts, grouped in a profit-centre-oriented sense.
- *Matrix* – featuring tables for measuring risks, operational costs, capital allocation, loan administrative issues and cost of funds.
- *Profit model* – targeting customer profitability information by selected reporting period, established according to management criteria.
- *Relationship audit* – containing images of all relationships. Anytime relationship maintenance is done, an image(s) should be created in this file for auditing purposes.

So much for databasing and datamining requirements. Equally important is the development of expert systems, agents, and simulators to automate the processes of computation and evaluation. Current profit models must be on hand to determine the profitability of active customers for the processing period under investigation. An interesting expert system I recently saw addressed peak commitment. Another expert system was looking after outliers in customer transactions.

Still other knowledge engineering artefacts should search the database for responsibility reporting – pertaining to branch, officer, trader, or investment adviser – on issues such as operational risks, actual *vs.* projected usage of funds, customer complaints, fees and other indices, for example, specific problems connected to customer accounts as far back as the databased information goes. Public databases may also have to be accessed on-line, for these and similar purposes.

To contribute to the improvement of quality of service other expert systems should be developed to keep operational risk under control, as well as to track operational risk events by customer profit centre. Figure 16.8 presents a framework for evaluation of operational risk and subsequent reporting to senior management. The building blocks in Figure 16.8 have been put in place with the objective of leading to an integrative operational risk structure that can serve to keep under surveillance both inhouse activities and outsourced functions.

8. General conditions characterizing a client's contract

Typically, a business relationship between a company and its clients is of a contractual nature. Every industry tends to have its own type of contract

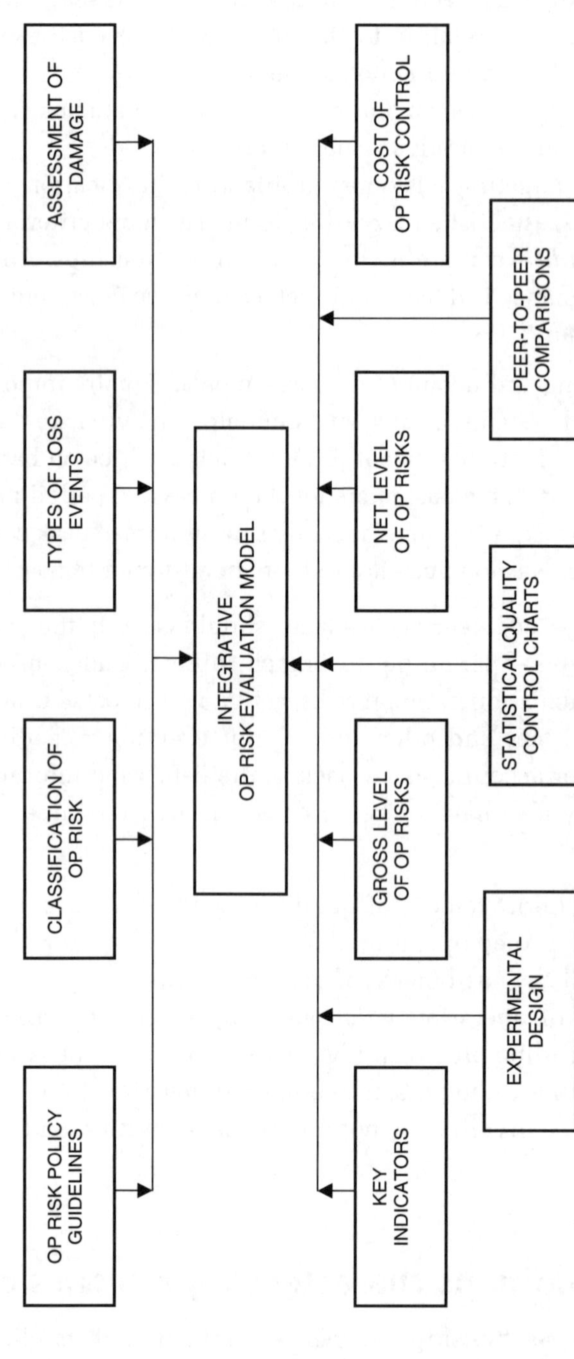

Figure 16.8 A framework for the evaluation of global operational risk

depending not only on the products and services it sells, but also on the law of the land, specific practices that prevail from the past, the thinking of its lawyers about protection from court action, and other factors.

As an example of contractual agreements, this section focuses on more or less general conditions applied by banking institutions. The 15 clauses that follow were assembled from different contracts. They have been deliberately chosen because such contracts need to be applicable to a significant number of circumstances. All contracts need to be carefully scrutinized by lawyers to strengthen the bank's defences.

Right of signature and authentication between the client and the bank are established and remain in effect until such time as the bank receives written cancellation from the client. In theory, the bank must always verify the authenticity of signatures by comparing them with the client's specimen signatures deposited with it. In practice, with high frequency items like cheques this is rarely done because of cost.

The contract usually states that the bank is entitled, but not required, to undertake more thorough verification of the client's order signature process. But the client typically bears all damages arising from failure to detect inadequate validity or forgeries, unless gross negligence on the part of the bank can be proved. (Note that 'gross negligence' is very difficult to prove.)

In case of *Incapacity to act*, the contract stipulates that the client shall bear all damages – specifically, damages arising from his or her own incapacity to act, unless such deficiency is announced in an official publication. The client also bears all damages arising from authorized representatives' or other third parties' incapacity to act.

Communications from the bank to the client are considered as duly effected if they have been dispatched according to the client's most recent instructions. Mail that the bank is instructed to hold is regarded as delivered on the day this mail is dated. Many contracts stipulate that the client shall bear all damages arising from delays, loss, errors, mutilation, or duplication in transmission or transportation, unless gross negligence by the bank can be proved.

Regarding *current account reporting*, the bank issues monthly statements, and at the client's request quarterly, semi-annual or annual statements. The bank reserves the right to charge the client for any expenses – as well as for taxes or fees – which may be incurred after closing of the account statement.

Assets of the bank corresponding to clients' *foreign currency accounts* credit balance are typically deposited in that currency. The client bears a proportionate part of all economic, legal, and other consequences that might arise from government measures, or political changes, affecting the bank's assets deposited in a given country or held in its currency.

In connection to *safe custody and trust accounts*, a client's securities, precious metals and other objects are held for safekeeping by the bank, subject to custodial fees. Barring explicit instructions from the client to the contrary, the bank deposits securities acquired abroad with foreign correspondent banks. Such deposits are made in accordance with local practices, in the name of the bank but for the account and *at the risk* of the client.

The bank effects the transactions due to *client orders* only on specific instructions by the client, or under the terms of a portfolio management discretionary rights authorization. Contracts stipulate that the client expressly acknowledges that upon placing orders or issuing instructions over the phone, such orders and instructions are to be carried out subsequently by the bank and are to be confirmed by the bank in writing.

In the event of late execution of *payment* transactions the contract typically stipulates that the bank shall be liable only for loss of interest, unless the bank's attention has been specifically drawn to the imminent risk of further damage.

In the event that *bills of exchange, cheques and other paper* that has been discounted or given to the bank for collection is not paid, or the payments reclaimed in accordance with applicable law, or should the bank be unable to freely make use of the proceeds therefrom, the bank is entitled to debit the client's account. Collections of drafts and similar negotiable instruments at subsidiary banking places are handled without liability on the bank's behalf.

Some of the most interesting of the contract's clauses concern *derivative* instruments such as *futures and options transactions*. Typically, contracts say that the bank agrees to undertake the following transactions on major exchanges and in the over-the-counter (OTC) market for the account and *at the risk* of the client:

- *Financial futures*: interest rate futures, foreign currency futures, stock index futures, precious metals futures, other types of financial futures.
- *Options*: options certificates and warrants, standardized and traded options, covered options, options on futures (interest rate, foreign currency, stock index, precious metals), and other options transactions.

All deals taken up must be adequately covered. In futures and option transactions, the bank shall only be bound by the client's instructions concerning prolongation or the exercise of options if such instructions are received by the bank before the stockmarket sessions of the last day the options can be exercised or extended.

Regarding *margins*, the contract stipulates that the minimum margins are set by the exchanges or by the bank, and are periodically adjusted to market conditions. As long as a position is open, the minimum margin must be available in the form of a credit balance or a credit line. If a loss incurred is not covered by that balance the client is required to put up additional collateral, immediately restoring the margin to its full initial level.

The bank has the right to *liquidate positions* if the margin falls below a certain maintenance level and such a level is not re-established by the client; or should the collateral decline in value, the bank is entitled to liquidate open positions.

Another contractual clause focuses on *pledging of collateral and assignment.* The client grants to the bank the right to fulfilment of all liabilities that arise or may arise in the future from business transactions with the bank – particularly but not exclusively: current account, bills of exchange and commodity transactions, stock exchange dealings, derivatives trades, deposit of securities, portfolio management, trust transactions. Derivatives trades include contingent liabilities, and those arising from other legal causes even though they are not yet validated in law, such as possible tax claims.

Contracts also feature *special conditions*, in addition to the general conditions. These pertain to special regulations issued by the bank applicable to the client account, particularly in respect of the use of chequebooks, deposit accounts, deposits of securities and other objects, rental of safe deposit boxes and vaults.

There is also a clause addressing *approval of statements of complaints.* In its common form, it specifies that objections to statements of account, or safe custody account, must be made within one month. After expiration of this period, the said statements will be regarded as approved, even if the client has not signed a confirmation.

Moreover, complaints by the client regarding execution or non-execution of orders of any description must be made immediately upon receipt of the advice concerning the transaction in question. Contracts specify that the client shall bear any damages arising from a delay in registering his or her complaint with the bank.

Notes

1 D.N. Chorafas, *Economic Capital Allocation with Basel II: Cost and Benefit Analysis*. Elsevier, Oxford, 2004.
2 D.N. Chorafas, *Operational Risk Control with Basel II: Basic Principles and Capital Requirements*. Elsevier, Oxford, 2004.
3 D.N. Chorafas, *Statistical Processes and Reliability Engineering*. Van Nostrand Co., Princeton, NJ, 1960.
4 D.N. Chorafas, *Reliable Financial Reporting and Internal Control: A Global Implementation Guide*. John Wiley, New York, 2000.
5 D.N. Chorafas, *Operational Risk Control with Basel II: Basic Principles and Capital Requirements*. Elsevier, Oxford, 2004.
6 D.N. Chorafas, *Management Risk: The Bottleneck Is at the Top of the Bottle*. Macmillan/Palgrave, London, 2004.

Strategic Mergers and Acquisitions

Mergers, Acquisitions, Takeovers and Their Deliverables

1. Introduction

Quoting E.M. Forster's *Howard's End*: 'It is a vice of vulgar mind to be thrilled by bigness.' Mergers and acquisitions (M&As) make the acquiring company bigger than it used to be, but not necessarily richer or better managed. Yet, M&As have merits, provided the proper homework preceded them. Generally, there are different forms of mergers:

- *Horizontal:* this is the case of two firms in the same business.
- *Vertical:* As happens when one firm is a supplier of the other.
- *Conglomerate:* usually product lines featured by the merging firms are unrelated.

Merger waves happen from time to time. Examples are those that took place at the turn of the 19th to the 20th century, the 1920s, 1967–9, 1980s, and 1990s. Some, though by no means all, M&As play an important role in business and industry, providing the means of consolidation and/or renewal. Mergers *might* be successful if the merging entities appreciate their aftermath, which may be at the same time:

- Product-oriented
- Market-oriented
- Political and social.

M&A history shows that corporate buyers usually overpay. This applies particularly to technology companies and mergers made for prestige or ego reasons. For instance, telecoms providers' market valuations are judged more on their perceived strength in service provision and their ability to migrate corporate customers to higher value services, than an objective evaluation on current fair value would have suggested (telecoms mergers are discussed in Chapter 18).

In the oil industry, too, an overriding reason for M&As has been size, though the acquisition of proven oil and gas resources is a potent reason, too. A study by Bloomberg suggests that returns are about four times as great on extracting oil from the ground than on refining it.[1] On the other hand, many major oil companies see acquisitions as a surer way to use their cash to raise stock price, rather than the longer-term investment in refining capacity, that could be unprofitable if oil and gasoline prices fall before new constructions are complete.

In terms of political and social impact, M&As have a long-lasting aftermath. This is one of the reasons why governments oppose some of them, like the French government's reaction to the takeover of Danone by PepsiCola, and the French, Spanish, and Luxembourg governments' response to the takeover of Arcelor by Mittal Steel.

Many companies on an acquisitions spree tend to forget that success with M&A can never be assured: Quite often, mergers present post-mortem surprises, as the law of unintended consequences is always at work. Diebold, a US firm that makes automated cash dispensers, found that out the hard way.

After the US presidential election in 2000, which featured a vote-counting fiasco in Florida, Diebold decided to expand a part of its business that made electronic voting machines by acquiring Global Election Systems (GES). This 2002 deal turned into a disaster when computer scientists and voting-rights groups educated the public about problems with electronic voting. Critics complained, not without reason, that GES's voting devices could not leave an audit trail because, among other flaws, they did not print paper ballots. Eventually, the media coverage generated widespread criticism and led several states to reject GES machines.

Like most mergers, this one suffered from lack of due diligence. After the electronic fiasco, it has been found that Diebold management had failed to do its homework prior to GES acquisition. Not only voting-rights activists were already calling attention to the GES machines' drawbacks in 2000–2002, but also blogs on the Internet highlighted the flaws. Diebold seems to have exercised traditional forms of diligence before buying GES, like examining the target company's balance sheet, but the risks embedded in its product line were skipped over.

Beyond the examples in the preceding paragraphs, mergers and acquisitions may, and often do, affect in an important way the human resources of both the acquiring and the acquired firm, as well as their technology. And because a key reason behind several mergers is eventual cost-cutting – which largely means wages and salaries – the management of acquiring companies should appreciate that:

- What it pays up-front for an acquisition is not necessarily the whole cost.
- Much more is usually necessary for reorganization, factory close down, restructuring, and plenty of downsizing to reduce the cost base.

Among other important issues, the acquiring company, should, in its homework, count both immediate and further-out costs, not only projected or expected benefits. Focusing on acquisition or merger costs is important because the economic logic of M&As has most often been to achieve profitability by significant:

- Synergies
- Restructuring, and
- Eventual cost cutting.

When the homework is superficial, many synergies do not materialize, while costs skyrocket. Restructuring, too, must be paid ex-ante attention, because many companies acquiring a competitor are typically reducing factors of production to acceptable levels by closing out factories, warehouses, offices, and other outfits; and also by sending home many employees and workers. All this entails additional costs and *if* there are government restrictions on laying off workers and shuttering factories, *then*:

- Efficiency suffers, and
- It becomes very difficult to turn the company around.

Consolidation aside, another major reason for M&As is diversification in product line, which often proves to be an elusive factor. Still M&As are seen as a way to provide much-needed injections of new products and expansion into new markets – as well as a means for transfer of management expertise. The message section 2 brings home is that it is always wise to look back at the most recent two or three decades, for evidence of 'pluses' and 'minuses' in M&A activities prior to engaging in mergers.

Caution should particularly be the order of the day when a merger wave swipes the industry. On 12 December 2005, a breaking news item in the *Wall Street Journal* had this to say about coming M&As: 'A handful of mega-buyouts are in the works. So naturally, investors anticipate juicy offers. They may be misguided. Shares in some of the most keenly anticipated buyout targets have risen to levels that make it hard to pull off a leveraged takeover. Boards may now have to consider bids below market or risk, seeing their share prices sink.'

2. Lessons from a quarter century of M&As

All told, mergers and acquisitions, like any other financial instrument, can have a brighter and darker side. The latter is often characterized by short-lived results, or pains beyond those originally foreseen. One of the ironies with M&As is that the acquiring company becomes itself the subject of an acquisition, or disappears in the next wave of mergers.

The financial industry provides an example. After World War II, New York banks entered a period of mergers which permitted them to significantly increase their financial power. By 1961, the five biggest financial institutions had 75% of all deposits in the state. Less than half a century down the line, of these five, now only two remain.

The Manufacturers Bank merged with the Hanover to create 'Manny Hanny'. Bankers Trust merged with a succession of smaller banks, but severe losses with derivatives led to its takeover by Deutsche Bank in the 1990s. Chemical Banking merged with the Corn Exchange, then with the New York Trust Company, and in the 1990s with Manufacturers Hanover; then with Chase Manhattan, taking on the latter's name, and with JP Morgan.

Well prior to that the latter acquisition, Morgan had merged with the Guaranty Trust, which had been the first American bank to go into the Middle East early in the 20th century. The merger matched Guaranty Trust's significant funds with Morgan's business expertise. Business strategy-wise, Morgan Guaranty first remained wholesale, dealing with august corporate clients. But when the Glass Steagall Act of 1933 was repealed, it branched into investment banking.

It is inevitable that across all M&As there will be both successes and failures. There are cases that demonstrate efficiency gains; and many other cases where the efficiency gain generated by the merger is limited, standing at about 1 percentage point. In still other cases, the merger results are negative; particularly when problem banks try to pull themselves up by their bootstraps. Still, looking, in retrospect, to the M&As boom of the 1980s, some economists regarded it as a positive development, which:

- Enriched stockholders
- While shifting control from complacent managers to more efficient executives.

Also present, opinion among economists and financial analysts has been that poison pills and similar gimmicks aimed at hindering takeovers were self-serving, adopted to protect management. But at least one of the M&A post-mortem studies demonstrated that poison pills and protective laws had little impact on the incidence of takeovers. By contrast, by giving added bargaining leverage to targeted companies, poison pills seem to have benefited their stockholders.[2]

All these are issues that any careful study on M&As should examine in depth, using both past precedents and the more recent aftermath from fairly similar types of M&As. Precedents provide a good basis for judging what might happen in the next case. It needs no explaining that every serious study should consider both the good news and the bad news from historical evidence.

Moreover, it should not escape the reader's attention that many studies which suggest that, in the general case, mergers don't pay off also point out that the reasons are not one or two, but several, and they vary from case to case. Professor

Michael Porter, of the Harvard Business School, made a study of merger behaviour in the 1950–80 timeframe, involving 33 large US corporations.

- As a group, these companies unloaded 74% of their acquisitions, many in fields unrelated to their main business line.
- But they also unloaded some of their acquisitions within their main product line(s), reaching, on average, the record of reselling one company out of two.

The conclusion reached by Michael Porter, as a result of these findings, is that mergers and acquisitions are a drug. Though in cases they seem to bring along certain advantages, they are no answer to management's strategic dilemmas. On the positive side, they may make the board feel good in the short term, but ultimately M&As sap the creativity and energy of the acquiring company. At least, this seems to be Porter's opinion.

McKinsey, the consultancy, made a similar study, which involved a larger sample of the top 200 corporations in America over the 1972–83 timeframe. This study documented that less than 1 out of 4 was successful in terms of increasing the acquiring company's value to shareholders. This went up to 1 of 3 when considering small acquisitions, but dropped to *1 out of 13* in the case of larger firms working in unrelated product lines. Let's keep these findings in mind when we discuss M&As in this and subsequent chapters.

Another interesting reference is the Hobart Papers, produced by the Institute of Economic Affairs at the end of the 1980s corporate takeover boom. These provide an interesting economic analysis of that decade's mergers, suggesting that the big chemicals, property and industrial mergers of the 1980s produced no new shareholder value – even if this was one of their stated objectives.

In terms of M&As' financial impact, as Figure 17.1 shows the high-water mark of the 1980s was $568 billion in 1989. This, however, was dwarfed by a record $2.5 trillion in takeover bids announced in 1998, compared to $1.6 trillion in 1997 and $1.1 trillion in 1996. Figure 17.1 clearly shows that both the pace and size of M&As has been higher in the 1990s.

Behind this wave of M&As has been a process of consolidation creating big entities of global dimensions, but also destroying the layer of small and medium-sized companies from which so many industrial, scientific, and technological breakthroughs have come. Boosted by the equity market's bubble of the late 1990s, the race has been to establish a position of power in the twenty-first century. Many chief executives, like Thornton of Litton Industries, followed the dictum: 'We don't buy companies, we buy time.'

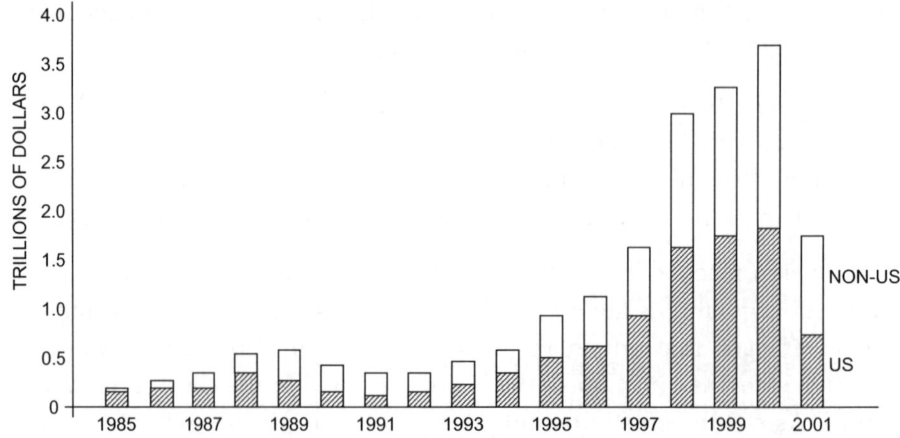

Figure 17.1 Value of announced mergers and acquisitions in the global market. Notice the spike in the late 1990s

Year 2000 was also most profitable to merger and acquisitions deal-makers, though not necessarily to companies that entered into M&A agreements, or to investors. The real winners were investment banks, law firms, and consultancies who advised corporate buyers and sellers. Advisory firms who focused on M&As in telecoms, in 2000, did great business:

- They shared work on about 1800 deals worth over $600 billion.
- But also found out, post-mortem, that their clients looked back on the year 2000 and wished they had not used their advisers' services.

Sliding stock prices in 2000 meant that deals had to be done at lower values than originally expected; yet, even so, many M&As were vastly overpaid. As equity values slid in all Group of Ten stock markets, a lot of people had regrets about mergers and acquisitions deals they did in 2000. They felt they either should have timed these transactions better, or that they should have offered a much lower price.

In the aftermath, as Figure 17.1 documents, 2001 was a lean year in M&As, with global transactions being less in value than US deals alone in 2002. The next few years have also been lean, though M&A activity picked up in 2004 and started to accelerate in 2005, as companies used the preceding years to restructure their balance sheet, and were again on the go.

American companies announced more than $144 billion worth of mergers and acquisitions in the first 40 days of 2005, the fastest start since the collapse of the equities market in 2000. Included in this number are SBC Communications' $16 billion deal for AT&T, followed by Qwest Communications' $6.3 billion bid for MCI – which fell through, with Verizon winning the MCI prize (see section 3). Also included are MetLife's offer to pay $11.5 billion in cash and stock for Travelers Life & Annuity, and Procter & Gamble's offer to buy Gillette for $57 billion in stock, with a $20 billion stock buyback to follow.

During the first seven months of 2005, deal activity in all major European markets has been up by about 50%. Analysts who a couple of years earlier advised great caution with M&As, changed their mind, suggesting there is great potential for value-creating deals within the EU, as fragmented national economies merge into a real single market. Activity in these markets has been driving the 2005 increase in mergers and acquisitions, other reasons being:

- Stronger corporate profits, and
- The fact that credit is cheap while shareholders are keen on takeovers once again.

According to some estimates made in mid-2005, Europe's telecoms could spend upwards of 80 billion euro in the 2006–2008 timeframe, consolidating their regional footprints. Shortly thereafter, Spain's Telefonica provided the evidence with its offer to acquire O_2 (see section 3 and Chapter 18). Most projections have been based on prognostication of the cumulative free cash flow for European telecoms operators: Estimates suggest it may reach as much as 183 billion euro in the years 2004–2008.

Sceptics answered these estimates with the argument that it is still to be proved how much of that money would be available for M&A. Not only has the telecoms sector dividend payout been rising in an attempt to attract equity investors, but also telecoms is a capital-intensive industry which has entered the broadband growth pattern, where significant capital expenditure (capex) increases are unavoidable.

3. Mergers in the United States, UK, and Euroland

There was a time when big buck mergers were an American company's speciality, followed by entities in the UK. By contrast, companies in Germany, France, Italy, Holland, Spain, and other countries in today's Euroland, were distant followers in both size and frequency of mergers and acquisitions. Since the last day of October 2005, however, this is no longer true. On that day, Spain's Telefonica made a 24.3 billion euro ($30 billion) all-cash offer for O_2 – one of the largest mobile phone operators in both England and Germany.

If it materializes, the merger of Telefonica and O_2 would create the world's second-largest phone company by number of customers, accounting for the fact that No. 1 is China Mobile. Through this takeover, Telefonica will have 170 million mobile and fixed-line users in Europe and Latin America. Experts say that in the background of this takeover-in-the-making is a combination of:

- rapid entrance of new, aggressive rivals
- The cost of third-generation wireless licences
- The still-felt after-effect of the technology bubble of 2000, and
- Technological breakthroughs obliging companies to look further afield.

Watchers of developments in Euroland's telecommunications markets suggest that if the Telefonica/O_2 deal goes through, it will sharpen competition in mobile telephones while, at the same time, threatening the incumbent fixed-line carriers. In the frontline are: British Telecom, France Telecom, and Deutsche Telekom. The reasons the incumbents face a challenge are that:

- Entry into the telecommunications market is increasingly through mobile phones, and
- Wireless technology is a substitute for both traditional copper-wire phone calls and, fairly soon, broadband Internet access.

The careful reader will notice that a similar method of consolidation in the phone industry is going on in the United States. In 2005 Verizon fought, and finally succeeded, in acquiring the formerly bankrupt WorldCom (renamed MCI, after one of its former subsidiaries). And SBC acquired AT&T, adopting its better-known brand name. (More on telecoms M&As in Chapter 18.)

Telecommunications is not the only industry sector experiencing an M&A revival. Since December 2004, in the United States, the mergers and acquisitions landscape has seen a significant pick-up of activity. Four large deals were announced within two weeks, including the $36 billion merger of Sprint and Nextel, the wireless carriers, and Symantex's purchase of Veritas, a $13 billion all-stock software acquisition.

Deals have been taking place across all industries. Gas Natural launched a £28 billion unsolicited bid for Endesa, a rival and bigger Spanish energy group. In technology, Oracle got a deal to buy Siebel Systems for $5.8 in stock and cash. Novartis, the Swiss pharmaceuticals firm, launched a $4.5 bid to buy all of the shares of Chiorn, the US vaccine maker, that it does not own.

Mid-November 2005 saw Swiss Re's proposed acquisition of GEIS, General Electric's insurance arm. Analysts gave mixed reviews to this $6.8 billion deal, which will catapult the Swiss reinsurer in front of Munich Re, its German rival, as the world's biggest reinsurer. Concerns were raised that buying GEIS could expose Swiss Re to too much risk.[3]

On Wall Street, some analysts suggest that the renewed interest in M&As defies prevailing uncertainty in the equity and bond markets because of the crude oil price spike and major natural disasters like Hurricanes Katrina and Rita. Ongoing merger deals show that companies continue to pursue M&As; therefore, the mergers market remains strongly aided by low interest rates.

When in 2005, Pernod Ricard, the French spirits company, launched a $7.4 billion bid for UK's Allied Domecq, one of the most striking aspects of the bid was the ease with which Pernod Ricard raised a 9 billion euro (over £6.0 billion; $10.8 billion) loan to finance the takeover. While precise details on pricing are always opaque in loan markets, insiders said that Pernod paid on average just 75 basis points over Euribor to raise the funds. This was noticeably lower than the 85 basis points Bacardi had had to pay a few months earlier to buy Grey Goose Vodka, in a fairly comparable deal.

E.ON, the German utility group, confirmed it was interested in buying Scottish Power, in a move towards consolidation among European energy firms before 2007, when the region's retail energy market is set to be fully liberalized. CMA CGM, France's largest container shipping line, said it had agreed the terms of its takeover of Delmas, a rival group specializing in routes to Africa, for $600 million. The merged company will surpass Taiwan's Evergreen to become the world's third-biggest shipper.

According to some economists, the No. 1 reason for M&A revival is neither big egos nor strong balance sheets. Rather, it lies in the fact that, in the 2002–2005 timeframe, the cost of borrowing money has fallen steadily for most companies, even if the Federal Reserve has raised interest rates in 2004 and 2005 13 consecutive times. This decline in cost of money partly reflects the fact that global financial markets have been awash with funds because of:

- Loose monetary policies in regions such as Euroland, and
- Huge savings held by many Asian central banks.

At the same time, however, low cost money also points to another trend. In recent years, most mainstream companies have been highly reluctant to raise their leverage because they were busy repairing their balance sheets in the aftermath of value-destroying M&As in the late 1990s. The surprise, several economists say, is that companies who went through the ordeal of cleaning their assets and liabilities are again in a merger mood.

Particularly European companies have been looking at M&A as a strategy to generate growth in an otherwise modest economic growth environment, which categorized continental Europe in the early years of the 21st century. It is true, however, that in spite of aggressive tactics reminiscent of the late 1990s, corporates have been much more disciplined in their evaluation of M&A than at the end of 20th century, and are not prepared to go to heady prices.

According to certain opinions, however, a more potent factor behind prudence in M&As, at least for American companies, has been reforms enacted by the US Congress, particularly the Sarbanes–Oxley Act. New accounting rules by FASB in the United States, and IASB in Europe,[4] as well as new and better focused rules by bank regulators, have made corporate boards more mindful of their responsibilities, including their review and approval of mergers and acquisitions deals.

In fact, as many recent M&A transactions tend to demonstrate, a lot of acquirers have become cautious about not overpaying. Gone is the 50% premium over market price, regularly paid in the past, particularly in the go-go 1990s. SBC offered AT&T virtually no premium over its market price, and the same is true of Comcast's offer for Walt Disney.

The aftermath of the Sarbanes – Oxley Act of 2002 prompted boards to question deals early, asking for detailed appraisals of individual assets that would be bought. Boards have also become more prone to stick with existing business instead of chasing new markets, and totally different product lines, whose integration with existing strategies does not come naturally. On the other hand, some CEOs point out that intensified due diligence can be a burden when market pressures are forcing a quick decision. The answer to this argument is that an incomplete examination of a contemplated merger or acquisition can come back to haunt an acquirer – and this is true no matter where the M&A deal is made, in North America, Europe or Asia.

Finally, as far as industry sector distribution of total value of M&As is concerned, the pattern in mergers and acquisitions is fairly different in Euroland, Britain, and in the United States. As Figure 17.2 documents, in the 1990–2002 timeframe, Britain led by far the whole pack in 2000, which was the peak year, as shown in section 2.

Statistics published in the 2002 Annual Report of the European Central Bank make interesting reading also in terms of the pattern of acquisitions of European

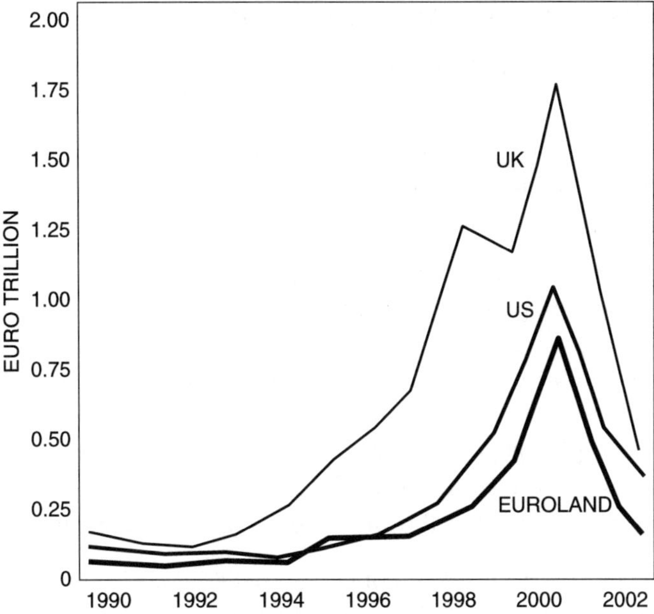

Figure 17.2 Value of M&A transactions in three areas, over 12 years. (Statistics from European Central Bank Annual Report, 2002)

Table 17.1 Percentage M&A investments in the 1997–2002 timeframe by US companies in Euroland and by Euroland companies in the United States

	Euroland companies investments in US	US companies investments in Euroland
Manufacturing	36%	58%
Services	29%	29%
Financials	25%	10%
Trade Firms	7%	2%
Natural Resources	2%	1%
Other	1%	Trivial

Source: ECB Annual Report, 2002

companies in the United States and of US companies in continental Europe. As Table 17.1 shows, in the 1997–2002 timeframe European companies had a greater appetite for financials in the United States, while more than half of acquisitions by US companies in Euroland were in manufacturing.

4. Friendly acquisitions and hostile deals

The dictum that 'Companies like people can make their own luck', fits hand-in-glove with mergers and acquisitions. Companies are made of people, and few chief executives appreciate that the corporate kind of marriages has a high failure rate, whether the deal was made on relatively friendly terms or was a hostile takeover. Study after study on M&As has been concluding that:

- Over half of them had destroyed shareholder value, and
- A further third had no discernible difference in value terms.

These are depressing statistics which, to a significant extent, document the fact many mergers are done without even the slightest study of synergy. One of the most glaring examples is AT&T's 1991 purchase of NCR. That was the second-largest acquisition in the computer industry, which was reversed after years of stress and enormous losses on the side of both the acquirer and the acquired.

Other mergers are the result of ill-conceived necessity, promoted by the government to cut down subsidies and hand-outs. A British example is that of computer companies promoted by the Wilson government in the 1960s. An American example is the McDonnell Douglas merger with Boeing, because the Pentagon was cutting spending by 50%. These are interesting case studies because they fall in the gap of what is considered to be:

- A friendly merger offer that may be put by the acquirer to the management of the company to be acquired, for its acceptance, and
- A hostile bid, where the raider buys the target company's shares in the stock market, or makes outright a public bid to equity holders (more on hostile bids in sections 5 and 7).

Some of the friendly mergers are made in the name of consolidation, and they are presented as a marriage of equals. Chrysler merged with Daimler–Benz because it was thought to be standing alone in a global market, having liquidated its European holdings in the early 1980s. Later on, it was revealed that this was not a merger of equals, though Kirk Kerkorian lost the legal action in which he demanded compensation for being misled (see the DaimlerChrysler case study in Chapter 21).

Typically, in a friendly merger, *if* the board accepts the suitor's bid, *then* a shareholder vote is taken to confirm the board's decision. Alternatively, the board may ask the acquirer for a higher price, look around for better alternatives in financial terms, or engage in horse trading to secure board and senior management positions in the resulting entity (see Chapter 20).

Sometimes projected mergers are a matter of management seeking glory, and the way to bet is that they will turn sour before they are consummated. An example is Deutsche Bank's projected merger with Dresdner Bank, followed by Dresdner Bank's projected merger with Commerzbank. None of them materialized. According to expert opinion, *if* these mergers had gone through, they would not have been successful.

Financial analysts in Frankfurt said that, most likely, the only synergy either of these mergers might have produced was found some years later, in November 2001. At that time, Deutsche Bank, Dresdner Bank, and Commerzbank announced a cost-cutting merger of their mortgage banking operations. This move created Germany's biggest property lender, with huge assets and an estimated 25% domestic market share.

The merger of three big bank mortgage operations came as Germany's credit institutions stepped up cost cuts and shed jobs at a time of falling profits. In parallel to the aforementioned event, pressure for consolidation mounted among Germany's Hypotheken (mortgage) banks which have been hit by:

- Shrinking margins, and
- Heavy loan losses, after a frenzy of lending in eastern Germany in the early 1990s.

A 2005 study by the Deutsche Bundesbank addressed the vital issue of how successful mergers, acquisitions, and consolidations in the banking industry have been.[5] This project used experimental design to measure the success of merging banks against two criteria characterizing the resulting entity:

- Level of cost-efficiency, and
- Change in cost-efficiency.

Prior to briefly describing the thesis of the Deutsche Bank discussion paper, let me bring two facts to the reader's attention. First, the use of *experimental design* in financial studies. In the 1950s, experimental design was the tool of excellence in applied experimental psychology. Over the past five decades I have successfully used it in engineering studies. It is therefore a pleasure to see that the significant analytical potential of experimental design is now applied in finance.

Second, the use of a *control group*. While this is an integral part of experimental design, it also constitutes an important concept in itself. The control group provides the needed reference level *as if* nothing has changed. We cannot measure the effect of change, such as the aftermath of a merger, without knowing what would have happened if that event had not taken place.[6]

Within this frame of reference, Dr Michael Koetter, the Deutsche Bundesbank's researcher, compared results obtained from merged banks with average values for a control group of banks. Members of this control group were institutions that did not merge in the period under review. Banks that have been affected by M&As were divided into four groups based on the extent to which the resulting entity was:

- Above or below the average level of the control group, in terms of cost-efficiency, and
- Above or below the average *change* of the control group, regarding overall efficiency.

After evaluating M&A results according to these criteria, Dr Koetter classified post-merger outcomes, up to nine years after they occurred. This classification into Groups 1–4 has been based on post-merger performance, along the line of the two aforementioned criteria.

Merged banks included into Group 1 have been characterized by a reasonably high level of post-merger achievement in connection to both criteria outlined in the above two bullets. In either case, the success rate was found to be about 50%. Group 2 was characterized by success in the first criterion, and failure in the second; Group 3 by failure, failure; and Group 4 by failure, success.

In the case of Group 1, the findings of this research project essentially mean that, in a way, every second merger is a success both in terms of level of, and of change in, cost-efficiency. At first sight, this result contradicts the statistics established by some US studies, discussed in the Introduction. In reality, however, the difference is not that big because in Group 1 have been included the best merger cases, after sorting results according to established criteria.

Moreover, as Dr Koetter points out in a private correspondence, despite mergers that 'beat' the control group simultaneously along the level and change dimension of post-merger cost-efficiency (precisely the 50% of entities in Group 1), the cost-efficiency differential is slim. It is a mere percentage point, which is too small in statistical terms to sustain a hypothesis of merger efficiency.

The reader should also pay attention to an interesting finding of the Deutsche Bundesbank study: that merging institutions with large *ex ante* efficiency differences boosts their efficiency only in the short term. Most likely because ex-ante efficiency differences provide a potential to transfer management skills. In the medium and longer term, the more successful mergers are those between similarly efficient banks.

Another interesting point confirmed by the study has been that in those mergers where a problem bank assumes the role of the surviving institution, this rarely results in sustained efficiency gains. By contrast, if a problem bank is taken over in a merger, the proportion of successes has been found to be comparable with mergers between two well-governed institutions.

Other M&A studies directed to the banking industry have revealed the interesting hindsight that bank takeovers are rarely hostile deals. There are several reasons for this, and most have to do with the nature of the financial industry. First and foremost, bank regulators have erected barriers that are high enough to deter all but the righteously determined to attempt a takeover. Regulators are also increasingly concerned with:

- Antitrust issues involved in mergers and acquisitions, and
- The need to assess whether a bank's managers can overcome the difficulties of merging different cultures.

Moreover not only does the scrutiny M&As in banking are going through discourage hostile bids, but also the threat of delays caused by regulators acts as a deterrent to a predator. Even friendly deals can take months to be approved, because in practically every state in which a target has a presence bank supervisory authorities must approve the deal.

The second barrier to hostile bids in banking can be just as important. Credit institutions are a special M&A case because what they do is quite opaque to outsiders. The acquiring institutions cannot truly examine the quality of a target bank's loan book until after a bid's completion. As a result, a bidder faces a unique risk: much of what the acquiring bank is paying may go up in smoke *if* the acquired entity turns out to have:

- Unexpected liabilities
- A huge amount of bad loans, or
- A portfolio heavily loaded with non-performing derivatives.

Even friendly deals that allow the two parties to examine each other's loan books, while minimizing the risk of nasty surprises, do not assure there will be no piles of non-performing assets. The merger of Bayerische Vereinsbank and Bayerische Hypo-Bank, to HVB (HypoVereinsbank), is an example we examine in Chapter 20. And there can be unforeseen restructuring costs.

A third reason for the unattractiveness of hostile deals in the banking industry has to do with accounting rules, particularly under US GAAP. When deals are friendly, banks generally use pooling arrangements to merge their balance sheets and avoid incurring goodwill costs that would have to be written off against earnings. To the contrary:

- Hostile deals offer no such escape route, and
- Financial reporting has to conform with purchase accounting.

Over many years prior to the change of rules by the Financial Accounting Standards Board (FASB), purchase accounting saw to it that goodwill was amortized against future earnings, creating a long-term drag on a bank's performance. In this case, the merger could be deemed successful *if* the resulting company is able to generate significant excess cash flow and first-class profits to offset the purchase accounting drag. (More on mergers of American banks in Chapter 19, and of European banks in Chapter 20.)

5. Big egos: case study on the RJR Nabisco takeover

One of the often touted but rarely realized goals with M&As has to do with 'combining world-class competencies and synergies'. Much less discussed is the fact that behind a great deal of M&A activity are big egos. Synergies turn out to be few, while the problems encountered in integrating different cultures and different products are real.

Take the merger of Molson and Coors as an example. The aim of the resulting company was to be the world's fifth-largest brewer, with $6 billion in sales. That's what management said. To the contrary, analysts' opinions have not been positive. 'The merger doesn't fix the company's core problems,' said Marc I. Cohen, analyst at Goldman Sachs, '[though] it makes each of the problems they face less significant'.[7] But is this enough of a reason for mega-mergers?

A British investments expert with whom I was talking about mega-mergers expressed the opinion that as the mass of post-merger industrial and financial aggregates grows, the rate of return tends to diminish. Yet, the merged companies:

- Have dividends to be paid out, and
- Their bonds have to be honoured.

Therefore, the merged firm must match the rate of return of its predecessors, which is not always done. Take the case of a leveraged buy-out (LBO). Company X takes over Company Y. Company X has $20 billion in debt. Company Y has $10 billion. But Company X borrows another $10 billion to go through the takeover of Company Y. So the merged entity now has $40 billion in debt. Chances are this is more than the combined company can sustain in its interest and principal repayments. (More on piling of debt in section 7.)

To serve its debt and pay dividend the resulting company has two options, neither of them being very appealing. One is continuing to leverage itself. The other is to sell divisions and subsidiaries, starting with those that attract bidders. Downsizing in people and product lines might even help the equity.

Rick Geiger, insurance broker in Jersey, beautifully described the market aftermath from downsizing through the allegory of two cows: 'You have two cows. You sell one, lease it back to yourself and do an IPO on the second cow. You force the two cows to produce the milk of four cows. You are surprised when one cow drops dead. You spin an announcement to the analysts stating you have downsized and are reducing expenses. Your stock goes up.' (Bravo, Rick!)

In investment terms, the RJR Nabisco takeover was a failure for Kohlberg, Kravis, Roberts (KKR), the takeover specialist, and for investors who put their money in the deal. Still, this was hailed as the epoch-making biggest takeover that had taken place at that time – and eventually it did make money for KKR by creating an excellent source of fees. Here is in a nutshell the story behind the RJR Nabisco case.

- KKR acquired RJR Nabisco in 1988 at $5.62 a share on an adjusted-cost basis.
- In March 1995 it unloaded its final 8% stake for only about $5.73 a share, with the bulk of its stake likely been sold for around the same price.

The company's takeover battle began on 19 October 1988, when RJR's own CEO, F. Ross Johnson, told his directors that he wanted to take the company private for $75 a share, or $17 billion. Johnson planned to do so through a leveraged buyout using Shearson Lehman, the investment bank, as adviser. Within hours of Johnson's announcement, plenty of investment bankers, lawyers, and commercial bankers rushed to get on the RJR deal, if they could find a way. Some of them focused their attention on KKR's New York office, where Henry Kravis was planning a counter bid. On Wall Street analysts said that, initially, KKR was an unwelcome outsider. But the takeover specialist had tremendous financial might as well as the skill needed to leverage it.

Within two days, Kravis began forming the nucleus of a group of big banks that would lend him billions. This included Manufacturers Hanover, Bankers Trust, Citibank, and Chase Manhattan. Kravis also hired a team of big-time Wall Street advisers who would eventually claim $100 million of the money that KKR planned to raise to buy RJR.

On 24 October KKR was in the bidding war with a $90-a-share offer. That bid, equal to $20.3 billion, was said to be staggering. The sheer size of this buyout, and the fees involved, brought a swarm of Wall Street deal-makers into the game. If starting price and ending price are used as the criterion, it should be appreciated that $5.73 a share is only 6% of $90 – which was the bid.

Post-mortem experts suggested that the biggest error in the RJR takeover battle was made by CEO Ross Johnson, who had started the ball rolling. Instead of proposing to share post-buyout ownership of RJR among as many employees as possible, he began to circulate a management agreement allowing the top seven RJR executives to own as much as 18.5% of the company for a mere $20 million. This was simply ridiculous because in bidding terms the value of that 'cheap stock' was nearly $4 billion. And it was over $500 million in market terms – making way for a mountain of personal profits. While Johnson's management agreement was self-destructive, Kravis and Roberts showed sure footing as the RJR auction proceeded, possessing the two crucial things needed to win:

- Money, and
- A post-LBO management plan.

To make matters worse for the Johnson party, contrary to KKR's finances, the Shearson–Johnson team seemed to be short of funding. Its bank syndicate was not as developed as KKR's – while its buyout was too small, and the steering team was not at ease in manoeuvrings in the junk bonds market. Moreover, KKR had a sure footing in running the competition against the management LBO:

- Its executives knew that every bidding contest is full of unexpected consequences, and
- These exist in deal-breakers and crises that have to be overcome in a resolute way if one wants to win.

The auctioneering of RJR finally came to a close only after the fifth round of bidding on 30 November 1988. For more than a week, night and day, KKR and the Shearson–Johnson team had been nudged to boost their bids so as to meet an elusive final deadline that soon gave way to yet another deadline as no party was willing to give in.

KKR carried off the prize, to the tune of over $25 billion – the largest takeover ever. Though this pales when compared to the Vodafone/Mannesmann transaction, which alone amounted to 204.8 billion euro ($245 billion), representing approximately 25% of the total M&A activity in 2000 in Euroland, it was still the first of that size. On Wall Street, analysts said KKR's victory over Shearson–Johnson reflected three time-honoured strengths of the buyout business firm – which the outside world took some time to recognize:

- Financial wizardry in developing a war chest
- Courting of outside directors, and
- At least theoretically, fighting for the interests of RJR's shareholders.

In terms of financial wizardry, while Shearson's final bid of $112 a share was nominally higher than KKR's offer of $109 a share, the crucial question in assessing both bids was how to value the $6 billion or so of low-grade securities that would be pushed into the hands of RJR shareholders. For many investors it boiled down to this: KKR's junk bonds were better than Shearson's junk bonds.

Post-mortem, however, it was said that as takeover battles progressed, mainstream investors benefited less and less. When it appeared time and again that bidders might drop out, ordinary shareholders rushed to sell equity and take profits, while arbitrageurs stepped in to make a fortune. They took their chances by:

- Buying the RJR shares, and
- Switching in and out of the takeover stock, typically owning it for six weeks or less.

At the end of the day, investors who bought into the 1987 buyout of RJR Nabisco found that KKR did not make any profits on the stock itself. Even the $126 million KKR partners themselves invested in RJR did not appreciate in value. Only *if* the nearly $500 million in transaction, advisory, and other fees KKR charged are accounted for, *then* its return on the RJR Nabisco takeover has been significant.

The takeover firm reaped a $75 million transaction fee from RJR Nabisco on the original deal, and an additional $60 million over the years for advising the company. Then there were the $2.3 million in directors' fees received by the KKR partners, who served on the RJR Nabisco board from 1989 to 1994. RJR needed management skill, and it had to buy it.

According to some opinions on Wall Street, the biggest chunk of the money stemmed from a 1.5% annual management fee assessed on the 1987 LBO fund until 1992, when the last of the fund's money was invested. Associated with the RJR Nabisco deal the portion of this fee alone added a further $279 million to KKR's coffers. All fees counted, KKR had a sweet deal, while investors (in its buyout fund) got the short straw.

6. A critical view of M&As and of some ironies behind them

A detailed analysis focusing on the wisdom of a merger, acquisition or takeover should consider not only the advantages that may come about but also the cost and, as the case study in section 4 has shown, the aftermath of the law of unexpected consequences. People and companies who remember only their successes and not their failures, don't have a bright future. Among the failures are disadvantages that have been, or may be, present. For instance:

- A clash of cultures, making difficult integration
- Incompatibilities resulting from the merger, including difficulties in combining technologies
- Duplication of different services, obliging considerable downsizing of parts of the combined business, and
- Cost of leverage associated to the M&A, which may go on for years and even make the resulting company a takeover target.

While cultural differences may be the subject that most frequently gets overlooked in a merger, the clash of egos at the level of senior management can have more devastating effects. The reader should be warned that, usually, too much emphasis is put on advantages that may result from a merger, acquisition or takeover – and too little on the negatives, which may include a whole range of issues ranging:

- From bureaucratic costs of transborder mergers
- To difficult-to-reconcile incompatibilities in information technology.

There is plenty of evidence to back up this second bullet, because very few people and companies pay due attention to the clash of technologies. Will the merged entity adopt one of the systems currently being used by either company? Will it lean towards selecting a new system? Or will both combined entities continue using their respective incompatible IT systems, as is so often the case?

Incompatibilities in IT solutions are highly counterproductive to one of the most frequently stated reasons for mergers: The notion that the resulting entity will be greater than the sum of its parts. Capitalizing on projected synergies and the hope the resulting entity will run like clockwork in spite of administrative scrutiny and bureaucratic costs, are pipe dreams as long as the infrastructure remains divided – and therefore inefficient.

Regarding bureaucratic costs, a 2005 study that focused on mergers in Euroland provided some interesting insights. Companies involved in large cross-border

M&As had to pay up to 10 million euro to have their deals scrutinized by a myriad of antitrust regulators, with the United States being home to the most expensive watchdogs. A fairly significant part of this cost came from the fact that even in the EU competition authorities failed to harmonize national rules and regulations. Wide differences in competition regimes give rise to:

- Unforeseen but significant costs, and
- Delays in the multi-jurisdictional merger process.

These have been the conclusions of a survey by PricewaterhouseCoopers, based on 51 companies that had been through 500 merger reviews in more than 50 countries. As is to be expected, legal fees accounted for more than 60% of the aforementioned cost, with the rest made up of regulatory charges and fees for other advisers.[8]

While in terms of absolute size this cost of 10 million euro per M&A is small relative to the overall magnitude of a cross-border bid, an average of 3.8 billion euro in the cases covered by the PwC survey, it is a burden that companies don't necessarily account for but cannot escape. Additionally, while the United States is an expensive regulator, the EU's initial merger probes are more expensive because the Brussels authorities want more information from the companies.

On the one hand, the European Union authorities say they want to promote cross-border mergers leading to true European companies. But on the other, they fail to provide the preconditions. Bureaucratic costs, unexpected consequences, system incompatibilities, and other imponderables aside, any party planning a business merger, acquisition or takeover needs to know the likelihood of seeing it through, and the cost this entails.

Other vital information concerns the company to be acquired. What is it doing well? What are the areas in which it performs best? Will these areas be promoted by the merger? Why? Strengths are always specific and always unique. Persons, companies, and nations survive on the basis of their strengths. Under 'expected advantages', management usually wants to know the answers to such questions as:

- Will the merger, or acquisition, result in operating or staffing economies? In tax optimization?
- Will it contribute to a more efficient system of sales and distributions? In improving the product range?
- Does it promote the company's goals by diversifying the markets, or the customers within markets?

- Can it give the company new management blood, which will enable it to build on to what it already has?
- Will the merger or acquisition give additional financial strength and earning power? Why? Where exactly?

Answers to these queries are never provided by the bureaucracy, but they could be revealed from reliable financial reporting documents – *if*, and only if, the terms and method of presentation are standard. This is why the adoption as of January 2005 of International Financial Reporting Standards (IFRS)[9] by all EU countries, instead of their practical accounting rules, has been a major step towards European integration.

This is written in the full understanding that the responses given to questions posed in the preceding paragraphs have to be factual and documented. A careful analysis must pay attention to the weaknesses characterizing both the acquirer and the entity to be acquired. One neither pays, nor should get paid, for weaknesses. Therefore, the exploratory study should always consider the negatives of a projected merger, acquisition, or takeover.

The reaction to M&As by companies targeted by an acquisition varies for many reasons, one of them being whether the merger is made on friendly terms, or is hostile. To counter unfriendly bids, the board of the company in danger of being absorbed may adopt *poison-pill* measures, such as taking on an inordinate amount of debt, designed to prevent the hostile takeover. Or, it may try to find a knight to come to its rescue.

Quite often, boards and CEOs have a habit of downplaying the risk of overleveraging to avoid a takeover. For example, in the case of Eastern Airlines, a formerly prosperous but now defunct US carrier, the board's action came at a time when Eastern's unions had been urging workers to buy more stock in an attempt to:

- Gain control of the company, and
- Oust the firm's incumbent management.

At the time, an Eastern spokesman strongly denied that the adoption of the poison-pill measures were intended in any way to frustrate plans by the company's unions, adding that any impact on the unions was 'coincidental'. This, however, proved to be a bad coincidence for everybody concerned – shareholders, managers, and unionized personnel alike.

To fence off a hostile merger, companies frequently use investment banking firms to recommend anti-takeover measures. At the beginning this was a fairly popular measure, but it has proved to be an expensive practice – not so much because of the fees of the investment bankers, but because of the aftermath of the strategy of gearing which has been widely employed.

Among other pitfalls in M&As is that the party or parties looking for an acquisition tend to overestimate its strengths. In the mid-1980s executives of Chrysler and Applied-Signal considered a $40 billion hostile takeover of General Motors, as Lee Iacocca, then Chrysler's chairman, has it in his book.[10] But Iacocca adds that he eventually concluded it 'might be easier to buy Greece.'

The Chrysler/Allied-Signal takeover discussions came while GM was reeling from a loss of market share and the turmoil surrounding H. Ross Perot's ousting from the board. As Iacocca relates the story, the idea of a bid for General Motors was raised by Victor Potamkin, who owns GM dealerships as well as Chrysler and Dodge franchises. Iacocca seems to have first dismissed the idea, but saw a potential in it after Edward L. Hennessy, Jr, then Allied-Signal's chairman, suggested that:

- They try to acquire GM jointly, and
- Afterwards split it into two, each taking the products lines closed to his firm's main business.

Iacocca says in his book that he was sceptical. After all, at the time GM's annual sales topped $100 billion, while Chrysler's were $25 billion and Allied-Signal's $11 billion. But Hennessy started running figures saying that he could take over all the party-supply divisions, and GMAC the finance company. (Incidentally, that might have been a good solution both for Delphi and for GMAC.)

The first irony of this whole deal, and in other oversized M&A targets, has been that had the GM takeover materialized, Chrysler/Allied-Signal would have needed 'only' $40 billion – just over one and a half times what KKR paid for the RJR Nabisco leveraged buyout, a much smaller company (see section 4). The second irony is that Chrysler itself could not survive after Lee Iacocca left and was swallowed up by Daimler. The third irony concerns the fate of GM, still to be decided at the time of writing, as 2005 comes to an end.

7. Buyouts, leveraged loans, and commissions

Besides payments in equity, leveraged loans and junk bonds have traditionally been the main forms of finance for leveraged buy-outs. In continental Europe, between 1998 and 2000 the combination of the projected introduction of the euro, which was thought of as enhancing the process of consolidation, and the boom in the stock markets, contributed to the boost in M&A activity. In turn, this led to a strong demand for funding, affecting both:

- The growth of bank loans, and
- The rush to the market for debt securities.

Non-cash payments, which are mostly exchanges of shares, were high in 1999–2001, but have fallen to around 10% in the first few months of 2003. In Euroland, this has contributed to the very low levels of equity issuance in 2002 and 2003, while adding its weight to the ongoing need to finance substantial cash payments for M&As. This trend is clearly shown in Figure 17.3.

In the United States, too, as the 2000/2001 financial crisis deepened cash became king while leveraged loans were both more expensive and taking longer to arrange. Sponsors of mergers and acquisitions activities have therefore been looking elsewhere for debt funding; for instance, to formerly niche products like:

- Mezzanine debt, and
- New market instruments, such as asset-backed securities.

Yet, in spite of the efforts to establish novel sources of funding, the leveraged loans market has been key to providing money for takeovers, as venture capitalists continued to rely on it both for financial immediate acquisition and for longer-term

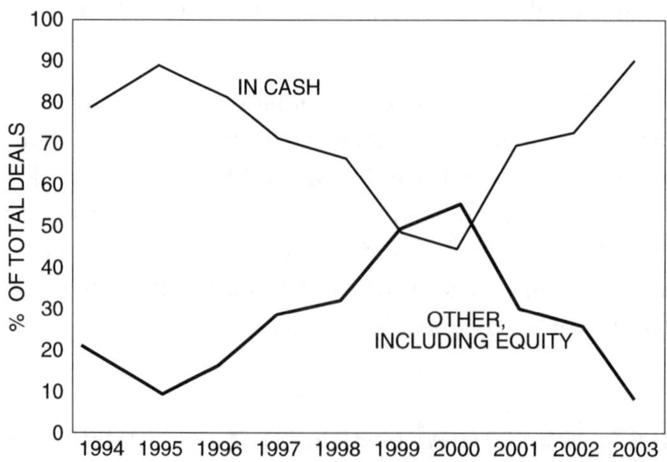

Figure 17.3 Types of payment of domestic M&A in Euroland over ten years. (Statistics from the European Central Bank, Monthly Bulletin, December 2003)

bank debt. For their part, banks have been re-examining their leveraged lending in response to:

- Fears of an impending recession, and
- Predictions of higher default rates.

Besides the reasons given in the preceding paragraph, the September 11, 2001 terrorist attacks on the World Trade Center and the Pentagon amplified the cautious mood that was setting in in lending. As a result, the syndicated loan market became tight, with the leveraged loans market increasingly driven by non-bank institutional investors.

The pros said that the leveraged finance market will always find ingenious ways to promote debt, but companies characterized by cautious management keep a close eye on liabilities in their balance sheet. Still, following the 1997 meltdown in East Asia, in 1998 Ford attempted to acquire bankrupt Kia Motors of South Korea, but was outbid by Hyundai Motor. A year later, Hyundai, which piled Kia's $8 billion in debt on top of its own imposing $6.6 billion, was looking for help to clean up its balance sheet.

In research I was doing in London at that time, financial analysts asked why American auto makers were eager to buy up Korea's bankrupt motor vehicle companies. As our meeting went on, they answered their own question with the statement that the reasons were: market share, prospects of recovery, and hope of capitalizing on economies of scale.

The Hyundai takeover of Kia was justified as having been made for reasons of economies of scale. Other leveraged deals are done because of economies of vertical integration, the expectation that financial results will improve by combining resources, as well as exploitation of tax shields. The latter range:

- From massaging transfer pricing
- To recovery of taxes paid by one of the merged entities, which allows it to pay off some of the acquisition's debt.

Sometimes, the prospects of recovery are a dream. After being taken over by Hyundai, when it collapsed, Kia's exports leapt more than 60% in 1999, allowing it to report its first profit in five years: $168 million on $7.7 billion in revenues. To turn Kia around, Hyundai boosted the acquired firm's productivity and saved $360 million on materials by purchasing them in bulk for itself and its new subsidiary. But:

- The aforementioned $14.6 billion in debt had to be serviced, and
- The company's severe financial problems persisted.

An unstated reason of some takeovers is that they provide a way to eliminate inefficient management. Another unstated reason is that they take place for monopolistic purposes. More rare is the case of an M&A done to lower debt cost, by renegotiating the combined company's loans with institutions characterized by a higher credit risk appetite.

Moreover, the socialization of debt sees to it that all sorts of investors, including institutional investors, are ready to buy collateralized debt obligations (CDOs). Not everybody has a sharp pencil when accounting for risks associated to derivative debt instruments and to equity derivatives.

Neither do acquiring companies always pay due attention to the weight of commitments the acquired firm's management has made to itself and to third parties. For instance, golden parachutes: high compensation to senior managers in case of takeover minus health care contracts, and so on. Still other risks come from the policy often followed after an LBO of selling off the crown jewels; and its inverse, the poison pill, making the stock unattractive to a raider.

Still other risks associated to mergers, acquisitions, and takeovers are the results of antitrust litigation, as well as very large compensation to be paid for environmental and other damages. Neither should M&A fees be left out of the profit and loss equation. For big ticket deals, fees are quite substantial, up to $100 million or more, depending on:

- Complexity, and
- Time taken to see the deal through.

Big advisory firms, the so-called *bulge bracket*, are typically international investment banks with extensive financial resources. Big banks, however, tend to leave marginal mergers and acquisitions activity to smaller institutions. Table 17.2 shows nine deals in the 1997 to 2001 timeframe where fees exceeded $100 million.

8. Deferred tax liabilities: case study with Gillette

One of the most interesting issues associated to mergers and acquisitions is *deferred tax liabilities* (DTLs), which should not be confused with deferred tax assets (DTAs).[11] For any practical purpose, DTAs are largely smoke and mirrors – a creative accounting gimmick.[12] DTLs practically mean that legal ways are being found to delay or downsize taxes because of capital gains or other reasons.

Table 17.2 Fees for M&A activity in the United States

Acquirer	Acquirer adviser(s)	Target	Target adviser(s)	Year of announcement	Value of merger ($ billion)	Disclosed fees ($ million)
America Online	Salomon Smith Barney	Time Warner	Morgan Stanley	2000	112	135
EchoStar Communications	UBS Warburg, Deutsche Bank, Alex. Brown	Hughes Electronics	Goldman Sachs, CSFB, Merrill Lynch, Bear Stearns	2001	29	123
Daimler–Benz	Goldman Sachs, Deutsche Bank	Chrysler	CSFB	1998	39	115
Comcast	JP Morgan, Morgan Stanley, Merrill Lynch	AT&T Broadband	Goldman Sachs, CSFB, Deutsche Bank	2001	72	110
Raytheon	Bear Stearns, CSFB	Hughes Electronics	Merrill Lynch, Salomon Brothers, Goldman Sachs	1997	10	109
AT&T	Goldman Sachs, CSFB	Tele-communications	Donaldson, Lufkin & Jenrette, Merrill Lynch	1998	52	105
Vodafone	Goldman Sachs	AirTouch Communications	Morgan Stanley	1999	5	102

* As the careful reader will observe, most fees are not proportional to the value of the merger.

On 28 January 2005 a novel two-step, tax-free deal for the acquisition of Gillette was revealed by Procter & Gamble. This M&A concerned Berkshire's Gillette share bought by P&G to the tune of $4.3 billion. The deal was done without triggering a giant tax bill of $1.5 billion – corresponding to the $4.3 billion of Berkshire's gain on the 96 million Gillette shares it has held since 1989.

By ploughing all of that gain into shares of the new company, P&G ensured the US taxman would have to wait for his piece of the profits. This case is a good example of the fact that tax authorities and supervisors are way behind the curve of risk and return with new financial instruments – because the smart people, the ones with lots of imagination, work for investment banks, not for the government.

It is not exactly known who suggested this DTL deal structure in the first place, but on Wall Street experts suggested it was indeed ingenious and it could become a model for future mergers and acquisition. What is known from the mechanism of the P&G/Gillette merger is that it has been worked out in two-steps:

- P&G paid for Gillette with nothing but stock, issuing 0.975 share of its common stock for each Gillette share.
- In the aftermath of this equity swap, Gillette investors will owe no tax since they are exchanging one stock for another.

If, instead, P&G had paid for Gillette with cash, Berkshire alone would have faced a whopping $1.5 billion tax bill because of the 35% corporate rate. The downside of a pure stock deal, however, is that it would have diluted the value of shares P&G's current investors hold and also slashed its earnings per share.

This has been corrected through the ingenious second step. P&G project to spend $18–22 billion over the next 12–18 months, buying back some of the stock it has issued for Gillette. After this second step has been completed, the result would be the same *as if* Procter & Gamble had paid for Gillette with a package of:

- 60% stock, and
- 40% cash.

The careful reader would compare the strategy followed with this DTL to that of using derivatives in financial planning (see Chapter 9, section 3). Both have been engineered by smart people working for investment banks, and both teach a lesson on what derivatives can do that classical financial instruments cannot.

If a 60–40 deal had been structured in the first place, this could have left many Gillette shareholders with an unwanted tax bill. Something like that happened to Berkshire in 1996, when Capital Cities/ABC, in which Warren Buffett held a

$2.2 billion unrealized profit, sold out to Walt Disney who agreed to pay partially in stock. But:

- When the Disney shares were divided among all Cap Cities shareholders who wanted them
- Berkshire ended up with half its money in cash and a tax bill of some $400 million, an experience Warren Buffet was probably not willing to repeat.

The great novelty of the DTL two-step deal has been that Gillette shareholders can keep as much stock as they want to be controlling, when their taxes come due. For instance, tax-exempt pension funds who want to cash out can sell the asset in the open market whenever they choose. And given that P&G will be spending millions on the buyback, there is less risk that a wave of investors selling out will weigh heavily on share prices.

Notes

1 Big Questions for Big Oil. 7 November 2005; http://money.cnn.com/2005/11/07/news/economy/oil-questions/index.htm.
2 *Business Week*, 26 July 1993.
3 *The Economist*, 26 November 2005.
4 D.N. Chorafas, *IFRS, Fair Value and Corporate Governance: The Impact on Budgets, Balance Sheets and Management Accounts.* Elsevier, London, 2005.
5 Deutsche Bundesbank, *Financial Stability Review*, November 2005; and Dr M. Koetter, *Evaluating the German Bank Merger Wave*, Deutsche Bundesbank Discussion Paper, Series 2, *Banking and Financial Studies*, 12/2005.
6 D.N. Chorafas, *Integrating ERP, CRM, Supply Chain Management and Smart Materials.* Auerbach, New York, 2001.
7 *BusinessWeek*, 21 February 2005.
8 *Financial Times*, 23 June 2003.
9 As per Note 4.
10 Lee Iacocca, *Talking Straight.* Bantam Books, New York.
11 D.N. Chorafas, *After Basel II: Assuring Compliance and Smoothing the Rough Edges.* Lafferty/VRL Publishing, London, 2005.
12 As per Note 4.

Case Studies on Mergers in Telecommunications, Computers, Oil and Air Transport

1. Introduction

Next to technology, the Internet, and the equity market boom, the biggest factor that characterized the late 1990s was the consolidation of a swarm of companies through mergers. Optimists say that this has created a seamless, borderless environment shifting attention away from policies traditionally followed in trading activities, which looked for diversification in risks being assumed.

Contrarians, however, have a different viewpoint. They say that because of mergers assumed risk is on the increase, as M&As lead into greater leveraging (see Chapter 17). They also add that there are seeds of instability in dealing with a handful of big entities, whose governance is not always Tier-1.[1] The argument is that bigger size requires much better management, and with anything short of it there is credit risk.

A core issue with concentration of credit risk because of a wave of M&As lies in the fact that crises can erupt at any time and take banks as well as industrial corporations down with them. This becomes even more likely as their counterparties go up in smoke. Risks are further amplified through market shifts in a globalized economy whose rules and regulations are still parochial:

- Too largely conditioned by the old national and diverse legal systems, and
- Too subject to nationalistic protectionism, in spite of paying lip service to the benefits of the global market.

Indeed, industrial nationalism is very much alive. In August 2005, news that Danone, a major French food company, might be taken over by America's PepsiCola led to French government assurances that the country's 'strategic' industries would be protected from foreign takeover. But at the same time, French businessmen have been snapping up companies elsewhere in Europe. In the first seven month of 2005,

- Pernod Ricard, a French spirits firm, bought its British rival, Allied Domecq
- Suez, a French utilities company, bought Electrabel of Belgium
- France Telecom took over Spain's Amena, a mobile-phone operator, and so on.

These were big to medium-size mergers that went through because the British, Belgian, and Spanish governments did not play the nationalistic card. The proponents of M&As point to the fact that takeovers prune the economic system. As an example one could mention the fate of startups from Internet firms to aviation and other industry sectors. After the airline industry's 1978 deregulation, the first startup airlines such as People Express and Air Florida emerged to take on the giants:

- At first they flourished quickly
- But then they succumbed to overexpansion and brutal competition.

Of 34 carriers that began scheduled jet service between 1978 and 1992, only two are still around. The others were either taken over or went bust. Characterized by low costs, low fares, high productivity, and, in many cases, non-union employees, the post-deregulation airlines were first seen as a nuisance by legacy airlines. However, after several years of rapid growth and sizeable gains in market share, carriers like America West and Southwest Airlines were beginning to seriously threaten the majors.

Once the dust had settled, most new entrants – Air Florida, Air One, Northeastern being examples – filed for bankruptcy or shut down. This story repeated itself in the 1990s with Value Jet, Western Pacific, and Kiwi International. In the 1990s analysts said that after dumping unprofitable routes and slashing costs in the early 1990s, the big carriers have been able to defend their turf by better and stronger operators:

- Creating lower-cost, low-fare routes, to directly challenge the startups, and
- Using sophisticated yield-management systems that allowed them to match low-cost carriers' fares selectively.

But were these traditional carriers better and stronger? Judging from the bankruptcy of the formerly prestigious United Airlines, two successive bankruptcies of US Air, the most recent bankruptcy of Delta (see section 9), and other events, this does not seem to be the case.

Similar issues can be raised with computer companies – for instance, the merger of Univac and Burroughs into Unisys (see section 5), and events taking place in other industry sectors, some of which have been the subject of case studies included in this chapter. A good example, on M&As that hurt the acquiring company, which is the focus of section 2, is telecommunications.

2. Strategy and aftermath of M&As in telecommunications

Chapter 17 brought to the reader's attention the Verizon takeover of MCI and the absorption of AT&T by SBC. (Both approved by the Federal Communications Commission.) What has not been said in this connection, is that neither of these two mergers gets close to challenging Japan's NTT for the No. 1 spot in the global economy's telecom industry, though both Verizon and SBC will make some progress up the rankings.

Moving up the scale of relative positioning in one's industry has been a frequent reason for M&As. But as Table 18.1 shows, with very few exceptions none of the most important mergers among telecoms of 2004/2005 has significantly changed the rankings in the telecommunications industry.

Positioning may also produce some unpleasant surprises. In November 2002, Comcast, the US cable operator, acquired AT&T's cable system for $58.7 billion; the deal led to a Comcast customer base of 22 million customers in 41 states.

Table 18.1 Most Important 2004 and 2005 telecoms mergers and acquisitions

Acquirer	Target
2004	
BT	Infonet
Cable & Wireless	Monaco Telecom, Bulldog Communications
Cingular Wireless	AT&T Wireless
KPN	Telfort
Level3	360networks, Sprint wholesale
Softbank	Japan Telecom
Sprint	Nextel
TDC	Song Networks
Tele2	Votec Mobil, UTA
TeliaSonera	Chess/Sense
2005	
Alltel	Western Wireless
Cable & Wireless	Energis
Cegetel	Neuf
France Telecom	Equant, Amena
Interoute	Via.networks
Mobilcom Austria	Mobitel
SBC	AT&T
Tele2	Versatel, Tiscali Denmark, Comunitel Spain
Telecom Italia	Telecom Italia Mobile
Telefonica	Ceskey Telekom, Moviles de Chile, Tele Centro Oeste, O_2
Telenor	Bredbandsbolaget

This was the biggest US media merger since the AOL Time Warner combination in 2001, transforming Comcast into the world's largest cable operator.

But the takeover of AT&T's cable system also brought problems. A big one was the huge difference in the acquired facilities' operating margin, which was 25% at AT&T compared with 42% at Comcast. Another challenge facing the acquirer was the need for big investment to upgrade AT&T cable.

- Bringing acquisitions up to standard to improve market share has many challenges attached to the task.
- The money paid for an acquisition may be nothing more than an entry price; M&As spring plenty of surprises.

The response can be made that at least some of these M&As are defensive, as telecoms are watching each other for fear of coming off worst in a wave of consolidation. Analysts, for instance, suggest that Telefonica's bid for O_2 is partly a reaction to the fact that its own home turf was invaded by France Telecom in July 2005, when it bought an 80% stake in Amena, Spain's second-largest mobile company. (More on this in section 3.)

Defensive strategies aside, many of the mergers, acquisitions, and takeovers by telecoms have a degree of irony in them. That SBC could buy AT&T, which gave it birth, turns regulation on its head. The seven Baby-Bells were spun off AT&T because Judge Green wanted to end the telephone monopoly.

Moreover, SBC stated it would use the AT&T brand, because it is better known. This is a reasonable move, which, however, makes fun of the 1980s court decision.

There are no rules in deciding which logo is best: that of the acquirer or of the acquired. France Telecom has done something similar to SBC's decision when it chose to capitalize on the international brand, Orange, of its acquired subsidiary – using it for all of its foreign operations. Notice that fixed-to-mobile convergence can be often found at the heart of a chosen branding strategy.

Wireless companies, too, consolidate. Mid-February 2004, Cingular Wireless agreed to pay nearly $41 billion in cash to buy AT&T Wireless. This was an acquisition that created America's largest mobile phone company, but it also raised concerns among consumer advocates that it might hurt competition and impede lower prices.

The Federal Communications Commission did not see it that way. The consolidated Cingular/AT&T Wireless controls about 30% of the US mobile market. Its nearest competitor is Verizon Wireless with 24.5%; followed by Sprint/Nextel nearly 20%; T-mobile (a subsidiary of Deutsche Telekom), 8.5%. The balance is controlled by different smaller operators.

Among major mobile operators with global presence, only Vodafone remains true to a pure wireless strategy worldwide. Most of the competitors in wireless business are old telecoms incumbents, attempting to sustain future profits through diversification. Vodafone is the:

- Is the number five telecoms operator world-wide
- But it is the top mobile operator globally.

A monolinear strategy, however, is not without problems. Back in 2002, slowing subscriber growth in Vodafone's key markets combined with little evidence of any upturn in average revenues per user of mobile telephony, damaged the company's equity. On 10 April 2002, with Vodafone stock 70% below its peak, Schroder Salomon Smith Barney:

- Issued a new lower price target on the stock based on an assumed sales growth rate of 4.5% annually, and
- Warned that in a scenario where there was no growth, its share price target range was between 80 and 113 pence.

Heavily weighting on Vodafone's balance sheet was the big money it had paid for several 3G licences. Writing them off would have been devastating. Correctly, then CEO Chris Gent refused to write-down any of the core mobile business or the company's 3G licences, which were on the balance sheet at their £13.1 billion cost.

In the years that immediately followed the equity bubble of the late 1990s, the market was deeply hit by slowing growth among mobile operators and worries that it wouldn't see a recovery in growth very soon. As an example, in April 2002 NTT DoCoMo, Vodafone's rival in Japan, warned that subscriber growth was likely to be 30% lower than expected. A sharp decline in the Japanese market hit Vodafone as the mobile operator derived close to 20% of its revenues from J-Phone, its Japanese subsidiary.

At about the same timeframe, Verizon, Vodafone's US partner, said it was incurring a $2.5 billion charge in relation to overvalued telecoms assets. An analyst at Bear Stearns warned, at that time, that Vodafone *could* report a loss of nearly £18 billion (then $25.2 billion), which would be the biggest in UK corporate history, including over £8 billion of goodwill and impairment charges. These were non-cash charges in the accounts to reflect the falling value of investments and other assets.

Over £2.3 billion of the charges, the analyst said, could relate to Mannesmann, the biggest ever cross-border hostile takeover. When that takeover had taken place, then CEO Chris Gent was praised for his move and he was (controversially) paid a £10 million bonus for pulling off the deal – but accepted half of it after bowing to pressure from the company's shareholders. The good news was that Vodafone avoided the mistakes of rivals such as British Telecom who ran up huge debt:

- It funded the Mannesmann purchase by issuing a massive 28 billion new shares.
- This lot was so huge that many investors have had difficulty digesting the new equity.

By contrast, 2005 was a good year for the telecoms (but not necessarily for Vodafone), which explains the flurry of M&A activity. Reported revenues have been growing at 8% a year, and some analysts projected the total market for network and IT services could continue growing at that pace. Other analysts, however, were of the opinion that intensifying competition puts profit margins in danger over the coming years of this decade. Therefore, operators will need to be careful as:

- They integrate their acquisitions, and
- Establish next-generation investment plans.

Another domain requiring extraordinary attention is service level agreements (SLAs), particularly with regard to the terms within the contract. Tough competition sees to it that it is a buyer's market, with users driving agreements allowing them to review performance quarter on quarter, or every half year. Additionally, big user organizations know how to build terms that drive the risk to the telecoms provider's side.

3. The acquisition of O_2 by Telefonica and credit ratings blues

Telefonica's chairman, Cesar Alierta, justified the projected acquisition of O_2, the former British Telecom subsidiary, as a way of broadening his firm's reach across different markets and technologies.[2] Behind this argument lies the fact that currently the majority of Telefonica's sales come from Spain and Latin America, and they are heavily weighted on the side of traditional fixed-line calls. At the same time, Telefonica has been unsuccessful in gaining a place in mobile technology through its own devices. Its Terra venture was largely a flop.

Standard & Poor's cut Telefonica's credit rating to A−, the lowest ever for the Spanish telecoms incumbent, when it agreed to purchase Britain's O_2 for $31.5 billion. S&P cited the aggressive nature of the purchase, the largest in Europe's phone industry in five years, and said the ranking might be reduced further.

Telefonica is not alone in trying to break out of the confines imposed by the fixed-lines market. Legacy phone companies, the so-called incumbents, are caught in a bind. On one side, they have to continue their huge investments in fixed line networks, and on the other they must buy mobile telephony assets, if they are to maintain their ranking. Experts say that:

- Scale, and integration of fixed and mobile operations is a formula that's hard to beat.
- But such integration is no easy feat, and it is bringing along new requirements that reverse past strategic moves.

In the late 1990s up to 2002, the strategy of incumbent telecom operators was to spin off their wireless and Internet divisions. By 2005 telecoms were putting these assets back together again, often acquiring them at a fraction of their spin-off price, as Telefonica did with Terra. In the United States, Sprint absorbed Sprint PCS, its former mobile subsidiary spun off a few years earlier, prior to merging with Nextel.

The irony of this switch largely lies in the fact that incumbent telecoms first dismantled themselves, then decided that it was better to regroup their spun-off businesses. To critics, this looks like a strategy that is lopsided, to which the proponents say that in the process the spin-offs get a chance to develop strength in their specific domain of mobile Internet access – which is only half true.

Critics add that the so-called incumbents, who are essentially formerly regulated state monopolies, don't have the culture and the people to implement the strategy they are aiming at. Critics also express concern about the fact that, as 2005 came to a close, the bond market has been reeling from declining credit ratings. The bonds of even France Telecom and Deutsche Telekom fell to the brink of junk status.

The way Bloomberg reported it in December 2005, as Telefonica, Vodafone, and Denmark's TDC planned to raise more than $45 billion in 2006, mostly in bonds (the first two to pay for acquisitions), yields of corporates have been rising at the fastest rate since 2000, compared with government debt. According to some estimates, altogether European phone companies need to sell an estimated $60 billion of bonds in 2006, almost double the 2005 total. This spark in borrowing is reminiscent of year 2000 when:

- Average yields on company bonds climbed more then 200 basis points, and
- There was a record number of credit downgrades with more than $27 billion in bond defaults by telephone companies.

Investors demand extra yield to hold Telefonica's 5¹/₈% euro-denominated bonds maturing in February 2013, rather than government debt. With the Spanish telecom company's O_2 deal in the making, by the end of December 2005 the spread jumped 19 basis points to 67 basis points (where it stood in late October 2005). The annual cost of insuring 10 million euro of Telefonica debt through credit default swaps (CDS) reached 54 000 euros, the highest in more than 2¹/₂ years.

'The memory is on investors' minds of what happened in 2000,' said Sajiv Vaid, who helps manage $21 billion of fixed-income assets at Royal London Asset Management, in an interview of 8 December 2005: 'The concern is that you get a frenzy and they go do stupid things.'[3] This is indeed the case with nearly all highly leveraged deals.

Mergers and acquisitions picked up 'more than we were expecting and at a faster pace than we had expected,' said Duncan Warwick-Champion, head of High Grade European Credit Research at UBS AG in London – as quoted in the same *Bloomberg News* release. Mid-November 2005 UBS lowered its recommendation for European phone company bonds to *underweight* after starting the year at *overweight.*

For its part Standard & Poor's let it be known it might lower credit ratings on nine phone companies in Europe, including British Telecom, Cable & Wireless, and Portugal Telecom, almost half the total it follows. A sign of the times is that the number of debt instrument issuers S&P is more inclined to downgrade than keep unchanged is the highest since December 2001.

Neither is Telefonica and the aforementioned other former government-controlled telecom companies alone in the credit risk challenge, which they have been facing. Bonds sold by TDC, Denmark's biggest phone company, lost more than 13% of their value in the 3¹/₂ months before it agreed to be bought by the so-called Nordic Telephone Company (NTC) – a newly formed entity established by hedge funds, directly or indirectly advised or managed by Apax, Blackstone, KKR, Permira, and Providence Equity Partners.

In the aftermath of these manipulations, on 30 November 2005 Moody's Investor's Service stripped TDC of its investment-grade status. That was about the time Copenhagen-based TDC said it would be sold for $12 billion in the largest leveraged buyout since the takeover of RJR Nabisco 16 years ago.

- The spread on TDCs 6.5% bonds due in April 2012 almost tripled in the months leading up to the acquisition, and
- It widened to 315 basis points on 8 December 2005, from 111 in August before talk of the deal began.

The irony is that the hunted TDC was itself a hunter. Prior to its fall to predators, the Danish telecom had been raising $14 billion to finance its proposed purchase of another telecom company. The reason given by Moody's in cutting the rating on TDC's debt was the expectation of a significant leveraging to fund its acquisition by the hedge funds.

All this has been taking place just five years after the great stock market crash of 2000, which resulted in a sea of damaged balance sheets and a long link of sunk firms. Speculators have a short memory, and 2005 has been the busiest year for telecommunications mergers in the 21st century, with 228 deals valued at $140 billion, according to some estimates. Therefore:

- There is no wonder that euro-denominated bonds sold even by investment-grade European phone companies have been underperforming the broader market for debt instruments.
- On the average, the yield gap has widened 10 basis points in 2005 to 62 basis points, while other European corporate bonds were little changed.

Several analysts suggested that in 2006 borrowing costs relative to government debt will rise another 7–8 basis points because of accumulating dark clouds ahead for telecoms. The irony is that telecommunications bonds were considered 'safe'. This was particularly true until the end of the 1990s, because the classical telephone companies were state-owned monopolies with steady cash flows. But:

- As governments sold their stakes, telephone industry executives began to concentrate on profit growth instead of steady returns, and
- The privatized telecom companies spent about $100 billion in 2000 and 2001 buying licences to provide 3G wireless services, borrowing to pay for most of these purchases.

Still another irony is that after the 2000/2001 disaster, where all hell broke loose even among the biggest and best-known telecom companies, and some like Dutch KPN and Finnish Sonera had to be saved with taxpayer money, phone companies spent three years or so reducing their debt. FranceTelecom and

Deutsche Telekom cut borrowings by a combined 33 billion euro in an effort to win A-ratings. In November 2001, British Telecom sold O_2 to decrease its debt.

By 2005, however, there has been a shift from a focus for debt reduction to exactly the opposite – a wave of M&As, many *without* specific purpose. Balance sheets were repaired, but right after this management posed itself the wrong question: 'What companies do with the cash' – without remembering the lessons taught by the very bitter experience of year 2000.

Only in Switzerland did the government, which still owns a majority stake in Swisscom, put a veto on its planned (silly) purchase of Ireland's telephone company. This would have been another deal whose only wisdom derived from the philosophy of the cancer cell – growth for growth's sake. Swisscom management had learned nothing from its unfortunate and costly foray in Thailand. Like other telecoms it had become a prisoner of an inappropriate growth mentality.

As a feature article in *Total Telecom* magazine aptly stated: 'There's simply nothing in the private equity sector's moves so far to suggest that telecoms company board directors have anything to fear – or their long-suffering shareholders anything to cheer. More likely, the private equity sortie into major telecoms management will degenerate into farce, leaving the "new masters" looking for all the world like circus clowns.'[4]

4. An M&A that turned on its head: Pirelli's acquisition of Telecom Italia

Many mergers and acquisitions in the telecommunications industry disappoint. Take as an example Olivetti's acquisition of Telecom Italia. In August 2001 disgruntled investors and bankers who in 1999 had financed the $45 billion hostile takeover of Telecom Italia by Olivetti's Roberto Colaninno were threatening mutiny. It did not take long for Milan's financial circles to leak news of chief executive Colaninno's frantic efforts to find fresh capital.

The moment had arrived for Marco Tronchetti Provera, the CEO of Pirelli, or at least it seemed so. The Pirelli CEO had been searching the global market for the right deal. Having grossed $5.6 billion in cash from the sale of two technology units, Tronchetti Provera considered nabbing part of Lucent Technologies fiber-optic business, but passed it over as too pricey. Then, the tantalizing opportunity of Olivetti Telecom Italia came along.

Tronchetti Provera had made a failed pitch for taking the Italian state-owned company private in 1994, and missed the boat when a takeover battle for the telecom company erupted in 1999 with Colaninno's Olivetti as the winner. But in 2004, together with ally Benetton and two banks, Pirelli took over Telecom Italia, whose market value (at the time) was $99 billion. To gain control, the partners put on the table only $6.4 billion, thanks to the complex chain of holding companies which were created by Colaninno.

- A good-size premium went to the handful of investors who owned 23% of Olivetti.
- By contrast, Telecom Italia's shareholders who found themselves outside that deal, got practically nothing.

At the time, experts said that Pirelli and its associates in the Telecom Italia takeover would find their nemesis in managing a telecommunications operator that was lagging in new technologies, was known to be customer-unfriendly, and had been chronically overstaffed. Additionally, Telecom Italia and Olivetti had $34 billion of debt, and Pirelli was taking on $2.7 billion of its own to finance the takeover. At the same time, analysts forecast that net profit at Telecom Italia was projected to decline as:

- Competition heated up, and
- The carrier had to do major investments to upgrade its network infrastructure.

For his part, Colaninno delayed going ahead with the deal, demanding a more lucrative handshake for a swift exit. People close to the transaction suggested that his former allies – essentially Brescia investors, Banca Antonveneta, and Chase Manhattan – agreed to pay him an extra $100 million dividend, plus $30 million in bonus payments. Then, with the golden parachute spread wide, on 30 July 2001, Colaninno resigned.

But his departure was only part of the problem. New boss Pirelli's Tronchetti faced analysts and the press as the chairman-in-waiting with his plans on Telecom Italia, pending a 30-day antitrust review by European Union officials. Those close to Tronchetti said he was anxious to work swiftly to:

- Address the company's huge debt
- Bolster investments in technology
- Promote innovation, and
- Transform the sleepy culture of Telecom Italia.

By contrast, financial analysts and the Milan market did not quite share that opinion, and what came next proved this pessimism to be right. Ironically, at the end of the day, even if he was pushed out of Olivetti/Telecom Italia, Roberto Colaninno seems to have been the winner of the M&A game. The deal did not go so well for the new raiders of the Italian telecommunications firm.

In 2001, when the Benettons joined forces with Marco Tronchetti Provera to take over the company through Olimpia, their acquisition vehicle, Telecom Italia had a rosy forecast for next year's profits, but this prognostication did not materialize. Rather, the result was red ink, and this struck a hammer blow because Olimpia itself was a highly leveraged company in dire need of cash.

The financial commitment the Benettons made was their 16.8% stake in Olimpia. By late 2004, that stake was worth only half its cost of 1.16 billion euro. 'It is an investment that gives less satisfaction,' Luciano Benetton remarked in an interview. At least the success of other investments saw to it that he could afford the loss.

The takeover of Olivetti/Telecom Italia by Pirelli, Benetton, and associates was a venture capital deal that turned on its head, as many of them do. Most investors and people who are managing investment funds are looking at whether to buy stocks or bonds and when to sell them. They look at a company from the *outside*. But venture capitalists are primarily hungry for *inside* news – precisely, how:

- A company runs
- Solves the problems of growth
- Faces the challenges of competition, and
- Attacks head-on the issues of technological change.

It is only natural that a venture capitalist should look at a business from the *inside*, because he does not have the leisure of an investor to examine a company's 5-year or 10-year track record and what the ratios are. When one is looking from the inside, one has to ask tough questions about market demand, cost factors, volume relationships, competitive positioning, and what financial resources are needed to assure staying in power. Tronchetti, Benetton, and their friends don't seem to have asked, let alone answered these questions.

Additionally, the inside look needs enough technical understanding of the targeted company's business to be able to translate concepts into relatively simple terms. Part of the process is talking with customers, users, and industry specialists to get a broad understanding of the dimensions involved. The next step in that sort of intense analysis is:

- Working with the firm's management to challenge business plan assumptions, and
- Following an evolutionary process, which would allow the opportunity to come up with a game plan on risk and return.

The innovative ways developed during the late 20th century for acquiring equity and know-how – which permit that sort of intensive analysis – can be classified in several directions. Strictly speaking, this is a process of *venture nurturing* involving high-grade managerial assistance from the investing entity as well as cash. The goal is to turn the company around and prepare it for an initial public offer (IPO), which furthermore requires a flourishing equity market.

The alternative is *venture merging*, in a deliberate attempt to piece together a deal with a deep pocket acquirer who really wants to expand and is not so inquisitive about the risks. Ironically, in its heyday, in the late 1990s, Deutsche Telecom was eager to buy Telecom Italia, but by the time Pirelli and associates took over Deutsche Telekom was a financial rag; it was far from having deep pockets.

Neither could Telecom Italia benefit from *internal ventures*, which occur when a corporation sets up an entirely separate greenhouse division within itself, to develop radically new products capitalizing on its leadership in high technology. And to make matters worse, Telecom Italia had no way to improve its profit margins because:

- It could not downsize its personnel, due to restrictive Italian labour laws, and
- It could not increase the price of its services because since the 1960s the Italian landscape was characterized by low cost telephony for households and high cost telephony for enterprises.

This absurd pricing structure had been used by successive Italian governments as a lopsided way for social policy. At the end of the day, the major benefit derived by Telecom Italia came in a curious way. Because of the different takeover troubles, which started in the boom years of the 1990s, it had kept itself out of the mergers and acquisitions stampede which wrecked France Telecom and Deutsche Telekom to the tune of 70 billion euro for each of them. And though Telecom Italia was deeply in debt, it was nowhere near the abyss of the French and German former state monopolies.

5. Strategic switch towards services: IBM's purchase of Monday

At the beginning of the 20th century, the company that later became International Business Machines (IBM) was born as an outfit specializing in scales, time equipment tabulators, and punched card equipment units. The first to go among these products was scales; it was followed, in the early 1960s by the time equipment line, as the company concentrated on data processing equipment, mastering a more than 60% share of the world market for mainframe computers.

As long as IBM's brand of 'big ... irons', as mainframes were called at the time, had universal appeal, the company was attributed almost unlimited staying power in its line of business. Its mainframes prospered largely due to the marketing wizardry of its people – which was most important because:

- IBM products were considerably more expensive than those of the competition.
- The company's renown and dependability meant that it could afford to charge what it liked.

Eventually, however, competitors caught up. Financed by the Japanese government (Project M), and emulating IBM's product line, Hitachi and Fujitsu developed good mainframes at much lower prices. At the same time, Digital Equipment Corp's minis and Vaxes provided customers with better and more cost-effective solutions. By the late 1980s, IBM felt the consequences of its blunders:

- Extremely low market sensitivity, and
- Blind faith that mainframes were everything.

Investment banks downgraded its equity, and whatever mainframes it did sell it sold them at nearly 50% discount. A full-scale computer price war had broken out, taking care of fat profits. At the end of the day, what was a tremendous strength in the 1960s and 1970s became a weakness in the 1980s and a disaster in the 1990s. Customers turned towards minicomputers, personal computers (PCs), local area networks (LANs), and client–server solutions. Critics attributed IBM's downfall to an inbred culture which:

- Accepted no dissent, and
- Based the company's future on layer after layer of bureaucracy.

The personal computers IBM brought out in the early 1980s used Microsoft's DOS. Then it changed the operating system to its own OS/2 proprietary software.

As a result its PCs would not sell. Clients went for what was the open software solution with Microsoft's DOS, then Windows. On the hardware side, the king of the PCs was Compaq, which began as a start-up and swept the market. IBM endeavoured to counter Compaq's low PC prices with a round of reductions, but its prices were still much higher than those of its competitors. In the aftermath of its $500 million fiasco with Westpac's CS90 system, of the late 1980s, IBM found it difficult to sell its new System Application Architecture (SAA), at a time when it was also being forced to slash its mainframe prices. The crisis cost IBM shareholders some $75 billion in equity value.

It is interesting to note as an aftermath, that after more than two decades of frustration, and a torrent of red ink, in mid-2005 IBM sold its PC division to Lenovo. This is a Chinese start-up originally financed by the Chinese Academy of Science to encode the country's script into punched cards. Lenoro branched into PCs, and with acquisition of IBM's PC division it became the No. 3 in global PC sales. By late 2005:

- Dell has 17%
- Hewlett Packard 15.2%, and
- Lenovo 7.4% of the global PC market.

This sale to the Chinese outfit ended IBM's ill-fated foray into PCs (it does retain, however, a 13.4% share in Lenovo). In retrospect, IBM PC business has been a poorly planned and even more badly executed project. It was a 'me too' strategy which joined the other financial hecatomb of System Application Architecture, arrogant warehouse pronouncements, and blind insistence on mainframe supremacy in a black list of management blunders.

Precisely because of these blunders, by the early 1990s, IBM was skidding fast downhill, collapsing under the weight of its own bureaucracy and inability to perceive the shift that had taken place in the market – and to capitalize on it. Neither was mismanagement limited to product planning. At the beginning of 1993, an estimated 26%, or 23 000 of its 90 000 employees in the Europe, Middle East, and Africa (EMEA) area of operations, were riding desks. They were assigned to 'support' as opposed to frontline functions.

To pull the company up by its bootstraps, in the late 1980s top management had split it up into dozens of independent fiefdoms, each with its own infrastructure and bureaucracy. This made matters worse rather than better. According to one estimate, there were 128 people who called themselves 'chief information officer' in this archipelago of multiplying, uncoordinated business units. Lou Gerstner changed all that when in 1993 he became the CEO.

- Gerstner refocused the company on technology services, and
- Decided to keep most of the company together, even if the previous management had decreed that vertical integration was finished in the computer industry.

This was a strategic initiative that proved itself right. Another of Gerstner's strategic hypotheses that turned out to be correct was that over time customers would become less interested in technological characteristics like chip speeds and proprietary operating systems. Instead, they will place much more value on *solutions*, with the computer industry becoming service-led rather than technology-led.

Putting in action a strategy to capitalize on this vision required a third major shift in IBM's history, after the disinvestment of non-data processing product lines and the switch from tabulators and electrical accounting machines (EAM) to computers. Targeting software and services rather than hardware as the income-earners on which the company bet its future also called for cultural change.

Concomitant to this Gerstner decision has been another one, which broke completely with past practices. In the years prior to and immediately following World War II, IBM distinguished itself from its competitors of that time, namely Remington Rand and Power-Samas (later ICT), by in-house-bred developments. Thomas Watson, Sr and Jr stayed away from mergers and acquisitions, but in 1993 this policy was no longer feasible. To survive, IBM had to:

- Buy time, and
- Bet its future on an acquisitions policy focused on consultancy services and software.

No better example can be given on this new strategy than IBM's purchase of Monday, nearly a decade after its acquisitions policy began. In the first days of August 2002, International Business Machines announced that it was buying PricewaterhouseCoopers Consulting, known as 'Monday', for $3.5 billion. The takeover made 'Big Blue' (as IBM is familiarly known) the biggest management consultancy by a margin.

Was this a high price, right price, or low price? To answer this query one has to recall that a couple of years earlier Hewlett–Packard had negotiated with Pricewaterhouse to buy its consultancy arm. At the time, the certified public accountant (CPA) demanded an staggering $18 billion, and the deal fell through.

In the aftermath of the fallen PwC/HP deal, analysts on Wall Street suggested that if PwC was less greedy and asked between $10 billion and $12 billion, HP would have gone along. But the business climate had changed and CPAs had become much more mindful of conflicts of interest, especially after the Arthur Andersen scandal, and the huge bankruptcies of Enron, Global Crossing, WorldCom and other big firms. Certified public accountants came under scrutiny for conflict of interest because of doing consultancy and auditing at the same time with the same clients.

- *If* $10–12 billion was the right price for Monday
- *Then* at $3.5 billion, in a fire sale, PwC's consultancy went for a mere 30% of what it *might* have been worth.

For Big Blue, Monday was a good acquisition. Just prior to it, in 2001, IBM Global Services, which includes consultancy and IT support, accounted for 41% of the company's $85.9 billion revenues. With the PwC advisory skills it added to its inventory, IBM had a chance of doing 50% or more of its annual turnover as a key player in the huge and growing service industry.

6. 'One plus one' can be 'less than two': mergers in the computer industry

Mergers and acquisitions are by no means the only way to become a leader, as IBM itself showed in the late 1950s and early 1960s, when it leapfrogged Remington Rand Univac, came up from under, and conquered about two-thirds of the global market in mainframe data processing. But M&As can be a powerful tool *if* and *when* they are properly used, as section 5 demonstrated.

The No. 1 reason why IBM shareholders should be grateful to Lou Gerstner is that he chose the right merger strategy. He did not acquire Digital Equipment, which had briefly been the No. 2 in the computer industry but by the early 1990s was going down the drain. Gerstner kept away from swallowing DEC, even if its famous Vaxes had ravaged IBM's mainframe installations. And he did not go after Compaq, to boost IBM faltering PC business. The lesson is that:

- In an M&A strategy, the 'don'ts' are as important as the 'do's'.
- Money should never be spent in pursuit of fancy objectives, for headline reasons, or on targets that would lead to a clash of cultures.

This is indeed a golden rule for M&As, which has been totally violated in an incredible number of instances, when big egos blur the logic of decisions. A classic example in the computer industry has been the merger of Univac and Burroughs.

- Unisys, the computer company formed in 1986 from Burroughs and Sperry (the Univac label), has been, on and off, awash with red ink.
- Apart from financial losses, substandard management also succeeded in losing the faith of investors and customers, who would have welcomed an alternative to IBM.

That merger was ill-conceived to start with. Burroughs and Univac had totally different product lines, as well as management cultures. Both their hardware and their software technologies were totally different, and it was clear that – short of abandoning the one or the other – their:

- Further development, and
- Continuing maintenance would have required that they double their costs.

It comes, therefore, as no surprise that the merged company's fortunes waned. While that happened, Unisys' senior management said it did not face an immediate cash crisis, but it aimed to sell off significant portions of the business. The sales finally included the merged company's most profitable operations, leaving Unisys a shadow of its former self.

It is appropriate to notice that Unisys's postmerger difficulties have not been unique. A similar story has repeated itself time and again in other cases: for instance, in the late 1960s when ICT took over English Electric's computer division to form ICL, and in the mid-1970s when Honeywell took over General Electric's computer operations, after GE decided that it had had enough challenging IBM.

Some years down the line, computer historians will probably write that the greatest blunder in computer-to-computer company mergers has been Compaq's series of acquisitions: buying Tandem to strengthen its client–server business, then taking over what was left by Digital Equipment, and finally being itself acquired by Hewlett–Packard – in another silly M&A decision. It is difficult to find so many management errors adding to one-another, in the same firm in one short decade.

True enough, mergers and acquisitions among computer companies never produced the expected miracle solutions. On one hand, since the mid-1980s almost every large computer manufacturer has had its troubles. Industry analysts, however, complain that the top management of companies in trouble:

- Does not assure its responsibilities
- It always blames the business climate, never its own shortcomings.

In all the cases mentioned in the preceding paragraphs the real problem has been bad planning, poor choices, and substandard execution by a highly paid but inefficient management. Precisely for this reason, Unisys is a good case study. The company's problems go back to the day of merger between two of the oldest names in computers.

- Michael Blumenthal, chairman of Burroughs and architect of the deal, hoped to create a 'giant' to challenge IBM.
- The hypothesis was that 'one plus one' would make 'more than two'. Combining Burroughs and Sperry would produce a company with a large customer base and lots of revenues.

Blumenthal, a former Treasury secretary, forecast that seven years down the line, by 1993, Unisys would have $20 billion in revenue. Instead, because of the reasons we already examined, Unisys's revenues have stagnated at about $10 billion, with a tendency to head south. There were two profitable years after the merger, then Unisys lost $639 million in 1989 and about half a billion dollars in 1990.

In less than ten years, Unisys's share of the mainframe computer market fell to 4.7% from a combined 8.2% at the time of the merger. Attempting to retain the loyalty of existing Sperry and Burroughs customers, Unisys continued development of the separate and incompatible computer systems offered by both companies. This was the wrong decision, which:

- Cut it off from hoped-for economies of scale, and
- Added significantly to research and development costs, with no commensurate return.

Critics blamed Blumenthal for failing to come to grips with this problem. But an even-more serious failure was that Unisys cornered itself. Like IBM, it continued betting on mainframes in the shrinking mainframe business of the late 1980s and early 1990s. It also paid lip service to the client–server market which boomed over that period.

When finally Unisys decided to look at its weaknesses rather than blame others, its plan to sort out the Babel of its incompatible products proved too little, too late. Its software strategy road map included a strong emphasis on open systems –

computers built to common industry standards in hardware and software. But like IBM, its underlying idea has been to 'serve open systems' through proprietary software – which is an absurdity.

This was a missed business opportunity because, at the time, the open systems segment of the computer market was growing at about 30% per year, much faster than other parts of the business; and surely faster than mainframes, which was a stagnant market. In its frustration, Unisys wanted to convert itself to a system integrator, but both technologists and financial analysts questioned whether it had the people to do so.

Even if it could have targeted open systems and the integration business Unisys could not do away with the fact that *open systems* computers were commodity products with lower profit margins. To make them profitable, Unisys had to find ways to reduce its manufacturing and distribution costs. Customer companies were also upset that Unisys was attempting to play both sides of the market by supporting both proprietary and standard software – with the result that it could succeed in neither.

7. Giant mergers in the oil industry: but no new departures

One year, 1999, saw two big mergers in the global petroleum industry: Exxon and Mobil, and BP and Amoco, which have created a new class of enterprise in terms of size and scale. Analysts characterized them as *mega-mergers*, and their aftermath contrasts starkly to the smaller integrated petroleum companies, as well as the mid-size ones with relatively broad product and geographic coverage. At play are factors such as:

- Corporate size
- Relationships
- Oil resources
- Political might, and
- Several structural considerations.

These bullets point to significant economic challenges in a number of domains. Such challenges are present not in one but in a number of countries where there are few competitors that can face up to entities resulting from mega-mergers – from owning or accessing reserves, to facing capital and risk requirements that cannot necessarily be met through current financial markets.

Acquisitions of resources in a market more competitive than ever is a fair enough reason for a merger. The December 2005 ConocoPhillips' takeover of Burlington falls in this class. Natural gas:

- Is used to heat a majority of US homes
- Generate about 20% of electricity, and
- Serves as a raw material for everything from plastics to fertilizers.

With all that, natural gas is a particularly hot commodity and its demand has surged as the US economy expanded, while North American production has been rather flat in recent years. This, analysts say, is a key reason why ConocoPhillips is in talks to buy Burlington Resources, a US natural gas producer, for some $30 billion.

On all the evidence, Conoco wants to rebalance its portfolio after taking a $2 billion stake in Russia's Lukoil in 2004. Burlington's assets are in the United States, and most are onshore. Additionally, ConocoPhillips suffers from the same problem dogging the rest of the oil industry.

- Capital expenditure is rising but volumes aren't.
- Therefore, buying reserves is a relatively easy way out.

Contrary to the computer industry, where big company mergers like Honeywell and GE's Computers, Univac and Burroughs (see section 5), and Hewlett–Packard and Compaq led to product line clashes and lots of overlaps and incompatibilities, oil industry mergers benefit from the fact that:

- As a product, oil is unique
- R&D skills are more easily transferable, and
- Mineral resources are not only precious but also dwindling.

Big company size, however, does create management problems – or at least serious management challenges – because mega-mergers lead to a new class of players, raising the bar for world scale and scope. Companies that result from mega-mergers require a view dimension in planning, organizing, staffing, and controlling (see Part 2) as well as a level of management skills able to keep the company as one entity.

Because, as is the case in most industry sectors, the attractiveness of a company depends on its pipeline of products, the results of oil industry mega-mergers have the advantage of broad portfolios. But they do not necessarily have lowest cost structures. Moreover, even if they can sustain substantial levels of investment in a number of growth projects, merged companies put their money where there is higher return on investment:

- In the 21st century this has been exploration rather than refining, and
- The result is that the American and other oil markets face shortages of refined oil products.

Analysts also point out that the existence of very big oil firms makes it more risky for medium-sized oil service companies to continue encroaching on the business of developing and operating wells. The challengers to the majors must run faster than ever before in order to survive, finding niche strategies and unique products that escape the very big firms (see Chapter 14 on product planning, and Chapter 15 on marketing).

Indeed, the emergence of specialist players on specific products or pieces of the oil value chain has been reshaping some markets and their players. The most capable among the independents are pursuing opportunities that were formerly the exclusive domain of major oil companies. They develop new parts of the energy industry value chain, including upstream exploration and deepwater developments, which have the potential of reshaping the oil industry.

Taking this into account it is reasonable to suggest that the rise of king-size oil firms has created difficult-to-beat monopolies. The silver lining is that this has also produced some opportunities for other companies, as the majors adjust their portfolios. Therefore, altogether it can be said that this led to two paths to distinctiveness in the oil industry:

Huge scale and scope, and
Specialization in products and processes.

Trends in capitalization, relative performance, and also in market-to-book values, reflect the degree to which majors and specialists stand. At the same time, however, the majors outdistance the rest of the pack, leaving more ordinary players and other oil industry competitors in search of a survival strategy. The planners should account for the fact that investors look at both:

- Share value attributed to near-term earnings and cash flow.
- Long-term growth prospects to gain perspective on future price-to-earnings ratios.

Big or small, practically all oil companies search for ways to leverage their intangibles – from equity to new marketing and risk management skills – and keep a close watch on other business opportunities. These range from gas exploration to gas and power marketing, which can create a momentum for more mergers and acquisitions.

According to at least some expert opinions, there is a historical precedent that continues to limit vision. For a very long time, the foundation of the oil business was a complex network of relationships among oil exploration and service firms, specialists, government organizations, and government-sponsored oil firms.

Alliances played an important role for companies that pursued the strategy of remaking these old relationships around the industry's competitive edges. But at the same time these alliances, and cosy connections, pulled down the shutters on the exploration of new, alternative sources of energy.

For instance, mergers or no mergers, no oil company distinguished itself in solar energy, or the exploitation of alcohol and common oil as alternative fuels. These have been left to start-ups: alcohol is now increasingly used in Brazil, while French farmers pioneered the use of a fuel for diesel engines containing one part oil from sunflower seeds to two parts diesel fuel.

In a way, this is a repetition of what happened more than a century ago in the transport industry. Rail companies were *not* an outgrowth of investment by the coach industry. Cars were *not* developed and launched by the then mighty and rich rail companies. In each case, there has been a new set of investors filling the gap and reaping the benefits.

Today, in spite of vast sums of money spent on R&D, or may be because of it, the oil industry has not yet produced anything similar to alternative fuels. Yet, time is pressing because the energy economy, as we know it, has reached its peak. Quite aside from questions about how much oil is still left, current solutions cannot provide answers for the future. The way Paul Roberts, an oil expert has it, by 2035:

- The world will use more than twice as much energy as today.
- Demand for oil will jump from the current 80 million barrels a day to 140 million, and
- The use of natural gas will climb by over 120%.[5]

Mergers or no mergers, oil companies should learn that business is moulded by its users and should adapt their strategy to that fact – something very few firms are prepared to do. Becoming extremely market-sensitive and far-sighted, oil firms should follow their customers into lots of other areas of energy usage. And they should direct their R&D labs towards finding solutions to future energy problems – rather than spending time reinventing the wheel.

8. Deregulation, consolidation, and shake out in air transport

The Introduction made reference to the swarm of new companies that sprang up in the late 1970s and early 1980s after President Carter's deregulation of the air transport industry. As the newcomers cut prices and attracted clients, the majors responded by significantly lowering their labour costs through the implementation of a separate pay scale, as well as:

- Building up their hubs
- Introducing sophisticated revenue-management systems, and
- Launching what has been one of the most brilliant marketing concepts, the frequent-flyer programme.

In terms of strategic business planning, all this has been necessary but not enough. To appreciate why, it is appropriate to bring into perspective that, as an after-effect of deregulation, air carriers faced four waves of fortune and misfortune, each lasting about five years: Consolidation, bankruptcies, rise of profits, bankruptcies again, and restructuring.

Consolidation has been the name of the game from the mid- to late 1980s. Those US airlines who successfully kept new entrants in check used their cash to consolidate their market share through mergers and acquisitions. In less than five years, there were a dozen business mergers in the airline industry, more or less with the aim of increasing the size of the network.

- Most of these acquisitions, however were funded with debt.
- Airlines took advantage of liquid junk bonds market to pile up liabilities.

Table 18.2 gives a snapshot of deals that went through in mergers and takeovers from 1985 to 1989, both by leveraged financiers and by competitors in the United States alone. In terms of money per transaction, they range from 70 million to over 3.5 billion – a big sum for that time. The keyword was *debt*, and debt had to be repaid with interest.

Unfortunately for the US airline industry, the years of the fatted calf did not last long. In 1990–91, the US economy as a whole took a turn for the worse, falling into a recession. This was followed by stress conditions in fulfilling assumed debt obligations. Moreover, war with Iraq resulted in great losses for the air transport industry, while many of the major carriers were:

- Reeling operationally from the mergers of the late 1980s, and
- Facing big financial burden from the leverage they had willingly incurred.

Table 18.2 M&As in the US air transport industry in mid- to late 1980s

Acquirer	Target	Equity value (in $ millions)	Year
Carl Icahn	TWA	910	1985
People Express	Frontier	310	1985
Southwest	Muse Air	70	1985
Northwest	Republic	880	1986
TWA	Ozark	240	1986
Texas Air	Eastern	615	1986
Delta	Western	790	1986
Texas Air	People Express	290	1986
American Airlines	AirCal	220	1987
USAir Group	PSA	385	1987
USAir Group	Piedmont	1560	1987
Donald Trump	Eastern Air Shuttle	365	1989
Wings Holdings	Northwest	3565	1989

In the aftermath, there were a number of Chapter 11 bankruptcy filings. Here is a short list: Eastern in 1989; Continental in 1990; Pan Am in 1991; TWA in early 1992. Eastern and Pan Am were not able to successfully reorganize and ultimately liquidated (see section 9 on the PanAm-Delta problems). Continental and TWA emerged from bankruptcy, but TWA filed for Chapter 11 again in 1995.

As is so often the case, the misfortunes of some of the major players were a business opportunity for others. While air transport capacity was withdrawn from the system because of bankruptcies, the financially stronger carriers like AMR (parent of American Airlines), Delta, Northwest, and United Airlines (UAL), cherry-picked assets.

- UAL had bought Eastern's Pacific Division in 1986. In 1991 it purchased the London Heathrow routes of Pan Am.
- American acquired in 1990 Eastern's Latin American Division, and the Miami–London run of Continental Airlines. In 1991, it bought the London Heathrow routes of TWA, as well as the Seattle–Tokyo link of Continental.
- Delta Airlines picked off the Atlantic Division and Frankfurt hub of Pan Am in 1991; while that same year Northwest Airlines acquired the Honolulu–Nagoya route of America West.

These acquisitions were thought to provide new income and more profits for the firms who made the purchases. Instead, they were faced with record losses in the early 1990s. This forced the financially stronger airlines to slow down their capacity growth. Only some years down the line, a more or less ill-fated attempt to restructure airfares allowed carriers to return to profitability.

This is the good news. From 1995 to 2000, the US air transport industry generated *net profits* of roughly $23 billion. Benefiting from a good economy, measured capacity growth and network breadth, American carriers were in good health for a few years. But the 2000 equity market crash brought an upheaval.

Matters were made much worse by the events of September 11, 2001, the increased terrorism concerns, and appreciating energy costs. US airlines, as a whole, reported some $30 billion in losses from 2001 to 2004, some 30% above the profits they had made in the previous 5 years. This was the industry's first-ever profitless recovery, exacerbated by new competitors, which were low-cost carriers (LCCs).

The best survival strategy available to the major US and other airlines has been that of slashing costs. Reducing expenses, however, was not enough to offset record-high energy costs, with jet fuel rising from $50/bbl to $120/bbl. As an after-effect, some of the older, legacy carriers like Delta and Northwest filed for Chapter 11 bankruptcy protection in September 2005. The bankruptcy of a formerly prestigious airline like Delta makes a very interesting case study (see section 9).

Some of the bankrupt airlines sought salvation in a merger. Swiss, which succeeded Swissair after its bankruptcy, was taken over by Lufthansa; and US Air by America West. As part of this merger, US Airways returned to GE Commercial Aviation Services, from which it was leasing its fleet, 25 more planes than originally planned.

Ending aircraft leases is part of the game of slimming-down the air transport industry. On 23 September 2005, Northwest Airlines, then newly in bankruptcy, announced that it hoped to eliminate, by abandoning or giving back, more than 100 aircraft in its fleet of 699 planes. It also told its Tennessee-based regional carrier, Pinnacle Airlines, to ground 15 of the 139 small jets it leases from Northwest; while its other regional carrier, Mesaba, had to return 35 regional jets to lease companies. These are essentially half-measures.

- Mergers made under distress conditions are no prescription for survival.
- As the saying has it, two things that are wrong don't make one that is right.
- Returning leased aircraft helps in cutting the carrier's bill, but there are also penalties and (most likely) the aircraft should not have been leased in the first place.

A better policy with cost-saving mergers is to enact them before reaching the breaking point. For instance, two major European airlines, Air France and KLM, have been toying with a link for years. Discussions were on and off for fear close ties would threaten Air France's alliance with Delta, and KLM's with Northwest. Only in mid-2003, after US regulators agreed to allow Delta, Northwest and Continental to press ahead with a marketing alliance, did merger talks accelerate, leading to a takeover offer from Air France for KLM.

Still, although they merged into a single holding company, the two air carriers continue to operate separately. This curious structure is reflecting in part national (French and Dutch) sensitivities and, in part, the need to meet US competition concerns. Another reason is to protect landing rights by continuing to compete against each other on the important North Atlantic route. But on the downside, this solution misses the cost-effectiveness of full integration.

Analysts say that it is not just arcane bilateral trade agreements that blow against airlines' consolidation. The importance of the US market to both AirFrance and KLM means US competition weighs heavily in their strategic plans. Moreover, with American carriers under pressure, everyone is eyeing benefits from transatlantic routes and, why not, for possible expansion into an internal US network if more American carriers go down into the abyss.

9. The bankruptcy of Delta Airlines: a case study

Delta Airlines was the United States' third-biggest carrier. In the 1980s and most of the 1990s, like Swissair, its also bankrupt international partner, Delta was a high flier. But in the 2001 to mid-2005 timeframe it lost $10 billion. By mid-August 2005 its shares fell sharply, as the troubled carrier delayed an SEC filing while negotiating a new contract with its personnel. A month later came the bankruptcy filing.

Had Delta lost its will to survive? Was its strategic business plan flawed? Was management not up to the task? Or were damages the airline had suffered irreparable? To better appreciate the answer to these queries, it is advisable to turn back a decade and a half, to the time when Delta Airlines:

- Was thought to have an unchallenged position
- Used its cash to buy up prized air routes, and
- Its management wielded a sharp knife to trim off fat all over the organization.

Delta's prominence was boosted when, in January 1991, Pan Am filed for bankruptcy, and sought to sell some of its operations in order to refloat. In August 1991, Delta agreed to a $1.7 billion deal, which included transfer of Pan Am's transatlantic routes and Northeast Shuttle. Analysts said that Delta's time had come.

A mistake Delta Airlines made at that time was that it proposed to finance a new carrier dubbed Pan Am 2. In December 1991, Pan Am ceased all operations after Delta declined to pump in millions, arguing that Pan Am's reorganization plan was doomed. Pan Am took the offensive and sued Delta for breach of contract, counting on the generally pro-debtor stance of bankruptcy courts.

Delta fought hard to avoid a jury. And with good reason. A jury consultant hired to conduct a series of mock trials found jurors especially susceptible to the emotional aspects of the case. PanAm did not give up easily, as it was fighting for its life. In a $2.5 billion battle between Delta and Pan Am the upcoming carrier spearheaded an elaborate three-year legal strategy that entailed everything lawyers could imagine for its defence. On Wall Street, analysts said:

- These manoeuvres were neither illegal nor unethical
- They merely took advantage of an imperfect, malleable system costing Delta, in the process, many millions of dollars for its team of lawyers.

The lawyers, however, delivered a stunning victory for Delta that saved the Atlanta-based carrier from life-threatening litigation. Pan Am had been counting on Delta to help foot the bill for its comeback. This did not materialize, and subsequently the $1.7 billion deal that was to finance Pan Am 2 in exchange for Pan Am's profitable transatlantic routes and Northeast shuttle was grounded and the company went into bankruptcy.

Six years passed by and things followed their course Delta was prospering, but costs ran up while the fleet was ageing. The next phase in the Delta Airlines drama was played in mid-1997 with a change in command. Gerald Grinstein, the board member who had led the ousting of long-time chief executive Ronald W. Allen a month earlier, met Leo F. Mullin as a candidate. Grinstein was looking for someone to shake the company. 'Is anything or anyone sacred?' Mullin asked.[6] Grinstein told him no – and Delta picked Mullin to take charge. The new CEO's 1997 strategy was based on four pillars:

- Rebuild morale
- Renew assets
- Redefine priorities, and
- Decentralize management.

To rebuild morale, Mullins met with employees all over the country, but had a hard time fighting his biggest threat: Pilots wanted more money. Renewing assets was expensive. To do so he had to speed up an upgrade of Delta's 559-plane fleet, ordering more new jets and revamping outmoded information systems.

An integral part of redefining priorities was Delta's transatlantic business and its flagging push into Asia and Latin America, while meeting the threat of low-cost carriers at home. As it should be remembered these further-out routes were the result of massive acquisitions. The chosen solution called for decentralizing management giving executives day-to-day decision-making power.

Thanks to the air transport's industry's healthy run during the Clinton years, in the late 1990s Leo Mullin had some breathing space. Fuel costs were down and Delta had plenty of business travellers. But Mullin was less successful in trimming Delta's overblown costs, and that weighed mightily with business confidence slackening after:

- The equity bubble blew up in 2000, and
- The dramatic events of September 11, 2001, sharply curtailed air travel.

Unwanted consequences can shatter any strategic plan. Between 2001 and 2005, as with so many other carriers, Delta was under stress. Finally, in September 2005, Delta and Northwest Airlines, the second and fourth largest US carriers, sought Chapter 11 bankruptcy protection to keep their creditors at bay. Their failure to remain solvent meant that four of the six largest US airlines were bankrupt.

Other airlines around the world were also suffering but the US carriers were deeper under water. The International Air Transport Association (IATA) estimated that in 2005 the aviation industry would make modest profits in Europe and Asia, but the global picture would be an overall loss of about $7.5 billion. With US carriers alone losing more than $8 billion, this means that even the profitable carriers in other countries will be earning peanuts.

As a postscript, Delta's bankruptcy may have achieved what Leo F. Mullin had tried to do and could not because of the labour unions' adverse reaction. In early December 2005, a new round of wage paybacks (tentatively agreed to by the pilots) underscored the weak bargaining position of pilots unions and other organized labour at major US carriers.

The payback has been a cut to wages by 14% as part of interim concessions valued at $143–150 million. A drop in the ocean given Delta's torrent of red ink, but still a welcome contribution to the carrier's salvage. US Bankruptcy Court Judge

Prudence Carter Beatty helped force the compromise, repeatedly urging both sides to make a deal. Meanwhile, Delta faced another looming showdown in the bankruptcy court, with its retirees.

The lesson to retain from this case study is that unlike startups that have no legacy costs to pay for, the better-established airlines are trapped in a downward spiral. Every move they make to cut costs, for instance by removing elements from their cabin service, brings them down to the level of service associated with low-cost carriers. The newcomers, by contrast, are helped by their youthful staff, simpler, point-to-point routes, and no appetite for mergers and acquisitions. Look at Ryanair.

Notes

1 D.N. Chorafas, *Management Risk: The Bottleneck Is at the Top of the Bottle.* Macmillan/Palgrave, London, 2004.
2 *The Economist*, 5 November 2005.
3 *Blooomberg News*, 20 December 2005.
4 *Total Telecom Magazine*, January 2006.
5 Paul Roberts, *The End of Oil.* Bloomsbury, London, 2004.
6 *Business Week*, 22 December 1997.

Case Studies on Big Bank Mergers in the United States

1. Introduction

In October 2004, Bank of America swallowed FleetBoston Financial for $47 billion. JP Morgan Chase offered even more for Bank One three months later in January 2005. On May 2005, Royal Bank of Scotland (RBS), the UK's second biggest bank, bought Charter One, a mid-sized, mid-western US institution, for $10.5 billion. This acquisition is RBS's 26th in America since 1988, when it bought Citizens Bank, in Rhode Island. With Charter One, RBS will be one of the top commercial banks in the United States.

These 2004 and 2005 M&As characterized the new wave in the banking industry. Over the past few years, European banks have increasingly been looking to America for growth. ABN Amro is already one of the US top ten banks. In March 2005 the French BNP Paribas acquired Community First Bankshares for $1.2 billion, adding to its already substantial presence on the west coast.

Analysts think this acquisition spree in the US banking industry is going to continue because many European credit institutions are flush with cash. Many experts reckon that European banks will generate some $80 billion in excess capital up to 2008, and they calculate that RBS alone is having some £3 billion a year in excess funds which it needs to invest in its line of business, provided it finds an opportunity.

It is only reasonable that European banks are after American financial institutions, because the United States is a strong economy that attracts plenty of financing (European bank mergers are discussed in Chapter 20). Other things being equal, bank profitability including return on assets (ROA) and return on equity (ROE) is also better in the United States than in Europe.

The financial industry's wave of M&As in the early part of this century seems to have a different pattern than that of the 1990s, which followed on the heels of deregulation of banking. As it will be recalled, world-wide the number of mergers and acquisitions among credit institutions increased most significantly in the 1990s:

- From 340 in 1990
- To nearly 980 in 1999, almost by 300%.

While many other companies were subject to mergers, acquisitions, and takeovers, in the United States banks represented the largest share of domestic, same-industry M&A. According to published statistics, bank mergers accounted for 68% or so of transactions, and 78% of the value of deals which led to substantial industry sector consolidation. Evidently, then as now, the net result is to reduce the number of players in the market.

While in the other industry sectors there are plenty of cross-industry mergers, among financial institutions cross-industry M&As have been the exception. In the 1995 to 2001 timeframe covered by a study I did on M&As in late 2001, about 70% of total activity, in a number of deals worth double-digit billions of dollars, involved firms in the same industry and from the same country.

The next most common type of M&A is between firms in the same country but different industries. In the aforementioned 2001 study, these accounted for about 15% of major transactions. Next in frequency were cross-border same-industry deals, while cross-industry, cross-border mergers have been the least common type, representing just 3% of transactions over the timeframe in reference.

Notice that this process of concentration in the financial industry has occurred in many First World countries. One of the after-effects has been that many of the banks that topped the list in 1985 have disappeared, acquired by others, which, sometimes, were their juniors in assets. More than anywhere else this is true in Japan, where credit institutions, already huge but not far from bankruptcy, have been merged into even larger but still not-that-stable financial giants.

The last ten years in Japanese banking provide an interesting case study. The first big bank merger took place in 1996 when Mitsubishi Bank took over the Bank of Tokyo to form Tokyo-Mitsubishi. Then Sumitomo and Mitsui formed SumitomoMitsui Financial; Dai-Ichi Kangyo Bank, Fuji Bank, and Industrial Bank of Japan merged into Mizuho, a new colossus; and the labels of other Japanese city banks disappeared into more mergers.

- The risk associated with this torrent of M&As comes from the volatility of reserves featured by many of the mammoth institutions.
- Some, like the Japanese Resona Bank, have been using smoke and mirrors, the so-called *deferred tax assets* (DTAs).[1]

As a list published by *Forbes* brought to its reader's attention, in 2003, these merged and remerged financial giants dominated the corporate world on a global scale. In 2003, of the top 50 companies in the world, ranked by assets, all but three were insurance companies or other financial entities. The three that are not – General Electric, General Motors, and Ford – are non-bank banks, with large financial arms that account for significant percentages of their assets.

Also interesting is the fact that some of the financial entities in the *Forbes* list have grown organically rather than through acquisitions. Examples are Fannie Mae, in 3rd position, and Freddie Mac in 13th. Both are highly troubled financial institutions, overexposed in mortgages (which is their charter), and in derivatives, which is neither their business nor a way to assure financial staying power. The same is indeed true of the majority of the other banks and non-banks in the aforementioned top 50 *Forbes* list.

2. Assets of US banks: case study with Citicorp

What has happened with Citigroup, and other mergers we will study in this and in the next two chapters, documents that, in real life, mergers and most particularly *mega-mergers* rarely work out smoothly. As an example, cross-selling to consumers often falls victim of turf wars among far-flung parts of a big organization's business empire. There are few examples of banks which:

- Have built their post-merger businesses into a textbook case of customer appeal and efficiency, and
- Have been able to master existing synergies in a way promoting shareholder value, while avoiding personal and cultural clashes.

In 1985, Citicorp was the biggest bank in America, with $174 billion in assets. At that time the top ten US banks had just $775 billion in combined assets. Twenty years down the line, in 2004, Citigroup had $1.26 trillion in assets, nearly a 725% increase, while the ten top US banks featured a combined $4.7 trillion in assets. This is an increase of 606%. Redimensioned for inflation which prevailed in these two decades,

- Citi's assets have grown by about 360%
- While altogether the assets of the top 10 American banks grew by 300%.

Through its merger with Travelers Insurance, Citi seems to have increased its assets faster than its peers in the top 10. This is, however, the wrong conclusion for the reason that of all individual credit institutions in the 1985 list only Citicorp, reborn as Citigroup after the merger, has survived as an independent entity. The top-10 list in 1985 included in line of assets value:

- Citigroup
- BankAmerica
- Chase Manhattan
- Manufacturers Hanover
- JP Morgan
- Chemical Banking
- Security Pacific

- Bankers Trust
- First Interstate
- First Chicago.

BankAmerica bought Security Pacific as well as Seattle First (see section 4) and Chicago's Continental Bank. But it was then itself bought by Nation's Bank (the former North Carolina National Bank) which adopted the better-known Bank of America trademark. As the reader will recall from the Introduction, in a drive to create a still bigger institution, in 2004 Bank of America bought Fleet Boston which was the result of other mergers, mainly in New England.

From the banks in the 1985 top 10 list, the more financially sound Chemical Banking bought Manufacturers Hanover (a bigger entity), then Chase Manhattan, retaining the Chase brand. Subsequently Chase bought JP Morgan to become JP Morgan Chase. Bankers Trust was bought by Deutsche Bank, and the label disappeared. First Interstate and First Chicago were bought by Bank One (which was not in the 1985 top 10 list), while in 2004 Bank One fell to JP Morgan Chase.

Because of its history and its evolution, Citigroup makes an interesting case study in mergers characterizing the American banking industry. In the mid-19th century, in New York, the forerunner of Citibank, Citicorp, and Citigroup, had been the City Bank which went nearly bankrupt in the bank's panic of 1837. (The 'National' was added to the name in 1865, as was the case with thousands of other American banks in many cities across the nation.)

The man who saved City and made it a sound institution was Moses Taylor, a merchant who became City's new chief after the troubles. Under his watchful eye, and that of his successor Percy R. Pyne, City gained deposits at the expense of its weaker competitors. The Taylor-Pyne principle, which saved City, is the most sound advice to all modern credit institutions:

- Have *ready money*, meaning enough cash to see the bank through in any emergency, and
- Keep your *equity capital*, not just any capital including hybrids and other fakes, at 16% of assets.

Not all bankers appreciate the wisdom of Taylor–Pyne principle, and they pay for that failure. Banks that cheat about their capital needs by manipulating correlation coefficients to reduce capital requirements – as happened with the 25% in connection to Quantitative Impact Study 4 (QIS4, November 2005) – should remember these two bullets from top bankers of the 19th century. In fact,

- They should gold-plate them, and
- Hang them on the walls of their offices and board room, because they are the best possible advice for the future.

In the mid-19th century at Big Apple there was another 'First National': the First National Bank of the City of New York. It was headed by George F. Baker, another great banker. As James Grant has it: '[Baker was] first in reputation, in conservatism, and in its refusal to bend to new ways.'[2] First National Bank and National City Bank merged at the end of 1954 to create First National City Bank (FNCB). The former was the institution which increased its prestige and prospered by raising:

- Quality of deliverables, and
- Specialization to a high degree.

The latter has been a bank better adapted to live in the post-World War II era of democratization of credit and socialization of risk.[3] In the 1970s the more sexy 'Citi' was promoted by its then CEO Walter Wriston, to replace FNCB. Wriston also created Citicorp, as a holding company, which permitted it to bypass some of Depression Era legislation, and engaged in a global mergers and acquisitions facility to make the institution a world leader in retail banking.

3. More growth, more mergers: from Citicorp to Citigroup

According to several financial analysts, today Citi has the only successful global brand in consumer banking. The institution:

- Features branches in about 100 countries, mostly serving better-off individuals
- It has become one of the world's leading credit card operators, and
- For many years it held a technological edge over its rivals, which provided it with strategic advantages.

After having nearly gone bust in 1991 because of bad loans, under John Reed Citibank established impressive lending controls. Travelers, its counterpart in the 1998 merger, was built up through a series of astute acquisitions to become an insurer and investment banker active from property insurance and mutual funds, to shares and bonds.

On paper, the merger between Citicorp and Travelers made sense. On 6 April 1998, when Citigroup was just created it had nearly $700 billion in assets, and aimed at reinventing banking by creating a full-service company for corporations and individual consumers. The downside, however, is that the concept of a global financial-services supermarket has yet to be proved a winner.

As a concept, the financial supermarket that can offer any type of goodies to everybody around is simplistic and it fails to consider inefficiencies of scale as well as risks. The process this concept contemplates is rather linear: two big institutions merge, combine operations, eliminate jobs, and produce a tidy and 'predictable' jump in:

- Earnings, and
- Share price.

But there is always a significant difference between theory and practice. Real life does not always work like that, as the events that followed the Citigroup merger demonstrate, including the sale of insurance and other assets of the merged company. (On 7 December 2005 Crédit Suisse announced it was preparing its Winterthur insurance subsidiary for sale. To the contrary, Holland's Rabo Bank said that it would focus on insurance.)

Initially articles published shortly after the announcement of the Citicorp/Travelers merger found nothing but praise: 'There is the central justification of the deal: cross-selling each other's products, mainly to retail customers,' said an article in *Business Week*, adding that: 'Over the next two years, Citigroup ought to be able to generate $600 million more in earnings because of cross-selling'.[4] Also in the news was that management hoped to double its $7.5 billion in revenue in five years. It did not happen.

Another complementary commentary made at the time of the Citigroup mega-merger stated that the arrangement could solve Citicorp's and Travelers' biggest problems. The given reason was that John Reed, Citicorp's CEO (and Citigroup's co-CEO) would get a stronger hand. Also, because a direct-sales force would market Citi chequing accounts, mutual funds, and credit cards, since Travelers had:

- 10 300 Salomon Smith Barney brokers, and
- 80 000 part-time Primerica Financial Services insurance agents.

For his part, the CEO of Travelers (and co-CEO of Citigroup), Sandy Weill, was supposed to gain control of Citicorp's 750+ branch offices outside the United States – including some 464 in Europe, 166 in Latin America, and 93 in Asia.

This was seen as the catalyst able to transform Travelers into an international player in the insurance industry – second to none.

But just eight months down the line from mega-merger time, it was no longer the same story. In late October 1998 long-simmering tensions came to the surface, while insiders were for some time saying that friction between various factions of Citicorp and Travelers origin had been wracking Citigroup for months. Then the bickering exploded into public view.

Acting together, as co-CEOs, John Reed and Sandy Weill asked for James Dimon's liquidation. At Travelers' Dimon had been Weill's heir apparent. Then Reed was ousted by Weill, and when the inside story was revealed it was found to involve biased investment opinions on AT&T. Beyond the executive shuffles, other events revealed that the 'the deal of the century' was in trouble. It was plagued by:

- Turf battles
- Cultural clashes
- Unsettled decisions on strategies, and
- A general malaise which put Citigroup at a disadvantage.

As one insider was to suggest, the merged financial institution was an organization of dukes and earls, adding that if your liege goes, unless you can quickly find a line of authority and loyalty to someone else, you are gone too. The way another insider put it, the real issue has been the rate of speed at which the merged company was put together. For Travelers to buy Salomon and then do the merger with Citicorp and Travelers within the same year, has been a very tough thing.

At Citigroup, senior management also had to cope with a sharp drop in capitalization, which unsettled shareholders. Back in April 1998, when Citicorp and Travelers announced their intention to merge, to form the new huge entity, the deal was valued at $70 billion. But by the time it was closed on 8 October of that same year, the price had fallen to $37 billion, reflecting the sharp declines in both institutions' stock prices.

As we will see in greater detail in section 8, a significant risk with mergers is that the taxpayer will be called to pay the damages if the merged bank fails. Citicorp's $3.1 trillion in notional principal amount in derivatives has been combined with Travelers' extensive holdings, mostly through its Salomon Smith Barney subsidiary.

- Some analysts estimated at the time of the merger that the new group had nearly $6 trillion in derivatives exposure.
- This was not the worst case, JP Morgan Chase had a multiple of it – but neither was it the only risk.

At merger time, Citigroup had about $700 billion in assets, meaning that a single mega-failure could bankrupt the US Federal Deposit Insurance Corporation (FDIC) and its fund. At just $30 billion, this deposit insurance fund suddenly looked inadequate, as Citigroup held roughly $50 billion in the US deposits, and

- Speculation by aggressive bond traders
- Faulty underwriting, or
- Large derivatives losses could cut deeply into the group's capital structure.

Finally, as fate would have, there has also been some personal irony in the Citigroup merger. Sandy Weill engineered it, and Sandy Weill managed to become the master of the merged entity after ejecting John Reed. On Wall Street, rumour had it that the ultimate dream of Weill was to become the CEO of the New York Stock Exchange. But it was Reed who got the Chairman's job at NYSE, after the Richard Grasso scandal (see Chapter 7).

4. Chemical Banking and Chase Manhattan

One of the interesting incidents in Chemical Banking's life has been that Hetty Green, the so-called 'Witch of Wall Street' but in reality a most successful and fabulously wealthy trader and investor, banked there. For many years, Chemical Banking was a well-to-do institution. When in the early part of the 20th century George Gilbert Williams, its long-time president, was asked for the secret of his success, he replied: 'The fear of God.'[5]

The pedigree of Chase National Bank, forerunner of Chase Manhattan, dates back to Salomon P. Chase, Lincoln's Secretary of the Treasury. In 1864, the bank was appointed an agent for the Union's 5% bonds. A hundred years later, in the 1960s, it prospered under the leadership of Dr David Rockefeller, but in the late 1970s and 1980s its fortunes waned.

Chase became the Chase Manhattan Bank when in the 1950s it took over the Bank of the Manhattan Company. In that decade, Chemical acquired New York Trust, and Manufacturers Trust merged with Hanover Bank. This has been one of the major merger waves during which about one-third of New York banks vanished.

During the years of his watch, David Rockefeller turned Chase Manhattan into a premier global bank. In his hey-day, in the early 1970s, he is reputed to have had direct access to 500 kings, prime ministers, senior government officials, and presidents of other banks around the globe. By means of one of the first on-line datamining systems in action, Rockefeller was able to retrieve on-line files on commitments made with any of the '500' – to provide information during a telephone conversation, without having to say 'I will call you later.' But in the 1990s, like many other commercial banks, Chase was stymied by sluggish revenues.

- In 1994 its interest revenue fell by 4.5%, to $3.7 billion
- While its non-interest revenue, primarily based on risky derivatives, rose by 3.5%.

In April 1995, it emerged that Heine Securities, an aggressive New Jersey investment firm that had never seen a business it did not want to break up, had taken a 6.1% stake in Chase. To safeguard its independence, the venerable New York credit institution raised its dividend again and promised cost-cutting. But cost-cutting alone could not do the turnaround.

As a result, Chase stepped up the search for a white knight. BankAmerica was apparently its management's first choice, but talks between the pair fizzled out in July 1995. The merger deal with Chemical was then put together in little more than a month, which speaks volumes about the urgency for capital injection.

Prior to the merger with Chase, Chemical Banking had swallowed Manufacturers Hanover, an institution loaded with derivatives. Chase Manhattan, too, was overexposed in derivative financial instruments, but somehow Chemical's management felt that bigger size would allow the merged banks to take still bigger bets, presumably with larger cushions, in fast-growing markets. Nor was it lost on management that:

- Big size made the bank too big to fail
- The Federal Reserve had acted to save Continental Illinois from bankruptcy, while it let smaller banks fail.

On 28 August 1995, the merger of Chemical Banking and Chase Manhattan was no longer top management's secret. The new Chase had an impressive $20 billion in equity, a sum exceeded by only three other banks in the world, but it also inherited lots of exposure in loans and in derivative financial instruments.

Contrary to the equity running, the combined financial institution ranked just 21st in assets worldwide, behind a host of giant Japanese and European competitors. But management probably felt that with more than $163 billion in overall deposits and some 4 million consumer accounts, Chase would be the dominant retail banker in New York.

The trouble is that in these days of fierce competition for clients and deposits, even in retail banking, size is only a starting point. At the time of the merger Wall Street analysts suggested that the only thing that matters about having a bigger customer base is if you segment it and do a first-class marketing job with each segment. Though size will make the bank a tougher competitor, if the product planning and marketing homework is well done:

- Size alone will not make much of a difference in survival terms.
- Instead, the No. 1 criterion is to administer, and continue administering, the level and type of services that customers want.

Experts also expressed the opinion that another danger with the merger and the sharp cut down in personnel, which was judged as being the right strategy, was that Chase management was going to be tremendously inwardly focused for about three years. A major hurdle, faced by so many other M&As, was in accommodating the gradual melting of the two corporate cultures as there was potential for cultural clash.

Furthermore, a critique heard on Wall Street has been that, when the Chemical/Chase merger took place, management practically focused on the strong points – but not on the weaknesses. The pros for instance emphasized the $20 billion portfolio of credit card balances making the merged entity fourth in America. Also, the fact that it will be global leader in emerging markets' underwriting and trading revenues, over and above $191 billion in loan syndication.

Critics said that Chemical Banking overextended its hand with the Chase Manhattan takeover, particularly so as it had not yet digested the acquisition of Manufacturers Hanover. Nor was the acquiring institution ready with streamlining the risk management system of the combined firm, something that critics judged as a 'must' given that Manufacturers Hanover had a large exposure in derivatives.

Moreover, after the Chase acquisition, the merged institution definitely needed to improve its bottom line, getting costs down close to 50% of revenues, which indicates a well-managed bank. It also needed to generate a return on equity of 18% or higher, which is far from being the case, and bring under control its mushrooming derivatives exposure – which stood at $4.7 trillion at the end of 1995 for the combined entity. An additional major problem was that before these goals were achieved, came the merger with the Morgan Bank.

5. JP Morgan Chase and Bank One

The story of the House of Morgan is too well known to be retold. Its founder had not only single-mindedness and deep knowledge of finance, but also the ability to make good use of his own relentless drive both in exploiting opportunities and in damage control. Prior to the institution of the Federal Reserve System, in the late 19th and early 20th century, J.P. Morgan, along with George Baker and a handful of other senior commercial bankers, orchestrated single-handedly the salvage of the US financial system, by exhibiting:

- Cool nerve in a crisis
- Risk-taking with own funds, and
- The attention to detail necessary in major restructuring operations.

Adversity was used as opportunity, and time was made to adapt to the work to be done. Crises were solved by a few men on the spot, with Dr Morgan the pivot point. After the death of the founder, however, and even more so after that of his son, who succeeded him at the bank's helm, the institution's fortunes waned.

In the years prior to and after World War I, the Morgan Bank kept a high profile in government business, with its senior executives having significant influence on the US Administration. As rumour had it, the younger J.P. Morgan pushed President Wilson to enter World War I because he was afraid that if Germany won he would lose the $1 billion in loans to England and France (big money at that time).

In the 1920s and 1930s, too, Morgan Bank executives kept close contact with the Administration in Washington, while the financial institution itself oriented its business largely towards investment banking. However, some of J.P. Morgan's intellectual and financial offspring, better known as 'the Trusts', proposed more than the bank that was once their parent. Therefore, in connection to this case study, it is important to briefly bring to the reader's attention the fact that at the end of the *first* decade of the 20th century, besides his own institution, Pierpont Morgan controlled several New York City trust companies. Financial history books say that the old trick of voting trusts amplified Dr Morgan's reach.

- The Trusts were instrumental in many of the master banker's deals, and
- Several became rich entities in their own right, surviving over several decades after their founder passed away.

Morgan's Bankers Trust, for instance, had taken over three other banks and prospered as a premier investment bank, till it wounded itself through derivatives, and fell to the Deutsche Bank. Also, in 1909 Dr Morgan had gained control of Guaranty Trust, which became the largest trust in the US and eventually merged into the Morgan Bank (more on this later).

In the early 1930s, following the Great Depression, the Glass Steagall Act obliged US banks to choose between commercial and investment banking. Morgan chose the commercial banking road, addressing a selective clientele, while a spin-off, Morgan Stanley, went after the investment banking business. After World War II, the fortunes of the Morgan Bank waned.

Over the same timeframe, however, while flush with money, Guaranty Trust – Morgan's former vehicle – became a sleepy, risk-averse institution. In 1959 the much smaller Morgan Bank merged with Guaranty becoming the surviving financial institution. A couple of decades later, it also became a leader in derivatives, after the repeal of the Glass Steagall Act. The next turning point came another couple of decades down the line.

Theoretically, the acquisition of JP Morgan by Chase Manhattan on 13 September 2000 formed a financial conglomerate with $670 billion in assets. This was a $36 billion deal, by far Chase's most ambitious push into investment banking. It also came on the heels of the $10 billion acquisition by UBS of PaineWebber, and Crédit Suisse First Boston's $11.8 billion deal to buy broker Donaldson, Lufkin & Jenrette (see Chapter 21).

While these were looked on by their proponents as great mergers, many Wall Street analysts doubted the wisdom of such mega-deals. And they were not accepting the arguments that such M&As were necessary for pairing investment banks with commercial banks, brokers, and market makers. UBS had already acquired brokers in the United States and the UK, while CSFB was an investment bank anyway.

Regarding the Chase Manhattan/Morgan Bank merger experts pointed to certain strange circumstances surrounding it. Attention was paid to the fact that the two institutions were the largest players on the global derivatives market. Also intriguing was the news that this acquisition followed by only a couple of weeks a report of late August 2000 that Deutsche Bank was going to buy up JP Morgan and become the world's largest bank.

The added flavour has been that according to some reports the Deutsche Bundesbank, Germany's central bank, had objected to the planned merger of Deutsche Bank and JP Morgan, because both institutions were massively exposed in gold derivatives contracts. Unconfirmed reports suggested that the responsibility for rescuing what would have been the largest banking group in the world would have fallen within the jurisdiction of the Bundesbank.

Golden Sextant, a financial newsletter associated with the Gold Anti-Trust Action Committee (GATA), which is battling against the manipulation of gold prices, reported on 19 September 2000 that as a consequence of failed derivatives gambles, JP Morgan was hard hit. The publication:

- Considered the takeover by Chase was nothing but a bailout, and
- Saw it also as the reason why Peter Hancock, chief of JP Morgan's derivatives department, resigned after the takeover by Chase.

Some financial analysts suggest that the merger of the two top global derivatives players was engineered at record speed to hide the fact that Morgan could no more go on as an independent entity. Others suggested that this acquisition was something like the takeover of Union Bank of Switzerland by Swiss Banking Corporation in the late 1990s.

On paper, JP Morgan Chase has been a premier global financial services firm with assets of $715 billion and operations in over 60 countries. The combined company offered investment banking, asset management, private equity, consumer banking, private banking, e-finance, custody, and processing services – serving some 32 million consumer and more than 5000 corporate, institutional, and government clients. But at the end of 2004, JP Morgan Chase also had:

- A whopping $45 trillion in derivatives exposure
- And this, when demodulated down to toxic waste (money at high risk), amounted to $9 trillion – or three-quarters the gross national product (GDP) of the United States.

It is appropriate to notice that this amount, which reaches for the stars, does not include the derivatives exposure of Bank One. Mid-January 2004, JP Morgan Chase announced plans to take over Chicago-based Bank One for $58 billion in shares. This has been another milestone in the wave of consolidation, but at the same time it brought JP Morgan Chase derivatives' exposure still further.

In several respects, Bank One could not be more different than JP Morgan Chase. Originally a Midwestern credit institution, with its roots in consumer and small business lending, Bank One had achieved most of its growth through acquisitions, which it found rather difficult to digest. In the mid-1990s it owned 88 different banks in the United States.

Bank One's philosophy, articulated by its founder John G. McCoy, was to be a leader in mid-market lending. Another McCoy principle was the need for understanding the business one is lending. As Caouette, Altman, and Narayanan have it, McCoy senior was once approached by his son (who eventually succeeded him at the bank's helm) to make a loan to Sweden. The father responded by asking the son to write down ten things he knew about Sweden. No loan was made.[6]

- Unfortunately, no such cutting questions are posed with derivatives exposure.
- If they were, then it would have been difficult to see how the JP Morgan Chase/Bank One merger has gone through – combining two totally different cultures and risk management philosophies.

Be that as it is, the combined Chemical Banking, Manufacturers Hanover, Chase Manhattan, JP Morgan, and Bank One new financial entity has $1.1 trillion of assets, second to Citigroup by a notch. But it also features over $46 trillion in notional principal derivatives exposure, which is a scaring height. At the same time, the Bank One merger, which followed that of Bank of America and Fleet Boston Financial, made analysts wonder:

- Who is next, and
- What's the real payoff.

Starting with the fact that the merger of JP Morgan and Chase Manhattan never achieved what was hoped, critics had several questions over what the Bank One merger could achieve. In retail banking, critics said, there *might* be few easy gains from eliminating overlapping operations. But the overhanging derivatives exposures will get bigger and bigger.

Another big question at Wall Street was whether JP Morgan Chase paid too much for Bank One. Some analysts suggested this is so, noting that in 2000, to buy JP Morgan, Chase Manhattan had paid 'only' $34 billion – or 58.6% the Bank One acquisition. Optimists said that while the Chase Manhattan/JP Morgan merger floundered after investment banking hit the wall in 2000,[7] improved economic conditions in 2004/2005 made the Bank One merger look better. At least its shareholders were better off as they received a takeover premium of about 14%.

6. Acquisitions under distress: case study with BankAmerica

In 1982, in the wake of the bankruptcy of the Penn Square Bank and the US government's takeover of Continental Illinois to save it from failure (more on this later), BankAmerica put on the table $400 million to buy Seafirst of Seattle. The Fed was eager to find a home for bankrupt Seafirst, and the low price was calculated to narrow the acquiring bank's potential losses from loan problems that were haunting the biggest bank holding company of the State of Washington.

The agreement making Seafirst and its principal unit, Seattle First National Bank, a subsidiary of BankAmerica was immediately followed by Seafirst's report that it had a $133 million loss in the first quarter of 1982. This was nearly triple the amount of red ink being forecast by analysts.

Seattle First National Bank went under because some years earlier, between 1980 and 1982, it scented the wrong bonanza in the energy-loan business. The early 1980s were the years when loans to real estate and oil companies soured. When hell broke loose, Seafirst wanted its money back, but this is easier to say than to do. Among other moves:

- Seattle First sued its client Clinton Manges for $100 million in a federal court in San Antonio, TX, accusing him of committing fraud by, among other things, posting as collateral ranch lands that were already pledged to other deals.
- Manges sued back, contending that Seafirst defrauded him by making false promises, and by disbursing money from his account without his approval.

Seafirst officials attempting to untangle the mess were not the only ones interested in how Clinton Manges received his loans. People familiar with the work of a federal grand jury in Seattle suggested investigators wanted to know more about the relationship between John R. Boyd, Seafirst's energy loans chief (subsequently fired from Seafirst) and Manges, to determine if there was anything improper about the loans. The grand jury was also scrutinizing other Seafirst energy borrowers in Texas.

The federal inquiry in Seattle into Seafirst's Texas energy loans represented the broadening of an investigation that began as a spin-off of an Oklahoma City federal grand jury investigation into the collapse of Penn Square Bank, and its ripple effect on credit institutions that had bought Penn Square energy loans. Seafirst had bought about $400 million of those loans, and most of them had gone bad.

This was the background, when Seafirst agreed to be acquired by BankAmerica. At the time, the Seafirst takeover was the largest acquisition of a bank-holding company by an out-of-state bank-holding company, and the transaction had to be approved by:

- The Federal Reserve Board
- The Comptroller of the Currency, and
- Most evidently, shareholders of Seafirst.

In addition, the Washington State Senate had to approve a bill needed for the BankAmerica/Seafirst combination. Its objective was to permit investments by out-of-state financial institutions in more than 5% of the equity of bank-holding companies based in Washington State. While these prerequisites were being fulfilled, the Fed was also confronted with the salvage of Continental Illinois.

The irony in this case lies in the fact that the run at America's seventh largest bank (in 1982) came at a time when the country was in the initial stages of a dynamic process of banking deregulation, whose detractors were at best fighting a rearguard action. Yet, at the middle of liberalization of the financial industry, the US government found itself obliged to nationalize a big bank.

On Wall Street, experts said that the July 1984 $4.5 billion rescue of Continental Illinois' National Bank and Trust was not the whole answer to the rescue solution. In their judgement, real salvage might take years, and much more US taxpayers' money would run down the drain, before the banking entity could survive without support. It did not; and Continental Illinois was eventually acquired by BankAmerica.

Aggressive lending to energy firms and other ailing borrowers had filled Continental's books with $2.3 billion in sour loans. After rumours that the bank was about to fail led to a run on the Chicago lender, Morgan Guaranty and 15 other big banks rushed to Continental's rescue with a $4.5 billion line of credit, the largest ever for an America credit institution. Its goal was to help avert what threatened to become the biggest collapse in US banking history.

But even that £4.5 billion effort proved too small to keep panicky corporate customers in the United States, Europe, and Japan from withdrawing $8 billion in deposits. Mid-July 1984 the Federal Deposit Insurance Corporation (FDIC), and some private lenders, had to pump $2 billion directly into Continental. Though it normally does not insure amounts of more than $100 000, the FDIC went so far as to pledge that all the bank's depositors and creditors would be 'fully protected'.

In addition, the Federal Reserve Board, which had also been supplying credit to Continental, promised to continue doing so until the bank's problems had been solved. And the Morgan Bank-led bankers, strengthened by the addition of 12 members to their group, put up $1 billion of fresh credit.

- The fact that all that good money was running after bad money, was initially considered to be a 'vote of confidence'.
- But as bad news piled up, US regulators acknowledged that it might be years before Continental Illinois could survive on its own.

Meanwhile, a new management was put in place with John E. Swearingen, a former Standard Oil (Indiana) chief executive, succeeding David G. Taylor as CEO. One of Swearingen's first announcements was that, quite likely, it would take a long time before FDIC would be able to sell the 80% stake it took in the company. No one should expect instant results, was the new CEO's message.

But FDIC suggested it should plan to sell its holdings in Continental as soon as the bank was healthier. It also said its outlays would come from the bank's assessments rather than from general taxpayer funds. This led to almost nonstop negotiations, clouded by strong objections to the rescue plan from the Treasury Secretary Donald Regan, who argued that it was poor policy, and possibly illegal, for the FDIC to rescue Continental bank's holding company as a vehicle for saving the bank itself. In fact,

- The downside of *deposit insurance* first became apparent in the early 1980s with this rescue effort.
- In Continental's case, almost all of its deposits were well in excess of the $100 000 deposit insurance ceiling.

FDIC's announcement that all accounts would be protected, no matter how big, brought Continental's bailout cost to $1.7 billion. For six long years, the Federal Deposit Insurance Corporation remained the largest equity investor in Continental Bank. John E. Swearingen was right.

Before the crisis really broke into the open, Continental had been working on a plan that would have created what several investment bankers called a 'good bank' and a 'bad bank'. The 'bad bank', nicknamed *Trashco* by Continental employees, would have been capitalized heavily by existing Continental shareholders, assuming most of Continental's bad loans, and some good assets as well – perhaps the bank's $1.8 billion of government securities.

Moreover, this 'bad bank' would not have been run by Continental, but by an independent banking house willing to take the risk, in the hope that it could make money collecting Continental's problem loans. The 'good bank' would have had a relatively clean loan portfolio but would have also needed to fund additional capital to replace the equity transferred to the 'bad bank'.

It did not turn out exactly that way. The Federal Deposit Insurance Corporation found itself obliged to accept most of Continental's bad loans, estimated at $4 billion, in return for the 80% stake in the wounded bank. This amounted to a huge bailout which represented a painful step for the Reagan Administration, who philosophically opposed government intervention to save failing firms.

At the Treasury, Donald Regan described the structure of the bailout as 'bad public policy', because it put a federal agency out on a limb to protect private investors. It also proved to be an unsuccessful exercise in trying to stop a failed bank from becoming outright bankrupt. Eventually, BankAmerica stepped in and carried home the remains of Continental Illinois.

Some analysts said this was an expensive exercise which, combined with others, was prejudicial for BankAmerica, which eventually lost its independence. The merger with Continental Illinois proved to be much more expensive than the money paid upfront – a case which repeats itself time and again with companies that have failed.

Another case where BankAmerica had difficulty in swallowing its acquisitions was the takeover of investment banking firms. At one time, the San Francisco bank faced itself with the challenge of combining two brokers firms with a long history of professional incompatibility: Montgomery Securities and Robertson, Stevens.

Nor was the September 1998 integration of BankAmerica into another organization, after the venerable bank of Amadeo Giannini became subject to a takeover, easy to consume. The No. 1 reason given when the merger of NationsBank (the former North Carolina National Bank, NCNB) and the old BankAmerica into the new Bank of America was announced, was to create a coast-to-coast institution and boost competitiveness. The new Bank of America, based in North Carolina rather than California, said that it can:

- Trim its $19 billion in combined expenses by 10%, and
- Cut up to 8000 positions nationwide resulting in big cost savings, the usual trickery of head count.

To ease analysts' concerns about exposure to derivatives and to hedge funds the new, $570 billion Bank of America was fast in making an announcement that the combined bank had less than $300 million in exposure to hedge funds. However, when the third-quarter 1998 results were released on 14 October, the bank reported a $372 million charge-off, on a $1.4 billion loan to D.E. Shaw and a $529 million trading loss – some $400 million of which came from the old BankAmerica and the rest from the old NationsBank.

Coming in the aftermath of a merger heralded for trimming and cost savings, this was not good news for investors. The fact that the Nation's Bank takeover of BankAmerica has given average results would not have been so surprising, if it were not for the fact that in the mid-1980s to mid-1990s NCNB grew into one of America's big banks by way of more than 50 acquisitions using the strategy of:

- Storming in
- Cutting costs, and
- Imposing *its* reorganization.

Over several years, that M&A strategy has worked because NCNB itself had been a very efficient, well-managed bank. At the time of its first major acquisition in the Republic National Bank of Texas, *The Economist* asked how could NCNB swallow a much bigger entity. And it answered its own question by stating that the North Carolina bank was very, very efficient, keeping overhead at below 50% when many of its competitors ran up to the 68–78% range. But as the size grows and grows, diseconomies of scale show up and management is no longer in charge as it used to be.

7. The merger of Citizen & Southern with Sovran: a case study on the downside of M&As

In 1990, the merger of Citizen & Southern (C&S) with Sovran Financial was supposed to be a model for joining forces in the banking industry. That was a time when mergers were being touted as the answer to banking woes, and the C&S/Sovran merger united two superregional banks into a new corporation with $50 billion in assets.

On paper, C&S/Sovran was well positioned to serve some of the fastest growing US markets, covering a territory sprawling from Baltimore to Key West, and from the Atlantic to the Mississippi. Moreover, this was announced as a merger of equals supposed to make everyone happy – starting with the two bank's senior management. That's precisely where the problems started.

As with the merger of Italy's Unicredit and Germany's HypoVereinsbank (see Chapter 20), all top executives of C&S and Sovran were supposed to get a seat in the executive suite. The boards were to be combined and few directorships cut. The institutions were also keeping headquarters in both Sovran's base, Norfolk, Va, and in Citizen & Southern's base in Atlanta. That was a very bad decision.

Both in the United States and abroad, other bankers watched this merger to see if it was indeed the model for the 1990s, a true step in the evolution of the banking industry. But what they saw was a disaster. The merged entity, C&S/Sovran,

was swamped in bad real estate loans – an unpleasant surprise from the Sovran side. Analysts said that while the combined institution was in no danger of failing, when compared to the most strongly capitalized US banks:

- Its performance plummeted
- Loan losses soared, and
- Profits plunged, making shareholders most unhappy.

Prior to their merger, both Sovran and C&S used to rank near the top of the list of southeastern regionals in terms of return on assets (ROA). Surprise, surprise: the merged company ranked next to last. The severity of the situation became clear in April 1991 when the financial institution reported a 72% drop in first-quarter earnings.

- Non-performing assets soared 57% to $1.11 billion, from the previous quarter, and
- The management of C&S/Sovran came under pressure to prove to shareholders that it could make the transition.

Investors and financial analysts asked themselves what had happened. The answer most frequently heard was that C&S/Sovran did not do much to solve the two banks' respective problems; rather, the combined entity multiplied them. Both institutions were still digesting many smaller banks they had acquired when this deal came along and added to the chaos. C&S and Sovran executives also continued to observe an old-fashioned etiquette in dealing with each other which:

- May be fine for the golf course
- But it impedes tough decision-making and cost-cutting.

An analysis of what did happen and *what did not*, but should have happened, indicates that more than anything else the case of C&S/Sovran illustrates how difficult it is for one bank to assess the health of another (see also the case study of the two Bavarian banks, in Chapter 20). In spite of millions of dollars worth of outside help, and its own scrutiny, each merging bank *missed the danger* lurking in the other's loan portfolio.

The market did not take kindly to these events and searched for parties to take the blame. One of the opinions I heard on Wall Street was that the merged entity's management was not market-sensitive. Another, better focused opinion was that management did not do its homework pre-merger. After the bad news hit the public eye, C&S/Sovran officials insisted the merger would, in the long run, produce a bank that is:

- Financially stronger
- More efficient, and
- More competitive

than the two separate entities ever were. To justify the merger post mortem, the merged bank's management said that C&S/Sovran was already cutting better deals with vendors and expanding services; also that it had a great franchise with 'tremendous potential'.

Such undocumented assurances did not slip down well. Many shareholders were disappointed and angry about the combined bank's deliverables, and its real estate problems. Other shareholders lamented that two years earlier C&S rejected an offer from North Carolina National Bank to buy the company for $39 a share. When the problems became public knowledge, C&S/Sovran closed on the New York Stock Exchange at $20.125 a share.

One of the interesting opinions heard on Wall Street was that the story of the Citizen & Southern, in the 1970s, repeated itself all over again. At that time the 100-year-old institution had played heavily during the Atlanta real estate boom. And when the market collapsed in 1977, it nearly did too.

The man who saved the day in the late 1970s was Bennett A. Brown. When he was appointed chief executive of C&S in 1978:

- He turned the bank around quickly, shedding problem real estate assets, and
- He enacted conservative policies to keep it from falling back into the same sort of trouble.

As a result, under Brown's watch C&S made mostly small and medium-sized loans, rather than opting for fast growth. Until its merger with Sovran, it had managed to maintain a relatively small problem-loan portfolio, making itself one of the more solid, if less exciting, of southeastern regionals.

Sovran had a different culture: Its strategy was that of acting like a go-go credit institution. Furthermore, like many other regionals born during the 1980s, it was little more than a patchwork of smaller institutions hastily stitched together during the US interstate banking boom.

Created in 1983 from the merger of Virginia National Bank, of Norfolk, and First & Merchants National Bank, of Richmond, Sovran quickly went about buying several other banks. For a time, it was highly profitable, but that profitability proved to be more a function of robust markets than of strong internal controls.

The opinion of some of the insiders has been that not only Sovran's risk management was wanting, but also the bank had done little to cut costs. And the job of merging the operations of several acquired credit institutions – which is a 'must' – was on the back burner. The bank was:

- Still using three different credit card computer systems
- Had not set a central, unified credit policy, and
- Had let the acquired bank in Washington, DC operate virtually untouched for three years.

Therefore it comes as no surprise that Sovran had become heavily exposed, to the tune of $2.21 billion, to real estate in the Washington area. First Boston, which served as investment banker for both companies during the merger, was paid $10 million to assess the fairness of the transaction to both sides. Shearson Lehman Hutton and Salomon Brothers were also paid $1 million each to scrutinize the proposed deal. No warnings seem to have been sounded from any side.

For their part, C&S executives had failed to find the problem loan in Sovran's portfolio. According to at least one opinion, their efforts had been coloured by wishful thinking. Other financial analysts however suggested that it is nearly impossible for one bank to truly evaluate the loan portfolio of another bank that does not share its territory and its accounting system. The rest was mismanagement:

- At first, the merger plan sounded like an elaborate, but not sound, ceremony.
- The gaps showed up later, and also consolidation at C&S/Sovran moved at a glacial pace.

One of the major flaws in the merger plan was the pre-merger compromise that C&S and Sovran would operate separately, exactly as before, except for the integration of some backroom chores and a few nonbank affiliates. That was a dumb idea, and that plan eventually had to be scrapped.

Management finally tackled the challenges of consolidation, but even then the job was done in a loose manner. Quite characteristic is the fact that this process began with a transition team of *equal numbers* of senior officers from each side. That team then set up *28 study groups* to mull everything from employee benefits to the handling of press releases.

Some 300 people, including many managers from the former C&S and Sovran, joined the process. In some cases, the panels took eight months to reach a conclusion. This is what is meant by killing an issue by committee. With all this procrastination,

- Time passed
- Costs mounted, and
- The merged bank continued to keep two headquarters.

Besides the many other negatives, this was an arrangement that kept the corporate air fleet busy. There were also hilarious incidents. The merged entity's board was so big that its 29 members could not fit comfortably around the directors' wooden conference table. The only plan to slim the board's size was to let it shrink through attrition and retirement – or through an earthquake when the time of complacency expired, which has indeed been the case.

8. Mergers, acquisitions, and the regulators' nightmare

In banking, as in many other industries, deregulation and globalization has been a major driver in many M&A initiatives. It is more or less a general consensus that the evolving financial landscape requires companies able to operate trans-border, communicate across language barriers, overcome cultural differences, and solve technological incompatibilities. Along with any-to-any networks that make improved coordination possible, come:

- Industry enablers that address customer needs in a more customized and personalized way than has ever been possible, and
- Innovative financial products and processes that provide for better and faster solutions on an ongoing basis, but also involve several unknowns.

That's the upside. One of the problems in the downside is that the grand vision of company leaders is not always shared by their subordinates. Another problem is the clash of personalities in a merger, as well as the lack of transparency in exposure, all the way from real estate deals to derivative financial instruments.

And there is, of course, the clash of personalities which makes the solution to other M&A problems so much more difficult. Sections 2 and 3 brought to the reader's attention the Weill–Reed drift. Another well-known case is that of Purcell–Mack at Morgan Stanley.

In the 1997 merger of Dean Witter and Morgan Stanley, the surviving bank was the former, but after some time of co-habitation of the two brand names; rebranding chose Morgan Stanley, a more prestigious label. Such rebranding came swiftly after the resignation of the merged bank's president, John J. Mack, leaving the chief executive, Philip J. Purcell, originally head of Dean Witter, fully in charge.

The way rumours had it, there were personal frictions, though officially the differences were strategic. Mack was keener on merging with a commercial bank, to fight off challenges from Citi and JP Morgan, by being able to 'lend' Morgan Stanley's balance sheet to big corporate clients. Purcell preferred Morgan Stanley to strengthen the investment bank's balance sheet by building up its own banking operations rather than merging.[8]

Mack left, joined CSFB as CEO, and eventually became co-CEO of the Crédit Suisse Group after the ousting of Lukas Mühlemann. Purcell won the day but in 2005 he faced a palace revolution within Morgan Stanley, which returned John Mack to the top job. Companies planning to merge should never forget that musical chairs are, fairly often, an after-effect.

Still another problem is that many financial companies don't have the resources, size, presence of spirit, or organization to take advantage of opportunities opened through mergers. And even when they do have some of these prerequisites, they are ill-prepared to handle the risks associated with new product lines and new territories added through the merger.

It needs no explaining that another major pitfall is the aggregation of risk. The NationsBank/BankAmerica merger (see section 6) combined the fifth- and sixth-largest derivatives-holding institutions in America. As for the Bank One/First Chicago NBD merger (which preceded the Morgan Chase takeover), Bank One had avoided getting on the derivatives disaster train, but with the acquisition of First Chicago NBD and its $1.4 trillion in derivatives, it found itself in the trillion-dollars exposure club.

For regulators, the trillion-plus dollars exposure is a nightmare. Examiners trained to monitor banks for loans may not be able to get their arms around a sea of derivatives red ink, or new mammoths like Citigroup, JP Morgan Chase, and Bank of America. 'The marketplace is moving so fast that the government is unable to keep up with it,' said William M. Isaac, former chairman of the Federal Deposit Insurance Corporation. 'Federal regulatory systems are 10 years out of touch.'[9] In other terms, legislators and regulators must rethink how banks are supervised by:

- Shifting more of the risk of failure to private investors
- Encouraging the banking industry to effectively police itself, and
- Establishing new rules of supervision, with a tight grip on ballooning risk.

Neither of these prerequisites would be easy. Investors don't like their capital to be a toss-up. And, so far, self-policing has not proven to be that successful, if for no other reason because, as several analysts argue, the complexity of big banks makes it harder to manage risks.

New rules of supervision are evolving, and Basel II is an example.[10] But this happens at a relatively slow pace, because there are many conflicting interests; few banks truly appreciate that regulators aim to protect them, rather than punish them; the non-regulated hedge funds loophole is still wide open; and several unknowns exist both prior to and after the merger.

For instance, the merger partner may be able to hide the fact of being loaded with junk bonds. Or, it may have lower investment grade bonds, which turn into junk at short notice. It happened with the leveraged buyout of RJ Reynolds Nabisco, and so many other LBPs. It has also been the case with the downgrading of widely held GM/GMAC debt to junk bond status by the rating agencies. This matters because:

- Investment grade corporate debt has an average cumulative default rate of 6.4% over 20 years.
- But junk bonds average 43%, while the worst grade of junk shows an average cumulative default rate of 66% over that timeframe.

Such high default rates mean exposure, but the associated risk figures are not necessarily considered, let alone revealed, in the case of bank mergers. In fact, the resulting mega-banks may not be banks at all, if by that is meant an institution that takes deposits in and then lends the money out in the form of home mortgages, credit card debt, and business loans.

The regulators' concern is real, because even medium-sized institutions that fail can lead to torrents of red ink. In August 1990, the US government sold National Bank of Washington (NBW) to Riggs National Bank for a paltry $33 million, in a transaction that ranked among the top 10 costliest US bank rescues ever.

At the time the Federal Deposit Insurance Corporation said it would cost US taxpayers at least $500 million to bail out NBW, which was officially closed and declared insolvent. The trouble with NBW, Continental Illinois, and the Savings and Loans debacle is that the guarantees are self-defeating.

- The more protection the government provides
- The higher risks financiers are willing to take, and the greater the likelihood of a very costly settlement.

Additionally, the red ink at Continental Illinois and NBW is a trifle compared to losses that can result from derivatives trading and hedge-fund lending. Let's not forget that some of America's, and Europe's, biggest banks have been prominent losers in investments and loans to a big hedge fund, Long-Term Capital Management (LTCM).[11] In the aftermath, in September 1998, the New York Fed obliged them to rescue LTCM with their money, but they don't seem to have learned much from that experience.

Lack of transparency, particularly when deals involve non-regulated entities like hedge funds, is one of the major problems with mega-mergers in the banking industry. Merged banks may be dealing with the same hedge funds, with the result that the consolidation of their balance sheets would double the level of exposure.

As these and plenty of other examples document, regulation has become more problematic than ever before. At the same time, consolidation is doubling the number of too-big-too-fail banks that in the past the central bank and regulatory authorities kept alive at a high cost to taxpayers. According to the Federal Reserve Bank of Minneapolis, there were 11 too-big-too-fail banks in 1984 with assets of $38.2 billion or more. Two decades down the line, this number has more than tripled.

Notes

1 D.N. Chorafas, *After Basel II: Assuring Compliance and Smoothing the Rough Edges.* Lafferty/VRL Publishing, London, 2005.

2 James Grant, *Money of the Mind.* Farrar, Strauss, Giroux, New York, 1992.

3 D.N. Chorafas, *The Management of Bond Investments and Trading of Debt.* Elsevier, Oxford, 2005.

4 *Business Week*, 20 April 1998.

5 James Grant, *Money of the Mind.* Farrar, Strauss, Giroux, New York, 1992.

6 J.B. Caouette, E.I. Altman and P. Narayanan, *Managing Credit Risk.* Wiley, New York, 1998.

7 *Business Week*, 26 January 2004.

8 *The Economist*, 3 February 2001.

9 *Business Week*, 27 April 1998.

10 D.N. Chorafas, *Economic Capital Allocation with Basel II: Cost and Benefit Analysis.* Elsevier, Oxford, 2004.

11 D.N. Chorafas, *Managing Risk in the New Economy.* New York Institute of Finance, New York, 2001.

Case Studies on Big Bank Mergers in Europe

1. Introduction

Since the late 1990s, in an effort to compete in the increasingly global marketplace, European banking and financial services companies have been rushing into mergers and acquisitions. Practically, however, a good deal of it proves to be wishful thinking, an example being the on–off merger of Commerzbank first with Deutsche Bank then with Dresdner Basnk, as well as several other rumoured deals that never saw the light of day.

It was the UK particularly which saw some notable M&A cases in European banking in the go-go 1990s. Royal Bank of Scotland took over National Westminster after the latter was wounded by huge losses from options at NatWest Markets. And a demutualized Halifax Building Society merged with the Bank of Scotland to create HBOS, and there were other deals like the acquisition of Midland Bank by HSBC, and of Abbey National by Santander.

In France, Banque Nationale de Paris merged with Paribas; Crédit Lyonnais was acquired by Crédit Agricole; and CIC, a privatized group of regional banks, became takeover targets. In late 1997 and 1998 there were the takeovers of Belgium's Banque Bruxelles Lambert by the Dutch banking group ING; and the merger of Swiss Bank Corporation with Union Bank of Switzerland (see section 3).

In Finland, Union Bank of Finland and KOP merged to create Merita, which became the country's biggest bank, and one eager to merge with Sweden's Nordbanken. Nordbanken (the former PK Banken), where the Swedish state held a 60% share, was once an emergency room patient. Nordbanken's turnover was slightly higher than Merita's, but it had 7000 employees while Merita had 15 000. Analysts said the restructured Nordbanken would show:

- A better net profit than Merita
- Its running costs would be lower, and
- It would be taking its profit from actual banking business, not from the proceeds of selling off assets.[1]

In a way different from that characterizing other mergers, both Nordbanken and Merita planned to hand over their assets to a holding company in a non-cash transaction, under the aegis of which both banks operated separately. The ownership of the holding company was divided in such a way that Merita and Nordbanken had equal voting rights, but the Swedish partner held 60% of the equity.

As with mergers, acquisitions, and takeovers in the US finance industry, which we studied in Chapter 19, not all mergers in European finance worked as planned. Neither were they free of management friction. Following the Bavarian marriage of Bayerische Vereinsbank with Bayerische Hypo-Bank, the new institution, known as HypoVereinsbank (HVB):

- Became Germany's second-largest, and
- Rapidly expanded abroad, particularly in Poland and in Austria, where it bought Bank Austria.

But the merged bank was hit by the twin forces of overstretching its financial resources and of discovering a swarm of bad loans in the books, particularly real estate loans at Hypo-Bank's side. As it should be expected, this created frictions on the board of management (more on this issue in section 2).

Neither did different sorts of partnerships and alliances between European credit institutions deliver as expected. In September 1999 Commerzbank, Germany's fourth-biggest, was negotiating the creation of a pan-European investment bank with Crédit Lyonnais in France, BCI Intesa of Italy and Banco Santander Central Hispano SA in Spain. 'We now are pursuing the enticing idea of building a joint investment bank,' said Martin Kohlhausen, chairman of Commerzbank, in an interview with the newspaper *Die Welt*, adding that a combined four-nation investment bank eventually could pave the way for a full merger of the parent-company banks.[2]

- *If* it had come about, that merger would have created a cross-border banking institution capable of taking full advantage of the European single currency.
- But it did not happen that way. Not even the investment banking plans materialized, nor was there a commercial banking alliance.

This failure should be judged in light of the fact that, in commercial banking, Commerzbank has, for three decades, been associated with Crédit Lyonnais, Hispano, and Banco di Roma in a loose alliance. What had changed with the 1999 plans, was the replacement of Banco di Roma (which after its merger with the Savings Banks of Rome Province merged into Capitalia), with BCI Intesa – Italy's largest bank. The lack of deliverables has shown that such cross-border alliances are easier said than done.

Notice should also be taken of the shopping spree of the west to the east. After the fall of the Iron Curtain, many Western European credit institutions aggressively pursued acquisitions of Eastern European banks. Polish, Ukrainian, and Romanian credit institutions are examples.

The 1990s saw a fire sale, but by 2005 the prices being paid for East European banks suggested that not everything there is a bargain. For instance, the cost of accounting a 61.9% stake in state-owned Banca Commerciale Romana (BCR), Romania's biggest bank, hit 3.4 billion euro ($4.2 billion), and the purchase of Ukraine's Aval Bank by Austria's Raiffeisen International was confirmed at $3.2 billion.

Experts suggested that the expected price for BCR, at 4.6 times book value, was fair, because the bank had assets of $9 billion and a profit of $200 million in 2004. The last two bidders, Austria's Erste Bank and Banco Comercial Portugueses, have been hoping that Romania's economy will grow fast enough to make the price worth paying, capitalizing on expected convergence of the region's economies with Western Europe.

2. The takeover of HypoVereinsbank by Italy's Unicredit

HypoVereinsbank (HVB) was born in 1997/1998, in the aftermath of a not so happy merger between Bavaria's Bayerischen Vereinsbank and Bayerische Hypo-Bank. This created Germany's second largest financial institution. Size, however, did not particularly help, and in a short span of years, in January 2003, there was a major change in management. A short flashback helps in appreciating the pains that came as an after-effect of the merger.

Both Vereinsbank and Hypo-Bank were primary lenders, mainly addressing the same market (Bavaria), and having plenty of overlapping operations. This was not a textbook case of synergies that might be derived from a merger.

Trouble erupted after an early November 1997 admission by the merged bank that it would have to take a DM 3.5 billion ($2.1 billion) charge to cover losses, mainly on property loans. These were made by Hypo-Bank in the early 1990s without (so it seems) due consideration of the different borrowers' creditworthiness.

The way it was reported in the press, Albrecht Schmid, the merged bank's chairman and formerly boss of Vereinsbank, suggested that former Hypo managers and auditors had shown negligence. This rattled Eberhard Martini, Hypo's former chairman, who was sitting on the merged bank's supervisory board. But the entity planned to capitalize on some of its strengths to overcome that adversity.

Because of its relatively small exposure to emerging markets and hedge funds, in 1998 HVB had hoped to outshine rivals, such as Deutsche Bank and Dresdner Bank, which had been badly hit by market turmoil. In a manner similar to that of C&S/Sovran however (see Chapter 19), internal friction had a negative effect. Adding to these frictions was the fact that the two banks' cultures are very different:

- Vereinsbank's bankers tended to be rather conservative.
- The risk-takers seem to have been on the side of Hypo-Bank.

Before HVB pruned its balance sheet, however, came the acquisitions spree in Austria and Poland. Shopping around in a big way satisfied egos and an expansion strategy, but it weakened HVB's finances. This led to a change in management, and hopes revived about a turnaround.

In the opinion of some financial analysts, on his accession to the banking group's top job, Dieter Rampl, HVB's new CEO, took on one of the toughest jobs in European finance. As the new CEO he had to grapple with:

- Mounting losses
- Tumbling credit ratings, and
- A share price less than half what it was a year earlier.

Additionally, Rampl had to deal with a massive $460 billion loan portfolio riddled with bad debts. At the positive side, HVB had more than $730 billion in assets, making it not only Germany's second biggest, after Deutsche Bank, but also 10th in the world. Also, on the 'plus' side was HVB Group's core business in Bavaria, from both Bayerische Hypo-Bank and Vereinsbank, as well as the fact that the bank:

- Owned Bank Austria, the biggest in Austria
- Had the largest presence of any Western bank in Eastern Europe
- Was a major player in the Dutch property market, and
- Had 8.5 million retail customers, while being Europe's largest mortgage lender.

Additionally, in Germany HVB was the leading lender to the *Mittelstand*, the small and medium-sized companies that form the backbone of the economy. Analysts and investors, however, wondered how, with all these assets, HVB was in danger of going under. Also, why did HVB's exposure skyrocket?

Much has been said about the loan problems brought along by the weaker partner in the merger, the Bayerische Hypo-Bank. In the early and mid-1990s, the mortgage company made real estate loans worth billions. When, after unification, Germany's 'eastern boom' went bust, and property in the rest of Germany tanked along with the economy, HVB was left with a load of bad debt which weighed on its balance sheet. Moreover, HVB made loans to plenty of German companies that went bankrupt:

- From big corporations such as the construction outfit Phillip Holzmann, the Kirch media group, and engineering firm Babcock Borsig
- To a lot of *Mittelstand* companies with weak balance sheets, where HVB lent most of its money.

In turn, this obliged the bank to make new bad-debt provisions of $1.25 billion in the third quarter of 2002, more than double its operating profit of $545 million. With the once mighty German economy remaining in the doldrums, the years that followed were no better.

With these statistics in mind, analysts expected the HVB's new management to make some bold moves. But they also foresaw the bank's loan losses could continue, leading to merger profits or even to pretax losses. This had to be compared to the Group's paltry market capitalization, which could make it the victim of a takeover bid – which happened in 2005, with the Unicredit takeover of HVB.

The Italians' has been by all accounts a rather friendly takeover. Critics have been sceptical, however, about the interpretation of the word 'friendly'. Some said that, in a manner resembling the merger of C&S with Sovran Bank in the United States, HVB management was more keen on negotiating board membership and executive positions in the merger entity than shareholder value.

There was, also, the regulator's consent to be acquired. This seems to have posed no major problem, neither in Germany, nor in Italy, though the governor of the Bank of Italy was venomously opposed to the acquisition of major Italian banks by other European Union financial institutions (see section 7 on the BPI scandal). Led by Alessandro Profumo, its CEO, Unicredit launched a public offer for HVB which in late October 2005:

- Reached 74.26% of subscriptions
- This was well above the pre-established minimum of 65%.

Much has been said of the weight, in that favourable stockholder reaction, of Munich Re, which controlled 18.3% of HVB, and of Bavarian foundations that contributed another 3.7%. What those who voted for Unicredit's takeover hoped to gain is benefits from a combined bank which:

- According to its top management's hopes could generate annual profits of nearly 1 billion (prior to taxes) *if* everything goes well.

- Would be present in 19 countries, with leading positions in Italy, Germany, and Austria, and with 126 000 employees, and
- Would have assets of over 300 billion euro (more than $350 billion), roughly divided 50–50 between the two banks, with an edge at Unicredit.

Nothing, however, is cast in stone. First the antitrust authorities of the European Union have been investigating monopoly risk that might result from combined Unicredit/HVB operations in Poland, Slovakia, and the Czech Republic. Though Brussels seems initially to have given the green light, nobody can guarantee what might happen further down the line.

A great deal of the Italian bank's motivation for this particular acquisition has been HVB's control of Bank Austria Creditanstalt – the jewel in its crown. There has been, and still is, tension in Vienna in regard to Unicredit's entry, regarding sharp reductions in head count and loss of the relative independence the Austrian bank has had so far.[3]

To overcome the tensions, Unicredit accepted that Bank Austria would maintain autonomy as a 'regional bank', as well as becoming the centre of management of controlled credit institutions in Eastern Europe. This, however, will make the new Unicredit an entity with three heads: Milan, Munich, Vienna – surpassing even the famous two-headed eagle of the Byzantines, Russians, and Austrians.

Worse yet is the concession made to the labour unions, offering them the possibility of blocking in a general assembly important strategic decisions of the banking group. This is a poisoned chalice, probably offered without due consideration of unintended consequences. All three main constituents of the banking group – Unicredit, HypoVereinsbank, Bank Austria – are known to be crowded with unnecessary personnel because of backward-looking European labour laws. Giving labour unions a veto on redimensioning may prove to be the nearest thing to a self-inflicted death sentence.

3. Swiss Bank Corporation and the new UBS

After the merger of the Union Bank of Switzerland (UBS) and of Swiss Bank Corporation (SBC), which at its time created the world's second-largest bank, United Bank of Switzerland (new UBS), analysts were quick to predict continued consolidation. Some analysts predicted that as the 20th century was coming to a close, European merger activity could become as intense as it was in the United States in the 1980s.

At time of the merger UBS was Switzerland's No. 1 big bank. SBC was third in the line, with Crédit Suisse in-between. The old UBS was a well-managed and more or less conservative bank, but it had made a couple of major mistakes as it expanded into derivatives. Bankers on SBC's side were like Spitfire pilots in strategic acquisitions, and rather ahead in derivatives following takeovers of US institutions specializing in exotic products.

The purchase in 1992 of O'Connor Associates, a Chicago firm whose *forte* was trading equity derivatives, had given the Swiss Bank Corporation a chance to push both into the Chicago and New York markets, and into the City of London, in an untraditional way. It did so by importing O'Connor's expertise into the other markets.

Rather than struggling to gain relationships with companies that already had chosen a merchant bank as their adviser, SBC capitalized on newly acquired know-how and built a trading business based on derivative financial instruments. Then, it used its edge in that particular market to devise innovative one-off deals for:

- Client companies, and
- Institutional investors.

After it realized that Swiss Bank Corporation simply did not have the sort of business relationships Warburg and Schroders had in the City of London, its management decided to make core profits by trading and mounting ambushes on the better-established investment banks, by means of corporate finance deals that often involved O'Connor expertise.

At the time, financial experts in London said that such an aggressive strategy hardly endeared SBC to the banks whose business it was raiding. For its part, SBC realized that it had little to lose from provoking such conflict, but much to gain from the image of being an outsider breaking into the City.

To become institutionalized as a London-based bank, mid-May 1995 Swiss Bank Corporation took over S.G. Warburg's. This acquisition provided SBC with plenty of skill and connections in investment banking operations. The bid also cleared the way for Mercury Asset Management, the fund manager controlled by Warburg, to become independent (eventually acquired by Merrill Lynch).

The SBC acquisition ended the private business life of Britain's leading investment bank. The deal had been engineered by Marcel Ospel, then head of international banking at Swiss Bank Corporation, who later became SBC's, and the new UBS's, CEO. That was SBC's third big acquisition in four years, following the purchase of trader O'Connor and asset manager Brinson Partners. In the City, the verdict was that S.G. Warburg failed to create a global investment bank as an independent entity.

The £860 million ($1.38 billion) price for S.G. Warburg, represented a 7.3% premium to net assets, reflecting the fact that during the previous few years Warburg's business had not performed so well. The failed merger attempt of Warburg with Morgan Stanley also had its impact. By contrast, Deutsche Bank's 1987 purchase of Morgan Grenfell had gone for 2.5 times book. In the one as in the other case, putting the businesses together as a well-functioning entity was no trivial task.

One of SBC's biggest challenges was to restore morale and stem the defection of top staff. SBC Warburg also had to work hard to develop a strong culture of its own, avoiding the risk of bitter infighting, which unavoidably results in the loss of clients and staff. These were also brand name challenges. In the end, some years down the line, all of its acquired investment banks, in the United States and the UK came under a single UBS banner.

According to insiders, the acquisitions in the United States and Britain brought a change in culture to SBC. As we saw, the purchase of O'Connor Associates helped the Swiss bank to concentrate on trading, and on derivatives. On the other hand, while buying Warburg weighed down SBC profits in the short term, this deal allowed SBC to become, in one strategic M&A deal:

- Europe's pre-eminent investment bank, and
- The world's largest underwriter of equities.

Moreover, besides being a top equities issuer, SBC Warburg was a force in foreign exchange and Eurobonds. Still, even with Warburg, SBC lacked the distribution network it needed to tap the big US market for corporate debt issues. And though it was expanding its foothold in Asia, SBC remained a second-tier player without another major takeover.

All told, the Warburg acquisition is a good example of positive results with M&As. Yet, immediately after, a big strategic question for UBS has been how to build a strong US presence. One option was to grow organically, using Warburg's outpost in New York and O'Connor in Chicago. But since no foreign institution has yet managed to crack the US market in this way, new acquisitions were another option.

On its side, the Union Bank of Switzerland had laboured diligently for more than a decade to build a first-class international network in investment banking – from New York and Los Angeles to Tokyo and London. This network was a prime asset, so much so that in the mid-1990s a takeover artist, who headed what was then Switzerland's only hedge fund, tried to acquire UBS, split its strong international banking network from the parent, spin-off the operations in Switzerland, and concentrate on managing the global investment business.

That plan failed, but UBS's defences, following the two derivatives' misfortunes, were not strong enough to repel SBC's approach. Along with the acquisition of the UBS global investment banking network there was profit projected from the sale of many UBS assets. This made a merger with UBS SBC's top target.

The integration that followed the merger between Swiss Bank Corporation and Union Bank of Switzerland resulted in the elimination of some 13 000 jobs worldwide, a large number being in Switzerland. Many analysts, however, thought that job cuts, though substantial, were not enough by themselves to cut costs quite substantially.

- The merged banks' overall cost structure needed to be remoulded, and
- Particular attention had to be paid to major expense chapters, information technology being an example.

Both SBC and UBS, the merged banks, provide an interesting example of the potential that exists for very significant cost-cutting in IT. Over 1997, for instance, UBS increased its (already high) spending on information technology by almost 150% – becoming one of the top ten IT spenders in Europe, ahead of rivals like ING and Deutsche Bank[4] – but also one of the top financial institutions in information technology.

For its part SBC had spent lavishly to buy a 25% interest in Perot Systems, then handed over to Perot Systems the responsibility for its information technology renewal. That project rolled on for about 4 years. Deliverables were scarce, but costs were high, as SBC's old and new IT infrastructure ran in parallel. SBS had much to gain by dropping this project and capitalizing on UBS's advanced system design.

What about the business prospects which followed the UBS/SBC merger? At the end of 1997, a *Business Week* article was to suggest that the nascent United Bank of Switzerland would have $910 billion under management, making it a world leader, at that time. The same article, however, pointed out that the bank's geographic distribution was uneven.

- 50% of that business was in Switzerland
- 25% in the European Union

- 10% in the United States, and
- 15% in other countries including Japan.[5]

Equally important was the proper balance of business and income. This required accurate identification of channels from which the merged banks' turnover will be coming. The same *Business Week* article suggested that in terms of profit generators the 'new UBS' depended for its income:

- 40% on private banking
- 28%, on investment banking
- 17%, on consumer and corporate banking
- 6%, on institutional asset management, and
- 9% on other channels.

These were prognostications rather than statistics, because after the mergers come relocations of strengths. In fact, immediately after the merger the combined operations of the two banks lost business, particularly so in private banking. This hurt the most given that 40% of the merged banks' income was in this channel. Table 20.1 presents statistics on this downsizing by comparing 2000 results to those of 1999. (From the 2000 Annual Report of UBS.)

Table 20.1 Loss of client deposits from 1999 to 2000 (CHF billion) at the New UBS

	31 December 1999	31 December 2000	% change
Assets under management by client type			
Institutional	376	300	−20%
Non-institutional	198	196	–
Institutional assets under management by client location			
Europe, Middle East, and Africa	185	160	−14%
The Americas	140	100	−29%
Asia-Pacific	51	40	−22%
Total	376	300	−20%
Institutional assets under management by client mandate			
Equity	125	89	$29%
Asset allocation	130	94	−28%
Fixed income	90	77	−15%
Private markets	31	40	+29%
Total	376	300	−20%

Source: UBS Annual Report, 2000

At the time, when the UBS/SBC merger took place, in Zurich's financial market, the City of London, and on Wall Street analysts suggested that as the big get bigger, medium-sized banks will have to merge or seek niche markets. They also prognosticated that the strategy of the big who want to remain at the top tier would be to build:

- A world-wide money management network, and
- An investment banking institution that can remain a global leader.

In all likelihood, this has also been the issue in the mind of the new UBS top management. On 12 July 2000 the then UBS President and CEO Marcel Ospel, and PaineWebber Chairman and CEO Donald B. Marron, made a deal to create a global investment services organization. More precisely, UBS picked up the American private client franchise from PaineWebber for $10.8 billion.

On paper, PaineWebber gained access to UBS's European research and global reach. But as the financial news indicated by late July 2000, the US broker suffered a haemorrhage of its best staff, as people got jittery about personnel reduction. For its part, Wall Street did not see the synergy of that particular merger. Merrill Lynch downgraded UBS to *neutral* from *accumulate*, while the acquirer's stock tumbled 9% in one day, to CHF 135.

- Since UBS agreed to buy PaineWebber at a 74% premium, the latter's stock rose by 34%.
- By contrast, UBS shareholders got burned because this acquisition magnified risks that were cultural, operational, and financial.

Neither did Wall Street experts count on the merger propelling UBS and PaineWebber into the major league of investment banks such as Goldman Sachs, or Morgan Stanley. PaineWebber had relatively weak investment banking, institutional, and asset-management operations. 'The UBS/PaineWebber deal seems to pose little risk to major US securities firms,' wrote Merrill analyst Judah S. Kraushaar in his report.[6]

UBS, however, continued to expand by courting both old and new financial markets. In October 2005 it gained a 20% holding and management control of Beijing Securities. This has been the first time a foreign investor has been granted a direct stake in a licensed Chinese domestic broker. That acquisition followed a 2004 coup by Goldman Sachs, who was allowed to set up a domestic investment bank in China, over which it claims future control rights.[7]

4. Deutsche Bank and its investment banking ambitions

German and other nations' banks who ventured with acquisitions abroad have neither been free of digestion troubles nor faced an easy transition to global investment banking role. An example is provided by the Deutsche Bank, which began life in 1870 with a licence from Kaiser Wilhelm I to conduct banking business of all kinds. As capital markets became internationalized, Deutsche struggled to keep up, and its takeovers did not have a very happy ending.

Critics say that while Deutsche Bank's international strategy was laudable, its management failed on two counts: It did not start by first building the necessary human capital, and it diverted too much money away from German company financing – its classical business mission. Deutsche is believed to have spent upwards of $3 billion since 1989 trying vainly to join the top league of global institutions. The money-letting started in 1989 when Deutsche bought Morgan Grenfell, a British merchant bank.

- It left Morgan Grenfell largely to its own devices, and
- Then, after five years, it decided to integrate its acquisition more fully.

With this, came numerous problems and defections. Evidently, a fund-management fraud did not help, raising questions about Deutsche Bank's internal controls. It also left the German credit institution with hundreds of millions of dollars worse off.

During the years of the British investment bank's free rein, Deutsche Bank had lavishly endowed its London-based daughter to buy itself a place in the global big league of investment banking. But this much-trumpeted foray by Deutsche Morgan Grenfell (DMG):

- Has been costly and disappointing, and
- It failed to reach its goals in many respects.

This and a series of other acquisitions (discussed in this section) have also threatened to put Deutsche at a disadvantage. Analysts both in the City of London and on Wall Street suggested that Deutsche had not only to pull off a major investment banking acquisition but also to gain some big name clients – if it really wanted to get out of the also-ran status as a deal-maker.

The need for a major acquisition might have been in the mind of Deutsche's top management in the early to mid-1990s, but substandard earnings frustrated the German bank's M&A strategy. As an example, Deutsche Morgan Grenfell's $492 million in earnings in 1996 amounted to only a 12% return on equity (ROE) – as contrasted to US investment banks which show a 15–30% ROE figure.

According to the opinion of some London City experts, until it was able to put its ROE act together, Deutsche Bank's management would find it difficult to justify putting roughly one-quarter of the entity's capital on the line for DMG and investment banking at large. At the time, unofficial reports in Frankfurt suggested that Deutsche's board:

- Has long been split on the wisdom of the DMG experiment, and
- Worsening conditions strengthened the hand of the sceptics.

Adding to Deutsche Bank's own management challenges were the prevailing criteria for beefing-up investment banking fortunes in the 1990s. The key trend was to pirate talent by overpaying, which, most evidently, had negative effects on the bottom line.

During 1997 and 1998 Deutsche Bank's strategy was to attract teams of investment bankers from top-name rivals, paying extravagant sums, quite disproportionate to results being expected. In parallel, there has been a change in brand names, with Deutsche Morgan Grenfell, the parent company's investment-banking arm, folded into a new unit: Deutsche Bank Securities (DBS).

Rumours had it that one of the reasons for rebranding was that Deutsche Bank had been actively looking for acquisition of an investment bank in America. Sometimes the Morgan Bank was mentioned as the target, and in other cases the name of Bankers Trust came up. Both US institutions, however, were wounded from losses in East Asia, in Russia and, most particularly, in derivatives.

- The search for an acquisition ended with a $9.2 billion purchase.
- This was hardly cheap, at 2.1 times Bankers Trust's book value (remember that SBC got Warburg at nearly book value).

On Wall Street many analysts doubted the wisdom of the Bankers Trust acquisition, which could simply promote Deutsche Bank from the third division of global investment banks to the second. This was no big deal; it was not worth $9.2 billion; and it could hardly promote the image of Deutsche Bank as an investment banker. Over and above spending big money unwisely, the German bank had indigestion problems.

Ironically, Deutsche might have escaped a bad deal without losing face by pulling out at the 12th hour because of a Holocaust hurdle. In New York, the city comptroller, whose threat of sanctions against Swiss banks helped persuade them to resolve Holocaust claims, said that Deutsche Bank's proposed purchase of Bankers Trust should be delayed until similar claims were settled by German banks.

When the US Federal government, and state governments, reviewed this proposed merger, they should consider how Deutsche Bank is dealing with Holocaust-related claims, said Alan Hevesi, the city comptroller, in prepared remarks. This position had weight, because the $9.2 billion deal had to be approved not only by the US Federal Reserve but by state banking officials as well. Deutsche Bank was struck with a golden axe, but its top management did not appreciate its luck as subsequent events showed.

- With the 1999 takeover of Bankers Trust, Deutsche became one of the three largest banks in the world
- But at the same time it became one with the largest derivatives exposure, and everything this means in terms of risk.

In the aftermath the German credit institution was almost unrecognizable in regard to its role as the bank of German industry created in 1871 by Georg von Siemens. Or in comparison to the vital role it played in such infrastructure projects as financing construction of the Berlin–Baghdad Railway.

Critics say that all that mega-merger achieved, at great cost, was that the then Deutsche Bank chairman Rolf Breuer turned his institution into one of the world's most aggressive derivatives players – a far cry from the strategy followed by his predecessors, Dr Abs or Dr Herrhausen. With this big switch, the German bank entered full speed into uncharted territory, evolving:

- From an institution traditionally tied to industry financing
- To a significant player in global derivatives which led it into the LTCM hedge fund debacle and Russian GKO bonds speculation.

Additionally, instead of expanding Deutsche Bank's investment banking activities and leading to the acquisition of some big name US customers, the Bankers Trust merger brought mainly troubles. There has been musical chairs as well, as the Deutsche management board let the Bankers Trust CEO go because his annual compensation was nearly equal to what all other Deutsche Bank board members were taking home – counted together.

Another mistake was relabelling the acquired institution. Bankers Trust was a *name* in the United States. Deutsche renamed it Taunus, a mountain near Frankfurt known to local residents but meaning absolutely nothing to the US market. Yet, it was the US market, and not some Frankfurt neighbourhood, to which the acquired entity addressed itself and its services.

Well beyond other major errors by the German bank's top management was the great dose of financial poison due to accumulated derivatives exposure that Deutsche Bank acquired with Bankers Trust. With it, Deutsche was ascending to the non-enviable position of No. 2 in the derivatives world of *toxic waste*, right after JP Morgan Chase.

Of course, it might have been even worse, because of a contemplated merger in 2000 which, happily for both institutions, never materialized. That would have brought together Deutsche Bank, the Morgan Bank, and two long, long lists of derivatives positions. Also discussed in 2000 was a merger of Deutsche Bank and Dresdner Bank. Were these mergers motivated by the existence of a similar culture? Of complementary strengths? Of thoroughly studied risk and return? Of the possibility to increase shareholder value?

- Existing evidence suggests that the answer to all these queries is: *No*.
- The most likely is that in the background of such on-again/off-again M&As was only *ego value*, and the risk that goes with it.

The good luck of some of the banks with such hit and run merger plans ensures that their ephemeral wishes go into the waste basket, rather than ending in disaster. In the Deutsche and Dresdner case, the No. 1 and No. 3 in Germany, neither institution was, or is, a strong investment banking player globally. And neither seems to have carefully studied, beforehand, whether the contemplated merger made sense.

5. Dresdner Bank and the takeover of Wasserstein Perella

Aside from the forays into investment banking, guided by *prestige* and the disastrous effect of *ego* power, several mergers between credit institutions are driven by domestic considerations in an overbanked retail market. As such, they might justify themselves *only if* costs are pruned ruthlessly, and the efficiency of the resulting institution is increased by leaps and bounds.

Mergers that expand the institution's product line and/or its geographic coverage outside its home country usually come under the umbrella of 'greater stockholder value'. In the general case, this is a weak argument, and the same is true of other given reasons: for instance, better service to corporate clients at home and abroad with intensified business relations to boost earnings. Only UBS, to my knowledge, provides positive results in regard to the latter concept.

Therefore, the jury on mergers that seek to achieve combined retail and investment banking operations is still out. Existing evidence is not positive. A case in point is the takeover of Kleinwort Benson, a British investment bank, by Dresdner Bank, the third largest in Germany. What many European banks targeting investment-type corporate activity in Europe, America, and Asia forget, when adopting a product line extension strategy, is that:

- US investment bankers are already on the spot, and
- They are confronted with overcapacity in their own business.

Moreover, for European banks entering the global investment banking arena the pressure is being increased by the growing competition not only from US investment banks like Merrill Lynch, Morgan Stanley, Goldman Sachs, JP Morgan, and others, but also Europe's own new entrants.

This is what Deutsche Bank discovered the hard way, and this is what in September 2000 hit this credit institution when Bruce Wasserstein sold it his investment banking boutique for $1.37 billion. Did the German bank, with $419 billion in assets, act foolishly? Wall Street thought so, as analysts have been negative on the deal, claiming that:

- Dresdner Bank overpaid, and
- It did not get what it really needed to become a world-class investment banking player.

Despite Wasserstein Perella's strong reputation as a mergers and acquisitions specialist, its purchase did not transform Dresdner into a universal institution, or into one well-encamped in American investment banking. Besides, after becoming one of Dresdner Bank's largest shareholders in the aftermath of the merger, Bruce Wasserstein left having being lured by Lazar Frères for that bank's top job.

At the end of the day, what Dresdner got for its money was a 12-year-old firm that made its name by advising companies in telecoms, media, and technology, like Time Warner. In Time Warner's case Wasserstein Perella worked out its $165 billion merger with AOL, which had the distinction of being one of the worst mergers ever.

The Dresdner takeover of Wasserstein Perella, which was much criticized by experts, came five years after Dresdner Bank bought London based-investment bank Kleinwort Benson, which it merged with the new acquisition to create the Dresdner Kleinwort Wasserstein (DKW) investment banking unit.

- Wrongly, Dresdner management believed DKW would be powerful enough to draw in new clients both in Europe and in the US.
- But on Wall Street, analysts were most sceptical about whether or not this game plan would work, and they were proved right.

According to experts, to cover the acquisition cost of $1.37 billion in Dresdner shares, the DKW investment banking division would have to earn a 10% return on equity. This meant increasing its earnings to $135 million, almost three times the $50 million in net income Dresdner projected for 2001 – a very difficult feat.

Critics also added that who gained most from the merger were not Dresdner's stockholders but Bruce Wasserstein, probably holding about a 3% stake in Dresdner's equity. At the same time, however, the irony was that Wasserstein was also a loser, because the capitalization of Dresdner caved in in the aftermath of mounting problems, many of them in the investment banking arena.

In Frankfurt, the sound of trumpets heralding the merger of the investment arm of Dresdner Bank with New York-based Wasserstein Perella had long died away when downsizing began in July 2001. After the high stakes of hiring new staff at inordinate prices, when the expected business did not materialize more than 1000 jobs were axed at Dresdner Kleinwort Wasserstein as a direct result of:

- Lack of investment banking clients, and
- A general market downturn which came after the 2000 equity market bust.

Staff cuts fell most heavily in the bank's operations outside Europe, especially in Asia, with slimming down representing at least 12% of DKW's 8500 employees. As with most other staff trimming, this move was part of a restructuring that accompanied the decision by Allianz Insurance, the owner of Dresdner Bank, to integrate DKW fully, abandoning its earlier plans to give it a separate stock market listing.

Bruce Wasserstein, then chairman of DKW, was said to have been in heated talks with Allianz, just days after the German insurer completed its takeover of Dresdner Bank. At about the time Allianz formally announced its takeover, in March 2001, senior management at Dresdner Bank said its investment banking arm would be made into a separate legal entity with the goal of taking it public.

This was bad timing. It also counted without the new owner's will. Subsequently, Dresdner management changed its mind, probably under Allianz pressure. It is also rumoured the insurer received some interest in DKW from potential

European and US bidders but none that was satisfactory. In the end, DKW stayed with Dresdner as a not-so-well performing business unit.

6. The ABN Amro and other merger strategies

ABN (Algemene Bank Nederland) and Amro (Amsterdam Rotterdam Bank) were both well-to-do and internationally active Dutch financial institutions. At the time of their merger, heralded as one of equals, experts said that this operation had a lot more to do with creating a bank big enough to discourage predators, than with any other single reason.

In August 1990 when ABN and Amro merged, one theory in banking circles was that the two banks hastily decided to join forces, with the encouragement of the Dutch Central Bank, because they faced takeover threats from West German, British, and Japanese financial institutions. In fact, the Japanese were already at home in both of them, albeit with a minor investment.

Nippon Life Insurance, Japan's biggest insurance concern, had taken a 2% stake in Algemene Bank Nederland. The purchase represented an estimated 2.4 million ABN shares. Nippon Life also held 2% of Amsterdam Rotterdam Bank, therefore becoming the biggest foreign stockholder after the merger of the two Dutch financial institutions. (Nippon Life's most notable stake in a foreign financial institution was its $300 million holding in American Express.)

In the opinion of analysts in 1990, a great deal of the merged companies' prospects hinged on making deep cost cuts at home so that they could boost profits and pay for overseas expansion. Another crucial task was to integrate a network of 1473 branches covering nearly every Dutch town, where ABN and Amro had competed with each other from opposite sides of the same street.

When the ABN Amro merger took place, senior management at both banks believed the integration process would take less than four years, but analysts estimated it might last 7–10 years. Seen with hindsight, the analysts were right – and they were also correct in forecasting that there would not be any quick savings from cuts in the bank's 42 500 domestic staff.

Fearing that deep job cuts could alienate customers in the Netherlands, ABN and Amro guaranteed trade unions that there would be no layoffs for four years. (Notice the similarity to promises given by Unicredit to labour unions regarding job cuts at Bank Austria, in section 2.) This, most evidently, did not permit cost savings for shareholder value – as was originally planned.

Also, at merger time, analysts suggested that the combined ABN Amro operations were likely to lose business from a core of Dutch companies who previously used both banks. This is practically true of all mergers. Many client firms prefer to maintain relationships with at least two separate credit institutions to ensure they compete, and will continue to compete, on price and service.

The good news for ABN Amro stockholders has been that management was able to overcome adversity and improve the merged bank's position. In retrospect, this merger has much in common with bank mergers that took place in Canada some years later with roughly similar results. For example, in April 1998 Canadian Imperial Bank of Commerce bought Toronto Dominion Bank for 22.7 billion Canadian dollars. At the time of merger, the new CIBC had combined assets of 460 billion dollars, 2350 branches and 69 000 employees:

- CIBC shareholders were to own 51.5% of the bank, and
- Toronto Dominion stockholders were holding the balance.

In a way that emulated the case of the two Dutch banks, the CIBC deal brought together Canada's big institutions (respectively, second and fifth largest banks), making the new CIBC slightly smaller than the 23 billion dollar combination of Royal Bank of Canada and Bank of Montreal, which preceded it in January 1998. Royal Bank of Canada and Bank of Montreal had combined assets of 481.4 billion dollars when they merged.

In the UK, the merger of Lloyds and TSB (Trustee Savings Bank, a former mutual) was of a totally different type. Its target has been the British retail market, and associated economies of scale. Slowly, very slowly, the combined credit institution attained its goals, after being able to overcome cultural difference that characterized the two entities before the merger, given their origin and prevailing philosophy of management.

The consolidation of Lloyds Bank and TSB was no mega-merger of ABN Amro, CIBC, or Royal Bank of Canada/Bank of Montreal type. It was one of more measured dimensions and the challenge mainly consisted in integrating retail operations, and slimming down the branch network. In the background lies the story of the transformation of the British Trustee Savings Banks into the TSB Group, which started with the recommendations of the Page Committee in 1972. These recommendations led to a series of mergers that eventually involved:

- A central savings bank, in Britain, and
- Eighteen regional savings banks.

From this transitional phase came the flotation of TSB as a public limited company, its acquisition of banking industry status, and abandonment of the traditional form of a savings banks in 1986. As a result of privatization, the new bank found itself with a surplus of capital, a drive to get involved in various acquisitions, and the hiring of people with experience in trading.

At first, the result was a fairly significant culture clash along with questions regarding structure as the institution tried to become a fully fledged commercial bank. The main lesson to be retained from this experience is that a purely retail bank cannot transform itself into a universal bank in a short space of time. This is particularly true in a period when:

- Competition from both clearing banks and the remaining building societies is relentless.
- While great changes take place in the retail banking market, as was the case in the 1980s.

In this connection, the Lloyds/TSB merger had advantages. While TSB lost its independence, it gained from Lloyds universal banking experience. The downside of Lloyds' merger with TSB has been slow progress in solving problems, which should have been attacked head-on. For instance, it took six years to the integrate data processing systems of the two institutions.

It also took some time to ease organizational frictions, to allow ex-Lloyds and ex-TSB employees to integrate into the new Lloyds TSB structure. Happily for the merged institution, its relatively medium size within the British banking market meant there was no great concern by the British regulator about monopolistic effects. Regulatory guidelines, however, do evolve over time.

Some years down the line, in November 2002, Derek Morris, chairman of the UK Competition Commission, signalled a shift away from the one-dimensional view of competition based on companies' market share, by presenting a new economic approach to merger regulation at a London seminar. In Morris's words: 'Where you find the main players [in a market] ... consistently achieving high profits, that is one signal that maybe it's not so competitive'.[8]

In my book, Lloyds TSB would have passed this test. In research I did in London in April 2005 on bank fees for company accounts, Lloyds TSB came out with the lowest fees structure, followed by HBOS, another merged company. By contrast, Royal Bank of Scotland was at top of the fee scale, with Barclays in the middle. Where most banks failed my test was in handholding.

Critics of Morris's thesis suggested that the downside of using profits as a criterion is that it is not easy to set a profitability benchmark, before deciding whether to approve mergers and takeovers. A spokesman for the British Bankers Association said the hurdle would be hard to define. Proponents responded that in the underlying position taken by the Competition Commission was the need to set out how regulators intend to handle mergers and acquisitions providing, at the same time, continuity and transparency in M&A activities.

7. Mergers and acquisitions in the EU: the BPI scandal

British authorities saw nothing wrong with Santander, the Spanish bank, buying Abbey National. Nor did the German authorities forbid the takeover of HypoVereinsbank by Italy's Unicredit. Two other banks whose home country is in the European Union (EU) have been interested in buying major foreign credit institutions:

- Bilbao Viscaya (BBVA) of Spain acquired a stake in the Rome-based Banca Nazionale del Lavoro (BNL) and expressed its intention of gaining a majority interest, and
- The Dutch ABN Amro has been after Banca Antoniana Popolare Veneta (Autonveneta).

Both ABN Amro and BBVA were frustrated in their efforts by Dr Antonio Fazio, governor of the Bank of Italy (the reserve bank), even if the takeovers were within the letter of economic, financial, and industrial agreements which, among themselves, underpin what is known as the European Union. The agent used to counteract ABN Amro's bid for Autoveneta has been Banca Popolare Italiana (BPI, formerly Banca Popolare di Lodi). In the constellation of Italian banks, BPI ranks tenth in assets; a smaller institution than Autonveneta, which it wished to swallow.

Several Italian bankers said that BPI was a weak institution in its capital base, and it simply did not have the financial resources for such a takeover. Yet in August 2005 Dr Fazio gave approval to the Lodi Bank to buy a major stake in Antonveneta. This was a blessing on a buyout effort, as BPI had been contesting control of Antonveneta since March 2005 – even if in capitalization the Venetian institution was about 300% larger than BPI.

Beyond that, at the time of the attempted takeover BPI's CEO Gian Pierro Fiorani was under criminal investigation, with magistrates having authorized interception of his telephone calls. His alleged offences included misleading the Bank of Italy, market-rigging connected to dealings in Antonveneta shares, and creative accounting practices.

Moreover, it was said that two senior executives at Bank of Italy were worried about the strength of BPI's balance sheet. Therefore, they refused to approve Fiorani's bid. For its part, Consob, Italy's stockmarket regulator, froze BPI's takeover offer for up to 90 days, allegedly suspecting that the offer documents lacked important information. And on 2 August 2005, a judge ordered that Fiorani and his finance director be suspended for the next two months.

Italian bankers say that Fiorani had been a successful operator in transforming the former Banca Popolare di Lodi from a regional credit institution into one with a nationwide branch network. BPI acquired 137 branches in Sicily after buying eight small local banks in just five years. It also has two quoted subsidiaries, one of which is Bipielle Investimenti (more on this later).

Statistics that came to the public eye indicate that between 2000 and 2004, BPI spent roughly 6 billion euro on acquisitions. But at the same time, this torrent of M&A money weakened its finances, raising serious doubts about whether it could afford to go after a big Italian credit institution.

Critics also questioned the fact that more than half the money used for these M&As came from shareholders and customers. Since 2000, BPI and its subsidiaries have raised 3.6 billion euro from six capital increases. The credit institution has also used its branches to promote its shares to its own customers, many of whom became shareholders. It is estimated that mid-2005 BPI had about 200 000 equity investors.

According to independent opinions, while there is nothing wrong with fund raising, old and new equity holders did not really get the company's true financial picture when they invested in BPI.

- The bank's accounts seem to have been characterized by aggressive accounting practices, and
- In its profit and loss accounting BPI was treating some costs, such as those of capital increases and extraordinary personnel expenses, as intangible assets.

As such these were written off over several years rather than in one, greatly improving the annual profit figures. There were also questions over the health of the bank's balance sheet.

Supervisors usually assess the solvency of a bank by the adequacy of its core capital, which must be kept above the minimum level at all times. There seemed to be problems with BPI's ability to maintain the required capital adequacy. The way an article in *The Economist* had it, among crucial issues have been:

- Provisions against loans, which were lower than average
- Off-balance-sheet commitments which, if valued at market prices, would reduce its net assets further, and
- BPI's 20% stake in Cassa di Risparmio di Bolzano, which was overvalued by 209 million euro when measured by the price that a purchaser paid for a 10% stake in 2004.[9]

In this '*serie noire*' of financial transactions, another of the questionable deals was that, in order to beautify its balance sheet, Banca Popolare Italiana had promised to pay Deutsche Bank 330 million euro in 2008 for 30 million shares of Bipielle Investimenti – which Deutsche bought for only 198 million euro in 2003. At the end of 2004, these were worth a mere 174 million euro, roughly half the commitment to pay the German bank – a silly move by the Italian credit institution, which came to light with IFRS financial reporting.[10]

Reportedly, BPI also had other similar commitments, particularly to holders of minority stakes in its subsidiaries. At the end of 2004, these amounted to more than 880 million euro, with 500 million euro payable in cash by mid-2005, further reducing the bank's core capital. And IFRS or no IFRS, intangible assets do not count towards core capital. With IFRS:

- Goodwill will be subject to an annual impairment test, and
- All off-balance-sheet commitments will have to be marked to market.

In the aftermath, nothing short of major recapitalization can correct the fragility of BPI's balance sheet. *If* indeed BPI has overpaid for its acquisitions, *then* substantial write-downs were not only necessary, but also they had the potential to bring down the whole house of cards. To critics, BPI's case started looking more and more like a second Parmalat – so far Europe's largest scandal.[11]

Moreover, according to the same issue of *The Economist*, to beautify its balance sheet and make up for shortfalls, BPI engineered an increase of 30 million euro in expenses recovered from customers' accounts through unusual entries in the final quarter of 2004. For instance, to their displeasure, customers found on their bank statements dated 31 December 2004 charges ranging from 30 to 125 euro for:

- 'Urgent commissions'
- Post and telephone expenses, and
- 'Extraordinary commissions'.

And like with so many other companies which have things to hide, there seems to have been a major concern about transparency in financial reporting. Allegedly, the bank's 2004 accounts failed to mention that BPI had an equity investment of 154 million euro in Victoria & Eagle Strategic Fund (VESF), based in the Cayman Islands, a fairly obscure special vehicle.

Not all Italian bankers, however, have been critical of BPI's drive to keep control of Antoveneta in Italian hands. Some mentioned the French government's very negative and angry reaction to the rumoured takeover of Danone by PepsiCola; and many made reference to the efforts of the US government to fence off China National Offshore Corporation, the state-owned Chinese oil company, from acquiring the US Unocal.

But there is a difference, and a major one for that matter. Though neither of the aforementioned two cases speaks well of globalization and free trade, neither involved European Union enterprises at both sides of the transaction. By contrast, this was precisely the case with both ABN Amro/Autonveneta, and BBVA/BNL. (Finally, ABN Amro was allowed to proceed with Autonveneta's acquisition.)

While the financial staying power of Banca Popolare Italiana, and its compliance to Basel II capital requirements under IFRS accounting should be a case for Banca d'Italia to watch, with all this entails for reputational risk – obstruction to M&As between European Union banks by Euroland's central banks is a serious matter for the EU.

What has been happening in Italy is further evidence that nobody, and no state, has in its heart the aim of building a united Europe. This irrational Italian reaction is particularly damaging in the light of Unicredit's takeover of HypoVereinsbank, and Santander's takeover of Abbey National in Britain.

* * * * *

There is an interesting post-mortem to this saga. While ABN Amro went ahead with its acquisitions plans, BBVA lost interest in BNL. In came BNP Paribas, the second biggest French bank by assets. In early February 2006 it announced that it was buying a 48% stake in Banca Nazionale del Lavoro, and it would bid for the rest. The offer valued BNL, Italy's sixth largest bank, at about 9 billion euro ($10.8 billion).

- If regulators approve it, this will be the biggest foreign acquisition ever by a French bank, and
- The fifth-largest cross-border takeover in European banking after Unicredit/HVB, Santander/Abbey, HSBC/CCF and Fortis/Générale de Banque.

One of the largest Italian banks, prior to the huge merger wave that came with privatization and deregulation, BNL has been seen as a takeover target for three years. Banco Bilbao Vizcaya Argentaria, which owned 15% of BNL and, as we have seen, wanted to buy the rest, was practically blocked by the Italian authorities. Then Unipol, an Italian insurer, tried its hand as a sort of 'national saviour'. But it saw its bid rejected by the central bank for reasons connected to its financial staying power, as it was rumoured.

Notes

1 *Business Week*, 29 December 1997.
2 *International Herald Tribune*, 4–5 September 1999.
3 *La Repubblica*, 23 October 2005.
4 *Information Strategy*, December 1997/January 1998.
5 *Business Week*, 22 December 1997.
6 *Business Week*, 24 July 2000.
7 *The Economist*, 5 November 2005.
8 *Financial Times*, 18 November 2002.
9 *The Economist*, 13 August 2005.
10 D.N. Chorafas, *IFRS, Fair Value and Corporate Governance: Impact on Budgets, Balance Sheets and Management Accounts*. Elsevier, Oxford, 2005.
11 D.N. Chorafas, *Economic Capital Allocation with Basel II: Cost and Benefit Analysis*. Elsevier, Oxford, 2004.

21 The Risk of M&As: Case Studies with Mergers that Went Sour

1. Introduction

In 1840, an English canal designer was working on a plan to link lakes Corrib and Mask, in western Ireland. While the construction work was being done it was found that the interlake canal rested on porous limestone. No sooner had the water been poured in than it drained away. This set the project back several months, but a solution seemed to have been found by laying a clay bed at the canal's base. However, with the work almost completed, it was further discovered that one of the lakes was several feet lower than the other. Suddenly it dawned on those responsible that they were asking water to flow uphill, and the entire project was abandoned.[1] This interesting incident of a double failure – and of late discovery of the most serious fault – is, to a significant extent, characteristic of many M&As.

Few merger-oriented bank presidents account for the fact that in the aftermath of M&As come diseconomies of scale and loss of clients. There may also be a shift in industry appeal. The Federal Reserve calculates that banks' share of household financial assets has fallen from 90% in 1980 to just over 50% at the beginning of the 21st century, while the mutual funds' share has grown from around 10% to more than 22%.

- Commercial banks now hold only a 26% share of consumer credit, versus 74% for 'nonbank banks', and
- The banks' share of business credit has fallen from nearly 50% in 1980 to around 33%, with the capital market picking up the slack.

While it can be stated, with reason, that this is a general trend rather than one exclusively resting on bank mergers, it is no less true that banking as a service does involve handholding and that usually, after the merger of two banks with overlapping branch networks, priority is given to elimination of duplicate offices. From a cost-effectiveness viewpoint this makes sense, but the other side of the coin is that customer contact is diminished – and with it handholding (see section 5).

Quite often, both same-country and transborder mergers take place without fully accounting for the consequences. In late August 2000 Credit Suisse chief executive Lukas Mühlemann said that his bank and its investment-banking arm, Credit Suisse First Boston (CSFB), wanted to expand but that the growth would be organic: 'The primary thing is to grow under our own steam because acquisitions usually come with significant goodwill and financial costs. In addition, the subsequent integration can lead to problems.'[2]

What Mühlemann said made sense. But straight afterwards he contradicted himself and two weeks later he acquired Donaldson, Lufkin & Jenrette (DLJ), the US investment bank, for $11.8 billion. This was a ruinous deal for Crédit Suisse. Both at the time and post mortem, many analysts said.

- Mühlemann overpaid for DLJ by at least $5 billion
- Considerable overlap existed between CSFB and DLJ, especially in underwriting and trading.

Several experts suggested at the time that the CEO of Credit Suisse was taken for a ride by a better player. The better player was AXA's chairman and CEO Henri de Castries, who has been trying to find a buyer for Donaldson, Lufkin & Jenrette. AXA, the French insurer, owned a 72% stake in DLJ, which it wanted to sell.

Whether they are in same industry or concern multi-industry deals, whether in the same country, or cross-country; whether big ticket transactions or small ones, mergers, acquisitions, and takeovers can be: hugely overpriced, right-priced, or a fire sale because the other party runs out of cash. A special type of fire sale bank merger has been engineered by the Federal Reserve, and other central banks, who look for an exit strategy from supporting a failing credit institution with taxpayers' money.

As these and plenty of other cases document there are many twists associated with mergers and acquisitions. Expected top-line gains and synergies, or cost-cutting hopes, never worked out as expected. Some deals have been troubled from the start. Wells Fargo's 1996 acquisition of First Interstate Bancorp took a long time to iron out, and at least $150 million in unexpected integration-related write-offs, as well as the loss of at least $5 billion in deposits, according to Wall Street rumours.

Whether in banking, manufacturing, merchandising or other industry sectors, serious analysts see the race for size at any cost as a dangerous excess; one that is driven simply by egos and inflated share prices. Others advise great caution because bigness creates its own problems. The case studies that follow document this thesis.

2. Reasons underpinning failed M&A deals

The list of failed mergers, acquisitions, and takeover deals from the late 1990s still resonates in their collective memory. They include Daimler's $39 billion deal for Chrysler (see section 4) and Conseco's $7 billion deal for Greentree Financial. Both were spectacular busts for shareholders. Among the outstanding examples of M&A failures is America On-line's $100 billion acquisition of Time Warner (see section 3).

As these and other epic mismatches, wiping out tens of billions of dollars of wealth, demonstrate, the risks of mega-deals should never be underestimated. Such risks were further underscored on 9 February 2005, when CEO Carleton S. Fiorina resigned under pressure from Hewlett–Packard's (HP's) board of directors. After pushing through the $19 billion Compaq Computer acquisition in 2002, Fiorina failed to achieve synergies she had promised, in order to promote HP's:

- Growth, and
- Profitability.

The irony with these frequently repeated wild promises and subsequent failures is that time and again acquiring companies say to their investors and to the market that 'this deal-making will be different'. Different in what respect? In failure reasons? The truth is that no acquirers appear to have learned some important lessons taught from failures of the past. In a nutshell, these lessons underline the need for:

- Giving more thought to strategic fit
- Paying lower premiums in an M&A, and
- Spending more time and attention on integration of the merged entity, rather than letting problems resolve themselves.

Study after study has shown that the majority of M&A deals result in worse returns for shareholders of *acquiring* companies than for their competitors – though they may benefit the shareholders of companies being *acquired*. The general trend is that about two out of three big deals hurt the buying company's investors, and half of the rest leave them dissatisfied. Dissatisfaction also characterizes most of the customers of merged firms.

Over the past few years, research results that have been published by McKinsey, Booz-Allen & Hamilton, the Boston Consulting Group, KPMG, Kearney, other consultancies and many academics, indicate that 60–75% of all mergers fall down against measures such as the acquirer's:

- Revenue growth
- Share price performance, or
- Meeting the targets announced when the deal was done.

The Introduction provided evidence that in the financial industry mergers have other negative after-effects. To those already listed should be added the fact that big bank mergers balloon the combined company's derivatives portfolio and increase by so much the toxic waste in it. Chapter 19 has provided the reader with case studies on the disastrous aftermath of accumulated derivatives risk.

Another very bad strategy is 'following the trend'. Many European acquisitions in the United States have gone sour because the 'trend' is to enter the lucrative US market, no matter what's the prospect and the cost. 'Follow the leader' is rarely the best advice, because between that dictum and real-life come cultural, organizational, financial, legal, and other differences. This is to a large extent the reason why many US acquisitions have largely been a disappointment for European financial firms.

Several European banks and insurance companies have had this negative experience. An example is Zurich Financial Services Group (the leveraged formerly prosperous Zurich Insurance), which brought itself to the edge of the abyss. The ups and down have not been alien to Zurich Financial, which in 1996 spent $2 billion to buy Chicago asset manager Kemper, and in 1997 bought Scudder, Stevens & Clark for $1.6 billion.

These were acquisitions based on hope rather than analytical facts. The resulting US money manager, which became known as Zurich Scudder Investments, with $290 billion in assets, caused many headaches to its Swiss parent. Critics said that Zurich Financial's successive acquisitions have led to a cultural mismatch characterized by the clashing managerial and investment philosophies of Scudder and Kemper. As an example:

- Scudder sold no-load funds directly to clients
- While Kemper marketed load funds via brokers.

Looking at it superficially, Zurich's purchase of Scudder and Kemper made strategic sense, but merging them under mainly Scudder management was a blunder. On Wall Street experts commented that the situation was made worse by the parent company's unwillingness to delegate authority over the asset management operations. As management theory suggests, one blunder rarely comes alone.

Clashing cultures and product lines, analysts said, were partly responsible for a mass exodus of money managers, particularly from Kemper. Many customers went with them. In 2000, institutional and retail clients yanked $5 billion out of the fund which pulled Zurich's overall earnings down by 5.5% in that one year, while most of its rivals made profits.

To come out of the abyss into which it led itself, Zurich Financial changed its top management and fought for its life. But even if this was a bad M&A failure, it may not be the worst case. Deutsche Bank seems to lead the casualties list, with its earlier acquisitions, all the way to that of Bankers Trust (see Chapter 20).

According to learned opinions, it has been mainly for damage control reasons that Deutsche was selling the on-line arm of New Jersey-based National Discount Brokers (NDB) to Internet brokerage Ameritrade, just a year after it bought it. NDB's business plunged after the US dot.com and technology crash, wiping out part of the Deutsche Bank's $888 million investment – just short of a billion.

That was not the only big money thrown down the drain by German credit institutions in their effort to 'be somebody' in the United States. Dresdner Bank, too, Germany's third largest, found out the hard way that its purchase of Wasserstein Perella, in 2000, could not generate new investment banking business as expected. And Commerzbank also stated, back in 2001, a short while after acquiring it, that it wanted to sell all or part of US-based Montgomery Asset Management in exchange for a partnership with a stronger US firm.

Sometimes mergers and acquisitions unravel before they are even consumed because of regulatory action or fear of it. This is often the case when the industry sector is most vital to the economy, and the projected M&A may result in a monopolistic situation. The KPMG/Ernst & Young merger that was called off is an example. Mid-February 1998, the $16 billion global merger of KPMG and Ernst & Young, two of the then six big certified public accountants, was abandoned abruptly ending plans to build the world's biggest accountancy firm. That deal:

- Would have created a firm dominating the sector on both sides of the Atlantic, and
- It would have monopolized accounting and auditing work, which was against public interest.

By contrast, the rival merger plan of PriceWaterhouse/Coopers and Lybrand went ahead, winning regulatory approval. Sometimes, regulatory response has its mysteries. If both mergers had materialized, international companies world-wide would have had little choice beyond this duopoly. The competition authorities seem to have balked at the idea of the Big Six becoming Four, and resulting potential conflicts of interest or monopolistic effects.

As far as public auditing firms are concerned, one major area of possible conflict has been the blurring of lines between the all-important audit and other services, such as consultancy. This case has been particularly dramatized by the Arthur Andersen scandal in the first years of the 21st century,[3] which has managed single-handedly to reduce the auditing firms to a Big Four.

3. IBM's acquisition of Rolm and other mergers with cultural discontinuity

Along the issues of monopolistic risk and conflicts of interest comes the subject of *cultural discontinuity* often associated with M&As. Cultural discontinuity is the opposite to cultural clash, though the latter may be a secondary effect. An example is what happened when Exxon bought one of the upcoming business systems companies, for diversification reasons. The acquired firm was mismanaged to the point of being killed, because:

- Exxon executives knew nothing about the way a business system company operates.
- Applying oil industry management principles in a fast-moving and upcoming business equipment firm proved to be a disaster.

Business discontinuity can also characterize M&As between business sectors. A classic example has been the 1969 purchase by Xerox of Scientific Data Systems (SDS) for nearly $1 billion, which was at the time big money. This has been one of the notable disasters due to cultural discontinuity and failed integration. Six years later, Xerox shut down SDS.

High-tech acquisitions have also backfired for IBM, which is a technology company but, for a long time, having a mainframe culture. General Electric and Schlumberger also provide interesting case studies on cultural discontinuity. In each case, fast-moving technology companies bogged down when they became divisions of major corporations characterized by a totally different culture.

IBM paid $1.5 billion for Rolm, a dynamic and successful telephone equipment firm. Analysts estimate that, consequently, IBM spent nearly $1 billion (including losses and research and development expenses) trying to turn Rolm around. Finally, it sold it for $1.1 billion – a big loss on its $2.5 total investment. For IBM, Rolm was the fourth false start in a decade, as it tried to become a leader in telecommunications.

- Correctly, IBM's management had seen the telecommunications business as crucial to the company future.
- But incorrectly it thought that its (then successful) model for selling mainframes through a trained, disciplined but unimaginative grey-suited sales force could fit any industry.

In the late 1970s, IBM's Satellite Business Systems (SBS) venture failed to win a chunk of the burgeoning market for private, corporate communications networks. So management swapped its SBS ownership for 16% of MCI Communications, then the No. 2 long-distance phone company. Subsequently, IBM bailed out of MCI before its recovery was complete – which proved to be the wrong decision.

Meanwhile, IBM's 1982 investment in Canada's upcoming Mitel fizzled out because of snags in a new Mitel voice-data switch, and the mainframer's impatience in having it fixed. Experts suggest that of all these failures, the Rolm debacle was the most shocking. According to some accounts, by the time IBM bought Rolm the firm had passed its peak and was already in decline.

- Insiders say that a 1983 IBM study showed this
- But, somehow, the executives who signed off on the deal, either did not get the message or underestimated it.[4]

As happens so often with acquisitions, it looks *as if* IBM was dazzled by Rolm. Here was a model startup whose computerized private branch exchanges (PBXs) revolutionized the industry in 1975, by routing calls faster and better than electromechanical switches. Rolm's sales rocketed to $295 million by 1981 as it captured 15% of the PBX market – second only to AT&T's 36%.

By 1982, Rolm had already developed promising new products like *voice mail* – heralded as PBX software that turns a basic office phone into an answering machine. But competition was no more as passive as it used to be in the earlier years, and Rolm encountered resistance to further market penetration. The cultural discontinuity added through IBM's acquisition crucified Rolm.

Not too different in terms of cultural discontinuity has been the case of Time Warner and America On-line (AOL). To this there has been a precedent. Having merged in 1999, Time Inc. and Warner remained distinctly unmelded over several years. This was a cultural clash, which also happened with the May 1998 investment by US West, to the tune of $2.5 billion for a 25% stake in Time Warner. That investment, too, yielded no synergies.

- Yet, theoretically at least, the merger of Time and Warner was a good match (marred by the speculators' interference), and
- There might have been some synergy in US West's investment in Time Warner, as many carriers try to get a party able to provide content.

The difference between theory and real life is that the former is based on assumptions, while the latter is based on evidence. In spite of all the talk of the 1980s and 1990s, vertical integration is not necessarily the best way of producing successful media companies. Experts had even pointed this out when they said that they had many doubts about a Time Warner merger with Turner Communications.

At the time of that particular M&A, Time Warner already owned *Warner Music*, the magazine of Time Inc., various Warner Bros film businesses and Home Box Office, a movie channel. It also had America's second-largest cable distribution network. Ted Turner's empire included not just its flagship Cable News Network (CNN) and other cable channels, but also businesses such as Hanna-Barbera Cartoons and two film production companies.

In short, there was considerable product line overlap, the stuff of which cultural clashes are made. Melding the two groups together was supposed to create a global cable-TV distribution business with no equal. Its sort of programming brand power hoped to overtake that of Disney/ABC. The way optimists looked at the Time Warner/Turner match:

- The resulting company was supposed to generate $18.7 billion in revenues in 1994.
- That would have outshone nearly merged Walt Disney and Capital Cities/ABC, with joint revenues at $16.4 billion in 1994.

Pragmatists, however, commented that this was to rush to conclusions, because Time and Warner were not really integrated, and rather than concentrating on ironing out several rough spots, management would have at the same time to cope with more rough edges created by the Turner merger. As if this was not enough, five years down the line AOL, an Internet startup, took over Time Warner. This changed the No. 1 problem from cultural clash to a cultural discontinuity. From the beginning, the $100 billion merger of America On-line and Time Warner has been battered by:

- Management turmoil, and
- Accounting scandals.

First, the capital market zoomed up the combined company's equity. But then, in about two years after the unwarranted acquisition of Time Warner by much smaller, and culturally different, AOL, the combined company has lost a staggering $40 billion in market value. And while in the 2003–2005 timeframe the stock of other companies' equities recovered, that of AOL Time Warner (renamed as Time Warner) stagnated at the $17–18 level.

The management turmoil also saw to it that some of the brilliant individuals who helped to make AOL left, while the combined firm's rather mediocre management just let time go by, uncertain about which course to follow. The effort needed to resurrect Time Warner was never really undertaken. In 2005, Carl Icahn, the takeover artist, tried to get hold of the company – but either the money he put on the table was not enough, or he had become too old to repeat his past successful takeover deals.

4. DaimlerChrysler: the merger of 'equals' and its unexpected consequences

On 22 August 2003, DaimlerChrysler said that it would pay $300 million to settle class-action claims that Daimler–Benz had deceived investors by characterizing the 1998 takeover of Chrysler as a merger. But while the settlement seemed to resolve fraud claims by Chrysler investors who sought as much as $12 billion, the company still faced a legal battle with billionaire Kirk Kerkorian, who opted out of the accord (Kerkorian finally lost his claim).

Kirk Kerkorian, who controls the Metro-Goldwyn-Mayer movie studio along with the MGM Mirage casino among other holdings, contended that then Daimler–Benz CEO Jürgen Schrempp misled investors by saying the combination with Chrysler was a 'merger of equals'. According to Kerkorian, Schrempp had done so to avoid paying a takeover premium for what was once the third-largest US automobile manufacturer.

The chairman stated that the takeover premium would have amounted to an additional $5–10 billion, for gaining control of the third largest US car company. That might or might not have been true. Generally speaking, investors should appreciate that mergers of 'equals' are fairy tales, and *if* they ever happen they become very bad deals because:

- Management infighting is at its worst, and
- Till the dust settles, which takes a long time, the company drifts because nobody is in command.

DaimlerChrysler has been a transborder merger with significant disparity in share value. Chrysler's stock, which traded at $41 prior to the merger, was valued at $63 through the share offer from Daimler. In a way, this was more than a 50% premium. Behind this huge notional premium, however, existed a much more complex calculation.

Chrysler's investors were giving up one of the best-performing US industrial stocks of the 1990s in return for a minority share in a foreign company that had been through some difficult times. Assessing the value of the new DaimlerChrysler shares, both in the short and in the long term, was complicated by the incompatible price/earnings (P/E) multiples accorded to automobile companies in different parts of the world.

- The typical US car company trades at a P/E ratio of 9.
- This compares poorly to a P/E of 18 in Europe and of 25 in Japan.

In fact, at the time of the aforementioned auto industry mergers, Daimler traded at about 22 times earnings, compared with 9 times at Chrysler. This was an intriguing gap in valuation of the two firms, and it had a certain effect on the stockmarket's valuation of the other two big US automobile manufacturers, General Motors and Ford.

Technical issues also appeared to be at work in connection to the Daimler/Chrysler affair. An example is the dividend Daimler planned to pay to its own shareholders. When the merger took place, the two companies said they intended to adjust the exchange offer to take account of the lower value of Daimler stock post dividend. However, the scale of the adjustment spent too long under discussion:

- Making analysts nervous, and
- Investors uncertain about the result on the equity's value.

According to US traders, the disparity in the stock prices also reflected technical obstacles in the way of capturing the arbitrage profit that could be made from buying Chrysler stock and selling Daimler. Traders said that the impending dividend payment had made it technically impossible to short Daimler's shares. Added to this was the law of unwanted consequences, whose effects are always present in mega-mergers.

As the careful reader has appreciated through the case studies in the preceding chapters, mega-mergers have implications that are huge, while the further-out aftermath is usually invisible and uncertain at merger time. Many analysts asked: will a Chrysler/Daimler merger work? Some said that when the deal was announced, Daimler chairman Jurgen Schrempp and Robert Eaton, his Chrysler counterpart, had sold it well by emphasizing the two companies were complementary in a geographical sense:

- Mercedes has been focused on the European market
- While Chrysler was very much a North American entity, after Lee Iacocca disinvested the company's European holdings.

But at merger time, Chrysler was not so much a car maker as a light truck producer. As far as private vehicles were concerned, in the US market Chrysler had been overtaken by Honda and Toyota. Mercedes had therefore to finance the new private car products, and provide plenty of assistance in quality improvements. Short of that, it could not bring back customers to Chrysler cars.

And as in all 'mergers of equals', a great impediment to good performance was the totally different management cultures of the two firms. While at the start Schrempp and Eaton seemed to be sharing the top jobs, their relationship degenerated, partly because of Schrempp's Mitsubishi Car *coup* (a very poor decision). Besides this, history shows that CEO-sharing is rarely a good idea.

- Everything really depends on the CEO's shared vision for the new group, and
- Time and again the evidence is that there is not any shared vision (see the case of Citigroup in Chapter 19).

All this was bad news for the post-merger company and its investors. Its future looked clouded, and financial analysts were passionate about what the two men, Schrempp and Eaton, planned to do. They also saw the co-CEO approach as an acknowledgement of the culture problem faced by the two co-CEOs, and by the company at large:

- Eaton stood down after three years
- While Schrempp carried off three prizes in the aftermath of the merger: 'Manager of the Year' (1998); 'Leadership Prize' (1998) and the chairmanship of the combined firm.

Of course, the prizes did not alter the fact that there were also other downsides. A wrong management decision was that the two brands, Chrysler and Daimler, were to be kept absolutely separate. To make matters worse, the same was true of the dealerships. Neither was there any plan that Chrysler cars would be made at Mercedes–Benz plants, or vice-versa.

The two-headed eagle was flying again, as is the case with so many other mergers. Careful analysts also pointed out that there were announced no job losses, either blue or white collar. On the contrary, both companies said the merger would *create* employment. Management expected rise in output and jobs, leaving aside evidence from other mergers that jobs are more likely to fall than rise.

Another downside was the fact of poor synergy between the merged firms. If the fact that both firms were car makers is left aside, the two of them differed in just about everything: language, markets, work traditions, and governance. And in the executive suite, Chrysler's sky-high American salaries and stock options sat poorly with the German structure of:

- Lower executive pay
- Employee representation, and
- Supervisory board functions.

Those who appreciated that merging cultures is possibly the greatest art of management doubted Schrempp's words that DaimlerChrysler would have a pre-eminent position in the global automotive market. While both companies had dedicated and skilled workforces, as well as good products, other basic ingredients were lacking. To further complicate matters, there was Schrempp's foray into the Japanese car market.

Yataro Iwasaki had started building the Mitsubishi business empire in the 1870s, with a steamship company. This happened at the time when Japan was transforming itself into one of the world's economic powers. The country's new *samurai* were businessmen who came to the forefront to help the economy in acquiring a sound industrial base.

At Mitsubishi, management skill and the ability to get results had been steadily built up in the 135 years since Iwasaki. But in the last couple of decades both these vital characteristics seem to have been somehow downgraded. Evidence is provided by the 450 billion Yen ($4 billion) rescue by the Mitsubishi *keiretsu* of the ailing Mitsubishi Motors (a company that should have never seen the light), after DaimlerChrysler walked away from its 37% stake in the Japanese auto firm.

This 37% participation was bought by Jürgen Schrempp, as CEO of DaimlerChrysler, because he wanted to acquire control of ailing Mitsubishi Motors, but was dissuaded from going further than a minority stake by Eaton. Such attempted expansion prior to having properly digested the previous big acquisition has a lot to say about what happens when:

- Egos are big,
- But management skills are wanting.

In retrospect, we know that the DaimlerChrysler merger has failed. But we also appreciate that the failure of the meaningless Mitsubishi Motors takeover has been an even bigger fault in terms of management decisions. This makes that whole deal an interesting case study in what happens when management does not know what it wants.

DaimlerChrysler made a bad deal in trying to enter the hugely competitive auto market. But the Mitsubishi Group did not fare better. After losing 215 billion Yen ($1.9 billion) in 2003, and after experiencing in 2004 further loss of market share, on 21 May 2004 the Mitsubishi Group decided to throw good money after bad and make the silly $4 billion handout.

- The Bank of Tokyo-Mitsubishi, along with Mitsubishi Trust Bank, swapped 130 billion Yen ($1.15 billion) of Mitsubishi Motors' debts for equity stakes.
- This is precisely the same sort of ill-considered swap the French government did, with taxpayers' money, to save the sinking Alstom from going under.

Neither was that $5.9 billion the last to go down the drain. At the time this announcement was made, it was said that Mitsubishi Motors would raise another 140 billion Yen (about $1.0 billion) by issuing of preferred shares to firms in the Group, including 40 billion Yen to each: Bank of Tokyo-Mitsubishi, Mitsubishi Heavy Industries, and the Mitsubishi Corporation. The latter is the Group's trading arm, which handles business ventures around the world.

Still another 70 billion Yen of good money running after bad was to come from Phoenix Capital, a venture fund started by former employees of the Bank of Tokyo-Mitsubishi.[5] The Group was also providing management skill to the badly wounded Mitsubishi Motors, including an executive from Mitsubishi Heavy Industries, to help oversee restructuring – *if* restructuring is doable. (The evidence from the DaimlerChrysler ownership years suggests that it is not.)

As will happen when the law of unwanted consequences has its way, the unsuccessful acquisition of a big stake in a fragile troubled company ended in court. Both DaimlerChrysler and Mitsubishi Motors accused one another of broken promises and other misdemeanours, simply forgetting the basic fact that they were co-responsible.

Moreover, in June 2004 DaimlerChrysler filed a lawsuit against Mitsubishi Motors, its Japanese partner, over worsening quality-control problems at Mitsubishi Fuso, a commercial-vehicle operation in which DaimlerChrysler had acquired a majority stake. Sometime after Japanese police arrested a former boss of Mitsubishi Motors and five former executives for suspected negligence over two deaths caused by faulty lorries ... and so on, and so forth. The rest is history.

5. Bank mergers may result in customer alienation

As the DaimlerChrysler case study in section 4 has demonstrated, the bigger the merging companies, the greater the temptation to throw more capital at the riskier side of the business. The end effect is that it becomes difficult to root out embedded problems characterizing the intricate financial and operational couplings that link large organizations.

Particularly in connection to the financial industry, Chapters 19 and 20 have documented that both in the United States and in Europe banks find it difficult to create long-term value for their shareholders out of mergers. In one country after another, typically, the biggest financial institutions have failed to harness their claimed merger synergies, after initial savings have been gained from stripping out duplicate costs.

The elusiveness of these 'expected synergies' over the longer run, more specifically those linked with boosting revenues from the combined banking group, has resulted in poor shareholder returns. As we have also seen, when domestic banks have made acquisitions in overseas markets the results have ranged from zero to disastrous, forcing institutions into doing embarrassing strategic U-turns. Few exceptions exist.

There are also conflicts of interest to account for. The big investment banks make much of their money from trading. But is it possible to reconcile giving advice on how to grow one's assets in a rapid fire way, with how to limit exposure being taken, and therefore losses?[6] The contradiction inherent in this task is best exemplified by loans granted by credit institutions to hedge funds and vulture funds – whose deal is to acquire distressed assets at lowest possible prices. Even the best-run institutions can get caught in this game, which has few, if any, rules.

Additionally, part of the problem from mega-mergers among financial institutions is *customer alienation* and the throwing away of valuable branding, as recent examples document. For instance, Philadelphians have not asked Wachovia or the Royal Bank of Scotland to guard their savings, clear their cheques, or lend them money. Yet, those two far-away institutions, the one from the Carolinas, the other from Scotland, have become the biggest banks in the city and its Pennsylvania suburbs.

Royal Bank's US arm, Citizens Financial Group, of Providence, RI, made a $2.1 billion bid for 316 Mellon Bank branches in Pennsylvania (including 128 in the Philadelphia area) and other 29 branches scattered through Delaware, Maryland, and New Jersey. Also, after its $14 billion bid to buy Wachovia, First Union scrapped its corporate identity and put Wachovia's name on more than 2000 branches, including 300 in the Philadelphia area.

As we saw in Chapter 19, this rebranding through the name of an acquired firm is not an exception. Nations Bank, the former North Carolina National Bank bought BankAmerica and put the latter's name to the combined enterprise; Chemical Banking bought Chase Manhattan and adopted its name; Northwest Corp. bought Wells Fargo and the combined enterprise became Wells Fargo. Lost in rebranding is the fact that bank mergers mean more than choosing brand names. They are often associated with:

- Office consolidation
- Staff cutbacks and turnover, and
- Changes in customer rules and prices.

Customers don't ask for those changes. Consumers, as well as small and medium-sized enterprises (SMEs), choose a bank for its handholding, its products, and its prices. Then, some other institution takes it over, alters (and in cases severs) the customer connection, ups the costs billed to the client, and damages the relationship.

In the Philadelphia area, First Union alienated at least part of the population by cutting staff, partly because of pressure to reduce expenses after costly acquisitions (see also section 6 on Hewlett–Packard's problems in France). Subsequently it lost market share and suffered steep share-price decline, adding to Wall Street's growing scepticism of bank mergers.

North Carolina's Wachovia, the bank that financed Reynolds Tobacco, is another interesting case. Both First Union, from the north, and SunTrust Banks, from the south, wanted to buy it, but only one could win. What has made this acquisition war so much fun is that, to buy Wachovia, First Union and SunTrust were offering stock, rather than cash. Therefore, each:

- Sought to increase its own stock price, while tearing down the other.
- But paid little attention to the fact that the acquisition would reduce competition and lead to substantial layoffs and branch closings in the state of Pennsylvania.

An important issue with diminishing competition, as one of M&As after-effects, is that the *cost of banking* goes up. Consumers care about the money their accounts would cost them in the future. Citizens Bank, for instance, did not establish at acquisition time its fees and account limits for the Philadelphia market. It did not even decide where its new Pennsylvania arm would be based. This made the local consumer and business community nervous.

Neither does this sort of customer alienation happen only in the United States. Here is a European example. Crédit Lyonnais, of France, has been for several decades a badly mismanaged bank. After its virtual bankruptcy in the early 1990s, to save its overblown personnel of 65 000 from unemployment, the Balladur government injected into the bank some 35 billion euro. But Crédit Lyonnais continued downhill, and was eventually bought by Crédit Agricole.

A poor decision has been to keep both Crédit Agricole and Crédit Lyonnais operating as separate entities, with overlapping branches. Another bad management decision was to overcharge clients, for instance for money transfers. A transfer from a client's account in Crédit Suisse, in Zurich, to the same client's account in Crédit Agricole in Nice, transits from the Crédit Lyonnais in the provincial city of Draguignan:

- This is totally unwarranted
- But in the process the client is charged a double commission for the same transfer: one by Crédit Lyonnais, the other by Crédit Agricole.

Like consumers, analysts have different reasons to worry about bank mergers. For analysts, one of the basic criteria is performance. Post-M&A performance was especially poor during the early 1990s when banks appeared to go into acquisitions with ill-defined merger objectives and fuzzy thinking. And as we already saw, through case studies, to placate egos and stop games of musical chairs, some institutions try to run dual systems, retaining both pre-merger labels and pre-merger headquarters.

Clashes because of cultural differences and huge technological problems see to it that the jury is out on whether banks are able to generate value from revenue-driven mergers. At the same time, investor tolerance of underperforming mergers has diminished. If they get the synergies wrong, let alone destroy value, merging entities are punished swiftly by the market. The bottom line is that for shareholders, the greatest value is always created by those banks that have got the revenue synergies right.

6. Fraudulent conveyance: a new thorn in M&As

In the early 1990, lawyers for the reorganized Kaiser Steel company were suing some 400 defendants, including Goldman Sachs, Merrill Lynch, Irwin J. Jacobs, and shareholders, over Kaiser's 1984 leveraged buyout (LBO) which had not gone as projected:

- The ammunition for legal action had been a bankruptcy-law provision from Elizabethan times called *fraudulent conveyance*.
- The suit argued that LBO payouts were fraudulent conveyances and, as a result, it sought over $200 million in compensation.

What this Elizabethan law says is that if a debtor who later goes bankrupt hides assets, gives away property, or takes other steps that hurt the company, the recipients of those assets, or beneficiaries, must return the assets or make up the lost value of creditors. This is due, even if the transactions were legal and made in good faith when they occurred.

For decades, fraudulent conveyance provisions were used quietly by creditors in ordinary bankruptcies. But in the 1980s and 1990s they have become quite a legal weapon. Some courts even have rules that the transactions forming a leveraged buyout can be challenged as fraudulent conveyances *after* the LBO files for bankruptcy.

Developed from a 1571 English statute, fraudulent conveyance was not intended to cover leveraged buyouts. Therefore, the stated claims have been unwarranted, if it was not for the fact that in 1986, a federal appeals court said that extending the law to certain leveraged buyouts is not clearly bad public policy.

- Different courts have since agreed, though no final precedents have been formed.
- In fact, experts say some rulings even suggest that courts may cast a wide net.

For instance, the Elizabethan law might cover events that took place as long as six years before a filing can be challenged. This is a new thorn in the side of mergers and acquisitions. In one case, fraudulent conveyance suits brought by labour unions led a court-appointed examiner to look into three years of transactions between Eastern Airlines and its parent, Texas Air Corp. On 1 March 1990, the examiner reported that he had found evidence that:

- Texas Air illegally siphoned off Eastern assets worth as much as $403 million, since the unit's late 1986 acquisition
- In the aftermath, Texas Air quickly agreed to pay $280 million to Eastern to get over the hurdle.

Along the same frame of reference, in late February 1990 Drexel's creditors asked a judge to name an examiner to collect information on bonuses and other outlays the company made prior to its 13 February (of that year) bankruptcy filing. A couple of weeks later, on 6 March, they dropped the request, but said they would seek the data directly from Drexel.

As the bandwidth of issues covered under fraudulent conveyance expands, lawyers are using it as a threat, on the premise that something will be found worth the challenge. This rests on the hypotheses that many deals rest on weak grounds, and they should never have been done in the first place. For instance, to take a company private, executives and bankers typically:

- Pile on debt, and
- Sell off assets.

The selling shareholders, and others partners in the game, often get rich. But the bondholders lose a great deal of money, and the company can end up crippled. Therefore, lawyers argue, when the board and CEO strip the company or mortgage it to benefit themselves, this is an insider play – and those parties engage in fraudulent conveyances.

On 15 January, the day Robert Campeau put his high leveraged retailing companies into the hands of a Cincinnati bankruptcy judge, bondholders and trade creditors of Allied Stores began talking about the $500 million in Allied assets that Campeau sold to buy Federated. On the hook, they argued, should be:

- Robert Campeau, and
- His advisers First Boston, including Bruce Wasserstein, and others.

Not everyone, however, is convinced that in the longer run fraudulent conveyance will turn out to play a big role in dissuading mergers, acquisitions, and takeovers. Several people think that the law does not apply to junk-financed LBOs, because investors buying them know very well these sort of bonds are risky. Hence, by taking legal action investors think they can both have their cake and eat it. By accepting credit and market risk, junk bond investors don't qualify for legal risk compensation. Yes, but legal risk and social risk are key elements in practically all M&A activities.

7. Legal risk and social risk with M&As

Even if the case of fraud was nonexistent (because of misrepresentation of financials and other reasons), there are plenty of other forms of legal risk relating to mergers, acquisitions, and takeovers: for instance, issues associated to downsizing of the company, which follows many M&As. Often, this particular legal risk is the aftermath of social risk with M&As.

For instance, in many countries, France being an example, hire and fire is virtually illegal; the size of financial penalties associated to it discourages such action. The government's response to the 2005 slimming down of Hewlett–Packard's operations in France (partly resulting from the takeover of Compaq a few years earlier) makes an interesting case study.

Job losses after a merger are not a problem in the United States. On 13 January 2003, Bethlehem Steel said as many as 4000 people would lose their job because of its buyout by International Steel Group (ISG). This figure amounted to 36% of Bethlehem's work force of 11 000, but there was no public uproar and no anti-management demonstrations.

In the aftermath of that acquisition, Robert Miller, Bethlehem Steel's CEO, told employees that the bankrupt company would work with ISG and union officials to determine the exact number of jobs to be cut. This was inevitable after the company's board voted to accept Cleveland-based International Steel Group's $1.5 billion offer (Bethlehem Steel, based in Bethlehem, Pennsylvania, had filed for Chapter 11 bankruptcy protection in October 2001).

ISG's chairman, Wilbur Ross, who specialized in buying distressed businesses, had said ISG would set aside $100 million for salaried and hourly employees, adding Bethlehem Steel's plants would make ISG the largest US steelmaker with an annual production capacity of 16 million tons.[7] The American government did not intervene. By contrast, when in the early 1960s General Electric bought Machines Bull, the French computer company, and wanted to pare down the personnel, the French government imposed a veto.

Things have changed little over the more than 40 years that have elapsed between General Electric's takeover of Bull and today. In 2005, in Hewlett–Packard's case, the French authorities had no right to impose a veto, but demanded HP return the sponsorship money it got to establish its labs near Grenoble – even if this money had mainly gone towards opening up and paving a road to make the lab building accessible.

The paring down of HP personnel in France was part of a global plan of the firm's new management to reduce costs and personnel. Years earlier, the acquisition of Compaq had oversized the local staff. But whether retained or thanked for their services HP employees demonstrated for several days in the streets. In other similar cases they went in interminable strikes, as if to bring the company the faster to its knees.

Demonstrations and strikes immobilizing and mobilizing, at the same time, are part of the 'social ballet' in France, and several other countries. The fact that the labour market is inflexible and highly regulated, sees to it that one cannot easily find a job after being fired. Even the unemployed go on strike of sorts, when the government does not give them an extra bonus for Christmas. All this is part of a destabilizing iron arm between:

- Employees
- Employers, and
- Government authorities.

At the same time, however, the strikes, demonstrations, and overt or covert government actions create a vicious cycle. Companies don't hire because they cannot fire. Or, they hire only temporary workers, for a few months, and fire them before they reach tenure and become untouchable.

This has been fully in the background of demonstrations and strikes because of Hewlett–Packard's slimming down. For his part, for evident political reasons, French president Jacques Chirac asked the European Union to intervene, and use all means at its disposal to stop Hewlett–Packard from firing French employees. The European Union Executive answered that:

- It has no such means at its disposal, and
- This is not an EU problem anyway, it is a French social problem.

Quite often, legal and social risk is augmented by the fact that the situation is mismanaged. Even if the law of the land allows hire and fire, shortsightedness of the restructuring plan sees to it that goals are never reached while employee pain and stress is always present. When LTV acquired Republic Steel, in 1984, its chief executive predicted the result would be:

- Huge cost savings, and
- Great efficiencies.

The then LTV's CEO also indulged in a little boasting. The company's dramatic increase in size, he said to shareholders, would not only make it the nation's No. 2 steel producer, but also No. 1 in key product areas. The result was a big company but not what the CEO had intended. LTV's acquisition of Republic ended in one of the largest bankruptcy filings in America. Barely two years after the deal:

- LTV defaulted on $2.6 billion in debt
- Filed for Chapter 11 protection, and
- Dumped $2 billion in unfunded pensions on the US government.

This is a good example of how poorly planned M&As become a social problem with huge consequences. Post mortem, Raymond A. Hay, LTV's CEO, insisted that the deal was an attempt to save two haemorrhaging companies that could not survive alone. But he gave no evidence about why Republic Steel's takeover was anything better than a hit and run affair.

Publicly, the way it has been reported in the press, Hay blamed the failure of the LTV/Republic merger, and subsequent bankruptcy, on unforeseen external forces – such as plummeting steel prices and Justice Department antitrust concerns. These allegedly delayed the deal by nine months. The way LTV's CEO put it: If he had known everything he now knows after the fact, there is no way he would have done the merger.

This, however, was not the opinion of financial analysts and steel experts. The latter said that, at best, the deal was shortsighted. While merging two members of a shrinking industry would theoretically create a better competitor, in 1984 steel defied convention.

- With foreign steel flooding the US market, *modernization* not size, was the answer, and
- While LTV took on Republic, its US rivals were slimming down. Moreover, years of mediocre management did not help.

During the 1970s and early 1980s, LTV (and other US steel producers) failed to invest in the latest steelmaking technology. Instead, LTV loaded up on debt acquiring everything from military vehicles to oil-field equipment. Then it merged with Republic for $714 million in stock. But also absorbed its $700 million in debt, adding $164 million in annual interest cost. This was in itself a recipe for failure. All sorts of companies who load themselves with debt in order to buy their competitors, should take notice.

8. The merger wave needs regulation to weed out seeds of disaster

Events that followed the 'bigger is better' trend of the late 1990s should be seen as a warning sign of possible disaster. This is particularly important as, in 2005, a new merger wave is about to start (see in Chapter 18 the case study on Telefonica). While deal-makers applaud big company consolidation, this process increases the risks resulting from synergy of existing exposures, cultural classes, and mismanagement. Particularly in the banking industry M&A failures can tear apart the financial fabric. Moreover,

- The greater is the degree of consolidation
- The less the resulting transparency, which is key to market regulation.

There have also been concerns about quality of financial reporting. In a 1999 letter to shareholders, Warren Buffett observed that 'growing number of otherwise high-grade managers have come to the view that it's OK to manipulate earnings to satisfy what they believe are Wall Street's desires'.[8] In the long run, creative accounting practices work to the detriment of stakeholders, including:

- The firms themselves, and
- The majority of their investors.

The pharmaceutical industry provides plenty of examples on how some mergers, acquisitions, and takeovers test existing limits. To appreciate the example that follows, it is important to notice that while not always recognized as such:

- Pharmaceuticals is a high technology industry, and
- To compete in global markets many firms are of the opinion they need to be bigger.

Not without reason, senior executives in the pharmaceutical industry say that given the high R&D expenditures they have to position themselves to make the most productive use of cutting-edge technology they develop. And they add that for this, too, they need to become bigger and bigger. Size is also seen as the way to keep up with fast-growing competitors.

Critics answer these arguments by pointing out the risks of M&As, as well as the fact that too many pharmaceutical mergers are leading to monopolies. Therefore, this is anti-competitive practice. Pragmatists, who find themselves between the two sides, point out that during the post-World War II years, the tendency to monopoly has been thwarted by the main forces:

- The first is through new entrants, coupled with the departure of acquired companies.

Capitalism has shown an immense capacity to renew itself, and new technology has provided a rapid succession of tools to do just that. As medical and health needs evolve, new drugs introduced by startups overtake those developed by established but slow-moving pharmaceutical laboratories of old firms.

- The other force is synergy, provided, albeit not always, by a curious combination of regulatory action and market forces.

Monopolies do show signs of forming, and when this happens, regulatory agencies and governments intervene and break them up. Within this duality of action, it is appropriate to point out that the question of size in the global market is not the same as it has been in each national market individually.

- When Glaxo Wellcome and Smith–Kline–Beecham went ahead with their merger, they formed a monopoly in England.
- But in the global market for pharmaceuticals the resulting company had just 7.5% of the world market for prescription drugs.

In terms of pure numbers, this 7.5% towered over Merck's 4.5% and Novartis' 4.3%. (Switzerland's Novartis was also the result of a merger involving Sandoz and Ciba-Geigy.) This, experts said, was not that crucial. More important was the fact that Glaxo Smith Kline's research budget:

- Became equivalent to a quarter of *total* private sector R&D spending each year in Britain, and
- At the time of the merger, the company boasted a market capitalization of over £100 billion ($165 billion), making it the second-largest company in the world after America's General Electric.

Investors seemed caught up in the excitement of it all. Nevertheless, the more cool-headed pointed out that in the drug industry real growth can come from combined research activity, though it will take some time to sort out conflicting egos and overlapping projects. A combined salesforce also helps in market leadership.

Up to about a decade ago, drug firms were reluctant to be seen as pushing their salesmen and assigning them quotas. They rather liked to see the public believing that doctors prescribe their medicines because they are the best. In reality, however,

- Doctors were more likely to learn of the results from clinical trials if these were brought to their attention, and
- It takes a well-trained salesforce to provide doctors with information about new research results concerning new drugs.

On 2 February 1998, in the first day's trading since Glaxo Wellcome and Smith–Kline–Beecham announced their merger plans, their combined value soared. This was good for their shareholders, provided they were timely in cashing in their paper profits. But it was no global monopoly by any means. Even if no supplier in the pharmaceuticals industry had more than 6% thus far, 7.5% was scarcely world dominant.

Besides this, there were still eight drug companies among the top 50 in the FT 500 alone. But in the mind of many analysts the Glaxo Smith Kline merger was a blockbuster which led to comparisons with what had happened, or was likely to happen, in other industries.

For instance, food manufacturing provided a good example of the concentration achieved by the dual effect of organizational growth and acquisition. Then (at Glaxo Smith Kline merger time) as now, the world's biggest producer was Nestlé. Within 10 years, 1987–97, its sales in dollar terms had risen 90%.

- In the same period, however, the world's nominal GDP has risen 75%.
- As a result, Nestlé's faster growth scarcely raised a worry about monopoly.

In fact, given the company's acquisitions of Rowntree, Buitoni, Perrier, and others, it was rather surprising that Nestlé has not grown faster. A different way to look at this issue is that the consolidation of the world food industry was not really happening. Sometimes consolidation:

- Is not a sign of overweening power
- Rather it is a defensive measure.

Whether or not it welcomes mergers and acquisitions of pharmaceutical companies, the market expects more and more from big firms. Because, however, of post-merger troubles with digestion and musical chairs, the merged companies cannot deliver what they promised. This is something the market does not forgive.

The pros point to the food industry and pharmaceuticals as two examples where, all told, M&As have been rather successful. This being said, they argue that therefore the problem is not with growing size, as long as this keeps at a single-digit share of the global market, but with regulation. Today's global markets require a global policeman in every industry, and no such entity exists.

The globalization of capital markets requires that there should be a way of clearing and policing mega-mergers between banks, chemicals, steels, oil, pharmaceuticals, food processors, telecoms, computers, entertainment, aviation, and other industries – along with setting tolerances and standards. Existing parochial competition law is not enough to protect consumers, or for that matter these industries from themselves. New regulatory powers are needed able to meet 21st century requirements – and they should be put in place on a global scale. All this should be done with wisdom: 'Wisdom is the son of experience,' said Leonardo da Vinci.

Notes

1 Geoff Tibballs, *Business Blunders*. Robinson, London, 1999.
2 *Business Week*, 11 September 2000.
3 D.N. Chorafas, *Management Risk: The Bottleneck Is at the Top of the Bottle*. Macmillan/Palgrave, London, 2004.
4 *Business Week*, 10 July 1989.
5 *The Economist*, 29 May 2004.
6 D.N. Chorafas, *Wealth Management: Private Banking, Investment Decisions and Structured Financial Products*. Elsevier, Oxford, 2005.
7 *International Herald Tribune*, 14 February 2003.
8 *The Economist*, 20 March 1999.

Index

ABC management teams, 214–18
Abetti, Pier A., 180
ABN (Algemene Bank Nederland), 570–1
ABN Amro, 570–1, 573
Account analysis, 427–9
Accountability, 146
  personal, 287
Accounting, 255–7
  disclosure about capital, 260–4
  financial accounting, 257–8
    virtual consolidated financial statement (VCFS), 274–8
  hedge accounting, 269–70
  IFRS as a strategic accounting initiative, 257–60
  management accounting, 258
  standards, 263–7
Acquisitions, *see* Mergers and acquisitions (M&As)
Added value, 24–6, 357
Agnelli family, 234–5
Air France, 519
Airline industry, 516–19
  consolidation, 516
  deregulation, 516
  United States, 493–4, 516–18
Alexander, Henry, 43–4
Alierta, Cesar, 498
Allianz Insurance, 569–70
Allied Domecq, 469, 493
Allied Stores, 598
Allied-Signal, 483
Ambiguity, accounting for, 89–93
America On-line (AOL), 587–9
American Airlines, 517
American Express (Amex), 383
American Federation of Teachers, 196
Amoco, 512
Amro (Amsterdam Rotterdam Bank), 570–1
Anticipation, 373, 374
Antonveneta, 573
Arthur Andersen, 22–3, 221, 584
Asian crisis, 280
Assets and liabilities (A&L) management, 229
  model based approach, 270–4
AT&T, 32–3, 422, 423, 472, 494–7
Avis Europe, 317

Baer, Raymond, 92
Baker, George F., 37, 44, 287, 529, 535
Banca Commerciale Romana (BCR), 555
Banca Nazionale del Lavoro (BNL), 573, 576–7
Banca Popolare di Lodi, 573, 574
Bank of America, 528, 542
Bank of New England (BNE), 280
Bank One, 537–8
BankAmerica, 528, 538–43, 595
Bankers Trust, 17–18, 566–7
Banking sector, 65–8, 77–80
  contractual agreements, 453–5
  cost control, 296–8
  liquidity strategy, 248
  mergers and acquisitions, 463–4, 473–6
    customer alienation, 594–6
    Europe, 553–77
    United States, 525–50
  product development, 383–5
    ECAPS, 386–90
  profit planning, 343–6
  profitability analysis, 350–4
    customer profitability, 434
  quality of service (QOS), 435–6
  strategic planning, 150–4
  see also Specific banks
Bankruptcy, 211
  Delta Airlines, 519–22
Barclays Bank, 168, 169
Barnes, Ralph, 380
Bayerische Hypo-Bank, 475, 554
Bayerische Vereinsbank, 475, 554
Benetton, Luciano, 504
Bennett, Phillip, 330–2
Berkshire, 488
Bernheim, Henry, 96
Bethlehem Steel, 599
Bilbao Viscaya (BBVA), 573, 576–7
Bipielle Investimenti, 574, 575
Bloomberg, 93–6
Blumenthal, Michael, 511
BMW, 307, 408
Bondi, Enrico, 160, 313
Boyd, John, 197, 539
BP, 512
BPI (Banca Popolare Italiana), 573–6
Branding, 420–3
Breuer, Rolf, 566
Bridgestone, 301–2
Brown, Bennett A., 545
Budgeting, 229
  budgetary model, 240
  flexible budgeting, 240–1
  zero-based budgetary policy, 241
Budgets, 149
  as financial plans, 237–41
  interest budget, 241
  lapsing budgets, 241
  line-item budgets, 241
Bundled rebates, 406

Burd, Steve, 293
Burlington Resources, 513
Burroughs, 510, 511
Business risk, management planning and, 166–70
Business strategy, *See* Strategy
Business unit (BU), 178
Buyouts, 483–4

Camco, 440–1
Campeau, Robert, 598
Canadian Imperial Bank of Commerce (CIBC), 571
Capital:
 allocation, 105–8
 circulating capital, 242
 debit capital, 247
 disclosure, 260–4
 equity capital, 247
 free-of-risk cost of, 318
 permanent capital, 242
 productivity, 81
Capital Cities/ABC, 488–9
Capital expenditure (capex), 356
Cash flow, 230, 242
 challenges, 242–7
 free cash flow (FCF), 242
 operating cash flow (OCF), 242
 statement, 243, 244–5, 246
Casio, 7
Castries, Henri de, 582
Catholic Church, 175–9
Chambers, John T., 16–17
Chase Manhattan, 437, 528, 532–4, 536, 595
Chemical Banking, 532–4
Chief Executive Officer (CEO), 59–60
 job description, 184–5
China, 26, 47–9
Chrysler, 180, 210, 211–12, 472, 589–93
Cingular Wireless, 496–7
Cisco, 15–19, 421
Citibank, 20, 61, 346
Citicorp, 67, 527–32
Citigroup, 527–32
Citizen & Southern (C&S), 543–7
City Bank, 528
Clausewitz, Karl von, 132, 186
Coca-Cola, 405
Colaninno, Roberto, 502–4
Comcast, 495–6
Commerzbank, 473, 554, 585
Committees, 60, 205
Commodity prices, 46–9
Compaq, 300–1, 507, 510, 583
Comparative advantage, 49
 knowledge workers, 49–52
Completeness check, 349
Computer industry, mergers and acquisitions, 509–12
ConocoPhillips, 513
Consolidation:
 airline industry, 516
 dealership networks, 406–7
 friendly mergers, 472
Continental Illinois, 540–2, 549–50
Contractual agreements, 451–5
Control, 218–22
 cost control, 230
 internal control, 220–2
 inventory control, 230
Controlling, 202
 management's controlling function, 218–22
Converium, 104–5
Coors, 476
Corporate governance, 222–4
 indices, 223–4
Cost control, 230, 287–8
 case studies, 289–92, 299–302
 in banking, 296–8
 profitability and, 342–3, 350
Cost of doing business, 21, 238–9, 347
Cost of staying in business, 21, 22–3, 238–9, 347
Cost-effectiveness, 287
Costs, 38, 287
 cost performance comparison, 292–5
 legacy costs, 208–11
 operating costs, 238, 350
 overheads, 297–8
 personnel/labour costs, 342, 356–7
 risk, 22, 311, 318–21
 social costs, 307, 357
 see also Cost control
Crédit Agricole, 596
Credit cards, 383–4
Credit equivalence, 278–81
Credit institutions, 74, 343–6
 client profitability estimation, 435
 See also Banking sector
Crédit Lyonnais, 596
Credit rating:
 importance of, 100–2
 strategic planning and, 102–5
Credit risk, 493
Crédit Suisse, 168, 169
Crédit Suisse First Boston (CSFB), 191, 311–13, 581–2
Cultural discontinuity, 586–8

Customer acquisition, 429, 433
Customer alienation, 594–6
Customer gateways, 381
Customer profit centre, 427, 428, 448, 449–50
  profitability analysis, 429–35
Customer profitability, 427–9
  analysis, 429–35
  technology for management of, 449–51
Customer relationship:
  contractual agreements, 451–5
  management, 429–32
  see also Know your customer (KYC) strategy

Dai-Ichi Kangyo Bank, 78
Daimler–Benz, 472, 589
DaimlerChrysler, 589–93
Danone, 493
Dashboards, 20–1
Databases, 449–51
Dealerships, 406
  consolidation, 406–7
Debit capital, 247
Debit cards, 383–4
Debt:
  fair value of, 266
  for company financing, 249–52
  undated, 157
Debt/equity ratio, 252
Deception, 99–100
Decision making:
  bad management decisions, 211–14
  day-to-day tactical decisions, 205–8
  strategic decisions, 37–8, 41–4
    macroeconomics and, 44–6
Deferred tax liabilities (DTLs), 486–9
Delphi, 208–10, 211, 213
Delta Airlines, 296, 517, 518
  bankruptcy, 519–22
Deming, W. Edward, 64
Dependability, 436–7
Depreciation, 245
Deproliferation, 299–301
Deregulation:
  airline industry, 516
  banking industry, 345
Derivatives, 234–7, 258
  risk management, 278–81
Deutsche Bank, 473, 564–7, 584–5
Deutsche Morgan Grenfell (DMG), 564–5
Development, 366
  see also Research and development (R&D)
Devil's advocate role, 111–13
Diebold, 462
Digital Equipment Corp. (DEC), 122, 509
Diners Club, 383
Directing, 201–2
Disintermediation, 344
Donaldson, Lufkin & Jenrette (DLJ), 582
Dray, Deane, 11
Dresdner Bank, 473, 567–70, 585
Drexel, 597–8
Drucker, Peter, 29
DVD recording standard, 24–5

E-commerce, 441
Eastern Airlines, 482, 597
Eaton, Robert, 590–1
ECAPS (Enhanced Capital Advantaged Preferred Security), 386–90
Ecomagination, 9–11
Economic capital, 105–8
Economic profit, 347
Enron, 256
Equity capital, 247
Equity swaps, 235–7
Ernst & Young, 585
Eurocheque, 383–4
Europe, 355
  mergers and acquisitions, 467–71, 483–4
    banks, 553–77
Exclusivity incentives, 405
Executives, 203–5
Expected losses (EL), 135
Expense control, 350
Experience curve, 11–15
Experimental design, 77, 473
Experimentation, 358–9
Experts, 203
Exxon, 512, 586

Fair value, 264–6
  hedging, 268
  tests, 329
Fancher, Brainard, 184
Far-out planning, 156, 375–6
Fast flow replenishment (FFR), 418
Fazio, Antonio, 573
Federal Deposit Insurance Corporation (FDIC), 540–1, 548, 549
Federal Reserve Bank of Kansas City, 44–6
Federated organization, 178
'Feels good' test, 109–10
Fiat, 63, 234–7
Fidelity Investments, 323–7
Financial accounting, 257–8
  virtual consolidated financial statement (VCFS), 274–8
  see also Accounting

Financial Accounting Standards Board (FASB), United States, 255–6, 262–3
Financial planning, 229–31
  budget as a financial plan, 237–41
  cash flow challenges, 242–7
  derivatives use, 234–7
  equity *vs* debt, 249–52, 387
  liquidity obligations, 247–9
Financial sector, *See* Banking sector; Credit institutions
Finsiel, 82–3
Fiorani, Gian Pierro, 573–4
Fiorina, Carly, 12–14, 583
Firestone Tyre & Rubber, 301
First National Bank of New York, 37, 44, 529
First National City Bank (FNCB), 529
First Union, 594–5
Ford, 61, 210, 211–12, 305, 380
  dealership consolidation, 407
  world product, 382
Forecasting, 119–25
  case studies, 129–35, 138–42
  forward-looking statements, 138–42
  models, 135–8
  pitfalls, 125–9
  unexpected losses, 135–8
Forward-looking statements, 138–42
France Telecom, 496
Fraudulent conveyance, 596–8
Free cash flow (FCF), 242
Friendly mergers, 472
Funds flow statement, 242

Gates, Bill, 69, 70–1, 124–5, 372
Geiger, Rick, 477
Geneen, Harold, 201–2
General Electric (GE), 7–11, 52, 189–90, 599
  far-out planning, 156, 375–6
  GEIS, 469
  Medical Systems, 442
  reorganization, 180–2
  Six Sigma approach, 77, 196, 437–9, 440–3
General Motors (GM), 61–3, 100–1, 161–2, 235
  dealership consolidation, 406–7
  legacy costs, 208–11
  poor management, 211–14, 297
  takeover bid, 483
  time-to-market target, 391–2
General Motors Acceptance Corp (GMAC), 100–1
Gent, Chris, 498
Gerstner, Louis V., Jr, 302–3, 508, 509
Gillette, 380–1, 488–9
Glaxo, 372, 603–4
Glaxo Smith Kline, 603–4
Global Election Systems (GES), 462
Globalization, 369, 604
Goals, 91
Goodwill, 258
  impairment, 261–2
Graham, Alastair, 167, 256
Grapevine, 173
Grasso, Richard, 191–3
Green, Hetty, 532
Greenspan, Alan, 44–6
Grinstein, Gerald, 520
Gruppo Cos, 82–3
Guaranty Trust, 535–6

Hamilton, Lyman, 201–2
Hartford Insurance, 132–5
Harvard Management Company (HMC), 327
Hay, Raymond A., 601
Hedge accounting, 269–70
Hedging, 267–9, 277–8
Hennessy, Edward L., Jr, 483
Hewlett–Packard, 11–15, 583, 599–600
Hitachi, 24, 403–4
Home entertainment standards, 24–5
HSBC, 169
Human resources, *See* Staffing
Hurricanes, 311, 312
  Katrina, 129–32
Hybrid bonds, 157
HypoVereinsbank (HVB), 475, 554, 555–8
Hyundai, 485

Iacocca, Lee, 180, 483
IBM, 122, 165–6, 174, 185, 506–8
  cost control, 302–5
  H Series, 159–60
  marketing, 407–11
  Monday purchase, 506–9
  product capitalization, 305, 307–8
  Rolm acquisition, 586–7
  Satellite Business Systems (SBS), 586–7
Impairment, 261–2
Inchon, Battle of, 38–41
Income tax expense, 242
Industrial loan companies (ILCs), 6
Inflation, 318
Infrastructure modernization, 14–15, 18–19
Innovation, 54, 83–4, 365, 372–3
  banking sector, 383–5
  bringing innovations to market, 382
  see also Research and development (R&D)
Intangible assets, 258
Intel, 421–2

Intellectual property, 372
Interactive computational finance, 317
Interbank Card Association, 383
Interest cover, 389
Interest expense, 242
Internal control, 220–2
International Accounting Standard (IAS) 39, 264–5
International Accounting Standards Board (IASB), 255, 256, 259
International Financial Reporting Standards (IFRS), 140, 162, 255–7, 482
  as a strategic accounting initiative, 257–60
  assets and liabilities management and, 270
International Steel Group (ISG), 599
Internet, 126–7
  e-commerce, 441
Inventory control, 230
Inventory management, 347–8
Inventory–shipment (I–S) ratio, 347–8
IPTV (Internet Protocol Television), 70–2
Isaac, William M., 548
ISS–FTSE index, 223–4
Italy, 337, 338, 365
ITT, 201–2
Iwasaki, Yataro, 592

Japan, 351, 354–5
  bank mergers, 526
  calculator industry, 7
Job description, 184–5
Johnson & Johnson, 371
Johnson, F. Ross, 477, 478
Johnson, Moira, 188
JP Morgan, 43–4, 67–8, 190, 437, 464
JP Morgan Chase, 528, 534–8
Julius Baer, 91–3
Just-in-time (JIT) strategy, 340–1

Kaiser, Henry, 250
Kaiser Steel, 596–7
KBC Group, 164–5
Kemper, 584
Kennedy, John, 109
Kerkorian, Kirk, 589
Kia, 485
KKR, 293, 477–9
Kleinwort Benson, 568, 569
KLM, 519
Know your customer (KYC) strategy, 427, 440
  statistical charts, 444–9
  see also Customer profitability
Knowledge, 50, 54–5, 187
  comparative advantage of knowledge workers, 49–52
  knowledge assets, 187–9
  return on knowledge (ROK), 55–6
Knowledge industry, 38
Kobayashi, Koji, 25
Koetter, Michael, 474
Koontz, Harold D., 219, 305
KPMG, 221–2, 585
Kravis, Henry, 293, 477–88
Kundenkreditbank (KKB), 346

Labour costs, 356–7
Leadership talent, 186–7
Lean organizations, 97–100
Legacy costs, 208–11
Lenovo, 507
Level scheduling, 341
Leverage, 319–21, 342, 389
Leveraged loans, 483–5
Licensing, 372
Liquidity, 247–9, 397
  measures of, 248
  obligations, 247–9
Lloyds Bank, 571–2
Lloyd's Insurance, 366–7
Long-Term Capital Management (LTCM), 550
LTV, 600–1

3M, 371
MacArthur, Douglas, 38–41
Macaulay, Frederick, 266
Macchiavelli, Nicolo, 108–9
McCoy, John G., 537–8
McCracken, William E., 303
Machines Bull, 599
Mack, John J., 547–8
McNamara, Robert, 185
Macroeconomics, 44–6
Macroinvesting, 320
Magellan Fund, 325–6
Management:
  ABC management teams, 214–18
  benefits from rigorous methodology, 439–43
  controlling function, 218–22
  decisions, *see* Decision making
  failure, 27
  span of, 173–4
Management accounting, 258
  see also Accounting
Management planning, 166–70
Managers, 203–5
Manges, Clinton, 539

Mannesmann, 498
Manufacturers Hanover Trust Bank (MHTC), 311
Manufacturing industry:
product planning, 377–83
profit planning, 346–50
Market capitalization, 302
Market differentiation, 397
Market potential, 416–17
Market research, 381
Market saturation, 399
Market segmentation, 398, 400
Market sensitivity, lack of, 28
Market share discounts, 405
Marketing, 397–403
branding, 420–3
case studies, 403–11, 420–3
planning, 411–16
sales office productivity, 416–19
Marron, Donald B., 563
Martini, Eberhard, 555
Mass customization, 178, 329
Mass market strategy, 402
Master Card, 383
Max Factor, 420
MCI Communications, 422, 494–5, 587
Mean organizations, 97–100
Mercedes, 590–1
Merck, 313, 372
Mergers and acquisitions (M&As), 461–3, 493, 547–50
airline industry, 516–19
banks, 463–4, 473–6
customer alienation, 594–6
Europe, 553–77
United States, 525–50
computer industry, 509–12
critical view of, 480–3
deferred tax liabilities (DTLs), 486–9
fraudulent conveyance, 596–8
friendly acquisitions and hostile deals, 472–6
goals of, 476–9
lessons from, 463–7
oil industry, 512–15
reasons for failure, 582–5
regulation, 548–50, 601–5
risks, 581–2, 598–601
telecommunications, 467–8, 494–505
Merita, 553
Microsoft, 68–74, 372
2005 Annual Report, 265–6
DOS, 506–7
embrace and extend policy, 74
Windows, 421
Xbox 360, 59, 69–70
Miller, Robert, 599
Ministry of International Trade and Industry (MITI), Japan, 125–7
MIT, 299
Mitel, 587
Mitsubishi Motors, 63, 592–3
Mobil, 512
Modigliani–Miller model, 249–50
Molson, 476
Monday, 508–9
Money, 231–4
Montgomery Asset Management, 585
Moody's Investors Service, 256
Morgan Bank, *see* JP Morgan
Morgan Grenfell, 564
Morgan, J.P., 535
Morgan Stanley, 383–5, 547–8
Morris, Derek, 572–3
Motorola, 370
Mühlemann, Lukas, 581–2
Mullin, Leo F., 520–1
Musashi, Miyamoto, 182–6

National Bank of Washington (NBW), 549–50
National Discount Brokers (NDB), 585
Nations Bank, 542, 595
NCR, 32–3
Nestlé, 216, 604
Net income to equity ratio, 351
Net interest margin, 345
New capitalism, 52–6
New product development, 373
banking sector, 383–5
ECAPS, 386–90
marketing, 391
timing, 391
see also Innovation; Research and development (R&D)
New York Stock Exchange, 190–3
Niche products, 401
Nippon Life Insurance, 570
Nissan Motor, 348
Nordbanken, 553
Nordic Telephone Company (NTC), 500
Normal distribution, 438
North Carolina National Bank (NCNB), 297, 542–3
Northwest Airlines, 518
Notional principal amount (NPA), 278–9
demodulation, 278–81
NTT DoCoMo, 497

O_2, 467–8, 496, 498–500
Objectives, 91, 184
  quantitative sales objectives, 407–9
  unclear, 28
O'Connor Associates, 559–60
Office automation (OA), 414
Oil industry, mergers and acquisitions, 512–15
Oil prices, 46–9
Olivetti, 365, 502–4
Olson, Ken, 122, 173
Openness, 355
Operating cash flow (OCF), 242
Operating characteristics (OC) curves, 444, 445
Operating costs, 238, 350
Operating income, 245
Operating profit, 141, 347
Operational risk, 446–8, 450–1
  evaluation, 451, 452
Orange, 496
Organization, 173–4, 175
Ospel, Marcel, 559, 563
Osram, 418
Outperformance, 82
Outsourcing, 26–7
Overhead costs, 297–8
Overstaffing, 296, 298

p charts, 444–8
PaineWebber, 563
Pareto's law, 75–7, 427
Parmalat, 160, 311–13
Patents, 372
Pattern analysis, 389–90
Patton, George, 31–2
Paycheques, excessive, 190–3
Pension Benefit Guaranty Corporation (PBGC), 101, 211
Pension liabilities, 258
PepsiCola, 493
Performance:
  cost performance comparison, 292–5
  sales force, 411–16
  sales office, 416–19
  short-term *vs.* long-term, 81–3
Pernod Ricard, 469, 493
Perot, H. Ross, 201
Perot Systems, 561
Personnel expenses, 342
Persuasion, 83
Peso problem, 124
Pfeiffer, Eckhard, 300
Phelps, Marshall, 372
Philips, 24
Pirelli, 502–5
Plan *See* Strategic plan
Planning, 145–6
  challenges of short-range planning, 159–63
  critical elements of, 147–50
  longer-range planning, 154–9
  management planning, business risk and, 166–70
  marketing planning, 411–16
  product planning, 75, 374–7
  profit, 338–43
  role of policies, 163–6
  see also Financial planning; Strategic planning
Policies, 204
  role in planning, 163–6
Porter, Michael, 465
Positioning, 397
Post Office, UK, 295
Power, 83, 188–9
  knowledge as, 187–9
Predictability, 83
Prices:
  key commodities, 46–9
  pricing strategy, 392
PriceWaterhouseCoopers Consulting, 508–9
Primerica Corporation, 292–3
Procedures, 204
Procter & Gamble (P&G), 421, 488–9
Product capitalization, 305–8
Product life management (PLM), 374–5
Product planning, 75, 374–7
  in manufacturing, 377–83
  product idea evaluation, 377
  product programme development, 379
  technical product definition, 378
Production patterns, 354–7
Production scheduling, 304
Products:
  maturity, 399
  new product development, 373
    banking sector, 383–5
    see also Product planning; Research and development (R&D)
  niche products, 401
  obsolescence, 28, 69
  profit patterns, 75
  quality, 441–2
  strategic, 72–5, 368
  tactical, 72–5, 368
  unique products, 401–2
  world products, 382

Professionals, 203, 205
Profit:
  economic profit, 347
  measurement, 347
  operating profit, 141, 347
  planning, 338–43
    banking industry, 343–6
    manufacturing industry, 346–50
Profitability, 337–8
  analysis, 230, 429–35
    longer term, 350–4
  cost control and, 342–3, 350
  customer profitability, 427–35
    technology for management of, 449–51
  income-based, 357–60
  measurement, 347
Prognostication, *See* Forecasting
Promoters, 214
Prospective payoff, 359–60
Purcell, Philip J., 547–8
Pyne, Percy R., 528

Quality:
  of products, 441–2
  of service (QOS), 435–7
Quality control:
  quality tracking, 350, 444
  statistical charts, 444–9
  total quality management (TQM), 436
Queuing heuristics, 349
Quotas, 407–9, 416

Rabobank, 434
Radar charts, 77
Rampl, Dieter, 556
Re-engineering, 53–4
Real World Computing project, 125–7, 128
Recovery-of-cost plus principle, 359
Reed, John S., 61, 530–1
Refco, 330–3
Regulation, mergers and acquisitions, 548–50, 601–5
Regulatory capital, 105
Relationship management, 429–32
Reorganization, 179–82
Republic Steel, 600–1
Reputational risk, 166
Research and development (R&D), 38, 365–6, 371–4
  budget, 238–9
  critical evaluation of deliverables, 390–2
  financial research, 386–90
  investment in, 367–8, 371–4
  knowledge economy and, 367–70
  laboratories, 369–70
  see also New product development
Return on equity (ROE), 350–1
Return on knowledge (ROK), 55–6
Reuters, 93–6
Reynolds, Jackson Eli, 37
Risk, 21–2, 311–14
  as a cost, 22, 311
  assessment, 317
  business risk, 166–70
  concepts, 314–17
  control of, 315–17
  cost of, 318–21
  credit risk, 493
  culture, 321–3
  experimental approach, 322
  forecasting, 123–4, 133–5
  mega-risks, 311
  mergers and acquisitions, 581–2, 598–601
  monetization of, 325, 327–30
  operational risk, 446–8, 450–1
    evaluation, 451, 452
  premium, 322, 323
  reputational risk, 166
  risk appetite, 313
Risk Adjusted Return on Capital (RAROC), 315
Risk management, 288
RJR Nabisco, 477–89
Roberts, George, 293
Roberts, Paul, 515
Rockefeller, David, 532–3
Roebuck, Thomas, 403
Rolm, 586–7
Root cause analysis, 77
Ross, Wilbur, 599
Royal Bank of Scotland (RBS), 525, 553, 594

Saab, 62
Saatchi & Saatchi, 80
Safeway, 293–4
Sales force:
  productivity, 411–16
  training importance, 408
Sales office productivity, 416–19
Sarbanes–Oxley Act (2002), 470
SBC, 494–5, 496
Scheduling:
  level, 341
  production, 304
Schmid, Albrecht, 555
Schrempp, Jürgen, 589, 590–2
Scientific Data Systems (SDS), 586
Scudder, Stevens & Clark, 584

Seafirst, 538–40
Sears, Roebuck, 96
Seattle First National Bank, 539
Self-knowledge, 50
Service economy, 54–5
Service level agreements (SLAs), 498
S.G. Warburg, 559–60
Sharp, 7
Shearson Lehman, 477–9
Six Sigma approach, 77, 196, 437–9, 440–3
'Sleep well' test, 110
Sloan, Alfred, 161–2, 177, 185, 212
Slotting fees, 405
Smith, Adam, 234
Smith–Kline Beecham, 603–4
Social costs, 307, 357
Solvency, 247–8
Sony, 24
Soros, George, 318–20, 322, 323
Sovran Financial, 543–7
Space Adventures, 80
Span of management, 173–4
  span of attention, 174
  span of control, 173, 175–8
  span of knowledge, 173
  span of support, 173
Sperry, 511
Sprint, 41–4, 423, 499
Staffing, 174, 190
  overstaffing, 296, 298
  personnel expenses, 342
Standards:
  accounting, 263–7
  setting, 23–5
Stock options, 259
Strategic customers, 75–81
Strategic decisions, 37–8, 41–4
  macroeconomics and, 44–6
Strategic goals, 37–8
Strategic plan, 83, 87, 147
  capital allocation and, 105–8
  developing alternatives to, 108–11
Strategic planning, 5–6, 19–20, 87–9, 119–21
  accounting for ambiguity, 89–93
  banking industry, 150–4
  credit rating and, 102–5
  mean and lean organizations, 97–100
  methodology, 111–13
  reasons for failure, 27–30
  tools of, 87–8
  see also Planning
Strategic products, 72–5, 368
Strategic switch, 9–10
Strategy, 15–16
  as master plan, 5, 12, 15–16
  commodity prices and, 46–9
  components of, 11–15, 83–4
Stress testing, 329
Sun Microsystems, 102
Sun Tzu, 30–2, 187
Supply chain management, 348
Swearingen, John E., 541
Swiss Bank Corporation (SBC), 22, 558–63
Swiss Re, 17, 131, 147, 469
Swisscom, 502
System integration, 54
Systems, 204

Tactical decisions, 205–8
Tactical products, 72–5, 368
Tartaglia, Nunzio A., 385
Taylor, Moses, 528
TDC, 500–1
Technology, 28, 176–7
  for customer profitability management, 449–51
Telecom Italia, 502–5
Telecommunications sector, M&As, 467–8, 494–505
Telefonica, 467–8, 496, 498–500
Texas Air Corp., 597
Time phasing, 359
Time Warner, 587–9
Time-to-market, 391–2
Toronto Dominion, 571
Toshiba/Time Warner DVD recording standard, 24–5
Total quality management (TQM), 436
Toyota, 61–5, 392
Training, 193–7
  sales force, 408
Transfer price, 306
Travellers, 529–31
Travellers cheques, 383–4
Tronchetti Provera, Marco, 502–4
TSB (Trustee Savings Bank), 571–2
Turner Communications, 588

Uncertainty, 314
Undated debt, 157
Underperformance, 82
Unexpected losses, 135
  forecasting, 135–8
Unicredit, 557–8
Union Bank of Switzerland (UBS), 22, 92–3, 102–4, 558–63
Unique products, 401–2

Unisys, 510, 511–12
United Airlines (UAL), 517
United Auto Workers (UAW), 209–10
United States, 47, 81, 351, 354–5
  airline industry, 493–4
  mergers and acquisitions, 466–7, 468, 471, 484
    banks, 525–50
  R&D investment, 368–9, 371–2
Univac, 510
Upton, Wayne, 146, 256, 259
Utilization check, 349

Value analysis, 291
Value differentiation, 398–9
VAR (value at risk) model, 136, 319
Vendor-specific objective evidence (VSOE), 265–6
Verizon, 468, 494–5, 497
Virtual consolidated financial statement (VCFS), 274–8
Virtual organizations, 178–9
Visa, 383
Vodafone, 497
Voice over Internet protocol (VoIP), 70

Wachovia, 594–5
Wal-Mart, 6, 53, 290–2
Walt Disney, 489
Walton, Sam, 31–2, 43, 53, 287, 289–92
Wasserstein, Bruce, 568, 569
Wasserstein Perella, 568–70, 585
Watson, Thomas J., Sr, 122, 403, 407
Wealth cards, 329
Wealth management, 327–30
Weather forecasting, 122–3
Weill, Sandy, 530–1, 532
Weill, Sanford Il, 292–3
Wells Fargo, 595
Welsh, Jack, 179–82, 189–90, 196
Welsh, John F., 52
Williams, George Gilbert, 532
World Wide Web, 127
Worldcom, 169, 468
Wriston, Walter, 20, 529
Wyfells, H.H.F., 434

Xerox, 586

Yaeger, Chuck, 197
Yanmar Diesel, 341

Zarrella, Ronald L., 406–7
Zurich Financial Services Group, 584